THE AMERICANS
The Democratic Experience

Daniel J. Boorstin has been senior historian of the Smithsonian Institution, Washington, D.C., director of the National Museum of History and Technology and Preston and Sterling Mortin Distinguished Service Professor of American History at the University of Chicago where he taught for twenty-five years. He has won many prestigious prizes for his work, including the Pulitzer Prize in 1974 for *The Democratic Experience*. He was also the Librarian of Congress from 1975 to 1987, during which period public use of the library more than doubled.

Dr Boorstin has spent a good deal of his life viewing America from the outside, first in England where he was a Rhodes scholar at Balliol College, Oxford, winning a coveted 'double-first'. More recently he has been visiting professor of American History at the University of Rome and at Kyoto University, consultant to the Social Science Research Center at the University of Puerto Rico, the first incumbent of the chair of American History at the Sorbonne, and Pitt Professor of American History and Institutions and a Fellow of Trinity College, Cambridge University, which awarded him its Litt.D. degree.

Also by Daniel J. Boorstin

Companion volumes in THE AMERICANS trilogy
The National Experience (Phoenix Press)
The Colonial Experience (Phoenix Press)

Other Works
The Creators (Phoenix Press)
The Discoverers (Phoenix Press)
The Seekers (Phoenix Press)

The Mysterious Science of the Law
The Lost World of Thomas Jefferson
The Genius of American Politics
America and the Image of Europe
The Image: A Guide to Pseudo-Events in America
The Decline of Radicalism
The Sociology of the Absurd
Democracy and its Discontents
The Republic of Technology
The Exploring Spirit
The Republic of Letters
Hidden History
The Chicago History of American Civilization (Ed.; 27 volumes)
An American Primer (Ed)
American Civilization (Ed)

Praise for *The Democratic Experience*

"Mr Boorstin tells the story of the invention of a new democratic culture and the reorientation of the national character through countless little revolutions in economy, technology, and social rearrangements . . . Illuminated by reflections that are original, judicious and sagacious . . ." Henry Steele Commager

"A huge, fascinating omnibus of a book . . . an exhilarating adventure that carries us along the highways and byways of a national history like no other." John K. Hutchens, *Book of the Month Club News*

"I have learned a great deal about the USA from Professor Boorstin's . . . He knows this country of ours as few historians know it . . . I read his book with delight and gratitude." Saul Bellow

THE AMERICANS
The Democratic Experience

Daniel J. Boorstin

'American life is a powerful solvent.'
GEORGE SANTAYANA

PHOENIX
PRESS

5 UPPER SAINT MARTIN'S LANE
LONDON
WC2H 9EA

A PHOENIX PRESS PAPERBACK

This paperback edition published in 2000
by Phoenix Press,
a division of The Orion Publishing Group Ltd,
Orion House, 5 Upper St Martin's Lane,
London WC2H 9EA

A CIP catalogue record for this book
is available from the British Library.

Printed in Great Britain by
Clays Ltd, St Ives plc

ISBN 1 84212 074 3

For Ruth

CHANGES

*In 1868, as the first transcontinental railroad was nearing comple-
tion, Charles Francis Adams, Jr., predicted the impending transformation of American experience:*

"Here is an enormous, an incalculable force . . . let loose suddenly
upon mankind; exercising all sorts of influences, social, moral, and
political; precipitating upon us novel problems which demand immediate solution; banishing the old, before the new is half matured
to replace it; bringing the nations into close contact before yet the
antipathies of race have begun to be eradicated; giving us a history
full of changing fortunes and rich in dramatic episodes. Yet, with the
curious hardness of a material age, we rarely regard this new power
otherwise than as a money-getting and time-saving machine. . . . not
many of those . . . who fondly believe they control it, ever stop to
think of it as . . . the most tremendous and far-reaching engine of
social change which has ever either blessed or cursed mankind.
. . . Perhaps if the existing community would take now and then the
trouble to pass in review the changes it has already witnessed it
would be less astounded at the revolutions which continually do and
continually must flash before it; perhaps also it might with more
grace accept the inevitable, and cease from useless attempts at making a wholly new world conform itself to the rules and theories of a
bygone civilization."

*The century after the Civil War was to be an Age of Revolution
—of countless, little-noticed revolutions, which occurred not in the
halls of legislatures or on battlefields or on the barricades but in
homes and farms and factories and schools and stores, across the
landscape and in the air—so little noticed because they came so
swiftly, because they touched Americans everywhere and every day.
Not merely the continent but human experience itself, the very
meaning of community, of time and space, of present and future,
was being revised again and again; a new democratic world was
being invented and was being discovered by Americans wherever
they lived.*

CONTENTS

BOOK TWO
THE DECLINE OF THE MIRACULOUS

Book One

EVERYWHERE COMMUNITIES

"When you get there, there isn't any there there."

GERTRUDE STEIN

A M E R I C A N S reached out to one another. A new civilization found new ways of holding men together—less and less by creed or belief, by tradition or by place, more and more by common effort and common experience, by the apparatus of daily life, by their ways of thinking about themselves. Americans were now held together less by their hopes than by their wants, by what they made and what they bought, and by how they learned about everything. They were held together by the new names they gave to the things they wanted, to the things they owned, and to themselves. These everywhere communities floated over time and space, they could include anyone without his effort, and sometimes without his knowing. Men were divided not by their regions or their roots, but by objects and notions that might be anywhere and could be everywhere. Americans lived now not merely in a half-explored continent of mountains and rivers and mines, but in a new continent of categories. These were the communities where they were told (and where they believed) that they belonged.

PART ONE

The Go-Getters

"Most of the time we were solitary adventurers in a great land as fresh and new as a spring morning, and we were free and full of the zest of darers."

CHARLES GOODNIGHT

"Money-getters are the benefactors of our race."

P. T. BARNUM

"To live outside the law you must be honest."

BOB DYLAN

THE YEARS AFTER the Civil War when the continent was only partly explored were the halcyon days of the Go-Getters. They went in search of what others had never imagined was there to get. The Go-Getters made something out of nothing, they brought meat out of the desert, found oil in the rocks, and brought light to millions. They discovered new resources, and where there seemed none to be discovered, they invented new ways of profiting from others who were trying to invent and to discover. Lawyers, who in the Old World had been the staid props of tradition, became a Go-Getting profession, profiting from the hopes of others, from the successes and frustrations of boosters and transients. Federalism itself became a profitable commodity, making business for lawyers and hotelkeepers and bartenders, and building improbable new cities. The moralism of Americans, even their high-minded desire to prohibit vice, itself became a resource, created new enterprises, accumulating fortunes for those who satisfied illicit wants. All over the continent—on the desert, under the soil, in the rocks, in the hearts of cities—appeared surprising new opportunities.

1

"Gold from the Grass Roots Up"

AMERICANS WOULD BECOME the world's great meat eaters. In the Old World, beef was the diet of lords and men of wealth. For others it was a holiday prize. But American millions would eat like lords—because of the efforts of American Go-Getters in the half-charted West.

The Western combination of desert, inedible forage, and unmarketable wild animals offered a puzzling, enticing opportunity to men in search of new wealth. It was seized by Western cattlemen and cowboys. Their great opportunity was to use apparently useless land that belonged to nobody. "There's gold from the grass roots down," declared California Joe, a guide in the gold-rich Dakotas in the 1870's, "but there's more gold from the grass roots up." Westerners took some time to discover that gold. But once they discovered it, a rush for the new gold was on. That rush would transform much of the West, would shape the American diet, and created some of the most distinctive American institutions and folk heroes—including the cowboy.

NOBODY KNOWS EXACTLY how it all began. Legend has it that sometime toward the end of the Civil War a heavy-laden government ox train traveling through the northern plains of eastern Wyoming was caught in a snowstorm and had to be abandoned. The driver returned the next spring to see what had become of his cargo. Instead of the skeletons he had expected to find, he saw his oxen, living, fat, and healthy. How had they survived?

The answer lay in a resource that unknowing Americans had trampled underfoot in their haste to cross the "Great American Desert" to reach lands that sometimes proved barren. In the Eastern parts of the United States the preferred grass for forage was a cultivated plant. It grew well with enough rain, then when cut and stored it would "cure" and become nourishing "hay" for winter feed. But in the dry grazing lands of the great West, that familiar blue-joint grass was often killed by drought. To raise cattle out there seemed risky or even hopeless.

Who could imagine a fairy-tale grass that required no rain and somehow made it possible for cattle to feed themselves all winter? But the surprising Western wild grasses were just like that. They had wonderfully convenient features that made them superior to the grasses cultivated by Eastern cattlemen. Variously known as buffalo grass, grama grass, or mesquite grass, they were not only immune to drought; the lack of summer and autumn rains actually preserved them. They were not juicy like the cultivated Eastern grasses, but had short, hard stems. And they did not need to be "cured" in a barn, but dried right where they grew on the ground. When they dried in this way they remained naturally sweet and nourishing through the winter. Cattle left outdoors to fend for themselves thrived on this God-given hay. And the cattle themselves helped plant the fresh grass year after year, for they trampled the natural seeds firmly into the soil to be watered by the melting snows of winter and the occasional rains of spring. The dry summer air cured them, much as storing in a barn cured the cultivated grasses.

In winter the drifts of snow, dissolving under the warm breath of the cattle, enlarged the range which in summer was limited by lack of water. Even when deep snow covered the grama grass, the Western range offered "browse feed" in the form of low shrubs. The white sage (*Eurotia lanata;* sometimes called winter fat) had, like other sages, its own remarkable qualities, for its nutritious value improved after it had been through a frost.

The Western cattle, too, had surprising virtues all their own. The great career of the Texas Longhorns had begun in Spain. Their ancestors had been brought over by the Spanish explorers and missionaries, who raised them for beef or for the bullfight. By the eighteenth century thousands of head, strayed from the missions, were roaming wild. When settlers from the United States came to the Mexican province of Texas in great numbers in the 1830's, they found large stocks of wild cattle bearing no brand or any other mark of ownership. To acquire a herd of Texas Longhorns required only the skill of the hunter. Texans, forgetting that these were descended from Spanish cattle, began to think of them as native wild animals— "wilder than the deer."

When the knowledgeable Army scientist Major William H. Emory was surveying the southern boundary of Texas in 1857 after the Mexican War, he reported that "hunting the wild horses and cattle is the regular business of the inhabitants of Laredo and other towns along the Rio Grande." But such hunting was no child's play. "The wild cattle of Texas, miscalled tame," were, according to an experienced hunter, "fifty times more dangerous to footmen than the fiercest buffalo." In the years after Texas' independence, they ranged over most of the state. This was the cow that made the cowboy.

Seldom has a wild animal so shaped the life of a civilized people. We read with incredulity how the buffalo dominated the life of the Plains Indians, yet the Texas Longhorn wielded a similar power over thousands of Western Americans. One consequence was, as J. Frank Dobie has explained, that "America's Man on Horseback" was "not a helmeted soldier, but a booted cowboy" who had his own kind of pride and insolence and self-confidence. The Texas Longhorn put the cowboy on horseback, kept him in the saddle, and fixed the rhythm of his life. The wildness of the Wild West, then, was in large part the wildness of the Texas Longhorn.

"In Texas," the saying went, "cattle live for the sake of man, but in all other countries, man lives for the sake of his cattle." Old World peasants were accustomed to coddle their cattle, and in harsh weather brought them indoors to sleep with the family. The "well-bred" Shorthorn cow of the East, as the cowboys remarked, had been spoiled by civilization. "Take her away from her sheltered surroundings and turn her loose on the range, and she is as helpless as most duchesses would be if left on a desert island." But since the Longhorns had preserved the wild animal's ability to fend for itself, the Western cattleman was saved much of the trouble of looking after them. Their long, sharp horns were no mere ornament, for the mother cows knew how to use them against wolves and others who attacked their calves. The Longhorns liked water and were ingenious at finding it. Ranging in solitude or in small groups, they did not require the large water source of a traveling herd. When a number of cows traveled together with their brood, they even developed their own lookout system. Two at a time would stand guard against the wolves while the other cows took the long trip to water, and then returned to refresh their own calves with milk.

The wild animal's sense of smell enabled the mother Longhorn to care for her own. Her bloodhound's nose could make the difference between life and death. Experienced cowboys driving cattle in desperate need of water would let the lead steer act as guide. Longhorns were said to be able to smell a shower fifteen miles away. Stories told how trusting cowboys were finally rewarded by a remote solitary lake or a hidden stream after a forty-mile trek.

The Longhorn's skill at finding food became a legend. Contrary to common report, his cloven hoofs actually made it impossible for him to paw snow or ice off the grass, but he was independent and resourceful in finding other food in winter. He had a remarkable ability to graze *up*. There was the apocryphal story of the dry cowhide (with bones inside) seen hanging high up in a tree. "Great browsers, those cattle of mine," the owner is supposed to have explained. "Spring of the year, and that old Longhorn clumb the elm like a squirrel to eat the buds, and jest accidentally hung himself." In sober fact, the Texas breed really did raise their forefeet on the cottonwood limbs to reach twigs and leaves, and they used their horns to pull down the long blossoms of the Spanish dagger. They could live on prickly pear, and where there was no grass, they browsed like deer on the shoots of trees and bushes. They were supposed to have the limber neck of a goat, a mouth that could chew and a stomach that could digest the thorns of cactus and chaparral—together with a barometric sense to warn of oncoming storms.

The Texas breed, destined to make so many men so wealthy, had been naturally bred to thrive "on air and scenery." What made them a rich resource was the vast unappropriated, unfenced West. In the scrubby, water-poor stretches thousands of miles northward of the Rio Grande, the Longhorns needed not tens or hundreds of acres, but hundreds of thousands of acres. The Longhorns required the bigness of Texas.

The fortunes of cattlemen were creatures of the public domain. While cattlemen sometimes called that "God's Country," they were reluctant to acknowledge their tenancy. Like the railroad builders, they believed themselves the rightful beneficiaries of the government. But while the railroad men received only particular parcels along their rights of way, cattlemen claimed a residual title to the whole undivided West. They made it theirs by ranging their cattle all over. "Free grass" was the foundation of their life and their living. "Our Eastern farmers are giving up the cattle-breeding," General James S. Brisbin explained in *The Beef Bonanza; or, How to Get Rich on the Plains,* in 1881. "They cannot compete with plains beef, for while their grazing lands cost them $50.00, $75.00, and $100.00 per acre, and hay has to be cut for winter feeding, the grazing lands in

the West have no market value, and the cattle run at large all winter
—the natural grasses curing on the ground and keeping the stock fat
even in January, February, and March." Brisbin could not imagine
"why people remain in the overcrowded East" when out West, fortunes were there for the taking.

THE RANGE-CATTLE INDUSTRY, then, seemed made for the
Go-Getter. The hero of the Western success saga was bright and
enterprising, housing a strong character in a sturdy physique—the
first American athletic idol. A hybrid of Davy Crockett and Horatio
Alger, he could not have won his fortune without the agility to dodge
Indian arrows, the stamina to ride for days, and the boldness to match
fists with all comers.

If he was as versatile as John Wesley Iliff he was a herd builder, a
trailblazer, and a city founder. Born in 1831 on a prosperous Ohio
farm, Iliff attended Ohio Wesleyan, a newly founded booster college
—one of the scores of optimistic little institutions founded in the
hope that cities would grow up to nourish them. In 1856 when his
father offered to give him $7,500 if he would settle on a good Ohio
farm, young Iliff refused, and (so the story went) asked instead for a
mere $500 so he could make his start in the West. His first stop was
a rendezvous in April 1857 with some friends in eastern Kansas Territory, where he helped lay out a new town, to be called Ohio City.
Lumber was hauled from Kansas City for the very first building—
characteristically a two-story hotel. Iliff, after raising money by popular subscription, built the first store, then secured some farmland.
Those were the days when Kansas was bleeding from its wounds in
the antislavery struggle. Murder was a common weapon of both pro-
and anti-slavery forces anxious to prevent the proposed state from
falling into the hands of the enemy.

In autumn, 1858, news reached Kansas of gold discovered in
Colorado. By early 1859 Iliff had sold his Kansas property, bought an
ox train and provisions, and joined the rush to Pikes Peak. There,
with two partners, he opened a store on Cherry Creek. By May there
were eleven thousand wagons on the plains moving toward Denver.
When these arrived along the South Platte River, in the neighborhood of Pikes Peak, their owners shed their belongings for the steep
trip through the mountains. Many sold their oxen or put them temporarily in charge of the new "cattle ranches." "Cattle Ranch!" read
an advertisement in the *Rocky Mountain News* on April 23, 1859.
"Our ranch is on the Platte River about three miles below the mouth
of Cherry Creek, where we have built a large and secure 'Correll' in
which the stock put in our care will be put every night. Terms $1 a

Head per month." These ranchers grazed their cattle on the plains, knowing from experience the winter before that their cattle could survive the winter fending for themselves on the native grasses. Iliff and his partners bought worn-out work cattle from the parties coming into Denver, fattened them on the free grass of the plains, and sold the beef at a substantial profit to the mining camps, to butcher shops, and to other wagon trains bound for points farther west.

When the Territory of Colorado was created in 1861, Iliff moved his operations north to the neighborhood of the already flourishing town of Denver. There, along the north banks of the South Platte River, he built a large-scale business reconditioning for sale the trail-weary cattle which the immigrants were only too glad to dispose of. "A great many of their cattle," one of Iliff's friends recalled, "became footsore traveling the sandy roads and had to be sold or traded to ranchmen or left with them. As traffic increased there were more cattle and more ranches, and trading in these 'footsores' became quite a business with the ranchmen, for it did not take long on good grass to rest up one of these steers and as soon as he was able to go to work he was traded for another footsore and sold and put to work." Then Iliff and a few others brought in cows and bulls and began breeding their own herds.

If you knew the range and could organize a crew of cowboys, your expenses were low and your profits could be high. The use of the range was free, and there was your year-round feed. Corrals were built from local materials that cost nothing, from adobe, or from poles found along the creeks. A few cowboys at $30 to $40 a month were all the labor required. Beef on the hoof sold by the living pound. Cattle fed on the native grasses of the range might gain one quarter of their original weight in a few months.

Risks also were there: some ranchers lost as much as one third of their herd on the range each winter. But the risks could be reduced by shrewd management, and Iliff succeeded in keeping his winter losses down to about 5 percent. The Indians, too, were a real and constant threat. When Iliff started his herd in 1861 he was lucky to have his own intelligence agency in the form of a neighboring fur trader whose family connections (he had married both the twin daughters of Chief Swift Bird of the Oglalas) enabled him to warn Iliff when Indians were about to attack. In 1862, when Indian raids had increased in Wyoming, the Postmaster General ordered the mail route up there abandoned and brought down along the South Platte, which meant more business for Iliff.

Iliff profited from the Indian menace in more ways than one. He made a small fortune by supplying meat to federal troops in remote outposts so they could fight the Indians. Then, after a region had been pacified and the local Indians were confined to reservations, he did just as well by selling beef to the federal troops to feed the Indians.

When the railroads came, the whole Eastern market was suddenly opened to Western cattle. And it took beef to build the railroads through the West. At the end of the Civil War when General Grenville Dodge, the road's chief engineer, decided that the Union Pacific would not go near Denver and through Berthoud Pass but through southern Wyoming, Cheyenne became a boom town. By November 1867, most of the town of Julesburg, Colorado, was moved to Cheyenne on flatcars. The foresighted Iliff boldly signed contracts to deliver cattle by the thousands to Union Pacific construction gangs and to the troops guarding them against Indians.

WHERE WOULD ILIFF find these thousands, and how would they be delivered? He needed help from another type of Western Go-Getter. The cattleman-trailblazer was as essential to the Western cattle business as the railroad builder was to the great industries of the East. Seizing the peculiar opportunity of unsettled, unfenced America, he made beef-on-the-hoof into its own transportation. The rewards were rich when steers, bought for $3 or $4 a head in Texas, sold for $35 or $40 a head up North.

Big money went to men who could organize the long drive. Charles Goodnight was such a man, and Iliff gave him his chance. Born in Illinois in 1836, Goodnight had lived in Texas since 1845; after the Civil War he began trailing cattle north. In 1868 Goodnight agreed to deliver $40,000 worth of Texas cattle to Iliff's camp near Cheyenne. Since there was no trail going up that way, and of course no railroad to carry them, Goodnight with his partner Oliver Loving made a new trail of their own. The Goodnight-Loving Trail started in northcentral Texas near Dallas, came through the valley of the Pecos, northward across eastern New Mexico and Colorado and ended just above the Union Pacific route in southern Wyoming. Goodnight delivered the cattle, which Iliff sold at a good profit: some to local butchers, some to railroad crews, and the rest in carloads on the new Union Pacific to dealers in far-off Chicago.

To deliver that first big herd of Texas stock to Wyoming, three thousand head of cattle across eight hundred miles, required no less skill than to command an ocean liner across the Atlantic in uncertain weather. The cattle, of course, moved on their own legs, but the vehicle that carried them was the organized drive.

The cowboy crew gave shape to the mile-long herd, kept the cattle from bunching up into a dense, unwieldy mass or from stringing out to a thin, discontinuous thread. At the front were two of the most experienced men (called "pointers"), who navigated the herd, following the course set by the foreman. Bringing up the rear were three steady cowboys whose job it was "to look out for the weaker cattle—the drags. Since the speed of the herd was determined by the drags, it was their duty to see that the stronger cattle were kept forward and out of the way, so that the weaker cattle would not be impeded. This was called 'keeping up the corners.' " The rest of the crew were stationed along the sides, the "swing," to keep the herd compact and of uniform width. The men were rotated from front to rear and back toward the front (the nearer the point, the lighter the work) to divide the burden on the men and the horses. Communication on the trail, where the rumble of hoofs smothered words, was by hand signals, mostly borrowed from the Plains Indians.

Controlling the speed of the herd called for experience. "The column would march either slow or fast, according to the distance the side men rode from the line [center of the trail]. Therefore, when we had a long drive to make between watering places, the men rode in closer to the line. Under normal conditions the herd was fifty to sixty feet across, the width being governed by the distance we had to go before resting. Narrowing the string was called 'squeezing them down.' Ten feet was the lowest limit, for then gaps came, and the cattle would begin trotting to fill up the spaces. The pointers checked them in front, for they were never allowed to trot. After a herd was handled for a month or two, they became gentler, and it was necessary to ride a little closer to obtain the same results." The horses (called the "remuda") which were brought along as spares to provide remounts were in care of a wrangler who kept them moving along together, just in front of the herd. To feed the men there had to be a chuck wagon, carrying food and utensils, which the cook would drive fast ahead to the next camping place so that food could be ready when the herd arrived.

At night, guards making their rounds would sing and whistle (the veteran cowman Andy Adams explained) "so that the sleeping herd may know that a friend and not an enemy is keeping vigil over their dreams." A well-serenaded herd would be less apt to stampede. Cowboy "hymns" they were called, because their tunes were compounded from childhood memories of church services. But their words told the exploits of famous horse races, addressed the cattle with endearment or blaspheming, repeated advertising slogans from coffee cans, or simply sprinkled profanity between nonsense syllables.

Apart from Indians, the great sudden peril was the stampede. And nothing was more terrifying than a stampede at night when three thousand cattle, which a moment before had been quietly dozing in the random postures of sleep, would suddenly rouse to become a thundering mass. They churned around, ever to the right, while the cowboy, trusting his life to his horse, joined with his fellows in a risky encircling tactic. By holding the cattle in the churning circle and pressing inward, the cowboys tried to squeeze the circle smaller and smaller until the herd became a compact "mill" and ground to a halt. If the cowboys failed to throw the herd into a mill, all was lost. The cattle would fly out like sparks, disappearing into the night. Even the toughest cowboys confessed that the stampede gave them a foretaste of hell. "The heat developed by a large drove of cattle during a stampede," Goodnight recalled, "was surprising, and the odor given off by the clashing horns and hoofs was nearly overpowering. Sometimes in cool weather it was uncomfortably warm on the leeward side of a moving herd, and to guard against loss in weight and muscular strength from the effects of this heat, the experienced trail manager always aimed to keep his cattle well distributed while they were in motion. Animal heat seems to attract electricity, especially when the cattle are wet, and after a storm I have seen the faces of men riding with a herd scorched as if some furnace blast had blazed against them." Cowboys found themselves riding blind through the night, unable to see the prairie-dog holes, the gullies, the precipices, which even in daylight would have been treacherous.

Sometimes, after weeks on the trail, the men were as jumpy as the cattle, and then it took a firm hand to prevent trouble. The foremen and owner, according to Goodnight, were "responsible for the lives of their men, not only against Indians so far as possible, but against each other in all cases." Before starting on a trail drive, Goodnight made it a rule "to draw up an article of agreement, setting forth what each man was to do. The main clause stipulated that if one shot another he was to be tried by the outfit and hanged on the spot, if found guilty." Since the successful drive had to be sober and orderly, drivers like Goodnight forbade liquor, gambling, and even swearing, on the trail.

Charles Goodnight achieved fame and fortune trailing cattle north by the thousands. In 1877 he joined with an Irishman, John George Adair, to build the JA Ranch, which soon counted one hundred thousand cattle and a million acres. He founded the first cattlemen's association to fight cattle thieves in the Texas Panhandle. He developed new equipment for the drive and the ranch—a newly designed stirrup that would not turn over, a new chuck box, a safe sidesaddle. In his effort to improve Texas Longhorns he bred them with the Eastern Herefords and Shorthorns, and he crossed the Polled Angus cattle with the buffalo to produce a new breed, called "cattalo."

After the death of his first wife, to whom he had been married for fifty-five years, Goodnight remarried at the age of ninety-one, and had a child by this marriage before his death in 1929 at the age of ninety-three. But more than anything else, he loved the life of a trailblazer and cattledrover. "All in all my years on the trail were the happiest I have lived. There were many hardships and dangers, of course, that called on all a man had of endurance and bravery; but when all went well there was no other life so pleasant."

COW TOWNS, A BY-PRODUCT of the Western cattle trade, were as American as the cowboys themselves. To build a cow town called for the ability to imagine that things could be very different from the way they were. One man who had this imagination in great measure was Joseph G. McCoy. In his *Historic Sketches of the Cattle Trade of the West and Southwest* (1874), McCoy left his own vivid record, which reeks of cattle and echoes the hopeful hyperbole of the West. Born in central Illinois of a Virginia farmer and a Kentucky mother, he went to Texas in 1867, a young man "with an earnest desire to do something that would alike benefit humanity as well as himself." Like Goodnight and others, he was impressed by the great numbers of cattle in Texas, and the much higher price of cattle up North, and he aimed to find a way to bring the cattle to market. What he imagined was not so much a new trail as a new destination. Why not establish a depot on one of the Northern railroads "whereat the Southern drover and Northern buyer would meet upon an equal footing, and both be undisturbed by mobs or swindling thieves." Up there the drover would be free to refuse an unreasonable offer, since from that spot he could always ship his stock east. McCoy imagined that such gatherings of thousands of head of cattle would awaken and enrich some sleepy Kansas town.

This was not an entirely original idea. In 1866, bold Texans had driven cattle north to Sedalia, Missouri, on the Missouri Pacific Railroad. Almost a quarter million Texas cattle arrived there that year. To drive cattle through southeastern Kansas or southwestern Missouri in those days took courage. Texas drovers found their passage blocked by hardy settlers who disliked having their crops trampled and feared having their own cattle infected. Thieves would stampede a herd under cover of night, and then offer to hunt up the cattle and return them for $5 a head. The cattle that survived to market were so thinned from hard usage that they brought little profit.

"There are few occupations in life," recalled Joseph G. McCoy, "wherein a man will hold by so brittle a thread a large fortune as by droving. In fact, the drover is nearly as helpless as a child, for but a

single misstep or wrong move and he may lose his entire herd, representing and constituting all his earthly possessions. None understood
this better than the mobs of outlaws that annually infested the cattle
trail leading from Texas to Sedalia, Missouri. If the drover had ready
money, and could obtain an interview with the leader of the mob,
it was not difficult to secure safe transmit for his herd, but it was
always expensive, and few drovers were disposed to buy a recognition of their legal rights; many of them had not the money." In that
very year of 1866, James M. Dougherty, a young man who had not
yet reached his twentieth birthday, was bringing up his herd of over
one thousand head of cattle from Texas, hoping to sell them profitably in the St. Louis market. In his memoirs McCoy reported Dougherty's experience:

> Soon after entering the State of Missouri, he was aroused from the
> pleasant revery of beautiful prospects and snug fortune easily won, by
> the appearance of a yelling, armed, organized mob, which ordered him
> to halt. Never in his limited experience had he seen such bipeds as
> constituted that band of self-appointed guardian angels. Dressed in
> coarsest home-spun pantaloons and hunting shirts, with under shirts
> spun of coarsest tow, a pair of rude home made cow-hide shoes, upon
> whose construction the broad ax and jack-plane had figured largely. All
> surmounted with a coon-skin cap of great antiquity and unmistakably
> home manufacture. To this add a score of visages closely resembling the
> orang outang, bearing evidence of the lowest order of humanity, with
> but one overpowering passion—a love for unrectified whisky of the
> deadliest brand. Young Dougherty was told that "them thar steers
> couldn't go an inch fudder. No sare." Dougherty quietly began to rea-
> son with them, but it was like preaching morality to an alligator. No
> sooner did they discover that the drover was a young man and probably
> little experienced in life, than they immediately surrounded him, and
> whilst a part of the mob attacked his comrade and shamefully mal-
> treated him, a half dozen coarse brutes dragged the drover from his
> saddle, disarmed him, tied him fast to a tree with his own picket rope,
> then proceeded to whip him with hickory withes in the most brutal
> manner.

Meanwhile others of the mob were stampeding the herd.

Such incidents as this inspired McCoy to seek a cattle depot farther
west on the railroads—so far west that drovers could bring up their
Texas herds without having to pass through the settled areas of Arkansas and Missouri. He set about trying to interest both the businessmen in the little towns along the Kansas Pacific and the Santa Fe
railroads, and the officials of the railroads themselves. From the president of the Kansas Pacific he received an incredulous smile and the
assurance that they were not willing to risk a dollar in the enterprise.

He next approached the president of the Missouri Pacific, the connecting road that went to St. Louis, who gave him a reception so pompous and contemptuous that McCoy (by his own report) "left the office, wondering what could have been the inscrutable purposes of Jehovah in creating and suffering such a great being to remain on earth, instead of appointing him to manage the universe." But the tireless McCoy finally secured a quotation of rates from the Hannibal & St. Joseph Railroad, which ran from Kansas City toward Chicago. Then he determined to pick the most convenient little town along the Kansas Pacific where he would build stockyards and facilities for loading large numbers of cattle. This would attract the drovers from Texas and so force the railroads to admit that there was good money in carrying cattle.

He proposed his project to leading citizens in Junction City, Solomon City, and Salina, all of whom, according to his own account, regarded him "as a monster threatening calamity and pestilence." But he did not give up. "Abilene in 1867 was a very small, dead place, consisting of about one dozen log huts, low, small, rude affairs, four-fifths of which were covered with dirt for roofing; indeed, but one shingle roof could be seen in the whole city. The business of the burg was conducted in two small rooms, mere log huts, and of course the inevitable saloon, also in a log hut, was to be found." The saloon keeper, the only noteworthy feature of the town, was known throughout the countryside for his colony of pet prairie dogs which he raised for sale to tourists who took them East as curiosities. Abilene was selected, according to McCoy, "because the country was entirely unsettled, well watered, excellent grass, and nearly the entire area of country was adapted to holding cattle. And it was the farthest point east at which a good depot for cattle business could have been made."

Within sixty days McCoy had transformed the village of Abilene into a well-equipped cattle capital, with a shipping yard to accommodate three thousand head, a pair of large Fairbanks scales, a barn, an office, and inevitably "a good three story hotel." McCoy then sent his publicity agent into southern Kansas and Indian Territory "with instructions to hunt up every straggling drove possible (and every drove was straggling, for they had not where to go), and tell them of Abilene." McCoy's agent rode his pony from Junction City for two hundred miles southwesterly across the Arkansas River at the site of the present city of Wichita, thence far down into the Indian country; then turned east until trails of herds were found. "The drove was overtaken, and the owner fully posted in that, to him, all-absorbing topic, to-wit: a good, safe place to drive to, where he could sell or ship his cattle unmolested to other markets. This was joyous news to the drover, for the fear of trouble and violence hung like an incubus over his waking thoughts alike with his sleeping moments. It was almost too good to be believed; could it be possible that some one was about to afford a Texan drover any other reception than outrage and robbery?"

The Texas herds turned toward Abilene. On September 5, 1867, when the first shipment—twenty carloads of cattle—went out from Abilene (which two months earlier had been only a prairie village), Illinois stockmen gathered in tents specially erected for the occasion to celebrate with feast, wine, song, and expansive speeches. By the end of December, thirty-five thousand head of cattle had been shipped through Abilene, and within a few years, the number totaled ten million. In addition to the moral satisfaction he was seeking of really having done something "for posterity," McCoy gained many-sided profits. When McCoy first picked Abilene he gave $2,400 for the whole townsite (with 480 acres). The managers of the Kansas Pacific Railroad had agreed to give McCoy one eighth of the freight on each car of cattle shipped. By the end of the second year, this gave McCoy a claim against the Kansas Pacific amounting to $200,000. The company then refused to fulfill their contract because, they now said, they had never actually expected that the business would amount to anything! But this did not dampen McCoy's enthusiasm. He became mayor of Abilene, and—booster that he was—produced for the census of 1890 an optimistic report on the livestock industry which brought large investments to his part of the West.

Abilene was only one example of this flourishing new subspecies of the American upstart community. Some, like Dodge City, which boasted herself "The Queen of Cowtowns," "The Wickedest Little City in America," eventually became famous in song and story and film and television. But there were many others: Schuyler, and Fort Kearney and North Platte and Ogallala and Sydney, in Nebraska; Pine Bluffs and Green River and Rock Creek and Laramie and Hillsdale and Cheyenne, in Wyoming; Miles City and Glendive and Helena, in Montana. Some were destined to become a new brand of ghost town. A few flourished for reasons that had nothing to do with the visions of their founders. In the 1870's and 1880's their great prosperity was still before them.

2

Rituals of the Open Range

THE CATTLE AND THE RANGE, there for the taking, invited Go-Getters to compete, but also brought them together. To make a living out of cattle you could not go it alone. We romanticize the "lone cowboy," communing with his horse, with the landscape, and with himself. But it was no easier for the lone cowboy to prosper safely in the West than it was for a lone immigrant to cross the ocean, or for a westward-mover to cross the continent by himself. The very landscape somehow led men to rely on one another, and to invent new community rituals to sort out their property and hallow each man's right to his own.

On the cattle trail, individual Americans who had recently faced each other on Eastern battlefields of the Civil War became reunited. "The Rebel," wrote Andy Adams in his *Log of a Cowboy*, "was a good bunkie and a hail companion, this being his sixth trip over the trail." It was a year before the two cowboys discovered they had been on opposite sides during the "late unpleasantness," and by then "the Rebel" was an amiable nickname like any other. In little metropolises like Abilene, Northerners and Southerners found the mutual respect needed to make business prosper. In 1874, when back East the sectional passions of Reconstruction were still bitter, Joseph G. McCoy reported that transactions involving many thousands of dollars were made orally only, and complied with to the letter. "Indeed, if this were not so they would often experience great hardships in transacting their business as well as getting through the country with their stock. . . . the Western Cattle Trade has been no feeble means of bringing about an era of better feeling between Northern and Texas men by bringing them in contact with each other in commercial transactions. The feeling today existing in the breasts of all men from both sections are far different and better than they were six years ago." Out West, beyond the force of settled laws, men were not bound by the political miseries of the more civilized East.

THE WEST WAS a good place for the refugee from older laws, but it offered no refuge from community. The cattleman's drive north—from Texas to meet the railroad at Abilene or Dodge City—

put cowboys under a near-military regime. A careless leader at the "point" or a sleeping sentry might mean disaster for the herd and death for the whole outfit. Men had to suppress their personal hatreds, confine their tempers, and submit to the strict law of the trail, otherwise they might find themselves abandoned or strung up or sent off alone hundreds of miles from nowhere.

The drives north were of course the longest and the most closely supervised of the cowboy's organized efforts. But they were not the only ones. The rhythm of every year was fixed by another organized communal effort, a kind of cowboy rendezvous. The Western cattle business would not have been possible without widespread faith in its own signs and symbols, and a willingness to observe its rituals. These arose out of the peculiar conditions of the American West and out of this novel form of property: wild cattle caught to be fed on wild grass on a no man's land.

Without benefit of law, ranchers had divided the range among themselves by a system that was informal, that had no standing in court, but was enforced by the cattlemen themselves. In the heyday of the cattleman—the two decades after the Civil War—each ran his stock on a portion of the range which he had taken for his own. Ideally one's range would run from a stream bed up to the top of a ridge where another cattleman's range began. The openness of the open range meant that no fence divided one man's range from another's, for in strict law it all belonged to everybody. These Great Plains "ranches" were measured not in acres but in square miles. Each rancher tried to keep his own stock inside his own pre-empted range by assigning a staff of cowboys to "ride the line" between his range and his neighbor's. Stationed in twos in remote "line camps," these line-riders patrolled the ranch borders, coaxing their owner's cattle inward toward the center of his holding, while drifting the neighbor's cattle in the other direction. But on the wide, unfenced range, the cattle did mix. There had to be a way of separating one man's cattle from another's, before they were driven to market.

Out of these needs of the open range, then, came the "roundup." A time of separating one man's property from another's, it became the harvest festival, when each rancher discovered how much his herd had increased. The importance of these two functions—of separating and of harvesting—varied, of course, with time and place. In the early days of the dry Southwest when ranches were far apart, when ranchers commonly bounded the land they called their own by some stream bed, the roundup was mainly a time of harvest. And then the roundup was a relatively simple operation. A couple of neighboring ranchers would agree on a time and place when they drove all the surrounding cattle to a common meeting point. Such a roundup was strenuous and inevitably required miles of riding over rough terrain, but it did not require elaborate organization, since only a few owners were concerned.

The Great Roundup—a community ritual in the days of free grass on the Great Plains—was quite another matter. Dozens of cattlemen had allowed their stock to intermingle on the open range, and there had to be a sorting time. Under these circumstances the spring roundup required far-reaching organization. The state or territorial cattle association divided the range into districts, each to conduct its own roundup. The arduous work of the roundup was distributed among crews supplied by the cattlemen concerned, each outfit providing a number of cowboys proportionate to the size of its herd. These cowboys, once brought together, worked under a roundup captain or boss, commonly elected by the cowmen of the roundup district, which might be forty miles wide and a hundred miles long. Split up into bands which covered the countryside under the command of lieutenants, they drove to the rendezvous all the cattle they encountered, and the gathered cattle might number several thousand. In some little valley, then, the assembled cowboys would do their work, "cutting out" the cows and calves from the rest of the herd, and giving each calf the brand of the mother it followed. Cattle which carried the brand of a distant owner would be separated out so the cowboys could "throw them over"—set them drifting in the direction of the range of their owner.

Chasing the cows and calves up and down ravines and across country wore down the horses even before it wore out the men, and each cowboy would bring his own string of eight or ten horses. A cowboy on roundup, riding scores of miles, had to keep a steady seat on frisky horses alive with the smell of spring and alert to a wild landscape. He had to know how to manage cattle by the hundreds and by the individual. He had to sit a jumpy bronc while he wielded the rope to down a lively calf. Much as the skills of the joust became the sport of medieval knights, these skills of the roundup became the sport of the cattlemen.

The first name used for roundup was "rodeo." It came from the Spanish *rodear* meaning "to surround," the purpose of the cowboys being to surround and bring in all the cattle on the ranges. Only much later, after the open range had disappeared, did the skills of the roundup come to be practiced for their own sake, and "rodeo" came to mean an exhibition staged for the amusement of spectators. A rodeo then was nothing but a show-off roundup, demonstrating for dudes the strength and grace and skill which in the heyday of the open range had been witnessed only by the cowboys themselves.

While the spring roundup was a harvest ritual, it was also a ritual of ownership. And its climax was the branding—burning an owner's mark into the hide of each recently-arrived calf. When the cattle had all been herded together, the mounted cowboy expertly "cut out" a cow and its calf, separating them from the herd. Then with his rope he downed the calf to drag it over to the branding men ready beside a fire. Glowing in the fire were a number of branding irons, each bearing the mark of one of the outfits in the roundup. The branding men glanced at the brand on the cow which the calf was following, then took the matching iron out of the fire. The smell and sizzle of the hide and the bawl of the calf announced that somebody's herd had grown by one. A "tally man," pencil in hand, recorded the numbers assigned by the roundup to each brand owner, and from this tally each rancher estimated his profits.

As spring brought the "calf roundup," so the fall brought another, commonly called the "beef roundup." Now the main purpose was to separate out the mature, fatted animals ready to be driven to the railhead to be turned into cash. In July or August, this would also be a cattleman's harvest. But when men thought of the verve and excitement of the roundup they usually thought of spring in the air and the bawling, leaping dogeys all about.

Those who idealize the cowboy find in the roundup the supreme symbol of cowboy justice. A cattleman's life was the years between his first and his last roundup. And the customs of the roundup showed a scrupulous concern to appropriate for each man his due. If the brands borne by a particular cow were too numerous or too confused to indicate one certain owner, its calf was not branded to any owner. Instead that calf was credited to the whole association, to help defray the common expenses. If one calf was mistakenly given the brand of the wrong owner, another calf was "traded back" in its stead, and given the omitted brand. If a cow was found with the brand of a remote rancher, it was "thrown over," drifted toward his proper range. The whole ritual was designed to make public, formal, and regular each man's appropriation of his own increase, clearly separating it from the intermixed herds which fed on the open range.

TROUBLED BY how to establish property in cattle if the land on which they roamed belonged to nobody in particular, cattlemen had fixed a new set of symbols, burned into the hide of each animal. They found a secure sense of property in these improvised documents of title. Where people and their cattle were on the move, far from courts and lawyers, paper documents were of little use. Who wanted to carry them? Where could they be safely stored?

Better make the cattle into their own documents of title. Then wherever a man took his cattle he could prove his ownership.

The technical literalism of a London chancery lawyer did not exceed that of a skilled cattleman interpreting the marks on a cow that bore many brands. The lore of cattle brands showed the technicality and subtlety that every society gives to its most sacred symbols. It was the cowboy's iconography. While of course each man recognized his own brands and marks, it took knowledge, experience, and skill to assign the ownership of a much-branded animal.

A calf, at its first roundup, was branded by a red-hot iron carrying a pattern and pressed against its hide. But there were other ways and times of branding. The "running iron," for example, was simply a straight poker, used like a pencil to draw any desired brand, which then was called a "running brand." The "stamp iron," shaped like a block of type, bore one particular "set brand" which was affixed with a single motion. Brands were of different sizes, but usually were not less than two inches high and four inches long, and not more than seven inches in either direction. Of course the brand grew with the animal, so that a brand which was only three inches high on a calf might measure twelve inches a few years later. Cattlemen, learning that too-large brands on the wrong part of the animal would reduce the value of the hides, burned their signs only on the hip, shoulder, or neck.

The particular design which a man chose for his brand was shaped by his own imagination and ingenuity, limited by choices already registered by others. At first there was only informal agreement on the assignment of brands, but by the 1880's, territories and states issued official brand books. These books illustrated the brands and the part of the animal on which they were to be affixed, and indicated the other accompanying marks (such as an "earmark," cutting off the left or the right ear, or both ears; or notching the dewlap). An owner might devise any combination of letters, figures, or doodles that struck his fancy, but since the brand was the hallmark of his ranch, he would have to live with it for years. At first the rancher might simply use his own initials, those of his wife or child, or of the name of his ranch, but after brands were registered by the hundreds, there were many interesting, whimsical, and cryptic combinations. One rancher, for example, adopted the brand "T M," which, he explained, meant that his ranch was "Twenty Miles" from a saloon.

But whimsy could not freely rule, for it was important to have a brand that a thief could not easily alter. For example, the letter "C" could easily be changed into the letter "O" or into a zero; the letter "I" could be made into any one of a dozen other letters, or seem to become the number "1" when a numeral was placed after it. Various devices in the design such as crowding letters together, framing them in lines, or inserting a short horizontal mark in the open end, would make alterations difficult.

Cattle rustlers elaborated techniques for modifying brands. If a rustler actually managed to get employed as a branding man at a roundup, he might imprint a "slow brand" on some of the calves, without others knowing what he was doing. A "slow brand" was a brand that was not registered, and which the rustler had invented because it belonged to nobody. Handling the branding iron himself, he would burn it into the hide so lightly that it would soon disappear; then at his later convenience he would claim the calf by burning on his own registered brand. A simpler device was the "hair brand"— any brand so lightly applied that over it the rustler could later apply his own brand.

Brands were described in an esoteric lingo, and reading the brands aloud became a highly skilled exercise. Just as any rancher could decide how his own name should be pronounced, so he could also decide the order in which the elements of his brand were to be described. But there were some well-recognized conventions. Thus "A2" was called the "Big A Two." "Lazy" was the word for an upended letter or one lying on its side; which made an "M" written vertically with a line underneath the "Lazy M Bar." A piece of a curve enclosing a letter was called a "quarter circle." A ring bisected by a vertical line was called a "buckle." A letter like a "W" when drawn in curves was called a "Running W." Two outward-curving lines on either side of a letter or numeral (say a 7) made it a "Flying 7." There was a copious lexicon of terms—"wallop," "whang-doo-dle," "hogpen," and others—which to the tenderfoot sounded like slang, but to the initiated cattleman had a precise technical meaning. "Ranch lingo is perfectly easy to understand," a cowboy once remarked. "All you've got to do is know in advance what the other fellow means, and then pay no attention to what he says."

The mystique of coats of arms was attached to the brands, which became subjects of an elaborate folklore. Take, for example, the principal brand of the great King Ranch—the Running W. No one knows precisely when Captain Richard King first put this brand on his stock, but he probably began using it in 1867, and it was officially registered in Nueces County, Texas, in 1869. While its technical name in the jargon of brands was the Running W, some preferred the more poetic Spanish name used by the local Mexicans— *Viborita*, or "Little Snake." This figure of a wriggly reptile (which implied *¡Cuidado!*— "Don't Tread on Me!") somehow kept away thieves and trespassers. A more prosaic explanation goes back to Captain King's purchase of the stock of a certain William Mann in 1862, when he acquired three of Mann's brands, one of them being the Running M. Trying to make the Running M distinctively his own, King simply inverted it into a running W. And this particular brand had a number of advantages:

it was open-spaced, without any crossing of lines (where a deep spot in the brand burn attracted screwworms and might heal into a wide blur); it was especially easy to draw with a running iron (if a stamp iron was not at hand), and yet its wriggly shape made it hard to alter. At the same time it was appealingly simple and attractive.

Interpreting the hide of a much-branded cow, then, called for as much familiarity with jargon as the interpretation of an abstract of land title. A brand might indicate not only a particular owner, but a particular kind of transaction, and from all the signs together a knowledgeable cowboy could read the animal's whole life history. Of course the first brand put on a cow, that of its first owner, had been burned on the calf at its first roundup. But often it was not easy to tell which was the first brand. The cow might also bear a "vent brand" or "counter brand," a different version of the original owner's brand, intended to be the first owner's admission of the sale. Then, of course, came the brand of the new owner. Animals which had been in a drive were likely to carry a "road brand," burned on at the beginning of the trip to help distinguish the herd from other animals encountered on the way. In Texas there were also special "county brands" (a different one for each Texas county) on the animal's neck, prescribed by law to make a thief's task more difficult. For then, unless the thief managed to alter the brand to another in the same county where the first brand was registered, he would have to change at least two brands on each stolen animal.

A skilled cowboy with the aid of brand books could know a lot about a cow without having to ask anybody any questions. He could tell in what Texas county the animal began its life, he could know how many different owners there had been, who they were and where they were located, he could see whether the animal had been driven north or had come by rail. It became a favorite Western witticism that "The critter didn't amount to much, but sure carried a lot of reading matter."

Many of the special problems of the West arose from those critters that bore no reading matter at all. These were commonly called "mavericks." They took their name from Samuel A. Maverick (1803–1870), a Texas rancher who, for uncertain reasons, would not brand his calves. Some say he was simply negligent or indolent, others that he aimed to create the presumption that all unbranded animals were his. Whatever the reason, the word "maverick" came to signify any unbranded calf found without an accompanying mother. In the beginning of the cattle trade in Texas these belonged, of course, to whoever found them and first affixed his brand. But later custom allowed a cattleman to brand a maverick only if found on his own

range. The temptation to create mavericks was hard to resist, and
nobody knows how many orphans were created in the "maverick
factories." On the remote range any cowboy with an easy conscience
and a six-shooter could quickly transform somebody else's property
into his own maverick by the simple process of shooting the calf's
mother.

The roundup, a public ritual, was designed to help cowboys resist
these temptations. Branding was usually done in the presence of men
from several ranches. Probably less theft was accomplished by mis-
branding mavericks than by altering the brands on mature animals.
Among the new skills of the American West, few were more highly
developed than those of the "brand artists" (also called "brand blot-
ters" or "brand blotchers"). Unlike the indoor forger of paintings or
antiques, the brand artist was in a wholesale business. While the
penalty for a single detection was death and the profit from each
individual forgery was small, a fast and skillful brand artist could
build a herd in short order, and his forgeries were soon consumed or
dispersed.

The incriminating instrument, the cattledom equivalent of a crow-
bar and burglar's tools, was the "running iron," the simple straight
poker that could be used to make any desired design. The suspicions
it raised were so general that Texas and some other states in the
1870's actually prohibited its use. Anyway, the running iron was
heavy and awkward to carry on the saddle, and prudent rustlers had
other tools. Almost any piece of metal when heated, even a piece of
a broken horseshoe, might serve to blot a brand and make it into
another. A favorite forging tool, light and easy to conceal, was a
length of baling wire or telegraph wire. When folded, it could be
tucked into a pocket, yet could be twisted into many different
brands, and the wire was thin enough to fit neatly into the healed
scars of the brand to be altered.

The skillful brand forger knew not only his brands, but when and
how to "work them over." His addition of a line or two was least likely
to be detected in the days after the roundup when many animals
bore fresh scars. By putting a wet blanket or buckskin over the
animal's hide and burning his brand through it, he could make his
marks match those legal brands that had been made in earlier seasons. Brand artists became so highly skilled that their misdeeds could
not be casually detected from the outside of the living animal. Some
states actually required butchers, on demand, to display the hides of
the animals butchered. A butcher might be in trouble if the hide did
not show, properly imprinted, the legal brand of a lawful seller.

Cattlemen and cowboys generally gave to the brand the combined respect owed to a totem, a hallmark, and a family crest. Ranches took their names from the brands their cattle bore, and cowboys identified themselves by the brand of their outfit. "I'm with the Circle Bar G."

3

PrivateWars for the Public Domain

WHILE THE "LAW OF THE RANGE"—the rhythm of the roundup and the lore of brands—had an appealing precision, answers to some basic questions remained tantalizingly vague. Since the land fed the stock, the ultimate source of all the cattleman's wealth was land. But who had a right to the land? Or to put his stock on the land? Such questions which the older world settled by centuries of custom, by ancient documents and long public acquiescence, in the American West were opened anew. The distinctive disorders of the cattleman's West did not arise because people refused to live by the Ten Commandments or to obey the simple rules of justice. The new problem was not dishonesty but ambiguity.

AMUSED AND UNCOMPREHENDING observers from more settled societies simply said that the naïve Americans had divided the whole world into Good Guys and Bad Guys. East Coast provincial Americans were inclined to accept this caricature. But nothing could have been further from the truth. The peculiar problem of Go-Getter Morality was not that it drew a clear line between Good Guys and Bad Guys. Quite the contrary. Traditional morality was inclined to do precisely that, but Go-Getter Morality was haunted by a New World uncertainty.

That uncertainty became a miasma enveloping the moral precepts and legal rules of the cattleman's West. It was a parable of continuing American moral and legal problems. And it had arisen out of the very opportunities of the West, out of novel resources and unprecedented forms of property. Many of the violent struggles of those days, explained far from the scene as a fight between "law" and "lawlessness," were in fact not that at all. On the scene both the rights and the wrongs seemed divided. And out of these uncertainties grew a novel Western version of civil war.

The ambiguities were never better dramatized than in the so-called Johnson County War in Wyoming in 1892. The celebrated Western feuds between cattlemen and the later invading sheepmen were mainly conflicts between the needs of two different kinds of livestock. Those had obvious parallels in the enclosure movement in western Europe, but the Johnson County War was something new. Here we see the full vagueness of Western morality, the mixing of legality and illegality, of honesty and thievery in a peculiar new concoction. The roots of this particular struggle lay in the Great Plains cattle boom which reached its height about 1883. Brisbin's *Beef Bonanza; or, How to Get Rich on the Plains,* along with many other books and countless rumors and legends, drew millions of pounds sterling from England and Scotland, and thousands of settlers from the eastern United States. "It does not matter where the emi-grant settles in the West, so he comes," urged Brisbin, "and he will almost anywhere soon find himself better off than if he had remained East." Within a few years the range was overstocked with cattle and overrun by people. British cattle corporations reported quick profits of as much as a third on their investments. Foreign speculators imag-ined there could never be too many cattle for the free Western range. But cattlemen on the spot knew better.

Fearing the overgrazing and depletion of the range, and distrust-ing the scores of small operators who had no registered brands of their own and hence were unlikely to respect the brands of others, the established cattlemen organized themselves. Their associations were of course intended to protect the cattle which bore their brands. But they were also protecting the large cattlemen's control over pieces of the open range—the public domain—which, without any legal title, they called their own. By the summer of 1885, cattle prices began to fall. The increased costs of fencing and the heavy dues to the association added to the troubles of a range overcrowded by reckless foreign investors. In addition there were the invading wool growers, whose sheep cropped the grass to extinction, and the invading farmers, whose living depended on keeping out the grazing cattle.

The climax of the cattlemen's woes came with two disastrous win-ters. The killing cold of 1885–86 foreshadowed what was to come, and the unprecedented blizzards of 1886–87 were a catastrophe. While the range was covered by the deepest snow in history, driving winds piled up the starving cattle against fences and tumbled them into ravines. A bad situation had been made even worse by President Grover Cleveland's proclamations under an act of Congress authorizing him to remove unlawful enclosures on the public domain. Ordering all cattle removed from the Indian reservations, he had sent in General Sheridan with federal troops to see that it was done. When government officials removed private fences from the Cheyenne-Arapaho public lands, over two hundred thousand head of cattle were added to the overcrowded range at the beginning of a killing winter. The "improvement" of the original Texas Longhorns, by crossing them with high-grade domesticated Eastern cattle, had made the animals beefier but had begun to deprive them of the hardy, rustling, self-preserving character of the pure Longhorn. Snow turned the range into a slaughterhouse. Carcasses by the thousands littered the range in the spring. For years the lifeless stalks of willows would record the desperate struggle of the animals during that winter to fend off starvation by eating bark.

Experienced Wyoming cattlemen, plagued by falling prices and increasing local hostility from new settlers on land they had thought was theirs alone, did not know where to turn. Their mainstay had been the Wyoming Stock Growers' Association. Another American example of community before government, the Association, when it was formed back in 1873, had only ten members owning altogether about twenty thousand head. But within a dozen years the Association had reached into the neighboring states of Colorado and Nebraska and the territories of Montana and Dakota, and counted four hundred members owning cattle to the number of about two million. Throughout a vast stretch of the West, nearly equal in area to all western Europe, the Association wrote and enforced its own law— its regulations for branding, roundups and cattle drives—where there was no other effective government. Mavericks were to be given the Association brand and auctioned off to help cover the Association costs. It was prohibited to brand any cattle found running loose between February 15 and the spring roundup. Association inspectors were stationed at the large markets and railroad depots, on the lookout for stolen cattle bearing brands registered to members of the Association. Such cattle were returned to their legal owners, or if the distance was too great, the agents sold the cattle and returned the proceeds. The laws of the Association became the law of the range.

In England the fundamental common-law distinction was between land and everything else: between "real property" (land and other forms of property which were attached to the land or had the character of land) and "movables" (personal property or chattels). That distinction seemed adequate to crowded, settled old England, where the basic fact was ownership of land, and where that ownership was anciently and most precisely defined. Medieval feudalism, in the age when the English common law was born, was at once a system of government and a system of land ownership. To own a piece of land meant to possess a fragment of government. But most of the land of the great American West was for all practical purposes at once ownerless and governmentless. You could not tell whose cow it was by seeing whose land it was on. For the land was everybody's. You could not tell whose cow it was by seeing whose custody it was in, for on the trackless range the herds were untended dispersed thousands.

In the American West the old distinctions would not fit. It was not good enough to adopt the jargon of the common law and say that cattle were "movables." Cattle out there were *mobile* property, self-moving property, that could care for itself and find its own way across the roadless expanse. This form of property was perfectly suited to Americans on the move. The cattle kept alive by moving, by seeking out the scant blades of grama grass; the cattle made money for their owners by moving, by taking themselves across no man's land to the railroad and the market.

THE WYOMING STOCK GROWERS' ASSOCIATION itself was a perfect embodiment of the special American ambiguity. For it gave to the big cattleman's extralegal appropriation of the range the color of law, while it gave to the small cattleman's and pioneer farmer's lawful appropriation of the land the color of lawlessness. The Association men had been there first, and they viewed later comers as enemies and overcrowders, agents of lawlessness and confusion. By the strict letter of the law, firstcomers actually had no better right to the range than anybody else, but they applied the transient rule which gave the best rights to those who were there earliest. The mere multiplying of owners naturally made anybody's brand harder to identify and harder to distinguish from anybody else's. By the end of 1891 in Wyoming alone there were five thousand different brands, and the number was steadily increasing. In Montana the six thousand brands listed in 1889 had nearly doubled by 1892.

The owner of any rapidly growing small herd was a man to watch. Everybody knew that the indiscriminate use of a branding iron was the quickest way to acquire a herd. "It's the fastest branders," the saying went, "who accumulate the largest stocks." Some of the large cattlemen, or their hired hands, had built their big herds in precisely this fashion. Knowing all the tricks of the business, and remembering the early days, they were not excessively trusting. Their Association, with its self-assumed powers of law, was not inclined to make subtle distinctions between the honest cattleman with a small herd, and the cattle thief who had not yet stolen more than a few head. It was always safer to be suspicious of unfamiliar persons whose cattle bore unrecognizable brands. What was the purpose of brand books and cattlemen's associations if not to help honest men prove their property, and to make it harder for thieves to prove theirs? In 1888 the Association, weakened by the catastrophic blizzards of 1886–87, transferred most of its powers to a new Board of Live Stock Commissioners created by the Wyoming legislature. But the board proved unequal to the work which the Association could no longer do.

By the spring of 1891, anarchy reigned on the Wyoming range. The Association had become too weak and the government of the new state of Wyoming (admitted to the Union on July 10, 1890) was not yet strong enough to govern. Cattle rustlers and maverick factories were everywhere, and the large herds of the old established cattlemen were now targets of a new barrage of Populist propaganda. "Men who before this year have borne and deserved good characters," wrote the Cheyenne *Daily Leader* on July 25, 1891, "are now openly engaged in preying upon the public ranges. . . . All their neighbors and acquaintances are perfectly aware of the fact and the practice is oftentimes not merely winked at, but applauded. . . . Efforts have been made by some of the larger cattle companies to bring the offenders to justice. In some cases the grand juries have refused to indict; in others petit juries have brought in verdicts of not guilty in the face of evidence as conclusive and convincing as any ever submitted in a court of justice." While cattle rustlers stole, farmers slaughtered. The laws appeared to require that a farmer fence his land to keep cattle out, but many a farmer preferred to save the cost of a fence, then wait until cattle came on his land, and with a shot or two secure a winter's supply of beef. While the big cattlemen insisted that God and Nature had decreed that theirs was "not a poor man's country," the federal land laws still limited the holdings of new settlers to 160 acres, too small an area for profitable irrigation.

Now on the defensive, the Association and its substantial members organized a counterattack. In the fall of 1891 they prepared a list of the rustlers' brands and took measures at the markets to stop the sale of all cattle bearing those brands. They seized and sold all such cattle and used the proceeds for their community purposes. In November 1891, in Johnson County in northcentral Wyoming, two suspected cattle rustlers were shot from ambush. Local opinion pinned the crime on two big cattle companies, and the stage was set for the Johnson County War.

In the spring of 1892 the small stockmen, defying the Association and the Live Stock Commission, which was its agent, announced they would hold a roundup a month earlier than officially scheduled. By the custom of the country this was a brazen act, since it showed an intention to put their own brands on whatever cattle they chose. The larger cattlemen decided it was now or never. If they could not revive respect for their laws of the range, they would be lost. They determined to make an example of the people of Johnson County, who, they said, consisted of only two kinds: "Ranchers, who rustled on the side; and rustlers, who ranched on the side." By a single dramatic act they would frighten the lawless into submission and reaffirm the laws of the range. The Association headquarters, the Cheyenne Club, was a favorite hangout for the big operators—English baronets attracted by romance and high profits; Eastern adventurers from the best families of Boston, Philadelphia, and New York; potent self-made Western cattle barons; and even a few literary men. Owen Wister, who had graduated from Harvard in 1882, went there to gather material for *Lin McLean* and *The Virginian*, and for other tales of the cattle country.

The Association collected a war chest, rumored at $100,000, from donations of $1,000 apiece. Secretly they organized an armed band of about fifty men. Twenty-six had been recruited by Tom Smith, a former cattle detective who had been indicted for murder for his work in Wyoming and who had served in Texas as a peace officer. To recruits from Paris and Lamar counties in Texas he offered pay of $5 a day and expenses, besides an accident policy of $3,000 and a bonus of $50 for each man they killed. A number of the recruits were former deputy U.S. marshals, who could be expected to know a thing or two about law enforcement. They were all told they were going to fight outlaws in Johnson County, Wyoming. One of the most interesting recruits was D. Brooks, later notorious as the Texas Kid, the only one of the group who would be executed as a result of his part in the Johnson County War. A year later, when the Texas Kid was hanged at Fort Smith, Arkansas, it was not for murder in Wyoming, but for killing his young wife, who nagged him for having joined the invasion. On the gallows he protested that he would never have gone to Wyoming if he had known what the Johnson County people were really like.

The Association recruits gathered in Denver on a special train which also carried saddle horses, wagons, and camping equipment. When the train arrived in Cheyenne the window shades of the passenger car were tightly drawn, and the mission remained secret. The party was given blankets and other equipment by a federal fort in the neighborhood. The train arrived in Casper, the end of the railroad line, early on the morning of April 6, 1892. After they unloaded they were joined by members of the Wyoming Association and their local recruits, including a correspondent of the Chicago *Herald* and a surgeon to treat their wounds, or more likely, those of the enemy. They mounted their horses and aimed for the county seat of Johnson County, the little town of Buffalo, reputed rustlers' citadel. The friendly collusion of the governor of Wyoming insured that the state's National Guard would not get in the way. Before leaving Casper, the invaders had taken the precaution of cutting the telegraph lines going north, so that the people down there would not be unduly alarmed.

En route to Buffalo they killed two men holed up in a remote cabin whom they assumed to be rustlers. One they shot from ambush as he went for water, then they burned the cabin and shot down the other as he fled. The delay for this little job gave time for the citizens of Johnson County to be alerted. On April 10, as the invaders approached the town of Buffalo, to their surprise they found their way blocked by an army of Johnson County citizens. Instead of attacking the town and exterminating the nest of rustlers, the invaders turned in quick retreat, finding refuge about twelve miles from Buffalo in the solid ranch buildings of Dr. Harris' TA Ranch, where they had spent the preceding night.

The citizens' army, two hundred strong, which now attacked them in the TA Ranch, confirmed their worst fears that the forces of lawlessness had captured Wyoming. Now they, the "law-enforcing" invaders, were the besieged. But the ranch house proved an effective temporary fortification, especially since the attacking citizens had no cannon, and the commander of the neighboring Fort McKinney refused to lend them one. Using wagons they had captured, the citizens improvised a movable breastwork which they called a "Go-Devil," designed to approach close enough to the embattled ranch house to allow use of their plentiful supply of dynamite. The Go-Devil was moving ahead when in the nick of time three companies of federal cavalry appeared. The acting governor of Wyoming, a friend of the Association, had appealed to President Benjamin Harrison to send these troops from Fort McKinney "to restore law and order" in Johnson County. In plain language this meant that Wyoming's leading cattlemen needed the intervention of United States troops if they were not to be lynched by an irate citizenry. The besieged invaders gladly surrendered to the commander of the federal troops, who took them to Cheyenne, where they were safely housed at Fort D. A. Russell.

Forty-six men surrendered. Of these, about half were the imported Texas gunmen, the rest were leading citizens of Wyoming, including a past president of the Stock Growers' Association, a Live Stock commissioner, the State Water commissioner, a deputy U. S. marshal, at least one Harvard graduate, and others equally respectable. The President of the United States had sent his federal troops on an errand of mercy to save some of the most substantial citizens of the West from the local law-enforcement officials.

The invaders were never actually tried. Eventually they were handed over to Johnson County authorities, but on the understanding that they would not be tried in Johnson County. Meanwhile President Harrison, urged by the Association, issued a special proclamation ordering all citizens of Wyoming to cease obstructing the courts and laws of the United States. The men who had witnessed the double murder by the invaders on their way into Buffalo were now arrested by the U. S. marshal for selling whiskey to the Indians, and they were never seen again. When it appeared that Johnson County actually did not have the funds to pay for a lengthy trial of forty-odd men, the District Court in Cheyenne released the invaders on their own recognizance. Despite all the shooting, the Johnson County War, then, left only three fatalities—the two men killed by the invaders before they reached their destination, and the Texas Kid, who was executed for a murder only indirectly caused by the war.

This was a war, like many others, in which both parties lost. The big stockmen did not succeed in re-establishing their kind of law and order on the range, nor in excluding the small cattleman or the nester. Cattle bearing the brands of any of the invaders, now less safe than ever, were promiscuously stolen and slaughtered without fear of redress. On the other side, the citizens of Johnson County and the small stockmen and small farmers had not really won. The state Republican organization, which had been closely allied to the invaders and the larger cattle interests, after only a two-year setback returned to power. Moreover, efforts to spread the true story of the invasion to the discredit of the big cattlemen were suppressed. When Asa Shinn Mercer (enterprising founder of the *Northwest Livestock Journal*) wrote and published a documented account in 1894 under the title *The Banditti of the Plains or the Cattlemen's Invasion of Wyoming in 1892: The Crowning Infamy of the Ages*, it was suppressed at once by a court injunction, and all copies were impounded for burning. A few copies were mysteriously rescued from the fire, but the plates of the book were destroyed. Mercer was charged with sending obscene matter through the mails, and he was forced to close his publishing business. The Association men even succeeded in extracting the copyright copies fom the Library of Congress. To try to give a true account of the cattlemen's invasion of Johnson County long remained a risky business. It was a full half-century before Jack Schaefer's novel *Shane* (1949), and the movie adapted from it, dared tell the story. Seldom before or since have the agents of law been so thoroughly confused with the agents of lawlessness. Even at this distance it is no simple matter to tell which were which.

4

Lawless Sheriffs and Honest Desperadoes

GO-GETTER MORALITY BROUGHT an age of Good Bad Men and Bad Good Men. While sheriffs and marshals were in the pay of rustlers and cattle barons, outlaws and vigilantes were taking oaths "to enforce the law." A Go-Getter's loyalty was his willingness to stick by his guns to avenge a friend, to defend his cattle, or to secure a fortune. It was a time of boon companions, of pals and "pardners," and of quick and mortal enemies. It was far easier to recognize a friend or an enemy, to tell a good proposition when you saw one, than to know whether or not the "law" was on your side.

THE PREVALENCE OF FIREARMS and the high value placed on the quick draw made a sure shot the test of manliness. From earliest colonial times, the needs of the wilderness and the threat of Indians had put firearms in the American household. The right to bear arms had been hallowed in the Constitution.

The six-shooter, a stepchild of the West, would for the first time provide a portable, rapid-shooting repeater which put "law enforcement" in the reach of any trained arm. The perfection of the six-shooter was a response to the special needs of Texan cattlemen in the treeless Great Plains. Menaced by the Comanche Indians, the settlers who went to Texas from the United States in the early nineteenth century, found themselves at a dangerous disadvantage. Their encounters with the Indians were commonly on horseback. But the skillful Comanche could ride three hundred yards and shoot twenty arrows in the time it took the Texan to reload his firearm once. Even if a Texan went the limit and actually carried two heavy single-shot pistols in addition to his rifle, he still had no more than three shots before he was forced to stop and reload. Anyway, the rifle could not be used effectively from horseback.

When Samuel Colt, a sixteen-year-old Connecticut sailor, whittled his first wooden model of a revolver on the long voyage to Singapore in 1830, he could hardly have been thinking of the needs of Texas pioneers. Two years later Colt sent a description of his revolver to the Patent Office in Washington. Employing the new techniques of interchangeable parts, Colt's company manufactured his revolvers, but the United States government refused to take these revolvers, nor were they extensively bought by private citizens in the East.

The new six-shooter did have great appeal out in the new Republic of Texas. In fact, so much of the demand came from there that Colt himself christened his first popular model "the Texas." The Captain of the Texas Rangers, Samuel H. Walker, went to New York to confer with Colt on improvements. Colt's new model, heavy enough to use as a club in close combat, and easier to reload, was then named "the Walker." The name "six-shooter" itself seems to have been introduced by the Texas Rangers. "They are the only weapon," Ranger officers insisted, "which enabled the experienced frontiersman to defeat the *mounted* Indian in his own peculiar mode of warfare ... your six-shooter is the arm which has rendered the name of Texas Ranger a check and terror to the bands of our frontier Indians." Probably the first use of the six-shooter in a mounted battle against Indians was at the Pedernales in 1840 when some fifteen Texas Rangers defeated about seventy Comanches.

But in the East the demand was so small that the Colt factory went bankrupt in 1842. The United States Army still could not see the value of the weapon. When war with Mexico broke out in 1845, the Texas Rangers at first used their own six-shooters, and then urgently demanded that the United States government provide a supply. Colt, who at the time did not possess even one six-shooter to use as a model, resumed production. "He had made a better gun," explains Walter Prescott Webb, eloquent historian of the Great Plains, "it had blazed a pathway from his door to the Texas Rangers and the Plains, and the world was now to pave that pathway with gold." The Mexican War established the six-shooter as the characteristic American weapon of the West and Southwest.

TO MANY OF the cattlemen and cowboys who gathered in the West in the late 1860's and '70's, the Civil War had given a new familiarity with all kinds of firearms. That bloodiest war of the century had accustomed them to the face of death and the smell of carnage. How all these experiences and opportunities came to focus among Western Go-Getters was illustrated in the remarkable career of Wild Bill Hickok.

As a boy James Butler Hickok loved to hunt, and he had a reputation for being the best shot in northern Illinois. In 1855, when he was only eighteen, he joined the Free State forces in Bleeding Kansas. Serving briefly as a town constable, he then found a job driving a stage across the Santa Fe Trail, which gave him further opportunity to test his fighting prowess. On one occasion he used his bowie knife to kill a bear. When driving on the Oregon Trail in 1861, he shot it out with the infamous McCanles Gang. His service as scout and spy for the Union in the Civil War was full of dangerous adventure and narrow escapes, which kept his shooting arm well practiced. In the public square in Springfield, Missouri, he killed a former friend of his, a fellow Union scout who had joined the Confederates. Then, after the war, as deputy U.S. marshal for a vast area around Fort Riley, Kansas, he became famous as a recoverer of stolen property and a killer of outlaws. As marshal of several rough Kansas cow towns, including Abilene, he proved faster on the draw than some of the most notorious desperadoes, until the number of men he had killed in single combat was reputed to be greater than that killed by any of his contemporaries. He became a public performer, touring the country with Buffalo Bill in 1872–73. Three years later when he returned to one of his old haunts, Deadwood, Dakota Territory, he was shot in the back of the head by a local citizen from whom he had won some money at cards earlier in the day. He was only thirty-nine years old. His murderer was tried and acquitted by the local court.

After Wild Bill's burial in Deadwood, the monument and railing around his grave were dismantled piece by piece by people who wanted a memento of so great a killer. Nobody knows exactly how many he actually shot down in open personal combat; some put the figure as high as eighty-five, but it was surely not less than thirty. He managed all these killings without once being brought into court even for a charge of manslaughter. During much of his active life Wild Bill Hickok wore the badge of the law. Still, a tantalizing ambiguity surrounded many of his killings, for his rule in doubtful cases seemed to be to shoot first and investigate afterwards. Admirers of Western ways have called Wild Bill "the greatest bad man ever in likelihood seen upon the earth." According to General Custer, "on foot or on horseback he was one of the most perfect types of physical manhood I ever saw. His manner was entirely free from all bluster and bravado. He never spoke of himself unless requested to do so. His influence among the frontiersmen was unbounded; his word was law. Wild Bill was anything but a quarrelsome man, yet none but himself could enumerate the many conflicts in which he had been engaged." If a willingness to take another's life on slight or half-proven cause was the sign of a *bad* man, Wild Bill was surely one. Yet if a willingness to risk one's life to defend the law and the right was the sign of a *good* man, Wild Bill was surely one of those, too.

"Desperado" was the name commonly used for the Western bad-man whose services often were not covered by the badge of the law. But in the world of the cattlemen, there were few if any notorious "bad men" who had not at some time or other worn the badge of the law, and risked their lives for what some men in their neighborhood called law and order. Beneath the widespread admiration for the "manhood" of the quick-on-the trigger desperado was a gnawing suspicion that the desperado himself was often (perhaps even more often than his opponents) on the side of the right. "The 'bad men,' or professional fighters and man-killers," wrote Theodore Roosevelt in 1888 after one of his trips out West, "are of a different stamp [from the common criminal, horse thief or highway robber], quite a number of them being, according to their light, perfectly honest. These are the men who do most of the killing in frontier communities; yet it is a noteworthy fact that the men who are killed generally deserve their fate." Some described desperadoes as simply engaged in a modern American version of the ancient trial by combat. "It was the undelegated right of one individual against that of another. The law was not invoked," observed Emerson Hough, who himself was a witness, "—the law would not serve. Even as the quickest set of nerves flashed into action, the arm shot forward, and there smote the point of flame as did once the point of steel. The victim fell, his own weapon clutched in his hand, a fraction too late. The law cleared the killer. It was 'self-defense.' 'It was an even break,' his fellowmen said; although thereafter they were more reticent with him and sought him out less frequently."

Was this perhaps another example of Americans' giving the law and the right to the man who "got there first"? Unwritten Law, so rigid and unbending in the static society of the older South, in another form thus came to rule the free-ranging West. But while in the South men could look to the traditional practices of the "best" people, and few dared doubt who those were, in the West there were no such people. Out there, the Unwritten Law showed all the vagueness and unpredictableness of a law each man chose for himself. It was in the lands of new property—of gold and silver and of cattle— that the peculiarly ambiguous American bad man flourished. Although the "ideal desperado" of course did not kill for money alone, in the early days most desperadoes were involved in or at least somehow were accused of "unlawfully" acquiring property.

UNEXPECTED SUBTLETIES, the classic confusions of Go-Getter Morality, appear in the careers of nearly all the eminent cattle-country desperadoes. We can examine them conveniently in the life of the most notorious of them all—Billy the Kid. William H. Bonney (his real name) was born in New York City in 1859 and as a boy was taken West by his family. His father died when they were living in

Kansas, and his mother moved to Colorado and then on to New Mexico. His character as a young man was described by his sometime friend and co-worker, later his assassin and biographer, Sheriff Pat Garrett:

> Bold, daring, and reckless, he was open-handed, generous-hearted, frank and manly. He was a favorite with all classes and ages, especially was he loved and admired by the old and decrepit, and the young and helpless. To such he was a champion, a defender, a benefactor, a right arm. He was never seen to accost a lady, especially an elderly one, but with his hat in his hand, and did her attire or appearance evidence poverty, it was a poem to see the eager, sympathetic, deprecating look in Billy's sunny face, as he proffered assistance or afforded information. A little child never lacked a lift across a gutter, or the assistance of a strong arm to carry a heavy burden when Billy was in sight. . . . Billy loved his mother. He loved and honored her more than anything else on earth.

At the age of twelve, Billy was reputed to have stabbed a man to death for insulting his mother.

Billy's first serious job was at the age of sixteen when he and a companion tried to persuade three peaceable Apache Indians on the reservation to supply them with horses. This is how Billy himself (reported by Garrett) described the venture:

> It was a ground hog case. Here were twelve good ponies, four or five saddles, a good supply of blankets, and five pony loads of pelts. Here were three blood-thirsty savages, revelling in all this luxury and refusing succor to two free-born, white American citizens, foot sore and hungry. The plunder had to change hands—there was no alternative—and as one live Indian could place a hundred United States troops on our trail in two hours, and as a dead Indian would be likely to take some other route, our resolves were taken. In three minutes there were three "good Injuns" lying around there careless like, and, with ponies and plunder, we skipped. There was no fight. It was about the softest thing I ever struck.

In the course of various adventures in Old and New Mexico, Billy was soon credited with a dozen more killings. All of which seemed qualifications for the job he found in 1877 when he arrived at the Pecos Valley.

At that time there was brewing in southern New Mexico a struggle, the Lincoln County War, destined to become the bloodiest of all the cattlemen's wars. This was not unlike the later Johnson County War in Wyoming in the readiness of both sides to hire gunmen and use the powers of "law-enforcement" officers. Here, however, the issue was not between the big and the small cattlemen. Rather, it was between two nearly equal factions of rich owners of large herds, both of whom were using all available means to secure contracts to supply the government posts and Indian agencies. Each faction accused the other of foul play and of stealing its cattle. From this distance it seems that they were both right. Soon nearly every cattleman in those parts was involved on one side or the other. In the late winter of 1877 when Billy the Kid started working for J. H. Tunstall on his ranch in Lincoln County on the Felix River, the feud had climaxed in a complicated lawsuit as a result of which the opposing faction, headed by Lawrence G. Murphy, sent a deputy sheriff and a posse of their own men to Tunstall's ranch to seize his cattle. Murphy controlled the wagon trains and dominated the finances of the region. On February 18, 1878, Murphy's men killed Tunstall in the presence of his foreman and Billy the Kid. The long-brewing Lincoln County feud now became open warfare.

This gave Billy the Kid a purpose from which he never relented —to punish the murderers of his friend Tunstall. Tunstall's foreman was sworn in as a "special deputy" by McSween, the leader of the anti-Murphy faction, and he gathered Billy the Kid along with a dozen others to wreak their revenge. Billy led several of the fights which followed. He and six cohorts ambushed and killed the sheriff of Lincoln County and his deputy, both of whom were partisans of the Murphy crowd. Then Billy and the other McSween men went on a law-enforcement spree of their own. Carrying a warrant issued by a justice of the peace authorizing them to recover stolen horses, they killed another of the Murphy men. The climax came in July 1878 when federal troops, summoned by a new sheriff of Lincoln County, who was a tool of the Murphy faction, brought up a company of cavalry to arrest McSween and his men. When they refused to surrender, the Murphy men set fire to McSween's house, but all except two of the party escaped in the night. The Lincoln County War did not begin to come to an end until General Lew Wallace (the Civil War hero who later wrote *Ben Hur*), carrying "extraordinary powers" from President Harrison, arrived as governor of New Mexico in August. He brought a truce to southern New Mexico, but he could not bring to justice the crimes of the past year. Someone suggested that the only way to give everyone his due was to hang the whole population of Lincoln County. But after many indictments, the cases were gradually dismissed, showing the inability of the official law to meet the needs of a society that lived by Go-Getter Morality.

Although more than sixty men had been killed, the only man actually brought to trial for a killing in the Lincoln County War was Billy the Kid. Governor Wallace summoned him to a meeting where, in the presence of witnesses, he asked Billy to lay down his arms and stand trial, promising that if Billy was convicted, the governor would give him a pardon. Some doubted the general's word and suspected that Billy was to be made a scapegoat. "There is no justice for me in the courts of this country now," Billy is reported to have replied as he refused to stand trial. "I've gone too far."

Billy the Kid now began a new chapter of desperate adventures. He had become too accustomed to the excitement of a professional gunman to settle for the cowboy routine of fence riding and round-ups. With a dozen old associates he roamed the countryside stealing cattle, killing old enemies, and seeking out new enemies whom he suspected of wanting to avenge his earlier killings. The courageous Pat Garrett, newly elected sheriff of Lincoln County, captured Billy the Kid, and managed to secure his conviction for his long-past murder of Sheriff Brady. But before the Kid could be hanged, he killed his guards and made another bold escape. It was two months before Garrett again found Billy the Kid, and as the Kid walked into the house of a friend, killed him under cover of darkness.

Theodore Roosevelt was so impressed by Garrett that he named him Collector of Customs at El Paso, but the President later withdrew his favors when he caught Garrett lying. Garrett himself was finally shot by one of his own tenants. The killer pleaded self-defense and the jury brought in a verdict of not guilty despite the fact that Garrett had been shot in the back of his head and had died with a glove on his trigger-finger hand. Ranchers in the neighborhood long remembered the barbecue offered by a prosperous local cattleman to celebrate the acquittal of Garrett's killer.

The gallery of Good Bad Men and Bad Good Men—of lawless sheriffs and honest desperadoes—could be lengthened indefinitely. It would include every shape and mix of good and evil. It would have to include mining-town Go-Getters like Henry Plummer, sometimes called "the gentleman desperado," who actually served as officer of the law while he led his band of road agents, then in disguise boldly joined the band of vigilantes organized to hunt him down. His commission as a U.S. marshal arrived while he was standing ready to be executed on the gallows. Of course, in those towns, too, there were a few, like Boone Helm, who seemed entirely without conscience (on one occasion when starving in the woods, he actually ate the flesh of a companion) and who never sought the cover of the law.

Alongside the authentic man of mixed motives and confusions, whose inner uncertainties reflected the uncertain possibilities of the American landscape, there arose a man of simpler stamp, the creation in large part of the telegraph, of the newly prospering, sensation-hungry daily press. He was the "Imitation Desperado—the Cheap 'Long Hair'" as the cowboy historian Emerson Hough labels him, "the counterfeit bad man . . . produced by Western consumptives for

Eastern consumption. . . . There always existed in the real, sober, level-headed West a contempt for the West-struck man who was not really bad, but who wanted to seem 'bad.' " He was the twentieth-century "Drugstore Cowboy." But the man really guided by Go-Getter Morality was a man who felt newly free, a man in the open air who still could not quite forget that society made discomfiting demands of him. The imitation bad man of the West, on the contrary, simply carried out West the criminal ways of a settled society.

Cowboy, cattle rustler, and cattle baron—Western sheriff and Western desperado—were all creatures of free land and the open range. They were all enticed by strange new opportunities and temptations. Men who had once made their living on free buffalo saw nothing odd about free cattle. The disappearance of the open range, the rise of the barbed-wire fences, and the selling and leasing of the West would put an end to many of the opportunities and temptations, and to the cast of characters of the cattleman's heyday. While counterparts might survive in the mountains, in a world of new flowing minerals, and later in the cities, the lawless sheriff and honest desperado would no longer roam the world of the stockman. These men, with their moral-legal ambiguities, would pass, but the Go-Getter Morality would survive.

5
Rounding Up Rock Oil

THE NEW WEALTH that the Western Go-Getters found growing from the grass roots up had a counterpart in the discovery of a new kind of gold deep underground. But while the world of the cattleman enriched American folklore and folk song, the roundup of rock oil left few folk heroes. Still, the discovery of oil, the invention of new ways to bring it to the surface, the organizing of ways to collect and transport it and deliver it to market—all these matched the achievements of cattledom.

THE MEDICINAL USE of natural oil was an old story in America. Seneca Indians, who found the black stuff floating on ponds and creeks, would soak it up with a blanket laid on top of the water and then wring out the blanket in a container. Before the end of the eighteenth century it was an item of trade with the Indians. When General Benjamin Lincoln's Revolutionary troops marched through western Pennsylvania in 1783, he allowed them to stop at a spring where they collected the floating oil and bathed their joints in it. "This gave them great relief, and freed them immediately from the rheumatic complaints with which many of them were affected. The troops drank freely of the waters—they operated as a gentle purge."

In those days salt was commonly produced from wells which brought up brine, to be evaporated for the market. In the late 1830's, a number of profitable wells were being spoiled by a black oily substance which came up with the salt. Some enterprising businessmen in Kentucky took over one of these "ruined" salt wells, formed the American Medical Oil Company and bottled the "American Oil" as a remedy for nearly everything. They sold their bottles by the hundreds of thousands. When Samuel M. Kier, the energetic son of a salt manufacturer, took over his father's wells in western Pennsylvania in the 1840's, he too was plagued by a black oily stuff, and he considered shutting down his wells. But after his wife became ill with consumption and the doctor prescribed "American Oil," Kier noticed that the fluid he bought in bottles was like that which was ruining his wells. When oil actually began to flow in quantity from his salt wells in 1846, he went into the medicinal-oil business.

Kier published leaflets with signed testimonials to the wonderful virtues of "Petroleum, or Rock Oil. A Natural Remedy! Procured from a well in Allegheny County, Pa. Four hundred feet below the Earth's Surface!" Rock oil, he said, had "Wonderful Curative Powers" for rheumatism, chronic cough, ague, toothache, corns, neuralgia, piles, urinary disorders, indigestion, and liver ailments. One of his fliers was printed like a state bank note featuring the numeral "400" (the number of feet below the earth's surface from which the marvelous mineral was drawn), signed by S. M. Kier and dated "A.D. 1848 discovered in boring for salt water: A.D. 1849 wonderful medical virtues discovered." He sent out salesmen in wagons ornamented with gilt pictures of the Good Samaritan ministering to writhing sufferers beneath a palm tree, and these emissaries relieved the rural monotony with their "Medicine Show." By 1858 he had sold nearly a quarter-million half pints of his wonderful Rock Oil at $1 a bottle. But the high cost of advertising and distribution together with the increasing flow of oil (far exceeding any possible medicinal uses) stirred Kier to find other uses for his product. What might these be?

The growth of American cities and of hundreds of new factories and the spread of railroads in the decades before 1850 had, of course, increased the need for better illumination. But the lighting in American homes had improved very little over that of ancient times.

Through the colonial period, homes were lit with tallow candles or with a lamp of the kind used in ancient Rome—a dish of fish oil or other animal or vegetable oil in which a twisted rag served as a wick. Some people used lard, but they had to heat charcoal underneath to keep it soft and burnable. The sperm whale, which was not tracked to its habitat until 1712, provided a superior burning oil and its spermaceti made the best candles, but these were expensive. In 1830 Isaiah Jennings of New York took out a patent for a new substance called "camphene," a redistilled spirits of turpentine which proved an excellent illuminant. But while camphene gave a bright light it too remained expensive, had an unpleasant smell and also was dangerously explosive.

Between 1830 and 1850 it seemed that the only hope for cheaper illumination in the United States was in the wider use of gas. In the 1840's American gas manufacturers adopted improved British techniques for producing illuminating gas from coal. But the expense of piping gas to the consumer remained so high that until mid-century gaslighting was feasible only in urban areas, and only for public buildings or for the wealthy.

In 1854 a Canadian doctor, Abraham Gesner, patented a process for distilling a pitchlike mineral found in New Brunswick and Nova Scotia which produced illuminating gas and an oil which he called "kerosene" (from "keros" the Greek word for wax, and "ene" because it resembled camphene). Kerosene, though cheaper than camphene, had an unpleasant odor, and Gesner never made his fortune from it. But Gesner had aroused a new hope for making an illuminating oil from some product of American mines.

Meanwhile, in Boston in 1852, some enterprising drug manufacturers in search of better lubricants had begun to produce "coal oil," distilled from coal tar. They discovered that their new oil was not only a lubricant, but would actually burn in a lamp, without an unpleasant odor. By 1859, coal oil, under the trade name of "kerosene," was making its way into the American home. Lard, whale and sperm oils were all rising in price, and the explosive qualities of camphene had given it a bad name. It was known that petroleum could be substituted for coal in the production of coal oil. Before the end of 1859 nearly two million coal-oil lamps had been sold, but Americans were still a long way from the ideal of "a lamp in every room." The raw materials for coal oil were still scarce, and the cost of producing illuminating oils from animal and vegetable oils or from coal was too high.

IN MIDSUMMER 1854 George H. Bissell, a Dartmouth graduate of 1845, visiting his old campus, happened to see a bottle of oil that had been left with one of the professors there by a doctor who had taken it from an oil spring in Titusville, in western Pennsylvania. The stuff excited his curiosity, which was possibly stirred also by having seen some of Kier's brochures touting the curative powers of his natural Rock Oil. Even before he knew precisely what he would do with the product, Bissell became interested in developing the springs that had yielded the oil in the bottle. He and a partner formed the Pennsylvania Rock Oil Company of New York (the first American corporation formed to take petroleum from the ground) optimistically capitalized at a half-million dollars, bought 100 acres of what they thought was oil land for $5,000, and secured the oil rights to an additional 12,000 acres. The oil was to be gathered by the only methods then used—receiving the natural flow of oil springs, collecting oil floating on creeks, or digging holes and ditches to increase the flow where oil had already been found.

Soon these costs of collecting the surface oil exceeded the company's returns from sale for medicinal purposes. Then the company enlisted expert aid. Professor Benjamin Silliman, Jr., of Yale was commissioned to do a full range of experiments on the Pennsylvania Company's rock oil to see what it might be good for. Silliman's report to the investors in 1855 (one of the first American examples of commissioned industrial research, billed for $526.08) was optimistic. He reported that the oil had wonderful lubricating qualities and was "chemically identical with illuminating gas in liquid form." "The lamp burning this fluid [distilled from the oil] gave as much light as any which they had seen . . . the oil spent more economically, and the uniformity of the light was greater than in camphene, burning for twelve hours without a sensible diminution, and without smoke."

Silliman's promise, however, still applied only to a meager product —the oil which had seeped up naturally to the surface. The idea of drilling deep into the ground for the express purpose of finding oil which could then be pumped to the surface—such an idea, if it had occurred to anyone earlier, must have seemed too far-fetched to justify any investment. We do not know who first had the idea of "drilling" for oil. It may have been Bissell, to whom it had possibly been suggested by Kier's brochure featuring the "400" feet below the surface where his panacea had been discovered in "A.D. 1848 . . . in boring for salt water." Or perhaps it was the New Haven banker James M. Townsend, who had taken over from Silliman as president of the Pennsylvania Rock Oil Company. "Oil coming out of the ground, pumping oil out of the earth as you pump water?" a friend exclaimed to him. "Nonsense! You're crazy." In 1858 most Americans would have reacted in this way.

Whatever their thoughts on how to harvest the oil, the investors in the Pennsylvania Rock Oil Company decided to take steps anyway to perfect their legal title to the land at Titusville where the rock oil was bubbling up into a stream, and also to see what else could be done to exploit the stuff. For reasons still obscure, in 1857 they engaged a man who was neither a lawyer nor a successful businessman, but a vagrant ex-railroad conductor then living in a New Haven hotel. Edwin L. Drake had clerked on the steamboat between Buffalo and Detroit, in a Tecumseh, Michigan, hotel, and in dry-goods stores in New Haven and New York. But he had only a grade school education, no technical training and no knowledge of mining. Drake's main qualification for the job appeared to be the railroad pass which he still held as an ex-employee, and which would get him to Titusville free of charge.

When Drake arrived there in December 1857, he found (according to his own account) "a population of about 125, no churches, two hotels." After settling the company's legal business with the local citizens, he visited the site where the famous medical oil, known in those parts as "Mustang Liniment," oozed up into a pool. There he witnessed the laborious process of harvesting the oil by spreading a blanket upon the pool and then squeezing the liquid out of the blanket into a container. Then and there, according to Drake's own later account, he had his inspiration. "The idea flashed upon him that there was a basin or spring of oil in the earth or rocks below, and . . . he then formed the resolution of sinking a well." "Within ten minutes after my arrival upon the ground with Dr. Brewer I had made up my mind that it could be obtained in large quantities by Boreing as for Salt Water. I also determined that I should be the one to do it." The popular idea in the region and even the scientific opinions of those whom Drake consulted were "that the oil was the drippings of the coal, imbedded in the contiguous hills—that it was idle to bore for it, and that the only method of accumulating it was by digging ditches leading to a vat." But Drake could not understand why the oil was under the creek "if it came from the Hills as it is so much lighter than Water that it would be impossible for it to go down of its own accord."

Not having enough expert knowledge to be confident that an oil well was impossible, Drake went ahead on his hunches. He now became obsessed by the novel notion of "drilling" for oil. He did not know whether rock oil, even if he could secure it in large quantities, was really superior to other substances for lubricating or for lighting. He had no notion of how or to whom the oil would be marketed. But here was a tantalizing new substance that just might be somebody's fortune. Why not try to collect it? Drake became president of his own new Seneca Oil Company, and he leased land from the Pennsylvania

Rock Oil Company. He would receive twelve cents for each gallon of oil he produced. Since there was nothing in the lease about "drilling" for oil, it appears that Drake at the time kept his obsession to himself.

Meanwhile Drake visited neighboring salt wells to see how they were drilled, and to find an experienced driller, someone who had shown that he knew how to bore for salt. Because drilling for oil was considered insane, he had trouble engaging a competent salt borer. The first salt borer who contracted to do his job never appeared, and later explained that since he believed Drake to be crazy, he "thought the easiest way to get rid of him was to make a contract and pretend that he meant to come."

Finally Drake found William A. ("Uncle Billy") Smith, who was not only an experienced salt borer (having drilled salt for Samuel Kier's father) but also a skilled blacksmith who knew how to make drilling tools. Uncle Billy, helped by his two sons, began drilling in June 1859. In salt boring in those days the usual procedure was to dig a hole and wall it around with a wooden "crib" until reaching bedrock; then an iron pipe was drilled into a hole. But when Uncle Billy tried this at the Drake well, water flooded the hole he dug long before bedrock was reached. So he tried the revolutionary new method of driving a pipe all the way down. After he reached bedrock at 32 feet, he went on drilling, making only 3 feet a day. By Saturday, August 27, 1859, Uncle Billy's hole reached a depth of 69½ feet, and (as Drake always required) drilling was stopped for the Sabbath. The next day Uncle Billy Smith went over to look at the well, and to his surprise he found it full of an oily substance. "What's that?" Drake asked. And Uncle Billy Smith replied, "That's your fortune!"

While that oily substance in the hole quickly dispelled Drake's reputation for insanity, making money out of the well was not quite so easy. The well did not flow but had to be pumped, and since Drake had not planned where to put the stuff, they had to use whiskey barrels, washtubs, and everything in sight. One day in October, Uncle Billy took a lamp to look down the hole, and the whole outfit went up in flames. But Drake rebuilt the derrick and pump, and he soon became the tool and the target of fortune hunters from all over. Leaving the oil country, he went to Wall Street, where he became a broker in oil stocks and lost everything. To save the "inventor" of the oil well from destitution, the Pennsylvania legislature finally gave him a pension of $1,500 a year, but in 1880, in an age of famous oil fortunes, Drake died in obscurity.

The oil mania, sparked by Drake and other Go-Getters, created still another new species of upstart town. The map of the far northwestern corner of Pennsylvania was soon dotted with names like Oil

City, Oleopolis, and Petroleum Center. These, and others, were built on oil, on the hope for oil, on the promise of oil, and in a few cases on a real oil bonanza. Oil towns prospered on the auxiliary services, the making of oil drums, oil derricks, and oil pumps, the trade in oil leases, and on the feeding, housing, clothing, and debauching of the thousands of oil prospectors.

We can trace their meteoric careers in the short life of a town called Pithole. In the spring of 1864 a lucky "oil finder," using a divining rod in the form of a witch-hazel twig, declared that a farm which spread on both sides of Pithole Creek held a fortune in oil. On January 7, 1865, the first completed well there was pouring out 250 barrels of oil each day. Thousands of the hopeful—some soldiers recently discharged from the Civil War armies, some investors with inflated greenbacks to spend, and some vagrants, wanderers, and adventurers—flocked to Pithole. When a second well struck oil, the fever became a mania. By the end of June the four wells flowing at Pithole were producing over 2,000 barrels a day, which was a third of the total production of Pennsylvania oil. The land that six months earlier had been nothing but a remote farm became a buzzing center of commerce. Three thousand teamsters were driving wagons carrying oil barrels back and forth from the wells to the river boats and to other shipping centers. A standard unit was a one-sixteenth interest in a well, which commonly sold for several thousand dollars. The "Working Men's Pithole Creek Oil Association" bought interests in wells and sold $10 shares to those who could afford no more. Adapting their techniques from earlier Western hoaxers who had "salted" their diamond mines with imported diamond chips to trap the unwary, some drillers avoided risk of a dry hole by "doctoring" their wells, through the simple process of pouring buckets of oil into their hole at night to appeal to buyers the next morning.

SCATTERED OVER northwestern Pennsylvania, scores of newly discovered oil wells every day poured up hundreds of gallons. Where would so much be stored? How to take it to market? Finding the rock oil and drilling for it were enterprises of a few bold Go-Getters willing to risk their time and money, and the ridicule of neighbors. To move it across the vast American spaces would demand the organized efforts of whole communities. Rock oil, like cattle, had its own ways of bringing men together.

One of the most remarkable of these was the "pond freshet." This was a way of using community organization to make navigable the small shallow streams which ran through the oil-rich countryside. Many productive wells in the early years were clustered near Oil

Creek, but during most of the year there was not enough water in the creek to float barges carrying the barreled oil to market. Instead oilmen had to haul their barrels by wagon the great distances to the railroad. Water transport was so much closer and so much cheaper that the enterprising oilmen in the neighborhood invented their own cooperative way of making their creeks navigable.

The pond freshet required long preparation, close coordination, precise timing, and skillful navigation. Here is how it was described by the superintendent of the pond freshet on Oil Creek on January 24, 1863:

> A Pond Freshet is a temporary rise of water in the creek for the purpose of running out boats, rafts, logs, etc. The water rises high enough to run out boats containing sometimes five hundred, and in some few cases, seven hundred barrels of oil. There are usually from one hundred and fifty to two hundred and fifty boats on each freshet. It lasts from one to two hours, and is caused by letting the water out from seven to seventeen dams on the principal branches of the Creek, so that the water will all meet together, making quite a flood upon which from seven thousand to thirty thousand barrels of oil are run to the river.

The preparations required that the oilmen upstream get together in building numerous dams, to collect the water in preparation for the planned dramatic moment. This might take weeks. The dams had to be specifically constructed so that their abutments could be quickly removed.

The climax of the work came when the water was to be released. Then, at precisely the right moment, beginning upstream the successive dams were opened, accumulating the water into a sudden rush large enough to raise the level of the creek for a few minutes all the way downstream. The boatmen along the stream had long been preparing for this moment. Having readied their boats and loaded the barrels of oil, they anxiously waited "for the flood which is to waft them to the much desired harbor at the mouth of the creek. About the time the freshet is expected the boatmen stand ready to let loose their lines. A cool, pushing breeze is the first sign of it, and soon after comes the swirling waters." It took sharp judgment to know the strategic moment, so as not to push off too soon and risk being grounded ahead of the current, and it took skill to keep the boat pointed ahead, to negotiate the narrows and avoid the piers of numerous bridges. The successful boatman brought his cargo swiftly to the wharf at Oil City, where he waited only long enough to prepare for the easier trip down the Allegheny River to Pittsburgh and to market.

The scene in the oil town resembled that in a cow town after the arrival of a large herd up from Texas on a drive. As the superintendent of the freshet reported:

> Our town is quite lively during the evening after a pond freshet. Shippers are busy paying off the boatmen, the citizens of the creek are laying in a stock of the necessaries of life, and all is bustle and business. You see men dripping with the oleaginous product. Our hotels are filled to repletion with these greasy men who are supplying light for the world. Oil is the only topic of conversation, and the air is redolent with its sweet perfumery.

OIL OFFERED FANTASTIC new opportunities, and the man who organized these opportunities was a Go-Getter of heroic proportions. His name was John D. Rockefeller. Since he has become part of the folklore of urban automobile America, we sometimes forget that he grabbed his fame and fortune and power back in the day of the kerosene lamp, when kerosene itself was a novelty. Like the Go-Getting Cattlemen and bold Cattle Drivers, like the Iliffs and Goodnights and McCoys, Rockefeller found ways to round up his new commodity, transport it long distances, and market it to the world.

When Drake made his strike at Titusville, in the wilderness of western Pennsylvania, John D. Rockefeller was a young man of twenty in Cleveland, Ohio, only about a hundred miles away. He had already done spectacularly well for his age, for in that year Rockefeller and his partner, by dealing in grain, meats, and other Western products, would gross nearly a half-million dollars. They were prepared for the business boom that would come with the Civil War.

In the fall of 1859 word came to Cleveland that somebody in western Pennsylvania had drilled a new kind of well that every day produced more than 300 gallons of an oil that sold for fifty cents a gallon. This news produced a miniature gold rush to the Pennsylvania oil fields, and some of the Cleveland businessmen whom Rockefeller knew hastened to the scene. Fantastic stories came back of overnight fortunes—oil-rich farmers, lucky oil-lease speculators, and the village blacksmith who "kicked down" a shaft in a defunct salt well, produced 25 barrels (31–42 gallons each) a day, and made his village into a boom town. Horror tales of unexplained explosions of the nitroglycerin used to "torpedo" failing wells, and of inextinguishable oil-well fires, added to the excitement. But by November 1860 the new black mineral was already a drug on the market. It came gushing from the oil fields, and since there was no place to store it, the Allegheny River was darkened by overflowing wells. The price of oil plummeted.

Rockefeller himself may have gone to the oil fields to see what was happening. But even from Cleveland he could have seen that oil was ruining as many men as it was enriching. Hundreds of barrels were hauled into the cities. Still nobody could see how it could be corralled into the homes that hoped for "a lamp in every room." How make rock oil into a stable commodity of commerce?

Rockefeller began to see his chance in the competitive chaos of the upstart West. Cities were competing for commerce, for railroads, and for citizens. Burgeoning railroads were competing for the traffic of cities and eagerly grasped for transportable new products. Cleveland itself, incorporated as a village only in 1814, had prospered from the traffic which came with the completion in 1827 of the first section of the Ohio and Erie Canal. Incorporated as a city in 1836, Cleveland annexed its rival, Ohio City, in 1854. During the Civil War, the new Atlantic & Great Western Railway, which connected with the Erie Railroad, tied Cleveland to the oil fields and became the biggest oil carrier in the country. Along the tracks in Cleveland, refineries sprang up to make the crude oil into marketable lubrication for machinery and kerosene for lamps. By 1863 Rockefeller had bought into a refinery, and in 1865 (at the age of twenty-six) he bought out one of his partners for $75,200. By the end of that year his refinery had grossed $1,200,000 (from a capacity of 505 barrels a day), more than double that of any other in the region.

Overproduction and the depression of 1867–68 brought down the price and killed off many smaller refineries, but Rockefeller survived. Railroads then competed harder than ever for the business of the remaining companies. There were no published freight rates, and the roads gave "special" rates to all their customers. Rockefeller was ingenious at playing off the competing roads against one another. He set up his own cooperage plants for making barrels, bought his own forests to supply the timber, produced his own chemicals for the refining processes, bought ships and railroad cars to carry his products, and yet watched every penny of cost. He found new markets for by-products. He used his large volume of shipments (promising to ship daily sixty carloads of refined oil by the New York Central–Lake Shore System) to secure the lowest rates.

But the fluctuations of the price of oil, due to unpredictable new sources, produced what Rockefeller called "destructive competition." He envisaged a huge combination to control the market, and called it the Standard Oil Company of Ohio. By 1872 his company was refining 10,000 barrels of kerosene a day—the largest operation of its kind anywhere. Then he went into the pipe-line business, which in the long run was essential if he was to perfect his monopoly. At his insistence one of his chemists devised a process for refining the cheap sulfur-base oil of Ohio, and so he opened up a whole new source of supply. By 1890 he had extended his marketing, and was using a fleet of tank wagons to deliver Standard kerosene to the consumer's door. As his organization reached out, his empty five-gallon cans were serving housewives in primitive huts and hovels on all continents. "Oil for the lamps of China" was a Standard product.

Rockefeller's grasp of public opinion was weaker than his understanding of rate negotiation and the competitive squeeze. He professed surprise at the well-documented attacks like Henry Demarest Lloyd's "Story of a Great Monopoly" in the *Atlantic Monthly* in 1881, and at the legislative hearings on the trusts. But these provided the basis for the Sherman Anti-Trust Act of 1890. When the Standard Oil Trust was dissolved by order of the Ohio Supreme Court in 1892, Rockefeller's lawyers proved more than equal to the challenge, and their newly invented "holding company" kept Rockefeller in the saddle.

The Standard Oil combination was one of the organizing achievements of the century. The price of oil products actually declined during the heyday of Standard Oil monopoly, but might it have declined still more if it had not been for Standard Oil? Rockefeller's ruthless tactics—his use of threats, his ability to make competitors "sweat," his willingness to employ strong-arm tactics, espionage (some even said murder)—became the reformist cliché of the century.

Rockefeller was a distinctively American breed. For he exploited a mysterious new mineral whose source was unknown and whose supply could not be estimated. He built his fortune in the Western vagueness. What was most remarkable and most New Worldly about Rockefeller was not his boldness in overstepping the bounds of common decency or of familiar business ethics. His methods had the authentic seductive stamp of a moral-legal ambiguity that flourished beyond precedent in America. The best lawyers of his day, men of the highest legal ethics, were employed by Rockefeller to devise his most dubious tactics. The trust—the notorious instrument of his ruthlessness—was one of the most ancient inventions of English law, devised centuries before in the moral laboratories of the Chancery and for the courts of Equity whose watchword was always a scrupulous concern for conscience. When the trust was made into an instrument to outrage the public conscience, it was only another symbol of the ambiguities that blessed and plagued the burgeoning West, that made possible both its worst and its best.

John D. Rockefeller was an American Cecil Rhodes, but in the

United States the empire was within. Rhodes's reckless unconcern for the African colonial was sanctioned by a pious faith in the "Anglo-Saxon" race. Rockefeller's unconcern for his American competitors was sanctioned by Baptist piety. But in England somehow the Victorian moral imperatives remained unclouded. Was not Africa a land of "natives"? And what about the White Man's Burden?

Since the American empire was inside the expanding nation, Americans somehow incorporated colonial ambiguities into widespread national ways of believing. Go-Getting Morality—the morality of lawless sheriffs and honest desperadoes—had a refreshing and energizing appeal. It spread easily from West to East, like other creative American tendencies. Historians have too long dazzled us with talk of a "Westward Movement." American civilization was just as much the product of an "Eastward Movement." A movement from the Western verges toward the respectable established East—of visions and uncertainties which would explain much that America had to offer the world.

Rockefeller, the ruthless philanthropist who gave no quarter to a weaker competitor, somehow considered himself a trustee for the poor everywhere. In an age of Wild Bill Hickoks and Billy the Kids he was a colossus of moral-legal ambiguity. The richest man of the age, he was one of its most conspicuously ascetic. After retirement from Standard Oil, Rockefeller (who ten years earlier had endowed a new University of Chicago) founded the Rockefeller Institute for Medical Research (1901); the General Education Board (1902), which conquered the hookworm in the South and helped reform American medical education; the Rockefeller Foundation (1913), "to promote the well-being of mankind throughout the world," which attacked yellow fever in Latin America and built medical education in China. Before his death Rockefeller's benefactions exceeded a half-billion dollars.

6

Generalized Go-Getters: Lawyers

THE RELATIONS BETWEEN the more and the less developed areas of the world everywhere provide a fertile field for lawyers. When there is a metropolis, a center of legislation and organization, a source of capital and knowledge and know-how which draws power and profit from lands at a great distance, there are all sorts of well-paid chores which require the lawyer's techniques. The multiplication of American lawyers in the colonial period was partly explained by the needs of novel colonial enterprises and by the expanding, unprecedented relations with the government back home in England. In London and Paris during the late nineteenth and early twentieth centuries, ambitious young colonials from Africa, Asia, and Australia could be found studying law to prepare themselves to return to places of wealth and power back home. When independence and anticolonial movements grew, these same lawyers, trained in the technical language of imperial relations, became constitution makers, government shapers, and political leaders of new nations.

The American West developed a relationship to the Atlantic-coast metropolises during the nineteenth century which was similar in many ways to that between British colonies like Australia and the metropolis of London. There, too—in Montana, Wyoming, Colorado, and the other states of the cattle-raising, mineral-rich West—the new investment capital had to be drawn from Eastern metropolises, thousands of miles distant. And this opened the way for enterprising lawyers who had new duties and opportunities as promoters, organizers, and intelligence agents.

In Old World empires, the enterprise and technical know-how of these agents of the metropolis were drawn off to the new countries, and so were subtracted from the national resource. In the United States, the federal system of a burgeoning rich continent kept these ambitious energies within the nation, and allowed them to be freely transplanted with shifting opportunities.

THE DEVELOPING WEST in the century after the Civil War was the scene of promising new careers in business and politics for young men who had the qualifications or the brashness to call themselves lawyers. Investors in the East employed local lawyers in small Western towns to advise them on the prospects for profit out there in cattle, mining, and railroads. And with this Eastern capital at his command, a young lawyer could do the favors which produced the Western fortunes. He could boost towns into cities, and could himself become a rich man or at least a potent vote getter.

The Wolcott brothers (descended from colonial settlers of New England) were a brilliant example. Edward Oliver Wolcott, the son of a Congregational minister in a small town in western Massachusetts, served when only sixteen as a private in the Civil War. He attended Yale College, received his LL.B. from Harvard Law School in 1875, then went out to join his brother Henry, who had settled in the village of Blackhawk, Colorado. After teaching school briefly there, Wolcott moved to the more promising Georgetown, county seat of Clear Creek County, just west of Denver. There he began to practice law. He became adept in the special mysteries of mining law, which were important to prospective investors in the East. Within a year (in 1876, the very year that Colorado became a state) he was elected district attorney and town attorney, he attracted attention by his work as public prosecutor, and two years later he was elected to the Colorado Senate. After moving to Denver in 1879, Wolcott was a power in Republican politics, and managed to be elected to the United States Senate (the state legislature still made the choice) in 1889 and again in 1895. The Wolcott firm had, by now, been named legal counsel to the Denver & Rio Grande Railroad, and to other large corporations. Wolcott himself was becoming prominent in national politics as an early champion of the silver interests. Meanwhile brother Henry, who had risen to wealth in the Colorado Smelting and Mining Company and the Colorado Fuel and Iron Company, was made president of the Colorado Telephone Company.

As Colorado prospered, the advice and collaboration of the Wolcott brothers became increasingly valuable to cautious Eastern investors, two thousand miles removed from the scene of promises. Henry Hyde, president of the Equitable Life Assurance Society of New York, was one of those who asked them for regular reports on "the political and business gossip." "I have greater faith than ever in this city," Henry Wolcott reported in 1895. "The right kind of people have come to make Denver a home and we have no rival for several thousand miles in either direction." Soon afterward Hyde invested insurance company funds in Denver to help build two pioneer skyscrapers. But the Wolcotts were not always so optimistic. They shrewdly warned Hyde against buying into the First National Bank of Denver because they had inside information that the management had been "placing too much confidence in the statements made to them by their customers," and within a few years their fears proved justified.

Out of the need for reliable financial information at a distance grew another American institution that made information its commodity. After the Panic of 1837, the enterprising credit manager of a New York silk jobber saw that many New York wholesalers needed reliable credit information on the country storekeepers who wanted to buy their goods. He suspected that they would be willing to pay a subscription fee for regular credit information. This man, the New England–born son of a devoutly Calvinist family, was Lewis Tappan. By 1849 Tappan's Mercantile Agency, as his credit-rating firm was called, had made so much money that Tappan could retire and devote himself to the abolitionist work that brought him fame. Just then, R. G. Dun, a twenty-four-year-old self-made merchant from a small town in Ohio, came to New York, where he joined Tappan's Mercantile Agency. Young Dun's talent for organizing expanded the business into a national enterprise, and by 1859 he was the sole owner of what became known as R. G. Dun & Company.

In 1861, when civil war came, Dun had offices all over the country, including the South. And after the war, his company flourished by supplying the businesses that were becoming more and more national with the reliable information they needed about faraway customers. Dun hired young lawyers in the small towns out West to make confidential investigations of local businesses. He paid as much attention to gathering information on the credit reliability of the proprietor of the Miner's Delight bar in South Pass City, Wyoming, as on the owner of the largest general store in Denver. Dun's long-range program for his clients included the detailed credit analysis of different regions: in 1872 it was Indian Territory (later Oklahoma); in 1873, southern and central California.

It was not easy to organize a continent-wide network of investigators who could secure small-town confidences, and yet not be tempted to put a good face on the financial condition of friends. "Age 32," went a typical report on a young lawyer-businessman, "a pretty fair lawyer but bears a bad reputation at one time threatened with criminal prosecution in debt now." Another read: "Fair habits, tho' he lives up to his income and is not believed to have much responsibility of his own." Dun's offices were among the first to use the typewriter, and in other ways, too, Dun pioneered in using new technology. By 1893 he had his own modern printing plant and was publishing *Dun's Review*, a weekly report on business conditions. As American business expanded over the world, Dun opened offices in Europe, Australia, and Africa. He died in 1900, but the firm lived on.

It became the famous twentieth-century Dun & Bradstreet in 1933 when it merged with a company which had been founded in 1849 by John M. Bradstreet, an enterprising Cincinnati lawyer-businessman.

EASTERN BUSINESSMEN EXPANDING into the half-known West needed counselors and advocates who knew their way around the laws and folkways of Montana, Wyoming, and Utah. Railroad builders retained "local counselors" along their Western routes. One small-town lawyer in Telluride, Colorado, was in charge of the mining interests of the wealthy Livermores of Boston. Others advised wealthy clients in Chicago, New York, or Philadelphia. The remoteness and geographic vagueness of the West which made it fertile of hoaxes and mining swindles also opened the opportunity there for an honest young man to secure the confidence (and sometimes, too, the capital) of powerful Eastern industrialists. It was the day of the organizer, the man who prospered by inventing new ways of drawing small units into more profitable large combinations. In the sprawling nation, the lawyer was apt to know how it could (and couldn't) be done. If he was clever, ambitious, and energetic, his know-how could serve him for capital.

Because the railroads touched so many questions of property—involving land law, public franchises, the law of common carrier and eminent domain, among others—the railroad builders especially needed lawyers. Railroad systems grew by adding one line to another, reaching out to new jurisdictions, across new states or territories. It was a great day for the lawyer-organizer.

One of the most brilliant of these was James Frederick Joy, who arrived in Detroit in 1837, the very year that Michigan was admitted to the Union. Having graduated from Dartmouth College and the recently founded Harvard Law School, he was unusually well prepared to seize the opportunities of the moment. The new state of Michigan had just authorized a $5 million loan to build three railroads across the state, but the Panic of 1837 intervened before much progress could be made. Joy persuaded the politicians to sell these railroads to private investors, and then induced some New York and Boston businessmen to put up the $2 million to buy the Michigan Central. In 1850 he helped push their line westward to Chicago by negotiating with the Illinois Central to use their tracks, enlisting the help in Springfield of a young lawyer named Abraham Lincoln. And from Chicago he moved farther west. In 1854 he engineered the liberal Illinois legislation to merge four small railroads into the Chicago, Burlington & Quincy, whose very name advertised the extension of the Joy lines westward to Iowa. Taking advantage of the

Panic of 1857, Joy bought at a bargain price another railroad, which had just secured a federal land grant of 350,000 acres.

By 1873 Joy's lines reached Kearney in central Nebraska, where they linked with the Union Pacific, which reached all the way west to the ocean. Joy then moved south toward the Gulf of Mexico, adding one little railway line after another, accumulating valuable state charters and federal land grants as he went. He founded canal companies to connect with his rail lines. And he became a pioneer bridge builder. The crucial weakness of his Burlington line between Chicago and Kansas City was the lack of a bridge across the Mississippi. He formed a company in 1868 especially to build the bridge at Quincy and defied critics by spending $1.5 million on the project. The Burlington's business in that area doubled the following year. He then went on to build the first permanent bridge across the Missouri, at Kansas City. When Joy retired from the presidency of the Burlington he was succeeded by another lawyer, who had made his start as the local attorney for the Michigan Central.

One of the most ingenious of the lawyer-organizers was Samuel C. T. Dodd, who had the good luck to be raised in a little town in western Pennsylvania near the first oil strike. In 1859, the year when Drake struck oil, young Dodd had just been admitted to the bar after obtaining a degree at Jefferson College and serving two years' apprenticeship in his native Franklin. Seeing that the growing oil business would require legal invention, he became an expert on corporation law when other small-town lawyers had barely heard of the subject. It was Dodd who developed the trust. He transformed that familiar device of English equity into Rockefeller's instrument of business combination, and then, as Rockefeller's confidant and as principal counsel to the Standard Oil Company when trusts came under attack, he devised the "holding company."

AMERICAN NEEDS for new devices to explore and exploit the continent, and the random quest for fortunes, produced myriad new techniques, machines, and gadgets. While the inventor himself might be a lonely, unworldly genius, there was commonly somebody else nearby who saw the chance to make a fortune. These calculating bystanders were often lawyers. There was hardly a major invention in the century after the Civil War which did not become a legal battlefield. While many battles were fought over patents, questions of patent law were inevitably confused with technicalities of contract, corporation law, taxation, and all sorts of common-law rights and duties. And these were entangled too with "interstate commerce," conflict of jurisdictions, and other mysteries of the Constitution.

The cast of characters in the American patent dramas varied, but the plot was remarkably uniform. Several men more or less simultaneously would devise a new machine or technique. Each wished to keep for himself or for his licensees all the profits of production. Meanwhile scores of businessmen would have entered the scene, having purchased fragments of the legal rights of the competing "original" inventors. Then, of course, every "improver" claimed that his version was the only one which really did the job. Legal battles went on for decades, but regardless of which inventor or businessman won a battle, the lawyers always won the war. They emerged not only with substantial fees, but also with expert knowledge of the company's rights and vulnerabilities that not infrequently left them in control of the firm. Beginning as pilots, they ended as captains.

This drama was reenacted with a familiarity that would be monotonous if the personalities had not been so flamboyant, the hopes so extravagant, the stakes so enormous, the products so unprecedented. There were the stories of the sewing machine (Elias Howe, Jr., against Isaac Merrit Singer and others) and the reaper (Cyrus McCormick's battles against Obed Hussey and others, engaging the legal talents of William H. Seward, Edwin M. Stanton, Judah P. Benjamin, Roscoe Conkling, and Abraham Lincoln), and the many legal battles surrounding the introduction of barbed wire, the telephone (Alexander Graham Bell against Elisha Gray, Thomas Alva Edison, Emile Berliner and others), and the phonograph. It was a sign that the time was ripe for an invention when a number of inventors were perfecting it simultaneously, and when the best lawyers had found it worth their while to organize the contending forces. The importance of any new technique in transforming American life could roughly be measured by the quantity of lawyerly energies which it called forth. It is not surprising, then, that while the century after the Civil War produced few legal classics and not many great American judges, there was a bumper crop of rich and famous American lawyers.

None of the legal battles was more prolonged, or more dramatic, than the Battle of the Automobile. The central figure in that battle was a man who, by the skillful combination of technical know-how and legal technique, dominated the production of automobiles in the early, formative years of the industry, but whose name never became a household word. George Baldwin Selden was a man with a bent for engineering and the inventor's capacity to be dominated by a single purpose. His father, a prosperous and strong-willed lawyer of Rochester, New York, had served as judge of the State Court of Appeals and as lieutenant governor, and he was determined that his son should become a lawyer. After a brief tour in the Union Army, young Selden studied classics at Yale, attended the Sheffield Scientific School, and then, obeying his father's wishes, entered his father's law office as an apprentice. According to Selden, a chance conversation he over-heard between his father and a client on the possibilities of a self-propelled road vehicle gave him the *idée fixe* of his life.

By 1871 he was admitted to the bar and opened his own office as a patent lawyer a few years later. George Eastman was his client, and in his Rochester office he prepared Eastman's application for a patent on the process for coating gelatine on photographic dry plates, which opened the way for celluloid film and the motion pictures. Mean-while, in off-hours in his basement workshop Selden tinkered with various inventions of his own. He made a device for attaching solid rubber tires to wheels, he patented new machinery for making bar-rel hoops, and he designed a typewriter. But his ruling passion was a self-propelled road vehicle. The "road locomotives," of which a few were already in use in the early 1870's, were boilers on wheels. Though they weighed three tons, they could be moved about for farm work. Enlisting the help of a Rochester model maker, Selden tried to perfect a light-weight engine. By 1873, when he was only twenty-seven, he decided that for his purposes an entirely different power source was needed. He intended, as he told a friend, "to work a revolution in locomotion upon common roads, and . . . his invention would be entitled to a place in industrial history analogous to that of the inventor of the steam engine, the locomotive, the cotton-gin and the telegraph."

Selden then began experimenting with internal-combustion en-gines. The earliest such engines, already in use in Europe by the 1870's, were stationary units fueled by pipes attached to the town gas system. When Selden and his partner went to the Philadelphia Cen-tennial Exposition in 1876 to demonstrate their patented machine for shaving and finishing barrel hoops, he studied the array of engines there displayed. Most promising for Selden's purposes was the Bray-ton engine, developed by an Englishman living in Boston. By con-trast to the others, which operated on illuminating gas piped to the machine, Brayton's engine used crude petroleum. But this machine, too, was impossibly cumbersome, taking 1,160 pounds of machine to develop 1.4 horsepower (828½ pounds of machine per horsepower). Selden imagined a way of redesigning the machine to reduce the weight of the engine so it might be the power source for a light road vehicle. By 1878 he had produced an engine weighing 370 pounds which developed 2 horsepower (only 185 pounds per horsepower).

From this time on, Selden diverted his energies from the effort to improve his vehicle to his attempt to secure the maximum legal protection of his imagined right to profit from all future self-propelled road vehicles. In 1879, instead of submitting a working model to the United States Patent Office, as the law required, Selden offered a model which only represented "in outline the general features," and relied mainly on a verbal description. This was a calculated tactic, for while the right to legal protection dated from the time of first *application* for a patent (in Selden's case, May 8, 1879), the expiration of the seventeen-year right to control a patent dated from the *granting* of the patent. Selden therefore applied for his patent as early as he could, but shrewdly delayed his actual receipt of the patent as long as possible. Meanwhile he took advantage of the inventor's option to amend his application, adding to his original design any improvements that later came to his attention.

Selden thus cleverly avoided risking his idea to the specificity of blueprints or working models until the manufacture of motor cars seemed to have become profitable. Not until November 5, 1895, sixteen years after Selden's patent application, did the U.S. Patent Office actually issue him patent No. 549,160 for a "road engine." This long delay had extended Selden's rights to royalties into a period when the financial community was willing to invest its capital in manufacturing "road engines." Thus, concludes William Greenleaf, the historian of the Selden patents, "an inventor who might have ranked as an honored automotive pioneer became instead a hawklike figure lying in wait."

But Selden's waiting was rewarded. In 1899, while reserving a royalty on each machine, he sold the patent rights to a group of financiers. In the following year they brought a successful lawsuit for infringement of the Selden patent. As a result of this suit, in 1903 ten leading automobile makers combined to form the Association of Licensed Automobile Manufacturers and purchased the right to use the Selden patent at a royalty of 1¼ percent of the retail price on each automobile sold. Within a few years, Selden was receiving a royalty on almost every car manufactured in the United States.

The challenge to Selden did not come from businessmen, who appeared willing enough to pay him their tribute so long as they could share the profits. Instead it came from another inventor who lacked the lawyer's expertise but who was securely clad in the armor of a primitive moralist. Henry Ford applied to the owners of the Selden patent for one of their usual licenses to manufacture automobiles. They refused for the reason, among others, that Ford was a mere "assembler" of the automotive parts made by others, and not truly a "manufacturer" at all, and so was not possibly qualified to receive the license which went only to competent manufacturers. Ford, confirmed in his Populist hatred of monopoly, went ahead anyway making his automobile, which he said was "the product of his own brain and no man on earth was entitled to any 'rake-off' from that particular car." He already had his vision of a car inexpensive enough to sell by the millions.

The Selden group started an infringement suit against Ford in 1903. It was eight years before the United States Court of Appeals settled the matter. The landmark decision by Judge Walter Chadwick Noyes provided a wonderfully legalistic anticlimax to what may have been the most expensive single litigation in American history. The Selden patent, said the court, *was* valid. But, Judge Noyes explained, showing a remarkable grasp of automotive engineering which he had acquired for the occasion, Ford had *not* infringed the patent! The Selden patent covered only automobiles modeled on the Brayton two-cycle engine, while Ford's cars (and nearly all others being manufactured at the time) used a form of the substantially different Otto four-cycle engine. Selden was given a dose of his own medicine. The judge showed how Selden could win on legal points, and yet lose the game.

By the time the decision was rendered in 1911, Selden's patent had only a few more months to run. His royalties stopped at once. When Selden himself turned to manufacturing automobiles, he could not make a go of it. In his last words on his deathbed in 1922, at the age of seventy-seven, Selden proclaimed, "Morally the victory is mine."

Henry Ford, of all people, became the champion of the view that all patents were immoral. Really, Ford was fond of repeating, there was "very little new under the sun." When he ran for United States Senate in 1918, he declared his intention to abolish all patent laws. "They don't . . . stimulate invention—that is an exploded theory. But they do exploit the consumer, and place a heavy burden on productive industry." He explained in 1921, "I have taken out 300 or 400 patents in all countries, and I undertake to say there is not a new thing in our car."

The long battle itself had been a victory for the lawyers on both sides. The total amounts paid in royalties under the Selden claim had been about $5.8 million. But after subtracting all the various fees and commissions for production, management, sales, and legal advice, the sum that had actually trickled through the numerous corporate and partnership agreements into Selden's own pocket was only about $200,000. Lawyers' fees from the pro-Selden Association of Licensed Automobile Manufacturers in the first three years of the litigation against Ford came to $225,000, and were matched by a similar sum in the next five years. Ford paid his lawyers about $250,000. Incidentally, too, since the case was front-page news for many years, the lawyers received priceless advertising and publicity which built several of their political careers.

In the century after the Civil War, American lawyers attained a new kind of power. While the fees paid to lawyers were never a measure of their influence, the increase in lawyers' incomes in the twentieth century was remarkable. In 1929, the first year for which Department of Commerce statistics are available, some $689 million was spent for legal services. In 1968, the figure had reached $5.2 billion. For each year the amount spent on legal fees amounted to about two thirds of all the sums spent by individuals in that period on religious and welfare activities. "It is almost unbelievable, but true," observed Martin Mayer in his popular survey of lawyers, "that nobody has any very precise notion of what is done for the money."

WITH THE WIDENING American opportunities for lawyers, it is no wonder that their numbers increased without precedent. And to supply men qualified to seize the opportunities, there flourished another American institution, the Law School. There was nothing quite like it in any other modern nation. In England, even into the twentieth century, the training of lawyers was left either to small self-perpetuating aristocratic guilds in London or to general undergraduate programs in "jurisprudence" (often chosen by students because they were reputed to be easy) at aristocratic universities. In America even in colonial times, there were signs that the guild monopoly was being broken. In the mid-nineteenth century, with the settlement of the West, the founding of new states, the building of canals and railroads, and the construction of modern industry, peculiarly American opportunities for the legal profession called into being American law schools. These became richly endowed, specialized postgraduate institutions to train lawyers.

In 1833, it was estimated, the students in the United States taking any kind of school instruction in the law numbered about 150. The American pioneering in legal education, not surprisingly, began in New England, where the spirit of enterprise, the closeness to English sources, and the presence of Harvard College and its many enlightened benefactors prepared the way. Harvard Law School came gradually into being in the early decades of the nineteenth century, after the appointment of the first professor of law there in 1816. By 1860 there were already in the United States 21 university law schools, of which 12 still required only one year's work. New norms were set when, in 1876, Harvard lengthened its course to three years, and required for admission either a college degree or three years in Harvard College. The number of law schools increased to 51 in 1880, 102 in 1900, and 190 by 1938. These institutions continued to increase their enrollments until, by 1970, they were granting over 18,000 law degrees each year.

A great nationwide change in American legal education appeared after 1870. The common-law way of thinking, perfected and applied by Chief Justice Lemuel Shaw in Massachusetts and by others elsewhere, was primarily a judge-declared law, which deftly bent ancient traditions and esoteric vocabularies to the new needs of the coming age of railroads. Before then, the lawyers who rode legal careers to national fame were men like Rufus Choate and Robert Y. Hayne and Daniel Webster and Judah P. Benjamin, noted for their oratory, their mastery of constitutional issues, and their skilled advocacy in such traditional subjects as contract and the law of land. James Kent, Joseph Story, and Nathan Dane built their reputations as shapers of the law on their legal treatises which expounded and clarified principles.

After the Civil War the peculiarly American challenge to ambitious young men hoping for a legal career came less from the mastery of grand legal principles than from an attention to minutiae, a concern for new nuances of fact, and an ability to negotiate and manipulate. Now the law seemed less a treasury of principles to be discovered than a set of instruments to be used. These uses could be discovered in schoolrooms only if somehow the law classroom became a laboratory of living situations. There the student might see how the legal tools had actually been used, and for what purposes.

A new approach to legal education, signaling a vigorous new American approach to the uses of law, was the invention of a dean of Harvard Law School, Christopher Columbus Langdell. He had been selected in 1870 by Charles W. Eliot, the new president of Harvard whose background as a chemist made him sympathetic to a new kind of laboratory approach to the law. Langdell's reform— the "case method" of instruction—was marvelously simple. The students, who formerly would have been required to read treatises expounding "general principles" of the law, were now exposed to the actual cases in which the principles had been applied. The traditional treatise was replaced by a new kind of legal laboratory manual: the "casebook." Langdell's own *Selection of Cases on the Law of Contracts* (1871) was the first. The casebooks collected examples of actual situations in which the legal principles had been applied. The attention of students was thus directed to factual minutiae and to the whole social context in which the case occurred. The object was not merely to acquaint the law student with the doctrines of law but, Langdell explained, even more to give him "such a mastery of these as to be able to apply them with constant facility and certainty to the evertangled skein of human affairs." By 1910 most American law schools had adopted this case method. English law schools, in the same common-law tradition, continued to use old-style textbooks.

While the training of lawyers was given a new academic dignity, law students were rapidly given a wide and usable knowledge of practical legal situations. The law, once a metaphysic, had become a social science.

"A town that can't support one lawyer," goes an old American proverb, "can always support two." Of the new opportunities opened by American civilization in the century after the Civil War, none were more striking than those for lawyers. The multiplying legislatures (by 1959 there were one hundred state lawmaking bodies, in addition to the Congress), the proliferating regulatory agencies, and the multiplying courts—federal, state, and municipal—provided opportunities, forums, and rewards for the nation's lawyers. By 1970 there were some ten thousand judges and a third of a million lawyers in the United States.

7

Exploiting the Federal Commodity: Divorce and Gambling

IN THE WOMB of the federal system itself there lay hidden some remarkable money-making opportunities. As novel as the cattle trade which prospered on the public domain, or the oil business which drilled rocks for a flowing black mineral to light the lamps of China and bring fortunes to businessmen in Cleveland and New York, was a new competitive American business of lawmaking.

The most spectacular scene of these unpredicted opportunities was Nevada. One of the largest states in the Union (2,500 square miles larger than the combined areas of Maine, New Jersey, Vermont, Connecticut, Massachusetts, Maryland, Delaware, West Virginia, New Hampshire, and Rhode Island), for most of its history Nevada had had the smallest population of any state. As late as 1940 the United States Census gave Nevada only 110,247, and in 1970 it still had the least population density of any state but Alaska. Except for the Colorado River, which runs a hundred miles along the extreme southeastern corner, and twenty-mile-long Lake Tahoe at the southwestern corner, Nevada was marked off by no natural boundaries. It was a vast and arbitrary geometric chunk for which there appeared no reason in geography.

THE REAL EXPLANATION for the extent and dimensions of Nevada lay hidden underground. The area later to become Nevada had been acquired from Mexico in 1848, and two years later became part of the new Mormon-controlled Territory of Utah. When, in 1859, the rich Comstock Silver Lode was discovered at Virginia City at the extreme western end of Utah Territory, newly arrived miners, distrusting the Mormon government, petitioned Congress, and a separate Nevada Territory was created in 1861. Many residents of the territory did not want statehood, for they assumed it would bring increased taxes. But President Abraham Lincoln needed the support of a new state, which would add two votes in the Senate and one in the House. Anxious for the congressional votes to pass the Thirteenth Amendment, Lincoln said bluntly that it was "a question of three votes or new armies." Also in the upcoming presidential election of 1864 a new state of Nevada would add three votes (almost certainly for Lincoln) in the Electoral College. The bill making Nevada a state was signed by Lincoln on October 31, 1864, one week before Election Day. With their usual talent for euphemism, Nevadans in the latter nineteenth century christened themselves the "Battle-Born State."

In fact, Nevada had been the creature not of freedom's battle, nor of tradition, nor of nature, but of politics and silver. For about twenty years, while the Comstock Lode held out, the state somehow prospered. But it was not a democratic prosperity. In California, the people who arrived to seek their fortunes found gold, if they were lucky, in the streams, where a pan and some hard work gave a man his chance. In Nevada, by contrast, the silver was sequestered deep inside a mountain in the heart of a desert. Large sums of capital and expensive heavy equipment were required to extract the ore from the rock and then to transport it to where it could be refined. From the very beginning you needed giant hoisting machines, pumps, stamps, and drills.

The great drama of the Comstock Lode was not a story of mining-camp justice, of unshaven fortune seekers or reckless claim-jumpers. Nevada silver was not the hard-won reward of penniless prospectors but the loot which wealthy bankers and businessmen, mostly from San Francisco, systematically drained from Nevada mines. In the twenty years after 1859, about $500 million in silver and gold was extracted. From the time of its discovery until the mid-1880's, the Lode was producing annually about half the silver being mined in the United States.

Then the Comstock, which had appeared like a comet, disappeared with hardly a trace. Other gold and silver deposits were found at Tonopah and elsewhere in the state, but they were nothing to compare to the Comstock. San Francisco bankers and businessmen went back to California with their Nevada profits. Between 1880 and 1903, when other mountain states were increasing their population threefold, the population of Nevada declined from 65,000 to 45,000. Nevada came to be described as a place you had to go through to get from Ogden, Utah, to California. There were some efforts to promote farming and cattle raising. The Southern Pacific Railroad, anxious to attract settlers, published cheery pamphlets ("The New Nevada: The Era of Irrigation and Opportunity"), but they persuaded very few. Eastern journalists began to call Nevada the nation's "rotten borough." And they asked whether a region once admitted to the Union ought not to be deprived of statehood when it ceased to have any considerable population.

But here they simply showed how little they understood of the West. The end of Nevada's Silver Age was the beginning of a New Nevada. The fewer the people, the greater the share for each in the benefits of "sovereignty." Nevada politics at the opening of the twentieth century, as Gilman Ostrander observes, had a kind of "town-meeting" air about it. Exploiting this advantage, Nevadans showed how enterprise and ingenuity could make a new resource out of statehood itself.

Under the federal system there was, of course, nothing new about a state that was "small" in area or in population using its "sovereignty" to exert a disproportionate power. Maryland, by staying out of the American confederation until 1781, had forced Virginia to yield to the whole nation her state's claims to the vast northwest. And Rhode Island had stayed away from the Constitutional Convention of 1787, hoping that her hold-out position would increase her power to bargain. But in the twentieth century, being a small state yielded a different kind of advantage. Not simply a disproportionately potent voice in the councils of the nation. This new advantage required a mobile population and depended on speedy, inexpensive transportation.

THE NEVADA LEGISLATURE'S first effort to outdo the other sovereign states came in 1903 with its passage of a new law of business corporations. Businessmen were to be enticed to set up their companies in Nevada because under Nevada's lax new rules there would be no annual tax on corporations, no troublesome supervision over the issuance of stock or the conduct of business. But other states quickly matched these advantages, and some states, such as California, tried to outlaw their competitors by making it illegal for any corporation to sell its stock within their borders unless the corporation had met their own strict requirements.

Nevada's first real opportunity for profitable legislative competition was found in a less prosaic branch of the law—divorce. Here was an area of ancient controversy where Nevada's other peculiar advantages would make it possible for her legislative ingenuity and enterprise to pay off.

Marriage, divorce, and celibacy had of course (long before Henry VIII!) been a battleground for competing jurisdictions. "Wherefore they are no more twain, but one flesh," Jesus had said, "What therefore God hath joined together, let not man put asunder" (Matthew, xix, 6). The Roman Catholic Church included marriage among the seven sacraments. Like the perpetual mystic union between Christ and his Church, a valid marriage of man and wife would never be dissolved. The Church therefore did not really recognize divorce at all. What was called divorce *(divortium a vinculo)* was really annulment, and in theory could be granted only for disabling causes (such as impotence or a legally existing prior marriage) which had prevented the supposed marriage from taking place at all. What the canon lawyers called *divortium a mensa et thoro* (divorce from bed and board) was only judicial separation, and carried no privilege of remarriage. Abuses in the Church's handling of matters of marriage had been among the arguments for the Protestant Reformation. Marriage, according to Martin Luther, was not a sacrament, but "a secular and outward thing, having to do with wife and children, house and home, and with other matters that belong to the realm of the government, all of which have been completely subjected to reason." Therefore the rules of marriage and divorce "should be left to the lawyers and made subject to the secular government."

The New England Puritans took Luther's distinction so seriously that they not only required marriages to be solemnized by a civil magistrate but in 1647 actually forbade the preaching of a wedding sermon. They feared the popish tendency to make marriage a sacrament. Before the end of the seventeenth century, the General Court of Massachusetts felt secure enough on this matter to allow ministers as well as justices of the peace to perform the marriage ceremony. During the colonial period, the New England colonies made their own laws of divorce. The Southern colonies followed English law, but this really left them without remedies, since they had no ecclesiastical courts. In the middle colonies, royal officials cracked down on attempts to pass divorce laws. While the grounds for divorce remained strict by modern American standards, they were generally much wider than those allowed in England. In the late eighteenth century, and especially in the 1770's as part of an effort to tighten control over the colonies, the British government (for example, in their instructions to royal governors, November 24, 1773) disallowed colonial laws "for the divorce of persons joined together in Holy Marriage." This must be counted among the minor irritations that stirred aggrieved American husbands and wives to fight for independence.

The winning of independence then, confirmed the freedom of each state to go its own way in the law of divorce. The spirit of the times, the enthusiasm for freedom, and the hatred of tyranny of all kinds which awakened in some quarters the movement to abolish Negro slavery, encouraged others to try to abolish domestic tyranny, to bring relief to those (in the phrase of one pamphleteer in 1788) "who are frequently united together in the worst of bondage to each other . . . relief to the miserable, hen-pecked husband, or the abused, and insulted, despised wife. . . . They are not only confined like a criminal to their punishment, but their confinement must last till death."

Between the Revolution and the Civil War, most states liberalized their laws of divorce. Generally speaking, the new states formed from the Old Northwest were more liberal, and the seaboard states more strict, New York and South Carolina being strictest of all. In nearly every state the movement was to regularize and standardize divorce procedure. By 1867, thirty-three of the then thirty-seven states had outlawed legislative divorce. This was an important step toward democratizing divorce, since the "Private Act" of the state legislature had been a device by which persons of wealth and influence obtained special treatment. But there remained a wide variety of rules because under the federal system, marriage and divorce remained the province of the states.

A result of the federal system, then, from the very beginning, was the practice of "migratory" divorce. A married person who found the laws of his own state inconvenient would go temporarily to another state to secure his divorce. Before the Civil War, unhappily married Easterners were going west to Ohio, Indiana, and Illinois in search of marital freedom. "We are overrun by a flock of ill-used, and ill-using, petulant, libidinous, extravagant, ill-fitting husbands and wives," the *Indiana Daily Journal* reported in 1858, "as a sink is overrun with the foul water of a whole house." Horace Greeley objected that a well-known New Yorker had gone to Indiana, secured his divorce by dinnertime "and, in the course of the evening was married to his new inamorata, who had come on for the purpose, and was staying at the same hotel with him. They soon started for home, having no more use for the State of Indiana; and, on arriving, he introduced his new wife to her astonished predecessor, whom he notified that she must pack up and go, as there was no room for her in that house any longer. So she went." In 1873 the Indiana legislature enacted a strict new law which destroyed the state's migratory divorce business. But Chicago remained a notoriously popular divorce center, and this business, like others, moved West with the population. Stories were told of how specially convened miners' meetings in Idaho would oblige one of their number by ceremoniously dissolving his marriage.

Among the enticements which Western states offered were their loose definitions of the admissible grounds for divorce. Some states actually enacted an "omnibus" clause allowing any cause the court might find proper. Equally important in the competition for the migratory divorce business were their vague, almost nonexistent, residence requirements. In Western states, where nearly everybody had arrived only recently, if there were to be any voters at all recent-arrivals had to be considered legal residents. Boosters for upstart cities, anxious to attract a population, made newcomers into full-fledged "residents" in short order. Territories and states that required only brief residence for the right to vote found that requirement suitable for other purposes as well.

Dakota Territory, with a three-month residence requirement, was attracting divorce seekers from the East before 1880. North Dakota and South Dakota, both admitted as states in 1889, preserved this hospitable residence requirement, and so laid the foundation for a thriving divorce business. Hotel owners, saloon keepers and merchants, and of course lawyers, all prospered from the free-spending visitors who had come for the quickest route from misery to bliss. "The notoriety South Dakota has got," a local lawyer boasted, "is doing us no harm. It advertises us abroad, brings thousands of dollars here, not only to pay expenses of divorce suits, but, for investment as well." For this promising new business, there arose a lively civic competition between Sioux Falls and Yankton. Sioux Falls, which already had two colleges, had the advantage also of a thirty-three-year-old judge, of "just that ardent and susceptible age when woman's distress appeals to man most strongly. In all the cases that Judge Aikens has heard where the fair sex has appeared in complaint, his course has been marked by the tenderest sympathy and the most delicate solicitude for their interests." But Yankton, although it still had only one college, had the compensating advantage of a new hotel which was advertised in an elegant brochure "sent by the hundreds to society in New York, Boston, and Philadelphia."

The two Dakotas themselves were also in competition for the

divorce business. When the Episcopal bishop of Sioux Falls in his New Year's sermon on January 1, 1893, delivered a jeremiad against the "consecutive polygamy" of quick remarriage after divorce and began lobbying in the state capital for stricter divorce laws in South Dakota, a hotel owner from Fargo, North Dakota, reportedly joined his campaign, in the hope that if South Dakota laws were stricter, the North Dakota divorce business would profit. But within a few years both Dakotas raised their residence requirements to one year, and so put themselves out of the competition.

This pattern—an early period of liberal divorce laws, followed by scandals, a conservative campaign for reform, and the tightening of laws, thereby spoiling the divorce business—was repeated all over the West. In the early years of the twentieth century, in addition to the Dakotas, several other Western territories and states (including Oklahoma, Wyoming, Texas, Nebraska, Idaho, and Nevada) counted the manufacture of divorce among their first local industries.

Their loose divorce laws were only the natural federal complement to the strict divorce laws of New York and South Carolina. The Nevada divorce mills thrived on the "morality" of New York. It was easier, too, for New York to retain its hypocritical chastity (and hence more difficult to change the laws of New York) because well-to-do New Yorkers always had the Reno alternative.

IN THE STATE OF NEVADA, divorce actually became a major force in the economy. And if there, more than elsewhere, the chronicle of divorce was spiced with scandal and romance, there too it bore vivid witness to the enterprising competitive spirit of the communities who built the West.

Until the beginning of the twentieth century, there were relatively few divorces granted in Nevada. For there were relatively few women residents in the state, and Nevada had not yet established its competitive advantage for migratory divorce. The first notorious Nevada divorce occurred in 1900 when Earl Russell, an English nobleman, after establishing the required six-month residence, secured his Nevada divorce, and promptly married another woman whom he took back with him to England. There his first wife, alleging that the Nevada divorce was invalid, sued for an English divorce on grounds of adultery. Earl Russell was indicted for bigamy, tried by his peers in the House of Lords, convicted, and eventually confined in the Tower of London. If this advertisement for Nevada divorces was somewhat ambiguous, it did at least publicize the brevity of the Nevada residence requirement and the laxity of its divorce laws.

The first "favorable" publicity in building this Nevada business came in 1906 when newspapers headlined the story of the unhappy

Laura Corey, who secured release from her adulterous husband by a Nevada divorce. William E. Corey was a self-made steel manufacturer who had risen from being a laborer in the Braddock, Pennsylvania, mills to become, at thirty-seven, president of the United States Steel Corporation. His colleagues described him as an "icicle in business." But outside the office he showed considerably more warmth, and in fact unceremoniously deserted his wife and family for the attractive musical-comedy singer, Mabelle Gilman. Then his wife, a poor miner's daughter whom he had married early in life, went to Reno for a divorce. Within nine months after the divorce, Corey married Miss Gilman. The press fumed with righteous indignation against Corey, but praised the laws of Nevada as the shield of the injured innocent.

The Nevada divorce business boomed, though not always for the benefit of violated innocence. Nevada lawyers advertised in Eastern newspapers that their state's six-month residence requirement was the shortest in the country. They described Nevada's numerous, easy-to-prove grounds for divorce, explained the state's convenient lack of requirement for corroborative proof of facts, and reminded readers that there was no Nevada bar to immediate remarriage. At least one lawyer was suspended briefly by the Nevada Supreme Court for such advertising. But the divorce practice grew, providing widespread financial benefits in the state. In 1910 (when Nevada divorces numbered three hundred per year), the familiar reform cycle began. Under pressure from clergymen and then from the Progressives, the state legislature in 1913 increased the residence requirement from six months to a year. But the lawyers, merchants, bartenders, hotelkeepers, and others quickly registered their protest. The Republican governor who had signed the divorce reform bill was defeated for reelection in 1914, along with some of the legislators who had supported the bill. At the very next biennial session of the state legislature in 1915, the bill was repealed and the six-month residence restored. The divorce business quickly revived, with the lucky assistance of a much-publicized visit from the movie queen Mary Pickford, who came for a Nevada divorce from her first husband so she would be free to marry Douglas Fairbanks.

Nevada still had competitors, and the legislature remained alert. In 1927, in the face of a growing threat from France and Mexico, and a rumor that Wyoming might reduce her residence requirement to three months, the Nevada legislature enacted a law requiring only three months' residence. Then again in 1931, when there were rumors that Idaho and Arkansas were about to enact the three-month residence, the Nevada legislature hastily reduced their residence requirement to six weeks.

"REVIVAL OF GOLD RUSH DAYS PREDICTED. BEAT THIS ONE, IF

YOU CAN" read the headline in the *Nevada State Journal*. The divorce business, as the historian Nelson Blake has pointed out, became increasingly confused with the tourist business. Instead of divorce seekers coming to establish residence to secure the desired legal result, and incidentally spending their money on entertainment, people came for fun, and incidentally found it convenient to get their divorce. It became hard to distinguish between fun-hungry vacationers and disconsolate divorce seekers. They all spent money in Nevada. In the early 1920's, when the six-month requirement was still in effect, Nevada had granted about 1,000 divorces each year; with the residence reduced to three months, the annual figure in 1928 reached 2,500; and the new six-week law in 1931 skyrocketed the number that year to 5,260. During the depths of the Depression the market for Nevada divorces, like that for other luxuries, declined. But the prosperity years of World War II brought new highs: 11,000 Nevada divorces in 1943, and three years later, 20,500. In the 1950's the number declined to an annual 10,000.

Nevada had also loosened its laws of marriage. In 1940, after California required a blood test and a three-day waiting period, Nevada was still offering (in Gilman Ostrander's phrase) "instant marriage, around the clock." This brought in a new crop of hasty honeymooners.

Tourism, too, stirred a lively new competitive spirit. Reno, which had been specially developed to accommodate divorce seekers, for several decades had almost all the divorce business. Of the 5,260 Nevada divorces in 1931, 4,745 were granted in Reno. But the day of the upstart town had not passed. Las Vegas, which was not even incorporated as a city until 1911, within twenty years had numerous neon-gleaming night clubs with a dazzling array of "chorus girls," comedians, and high-priced celebrities of stage and screen. "Getting it is half the fun." Divorce seekers from Los Angeles and elsewhere were soon persuaded that it was more fun to get unhitched in Las Vegas. By the late 1950's Las Vegas was granting nearly half the state's divorces. The divorce business and the entertainment business stimulated each other. In Nevada, in the two decades after 1950, the annual number of divorces per 1,000 of resident population was about ten times the national average, and the number of marriages about twentyfold. Nevada's divorce rate was five times that of any of the closest competitors (Florida, Oklahoma, Texas, Arizona, Idaho, Wyoming, and Alaska); and its marriage figure was ten times that of its closest competitor (South Carolina).

DIVORCE WAS NOT the only business by-product of the federal system. Another was gambling. Here, again, an unpopulous state like

Nevada was peculiarly well qualified to profit. Some historians have observed that Nevada's whole history was nothing but one long gamble. A less metaphorical explanation lies in the working of the federal system and in the legislated prudery of Nevada's sister states. Horse racing, for reasons of tradition, tended to be excepted from those common-law prohibitions brought over from England which made the keeping of a common gambling house indictable as a public nuisance. In 1887 New York, for example, allowed betting under special legal regulation at the race tracks. But in the early twentieth century, in some states, because of the rise of "bookies" (the first recorded use of this Americanism is 1909) and other abuses, race tracks were closed. Then, in the late '20's and early '30's, the legalized parimutuel system (facilitated by the completely electrical "totalizer" introduced in 1933), which used automatic vending machines to sell betting tickets, gave horse-race betting a new popularity. Still, legalized betting was tightly restricted: off-track betting was generally not allowed, and public gambling houses remained illegal. The states commonly outlawed gambling devices, and either regulated or prohibited pool halls, slot machines, and punch boards. The opportunities for gambling which were offered by boxing led some states to outlaw that sport, and led others to regulate it strictly under a public commission.

When the Depression hit Nevada in 1931, the divorce market lagged and there was widespread fear that other states might liberalize their divorce laws. Nevadans felt that merely reducing the divorce-residence requirement to six weeks might not be enough to insure economic recovery. The Nevada legislature in 1931, then, partly as a recovery measure, legalized gambling. But the tradition of clandestine gambling, from the days when it was illegal, was hard to overcome. Since gambling, when illegal, had been a discreetly private activity, there was no established pattern of promotion or advertising to widen the reach of the newly legalized gambling houses. Nevada's new laws opened the door for a new brand of Go-Getter.

Raymond Smith was the pioneer. With no experience as a professional gambler, Smith, bringing his two sons, came to Reno from California during the Great Depression in search of a living. Drawing on his earlier experience as a carnival barker, he used his native flair for organization to make gambling into a popular public entertainment. While illegal gamblers had survived by keeping their operations quiet, Smith saw that the success of legalized gambling would depend on advertising. From the day when he opened his first small casino on Virginia Street in Reno, he began an advertising campaign which culminated in thousands of billboards along the highways of the country. And he made "Harolds Club" (named after Raymond

Smith's son Harold; the omitted apostrophe was part of the trade-mark) into a national brand. He persuaded timid and suspicious middle-class Americans all over the country that they could put the same confidence in Harolds Club that they put in other nationally advertised products and services.

In short order Raymond Smith (whose career is delightfully chronicled by Gilman Ostrander) succeeded in democratizing gambling, "as Henry Ford had democratized the automobile." Before Smith, gambling casinos had thrived on the "high rollers" (the flamboyant sports of Mississippi river boats and of American folklore), the professional male gamblers who played for big stakes. A casino's profit or loss might depend on the draw of a card or a throw of the dice. Raymond Smith changed all this. By lowering the stakes and so enlarging his clientele, he aimed to produce a Woolworth's of the gambling business. Harolds Club was as different from the old gambling casino as the five-and-ten-cent store was different from the élite specialty shop.

To attract his Depression-stricken customers, Smith offered penny roulette and other stunts such as mouse roulette, in which a live mouse picked the winning number. And he set up rows of slot machines which enticed nickels, dimes, and quarters from people who did not even know the rules of poker or dice. (It was twenty years later that the slot machine acquired the American nickname of "one-armed bandit.") To make women feel at home and attract them to the gambling tables, he employed women dealers and women shills drawn from the past or prospective customers of the quickie divorce courts. These friendly feminine dealers were instructed to play according to fixed rules set by the house so that they never matched wits against the players. Part of their job was to advise inexperienced customers how to play. Smith even provided baby-sitters so that mothers would not have to leave their children unattended in motel rooms while they enjoyed Harolds Club.

True to the booster pattern, Raymond Smith became a notable local philanthropist. He built a museum of Western Americana for his customers, and offered scholarships to needy students at the University of Nevada. To customers of Harolds Club who had not heeded Smith's warning that they gamble no more than they could afford to lose, Smith actually lent small sums to help them get back home.

Harolds Club set the pace, and others followed. The Nevada Club prospered, and then came Harrah's Club (named after its proprietor William Harrah, who profited from the convenient confusion of names), and many others.

NEVADA GAMBLING FLOURISHED as a border industry—just over the border from illegality and from other states. None of the Nevada gambling resorts was located near the center of the state. Reno in the west was a scant dozen miles from the California boundary. Las Vegas in the southeastern tip was close to California, Arizona, and Utah; and Lake Tahoe actually marked the state's southwestern border with California. The Las Vegas town site, bought by the railroad back in 1903, had been headquarters for construction of the nearby Hoover Dam and was ready for the gambling boom created by the new Nevada laws in 1931. It had the advantage over Reno of being within easier driving distance from Los Angeles, San Diego, and other fast-growing centers in Southern California. After World War II, Las Vegas set a new pattern. If Reno was offering a five-and-ten for gambling customers, Las Vegas would provide grand new department stores of gambling. Just outside Las Vegas a new luxury gambling-and-entertainment development sprang up on "the Strip," a street in a new unincorporated area which called itself by the booster name of Paradise. Within a decade there appeared a galaxy of de luxe chromium-plated hotel-motel-night-club-casinos boasting extravagantly romantic names: the Desert Inn, Sahara, Showboat, Royal Nevada, Riviera, Moulin Rouge, Stardust, Martinique, Tropicana, Vegas Plasa, Casa Blanca, San Souci. Even the more modest of these cost $5 million. Drawing on Hollywood only two hundred and fifty miles away, they competed in Big Names to draw the Big Spenders. By 1955 it was estimated that $20 million was being spent annually around Las Vegas for entertainment offered free to patrons of the gambling tables.

Then in the 1950's came Lake Tahoe, pioneered by William Harrah from Reno, who had bought the especially desirable Nevada acreage just adjoining the California border. Casinos located there would be most inviting to Northern California gamblers. Finding that the five-hour car drive from San Francisco to his casinos was keeping customers from coming for the day, Harrah planned his own bus line. For advice he turned to the Stanford Research Institute, which, for a fee of $16,000, provided "An Investigation of Factors Influencing Bus Scheduling," along with valuable insights into Harrah's potential clientele. His most likely customer, the Institute predicted, was "elderly, in low occupational status, unmarried, a renter rather than a home owner, and without a car. . . . an unusual segment of the total population." Harrah then aimed his advertising at these customers in the smaller cities around San Francisco. He did everything to make their trip to his casino easy, to keep them happy there, and to keep them spending. When others followed Harrah's lead, Lake Tahoe grew into a potent competitor to Reno and Las Vegas.

After World War II, Nevada became a refuge not only for the activities, but also for the people outlawed in other states. In 1946, at a cost of $7 million, a racketeer, "Bugsy" Siegel, who controlled the local use of Al Capone's racing wire service, built the Flamingo Hotel on the Las Vegas Strip. Within a year Siegel was murdered by gangster rivals, and the battles of the gangs for control of Nevada gambling had begun. Senator Estes Kefauver's hearings on organized crime exposed a network of criminal control over the state's profitable new industry. The state tightened its laws for licensing casino owners, but Nevada laws could not keep out the gangsters.

While ex-convicts, refugees from the law and from unsavory reputations, seeped into Nevada as another by-product of the federal system, the state's growing population created a host of new problems. At Stateline on Lake Tahoe, two of the new casinos every day produced an estimated half-million additional gallons of effluvium. At first the Nevadans tried to dispose of this surplus sewage by treating it and then spraying it on the trees, but the runoff into the lake began to turn the pure waters of Tahoe a dirty green and bred algae that spoiled the swimming. It was then found more convenient and more economical to pipe the treated effluvia directly into Tahoe. As the polluted waters of the lake flowed across state lines, the neighboring Californians were warned not to "drink, fish, swim, or wade in this water." Californians were paying for Nevada's federal opportunities.

IN FAR-OFF WASHINGTON, D.C., unpopulous Nevada reaped still another, more predictable, advantage of the federal system. Senators from Nevada came to play a disproportionately large role in the legislative counsels of the nation, for the Senate had organized itself in a fashion which gave states like Nevada a good deal more than equality. "Small"-state senators could be more certain of reelection back home and so they became more effective in securing what they wanted in the Senate. Since they represented fewer major economic interests, they were in a better position to trade votes to secure what their constituents really wanted. And in proportion to the population of their states, they usually had at their disposal a larger federal patronage than other senators. In Nevada after 1889, few elected senatorial incumbents were defeated for reelection. As a result of the senatorial seniority system, then, Nevada senators had a leading, and often a decisive, voice in powerful committees. Senator Pat McCarran of Nevada became, by seniority, the chairman of the Senate Judiciary Committee; Senator Key Pittman of Nevada became chairman of the Foreign Relations Committee. These elected representatives from the least populous state were quietly altering the balance of forces in the representative system. The American people might rush to the cities, but the Constitution continued to provide new resources of wealth and power, and powerful voices, for the interests of a new West.

8

Crime As a Service Institution

"THE HIGH LEVEL of lawlessness," Walter Lippmann observed in 1931, "is maintained by the fact that Americans desire to do so many things which they also desire to prohibit." This observation, which might have been truthfully made in the United States at almost any time after the Civil War, was occasioned by the report of President Herbert Hoover's National Commission on Law Observance. The commission had been charged to look into the whole federal system of law enforcement, and especially to investigate the enforcement of the Eighteenth Amendment, which prohibited the manufacture, sale, or transportation of intoxicating liquors. After nineteen months of work and the expenditure of a half-million dollars of federal funds, the eminent commission, headed by former Attorney General George W. Wickersham, offered its report on January 19, 1931. Public interest focused on the commission's conclusions on Prohibition.

Whatever its strengths in promoting reforms of police and correctional procedures, the Wickersham Report was a wonderfully accurate self-portrait of the national confusion. The commission (by a vote of 10 to 1) opposed repeal of the Eighteenth Amendment. But they reported that public hostility and the profits of bootlegging had made the Prohibition laws unenforceable. Individual commissioners salved their consciences in separate reports, each with its own kind of equivocation. "A perfect picture of the public mind," the San Francisco *Chronicle* called it. President Hoover said that he agreed with the commission, which led Heywood Broun to note the President's "apparent intention to fuse the Anti-Saloon League and the Republican Party, retaining the worst features of each." The best summary was Franklin P. Adams' poem in the New York *World*, entitled "The Wickersham Report":

Prohibition is an awful flop.
　We like it.
It can't stop what it's meant to stop.
　We like it.
It's left a trail of graft and slime,
It don't prohibit worth a dime,
It's filled our land with vice and crime,
　Nevertheless, we're for it.

But this was not the first time that Americans had found the means to preserve both the satisfaction of forbidding vice and the opportunity for its profitable enjoyment.

THE AMERICANS' DESIRE to gamble had been equaled only by their desire to see that gambling was legally forbidden. They loved the moralistic witticisms of Elbert Hubbard, who observed that "the only man who makes money following the races is the one who does so with a broom and a shovel." But there was an element of gamble in all American life, whch made it hard to distinguish the prudent planner from the man who won by taking chances—on the fertility of unknown land, on the salability of half-known new minerals, on the prospects of unbuilt railroads and unpopulated cities.

Individual professional gamblers of great wealth were known here as they were in Europe. The elegant "Dick" Canfield, for example, built a gambling club furnished with works of art next door to Delmonico's in New York, helped make Saratoga into the "Monte Carlo of America," and died a respected millionaire-philanthropist. But what made gambling an American enterprise were the peculiarly American opportunities to organize illegal activities into nationwide big business. Several circumstances made this possible: a federal system with a confusing variety of state regulations, and each state's jurisdiction locally confined; a national government with powers so circumscribed that it was compelled to use control over "interstate commerce" and the power to tax as a substitute for a national criminal code; the continuing influx from abroad of new Americans, energetic and ambitious, of various religions, ignorant of and indifferent to local mores; a national tradition of golden opportunities for everybody, but where lawful and respectable opportunities appeared to have been preempted by earlier comers; a mobile people in a fluid society, where social position could be bought with money; a vast continent with speedy techniques of communication and transportation, and lots of places to hide. Brooding over all was the national tradition, opportunity, and challenge to *organize*. Moralistic and unrealistic laws, as Walter Lippmann explained, provided the under-world with its own effective protective tariff. The result, in the twen-tieth century, was perhaps the most flourishing array of outlaw enter-prises ever found in a modern nation.

Long before the Nevadans decided to change their laws so they could profit legally from the widespread desire to gamble, Go-Get-ters elsewhere had organized gambling into a remunerative busi-ness. They, too, had tried to draw customers from the whole nation.

Chicago, a center of national enterprises in railroad building and meat packing, was to be a center, too, for the new business of gam-bling. Mont Tennes, destined to become the biggest gambling opera-tor in the nation before World War I, started modestly in Chicago. Ostensibly a real estate man and owner of a cash-register company, he achieved success from his talent as an organizer. By 1904 Tennes owned a few saloons, a cigar store at 123 North Clark Street, and a string of race horses, and was already known in the gambling world as King of Chicago's North Side. His places were raided by police about once a week, but they promptly reopened. From time to time Tennes announced his retirement, which one newspaper called "re-peated swan songs sung for the benefit of the police." A war between rival gambling "syndicates" (in this sense an Americanism just com-ing into use) began with six bombings in 1907. "I am a marked man," Tennes told the Chicago *Evening American.* "A price has been set upon my life and I am more liable to be assassinated than Alfonso, the Spanish King." At the end of the war, Tennes had established himself as the nation's king of gambling.

Applying a chain-store idea to his illegal gambling establishments, he soon had thirty handbook operations in saloons and poolrooms in Chicago alone. His leadership came from his organized control of the telegraph services that brought in daily returns on races from tracks throughout the country. The racing wire news service was essential to the bookie's operation. For it gave him information on the odds at the track up to the last minute, facilitated his own bets, and made possible the rapid and accurate settling of betting accounts. Tennes paid the Payne Telegraph Service of Cincinnati $300 a day for exclu-sive control of the service in Chicago; then he used fire, dynamite, and sometimes the police themselves, to persuade other gamblers to use his service. Later, at considerable personal risk, Tennes set up his own nationwide General News Service, to bring "more reliable" information from the race track. He warned that competitors were trying to break up his business by sending out "wrong winners." With the support of Chicago's three most influential aldermen—Hinky Dink Kenna, Hot Stove Jimmy Quinn, and Barney Grogan—he suc-ceeded in forestalling an investigation. Trying to satisfy the reformers, Chicago's Chief of Police John McWeeney announced a vigorous new police campaign against the slot machines in which "children wager pennies for candy" and against gambling with dice for drinks and cigars. Meanwhile the Interstate Commerce Commission had decided that the transmission of race-track results was legal.

In 1923 Tennes was said to be netting $364,000 per year from his two hundred handbook "joints" in Chicago alone. Although periodically, after reform campaigns and ostentatious raids, the police would declare that they had shut down his operation, Tennes continually protested that he was nothing but an innocent dispenser of sporting news, and he was never himself arrested. What finally forced Tennes' retirement about 1928 was not the activities of the police, but the rise of the powerful Capone gang.

Tennes was only one of an impressive gallery of Go-Getters on illegal frontiers. They prospered by selling to Americans something that Americans wanted to prohibit by law. In 1910 Congress passed the Mann Act ("White Slave Traffic Act"), which prohibited the interstate transportation of women for immoral purposes. In 1913 the Supreme Court ruled the act constitutional on the grounds that the illegalizing of prostitution properly fell within federal control over "interstate commerce." But five years later, in 1918, the Court ruled in Hammer v. Dagenhart that control of the products of child labor fell outside federal powers over commerce.

Meanwhile Big Jim Colosimo was making his fame and fortune by organizing prostitution into big business in Chicago. After his murder by business competitors in 1920, Colosimo's spectacular funeral attested to public gratitude for the man and his works. Archbishop George Mundelein refused a Catholic burial to Colosimo, but a priest tactfully explained that "it cannot be assumed that the fact of one's being a gangster or bootlegger is alone the cause of his being refused Christian burial, for each individual case must be considered." Five thousand mourners witnessed what, in the words of the Chicago *Tribune,* was "a cavalcade such as moved behind the funeral car of Caesar . . . to pay homage to the memory of the man who for more than a decade has been recognized as the overlord of Chicago's underworld." The public list of honorary pallbearers included three judges, eight aldermen, an assistant state's attorney, two congressmen, leading artists of the Chicago Opera Company, along with gamblers, associates, and ex-associates in Colosimo's business of prostitution.

THE GREAT OPPORTUNITY for illegal enterprise had come, of course, with Prohibition. On December 18, 1917, Congress approved and submitted to the states a constitutional amendment prohibiting "the manufacture, sale, or transportation of intoxicating liquors within, the importation thereof into, or the exportation thereof from the United States and all territory subject to the jurisdiction thereof for beverage purposes." Ratified as the Eighteenth Amendment by the required number of states on January 29, 1919, it went into effect one year later. Only Connecticut and Rhode Island had failed to ratify. To enforce the amendment, Congress passed an act (October 28, 1919) shaped by Congressman Andrew J. Volstead from rural Minnesota. The Volstead Act defined "intoxicating liquor" as any beverage containing more than one half of 1 percent of alcohol, and put enforcement of the law under the Bureau of Internal Revenue in the Treasury Department. To perfect the law's high purpose, Congressman Volstead soon offered another act, which prohibited the sale of beer to the sick on medical prescriptions.

Historians disagree over what forces were mainly responsible for passing the Eighteenth Amendment. The voting in the legislatures of the forty-six states that ratified showed that in the upper houses about 85 percent of the members and in the lower houses about 78 percent favored passage of the law. By 1917, even before the amendment was introduced, state-wide prohibition of some sort had already been enacted in twenty-three states, and thirteen were totally dry. Among explanations for passage of national prohibition, we must include the long-standing abuses of the saloon, the wartime concern for conserving grain for food, chauvinistic feeling against the German-Americans who were prominent in brewing and distilling, and the disproportionate political influence of the Anti-Saloon League at a time when large numbers of men were absent in the armed forces. Topping all was the moral fervor inspired by a War to Make the World Safe for Democracy. But whatever the causes of national prohibition, there can be little disagreement about the consequences. It created the greatest criminal bonanza in American history, and perhaps in all modern history.

"Prohibition," the generic word that might have described vast areas of American legislation, now came to mean specifically the prohibition of alcoholic beverages. The Prohibition Party, still in existence in the late twentieth century, is sometimes described as the oldest of American "third" parties, and so is symbolic of even more than its founders intended. No earlier piece of federal legislation, not even the Fugitive Slave Act, was so productive of widespread illegal enterprise or became so prominent in presidential politics. For no earlier legislation of the federal government had so touched the intimate habits of so many Americans, nor so flagrantly violated their daily customs, habits, and desires.

Among the clues to the impotence of Prohibition to prohibit what it legally forbade, none is more revealing than the history of the American language. No legislation could prevent Americans from talking about what interested them most, and American speech showed its usual expressive fertility. *Drunk,* according to the scholarly *Dictionary of American Slang* (1960), by Harold Wentworth and Stuart Berg Flexner, is the subject of 331 slang synonyms which is the largest number for any activity, condition, or concept, including sexual acts. Some expressions (such as *half-seas over,* or *oiled*) go back to colonial times. Others date to the period of first adjustment of the various immigrant groups when, editors Wentworth and Flexner explain, "a fair number turned to whiskey as a compensation for the rejection they suffered as newcomers in a strange land." But most of the words for *drunk* originated or became popular during Prohibition.

During this same period the American language was being enriched, also largely as a result of Prohibition, by a whole new vocabulary of crime. *Gangster,* for example, which in the last years of the nineteenth century had come into use to refer disparagingly to crooked politicians who formed gangs, became obsolete in that sense and by about 1925 referred to criminals. *Moll,* a respectable old English word which originally meant simply a girl or sweetheart, became obsolete in that sense, and in the Prohibition Era, came to mean a gangster's female accomplice. *To take someone for a ride* during these same years came to describe a new institution of American criminal life requiring the automobile.

In other ways, too, the automobile was essential to the day-to-day operations of the well-organized criminals on urban frontiers. Gangsters were often better equipped than the law-enforcing agencies that had to operate within limited budgets and had to persuade public bodies of the reasonableness of their requests. The automobile gave the Prohibition gangsters the "getaway car" in which they could elude the police, dispose of their enemies, and quickly move to another jurisdiction where the pursuing police had no authority. The automobile also made their customers more mobile, and this enabled them to disperse their illegal activities into roadhouses far out in the countryside, or when more convenient to concentrate their gambling resorts, houses of prostitution, and speakeasies in suburbs like Chicago's Cicero. It is hard to imagine how bootleggers of beer and liquor could have prospered by relying on the slow-moving horse and wagon or on the inflexible routes of the railroad. For their purposes the truck was perfect. And it took some time before the radio actually gave any advantage to the police. When radio station WGN in Chicago first began its police broadcasts, the word went out over the public wavelengths, which meant that well-equipped gangsters often had the information as soon as the police. It was 1930 before the police installed special radio systems.

THE TOWERING FIGURE of crime in the Prohibition Era was, of course, Al Capone. But he was only one in a succession of giant criminal entrepreneurs—from Tennes, through Colosimo and his successor John Torrio, to Capone himself. Each followed and improved on the organizing techniques of his predecessor. By the time Capone arrived in Chicago from the New York slums in 1920, there was a gangster tradition with its own folkways and loyalties. Capone's task was not so much to invent as to develop, elaborate, and organize. And for all these roles he proved superbly competent.

In 1925 Al Capone took over from John Torrio, who had been the leader of organized crime in Chicago since the murder of Colosimo five years before. Capone's organization differed from that of some other Chicago gangs (as the sociologist John Landesco's delightful understatement explained) "in that it is not an outgrowth of a neighborhood play group. The Capone gang was formed for the business administration of establishments of vice, gambling and booze." Within two years Capone dominated the establishments that were providing Chicago's citizens the illegal services and commodities they were willing to pay for. Capone, preferring not to risk his own capital, allowed others to own the speakeasies, the houses of prostitution, and the gambling casinos. Instead he elaborated his profitable system of "protection," a blackmail scheme which brought him a regular income from these establishments in return for his guaranteeing their immunity from police raids and from arson, bombings, or murder by his own or rival gangsters. To enforce this system of protection Capone had to find, train, and organize a large and loyal personnel with special qualifications. Wealthy customers could receive from him their choice imported liquors because he had established a nationwide organization that smuggled from Canada, Atlantic ports, and Cuba. Capone's system required the organized cooperation of law-enforcement officers. For the revolvers they carried, Capone's men secured permits from friendly judges, and Capone controlled the elections in Cicero, his suburban headquarters outside Chicago. Chicago's Mayor Big Bill Thompson had helped Capone lay the foundation of all his enterprises. In the late 1920's some national political leaders were reportedly enlisting Capone's aid in the management of federal elections.

Following the practice of his predecessors, Al Capone was careful to keep himself "clean," which meant avoiding any legally detecta-

ble ties to the acts of blackmail, kidnapping, and murder committed
by his subordinates. But there was no secret about Capone's business
or the methods which made him prosper. "The John D. Rockefeller
of some twenty-thousand Anti-Volstead filling stations" (as one biographer characterized him) by 1929 was worth at least $20 million, but
there was no way of estimating his power. Capone himself insisted
that he was just another Go-Getter seizing his peculiarly American
opportunities. "I make my money by supplying a public demand. If
I break the law, my customers, who number hundreds of the best
people in Chicago, are as guilty as I am. The only difference between
us is that I sell and they buy. Everybody calls me a racketeer. I call
myself a business man. When I sell liquor, it's bootlegging. When my
patrons serve it on a silver tray on Lake Shore Drive, it's hospitality."
Reformers thought the supply of liquor could be suppressed without
reducing the demand, but Capone knew that it was the mores of the
time that provided him his opportunities. After he retired to Florida
in 1929 he was finally convicted and jailed in 1931 for failing to pay
his federal income tax. Sentenced to eleven years in prison, he was
released because of poor health in 1939, and died in Florida in 1947.

THE REMARKABLE RISE of organized crime in the twentieth
century is only another episode in the saga of restless new Americans
reaching for opportunities to enlarge their fortunes and to rise in the
world. On the list of the most successful organizers of crime as a
service institution were a striking number of recent Italian immigrants. Tennes, Colosimo, Torrio, and Capone were all born in Italy
and were brought here at an early age. Despite the strong anti-
immigrant and anti-Italian bias of the lengthy congressional investigations and voluminous reports on the immigrant record in the early
twentieth century, there was no convincing evidence that any immigrant group had a criminal bent. The prominence of Italians in the
annals of organized crime in the early and mid-twentieth century
tells less about the Italian immigrants themselves than about the
situation they found when they arrived. They were the last of the
major immigrant groups to reach American shores. Consequently,
the sociologist Daniel Bell has pointed out, they found the more
obvious and more respectable paths to success preempted by the
earlier comers.

Most of the Italian immigrants of the late nineteenth century were
peasants with few of the skills that could help them rise in an urban,
industrial world. The Italians, Jacob Riis observed, had "come in at
the bottom." Even within the Catholic Church, where they comprised a considerable proportion of the communicants, they found

little opportunity for leadership. As late as 1960, when Italian-Americans numbered one sixth of American Catholics, there was not one Italian-American bishop of the hundred Catholic bishops, nor one Italian-American archbishop of the twenty-one Catholic archbishops. The Irish-Americans, who had arrived in large numbers a half-century before the Italians, were in charge of the American Catholic hierarchy.

The Italian community, then, as Bell observes, had to find their opportunities in the interstices, in enterprises not already pre-empted, in those which required neither capital nor specialized training. The success of some of their number in organizing to supply outlawed products and services attested to their determination to find here the opportunity to rise which for generations had been denied them in their Old World homeland. Al Capone's complaint had a historical foundation: "Why, I tried to get into legitimate business two or three times, but they won't stand for it."

Historians have been tempted to facile analogies between the Sicilian secret terrorist organization, the Mafia, which was originally founded to defend the poor and oppressed peasants against their ruthless landlords, and the twentieth-century gangs in American cities. Although Senator Estes Kefauver's televised hearings of the Senate Crime Committee aimed to prove the existence of a national and international Mafia, the main product of the hearings was a new kind of TV spectacular and a vice-presidential nomination for Senator Kefauver.

The Mafia became more vivid and more credible than ever after World War II. For instance, during the Allied invasion of Sicily in July 1943—so the story went—Lucky Luciano (allegedly the head of the Mafia in the United States, at that time serving a thirty-to-fifty-year prison sentence on sixty-two counts of compulsory prostitution) who was a native of Lercara Friddi, a village on the Allied invasion route to Palermo, planned collaboration with the Sicilian Mafia to aid the Allied invasion. The naval intelligence officers who testified at Luciano's parole hearings in 1945 refused to confirm the story, but by 1946 Luciano had been released and returned to Italy, where he was living in a Palermo hotel suite next door to Don Calò, the acknowledged leader of the Sicilian Mafia. How much he was able to add to the repertoire of the Sicilian Mafia from the lessons learned on the illegal frontiers of the New World will never be known.

The Sicilian Mafia experience may have been informally transplanted to America, just as a century earlier the Irish immigrants had adapted their techniques of organizing against the oppressive English landlords to the new politics of the American city. Some features of Italian institutions—the close family ties, and the intense quasi-tribal feeling among residents of particular parts of Italy—played a part in the success of the criminal organizations in some American cities. That Capone's men, held together by tribal loyalties, were willing to die for him gave him a great advantage over gangs united only by moneymaking. A potent competitor of the Capone gang in Chicago in the late 1920's was the O'Banion gang, whose leaders (in addition to O'Banion, who was Irish) included a Jew, an Italian, a Pole, and still others. Ethnic balance could add power to a political ticket, but did not similarly strengthen a criminal gang. The gang depended more on personal loyalties than on a public appeal, and the O'Banion gang eventually lost out.

American gangsters, who only recently had arrived as downtrodden peasants, became rich businessmen and mayor-makers. And these quickly took their place in the iridescent American folklore of adventuring Go-Getters. For the earlier tales of Western sheriffs and desperadoes, American moviemakers in the twentieth century found counterparts on the urban frontier in tales of loyal, smart, ambitious gangsters and corrupt, stupid, indolent cops.

The hesitation of Americans to abandon their virtuous prohibitions appeared in the shrewd reluctance of presidential candidate Franklin Delano Roosevelt in the campaign of 1932 to take a firm stand for repeal. But Depression and unemployment and the need for jobs in a legalized liquor industry made moralism a too-costly luxury. In February 1933 Congress approved a resolution calling for a constitutional amendment to repeal Prohibition. Within less than a year, the Twenty-first Amendment to the Constitution was adopted by the necessary number of states, and alcoholic beverages were legalized.

Even after the nation as a whole had abolished the nationwide prohibition of alcoholic beverages, separate states kept their own prohibition laws. As late as 1959 two states, Oklahoma and Mississippi, still outlawed alcoholic beverages. An allegory of American history was lived out in April of that year when citizens of Oklahoma once again faced a referendum on changing their state constitution to legalize liquor. In the last hours before the citizenry went to the polls, bootleggers (who had found Oklahoma a refuge of their former prosperity) and Protestant ministers joined in futile all-night prayer, meetings against repeal. It was 1966 before Mississippi adopted a local-option liquor law and so became the last state to abandon the luxury of prohibiting what its citizens desired.

After Repeal, the most promising business opportunities created by law were no longer in alcohol. Street prostitution, which had been a rich resource for illegal enterprise in the late nineteenth century, also was losing its commercial promise. The telephone, which had facilitated violations of Prohibition, also brought into being the high-priced "call girl" (an Americanism which had entered the language by mid-twentieth century) and made her less conspicuous and so less subject to arrest. At the same time loose tax laws provided ways of charging off her services as a business expense for "entertaining customers." Changing sexual morals, looser as the century advanced, and medical innovations reducing the risks from casual sexual encounters, made the sexual commodity so available that it was harder to sell. As Alexander Woollcott complained, prostitution, like acting, was being "ruined by amateurs."

The profits of illegal gambling, however, increased with the years. By the late 1960's, informed observers agreed that it was a multibillion-dollar business, and probably the largest single source of income for organized crime. In 1967 the President's Commission on Law Enforcement estimated the annual profits of illegal gambling at somewhere between $7 billion and $50 billion.

By mid-century, organized crime had turned successfully from bootlegging alcoholic beverages to pushing narcotics. While in the days of Prohibition the bootleggers had aimed to satisfy a demand that was already there, when organized crime turned to narcotics it also undertook to stimulate the demand. This in turn created problems of new proportions, without precedent in American history.

PART TWO

Consumption Communities

"Because you see the main thing today is—shopping. Years ago a person, he was unhappy, didn't know what to do with himself—he'd go to church, start a revolution—*something*. Today you're unhappy? Can't figure it out? What is the salvation? Go shopping."

Solomon in *The Price* by ARTHUR MILLER

"Pappa, what is the moon supposed to advertise?"

CARL SANDBURG, *The People, Yes*

INVISIBLE NEW COMMUNITIES were created and preserved by how and what men consumed. The ancient guilds of makers, the fellowship of secrets and skills and traditions of fabricating things—muskets and cloth and horseshoes and wagons and cabinets—were outreached by the larger, more open, fellowships of consumers. As never before, men used similar, and similarly branded, objects. The fellowship of skill was displaced by the democracy of cash.

No American transformation was more remarkable than these new American ways of changing things from objects of possession and envy into vehicles of community. The acts of acquiring and using had a new meaning. Nearly all objects from the hats and suits and shoes men wore to the food they ate became symbols and instruments of novel communities. Now men were affiliated less by what they be-

89

lieved than by what they consumed. In the older world almost every-thing a man owned was one-of-a-kind. In the newer world the unique object, except for jewels and works of art, was an oddity and came to be suspect. If an object of the same design and brand was widely used by many others, this seemed an assurance of its value.

And there were created many communities of consumers. Men who never saw or knew one another were held together by their common use of objects so similar that they could not be distinguished even by their owners. These consumption communities were quick; they were nonideological; they were democratic; they were public, and vague, and rapidly shifting. Consumption communities pro-duced more consumption communities. They were factitious, malle-able, and as easily made as they were evanescent. Never before had so many men been united by so many things.

9

A Democracy of Clothing

IN THE MIDDLE of the nineteenth century, European travelers to the United States were struck by a new American peculiarity. Just as travelers before them in the eighteenth century had noted the difficulty of distinguishing between American social classes by the habits of speech, and had noted that master and servant, even in the South, spoke in accents far more similar than did their English counterparts, they now noted the strange similarities of clothing.

In America it was far more difficult than in England to tell a man's social class by what he wore. The British consul in Boston in the early 1840's, Thomas College Grattan, complained of American equality; he found servant girls "strongly infected with the national bad taste for being over-dressed, they are, when walking the streets, scarcely to be distinguished from their employers." The Hungarian politician Francis Pulszky, traveling the country in 1852, missed the colorful Old World distinctions. In Europe there was "the peasant girl with the gaudy ribbons interlaced in her long tresses, her bright corset, and her richly-folded petticoat; there the Hungarian peasant with his white linen shirt, and his stately sheepskin; the Slovak in the closely fitting jacket and the bright yellow buttons; the farmer with the high boots and the Hungarian coat; the old women with the black lace cap in the ancient national style, and none but the young ladies appareled in French bonnets and modern dresses." He lamented that in New York, "no characteristical costumes mark here the different grades of society, which, in Eastern Europe, impress the foreigner at once with the varied occupations and habits of an old country." No wonder that the snobbish British merchant W. E. Baxter was irritated in 1853–54 to find common workmen so overdressed by English standards. "You meet men in railroad-cars, and on the decks of steamboats, rigged out in super-fine broadcloth and white waistcoats, as if they were on their way to a ball-room, and common workmen you find attired in glossy black clothes while performing work of the dirtiest description. . . . The farmers are the only class who wear rough garments. . . . The people have yet to learn that apparel should be chosen for use not show, that shabby broadcloth is the most pitiful of all costume, and that it is no mark of gentility to wear a dress unsuitable to one's means and employment."

Before the end of the nineteenth century, the American democracy of clothing would become still more astonishing to foreign eyes, for by then the mere wearing of clothes would be an instrument of community, a way of drawing immigrants into a new life. Men whose ancestors had been accustomed to the peasant's tatters or the craftsman's leather apron could show by a democratic costume that they were as good as, or not very different from, the next man. If, as the Old World proverb went, "Clothes make the man," the New World's new way of clothing would help make new men.

IN THE TWENTIETH CENTURY Americans would be the best-clothed and perhaps the most homogeneously dressed, industrial nation. It is hard to imagine how it could have happened without the sewing machine.

The sewing machine, however, like the system of interchangeable parts, was not first conceived in America. In England, in 1770, Thomas Saint had been granted a patent for a machine to sew leather. By 1830 Barthélemy Thimonnier, a French tailor who had long been obsessed with the idea, had patented and perfected an effective sewing machine. When eighty of his machines were making uniforms for the French army, Paris tailors, alarmed at the threat to their jobs, smashed the machines and drove Thimonnier out of the city.

Perhaps the first of many American sewing-machine inventors was Walter Hunt. He was pure inventor, so obsessed by inventing and so bored by the prosaic tasks of exploiting his novelties that his very genius was destined to deny him a place in the history books. His inventions included a flax-spinning machine, a knife sharpener, a yarn twister, a stove (some say the first) to burn hard coal, a nail-making machine, ice plows, velocipedes, a revolver, a repeating rifle, metallic cartridges, conical bullets, paraffin candles, a street-sweeping machine, a student lamp, and paper collars. According to his draftsman friend who had been making drawings to accompany Hunt's numerous patent applications, Hunt designed a patentable safety pin quickly in order to get the money to pay him a debt of $15. Within three hours Hunt worked out the idea, made a model from an old piece of wire, and sold the patent rights for $400.

By the early 1830's in his workshop on Amos Street in New York City, Hunt had made several machines that actually sewed. Although they were rudimentary, sewing only a straight seam and requiring readjustment of the cloth every few inches, they did include the basic features that later would make a fortune for others. Hunt's revolutionary new idea was an eye-pointed needle moved by a vibrating arm and a shuttle which carried a second thread to make an interlocking stitch. This was the great stroke of imagination that liberated sewing-machine inventors from the temptation to imitate the seamstress' hand. But Hunt had neither the capital nor the organizing talent to make money out of his idea.

Others did. And there was enough money in the sewing machine to enrich scores of inventors, would-be inventors, lawyers, promoters, salesmen, and businessmen. The two giants in the War of the Sewing Machine, which climaxed about 1850, were Elias Howe, Jr., and Isaac Merrit Singer. They battled not merely for money but for the honor of having been "the principal inventor" of the sewing machine.

Elias Howe, born in 1819, was the son of a Massachusetts farmer. At the age of twenty, when he was working as a journeyman machinist for a Boston scientific-instrument maker, his interest was awakened by a customer's effort to perfect a knitting machine. Some years later, under pressure to support a wife and three children and desperately casting about for some way to add to his salary of $9 a week, he decided to try to make his fortune from a sewing machine. After many false starts, in 1844 he too was inspired by the idea of an eye-pointed needle, using a second thread on a shuttle, on the analogy of the loom. By April 1845 he was actually sewing a seam on his machine. In 1846 he received a patent.

To persuade the public that his machine would really work, Howe took it to the Quincy Hall Clothing Manufactory in Boston, seated himself before it and offered to sew up any seam that anyone would bring. For two weeks he astonished all comers by doing 250 stitches a minute, about seven times the speed by hand. He then challenged five of the speediest seamstresses to race his machine. The experienced tailor whom he had called in as umpire announced Howe's victory and declared that "the work done on the machine was the neatest and strongest."

Even these demonstrations did not persuade people to buy Howe's machines. Some objected that it was still imperfect, because it did not make a whole garment; others feared it would put tailors and seamstresses out of work. All were discouraged by the cost of a machine, at that time about $300. Howe determined to try the English market. When his brother, Amasa, took the machine to London, he awakened the interest of a shrewd corset manufacturer who bought the English rights for a song, and then persuaded Elias Howe to come to London to adapt the machine to the needs of corset making. By working hard for eight months, Howe accomplished the difficult assignment, whereupon his employer (who proved to be a Dickensian villain) fired him. Suffering from the tragedy of his wife's death (he had to borrow a suit to attend her funeral!) and the loss of all his household goods in a shipwreck off Cape Cod, in 1849 Howe returned penniless to New York.

In Howe's absence, the sewing machine had become a popular curiosity. A machine was actually being carried about western New York and exhibited as "A Great Curiosity!! The Yankee Sewing-Machine," for an admission fee of twelve and a half cents. Ladies carried home specimens of machine sewing to show their friends. Machines were now being made and sold in considerable numbers by persons Howe had never known, many of these using features that Howe had patented. Determined to protect his legal rights, Howe sent to England to recover his original machine and the Patent Office papers he had pawned.

Howe then warned the infringers, offering to sell them licenses for a royalty fee. All but one agreed, but that one organized the rest, and Howe had to fight his case in court. For this purpose Howe needed money, which he finally secured from a Massachusetts lawyer who financed the infringement suits, but was secured against loss by a mortgage on Howe's father's farm.

The stage was set for one of the decisive industrial battles of the century. It might have been planned as an allegory, for there were the figures who would reappear with monotonous regularity: the competing "first inventors" and the Go-Getting lawyers. The dramatic struggle produced a mass product and eventually created a new consumption community. Incidentally, the prolonged and sensationalized courtroom struggle helped fill the new mass-circulating newspapers, and awakened consumer interest in the sewing machine by the public debates over its remarkable new features.

Isaac Merrit Singer, Howe's antagonist, also had inventive talent, but his flair for salesmanship made him a man of quite another stamp. Raised in upstate New York as the son of a millwright, he had, while still a young man, secured a patent for a rock driller and a carving machine. But he had also been an actor and a theater manager. In 1850, when he happened to see a sewing machine, he determined to improve the machine so it could do a greater variety of work. According to Singer's own account, after eleven days and nights of intense work during which he slept and ate only irregularly, he produced his improved model. Immediately he began manufacturing, selling—and, above all, promoting—this machine. In one way at least Singer's machine was superior to Howe's, for it could do continuous stitching. But what explained Singer's success was his genius as advertiser and organizer, and his determination to sell sewing machines to the millions.

Singer refused to pay Howe a royalty. For, he claimed, Howe had not in fact been the inventor of the sewing machine. Singer tried to prove in court that fourteen years before Howe's 1846 patent, Walter Hunt had actually made a working sewing machine; that Howe's machine was nothing but a copy of Hunt's. After a long search, Singer and his lawyers located Walter Hunt, and some fragments of Hunt's early machine were finally discovered in a garret. In 1854, after a costly three-year trial, the court held in favor of Howe. Though Hunt had been on a right track, the court said, Hunt had never patented his invention, nor had he made a practical, salable machine. "For all the benefit conferred upon the public by the introduction of a sewing-machine, the public are indebted to Mr. Howe." Howe's fortunes abruptly changed. He obtained $15,000 from Singer, and soon was receiving a $25 royalty on every sewing machine made in the country.

This bonanza did not last long. Other sewing-machine inventions forced Howe to compromise. To keep his own machines salable in a competitive market, he had to incorporate improvements patented by others. Soon three other large manufacturers, each controlling some essential patent, were suing one another.

The upshot of these and other widening disputes, which now involved another half-dozen large manufacturers, was the great Sewing Machine Combination in 1856. The patent owners pooled all their patents on the essential features of the sewing machine into a single franchise for a single fee, and the owners of the different patents shared the franchising fees. Before signing, Howe insisted that at least twenty-four manufacturers be franchised. Howe himself received $5 for each machine licensed to sell in the United States and $1 for each machine exported, which eventually brought him about

$2 million. Numerous manufacturers, willing to pay the costly licensing fees, now entered the race for sales.

By 1871 the sewing machine, which only twenty years before had been a curiosity to be exhibited at fairs for twelve and a half cents' admission, was being manufactured at the rate of 700,000 a year. The machine was constantly being improved; before the end of the century nearly eight thousand patents had been issued on the sewing machine and its accessories. American manufacturers sent their machines all over. Competing in their claims for creating a new worldwide consumption community, the I. M. Singer Company asserted that by 1879 three quarters of the machines being sold were Singers. An 1880 Singer brochure, immodestly entitled *Genius Rewarded; or, the Story of the Sewing Machine,* proclaimed:

> On every sea are floating the Singer Machines; along every road pressed by the foot of civilized man this tireless ally of the world's great sisterhood is going upon its errand of helpfulness. Its cheering tune is understood no less by the sturdy German matron than by the slender Japanese maiden; it sings as intelligibly to the flaxen-haired Russian peasant-girl as to the dark-eyed Mexican Senorita. It needs no interpreter, whether it sings amid the snows of Canada or upon the pampas of Paraguay; the Hindoo Mother and the Chicago maiden are to-night making the self-same stitch; the untiring feet of Ireland's fair-skinned Nora are driving the same treadle with the tiny understandings of China's tawny daughter; and thus American machines, American brains, and American money are bringing the women of the whole world into one universal kinship and sisterhood.

The new machine was supposed to relieve drudgery. "Now," *Godey's Lady's Book* rejoiced in 1860, ". . . what philanthropy failed to accomplish, what religion, poetry, eloquence and reason sought in vain, has been produced by—The Sewing Machine." But there is little evidence that the sewing machine much eased the lives of seamstresses, or that the housewife actually spent less time on sewing. "Where is the woman," James Parton asked in the *Atlantic Monthly* in 1867, "who can say that her sewing is less a tax upon her time and strength than it was before the sewing machine came in? . . . As soon as lovely woman discovers that she can set ten stitches in the time that one used to require, a fury seizes her to put ten times as many stitches in every garment as she formerly did."

In the 1860's, styles changed. Just as the improvement of wood-carving machinery produced ever more ornate furniture, now the sewing machine produced elaborately draped overskirts, a new opportunity to display fancy sewing and intricate trimmings. In this way, too, a use was found for the numerous sewing-machine attachments: hemmers, fellers, binders, tuckers, rufflers, shirrers, puffers, braiders, quilters, hemstitchers, and even an etcher adept at "beautiful machine embroidery in imitation of the Kensington hand stitch."

The consequences of the sewing machine were not merely aesthetic or humanitarian. In America the sewing machine helped change the social meaning of clothing: a larger proportion of people than ever before could wear clothes that fit them, and could look like the best-off men and women. "The sewing-machine," observed Parton, "is one of the means by which the industrious laborer is as well clad as any millionaire need be, and by which working-girls are enabled safely to gratify their woman's instinct of decoration."

IN THE LATTER HALF of the nineteenth century the United States experienced a Clothing Revolution—more far-reaching, perhaps, than any that had occurred since the birth of modern textile technology. Alexander Hamilton had noted in his *Report on Manufactures* (1791) that four fifths of the American people's clothing were made in their own households for themselves. Only the rich could afford to employ tailors. At first these tailors traveled the countryside working on material supplied by customers, and eventually they settled down in the cities.

A ready-made-clothing industry did not begin to develop until the early decades of the nineteenth century. At first only the cheapest grades of clothes could be bought in stores. Shops in New Bedford, Massachusetts, for example, supplied sailors with the clothing they needed quickly when they had just returned from a long voyage or when they were hastily preparing to sail again. Sailors put these store-boughten clothes in their sea chests, generally known as "slop chests" (after the Old Norse word for the loose smock or the baggy breeches of the kind sailors wore). The clothes they bought were therefore called "sailors slops," and the places where these were sold were called "slopshops." "Slop clothes" or "slops" became a synonym for ready-made clothes. Cheap ready-made clothing was also in demand in the South for Negro slaves, and in upstart Western towns for newly arrived miners who had no household to make clothes for them.

All over Europe in the eighteenth century there were depots for renovating and distributing castoff clothes. Until well into the nineteenth century almost the only kind of ready-made clothing for sale was secondhand. Before the rise of a clothing industry, before machine manufacture had made textiles cheap, the clothing which had originally been tailor-made for the rich was the main source of ready-made clothing for the poor. "In this Country," the English economist Nassau Senior wrote in 1836, "the poor are, to a great extent, clothed with garments originally provided for their superiors." Around this fact Senior actually built a whole theory of expenditure.

In those days neither the buying nor the selling of secondhand clothes was disreputable; and even today in poorer nations castoff clothing is a staple of country fairs and cheap city shops. In the United States, too, before the Civil War, there was a sizable trade in castoff clothing, much of it destined for the South and West. Metropolitan newspapers like the New York *Herald* printed scores of advertisements for secondhand clothing.

Work clothes for Negroes and for sailors long remained the only clothing manufactured in quantity. A few ready-made garments were turned out as a sideline by the custom tailor. The demand for ready-made clothing grew fastest in the South and West, and establishments grew on the eastern seaboard to satisfy these needs.

The American revolution in clothing, which was well under way before 1900, was a double revolution: in the making of clothing (from the homemade and the custom-made to the ready-made or factory-made) and in the wearing of clothing (from the clothing of class display, by which a man wore his social class and his occupation on his sleeve, to the clothing of democracy, by which, more than ever before, men dressed alike). In Western mining camps, on wagon-train journeys west, on long sea voyages, men could not carry elaborate wardrobes. Specialized skills were few, and qualified custom tailors scarce. At the same time that wealthy Americans found it hard to dress as elegantly as wealthy Europeans, the new technology of the garment industry was making it easier for Americans in moderate circumstances to dress well.

By mid-century, the sewing machine was being used in the factory production of clothing. When the chain stitch, which unraveled if the thread was broken at any point, was displaced by the lock stitch, machine sewing was as strong as that by hand. Improvements and attachments, like the buttonholer, made the machine versatile enough for most sewing tasks. And new cutting machines which could slice through eighteen thicknesses of cloth made it easy to prepare numerous garments of the same size.

Then the Civil War brought an unprecedented demand for large quantities of men's wear. In mid-1861 the need was for uniforms to outfit an army of hundreds of thousands; in the fall of 1865, for civilian clothing to outfit the demobilized hundreds of thousands. The clothing business suddenly became attractive and profitable. The demand for uniforms had encouraged standardization. When the government supplied measurements for the uniforms it required, it had given manufacturers the most commonly recurring human proportions. With this information, manufacturers developed a new science of sizing and began to make garments in regular sizes. Between 1880 and 1890 the total value of the products of manufacturing industries that used the sewing machine increased by 75 percent, to well over $1 billion. This was due largely to the sudden growth of the ready-made-clothing industry, including shoes, which accounted for 90 percent of sewing machine products.

The wearers of all sorts of factory-made clothing increased by the tens of thousands. As early as 1832 there had been an American shirt factory; the manufacturing of men's detachable collars grew about the same time, and within a few years there was a thriving business in shirts and collars. The value of manufactured men's garments nearly doubled between 1860 and 1870. In the next two decades the business was still one for pioneers. As late as 1880 less than half of men's clothing was purchased ready-to-wear. But by the beginning of the twentieth century it had become rare for a man or boy not to be clothed in ready-made garments. Now even the wealthy, who had once employed tailors, were buying clothes in the better shops. By 1890 the value of clothing sold in shops amounted to about $1.5 billion; about three quarters of the woolen cloth made in the United States were being consumed in the manufacture of ready-made clothing.

Alexander Hamilton's statistics had been reversed. Now, according to the best estimates at the time, nine tenths of the men and boys in the United States were wearing clothing made ready to put on. "Little by little," William C. Browning, a pioneer in the business, boasted in 1895, "the early prejudice, founded upon the character of 'slop' clothes first introduced, was overcome. Men who had fancied that they would never wear 'hand-me-downs,' as they were vulgarly called, soon found that neither in respect of style nor materials was the best ready-made clothing inferior to the handiwork of the merchant tailor.... there was a wonderful advance in the quality of goods manufactured." The Americanism "hand-me-down" (in England it was "reach-me-down" to signify clothing that was simply reached down from a rack) had come into general use to signify shabby clothing. New expressions were needed for the good-quality new clothing now sold in shops. "Ready-to-wear" in the early twentieth century began to supplant "ready-made" with a significant new emphasis not on the maker but on the wearer.

Not only suits and coats, but everything else that people wore—hats, caps, shirts, undergarments, stockings, and shoes—were now for the first time generally beginning to be bought ready-made. Until the mid-nineteenth century, the shoes that could be bought ready-made in shops were "straights"—that is, there was no difference between rights and lefts. Then American manufacturers began to turn out "crooked shoes," specially cut to fit the right or the left foot, and the increase in the mass production of shoes in the decade before 1860 brought (in the language of the Census Report of that year) a "silent revolution" in footwear. By 1862 Gordon McKay, a Massachusetts industrialist, had perfected a machine that sewed the soles to the uppers, just in time to help supply the Union demand for army shoes by the thousands. After the war the working class was buying factory-made shoes, but it was several decades before the middle classes and well-to-do were provided with factory shoes to their taste.

It happened, too, that the character of immigrants who came in the last twenty-five years of the nineteenth century stimulated the clothing industry. Many from Germany, Russia, Poland, and Italy were tailors. Among the four hundred thousand Jewish immigrants in the first decade of the twentieth century, more than half were in the needle trades. At the same time the new sewing machine, requiring very little skill, attracted into the work many wives and sons and daughters of the immigrants in the Eastern cities.

An infamous by-product of the sewing machine was the "sweatshop" (an Americanism first noted about 1892), where women and children worked long hours at piecework for low wages. But in the clothing industry, too, where the business unit was small and the machinery inexpensive, it was less difficult than elsewhere to move up from wageworker to employer. In many unpredicted ways, then, the nation's new clothing industry could be an agent of democracy. "The multitude is clothed by the clothier, not by the tailor," a pioneer American merchant-clothier boasted at the turn of the century. "And if . . . the condition of a people is indicated by its clothing, America's place in the scale of civilized lands is a high one. We have provided not alone abundant clothing at a moderate cost for all classes of citizens, but we have given them at the same time that style and character in dress that is essential to the self-respect of a free democratic people."

Ready-made clothing instantly Americanized the immigrant. When David Levinsky, the hero of Abraham Cahan's Yiddish novel, arrived in New York from Russia in 1885, his benefactor, eager to make him at once into an American, took him to store after store, buying him a suit of clothes, a hat, underclothes, handkerchiefs (the first white handkerchiefs he ever possessed), collars, shoes, and a necktie. "He spent a considerable sum on me. As we passed from block to block he kept saying, 'Now you won't look green,' or 'That will make you look American.'" Nothing else could so rapidly and painlessly transform the foreigner into one who belonged.

10
Consumers' Palaces

BETWEEN THE CIVIL WAR and the beginning of the new century there appeared grand and impressive edifices—Palaces of Consumption—in the principal cities of the nation and in the upstart cities that hoped to become great metropolises. A. T. Stewart's, Lord & Taylor, Arnold Constable, R. H. Macy's in New York City; John Wanamaker in Philadelphia; Jordan Marsh in Boston; Field, Leiter & Co. (later Marshall Field & Co.) and the Fair in Chicago. And even smaller cities had their impressive consumers' palaces—Lazarus in Columbus, Ohio, and Hudson's in Detroit, among others.

The distinctive institution which came to be called the department store was a large retail shop, centrally located in a city, doing a big volume of business, and offering a wide range of merchandise, including clothing for women and children, small household wares, and usually dry goods and home furnishings. While the stock was departmentalized, many of the operations and the general management were centralized. If the department store was not an American invention, it flourished here as nowhere else. "Department store" was an Americanism in general use before the opening of the twentieth century.

The grand new consumers' palaces were to the old small and intimate shops what the grand new American hotels were to the Old World inns. Like the hotels, the department stores were symbols of faith in the future of growing communities. For citizens of the sprouting towns the new department-store grandeur gave dignity, importance, and publicity to the acts of shopping and buying—new communal acts in a new America.

ALEXANDER TURNEY STEWART, at the age of seventeen, came to New York City from Northern Ireland and began his business with a stock of Irish laces. Only fifteen years later, in 1846, he built an impressive structure at Broadway and Chambers streets, known as the Marble Dry-Goods Palace. Like many another earlier palace, it expanded with addition after addition until it extended along a two-hundred-foot frontage on City Hall Park and covered the whole block on Broadway. In 1862, when Stewart's outgrew these premises, it moved into another palace—this time eight stories high and no longer of marble. This building, which became famous as Stewart's Cast Iron Palace, was reputed to be the largest retail store in the world.

The new department stores, unlike the elegant exclusive shops of Old World capitals, were palatial, public, and inviting. Cast iron made it easier than ever to make buildings impressive on the outside, and on the inside to offer high ceilings, and wide, unbroken expanses for appealing display. In the five-story E. V. Haughwout Department Store, built in 1857 at Broadway and Broome Street in New York City, Daniel Badger, pioneer in manufacturing iron for buildings, offered his most impressive work. The intricate façades of the Venetian *palazzos* were easily reproduced in cast iron. Their elegant patterns of columns, spandrels, and windows could be endlessly extended around a building, and the architectural orders could be piled one above another indefinitely.

When James Bogardus (the prolific inventor whose works included a metal-cased pencil with a lead "forever pointed," improvements in the striking parts of clocks, a new machine for making postage stamps, and an improved mill for making lead paint) turned his genius to finding new uses for cast iron, the needs of the department store excited his imagination. These new iron structures, he exulted, could be raised to a height of ten miles. Bogardus would exploit qualities in the cast-iron frame—lightness, openness, adaptability, and speed of construction—similar to those which three decades before had given the balloon frame its special American appeal.

The climax of this new Iron Age was the Cast Iron Palace which Bogardus built on Broadway between Ninth and Tenth streets for A. T. Stewart. It was the largest iron building of its day, one of the largest of any kind. On the exterior, the molded iron panels were painted to resemble stone; the repeating column-and-beam design added dignity and expansiveness. Each floor took the weight of its own outer walls, in the structural scheme which would make possible the skyscraper. The thin walls at the ground floor produced a spacious, open lobby, and the slender iron columns kept vistas open on every floor, vistas of appealing merchandise of all shapes, color, and description, objects one had never thought of seeing, much less of buying. And one could see out there among the merchandise the enticing crowds and clusters of buyers, shoppers, and just lookers. The palatial ground floor was dominated by a grand stairway and a great rotunda brightened by daylight which streamed through an overarching glass dome. Up and down these stairs, frequenting the high-ceilinged grandeur of these consumers' palaces, came the lords and ladies of these domains by the thousands and tens and hundreds of thousands.

The traditional elegance of the grand stairway was complemented by the modern charm of the elevator, which made the upper floors more easily accessible. Incidentally, the elevator car pushed together in sudden intimacy random members of the public who had the same destination. Elevators had been tried before for freight, and there had been experiments in using them for passengers in hotels. But the department store gave everybody a chance to enjoy them.

The essential problem was to combine speed and safety. The old freight elevators, in which the cage was counterweighted by a plunger that descended into the ground to a depth equal to the height of the building, was relatively safe but slow. To obtain faster movement it was necessary to use a system of pulleys, which increased the wear on the ropes holding up the cage. This increased the danger of a plummeting cage. Then, to insure against such accidents, Elisha Graves Otis, an ingenious New Englander who had been born and raised on his father's Vermont farm, invented a safety device. He set up ratchets along each side of the shaft and attached teeth to the sides of the cage. These teeth were held clear of the ratchets by the rope which held up the cage, but when the rope ceased to be in tension, the teeth were released against the sides of the shaft and gripped the cage safely in place. Otis himself sold the public on his device at the Crystal Palace Exposition in New York City in 1854. He had his elevator drawn up, then he melodramatically cut the supporting rope and displayed himself in the cage safely held in place.

It was in the Haughwout Department Store in 1857 that Otis first put his safety elevators into permanent use. Experiments with the elevator had been made in hotels as early as 1833, and the old Fifth Avenue Hotel in 1859 installed a practical passenger elevator. When Strawbridge & Clothier in Philadelphia carried its customers up and down in an elevator in 1865, anybody could enjoy free of charge this novel sensation. Otis patented a steam-powered elevator in 1861. By the time the Eiffel Tower was built for the Paris Exposition of 1889, three hydraulic elevators (one made by Otis) arranged in stages carried a visitor to the top in seven minutes. Even faster were the new electric elevators, which first appeared that year and which soon were carrying the public in Macy's and Wanamaker's.

Glass would play an important new role in this new consumer's world. Before the introduction of electric lighting, large windows were needed to bring daylight into the extensive buildings. But at least until the mid-nineteenth century, large sheets of glass were costly and difficult to make. "Plate glass" (the word came into English about 1727), a flat sheet smooth and regular enough for mirrors or large windows, was made from a rough sheet of glass which was then laboriously ground and polished. At first the rough sheets were produced by blowing (which could make a plate no bigger than about 50 inches by 30 inches); then, in the early eighteenth century, the French perfected a system of casting glass in sheets. In 1839 an Englishman simplified the process for removing irregularities. Further improvements pointed the way to the continuous plate-glass process using rollers, which could make sheets of any length with the transparency of the old plate.

The larger sheets of glass, combined with the light cast-iron frame of the building, transformed the ground floor of department stores. The windows at street level were no longer merely openings to admit light and sun, but vivid advertisements—literally "show windows," an Americanism which came into use about the mid-nineteenth century for a shopwindow in which goods were displayed. The shop itself, the stock, and the goods themselves had become a powerful new form of advertising. Now for the first time the society's full range of material treasure would be laid out for all to see. "Window-shopping" was the name for a new and democratic popular pastime. The effectiveness of a building, the desirability of a retailing location, were now measured by the numbers in the passing crowds.

THESE URBAN CROWDS were brought to the city center by two important devices, neither of them quite new, but both newly flourishing in the United States after the Civil War. One made it easier for people to come to the department store; the other stirred them with the latest merchandising news, arousing their desire to come.

Public transportation did not appear in American cities until the second half of the nineteenth century; until then the ordinary citizen commonly shopped within walking distance, that is to say, within a radius of about two miles. Except for wealthy customers who could afford their own carriages, or for visitors from afar, a city merchant drew his customers from those who could walk to his shop from their house. This helped explain the importance of the neighborhood community. Almost all a man's activities, including his buying and selling, were with people who lived nearby and who as neighbors were very likely known to him personally. A neighborhood community was a walking community: of passers-by, of casual streetcorner encounters, of sidewalk greetings and doorway conversations.

Streetcars in the cities helped change all this. The early alternatives to walking were the omnibus (a kind of city stagecoach which held few passengers, was expensive, appeared infrequently, and lumbered slowly over the streets of cobblestone or mud) or the steam-driven railroad. Although the railroad was speedy, the noise, smoke, and embers from the locomotive made it a menace on the streets, and it was not suited to a line with frequent stops. The first effective public transportation within cities was the horse railroad, whose level tracks made the ride more comfortable, and which was well adapted to stop at any corner. We have become so accustomed to public transportation in our cities that we forget what a revolution in city life came with the first cheap public transportation.

The revolution occurred in many places at about the same time. As good an example as any other is the story of Boston, which has been admirably told by Sam B. Warner, Jr. In 1850, congested urban Boston extended out only about two miles from City Hall. By 1872 the horse railroads had pushed the radius out another half-mile. By 1887 the horsecar had pushed on for still another mile and a half, doubling the 1850 radius, and incidentally, of course, quadrupling the area of dense settlement. When by the 1890's the horse car was displaced by the electrified trolley, which moved twice as fast and could carry three times the number of passengers, public transportation reached out for at least another two miles, now making a greater Boston that reached six miles from City Hall.

The profits and enthusiasms of suburban investors and streetcar builders accelerated the process. The first street railway in Greater Boston, a single car in 1852 running between Harvard Square, Cambridge, and Union Square, Somerville, was so profitable that it invited imitation by other investors. It seemed simple enough to lay tracks on the roadbeds already provided by the city, to mount a coach on the rails, and buy a horse or two to provide the power. Booster real estate men who had bought tracts on the edge of the city had as much interest in linking their lots to the city centers as the earlier boosters of upstart towns had in bringing the railroad their way. Optimistic businessmen like Henry M. Whitney, the steamship magnate who consolidated the Boston lines in 1887, tried to attract more passengers by a standard five-cent fare and free transfers.

Meanwhile the boosters for streetcar monopolies urged the great "moral influence" of street railways. At long last, they said, the workingman who had been crowded into a multifamily tenement in the congested center of the city could buy his own lot, build his own house, and enjoy the wholesome delights of the rural suburb. The rapid expansion of street railways brought a scramble for franchises and entangled urban politics in the quest for monopolies, what Lincoln Steffens called *The Shame of the Cities* (1904). But regardless of the motives, the result was to draw more customers into the orbit of the city.

Streetcar tracks were rigid channels. A man in a streetcar had to go where it took him. And the streetcar, in almost any city, was likely to take him into the center; there were the great consumers' palaces.

ALONG WITH the centralizing influence of the streetcar, which brought city dwellers to department stores, came a new indrawing power over customers' minds and desires: the daily newspapers with large circulation concentrated in the cities. The department store, through its heavy newspaper advertising, contributed substantially to the success of these papers, and so helped keep them independent of subsidy by political parties. In this way the department store, like other large advertisers, indirectly contributed toward the political impartiality of American news reporting that would contrast sharply with the partisan-dominated press of France, Italy, and some other countries. The urban dailies also did much to help the great consumers' palaces to attract their vast constituencies. Just as the rise of the suburbs in the late nineteenth century was inseparable from the story of the streetcar, so the rise of the department store was one with the rise of newspaper advertising. The department-store pioneers were pioneers in the art and science of advertising.

R. H. Macy, like the mail-order pioneer Richard Warren Sears, was a bold and ingenious advertiser in the days before merchants had made advertising a part of their regular operations. Macy used repetition, composed bad verse, and combined hundreds of tiny agate-sized letters (the only kind which newspaper editors tolerated at the time) to make the Macy star or to produce larger letters. Beginning in 1858, he dared to leave large white spaces in the expensive columns; he advertised frequently, and put his ads in four or five different papers at the same time, to overshadow his more conservative competitors. John Wanamaker of Philadelphia was another vigorous leader. He pioneered in 1879 with his first full-page newspaper advertisement; within ten years Wanamaker's full-page advertisements were appearing regularly. Other department stores followed, and big-city dailies all over the country profited. In 1909, when Wanamaker's in New York City began putting full-page advertisements in the evening newspapers daily, this gave the lead to the evening over the morning newspapers in advertising linage. In Chicago, too, Marshall Field had become a big newspaper advertiser. Mandel Brothers made news when it contracted with the Chicago *Tribune* to run its full-page advertisement six days a week throughout 1902, for an annual fee of $100,000.

By the beginning of the twentieth century, the department store had become a mainstay of the big-city daily newspaper throughout the country. And as the circulation of dailies increased, the dailies became the mainstay of department stores, the increasingly powerful enticers of their hundreds of thousands of customers. City newspapers had become streetcars of the mind. They were putting the thoughts and desires of tens of thousands of people in the new cities on tracks, drawing them to centers where they joined the hasty fellowship of new consumption communities.

THE DEPARTMENT STORE, as Émile Zola observed in France, "democratized luxury." We have forgotten how revolutionary was the new principle of free admission for the whole public. In the old fairs and bazaars, the stall keepers had of course shown off their goods to the passing crowds. But the goods displayed to the common view were of the familiar sorts, to satisfy familiar wants. Any passer-by could look at the fruits and vegetables, at the sides of beef or the slabs of pork, at pots and kitchen utensils, at a basket or a length of cheap cloth. The costlier textiles or home furnishings were kept in an inner room, to be brought out only for serious customers who could afford such goods. In the great cities of the world, the better shops hung their symbols over the door, but they boasted their exclusiveness, displayed the coat of arms of the noble family who had appointed them to be their supplier, and exhibited little or none of the merchandise to the casual passer-by. The less expensive shops, too, were specialized, and their stocks of ready-made goods were small. In the latter part of the eighteenth century "shop" became a verb: then people began to "go shopping"—that is, go to the shops to see what they might buy. But still, common citizens might spend their lives without ever seeing a wide array of the fancy goods that they could not afford.

The department store helped change all this. Now a flowing, indiscriminate public wandered freely among attractive, open displays of goods of all kinds and qualities. One needed no longer be a "person of quality" to view goods of quality. Anyone could enter a department store, see and handle the most elegant furnishings. In this new democracy of consumers it was assumed that any man might be a buyer. Just as standard of living, by contrast with wealth, was a public and communal fact, so, too, buying and "shopping" became public. In the department store, as in the hotel, the distinction between private and public activities became blurred.

An urban shopper now could stroll through the world of actual goods as casually as a farmer soon would be leafing through the mail-order catalogue. Architects now aimed to make goods into their own advertisement: a permanent exposition for consumers and would-be consumers. Formerly merchandise had remained mostly dispersed into its raw forms, awaiting a customer's command or design. But this world of the ready-made was now a world of "consumers." Goods that had been assembled in advance into shoes, suits, or furniture were offered enticingly to the whole milling passing public. In these palaces of awakening desire, the new merchandisers hoped to offer something near enough to what the customer might already have wanted, and to stir him to wants he had never imagined.

In other, subtler ways, the market was homogenized and democratized. One of the most interesting, and least noticed, was the fixed-price, one-price policy of the great new department stores. The old practice, still a spice of life in the world's bazaars, was for the seller to bargain individually with each buyer, asking a price determined by that particular buyer's social position, his need, and his desire for that particular item. Some merchants marked each item with its cost (in private symbols), and then sought to secure from the customer the highest price above that which he could manage to extract. The refusal to bargain was considered churlish or unsociable, and it surely made life less interesting. The price actually paid for an item varied with the bargaining ability of each customer.

It is not surprising, then, that doctrinaire egalitarians had objected to this way of pricing. George Fox, founder of English Quakerism, as early as 1653 urged his followers to refuse to haggle, and advised merchants to fix the one fair price for every item and for all customers. Like some other Quaker principles, this was considered odd, but it had its business compensations. Customers who distrusted their own bargaining ability, Fox himself explained, would be reassured by the thought that "they might sende any childe and be as well used as themselves at any of these [Quaker] shopps."

The progress of the fixed-price policy had been slow, but department stores were quickly committed to it. The pioneering Paris department store Bon Marché had a fixed-price policy as early as 1852. For the large American department stores the policy was inevitable. In 1862, when Stewart's already had a staff of about two thousand, most of them on meager salaries and personally unknown to the store owner, it was not feasible to entrust bargaining to the individual salesman. A consequence, then, was the democratization, or at least the equalization, of prices. One price for everybody! Regardless of age, sex, wealth, poverty, or bargaining power. The price was marked for all to see. As the merchandise itself had become public and the intimate shop had been transformed into a palatial lobby where the best merchandise was open to vulgar eyes, so, too, the price was no secret.

Goods were priced for mass appeal, and department-store services were offered to the general public: free delivery, freedom to return or exchange goods, and charge accounts. These services, like "Satisfaction guaranteed or your money back" (an early department-store slogan), were not a product of private promises between shopkeeper and customer, but were part of a "policy," publicly proclaimed and advertised, from the firm to all consumers.

In a new sense now every sale and every purchase became a public act. The consumer was accepting an offer made, not only to him, but to anyone, usually in advertising. And advertising developed into the characteristic commercial relationship of the new age. Now it was no longer buyer and seller, the custom maker and the customer. It was advertiser and consumer: much of the advertiser's appeal was in his bigness; the consumer was a numerous horde whose strength was in numbers. The consumer now was being persuaded not merely to become a customer but to join a consumption community. He was being offered something that was not just for him but for everybody like him, and as both advertiser and consumer knew, there were millions.

11

Nationwide Customers

JUST AS DEPARTMENT STORES drew together thousands within the city in their consumers' palaces, other new enterprises reached out from city to city, creating nationwide consumption communities. Chain stores, pioneers of the everywhere community, built communities of consumers across the land. The expression "chain store," an Americanism firmly settled into the language by the beginning of the twentieth century, described one of a group of similar stores under common ownership. This was not, of course, a new idea, nor an American invention. But in the United States in the century after the Civil War, the chain store became a newly powerful institution.

"CASH-AND-CARRY," an Americanism added to the language by the early twentieth century, would become the motto of the chain stores. An affirmative way of saying "no credit and no deliveries," it would be an advertising slogan to inform all would-be customers that here was a shop with no frills, where the customer could save money. The department stores, oddly enough, had succeeded by offering some of the personal conveniences traditionally associated with the small neighborhood shop and the friendly reliable shopkeeper.Their developing systems of credit and installment buying and their numerous incidental services would actually provide a foil for the sales pitch of the new chain stores, which usually featured price and made a public virtue of their economies.

The first unit of what by mid-twentieth century was to be the chain-store system with the largest annual volume was founded in 1859. In that year George F. Gilman and George Huntington Hartford, both from Maine, opened a small store on Vesey Street in New York City under the name The Great American Tea Company. By cutting out middlemen, by buying tea in quantity and by importing it themselves from China and Japan, they offered tea at the spectacularly low price of 30 cents a pound when others were charging $1. They attracted customers by Barnumesque showmanship: premiums for lucky customers, cashiers' cages in the shape of Chinese pagodas, a green parrot in the center of the main floor, and band music on Saturdays. They sent eight dapple-gray horses pulling a great red wagon through the city and offered $20,000 to anyone who could guess the combined weight of the wagon and team. They gradually added other grocery goods—spices, coffee, soap, condensed milk, baking powder—and by 1876 had multiplied their stores to the number of sixty-seven.

With a booster enthusiasm worthy of an upstart Western town, they anticipated greatness by adopting the name The Great Atlantic & Pacific Tea Company in 1869. Perhaps the notion was that this chain of stores would unite the two oceans as did the Union Pacific Railroad, which had been completed that same year. The number of stores increased and the distinctive red-and-gold façade became familiar across the land. By 1912 there were nearly five hundred A & P stores. While they offered the advantages of lower prices which they claimed came from large-scale purchasing and from the elimination of middlemen, they still provided charge accounts and free delivery.

Led by John Hartford, son of the founder, the great expansion of the A & P chain came in 1912. Between 1912 and 1915, a new A & P store was opened every three days, to a national total of one thousand stores. Expansion was based on the cash-and-carry idea and on reduction of staff to make the one-man "economy" store. Meat, which soon became the largest single item, was not added till 1925. For the year 1929, total A & P sales exceeded $1 billion; in the following year, A & P stores numbered 15,709. By 1933, A & P was doing over 11 percent of the nation's food business. After that year, there was a trend to larger stores, and the number of individual stores gradually decreased. But by 1971 the 4,358 A & P stores reached an unprecedented annual sales volume of nearly $5.5 billion.

The builders of these new nationwide consumption communities met bitter opposition from local merchants, hometown boosters, and champions of neighborhoods who stood for the *local* community. The keepers of the old general stores had fought the big-city department stores; they would also fight RFD, they opposed parcel post, and they attacked the mail-order "monopolies." The menace of "chain stores," they said, was a threat to the whole American way of life. By the early 1920's, when a number of chains were prospering, the opposition of small, independent retailers became organized. The National Association of Retail Grocers in their annual convention in 1922 urged laws to limit the number of chain stores in any community. In defense of the neighborhood store they proposed various legal devices, such as special escalating taxes on every store beyond the first under the same ownership in a given state, and special taxes on merchandise purchased by chain stores.

At one time or another most states enacted some type of anti-chain-store tax. The most extensive effort at controlling chain-store merchandising was the Robinson-Patman Act of 1936 (sometimes called the Federal Anti-Price Discrimination Act), a New Deal measure amending earlier antitrust legislation. It aimed at the chain-store practices of "price discrimination" which were said to destroy competition or promote monopoly, and it gave the Federal Trade Commission important, if vague, supervisory power. The chain stores, like other large enterprises, had been guilty of some abuses. But they were unstoppable institutions in the movement to larger and larger consumption communities. The anti-chain-store movement, like the anti-RFD and anti-parcel-post movements, was a rear-guard action. Its spokesmen spoke for the dying past of the general store, the village post office, the one-room schoolhouse and the friendly corner drugstore.

Jeremiads against the chain store really expressed bewilderment at the dissolving of the neighborhood community. "The chain stores are undermining the foundation of our entire local happiness and prosperity," lamented the Speaker of the Indiana House of Representatives in a letter to his constituents in the late 1920's. "They have destroyed our home markets and merchants, paying a minimum to our local enterprises, sapping the life-blood of prosperous communities and leaving about as much in return as a traveling band of gypsies." Senator Royal S. Copeland of New York declared, "When a chain enters a city block, ten other stores close up. In smaller cities and towns, the chain store contributes nothing to the community. Chain stores are parasites. I think they undermine the foundations of the country."

A hysteria which paid heavy political dividends seized the congressional representatives from the rural and small-town world. "A wild craze for efficiency in production, sale, and distribution has swept over the land," warned Senator Hugo L. Black of Alabama in 1930, "increasing the number of unemployed, building up a caste system, dangerous to any government. . . . Chain groceries, chain dry-goods stores, chain clothing stores, here today and merged tomorrow— grow in size and power. . . . The local man and merchant is passing and his community loses his contribution to local affairs as an independent thinker and executive."

The response of the chain stores was multiplex. Their owners tried to answer the accusations that they lacked old-fashioned community loyalty by going to great lengths to advertise locally and to reward examples of community leadership among their managers. In 1939, under the very shadow of the Robinson-Patman Act, the trade journal *Chain-Store Age* announced awards for "Community Builder of the Year" to advertise the hometown services of chain-store managers. The local manager, they argued, actually did support the Community Chest and the Red Cross, he helped local students, he served his local church, and he cooperated with local merchants.

But both the accusation and the response were beside the point; the chain store announced and symbolized a new kind of community. The new consumption communities were, of course, shallower in their loyalties, more superficial in their services. But they were ubiquitous, somehow touching the American consumer at every waking moment and even while he slept. Senator Black was right in his alarums that the "local man" was passing. Man was no longer local. As the American population adopted mobility as normal, the new arrivals in a new suburb or city who might not know their neighbors would at least feel somewhat at home in their A & P (where they knew where to find each item) or in their Walgreen's (where familiar brands abounded). Had these enlarging communities of consumers provided some slight solace and substitute for the declining neighborhood community?

12
Goods Sell Themselves

"GOODS SUITABLE for the millionaire," R. H. Macy's advertised in 1887, "at prices in reach of the millions." The fixed price had helped democratize the marketplace, and the new impersonal way of pricing had far-reaching effects on the consumers' world. Consumers with money to spend were eager to find something to buy. But they were more uncertain than ever about what they "needed," what was really essential to their style of life or to their station in life.

New classes of merchandise came into being, characterized not by their quality or function, but by their *price*. One of the most spectacular careers in American history and some of the nation's most distinctive institutions were built on this simple new notion.

TO CALL the five-and-ten-cent store the poor man's department store tells only part of the story. The department store was a consumers' palace; the five-and-ten was a consumers' bazaar. Both were places of awakening desire. The department store displayed items of all prices and shapes and sizes and qualities; and the five-and-ten displayed a tempting array of items which one could buy for the smallest units of cash. If an attractive item was offered at a low enough price, the customer would buy it if he needed it—but if the price was low enough and in convenient coin, perhaps the customer would buy it anyway on the spur of the moment, whether or not he "needed" it. In a world where the fixed price and the public price were only beginning to be known, where haggling was still a social pastime, it required a bold imagination to conceive the five-and-ten way of merchandising. If the fixed price was low enough, could people somehow be induced to buy *because of* the fixed price? Even before the fixed price was a firmly established institution, a clever merchant built an empire on this experiment.

The man who, more than any other, helped give commodities this price-focused quality was F. W. Woolworth. He conjured up a new world of five-cent items and ten-cent items. Hating the drudgery on his father's farm in upstate New York, young Woolworth had found work in the general stores of neighboring country towns. But, significantly, he had no knack as a salesman. In one of his early jobs his salesmanship was so poor that his employer reduced his wages from $10 to $8.50 a week. He did have a flair for display. His first success, in a small dry-goods store in Watertown, New York, was in using remnants of red cloth to make an attractive window display. His employer, hearing of another merchant's success in selling handkerchiefs at five cents apiece, decided to try a "five-cent counter," and bought a hundred dollars' worth of miscellaneous five-cent items: crocheting needles, buttonhooks, watch keys, safety pins, collar buttons, baby bibs, washbasins and dippers, thimbles, soap, and harmonicas. Woolworth arrayed them on a long table surmounted by a placard advertising the price. On the first day they were all sold.

Profiting from this experience, in 1879 Woolworth went off on his own (first in Utica, New York, then in Lancaster, Pennsylvania), trying out the idea of a "Five and Ten Cent Store." His first problem was finding enough different items to sell at his price. In the long run Woolworth would secure a large enough stock of five-and-ten-cent items by multiplying his stores and increasing his volume. By 1886 Woolworth controlled seven stores; by 1895 there were twenty-eight; by 1900, fifty-nine. Even though each store was small, with a chain of them he could buy on a large scale. He attracted new kinds of merchandise, he invented some items himself, and he bought in large quantities. In this way he gave to all buyers, even in small towns, the advantages of membership in a vast consumption community.

"Price lining"—the production of items to sell at a predetermined price—expressed a new way of thinking. And it expressed a new extreme of buyer passivity, perhaps the last stage in making shopping into a spectator sport. In the new world of the fixed price, Woolworth gave modern form to the traditional notion of a "fair price," long since elaborated by Aristotle and the medieval moralists. Was price somehow not a product of individual bargaining, but a quality of the commodity itself?

Woolworth from the beginning was bold in using red and he showed lots of red jewelry. In 1900 he standardized on the brilliant-carmine-red storefront (probably borrowed from The Great Atlantic & Pacific Tea Company), with gold-leaf lettering and molding.

For his advertising, Woolworth relied not on the newspapers or magazines, but on architecture and on the self-advertising qualities of his merchandise, which had not been widely exploited until the recent improvements in plate-glass manufacturing. "No, you don't have to bark for customers," Woolworth advised his store managers near the beginning of the century. "That method is too ancient for us. But you can pull customers into your stores and they won't know it. Draw them in with attractive window displays and when you get them in have a plentiful showing of the window goods on the counters. . . . Remember our advertisements are in our show windows and on our counters."

Goods that carried a tag announcing their price actually "sold" themselves. The only function of salesclerks was to wrap packages and make change. This helped Woolworth keep costs and prices low, since he could conduct his business successfully by employing young girls at low wages. In the early days they received $1.50 a week. "We must have cheap help," he wrote his store managers in 1892, "or we cannot sell cheap goods. When a clerk gets so good she can get better wages elsewhere, let her go—for it does not require skilled and experienced salesladies to sell our goods . . . one thing is certain: we cannot afford to pay good wages and sell goods as we do now, and our clerks ought to know it." Following the examples of John Wanamaker and Marshall Field, who would not allow a clerk to approach a customer, Woolworth boasted that his managers "make their stores Fairs and a person can go entirely through them without once being pressed to buy anything."

And Woolworth's flourished. By 1900 his volume was over $5 million a year; in another five years it had trebled. For more customers he reached up into the middle classes. Then he crossed the Atlantic and opened a chain in England. By 1913 F. W. Woolworth, who made a fetish of simplicity and directness, who believed his five-and-ten-cent merchandise should be its own advertisement, had built the most spectacular piece of architectural advertising in history. President Woodrow Wilson pressed the button in Washington which lit up in New York City the tallest habitable building in the world, the Woolworth Building.

PRICE LINING was only one of many inventions and institutions which made it ever harder for Americans to define the limits of their needs and wants. Was it possible that every step to the cheapening of things would somehow impoverish people by increasing the disproportion between their newly awakened desires and the satisfactions they could afford?

In 1916, soon after A & P had inaugurated its accelerated expansion with "economy" stores, Clarence Saunders of Memphis, Tennessee, opened his first new-style grocery store under the enticing name of Piggly Wiggly. The novel feature of Piggly Wiggly was a floor plan which let the customers in through turnstiles, channeling them back and forth through a maze which required them to follow a prescribed path, in the course of which they saw all the merchandise displayed before reaching the only exit, which was the check-out turnstile at the end. By this ingenious scheme the customer, once in the store, could not find his way out except by exposing himself to the appeal of all the merchandise, including, of course, the things he had not come to buy. This plan for forcibly exposing a customer to the storekeeper's whole stock came to be called, somewhat eu-phemistically, "self-service." While this popular term emphasized the absence of a salesman, the revolutionary significance of the in-vention was that by making the goods "sell themselves," it estab-lished a new relation between each buyer and everything offered for sale.

In stores of this type the attendant was needed to service the goods, not the customer. The "customer" had become less a willing consumer with specific demands than the unwitting target of the seller's packaging and display. The seller had entrapped the buyer, not by any immoral or illegal device, but by the new architecture and technology of distribution.

An obvious consequence was the increased importance of packag-ing and the rise of "impulse buying." The buyer had a new au-tonomy, a new isolation, forced on him. Alone, without a friendly or persuasive salesman, he confronted packaged goods in vast array. If he would indeed join the consumption community of Borden's, Campbell's, Del Monte, or Morton's Salt, it was now his own "volun-tary" act. But as the decision was forced back on him, he became less and less sure of what he really wanted and whether his decision to buy was really his own. Was he in fact choosing to purchase this instead of that because of some irresistible, Machiavellian, scientific techniques of persuasion that he did not even understand? Ameri-cans were drawn to perform acts of faith (hallowed and sealed by the price they paid) in the brands of goods in which other Americans by the millions were also expressing their faith.

Thousands of stores adopted "self-service." Some secured fran-chises to operate under the Piggly Wiggly name, others invented variations. In California in the 1920's the spread of the automobile produced the "drive-in" market. This motorized form of self-service was designed to draw people from a wider area and to make it more convenient for the customer to shop by car. Along with the automo-bile, the spread of home refrigeration encouraged people to buy in larger quantities. In 1921 only five thousand household refrigerators were sold in the United States; in 1931 sales exceeded one million. The 1950 census showed that over 90 percent of the dwelling units in the United States had refrigeration. The incentive to buy for home storage was increased with the arrival of the home freezer (hardly known in 1940) after World War II. By 1972 one household in three had its home freezer.

THE SELF-SERVICE IDEA was elaborated, and clever merchants found other ways of establishing newer and more direct relations between the consumer and all sorts of goods. What is sometimes called the first super-drugstore was opened by Walgreen's in Tampa, Florida, in October 1934. "A revolutionary new kind of drugstore," the company explained, "which not only provided the space for additional lines but took merchandise out of the traditional show-cases and presented it instead on open display counters where customers could see it, touch it and buy it. The success of this new type of drugstore sounded the knell for the old-fashioned kind of 'small corner drugstore.'" One of the largest was Walgreen's gigantic Chicago store, which opened in 1949 at State and Madison streets comprising thirty thousand square feet on two floors.

Charles R. Walgreen's success story was similar to that of F. W. Woolworth or George Huntington Hartford. He was the father of the modern American drugstore, one of the most characteristic American institutions of the twentieth century, an institution as bewildering to foreign visitors as it was expressive of the new American consumption communities. Born on an Illinois farm of Swedish immigrants, Walgreen began life as a bookkeeper in a general store. Later, when working in a shoe factory in Dixon, Illinois, he suffered an accident which cost him part of a finger; the doctor who treated him persuaded him to become a druggist's apprentice. Walgreen found a job in a Chicago drugstore, which he eventually bought. Then Walgreen multiplied his stores, offering a vast range of nonpharmaceutical services. He developed lunch counters in connection with soda fountains, then manufactured his own brands of ice cream and candy. Walgreen's drugstore became a modern version of the old general store, but it bore almost no resemblance to the English or continental chemist's shop which was its predecessor, and which still survived on the other side of the Atlantic. In 1916 Walgreen had seven stores, and by 1927 they numbered over a hundred. By the time of Walgreen's death in 1939, he had some five hundred stores with twelve thousand employees in two hundred cities in thirty-seven states.

"Supermarket" was the American booster name for still another new institution which first became widespread in the 1930's. The supermarket combined self-service, cash-and-carry, a wide assortment of goods (at least grocery, meat, produce, and dairy products) and a large volume of sales. By about 1950 the trade had defined a supermarket as such a store with an annual volume of at least a half-million dollars. As if to demonstrate the wonderful flexibility of the American language, and the American reluctance to avoid hyperbole, a supermarket with a smaller volume was now called a "superette."

Supermarkets had first been tried not by the big chains but by the independents, who were freer to change their pattern. A & P, beginning about 1937, gradually converted from their small "economy" stores, each staffed by one man with minimum fixtures and facilities, to the supermarket. And they made the enormous volume of the supermarket another opportunity for pioneering. For example, in 1940 they opened a new era in food merchandising with the experimental sale of cellophane-wrapped meat. In one place after another A & P consolidated three or four of their smaller stores into one supermarket. The nearly sixteen thousand stores of the year 1930 had been combined into some four thousand by the early 1950's. Other leading food chains went in the same direction. As the supermarket, like the drugstore, moved beyond its original province, as new techniques of merchandising grew, the consumption communities overlapped. There was more similarity than ever before between the stores where the consumer bought his groceries, his hardware, his household cleaners, and his toilet needs. The faith and loyalties of consumers were less in the people who sold him the goods, and more than ever in the promises of unseen merchandisers, in familiar packaging and in trusted national brands.

13

How Farmers Joined Consumption Communities

IN THE LATE NINETEENTH CENTURY, the great American railroad network combined with other forces to draw the remote farmer and his family into the new consumption communities. The new American institutions which accomplished this were the mail-order houses. The expression "mail order," applied to retail merchandisers and catalogues, was an Americanism that had come into general use by the beginning of the twentieth century. The consumption communities of Montgomery Ward or Sears buyers, which had not even existed at the end of the Civil War, a bare half-century later numbered millions. By the mid-twentieth century, Sears, Roebuck and Company would be the nation's largest retailer of general merchandise. This was a movement from the general store, with its gathering of a half-dozen local pundits around the cracker barrel, to the mail-order firm, with its dispersed customer-millions hungering through the half-thousand pages of vivid advertising copy, or waiting at their mailboxes: customer-millions who would never see one another but who still somehow leaned on one another. This was a vivid allegory of how America moved from cluster communities of transients and upstarts, of individuals calling one another by their first names, to a nation of everywhere communities of consumers and national-brand buyers who would never meet.

THE AMERICAN FARMER especially needed some kind of community because certain facts of American life had tended to keep him from living close to his neighbor. The Homestead Act of 1862 required a settler to live on his claim for five years in order to perfect his title. This gave a character to American farm life very different from that of the Old World peasant, who lived in a village and then went out every day to the plots that he cultivated. Even if every homesteader had had no more than a quarter-section (160 acres), and every quarter-section was actually homesteaded, under the rigid rectangular system of surveying public lands for sale, the average distance between farmhouses would still be at least a half-mile. But many settlers had larger tracts, some sections were reserved for schools, and there were large unsettled areas that had been abandoned by Eastern speculators—all of which separated a homesteading farmer from his neighbors.

The isolation varied from place to place, with the climate and the terrain. The lonely prairies of the great Northwest, in the Dakotas or Nebraska, taxed the endurance of sociable men and women. "The reason is not far to seek," E.V. Smalley, the observant editor of the *Northwest Illustrated Monthly Magazine,* who knew that land personally, explained in 1893. "These people came from cheery little farm villages. Life in the fatherland was hard and toilsome, but it was not lonesome. Think for a moment how great the change must be from the white-walled, red-roofed village on a Norway fiord, with its church and schoolhouse, its fishing boats on the blue inlet, and its green mountain walls towering aloft to snow fields, to an isolated cabin on a Dakota prairie, and say if it is any wonder that so many Scandinavians lose their mental balance." The climate and topography made the loneliness harder to bear.

If there be any region in the world where the natural gregarious instinct of mankind should assert itself, that region is our Northwest prairies, where a short hot summer is followed by a long cold winter, and where there is little in the aspect of nature to furnish food for thought. . . . No brooks babble under icy armor. There is no bird life after the wild geese and ducks have passed on their way south. The silence of death rests on the vast landscape, save when it is swept by cruel winds that search out every chink and cranny of the buildings, and drive through each unguarded aperture the dry, powdery snow. . . . A barbed-wire fence surrounds the barnyard. Rarely are there any trees, for on the prairies trees grow very slowly, and must be nursed with care to get a start. . . .

Neighborly calls are infrequent because of the long distances which separate the farmhouses, and because, too, of the lack of homogeneity of the people. They have no common past to talk about. They were strangers to one another when they arrived in this new land, and their work and ways have not thrown them much together. Often the strangeness is intensified by differences of national origin. There are Swedes, Norwegians, Germans, French Canadians, and perhaps even such peculiar people as Finns and Icelanders, among the settlers, and the Americans came from many different states. . . . An alarming amount of insanity occurs in the new prairie States among farmers and their wives.

Some, like Smalley, said the only remedy was to abandon the isolated farmhouses and draw farmers together in villages. But by the 1880's it was already too late to alter the pattern of American farm settlement.

American railroads, the connecting ligaments of the great West, had appeared in a peculiar way. In England, for example, they were commonly built to connect one city with another, to carry an already heavy traffic for people who were already there. Nineteenth-century America had seen the booster railroad arise to match the booster press, the booster college, and the upstart town. Running often from "Nowhere-in-Particular to Nowhere-at-All," the American railroad was commonly built in the hope that it would call into being the population it would serve. If American railroads had not grown in this anachronistic way, there might never have been an opportunity or an incentive to enlist isolated farmers in the city-bred consumption communities.

In the years just after the Civil War, railroads covered the West with spectacular speed. In 1865, when there were 35,085 miles of railroad in the whole United States, only 3,272 miles were west of the Mississippi. By 1890, when the total national mileage had reached 199,876, the mileage west of the Mississippi came to 72,473, over twice that of the whole nation twenty-five years before. But the West was still sparsely populated; large areas still averaged under two inhabitants per square mile, and hardly a Western state came up to the national average of 21.2 per square mile. By 1910 the United States possessed one third of the world's railroad mileage, and the mileage was continuing to grow. The excessively expansive, optimistic spirit of those earlier days (which, of course, did not foresee the competition of the automobile and the truck, much less the airplane) was evidenced in the fact that in nearly every year between 1916 and 1960, more mileage was abandoned than built, and in the period as a whole the total operating mileage actually declined.

The railroads did, of course, succeed in attracting people; by carrying what the people needed and what they produced, the railroads prospered. In America then, as the English economist Alfred Marshall observed in 1919, the opportunity to widen the market for any item was unlimited. The United States would be the land of "massive multiform standardization." He noted "the inevitable preference given by great railways to large consignments traveling long distances, by which a giant business, even if far off, is at an advantage in competition with a smaller business near at hand." Marshall was struck by "the homogeneity of the American demand for manufactured goods. Even those race differences, which have become almost a dominant factor in American life, lessen this homogeneity very little. Widely as the Scandinavians are separated from the Italians, and the native Americans from the Poles, in sentiment, in modes of life, and even in occupations they are yet purchasers of nearly the same goods. Allowance being of course made for differences of climate, they buy similar clothes, furniture, and implements." We have already seen the significance of what Marshall called "homogeneous consumption" for Americans in cities and towns.

CHICAGO, THE RAILROAD CENTER of the nation, was the natural place from which to reach out to the vast rural hinterlands, and Chicago became the capital for the great nationwide enterprises of absentee salesmanship. The pioneer there was an energetic young transient, Aaron Montgomery Ward. Born in a small New Jersey town in 1843, Ward moved with his parents to Niles, Michigan, where he attended public school until he was fourteen, then worked in a barrel-stave factory and later in a brickyard. His first merchandising experience was in a general store in nearby St. Joseph, until he secured employment, about 1865, with young Marshall Field's firm in Chicago. Moving on to St. Louis, he became a traveling salesman for a dry-goods wholesaler; covering the rural West, he learned the problems of the farmers who bought from a general store. Ward saw that he could reduce retail prices if he purchased large quantities for cash direct from manufacturers and then sold for cash direct to the rural consumer. This was the seed of his mail-order idea. Returning to Chicago, he began to lay his plans. The great Chicago fire of 1871 nearly consumed his savings, but by the spring of 1872 he had scraped together $1,600 of his own, to which a partner added $800.

Starting in a loft, 12 feet by 14 feet, over a livery stable, Ward issued a single price sheet which listed the items for sale and explained how to order. Within two years the price list became an 8-page booklet and then a 72-page catalogue. By eliminating the middleman, Ward promised savings of 40 percent: on fans, parasols, writing paper, needles, stereoscopes, cutlery, trunks, harnesses, and scores of other items. The catalogue grew and grew, at the same time becoming more vivid and enticing through illustrations. By the 1880's a wood-cut illustrated nearly every item. In 1883, only a decade after the founding with a capital of $2,400, the catalogue boasted goods in stock worth a half-million dollars. The catalogue for 1884 numbered 240 pages and listed nearly ten thousand items.

Montgomery Ward's business depended on the confidence of a buyer in a seller whom he had never seen. From the beginning, Ward's had the advantage of being the official supply house for a widespread farmers' organization, the Patrons of Husbandry, popularly known as the "Grange." Founded in 1867, the Grange aimed, among its other purposes, to reduce the cost of goods to the farmer by fighting "monopoly" and by eliminating middlemen. Ward's fitted perfectly into this scheme. From 1872 through the 1880's, Ward's described itself on the catalogue cover as "The Original Grange Supply House," and offered Grangers special privileges. While everybody else had to pay cash in advance or on delivery, orders from Grange officials or countersigned with the Grange seal were allowed ten days' grace. The very first catalogue illustration was a picture of the official "Granger hat," and early catalogues featured Granger regalia. Testimonials from Grange officials appeared regularly in Ward's catalogues, and some Granges actually sent representatives to Chicago to inspect their supply house.

Everything was done to build up the friendly confidence needed to induce farmers to buy goods sight unseen from a distant warehouse run by strangers. For it had been the farmer's custom to buy his store goods from an old acquaintance, the country storekeeper, and even then only after close inspection. A. Montgomery Ward built his business on his hope for a revolution in farmers' buying habits.

In other words, this meant creating a new consumption community of rural Americans. Soon Ward's announced that the same savings given to Grangers would be offered to all buyers. Hesitant customers were attracted and reassured by Ward's ironclad guarantee: all goods were sent "subject to examination," and any item found unsatisfactory could be returned to the company, which paid for the transportation both ways. Signed testimonials from the secretaries and masters of Granges all over the West, were printed in the catalogues. And just as the customer had to have confidence in the unseen seller, so, too, the firm had to have confidence in the unseen customer—to believe his complaints in order to refund his money or to replace his goods without delaying to investigate. Even after Ward's community of customers had grown to hundreds of thousands, the firm took pains to reassure each of them that the company was his friend. This helps us understand why early catalogues showed pictures of the founders, of company executives, and even of the buyers for individual departments; these men personally signed catalogue guarantees for the goods. Customers wrote in to say how pleased they were to deal with such "fine looking men." Some, who had named their babies after Mr. Ward, requested photographs, which might be an inspiration to the child.

Correspondence from customers received close personal attention. One husband asked Mr. Ward to select a hat to be a birthday present for his red-headed wife. Another customer asked him to help her find some summer boarders. A single mail in 1908 brought inquiries about the reliability of Field's and Wanamaker's and about procedures for proving land claims, along with requests for the name of a good lawyer, for an honest hired girl, and for a baby to adopt. Some customers asked if they could pay in produce instead of cash; some tried to sell Mr. Ward their secondhand furniture or their livestock. Others asked help in finding runaway boys, sought advice on how to discipline disobedient children, how to regain a husband's love. Still others wrote to assuage their loneliness or simply because they had nobody else to write to.

Many of these letters show the remote farmer relying on Mr. Ward much as their Southern colonial predecessors had relied on a London (or later a Baltimore, New Orleans, or Charleston) factor. In colonial days it was not unheard of for a planter to ask his London factor to select his books or to ship him a suitable wife. Now Mr. Ward received hundreds of letters annually from men seeking wives and even a few from women seeking husbands. We are not surprised to find a lonely farmer proposing marriage to the "girl wearing hat number———on page 153 of your catalogue." A blacksmith wanting a wife promised that he was a total abstainer from tobacco, cards, and whiskey. "As you advertise everything for sale that a person wants," one customer from the state of Washington reasoned, "I thought I would write you, as I am in need of a wife, and see what you could do for me." While some bachelors were vague ("Not particular as to nationality") or simply asked for pictures and prices of good wives, others knew precisely what they wanted:

> Please send me a good wife. She must be a good housekeeper and able
> to do all household duty. She must be 5 feet 6 inches in height. Weight
> 150 lbs. Black hair and brown eyes, either fair or dark.
>
> I am 45 years old, six feet, am considered a good-looking man. I have
> black hair and blue eyes. I own quite a lot of stock and land. I am tired
> of living a bachelor life and wish to lead a better life and more favorable.
>
> Please write and let me know what you can do for me.

Ward's, instead of treating these as crank letters, shrewdly advised
that it was not wise to select a wife by mail, but added that "after you
get the wife and you find that she needs some wearing apparel or
households goods, we feel sure we could serve both you and her to
good advantage."

Customers sometimes felt bound to explain why they had not
recently written to Mr. Ward:

> I suppose you wonder why we haven't ordered anything from you
> since the fall. Well, the cow kicked my arm and broke it and besides my
> wife was sick, and there was the doctor bill. But now, thank God, that
> is paid, and we are all well again, and we have a fine new baby boy, and
> please send plush bonnet number 29d8077. . . .

This friendly customer received an equally personal reply: regrets
about the broken arm, pleasure that the wife was recovered, congratulations on the son with hopes that he would grow up to be a fine
man, acknowledgment of the order for the bonnet, plus an inquiry
whether the customer had noticed the anti-cow-kicker shown in the
catalogue.

WARD HAD ALREADY proved the success of the mail-order idea
when another young man, apparently uninfluenced by Ward's example and taking a path quite different from Ward's, began to develop
a mail-order business destined to be even vaster than Ward's. Without the advantage of the Grange name and with almost no capital
himself, young Richard Warren Sears had a sharp eye for how to use
other men's capital, and how to make the most of the organizations,
especially the railroads, which others had been building. From an
early age Sears, who had been raised in rural Minnesota, had to help
support his family. He learned telegraphy, which was then a qualification to be a railroad station agent, and he secured the job managing
the railroad and express office of the Minneapolis and St. Louis line
at North Redwood, Minnesota, a village of three houses. Since his
duties as agent took little of his time, he made a business of selling
wood, coal, and lumber to the farmers and the Indians. He could offer
these at an attractively low price because of the special freight rates

he could secure; and he bought the farmers' meat and berries which he shipped out at a profit.

In 1886 when a package of watches sent by a Chicago jewelry company was refused by the addressee in nearby Redwood Falls, station agent Sears saw his opportunity. In those days it was common for wholesalers to ship on consignment to retailers; in fact, they sometimes tried to unload stock by shipping goods that had not been ordered. Or they would deliberately ship to fictitious addresses. Then, when the railroad station agent informed them that the goods were undeliverable, the wholesaler would offer the goods to the station agent at "half-price" suggesting that this would save the shipper the cost of return freight, and that by reselling them, the station agent could make a good profit. Following this pattern, the Chicago company offered these undeliverable watches to Sears for $12 apiece. They were of a stylish type, gold-filled, so-called "yellow watches" with a hunting case, which retailed for about $25.

Instead of paying for the watches himself, Sears took advantage of his location on the railroad to offer them by mail to other agents along his line for $14 apiece. He offered to send them C.O.D. subject to examination, and since the station agents were bonded, there was little risk. The other agents along the line would then be in a position to sell these popular watches profitably at less than their price at the local jewelers. From this casual beginning, using the stock furnished by a Chicago wholesaler, Sears soon built a flourishing watch business. Sears himself extended his business by the old-fashioned techniques of sending his watches to nonexistent persons and then offering a moneymaking opportunity to the lucky agents who held the unclaimed parcels.

Having made about $5,000 in six months, Sears gave up his station-agent job and, in 1886, set up the R. W. Sears Watch Company in Minneapolis. From an office renting for $10 a month, equipped with a kitchen table, a fifty-cent chair, some record books and stationery, he now reached out beyond the market of station agents by advertising in the newspapers. In 1887 he moved to Chicago, which was already the railroad capital of the nation. There he enlisted the help of Alvah Curtis Roebuck, a watchmaker of about Sears' age, who had also run a job-printing business, and Sears quickly showed his flair for advertising. His ingenious selling schemes included a "club plan" under which thirty-eight men clubbed together, each paying $1 a week into a pool; each week one man would win a watch by lot, until at the end of thirty-eight weeks all the members had their watches.

Sears' market was still primarily among station agents, but there were about twenty thousand of these in the country at the time. And, of course, they were a select clientele, not only because they were all bonded, but also because they tended to be steady men of good character. Sears' ironclad guarantee made it easier for him to attract customers from the general public. From the beginning he planned for low profit margins, but aimed at large volume and rapid turnover. All this was to be made possible by extensive advertising to attract an ever-widening community of customers. In 1889 Sears sold his young watch business for about $70,000. But within a few months he was back again in the mail-order business, still featuring watches, watch chains, and other jewelry. His business was built around a catalogue which combined scrupulously honest guarantees ("Satisfaction or Your Money Back") with flamboyant unprovable claims (goods were "The Best in the World" and would "Last Forever").

In the early days, especially when Sears was still relying heavily on newspaper advertising, his ingenuity and his remoteness from the customer occasionally tempted him into the tradition of Western hoaxes. "An Astonishing Offer" which he announced in rural weeklies in 1889 was illustrated by a drawing of a sofa and two chairs, all of "fine lustrous metal frames beautifully finished and decorated, and upholstered in the finest manner and with beautiful plush" which "as an advertisement only" and only for the next sixty days would be sent to anyone who remitted ninety-five cents "to pay expenses, boxing, packing, advertising, etc." Customers who sent in their money received a set of doll's furniture exactly as specified; they had not noticed in the first line of the advertisement, in fine print, the word "miniature." Sears' clever advertising became proverbial. There was the story, for example, of a Sears advertisement which offered a "sewing machine" for $1—for which the customer duly received a needle and thread.

By the time the firm name of Sears, Roebuck and Company came into use in 1893, the business had moved into a wide range of merchandise, including clothes, furniture, sewing machines, baby carriages, and musical instruments, described in a catalogue of 196 pages. As the firm grew, Sears made a special effort to keep the personal touch. For some time, even after the typewriter had come into general use, letters sent out by the company were handwritten, out of respect for the feelings of the farm clientele who were sometimes offended to receive a letter that was "machine-made."

And Sears' business grew, increasing in volume even during the depression years of 1893–94. "We will forfeit ten thousand dollars ($10,000.00) in cash to any worthy charity," the cover of Sears' 1907 catalogue announced, "if anyone can prove that any other five (5) catalogue houses in the United States, selling general merchandise exclusively to the consumer, the same as we do, can show combined sales for the twelve months ending July 30, 1907, aggregating as much as [Sears'] \$53,188,901.00."

WHILE THE CITY MERCHANT used newspaper advertising to entice customers to come see his merchandise, for the mail-order merchant the catalogue (which was his advertising) was also his only merchandise display. The catalogue *was* his shop window, his store counter, and his salesman. It would have been hard to imagine a way of selling that was more dependent on advertising. In the early days before 1890, Sears was still doing considerable advertising in certain periodicals, then known as "mail-order" magazines, which circulated in the rural market. Such advertisements aimed, by popularizing the Sears name, to increase the demand for catalogues. Newspapers, under pressure from the local merchants who were fighting for their lives against the "Mail-Order Trust," often refused to sell advertising space to Sears. Meanwhile the *Ladies' Home Journal,* which would have been a natural medium, refused to take Sears' copy because its editor, Cyrus H. K. Curtis, thought Sears' copy was extravagant in its claims and undignified in its make-up.

In the mail-order business, the catalogue was the thing. And in the form that great mail-order houses developed, the catalogue was something new under the sun, a kind of booster press for an upstart community of consumers. And what it brought was more than news, for it sought to persuade and attract. The first object was to get the catalogue out into people's hands. Rural Free Delivery, as we shall see in the following chapter, was the great boon.

One successful Sears plan was to send the catalogues in batches of twenty-four to persons who agreed to distribute them. A record was kept for thirty days of purchases by the new customers to whom the "distributor" had given catalogues. The distributor then received a premium which increased in value with the size of the purchases he had stimulated: at one time, for example, total orders amounting to \$100 would earn the catalogue distributor a bicycle, a sewing machine, or a stove.

Richard W. Sears was a fanatic for the catalogue, and for years he wrote nearly all the copy himself. The basis for the Sears business, he insisted, was the widest possible distribution of catalogues to the most likely customers. Policy varied from year to year on whether to charge for the catalogue; when it was not offered free, the price varied from five cents in 1893 to fifty cents in 1901, but the best customers always received their catalogues free. As a reward for their loyalty they sometimes were sent a deluxe edition on better paper bound in red cloth.

The circulation of the general catalogue increased phenomenally: from some 318,000 in 1897 (the first year for which figures are available) to over 1 million for the spring catalogue in 1904, to over 2 million for the spring catalogue the very next year, and over 3 million for the fall catalogue in 1907. Since there were two annual editions, one in spring and one in fall, the total number of general catalogues distributed each year was about double these figures. Circulation figures for the general catalogue climbed steadily, reaching 7 million in each of the two seasons by the late '20's. In 1927 Sears, Roebuck sent out 10 million circular letters, 15 million general catalogues, 23 million semiannual sales catalogues and other special catalogues, to a grand total of 75 million.

As circulation spread, the book became bigger, more vivid, and easier to use. By 1894 it exceeded 500 pages; in 1898 a detailed index was provided. In 1903 Sears set up its own printing plant, and improvements in the quality of the catalogue came year after year. Sears turned to linotype, then to four-color printing, which required an improved ink to dry rapidly without smearing. The company then had to produce new paper which would take color printing and would still be light enough for cheap mailing. As late as 1905, more than half the illustrations were still woodcuts; and art historians have suggested that it was the mail-order catalogue that kept alive the art of wood engraving.

The mail-order catalogue pioneered in other techniques of illustration. Since Ward's and Sears' could not show the customer the actual product they wanted him to buy, they obviously had to depend on the catalogue to give him an accurate and enticing view. The extent of their market and their control over catalogue circulation gave them an opportunity to experiment. They are credited with the "discovery," for example, that four pages in color would sell as much of the same goods as twelve pages in black-and-white.

SOME HAVE CALLED the big mail-order catalogues the first characteristically American kind of book. Since colonial times, Americans had been more notable for their almanacs, newspapers, magazines and how-to-do-it manuals than for their treatises: the relevant, the topical, the ephemeral, had been more expressive of American life than the systematic and the monumental. The Sears, Roebuck Catalogue was the Bible of the new rural consumption communities. The newer gospels would be more dispersed, and would include sounds and living pictures going into a thousand places, on billboards, over radio waves, in television images.

It was not merely facetious to say that many farmers came to live more intimately with the good Big Book of Ward's or Sears, Roebuck than with the Good Book. The farmer kept his Bible in the frigid parlor, but as Edna Ferber remarked in *Fanny Herself* (1917), her novel of the mail-order business, the mail-order catalogue was kept in the cozy kitchen. That was where the farm family ate and where they really lived. For many such families the catalogue probably expressed their most vivid hopes for salvation. It was no accident that pious rural customers without embarrassment called the catalogue "the Farmer's Bible." There was a familiar story of the little boy who was asked by his Sunday School teacher where the Ten Commandments came from, and who unhesitatingly replied that they came from Sears, Roebuck.

Just as, three centuries before, New England schoolchildren had learned the path to salvation along with their ABC's and had learned how to read at the same time that they learned the tenets of their community, so farm children now learned from the new Bible of their consumption community. In rural schoolhouses, children were drilled in reading and spelling from the catalogue. They practiced arithmetic by filling out orders and adding up items. They tried their hand at drawing by copying the catalogue models, and acquired geography by studying the postal-zone maps. In schoolrooms that had no other encyclopedia, a Ward's or Sears' catalogue handily served the purpose; it was illustrated, it told you what something was made of and what it was good for, how long it would last, and even what it cost. Many a mother in a household with few children's books pacified her child with the pictures in the catalogue. When the new book arrived, the pictures in the old catalogue were indelibly fixed in the memory of girls who cut them up for paper dolls. Just as Puritan children were supposed to think of their Bible as an exhaustive catalogue of the "types" which provided the pattern for all the actual happenings of the world, so the children of rural America thought of the big books from Sears' and Ward's as exhaustive catalogues of the material world.

14
Citifying the Country

IN THE DAYS before telephone, radio, and television, the only network of public communication which could reach remote farmers was the mail. But the postal network, essential to the making of consumption communities, had spread over the nation only slowly and unevenly. Although the Federal Constitution in 1787 had given the Congress the power "to establish Post Offices and post Roads," not until the era of the Civil War did the outlines of the modern system appear.

In the beginning, postal charges were paid by the recipient, and charges varied with the distance carried. Then, in 1825, Congress permitted local postmasters to give letters to mail carriers for home delivery, but these carriers received no government salary and for their whole compensation depended on what they were paid by the recipients of individual letters. This meant, of course, that the carrier would not leave letters in mailboxes, but had to find each recipient in person or lose his fee. People who did not want to pay these fees could instruct the postmaster to keep their mail at the post office. This system lasted for about forty years, down to the very era of the Civil War.

In 1847 the Post Office Department adopted the idea of a postage stamp, which of course simplified the payment for postal service but caused grumbling by those who did not like to prepay. In Philadelphia, for example, with a population of 150,000, people still had to go to the post office to get their mail. The confusion and congestion of individual citizens looking for their letters was itself enough to discourage use of the mail. Besides, the stamp covered only delivery to some post office and did not include carrying to a private address. It is no wonder that during the years of these cumbersome arrangements private letter-carrying and express businesses developed, some delivering a letter anywhere in the city for a penny. Although their activities were semilegal, they thrived, and actually advertised that between Boston and Philadelphia they were a half-day speedier than the government mail. The government postal service lost volume to private competition, and was not able to handle efficiently even the business it had.

Finally, in 1863, Congress provided that the mail carriers who delivered the mail from the post offices to private addresses should receive a government salary, and that there should be no extra charge for that delivery. But this delivery service was at first confined to cities, and free home delivery became a mark of urbanism. As late as 1887, a town had to have 10,000 people to be eligible for free home delivery. In 1890, of the 75 million people in the United States, fewer than 20 million had United States mail delivered free to their doors. The rest, nearly three quarters of the population, still received no mail unless they went to their post office.

FOR THE FARMER, then, regular trips to the village post office were part of the rhythm of his life. And the village postmaster was commonly the keeper of the village general store where the post office itself was located. The trip to town to get the mail was also a shopping trip to pick up supplies. The role of the postmaster, ever since colonial times, had been peculiarly important in this newly settled, sparsely populated country of great distances. Colonial postmasters (who commonly were also the "Publick Printers," who printed legal notices and the official texts of statutes) had used their control of the channels of communication to gather information for the newspapers which they published. Now, similarly, the postmaster-storekeeper used his privileged position to draw in customers. And there were thousands of small merchants all over the country who had a vested interest in the old postal system, and especially in the nondelivery of mail to rural addresses. Other villagers, too, liked the old system, for it brought business from farmers who loitered before and after the arrival of the irregular and uncertain mail. Some bluenoses actually made this an argument for free delivery direct to the farms. "Our men and boys," a seventy-year-old lady Granger complained in 1891, "would not so often be tempted to spend time and money in the billiard rooms and other similar places while waiting for the mail."

After free delivery was tried in the cities, the farmers began to ask the same for themselves. But the economy-minded found the proposal outrageous. What could be more ridiculous than hiring an army of federal employees to travel miles across the countryside to deliver an occasional letter to a farmer who would probably not even be interested in its contents? *"The Farm Journal* wants, and the people want . . . 1-cent postage. We don't want our country roads overrun with half paid federal officials delivering 2-cent letters at a cost of 10 cents a letter." Not until the energetic Philadelphia merchant John Wanamaker became Postmaster General in 1889 did the movement for rural free delivery gain momentum. After local experiments,

Wanamaker decided that nationwide rural free delivery was feasible. Endorsed by the National Grange in 1891, rural free delivery was supported by scores of petitions to congressmen for their rural constituencies.

The demand for free delivery to the farm—RFD—became the suffering farmer's battlecry, and before long, rural politicians were competing to be called "Father of RFD." The man who made the biggest political capital was Tom Watson, the "agrarian avenger" from rural Georgia who during his single term in Congress introduced the first resolution to be passed (1893) providing for rural free delivery. But the struggle was only beginning. Those were the days of "In God we trusted, in Kansas we busted" chronicled by Hamlin Garland in the bitter pages of *Main Travelled Roads* (1891) and *A Son of the Middle Border* (1917). It took a shattering farm depression, when "more midland farmers' wives died of mortgage than of tuberculosis and cancer together," to rouse Congress to favor the farmer with a service long since provided to the city dweller. How or why RFD would fundamentally improve the farmer's lot was not quite clear. But it was a desperate time when the new People's Party was threatening "not a Revolt but a Revolution," and RFD was the safest kind of radicalism.

The system was haphazard until 1898, when it was announced by the Post Office that RFD would be provided for groups of farmers who petitioned their congressmen. The elaboration of the system was, of course, hastened by this vast new opportunity to enlarge party patronage. In the postal bureaucracy, rural agents, route inspectors, and rural mail carriers multiplied, and in one year they actually laid out nine thousand new routes. The "rural agents," who gathered the information for laying out the RFD routes and then supervised them, were a valuable new source of up-to-date facts of rural life for government officials, sociologists, and reformers. At this time, too, the Postmaster General, after a struggle against the lard pails and soapboxes that farmers put out for their mail, and against the usual charge of "monopoly," approved the familiar design for the rural mailbox, which has remained a symbol of farm life. The successful organization of RFD was one of the great administrative achievements of the later nineteenth century. By 1906 the essential routes had been set up, and rural agents were incorporated into the general postal service.

THIS WAS THE LEAST HERALDED and in some ways the most important communications revolution in American history. Now for the first time it was normal for every person in the United States to be accessible by cheap public communication. For the rural American (more than half the nation's population by the census of 1910), the change was crucial. Now he was lifted out of the narrow community of those he saw and knew, and put in continual touch with a larger world of persons and events and things read about but unheard and unseen. RFD made these everywhere communities possible. From every farmer's doorstep there now ran a highway to the world. But at the price of dissolving some of the old face-to-face communities.

RFD led to the combining of post offices and the abolishing of many of the little fourth-class post offices which had given their name and their focus to hundreds of village communities. In Reno County, Kansas, for example, sixteen post offices disappeared in ten years. With the village post office often went the general store that had housed it, and there was commonly nothing left. Across the country RFD created ghost villages. For example, about 1900, in the southern half of Cortland County in central New York, there were some fifteen active neighborhood-communities known by such flavorful rural names as Texas Valley, Barry Hollow, Merrill Creek, Quail Hollow, and Hunts' Corners. At least five of these neighborhoods had their own post offices, stores, and social organizations. Then, after the turn of the century, RFD was introduced and all the rural routes for that region went out of the town of Marathon. Within twenty-five years almost all the other neighborhood communities of the area had lost their post offices and their stores. Attendance at their separate churches and Granges declined, and the villages disappeared. Marathon had become the postal and shopping center for people who no longer saw one another's faces.

"The regular arrival of the papers and magazines. . . .," Postmaster General John Wanamaker urged in 1891, "will not only keep many of the boys and girls home and make them more contented there, but add to their ambition and determination to make the old farm pay." Extending rural free delivery, a congressman argued in 1902, would "destroy the isolation and loneliness of country life and stop the constant and deplorable drift from country to town. We can never do too much for the rural sections of this great country, whose people feed and clothe the world." These enthusiasts forgot that breaking down the "isolation" of the farm also meant introducing the farmer to the charms of the city. While the isolated farmer may have been an unhappy farmer, the unisolated farmer often ceased altogether to be a farmer.

In 1908 President Theodore Roosevelt appointed a Commission on Country Life to see what could be done to improve the living conditions of the farmer, "to do away with the disadvantages which are due to the isolation of the family farm, while conserving its many and great advantages." This nice balance proved impossible. There would be no greater forces drawing farmers off the farm than the efforts of the well-intentioned champions of rural life, through RFD, through improved highways, and through increased farm circulation of newspapers and magazines, to make farm life more pleasant. The Country Life Commission commended RFD and recommended its extension. For a time, a back-to-the-farm movement gained momentum. Newspapers and magazines rang with declarations and stories of the virtues of farm life—often by romantic urbanites who were disgusted with city life and who liked to believe that what they could no longer find in the city they might still find down on the farm. But "farmers' sturdy sons" kept moving in ever larger numbers to the cities.

Another innovation that aimed to reduce the farmer's isolation eased the farmer's way into nationwide consumption communities. Even after RFD brought letters and printed matter to rural mailboxes, the farmer still had to pick up any but the lightest parcels from the nearest railroad freight station. We forget how difficult it was to send a package before parcel post. Before 1913, the maximum weight for an individual parcel in the domestic mail was four pounds; if you wanted to mail twelve pounds of goods you had to send three separate packages, and the charge was $1.92 regardless of distance. The profitable business of carrying the nation's parcels was conducted by private express companies—Adams Express, American Express, United States Express, and Wells, Fargo—which went back to pre–Civil War days.

Postmaster General Wanamaker repeatedly, and unsuccessfully, urged a government parcel post. "In point of fact," he reported to the President in 1891, "there are but four strong objections to the parcel post, and they are the four express companies." This issue remained politically explosive. At the turn of the century, despite the efforts of the single-minded James I. Cowles, "The Fighting Father of the Parcel Post," and of Populist politicians, congressmen and senators were still wary even of allowing any article that advocated parcel post to be printed in the *Congressional Record*, to which no folly had been alien. Opponents warned that for the government to deliver packages "is likely to change fundamentally our conception of government."

But the farmers' lobby eventually prevailed. And within a month of the inauguration of parcel post on January 1, 1913, the Postmaster General pronounced it a success—"the greatest and most immediate ever scored by any new venture in the country." Within twelve months, packages were being mailed at the rate of three hundred million a year. The main argument for the system, oddly enough, had been to help the farmer by promoting shipments of his produce to the city. As his first parcel post package President Woodrow Wilson received eight pounds of New Jersey apples. This "farm-to-table" movement did not flourish, but the factory-to-farm movement did. The mail-order houses, introducing farmers to the ways and things of the city, prospered as never before. In the first year of parcel post, Sears received five times the number of orders it had the year before, and the increase at Ward's was nearly as dramatic.

Parcel post sealed the doom of the rural merchant. There were desperate efforts to save the old country store—including a widespread "buy at home" movement, an "antimonopoly" movement, and a last-ditch campaign in the era of World War I, which actually tried to make buying at the local store a touchstone of "loyalty" and labeled the catalogue buyer a "traitor" to his community. But soon the old general store was as romantic (and as unrealistic) a symbol of the vanished charms of rural life as the saloon was of the evils of the city.

THE TRIUMPH OF MAIL ORDER, and its new literature, brought visions of new ways of living which were a triumph of a larger over a smaller community. It was a victory of the market over the marketplace. And it spelled the defeat of the salesman by advertising. In a word, it was a defeat of the seen, the nearby, the familiar by the everywhere community. It depended on a new confidence of the rural American in the city businessman. And the Iowa corn farmer who sent his money to Mr. Sears in Chicago was not merely putting his faith in the faraway merchant; by doing that he was joining with the Georgia orchard grower and the Arizona rancher.

In the century after the Civil War, mail-order enterprises using the power of their Big Book became another of the unplanned forces of attenuation, thinning out the differences between all places and times and seasons, assimilating the ways of the country and of the city. Americans were coming to think of the improvement of life as whatever made life where they were more like life everywhere else. And by the turn of the century that everywhere else was the city.

RFD gradually citified the country, and changed the pace of the farmer's life. When a weekly trip to the village post office was the farmer's only way of receiving mail, it was pointless for him to subscribe to a daily newspaper and periodically receive an armful of stale news. Then his needs were best served by the country weeklies. As early as 1902, *Editor and Publisher* noted that "the daily newspapers have never had such a boom in circulation as they have since the free rural delivery was established." Areas with RFD were quickest to subscribe to dailies. Some farmers who never before had a chance to receive a daily ration of fresh news from the city, gorged themselves with two or even three daily papers. In 1911 more than a billion newspapers and magazines were delivered over rural routes; by 1929 the figure had reached nearly two billion.

Some of the new country dailies, like the Emporia *Gazette* (edited after 1895 by William Allen White), were daily versions of the old country weeklies. But for the most part, the city dailies which now reached the farmer for the first time brought him the news and advertisements of a wider world. This was a more cold-blooded world, where the happenings concerned people the farmer never knew and would never see. The country weekly which he had once picked up himself at the rural post office had brought him what William Allen White called "the sweet, intimate story of life." And White was not merely being sentimental in 1916 when he described the dissolving world of the country newspapers:

> When the girl at the glove-counter marries the boy in the wholesale house, the news of their wedding is good for a forty-line wedding notice, and the forty lines in the country paper gives them self-respect. When in due course we know that their baby is a twelve-pounder named Grover or Theodore or Woodrow, we have that neighborly feeling that breeds real democracy. When we read of death in that home we can mourn with them that mourn. . . . Therefore, men and brethren, when you are riding through this vale of tears upon the California Limited, and by chance pick up the little country newspaper . . . don't throw down the contemptible little rag with the verdict that there is nothing in it. But know this, and know it well; if you could take the clay from your eyes and read the little paper as it is written, you would find all of God's beautiful, sorrowing, struggling, aspiring world in it, and what you saw would make you touch the little paper with reverent hands.

The old world, where so much of "news" concerned people one knew, the world of the neighborhood community, was slipping away. In its place there was forming a world where more of the communities to which a man belonged were communities of the unseen.

15

A New Freedom for Advertisers: Breaking the Agate Rule

ADVERTISING, DESTINED TO BE the omnipresent, most characteristic, and most remunerative form of American literature, did not come into its own until the second half of the nineteenth century. This new subliterature was destined to have an intimate popular appeal and a gross national influence without parallel in the history of sacred or profane letters. In mid-twentieth-century America the force of the advertising word and image would dwarf the power of other literature.

While advertising was not, of course, a modern invention, the American elaboration and diffusion of advertising, and its central place in the consciousness of the community, were new. The proportion of the national ingenuity, energy, and resources that went into advertising was unprecedented. We have seen how, within two decades after the end of the Civil War, Montgomery Ward and Sears, Roebuck, among others, had built their vast communities of consumers on the advertising in their skillfully composed catalogues. This advertising went to millions of readers, not sandwiched between news or fiction, but exclusively to offer specific merchandise in the best light, and so to persuade people to buy. Even before advertising had become a major American art and a developed American science, Sears, Roebuck's Big Book had become the characteristically American book.

"Everything is against distinction in America," explained the English pundit Matthew Arnold in 1888, as he condescendingly cited Abraham Lincoln. "The glorification of the 'average man,' who is quite a religion with statesmen and publicists there, is against it. The addiction to the 'funny man,' who is a national misfortune there, is against it. Above all, the newspapers are against it." And, he might have added, advertising was against it.

Nothing loosened up the world of the word quite so much as advertising. Another symbol of how the New World dissolved distinctions, it blurred the line between word and picture, between word and gesture. It showed an aggressive, sometimes belligerent, democracy that had been rare in printed matter before that time. For it ruthlessly and relentlessly sought to widen the audience and to broaden its appeal. There is no better example of the power of new American circumstances to break up old rigidities, to allow the world to flow.

IN THE MID-NINETEENTH CENTURY, even after American daily newspapers prospered and became enterprising in other ways, their advertising was dull. Monotonous solid columns of small type were the rule. The front page of most dailies was given over to advertisements, which were usually not even classified. (The very notion of "classified" advertisements, and the Americanism "classified," did not exist until after the Civil War.) Page one of the Boston *Evening Transcript,* for April 9, 1840, jumbled together three-line notices for Italian Cravats, Money to Loan, Potatoes, two seventeen-year-old lads wanting to help in a public house, the Cincinnati Almanac, and shares of bank stock. The only relief was an initial capital letter or a crude minuscule standard cut of a sailing ship, a horse, or a runaway servant. Yet, from the beginning, the profits of American newspapers depended on just such advertisements, which, even in the colonial period, might run to as many as five pages.

From time to time, even before 1790, an adventurous or flamboyant publisher would offer a double-column spread, a big, specially drawn cut, or large type. But this was uncommon. Shortage of paper, for example during the Revolution and in the early years of the Republic, sometimes forced the abridgement of advertisements, the omission even of the minute stock cuts, and so put the development of display advertising entirely out of the question. In 1833 the Boston *Evening Transcript,* then printed on small tabloid-size sheets, changed its advertising from the customary small agate (5½ point) type to the even smaller diamond (4½ point) type; the paper explained that this was the only way it could increase its advertising.

Until about the time of the Civil War, experiments in display advertising and in use of the double-column measure were only sporadic. Publishers thought bigger advertisements were a waste of space. They urged, also, that to allow the large advertiser to attract attention by display type or large cuts would be "unfair" to the daily small-space advertisers. And there were technical problems in breaking a column. The markers or "rules" which separated the columns came only in full-column lengths. Therefore in order to print an advertisement stretching across two or more columns, and still keep the rest of the page neatly divided, the printer had to go to the trouble of sawing off the column rule. At best this was a nuisance, but many print shops did not even have the right kind of saw. As a result, agate type and single-column measure became a rigid custom.

Although the more primitive Western papers and weeklies some-times tried larger type and occasionally broke their columns, the larger and more influential Eastern papers stayed with the Agate Rule. They required advertisements to be set in agate type, which was this size. James Gordon Bennett, of the New York *Herald,* an innovator in many other ways, only briefly tried a liberal policy in the typography of advertisements in his paper. By 1847 he had returned to a strict typographic democracy among his advertisers, banning even the ornamental stock cut or the two-line initial. Bennett's highly intellectual rationale was that an advertiser should gain his advantage only from *what* he said, not from how it was printed. Bennett, with others, made rigid enforcement of the Agate Rule, single-column measure a journalistic principle. As Frederic Hudson, who worked for thirty years for Bennett during the heyday of the Agate Rule and who was managing editor of the *Herald,* explained in 1872:

> The advertisements in the *Herald* increased with its enterprise and its circulation. It had been the custom of all newspapers in the United States to illustrate the business notices of their patrons with pictures representing the character of the advertisements—of ships, race-horses, houses, stage-coaches, railroad trains, dogs, birds, runaway apprentices and slaves with packs on their backs, wagons, steam-boats, cattle, and the Muses. Typographically, the plan was not a good one. In a business point of view, it was unfair to those not represented pictorially. The *Herald* in 1847 omitted all cuts and all display. All advertisements were printed in the same style, but neatly and systematically arranged. They gave a thorough business appearance to the paper. Since then no pictures have appeared. There has been no typographic splurge for one to the injury of another. The new plan worked well from its initiation, and the public and the advertisers were alike pleased.

BUT HUDSON WAS not quite accurate. For energetic and imaginative advertisers felt bridled by the old Agate Rule and made it a challenge to their ingenuity. They showed how pieces of the small agate type could be combined into a new kind of display. The Agate Rule, like other efforts at leveling, could not take away the special advantage of the especially clever.

When the pioneer photographer Mathew B. Brady in 1856 advertised "Brady's Gallery—Photographs, Ambrotypes and Daguer-rotypes," in Bennett's *Herald* he arranged the pieces of tiny agate type to form the inch-high numerals "359," his address on Broadway. A clothing merchant announcing a sale at the Christmas season repeated and rearranged the word "overcoat" into the shape of a Christmas tree. And there were other ingenious variations.

The hero of the battle against the Agate Rule was the flamboyant Robert Bonner. While he dramatized the folly of the Agate Rule, he foreshadowed the power of the advertiser in American life. Considering the future of American advertising, Bonner's first engagement was fought in a most unlikely cause—the popularizing of sentimental literature. Bonner, born in Ireland, had immigrated in 1839 at the age of fifteen, and began as a typesetter on the Hartford *Courant,* where he showed a talent for fast composing and a taste for fast horses. In 1851 he paid $900 for the New York *Merchant's Ledger,* a dull journal of the dry-goods trade. By 1855 he had discarded the drab commercial matter, had shortened the name to the New York *Ledger,* and his weekly now offered sentimental stories, serials, moral essays, heartwarming doggerel, and advice to the lovelorn.

One of Bonner's great services to advertising, as Frank Presbrey, the advertisers' historian, observes, was to help build an audience of women readers "for the benefit of future advertisers." The *Ledger* featured the most popular writers of the day: "Fanny Fern" (the pseudonym of Sara Willis, wife of the biographer James Parton), whose edifying "Fern Leaves" were so successful and so full of amiable buncombe that one reviewer said she should have married P. T. Barnum, and whom Bonner paid the amazing price of $100 a column; Sylvanus Cobb, Jr., whose thriller "The Gunmaker of Moscow" and other items (in the *Ledger* alone, 130 novelettes, 30 "Forest Sketches," 72 "Forest Adventures," 102 "Sketches of Adventure," 57 "Scraps of Adventure from an Old Sailor's Logbook," 573 other stories, and 2,305 other short pieces) earned him the title of the Father of Mass Production in American Fiction. And he offered other masters of the lurid and the sensational—Mrs. Emma Southworth of *The Hidden Hand,* John G. Saxe, T. S. Arthur, and others—who are now remembered only for having been the forgotten authors of that age.

Bonner published work by names he could advertise. These included General Grant's father (who wrote the life of his son), William Cullen Bryant, Henry W. Longfellow, George Bancroft, and Harriet Beecher Stowe, besides "the twelve leading clergymen" and "the presidents of the twelve chief colleges of the United States." To everybody's astonishment Bonner actually secured articles from his leading journalist-rivals in New York: Horace Greeley of the *Tribune,* Henry J. Raymond of the *Times,* and James Gordon Bennett himself; then he splurged them all in one issue. He enlisted the eminent Edward Everett by helping him raise money to buy Mount Vernon to be a public monument, and offered Everett $10,000 for a series to be called the "Mount Vernon Papers." Bonner reputedly bought from the already notorious Henry Ward Beecher the serial rights to his novel *Norwood* for $30,000. Among his more conventional acquisitions were a short poem by Tennyson and a short story by Dickens (at $5,000 each).

All these items were themselves a new form of advertising, of which Bonner was well aware. His confidence in the power of advertising led him to risk ever larger and larger sums. The bold gambling spirit which Bonner shared with his contemporary P. T. Barnum made Bonner one of the leading race-horse owners of his day. He spent more than half a million dollars on racehorses during his lifetime; but once he owned a horse, he never allowed it again to race for money. One of his prizes was the famous trotter Dexter, the envy of Cornelius Vanderbilt, and said to be one of the few of Vanderbilt's desires that he was not able to buy.

While Bonner's *Ledger* did not accept advertising, nevertheless it was built on a foundation of advertisements. By advertising in other publications, Bonner gained the attention of the world and secured the large circulation needed to repay the high stakes he had invested in his writers. And his passion for advertising stirred him to bold experiment.

When James Gordon Bennett refused to let Bonner use display type in the New York *Herald*, Bonner took a cue from the London *Times*, where he had observed the effect of repetition. There auctioneers, instead of taking a single long advertisement, would run in the same column numerous short announcements of equal length, each beginning with the same large initial letter and the name of the firm. Bonner observed that these repetitive items caught the reader's attention more than a similar number of miscellaneous items inserted by the same advertiser. He then elaborated his own techniques of repetition, which got around the Agate Rule and put new power in the printed page. Bonner began by filling a whole column with ninety-three repetitions of a single announcement: "Orion the Gold Beater is the title of Cobb's sensational story in the New York Ledger." Soon after, he tried filling two columns with his repetitions. He created the advertising sensation of 1856 when he took a full page and repeated his message six hundred times.

"Iteration copy," as this came to be called, was ingenious form repeating commonplace content: "See the New York Ledger with Cobb's new story," or "Don't go home to-night without the New York Ledger," or "Let the news go forth that the New York Ledger is out." Or Bonner would take six columns to make such a message into an acrostic. The two-line-high initial letter "L" of "Let the news go forth . . ." in the first column would fit with the initial "E" in the second column of "Everyone is reading Cobb's new sensation story in the New York Ledger" and so on to spell "L-E-D-G-E-R." Lest any reader should miss the point, each column bore the heading "Ledger

Acrostic." The climax of iteration copy was reached on May 6, 1858, when Bonner produced what was said to be the largest advertisement yet to appear in any newspaper. In the *Herald* he announced a new adventure serial by the prolific Emerson Bennett, with iterations that filled seven pages.

Bonner soon secured nearly as much publicity from the rumors about his advertising budget and his advertising stunts as from the printed advertisements themselves. The *Ledger* was reputed to have spent as much as $27,000 on advertising in a single week; its annual advertising budget ran to $150,000. This paid off when Bonner managed to bring the circulation for his four-cent weekly of "choice literature and romance" up to nearly 400,000. He had shown American advertisers how to break the shackles of a stodgy tradition. Bonner's iteration style, as historians of advertising suggest, may have been the parent of the advertising slogan. Advertisers later in the century, when they attacked the eyes of Americans everywhere with "Use Sapolio" and other unforgettable refrains, were profiting from Bonner's early successes in the battle against the Agate Rule.

BONNER'S ITERATION STYLE was widely imitated. The built-up large letters compounded of numerous small agate letters actually became a trademark of Bennett's *Herald*. The Agate Rule had proved futile as a way of preserving a paper's "dignity." But the great liberation of advertising typography, by the widespread use of large and varied display type and the freeing of the newspaper page from rigid columns, was surprisingly slow in coming. Brady, Bonner, and others had unintentionally begun to show the attention-getting value of white space on the printed page. Although early patent-medicine advertising and theater handbills had occasionally used large type and illustrations, the freer new techniques were not common until near the end of the nineteenth century.

It was no accident that the largest and most enterprising department stores were the pioneers of newspaper display advertising. Their need to attract crowds within a small geographic radius made the city dailies their perfect medium. And before long, as we have seen, the department stores had become the mainstay of the big-city dailies. The American leadership was taken by Macy's, Lord & Taylor, and Wanamaker's. The *Journal des Débats*, published in Paris in the 1850's, had carried advertisements in type three inches high (72 point), a font larger than any found in American newspapers. But for some time the five-pointed star that headed Macy's advertising columns and became its trademark was composed of numerous pieces of agate type. By 1865 Macy's had begun to use display type in its advertisements. Lord & Taylor (by now using 30-point type for its signature) joined Macy's in revolt against agate type for general newspaper advertising, and they both broke the column rules with advertisements that regularly appeared in an undivided double column. In 1879 Wanamaker placed what is said to be the first full-page American daily newspaper advertisement for a retail store. By the 1880's, full-page newspaper advertising, with liberated type, including display, was common practice for department stores.

Another break in the stodgy pattern of agate advertisements came in 1870 when Sapolio (a soap powder) introduced the human-interest illustration. A cut that had been used in magazine illustrations, showing a man looking contentedly at his own reflection in the bottom of a pan made mirror-shiny by Sapolio, finally appeared in a general-circulation newspaper. But pictorial representation entered the advertising columns of newspapers only gradually. And then it was not the department stores but the manufacturers, especially the sewing-machine firms, who took the lead.

UNTIL THE 1830's the common newspaper practice was to sell to advertisers the right to insert a daily advertisement at a flat fee for the whole year. For about $32 an advertisement would appear every day in a big-city newspaper, and the advertiser was not closely restricted in space or linage. This practice, together with the cheapening of paper by the Fourdrinier paper-making machine in the 1820's, encouraged the printing of larger and larger papers. By the 1830's the New York *Journal of Commerce* stretched across eleven columns on a sheet 35 inches wide and 58 inches high. This unmanageable expanse, nearly six feet wide when opened, came to be called the "blanket sheet." The inconvenience of such a paper explained the special appeal of the new tabloid format, and when the New York *Sun* first appeared in 1833, it was only 9 inches by 12 inches. A paper shortage in the mid-1830's was another incentive for smaller-size sheets.

Dailies changed their policy, and instead of receiving unlimited space, an advertiser now had only ten lines a day for his small annual fee. For the first time, then, daily newspapers generally fixed daily rates by the line. Of course, this economized advertising space. But the "standing ad," the fixed text which did not need to be reset and which remained unchanged month after month, or even year after year, was still common.

James Gordon Bennett of the New York *Herald,* who had stuck by his rigid Agate Rule to keep his advertising columns "dignified" in form, showed more imagination in improving the advertising content. Advertising, Bennett said, like all the rest of a newspaper, should be newsy. At first, early in 1847, he required that the text of all advertisements be changed every two weeks. Then he made the sensational announcement that beginning on January 1, 1848, all advertisements would have to be renewed daily. The top of his front page proclaimed: "Advertisements Renewed Every Day." As Bennett's long-term managing editor, Frederic Hudson, boasted:

> The advertisements of the *Herald* are a feature. They are fresh every day. It is intended, by its system, that they should be. Its proprietor would prefer to have every business notice freshly written daily. On this plan the advertisements form the most interesting and practical "city news." They are the hopes, the thoughts, the joys, the plans, the shames, the losses, the mishaps, the fortunes, the pleasures, the miseries, the politics, and the religion of the people. Each advertiser is therefore a reporter—a sort of "penny-a-liner," he paying the penny. What a picture of the metropolis one day's advertisements in the *Herald* presents to mankind!

This extravagant puff for advertising was already beginning to be sober fact when Hudson composed it in 1872. Advertising, with its spreading power and its new freedom from pedantic and typographic bonds, was already evolving a democratic genre of literature. Within the next century, advertising would shape the American language, would make new demands of writers and would offer a kaleidoscope of bizarre and staccato trivia to listeners and readers.

The commercial motive, aiming to reach everybody's pocket book, to enlist as many as possible in the new consumption communities, like the religious motive of the New England Puritans two centuries earlier who aimed to enlist as many as possible in communities of the converted, now produced a new kind of "plain style." Something like what rising Protestantism had done for the spiritual world, the democratized American consumption communities now did for the material. Everybody was now a potential buyer, to be reached by an advertising appeal directed to him.

"The commonplace is the proper level for writing in business," explained John E. Powers, the dean of early American advertising writers, "where the first virtue is plainness, 'fine writing' is not only intellectual, it is offensive." The pioneer advertising agent George P. Rowell advised, "You must write your advertisements to catch damned fools—not college professors, and you'll catch just as many college professors as you will of any other sort." Or, as his disciple Claude C. Hopkins in the 1920's still urged, "Brilliant writing has no place in advertising. A unique style takes attention from the subject. Any apparent effort to sell creates corresponding resistance. . . . One should be natural and simple. His language should not be conspicuous. In fishing for buyers, as in fishing for bass, one should not reveal the hook."

In the new literature of advertising, alongside the tradition of forthright plain talk, another American tradition flourished anew. This was the tradition of Tall Talk. Boosters for new consumption communities discovered extravagant possibilities in the language of the commonplace. Advertising men, like the publicists for imaginary Western towns, freely used the language of anticipation, and they, too, were seldom inhibited by the fact that something had not yet "gone through the formality of taking place." Any Western tall-talker would have been proud to call a shampoo "Halo" or to name an automobile the "Fury."

16
Building Loyalty to Consumption Communities

ADVERTISING COULD NOT be understood as simply another form of salesmanship. It aimed at something new—the creation of consumption communities. As advertising displaced salesmanship, different arguments became effective and different satisfactions were felt by everyone concerned. The primary argument of the salesman was personal and private: this hat is perfect for *you* (singular). His focus was on the individual; he succeeded when he cajoled, flattered, managed, and overwhelmed a particular buyer's ego. The primary argument of the advertisement was public and general: this hat is perfect for *you* (plural). While the salesman persuaded the customer that the item was peculiarly suited to his unique needs, the advertisement persuaded *groups* of buyers that the item was well suited to the needs of all persons in the group. The advertisement succeeded when it discovered, defined, and persuaded a new community of consumers.

And an advertisement was, in fact, a form of insurance to the consumer that by buying this commodity, by smoking this brand of cigarette, or by driving this make of car he would not find himself alone. The larger the advertising campaign, the more widespread and the more effective, the more the campaign itself offered a kind of communitarian seal of approval. Surely a million customers can't be wrong! An advertisement, then, announced that in the judgment of experts, some kind of consumption community probably existed. Won't you join?

The arts and sciences of advertising, then, were the techniques of discovering consumption communities, of arousing and preserving loyalty to them. Toward this end there developed a new iconography of consumption communities, which transformed the old world of brand names and trademarks.

The inconspicuous "hallmark" of silversmiths and goldsmiths had been discreetly placed to assure the buyer of the purity of the materials, and later of the quality of the workmanship. In America, the discreet "hallmark" became the blatant nationally advertised trademark. The first federal trademark law was passed in 1870, but a decade later was declared unconstitutional because it purported to restrict commerce within the states. A new law passed in 1881 (and frequently amended) became the basis for the registration and protection of trademarks used in interstate and foreign commerce. Brand names acquired a new power and a new meaning. By 1972 the number of trademarks registered with the United States Patent Office came to nearly one million.

Brand loyalty became one of the most important concerns of the commercial world. Advertising researchers aimed to discover the strength, the reach, and the volatility of these loyalties to consumption communities. The multiplied opportunities for loyalty to so many different communities made advertisers ask whether some consumers were more "loyalty-prone" than others. But however tenuous and hard to measure these loyalties were, American businessmen spent increasing sums trying to develop them.

AFTER THE CIVIL WAR, the volume of national expenditure on advertising increased spectacularly and regularly, interrupted only by the deeper business depressions. In 1867 the total national figure was only some $50 million; by 1900 it had increased tenfold to $500 million; by 1950 it had reached $5.5 billion; by 1972 it amounted to $22.4 billion.

Brand names first flourished about the time of the Civil War with patent medicines, soaps, and cleaning powders. By the time of World War I, people were asking for national brands in chewing gum, watches, hats, breakfast food, razor blades, and pianos. Advertising was becoming a technique, a science, and a profession. In 1869 appeared Rowell's *American Newspaper Directory*, the first serious attempt to list all newspapers in the United States with accurate and impartial estimates of their circulation. Ayer's *American Newspaper Annual* followed in 1880.

The advertising agency then was organized to give expert and imaginative advice on how to build brand loyalty. Here, too, N.W. Ayer & Son of Philadelphia was a pioneer, with accounts that included Hires Root Beer, Montgomery Ward, Procter & Gamble Soaps, and Burpee Seeds. By 1900 the advertising of foodstuffs held first place in the firm's volume. What was perhaps the biggest single advertising push until then was Ayer's campaign, beginning in January 1899, for the new National Biscuit Co. This was one of the first campaigns to feature a staple food that was nationally branded, boxed in individual packages, and ready for consumption. The campaign required the perfecting of an airtight package, and above all the popularizing of a distinctive trademark and brand name. Ayer reached consumers through newspapers, magazines, streetcar ads, posters, and painted signs. Overnight, people all over the country were demanding the "Uneeda Biscuit."

Of course, "communities" of Uneeda Biscuit buyers and of other brand-name consumers were held together by much thinner, more temporary ties than those that had bound earlier Americans. But they drew together in novel ways people who might not otherwise have been drawn together at all—people who did not share a religious or political ideology, who were not voyaging together on the prairie nor building new towns. The peculiar importance of American consumption communities made it easier to assimilate, to "Americanize," the many millions who arrived here in the century after the Civil War. Joining consumption communities became a characteristic American mode of acculturation.

For a consumption community, like other communities, consisted of people with a feeling of shared well-being, shared risks, common interests, and common concerns. These came from consuming the same kinds of objects: from those willing to "Walk a Mile for a Camel," those who wanted "The Skin You Love to Touch," or who put their faith in General Motors. The advertisers of nationally branded products constantly told their constituents that by buying their products they could join a special group, and millions of Americans were eager to join.

These consumption communities, even while they became ever more significant in the daily life of the nation, were milder, less exclusive, and less serious than the communities that had held men together in an early New England Puritan village or in a westward-moving wagon train. These myraid new "communities" of men and women not in one another's presence were diffused and dispersed over the country—communities of Lucky Strike smokers and Chevrolet drivers—or, more broadly, of cigarette smokers and car owners. Their members recognized one another, sharing certain illusions, hopes, and disappointments. These were trivial, to be sure, compared to the shared beliefs of the Visible Saints of Massachusetts Bay Colony. But while the seventeenth-century New Englanders were members of only a few intense communities, twentieth-century Americans led more attenuated lives, as members of countless more casual communities.

The modern American, then, was tied, if only by the thinnest of threads and by the most volatile, switchable loyalties, to thousands of other Americans in nearly everything he ate or drank or drove or read or used. Old-fashioned political and religious communities now became only two among many new, once unimagined fellowships. Americans were increasingly held to others not by a few iron bonds, but by countless gossamer webs knitting together the trivia of their lives.

17

"The Consumer Is King"

WHEN THE SELLER no longer met the potential buyer face-to-face as craftsman or seller, but only indirectly through advertising, it was harder than ever for him to know what the buyer wanted, or even to know who the buyer was. The old direct democracy of demand—the customer telling the cobbler the style of shoe to make for him—had disappeared. In the everywhere market the merchant had to find indirect ways to answer his urgent questions. And manufacturers and merchandisers democratized the market by inventing ways for the consumer to vote his preferences. The vast market of unseen buyers gave rise to a new science for sampling the suffrage of consumers.

IN ITS BEGINNINGS, Market Research was directed simply to answering magazine advertisers' questions about whom they were reaching. For in the early days of American advertising there was no generally reliable information about the circulation figures of newspapers and magazines. Since the advertising agent supported himself by buying space at wholesale rates and then retailing it to advertisers, the agent was always trying to sell space which he himself had already bought. Especially since there were no authentic figures, he was understandably tempted to exaggerate the reach of his advertisements. Unchecked by any impartial source, the publications themselves commonly issued circulation figures that were inflated.

From the point of view of the advertiser, then, buying advertising space was like buying a lottery ticket. Not only did he not know how readers were responding to his paid message; he had only the vaguest notion even of how many subscribers or purchasers or readers there were. Detailed questions about the character of the audience to whom the publication circulated were far outside anybody's realm of knowledge.

An enterprising New Englander saw the advertisers' need and aimed to make a business of providing them reliable information on what they were getting for their advertising dollars. In 1869 George P. Rowell, founder of the trade journal *Printer's Ink*, who had got his start in Boston by a scheme of theater-program advertising, published the first extensive and impartial directory of American newspapers. He listed geographically and by class 5,411 United States publications and 367 periodicals in Canada.

After reliable circulation figures were available, it became more difficult to persuade advertisers to buy space which reached an undefined audience. Advertising in America was challenged to become a science. The decisive step was taken by Francis W. Ayer, a former schoolteacher who, with his father, had founded N. W. Ayer & Son in Philadelphia. Their main business was selling advertising space in religious papers. Soon after his father's death a friend urged that since he was much too good a man to be "nothing but a drummer" for a product of dubious value sold to ill-informed customers, he should get into some honest business. "I will not be an order taker any longer," Ayer determined. "I will not take orders for these lists of magazines and lists of newspapers and get my commission out of them and be satisfied just to make money. I will have a business, I will mean something to somebody every time I take any business, and I will have clients rather than people who just give me orders."

In 1875 Ayer signed the first "open contract" (with a firm of rose growers in West Grove, Pennsylvania) and so gave a new character to American advertising. Under the open contract, the advertising agent became the agent solely of the advertiser. He offered expert advice on where, when, and how to place advertising. He shared with the advertiser all information about the price he was paying for the space, and he committed himself to secure space at the lowest possible price. In return, the advertising agency received a fixed commission (at first 12½ percent) and a contract to service the advertiser for a definite period. The advertiser then would not judge the agent in advance by the few cents' difference between his bid and that of a rival agent for a particular advertising space, but would wait to see the effectiveness of the agent in increasing sales. In this way Ayer gave the advertising agency a new role in American life, and set a pattern which lasted into the late twentieth century.

Within twenty years, newspaper publishers, soon to be followed by magazine publishers, recognized the independent advertising agencies by announcing that they would give no special discount to direct advertisers. In return, the advertising agencies agreed not to try to beat down the publishers' announced rates on behalf of their advertisers.

Advertising space in newspapers and magazines became a commodity in the open market, and publishers were finally under pressure to give full and accurate facts about the circulation and character of their publications. By 1914 the publishers themselves were subsidizing the new Audit Bureau of Circulation, fortified with authority to examine publishers' records and to verify publishers' statements. By the 1930's about half the daily newspapers were members of the Bureau, and they accounted for some 90 percent of daily circulation.

NOW AT LAST the advertising agencies could be judged by the cost for reaching a customer. And the seller, for the first time, had expert help in the advertising he was paying for. In 1911, R. O. Eastman, advertising manager of the Kellogg Company, manufacturer of breakfast foods in Battle Creek, Michigan, persuaded fifty other national advertisers to support his postcard-questionnaire survey of magazine readership. He turned up some important new facts, for example on duplicate circulation, and so persuaded advertisers that they needed still more facts about what they were getting for their advertising dollar. When Eastman opened his own market research agency in 1917, his first client was the General Electric Company, for whom he tried to find out what the "Mazda" trademark meant to the consuming public.

Publishers now tried in earnest to discover what they were really selling. Circulation figures, they began to see, were not enough. They asked who bought their paper, where they lived, what they did for a living, and what they wanted to buy. This knowledge, destined to

affect not only American advertising but even the products themselves and the development of new products, made the relationship
between seller and buyer more self-conscious. The seller set up his
own "intelligence agency," and planned his strategy to conquer the
market. The buyer meanwhile began to see himself as a significant
unit in the mass of "consumers" who had a power to affect the flow
of goods.

Cyrus H. K. Curtis, as publisher of the *Ladies' Home Journal* and
the *Saturday Evening Post,* had shown a remarkable talent for building magazine circulation. When he bought the "elderly and indis-
posed" *Post* in 1897 (price: $1,000), it had a circulation of less than
2,000, but within ten years he lifted its circulation to 1 million, and
the circulation soon thereafter reached nearly 3 million. Like Bonner
before him, Curtis enlisted the leading writers of the day by paying
the highest prices for their work, and he succeeded in making the
Post weekly fare for the great mass of Americans who considered
themselves middle class. In the heyday of the *Post,* an age of optimism for "American business," he gave to advertising about 60 percent of its 125 pages. Then in 1911, one of his advertising representatives persuaded Curtis that he lacked the information he needed
about the wants and habits of consumers and about the dealers who
sold the products that were advertised. A salesman for advertising
space in the *Post* could talk glibly about the Curtis publications, but
he knew very little about the customers whom their advertisers
wanted to reach. Curtis agreed that more facts would make better
salesmen. And he looked for a man "who could not only collect facts,
but who knew one when he saw it."

A young schoolteacher from Wisconsin was willing to take on this
ill-defined task. When Charles Coolidge Parlin was hired in 1911, the
name he invented for what he was trying to do was "commercial
research." ("Marketing research," a more focused phrase, did not
come into use until later.) Curtis had recently purchased *Country
Gentleman,* but no one in the firm knew much about agriculture, so
Parlin decided to begin by collecting facts about the agricultural-
implement industry, which was buying much of the advertising in
this magazine. By interviewing manufacturers, retailers, and farmers, within six months he had compiled a 460-page survey of the
industry that revealed unsuspected facts about where agricultural
tools were made, to whom they were sold, when, and where.

Parlin moved on to an ambitious study of the market for almost
everything in the nation's one hundred largest cities (at the time,
cities of over 54,000 population). After 37,000 miles of travel and 1,121
interviews, he organized his information on the volume of business
and on the kinds of merchandise in every department store, dry-

goods store, and principal men's ready-to-wear store in all these cities. *Department Store Lines* (1912), his pioneer report, withstood the scrutiny of Marshall Field and other large-scale merchants of the day, and produced some useful distinctions:

> Woman is a shopper. Out of that fact has come the modern department store. Partly by nature and partly by education, woman is a comparer of values. . . .
>
> A woman's purchases may be divided into three groups: convenience goods, emergency goods, and shopping items.
>
> Convenience goods are articles of daily purchase, such as groceries, aprons, children's stockings and, in general those purchases which are insignificant in value or are needed for immediate use.
>
> Shopping goods include all those purchases which require thought and will permit delay, such as suits, dress goods, high grade underwear, in fact high grade dry goods of all kinds. Values are compared and a serious effort is made to secure the best value for the money.

Parlin thus showed the manufacturer that if his product was a "shopping line" the number of stores which could carry his goods profitably might be so small that he could cover the market with his own salesmen; but if it was a "convenience line" the diffusion of the suburban and rural markets would require a jobber.

Parlin's most remarkable product was his five-volume study *Automobiles* (1914). In the United States there were still fewer than two million automobiles, but one hundred widely sold makes. Parlin collected facts on manufacturing and distribution, on the influence of women on automobile purchase, and he asked questions which proved prophetic for the coming automobile age. He foresaw the tendency to reduce the number of grades and makes, he envisaged the dimensions and even the shape of the automobile market. As a result of his persuasive predictions, the automobile manufacturers increased their advertising in national magazines, and the *Saturday Evening Post* received a good share.

IN 1916 THE *Chicago Tribune* used house-to-house interviews to gather the marketing facts all over Chicago. By 1929 the United States Department of Commerce recognized the need for these facts with its first Census of Distribution, and then itself began regularly collecting facts on wholesale and retail establishments, on their size, and on the character and quantity of goods and services sold.

In the 1930's a picture frequently reproduced in magazines showed a pile of hairpins which had been dumped on a vacant lot by a bankrupt manufacturer who had not kept up with the times. The promoters of the new science of market research argued that the manufacturer might have averted this fate if he had listened to the shrewd market researchers around 1920 who, when they saw the musical comedy idol Irene Castle featured on front pages with bobbed hair, forecast the change in hair styles and would have shifted their clients to making other products.

Some manufacturers used market research to go direct to the customers for their preferences. The design of the old-fashioned alarm clock had been so standardized as to become a comic-strip symbol. Then in the late 1920's the Western Clock Company, drawing on recently discovered consumer preferences, offered a new model: smaller, thinner, of lustrous black and nickel, with svelte figures and graceful pierced hands. It was an immediate commercial success. But the makers of Listerine at first did not research the market and simply assumed that customers who liked Listerine mouthwash would like the same taste in a toothpaste; the toothpaste did not sell. Then, with market research, they discovered the consumer preferences in toothpaste flavor, which could have saved them large losses if known earlier.

Manufacturers had begun the practice of counting the market research ballots to discover the whims of their customers. "The consumer is king," concluded C. C. Parlin. "His preference is law and his whim makes and unmakes merchants, jobbers, and manufacturers. Whoever wins his confidence controls the mercantile situation; whoever loses it, is lost."

The efforts of craftsmen to please monarchs were crude beside those of modern American market researchers to anticipate the tastes, habits, and desires of their majesties The Public. In 1920 the Curtis Research Department sent investigators to the little town of Sabetha, Kansas, and interviewed all but twenty families in the 144 square miles surrounding. They secured information from these families about their buying habits and brand preferences. A few years later they took the first national pantry survey, based on inventories in 3,123 homes in eighty-five neighborhoods in sixteen states. Then, in Watertown, New York, they made the first "every-house-and-every-outlet" survey. Detailed reports on 28,203 of the town's 28,930 homes provided a "sample" of 97 percent.

In a desperate effort to verify interviews and questionnaires on grocery consumption, the Curtis Publishing Company made a "Dry Waste Survey," popularly known as the Ash and Trash Survey. Fifty-six Philadelphia families, fourteen in each income quartile, cooperated by agreeing to allow the Curtis researchers to collect and analyze their trash for a four-week period in July and August 1926. The families were instructed not to burn or destroy any containers and to keep a record of any wrappers or labels saved for premiums. Once a week Curtis researchers picked up all the trash from each of the fifty-six homes, then separately packaged and labeled the batch from each family. This packaged trash, finally totaling six thousand packages and containers, was taken to a nearby warehouse where it was studied and classified. The puzzled neighbors came to describe the work as that of the "Curtis Rubbishing Company."

THE RISE OF radio made the relation between seller and buyer more indirect than ever, and deepened the mystery of who was receiving the advertiser's message. In the 1920's when David Sarnoff urged his associates to invest in the new wireless "music box," they objected that it had no imaginable commercial future, because it depended on "broadcasting." That meant, of course, sending out messages "broadcast" to persons who could not be identified, counted, or located. Since no visible connection was required between broadcaster and receiver, who could tell who was receiving the message? And who would pay for a message sent to nobody in particular? But there proved to be enough advertisers willing to send out their messages to everybody in general, taking their chances on who might be listening. Then, as the cost of radio advertising rose, advertisers, educated by market researchers, expected to know whom they were reaching.

Advertising on the airwaves offered the market researcher a puzzling new problem. While a publisher could identify his subscribers and could locate his newsstand sales, the radio broadcaster could only guess who might be listening.

The pioneer in this new field of audience research was Arthur C. Nielsen. Son of a Danish immigrant, and an engineering graduate of the University of Wisconsin, he devoted his life to unraveling the mysteries of the market. In 1933 he introduced a novel scheme of retail-sale indexes for druggists, who allowed him to collect the figures from their own records; then he went on to a "Food-Drug Index," and to still others. Within four years he was receiving over $1 million annually from selling this information.

To test the audience for radio advertising Nielsen used the Audimeter, a device invented by two M.I.T. professors which could be attached to a radio receiver to record the times when the set was actually in operation, and the frequencies to which it was tuned. By 1950 he had applied this system to television. In a scientifically selected sample of homes, Audimeters were attached to television sets to record when the TV receiver was on or off, and to which channel it was switched; the records went to Nielsen in Chicago, where the information was correlated with the programs which had been broadcast, and was compiled into a report every two weeks. Each Audimeter family received a nominal sum for its trouble, and Nielsen agreed to pay half the cost of repairs if anything went wrong with the TV set. Since the machinery was expensive, only a small part of the audience could be monitored, and a great deal of effort went into making the sample representative. By the 1960's the Nielsen Television Index Service annually offered 840 different reports with 14 million new figures, including estimates of the number of families viewing each broadcast, the number of different families viewing one or more of a series of broadcasts, each program's share of total television viewing, and minute-by-minute fluctuations in the audience of each program. To establish this service on a break-even basis required seventeen years of work, and investments of $15 million. Just as Americans spoke of Dow-Jones averages on the stock market or Dun & Bradstreet ratings in the world of commerce, they now spoke of Nielsen ratings.

But there still remained mysteries about which of the listeners were really listening. Archibald Crossley's studies in 1939 had shown that at any time as many as 25 percent of the radio sets left on were playing to an empty room. Later studies showed that during the day as many as 40 percent of housewives were not watching their turned-on television sets. More and more Americans were not listening to what they "heard," nor looking at what they "saw."

THE NEW TECHNIQUES for polling consumers were obviously useful, too, in polling voters to predict their opinions on issues and on their tastes in candidates. By the early twentieth century, academic students of politics had shifted their interest from "political philosophy" or "political economy" to "political science." Now they aimed, in Harold Lasswell's phrase, to predict "Who Gets What, When, How." By the time Eastman and Parlin had begun to develop a science of "market research," political scientists were ready and eager to develop their own predictive science of political opinions. As the century wore on, this new political science became more and more assimilated to merchandising, and shrewd politicians increasingly borrowed the techniques of market research so they could make themselves an attractive package for the democratic millions.

The first "social-scientific" survey of the opinions and attitudes of large numbers of Americans was the *Pittsburgh Survey* (1907–08) supported by the Russell Sage Foundation. By 1928 a bibliography of social surveys in the United States listed nearly three thousand titles. Alongside the social survey came the opinion survey. At first these had been amateurish, and the popular *Literary Digest* poll was taken from names listed in the telephone book. But after 1936, when the *Digest* poll predicted a landslide defeat of Franklin Delano Roosevelt by Alf Landon, the political-opinion surveys which commanded public confidence came to be based on scientifically selected samples.

The true ancestor of the modern scientific opinion poll was not the old straw poll but the market survey, which, in the early years of the century, had done much to improve the techniques of sampling. Elmo Roper's first public-opinion survey, based on a carefully selected representative sample, appeared in *Fortune* magazine in July 1935, and from then on he regularly offered the results of his findings of public opinion about many issues. George Gallup founded the American Institute of Public Opinion, followed by the National Opinion Research Center, the enterprises of Louis Harris, and many others. The polls spread, their results were soon syndicated and became a popular feature of the daily papers.

John F. Kennedy's possession of the resources, financial and intellectual, to employ opinion polls to the best advantage, was a major factor in his victory in 1960. With the constant advice of Louis Harris, a brilliant public-opinion analyst, in one episode after another Kennedy took shrewd advantage of the information he had obtained from the polls. After each of the TV debates, the polls enabled Kennedy to see which issues were likely to pay off in votes, and where opinion was most mobile. This knowledge had a good deal to do with his crucial decisions in the last ten days of the campaign.

But this role of opinion polls in American political life was something new. As late as 1935 a bill (H.R. 2729) was introduced in Congress which aimed to stop the "vicious practice" of opinion polling by prohibiting the use of the mails for taking polls. As the scientific polls became increasingly accurate they gained the confidence of voters and candidates. In the election of 1944, the predictions of none of the major polls differed by more than 2 percent from the popular vote actually cast. Elmo Roper's *Fortune* poll predicted that President Roosevelt would win with a popular majority of 53.6 percent; the election figure was 53.4 percent. The errors of the pollsters in not predicting the election of President Truman in 1948 and the Gallup poll's 5 percent margin of error in 1952 gave some support to critics. But in later elections, the polls showed such accuracy that in 1966 President Lyndon B. Johnson urged increasing the terms of congressmen from two to four years since public-opinion polls kept them so constantly and effectively informed of the wishes of their constituents.

18

Christmas and Other
Festivals of Consumption

IN 1939, WHILE the nation's business still suffered from the Depression, the month of November happened to have five Thursdays and Thanksgiving Day was scheduled to fall on November 30. But celebration of the holiday on the traditional last Thursday would have been unfortunate for the nation's merchants. With business lagging, they needed every fillip they could find, and by tradition the Christmas shopping season did not begin until the day after Thanksgiving. In New York City, Detroit, and elsewhere, the opening of the season was customarily marked by a Christmas-oriented Thanksgiving Day parade. It is not surprising, then, that under the circumstances an enterprising Ohio department-store owner, Fred Lazarus, Jr., proposed that the nation move the celebration of Thanksgiving to the earlier Thursday, November 23, which would add a whole week to the "Christmas shopping" season. The Ohio State Council of Retail Merchants and the Cincinnati *Enquirer* endorsed the idea. In Washington, President Franklin D. Roosevelt greeted the suggestion with enthusiasm, and proclaimed that in 1939 Thanksgiving should come on November 23.

President Roosevelt's "tampering with the calendar" (like the establishing of Standard Time a half-century before) was labeled by some as an interference with the divine order, but within a few years, all the states had fallen in line by enacting Thanksgiving as the fourth Thursday. Only a few continued to declare their independence from federal fiat by authorizing a Thanksgiving holiday on both the fourth and the last Thursday.

It was a little-known oddity of American life that the United States, unlike other nations, actually had no "national" holidays established by law. Under the federal system the legalizing of holidays had been left to the states. The President's only power over holidays was to issue proclamations focusing national attention and to give a day off to federal employees in the District of Columbia and elsewhere. Thanksgiving had grown up simply as a national custom. President Lincoln in 1863 was the first to issue a presidential Thanksgiving proclamation, and then the legal holiday was created by separate laws in each of the states. This trivial shift in the date of President

Roosevelt's proclamation of a national Thanksgiving was significant mainly for what it revealed of the American Christmas; and for what it told of the transformation of this ancient festival into an American Festival of Consumption.

IN THE EYES of the early New England Puritans, Christmas was a menace to the pure Christian spirit. Fearing "popish" idolatry, the General Court of Massachusetts in 1659 passed an act punishing with a fine of five shillings for each offense "anybody who is found observing, by abstinence from labor, feasting, or any other way, any such days as Christmas day." By 1681 they felt secure enough against "popery" to repeal the law, but they still feared giving the day any ritualistic significance. In his diary for 1685, Judge Samuel Sewall, for example, expressed his satisfaction that on Christmas day he saw everybody conducting business as usual. During the next two centuries, while Christmas was somehow Americanized, it still remained a simple folk holiday marked by no grand religious observance and with little commercial significance. The season is hardly recognizable, for example, in the pages of the New York *Tribune* for the month of December 1841, which are barren of flashy Christmas advertising and simply repeat the unchanging copy which merchants had run for months. In a few instances when gifts are mentioned, they are referred to as "Christmas and New Year's" presents; Santa Claus has not yet entered the Christmas scene.

By the era of the Civil War the old festival, characterized by folksy conviviality, was beginning to be transformed. There were signs that the holiday was on its way to becoming a spectacular nationwide Festival of Consumption. On December 24, 1867, the first Christmas Eve when R. H. Macy's remained open until midnight, the store set a record with one-day receipts of $6,000. In 1874 Macy's offered its first promotional window displays to have an exclusively Christmas motif, featuring the Macy collection of dolls, and from then on the Christmas windows became an annual institution. During the next years, those Macy departments whose volume depended heavily on the Christmas trade increased their share of the store's total sales. Other department stores, too, began the practice of staying open late during the last two weeks before Christmas. December began to become the big month for retailers, and by 1870, December sales were already double those of May, the next best month.

Still, in 1880 Christmas was so undeveloped that a manufacturer of Christmas-tree ornaments had difficulty persuading F. W. Woolworth to take $25 worth of his product. Within a few years Woolworth's annual order of Christmas-tree ornaments from this supplier alone came to $800,000. In the next half-century, he drew on numerous suppliers and his orders totaled $25 million. "This is our harvest time," Woolworth instructed his store managers in December 1891. "Make it pay."

> Give your store a holiday appearance. Hang up Christmas ornaments. Perhaps have a tree in the window. Make the store look different. ... This is also a good time to work off "stickers" or unsalable goods, for they will sell during the excitement when you could not give them away other times. Mend all broken toys and dolls every day.

By 1899 Woolworth's Christmas trade was reaching a half-million dollars. In order to avert a strike at that crucial time of year, Woolworth introduced a system of Christmas bonuses ($5 for each year of service, with a limit of $25).

The mail-order houses began to issue special Christmas catalogues. At the 1939 Christmas season Montgomery Ward and Company gave away 2.4 million copies of "Rudolph the Red-Nosed Reindeer," a versified story written by an employee in their advertising department. Gene Autry's singing version became a runaway best-selling record.

Display type was used for Christmas advertising even before it became common for other purposes. Newspaper advertising peaked in December, and then fell off sharply after Christmas. By 1910 more than one third of the nation's annual output of books was being delivered in the six weeks before Christmas. Before mid-century, one quarter of the whole year's jewelry purchases were being made in December.

The Christmas Club, which first appeared in 1910, was an arrangement by which a person deposited a specified amount every week during the year, to be accumulated in a special savings account for withdrawal at Christmas time. By 1950 there were more than 10 million members of such clubs in 6,200 banks, in all states of the Union; and their deposits for the year exceeded $950 million.

With the passing decades of the twentieth century, Christmas became overwhelmingly a season of shopping. Gifts which first had the force of good manners actually acquired the force of law. The Christmas bonus (soon "expected but not appreciated") became a part of the anticipated compensation of employees. In 1951, when a firm reduced its Christmas bonus and the union appealed to the National Labor Relations Board, the board ruled the "Christmas" bonus to be not in fact a gift at all. The employer, they said, was not free to discontinue this practice. Christmas gifts to policemen, mailmen, janitors, and others tended to become a kind of insurance against poor service during the coming year. And the "executive gift" some-times became a convenient device for evading the laws of bribery.

ONE OF THE most distinctive features of the American Christ-mas was Santa Claus, who was speedily transformed out of all recog-nition from his Old World character. There had been a real St. Nicho-las, a fourth-century bishop of Myra in Asia Minor, who became the patron saint of Russia, and of mariners, thieves, virgins, and children. According to legend, St. Nicholas had saved three poor virgins from being forced to sell their virtue, by throwing a purse of gold through their windows on three successive nights.

In the United States, St. Nicholas early became a familiar figure of folklore and pseudo-folklore. His earliest conspicuous appearance in American literature was in Washington Irving's *Knickerbocker's His-tory of New York* (1809), where St. Nicholas traveled through the skies in a wagon, and began to acquire some of his other features. The American Santa Claus's rotund figure, jolly mien, and white beard were conferred on him by Thomas Nast in his series of Christmas drawings for *Harper's Weekly* beginning in 1863. By the late nine-teenth century, "belief" in Nast's Santa Claus had become a symbol of childhood innocence and adult warm-heartedness.

No sooner had Santa become the patron saint of a Saturnalia for children, "bringing treasures for the little rogues," than he was ele-vated to patron of a nationwide Saturnalia of consumption. The de-partment store was the proper habitat of *Santa Claus Americanus*. And he above all others was responsible for moving the primary scene of the festival from the church to the department store. By 1914 a well-organized Santa Claus Association, with headquarters in New York City, had as its object "to preserve Children's faith in Santa Claus." The association aimed to secure from the post office the letters addressed to Santa Claus and then reply to them in the name of Santa with letters or gifts. When there was public objection, postal authorities intervened. "All I ask," the founder of the association urged, "is that these people don't sock it to us at this time of the year and spoil the faith of little children."

Widespread demand led to the founding of "schools" for "real" Santa Clauses. The curriculum of the first such school (in Albion, New York) included indoctrination in the history of Santa Claus, dressing for the role, wearing beards, handling children, and other special techniques. A firm called Santa's Helpers rented out trained Santas for special occasions. In 1948 the City Council of Boston, acting on the complaint of a council member that "there is a Santa on every corner and children are beginning to wonder," formally requested the mayor to "permit only one Santa in the city in 1949 and to station him on the historic Boston Common." A bill in the California Senate in 1939 (required, a senator explained, by the sight of Santas "selling everything from bottled beer to automobiles") aimed legally to restrict the use of Santa's image.

"Belief" in Santa Claus was widely defended. A sentimental editorial, "Yes, Virginia, There Is a Santa Claus!," became the classic declaration of faith for agnostic Americans. When a savings bank in Muskegon, Michigan, displayed a sign in 1949 declaring "There Is No Santa Claus—Work—Earn—Save," local parents protested. And when the sign was removed, the bank president wryly commented, "The myth of Santa Claus is far-reaching and implies a nation of people who seem to accept a Santa Claus with headquarters at Washington." Judges issued facetious opinions from the bench *(ex parte Santa Claus)* to defend Santa, and held in contempt of court those who impugned him.

A few dared to put Santa Claus in the tradition of the great American hoaxes. But psychiatrists, the new authorities on national myths, could not take him so lightly. One solemnly declared that "any child who believes in Santa Claus has had his ability to think permanently injured." Others diagnosed the Santa myth as a symptom of parental insecurity, although some, including the influential Dr. Arnold Gesell, were not unduly alarmed.

THE CHRISTMAS TREE, too, acquired a special American character, and with its numerous accessories it became a significant seasonal industry. One story is that trimmed trees were first introduced to the United States during the Revolution by Hessian soldiers trying to recreate here the holiday of their homeland. In the nineteenth century the Christmas-tree custom was widespread in northern Europe. But the elaboration and electrification, and finally the syntheticizing of the Christmas tree, were reserved for the United States. By 1948 about 28 million Christmas trees were being distributed annually in the United States. The 100,000 acres devoted to Christmas trees were producing a crop valued at $50 million annually. At least after Woolworth began featuring Christmas-tree decorations in the 1880's, the business of decorations, ornaments and accessories flourished. The Christmas tree was officially recognized in 1923 when the President began the practice of lighting a tree on the White House lawn. Raising trees became more profitable with the development of the ingenious technique of "stump-culture" (by which the tree was severed above live-branch whorls, leaving a pruned number of these to grow, in turn, into trees for the next season). But the rising prices of trees, together with fire hazards and a growing interest in forest conservation, combined to create a new market for synthetic, plastic reusable Christmas trees.

Another thriving American industry—greeting cards—was a by-product of the American Christmas. Louis Prang, a sixteen-year-old refugee from the German revolutions, came to New York in 1850, acquired a reputation as a lithographer, and pioneered in making colored lithographs of famous works of art (he christened them "chromos" and the name stuck) which he sold for $6 apiece. In 1875 he applied his techniques to producing colorful cards for Christmas, and these came to be esteemed as works of art. Prang's elegant eight-color chromos of the Nativity, of children, young women, flowers, birds, and butterflies (a few, too, of Santa Claus) gave a certain tone to the practice of sending greeting cards at Christmas and dominated the market until about 1890. When the Christmas card was democratized by the import of cheaper cards from Germany, Prang retired from the business, but even less expensive cards of American make recaptured the market within another twenty years. By the early twentieth century the practice of sending Christmas cards, and then other greeting cards, had become widespread. By mid-century, about 1.5 billion Christmas greeting cards were being sold each season.

As the custom became more widespread, cards tended to become less and less religious in motif. The message, even in Prang's first de luxe items, had never been predominantly religious. The friendly secularized texts became acceptable to Jews and others who did not subscribe to such theological message as still remained in the American Christmas.

Americans found other ingenious ways to elide religious issues in order to share in the national Festival of Consumption. While the Rabbinical Assembly of America in 1946 protested the school practice of singing Christmas carols as an infringement of freedom of religion, the Jews themselves helped "solve" the problem. They promoted Chanukah, historically only a minor Jewish festival, into a kind of Jewish Christmas, with *eight* gift-giving days. More than one Jewish child probably asked, "Mother, dear, are we having Chanukah for Christmas this year?"

IN A NATION of consumption communities, there was a tendency for all festivals somehow to become Festivals of Consumption. Mother's Day was an example.

Something like a Mother's Day—the fourth Sunday before Easter, a day to honor Mary, the mother of Jesus—had been observed in

European countries. "Mothering Sunday" was when servants and apprentices were given a day off to "go a-mothering," to go visit their mothers. Sometimes the eldest son would bring his mother a "mothering cake," which was then shared by the family. There appears to be no evidence that Mother's Day was an American holiday before 1907. In that year an enterprising young lady from West Virginia, Anna Jarvis, much attached to her mother who had died two years before, consulted the Philadelphia merchant John Wanamaker about a suitable way to honor the nation's mothers. He advised her to campaign for a national observance. Helped by evangelists, newspaper editors, and politicians, the campaign for a nationwide Mother's Day quickly succeeded. The governor of West Virginia issued the first Mother's Day proclamation in 1912, and the Mother's Day International Association was founded. On May 9, 1914, pursuant to a Congressional Resolution, President Wilson issued the first presidential Mother's Day proclamation urging that the flag be flown on that day.

The simple old "mothering cake" was transmuted into a whole range of Mother's Day gift merchandise. The practice of noting the day by going to church (wearing a red carnation for a living mother or a white carnation for one deceased) blossomed into a bonanza for telegraph and telephone companies, candy shops, florists, jewelers, and cosmetic manufacturers. Like other American festivals which had originated in church, Mother's Day too ended in the department store.

In 1934, when retailers needed every possible stimulus to business, Postmaster General James A. Farley ordered a Mother's Day stamp showing Whistler's "Mother." The stamp, said to have been personally designed by President Roosevelt, actually offered a cropped and barely recognizable version of Whistler's well-known painting, which had been improved for the purpose by a vase of carnations prominently added in the lower left-hand corner. While the American Artists' Professional League objected to this "mutilation" of Whistler's painting, Anna Jarvis, the mother of Mother's Day, went personally to the Postmaster General to protest the transformation of her holiday into an advertisement for the florists' trade. She finally secured an apology. On the occasion of Mother's Day 1961 (according to a retail association estimate), more than 55 million families bought Mother's Day gifts for a total of some $875 million.

It is not surprising, then, that there was also to be a Father's Day, and the authorship of this idea was claimed by many. In 1910 a lady in Spokane, Washington, supported by William Jennings Bryan, began to campaign for a Father's Day; in 1916 President Wilson pressed a button in Washington to open the Spokane celebration. In June 1921 the governor of Virginia was persuaded to proclaim a Father's Day by a young lady who in 1932 registered the name "National Father's Day Association" with the United States Patent Office. Then, in 1935, a National Father's Day Committee was established "dedicated to building a democratic world through wholesome child upbringing." The prime mover for this holiday, Mrs. John Bruce Dodd, unlike the founder of Mother's Day, was not troubled by the danger of commercialization or the practice of making the day a time for gifts. "After all," she observed, "why should the greatest giver of gifts not be on the receiving end at least once a year?" The gift idea, she explained, was "a sacred part of the holiday, as the giver is spiritually enriched in the tribute paid his father."

PART THREE

Statistical Communities

> "The science of statistics is the chief instrumentality through which the progress of civilization is now measured, and by which its development hereafter will be largely controlled."
>
> S.N.D. NORTH

> "I feel like a fugitive from th' law of averages."
>
> Willy in *Up Front* by BILL MAULDIN

A DEMOCRATIC NATION, like any other, needed some way of distinguishing its groups of citizens. While Old World class distinctions would not do, there were certain obvious advantages to numbers. Statistical communities, creatures of the new science of statistics, provided ways of clustering people into groups that made sense, without necessarily making invidious distinctions. Numbers were neutral. No number was "better" than another. The numbering of people (one person, one vote) itself seemed to symbolize the equality at which a democratic society aimed. From their very nature, numbers offered a *continuous* series, a refuge from those sharp leaps between "classes" found in other societies. And, unlike the traditional categories of social class which had been topped by a divinely anointed monarch, statistical categories could be extended upward indefinitely. They were thus admirably adapted to a New World booster optimism: "The sky's the limit!" The direction of numbers, like the aims and hopes of American society, could go endlessly *up*.

But statistical communities had their own problems. The social "science" which brought these communities into being could reassure the citizen that he was average or normal. But while the neutral language of numbers made no invidious distinctions, neither did it help the man who needed a moral guide. In the world of measuring and counting, of correlated numerical indices, the citizen was thrown back on himself, left alone in a supermarket of statistics. There he had to decide for himself what the numbers meant and how to translate facts into rules. The most ancient and sacred of human relations—rich and poor, parent and child, husband and wife—were antisepticized into percentages. After mid-twentieth century the nation which had grown in an effort to fulfill the rule of the "majority" gave a politically potent new meaning to the numerical word "minority." And Americans went in desperate, sometimes futile, quest of moralistic meanings for what were once purely statistical terms.

19
A Numerical Science of Community: The Rise of the Average Man

A WHOLE NEW SCIENCE was coming into being for the quantitative analysis of society. The application to New World needs of theoretical tools from western Europe was creating a new Numerical Science of Community.

The words "statistics" and "statistical" entered the language in England about 1790, probably from the German. These new words, built on the word for "state," expressed expanding nationalism and also the universal quest for new "sciences," both of which bred a new faith in measurement. For a while the word "publicistics" (from "publicist") competed in literary use. In 1797 the *Encyclopaedia Britannica* (3d ed.) defined: "*Statistics*, a word lately introduced to express a view or survey of any kingdom, county, or parish." Its usage quickly broadened. "The Idea I annex to the term," the far-sighted Sir John Sinclair wrote in his *Statistical Account of Scotland* in 1798, "is an inquiry into the state of a country, for the purpose of ascertaining the quantum of happiness enjoyed by its inhabitants, and the means of its future improvement." To help increase agricultural production, Sinclair developed a system of county reports for the whole of Britain.

The great European pioneer in the practical science of statistics was the Belgian mathematician and astronomer Adolphe Quételet. Instructed in the theory of probability by Laplace in Paris, Quételet used census statistics to test probability theory. From his experience in organizing the census of 1829 in Holland, and in collecting statistics for Belgium, he came to the enticing new notion of "moral statistics." This was his name for the effort to quantify psychological facts and social customs. When he observed that if the height of a large number of men was charted on a graph, the distribution of human statures followed the normal-distribution curve, he came to his theory of the *homme moyen,* or average man. And from this concept he developed his "social physics," which sought the "laws" of such phenomena as marriage, suicide, and crime. Statistics had become the data of a new social "science."

FEDERAL POLITICS HAD committed us, from our national beginnings, to a special interest in numbers. One of the Great Compromises at the Philadelphia Constitutional Convention of 1787, when the large and the small states agreed upon a two-branch federal legislature, established a House of Representatives where the people would be represented in proportion to population. And this, of course, required that the people be counted. "Representatives and direct Taxes shall be apportioned among the several States . . . according to their respective Numbers. . . . The actual Enumeration shall be made within three Years after the first Meeting of the Congress of the United States, and within every subsequent Term of ten Years, in such Manner as they shall by Law Direct" (art. I, sec. 2, para. 3). The federal census was not the first such head count, for there had been official counts in Virginia, in New France (later Quebec), in Sweden, and elsewhere; but our periodic national census was probably the first in modern times to become institutionalized, and this American example influenced the world.

The census of 1790 counted only total population, divided into white (male and female) and colored (free and slave); white males were divided into those above and those below sixteen years of age. Even before the second census, a movement headed by the American Philosophical Society and led by Vice-President Thomas Jefferson urged a more detailed census to discover the facts about the life span of Americans so these could be used for social measures to increase longevity. Consequently the census of 1800 broke down the white population (male and female) into five age groups. For the next half-century, census data continued to be gathered according to judicial districts by federal marshals who had no experience in such matters. The unit for gathering information was not the individual but the family.

Th epoch-making seventh census of 1850, when the official statistics of the United States began to enter the modern era, was the product of a symbolic collaboration between two able champions of statistics, one from the South and one from the North. James D. B. De Bow, who had been born in Charleston, South Carolina, was only thirty when he was named to superintend the United States census of 1850. He was already noted for his influential *Commercial Review of the South and Southwest* (founded in 1846), the largest circulating magazine in the South, which urged industrial development and diversification. An admirer of John C. Calhoun, a defender of Negro slavery, and a fervent Southern partisan, he had a warm feeling for his section and his past. And he saw statistics as an indispensable new tool. As professor of political economy (probably the first in the nation) in the new University of Louisiana in 1848, he also headed the new Louisiana Bureau of Statistics.

To advise him in Washington on the census of 1850, De Bow brought Lemuel Shattuck, who had recently succeeded in giving statistics a new prominence in the public life of Massachusetts. Like De Bow, Shattuck believed that the answer to all public questions lay in more facts, more precise facts, more up-to-date facts. A New Englander, Shattuck had briefly attended a preparatory academy, but he never went to college. After a short tour as schoolteacher he settled in Concord, Massachusetts, where he became a prosperous merchant and a leading citizen. On the Concord School Committee, Shattuck insisted that to provide better education, the committee needed more facts, and he tried to provide these facts in an annual report on the schools, which he himself prepared and published. As a result of Shattuck's work, such reports were required by law throughout the state. After he moved to Boston in 1836, Shattuck was so successful as bookseller and publisher that at the age of forty-six he could retire to devote himself to public affairs. One of his projects, a history of Concord, convinced Shattuck of the need for better vital statistics; at that time births, deaths, and marriages were only haphazardly recorded.

Prodded by these experiences, Shattuck became a founder of the American Statistical Association; he then helped the Massachusetts Medical Society and the American Academy of Arts and Sciences to develop a new system for registering vital statistics. And he secured passage of the pioneer Massachusetts law in 1842 which required the uniform registration of vital facts.

In all this work Shattuck was bringing to fruition New England efforts reaching back to colonial times. Their remote New World situation had offered opportunities to experiment, and ever since the early eighteenth century, New Englanders had shown a special interest in public health. During the Boston smallpox epidemic of 1721–22, Cotton Mather had collected statistics which showed that the calculated risk of death from the new technique of inoculation was far less than from cases of smallpox naturally contracted. This had opened new vistas for statistical analysis of public-health problems. Later in the century, Jefferson's *Notes on Virginia* (1784) used rudimentary statistics, which he displayed on a chart, to refute the unfounded European notion that in America, animals and men were stunted. The booster enthusiasms which once nourished legends of an American Fountain of Youth tempted latter-day city promoters to use figures, real or imaginary, to prove that in their Lexington, their Cincinnati, or their Denver, people lived longer and all things desirable were bigger and more numerous.

Others used figures to assess the actual probabilities of health and prosperity in different parts of the continent. Dr. Daniel Drake, for example, infected by booster enthusiasm for his Cincinnati, produced a pioneer *Systematic Treatise, Historical, Etiological and Practical, on the Principal Diseases of the Interior Valley of North America, as they Appear in the Caucasian, African, Indian and Eskimoux Varieties of its Population* (1850; 1854). About the same time, in Boston, Lemuel Shattuck was doing the best he could with the meager facts to help citizens understand their public-health problems.

The American Statistical Association, upon its founding in Boston in 1839, had set itself the task of collecting, interpreting, and diffusing statistics "as general and as extensive as possible and not confined to any particular part of the country." In that year President Martin Van Buren had declared that the nation was not apt to legislate more intelligently until the census provided better statistics. The scholars of still another new science, attacking the nation's "utter ignorance" of the simple facts of "longevity, social happiness, or domestic habits," declared that political economy (later called "economics") could never become scientific without a solid new base in statistics.

THE BOSTON CENSUS of 1845, which Shattuck himself directed, opened a new era in American statistics. As Shattuck explained, the census reported "the name and description of every person enumerated . . . among other characteristics specifying the birth place of each, and thus distinguishing the native from the foreign population." And he prefaced these statistics with an important interpretive introduction. The new funds of facts like those which Shattuck gathered would make possible modern programs in public health. In 1849 Shattuck became chairman of a pioneering commission for a "sanitary survey" of Massachusetts. The commission's report, written by Shattuck, used the newly gathered statistics as the basis for its fifty far-sighted recommendations for the improvement of public health.

Shattuck's Boston census of 1845, then, became the prototype for the greatly enlarged federal census of 1850. And that seventh federal census marked an epoch in many ways. For the first time statistics for the whole nation were reported not by families but by individuals. The facts were no longer collected by local federal marshals who were not competent to evaluate the material and whose methods of tabulation were not uniform. Now the local "census takers" (an Americanism) merely filled out forms, which were then forwarded to the central office in Washington for uniform classification. The first six federal censuses had been confined, for all practical purposes, to a counting of the population. Now facts were gathered on the whole social and economic life of the nation: on agriculture and industry, on schools and colleges, churches, libraries, newspapers and periodicals, pauperism, crime, and wages. The seventh census schedules actually returned to the office in Washington were an unprecedented mass of 640,000 pages, which when bound came to some eight hundred volumes. The census had become a national inventory.

The bitter sectional debate over slavery was a battle not only of lawyers, ministers, moralists, and novelists, but also of statisticians. Numbers seemed somehow to offer self-evident answers to complicated social questions. From the raw material of this census of 1850, Hinton R. Helper, a North Carolinian, shaped his *Impending Crisis of the South* (1857), probably the most influential antislavery work of nonfiction. Helper aimed to prove with statistics that the South as a whole, and especially the free white laborer, was being impoverished by slavery. He therefore attacked slaveholders as the enemies of Southern prosperity. Because Helper was a Southerner, his book created a stir even greater than that of *Uncle Tom's Cabin* five years before. And the Republican Party ordered one hundred thousand copies to support Lincoln in the campaign of 1860.

Helper's cold-blooded use of statistics in a controversy where moral passions ran so high made his book all the more effective. But a parable of the perils of the new statistical morality appeared in Helper's own career. After the Civil War he shifted his target away from the institution of slavery, and his later books were fanatically anti-Negro. He aimed (in his own words) "to write the negro out of America . . . and out of existence." In another of his projects, he juggled statistics to prove that the salvation of the New World would be a railroad to run from Hudson's Bay to the Strait of Magellan. He spent his private fortune on prizes for the best essays and poems on the subject, and he lobbied with monomaniacal zeal for the enterprise, which, he said, would make him "the new Christopher Columbus." When the project came to nothing he was reduced to poverty and despair; he committed suicide and was buried in Washington, D. C., by strangers.

IN THE LATER DECADES of the century, American statistics became more copious and the new science grew in prestige. At the seventy-fifth anniversary of the American Statistical Association in 1914, Dr. S. N. D. North, the first head of a permanent census office (founded in 1902), divided all modern history "into two periods, the non-statistical and the statistical; one the period of superstition, the other the period of ascertained facts expressed in numerical terms. ... The science of statistics is the chief instrumentality through which the progress of civilization is now measured, and by which its development hereafter will be largely controlled."

Meanwhile, although Americans had made few significant contributions to statistical theory, they were showing themselves adept at developing new tools for collecting and correlating statistics. A crucial invention, without which the proliferating statistical communities would hardly have been possible, was made by an unsung American pioneer, Dr. Herman Hollerith. His new system translated statistics into punched holes in a nonconducting card, then counted and correlated the items by allowing an electric current to pass through the holes that were identically placed. His scheme, first used in the federal census of 1890, was not only a great labor-saver, but for the first time made possible quick and complex correlations. Now it was as easy to tabulate the number of married carpenters 40 to 45 years of age as to tabulate the total number of persons 40 to 45 years of age. Hollerith's simple invention was the grandparent of the modern computer industry. His enterprise became part of the International Business Machines Corporation (IBM), which, with other similar firms, by the mid-twentieth century had made the hum of the computer heard throughout the land.

Numerous techniques for visualizing and dramatizing statistics for a still wider public were developed at the same time. Dr. Henry Gannett, a geographer, used novel devices for symbolizing census results in his *Statistical Atlas for the Censuses of 1890 and 1900.* Further advances were made by cartographers, especially those working for news magazines in the early twentieth century. A growing popular demand for current statistics on all sorts of subjects, from railroads to books, produced new statistical almanacs for every conceivable business, industry, trade, or profession. One of the most useful and influential of these, after its first appearance in 1878, was the *Statistical Abstract of the United States,* which appeared annually and became the standard national inventory. On the desks of men of affairs it now took its place beside a dictionary and a collection of familiar quotations as an indispensable new lexicon of American statistical communities.

20

Communities of Risk

OF THE NEW statistical communities, none were more widespread or more potent than the communities of the insured. By the mid-twentieth century, insurance touched the lives of all Americans, was a major item in the family budget, and shaped the American's vision of his future. In 1840 there was less than $5 million of life insurance (issued by a total of fifteen companies) in force in the whole United States. Within twenty years the face value of life policies exceeded $150 million; within another decade they reached $2 billion, and a century later totaled a staggering $1,284 billion. By 1970 there were 351 million life policies in force with an average coverage per family of $19,500. The assets of the fifty largest life insurance companies were valued at $164,555 million, and insurance companies had become a large factor in the investment and securities market and in the process of capital formation.

The prominence of insurance in American life, which historians seldom noted on paper, was starkly revealed on the American skyline. Insurance buildings rose in cathedral eminence. The history of the American skyscraper could have been illustrated by monuments to the growing insurance industry, from the Equitable Life Building (1868–70) in New York through the Home Insurance Building (1883–85) in Chicago (the first skeleton-frame tall building, sometimes called the first true skyscraper), and the New York Life Insurance Building (1890) in Kansas City, and many others. "The idea is to construct a building," Prudential's president explained of the structure which opened in 1892, "which shall typify and symbolize the character of the business of the Prudential, exemplify its all-pervading spirit of beneficence and its ingrained love of the golden rule." The New York Life Building at 346 Broadway had an entrance which resembled "an ancient temple—and a temple it is—a Temple of Humanity." The new building of the Metropolitan Life Insurance Company on Madison Square (the first part of which was opened in 1893) offered a main staircase imitating that of the Paris Opera and a tower which when completed in 1909 was reputedly the tallest in the world.

INSURANCE, OF COURSE, was no American invention. Even in ancient times the risks of merchants and mariners, the dangers from disaster at sea and fire on land induced people who had large stakes to lose to pay others to share their risks. But only in the United States after the mid-nineteenth century did insurance become a democratic, universal institution. Mass-produced, democratized insurance —insurance for everybody and against almost anything—came in the century after the Civil War and was a product of American civilization.

While not all citizens had property worth insuring, every citizen had a life. In one sense, of course, death was not a "risk," for it was the one certainty in life and insurance could do nothing to prevent it. Though for any individual nothing was more uncertain or democratic than the time of his death, it was within human power, by accumulating funds, to cushion the shock of death for those who remained. Life insurance, then, if spread among those who were not wealthy, was actually a welfare institution: a way to help the needy, the widows, and the orphaned. And for this reason insurance on lives was one of the last forms to develop. Insurance against commercial risks had become a profitable enterprise long before life insurance was common.

In western Europe, life insurance was at first a form of gambling. Anyone could take out a policy on the life of any other person. Since this created incentives to murder, by the end of the eighteenth century English laws required that the person who took out the policy should have an "insurable interest"—a substantial interest in the insured person or event entirely apart from the insurance itself. The progress of mathematics (through the work of Pascal, Halley, and others) and the accumulation of statistics produced some crude life-expectancy tables. Religious sects and certain professions formed "mutual friendly" societies to pool their risks and help members in need. The first American life insurance enterprise, the Presbyterian Ministers' Fund of Philadelphia, appeared in 1759, but not until a century later did life insurance become widely available.

When communities were local, friends and neighbors were nearby, ready and willing to help in disaster. The church tried to look after widows and orphans. Neighbors who had gathered for a barn raising were likely also to gather to rebuild the barn that had been burned. But the attentuation and the stretching of communities created new needs. People who could not confidently rely on their neighbors, people whose relatives had moved to remote parts of the continent, had to find other security. And insurance became a kind of substitute for family, for neighborhood, and for community. Again, insurance handled the problem by creating a centralized source of supply, on which an individual could draw as he needed. Just as with the growth of city plumbing, with electricity, and later with television, this opportunity to draw on a large central source tended to isolate the individual citizen. A man's insurance was his own business. The well-insured man had less need of his neighbors, and received the benefits of his insurance without their consent or their knowledge.

By its very nature, insurance—a new kind of consumption community—was a large-scale institution with a democratic reach. "While nothing is more uncertain than the duration of a single life," observed Elizur Wright, "nothing is more certain than the average duration of a thousand lives." Since insurance would not work for small numbers, it was necessarily a democratic commodity. So it was not surprising that the first flourishing of insurance into a gargantuan institution, rivaled in economic power only by government itself, came in the first large-scale democratic nation.

THE "FATHER OF LIFE INSURANCE," Elizur Wright, came to the enterprise not as a businessman, but as a reformer. We do not ordinarily think of life insurance as an outlet for the passionate crusader. But Wright was a passionate man, and the evangelical fervor which he at first directed against slavery he later turned to support insurance. He saw insurance as both a humanitarian institution to serve widows and orphans, and a social invention to multiply a man's resources and extend them after his death. In 1810 his father had gone west from Connecticut to Ohio, where he cleared a farm and opened an academy, and there young Elizur prepared for college. Working his way through Yale, he graduated with distinction in mathematics in 1826. Fired by the antislavery evangelist Theodore Weld, Wright himself became an antislavery organizer and publicist, and edited the *Massachusetts Abolitionist*. To support his growing family (eventually his children numbered eighteen, of whom six died in infancy), he solicited subscriptions for an elegant and improbable project, an English verse translation of La Fontaine's *Fables*, to be published in a de luxe illustrated two-volume edition. He paid for printing one thousand sets, which he went about peddling.

During a book-selling trip to England his translation of La Fontaine, together with his interest in statistics, gave him entrée to London literary circles. One morning in 1844 at breakfast with Elizabeth Barrett, Robert Browning, and their friends, he was asked which London sights had interested him most.

> "The Thames Tunnel," I replied, "is the largest, but the most interesting to me has been the Sun Life Office, where I have learned a good deal about life insurance that was new to me." "Life insurance," broke out Mr. Procter, "it's the greatest humbug in Christendom." I was quite thunderstruck, but managed, after a little hesitation, to say, "You surprise me, Mr. Procter. If I had not taken a policy from a life company just started in Boston, I should not have dared to cross the water, leaving a wife and five children on the other side." "Go to the Royal Exchange," said Mr. Procter, "Thursday afternoon at three o'clock, and you will see what I mean." I assured him I would do so, and did. What I saw at that sublime center of trade was a sale of several old policies on very aged men to speculators apparently of Hebrew persuasion, to be kept up by them by their paying annual premiums to the company till the decease. This was done, I was told, because the companies made it a rule *"never to buy their own policies."* A poor rule it seemed to me! I had seen slave auctions at home. I could hardly see more justice in this British practice. If I should ever become old myself, I thought, I should not like to have a policy on my life in the hands of a man with the slightest pecuniary motive to wish me dead. This then is what had disgusted the sweetest song writer in England with life insurance. . . . I resolved, if I ever returned to America, it should be otherwise here, if my voice could avail.

The abuse which Wright witnessed in London came from the refusal of insurance companies to give a cash-surrender value to policies. It was thirty-six years before Wright managed to remove this abuse from the laws of Massachusetts. Meanwhile he labored to make life insurance a cure for the worries of the common man.

Life Insurance, when Elizur Wright first turned his mind and heart to it, was, he complained, "the most availably convenient and permanent nidus for rogues that civilization had ever presented." Of course, there were a number of honest companies. But the temptations to charlatanry were overwhelming. Swindlers set up impressive offices, enlisted unsuspecting solid citizens to serve as front men, collected lifetime savings in premiums and then dissolved their companies into bankruptcy or absconded.

"Dear Wright," one of his friends observed, "has every kind of sense but common sense." But his peculiar combination of mathematical talent and reforming zeal actually qualified him to shape insurance into a grand new democratic institution. "Life insurance," Wright explained, "comes in as a financial invention by which capital in the shape of a productive life . . . can perpetuate itself. . . . It gives to an energetic young man, who has not a spare dollar to bequeath, the power of making a will good for several thousand dollars in case of his death the next day." This invention multiplied human resources as the steam engine had multiplied power or the telegraph conquered distance, and it should be made available to all citizens in a democracy. To young people just assuming the responsibilities of a family, life insurance was "as great a blessing as sound sleep. But it must be sound life insurance."

The "facts" required to run a prudent life insurance company were complicated beyond the comprehension of the ordinary policyholder, and even beyond the resources of information then available to insurance executives. A company should charge a sufficient annual premium to cover its current risk on a policyholder's life, while accumulating sufficient reserves to pay off its accrued policies. Yet the company should not require excessive premiums, nor, on the other hand, should it offer "bargain" rates which left it without a sufficient reserve. These computations were further complicated if the company wished to offer a "level premium," which would allow the policyholder to continue over an extended period to pay the same annual amount despite the company's increasing risk. And what was the proper surrender value of a policy, should the holder wish to cancel at any time? All these sums had to be figured in dollars and cents despite the fact that the company, of course, could never know the precise number of death claims it would have to settle in any one year. No wonder, then, that life insurance was a happy hunting ground for charlatans, swindlers, and high-pressure salesmen. The holder of a life policy was apt to be gambling as much on the solvency of the company as on the length of his own life.

Wright attacked some of the more obvious abuses in the columns of his crusading *Chronotype*. In order to sell more insurance, for instance, some companies were accepting personal notes signed by the insured for as much as three quarters of the premium. As a result, these companies' "reserves" consisted largely of promissory notes from the very persons they were supposed to protect. And on the death of the insured the widow would receive nothing but the promissory notes of the deceased. Wright aimed to reduce the understanding of insurance "to the range of ordinary mathematical ability and freed from unnecessary expense. Thus far, to the millions, it has been enveloped in considerable mystery . . . a hieroglyphic veil." Under this veil, fraudulent companies "bled the confiding" and charged policyholders with the high salaries of " 'eminent mathematicians' to pilot them annually across the unknown depths of the logarithm table." Wright's great success, as *Hunt's Merchant's Magazine* observed, was in "unmystifying" the subject.

WITH HIS ZEAL for reform, his talent for mathematics—and his numerous children to whom he could assign the thousands of necessary simple calculations—Elizur Wright was well equipped for the job. Six insurance companies hired him to prepare "Valuation Tables on the Combined Experience, or Actuaries' Rate of Mortality." Using the English "Combined Experience Tables," after a year's intense work Wright completed his tables in 1853. For each of 268 different kinds of policies, the tables showed the precise reserve which the company should hold each year from the date of the policy until its termination; each of the 203 pages of Wright's Tables required a thousand separate computations, which, of course, had to be accomplished without calculating machines. For this monumental labor, including ten handwritten copies, six of which were delivered to the subscribing companies, Wright received $2,200.

With these tables, then, any businessman without special training could determine the solvency of an insurance company. Now there was no excuse for a company's not keeping a sufficient reserve to pay death claims, and the fair surrender value of any policy could be figured at any time. But there was no law yet to require a company to set aside such reserves, nor were insurance companies regulated in other ways to protect the rights of the insured. What solace was a lawsuit against a defunct company to the widow or the orphan whose family's savings had gone into a life insurance policy?

Wright, whose years as an abolitionist had made him impervious to ridicule, began "lobbying for the widow and orphan." At the Boston State House he crusaded for laws to require every company chartered by Massachusetts to keep the necessary reserves, which were now defined in his valuation tables. Finally, on the last day of the session of 1858, as much to be rid of Wright as for any other reason, the Massachusetts legislature in exasperation enacted "that everlasting Wright bill," and Wright personally supervised the unenthusiastic governor's signature. There were to be two insurance commissioners charged with enforcing the law, but Wright's Act was so complicated and so full of technical mathematical terms, and the enforcement of the law was so unpalatable to business interests that the governor's political friends refused to accept appointment. The governor had no alternative but to appoint Wright, who reputedly was the only person who could understand the act, as one of the commissioners.

Commissioner Wright collected facts on every company in Massachusetts and compiled a Life Insurance Register, recording the amount of each policy, the premium paid, and the reserve required. He asked policyholders to bring him their questions. By referring to his Register, Wright informed the policyholder whether he was getting his money's worth, and told him the surrender value of his policy. In a single year this job (according to Wright) required 250,000 separate calculations. To help in his work Wright invented a calculating machine, which he called the "Arithmeter." This device, based on the principle of the slide rule, showed the natural numbers separated by logarithmic distances; by putting these numbers on the surface of a cylinder in a continuous spiral, he provided a compact machine with the accuracy of a slide rule eighty feet long.

Wright's investigations, his published studies of particular companies, and his Annual Reports as commissioner made him few friends among insurance executives. They called him their persecutor. "Rosewater is good," he replied, "but it never built pyramids or machine shops." Armed with the facts, he drove fourteen shady companies out of Massachusetts. This required a courageous disregard for social amenities, since the dubious enterprises had paraded respectable names in their lists of officers and trustees. One such company—which, Wright found, was spending fifty cents of each dollar on "expenses" and was insuring anybody regardless of health, had cut its reserves and was publishing false financial statements— had for its president the eminent Yale scientist Benjamin Silliman, Jr., with Silliman's son-in-law as manager. Another swindling Massachusetts company listed English noblemen as trustees and for its actuary had hired a Fellow of the Royal Astronomical Society. Wright's crusade against the swindlers strengthened public confidence in those firms which he endorsed, and the honest life insurance business flourished. During Wright's eight years as commissioner, life policies issued in Massachusetts increased fivefold, to a figure of a half-billion dollars.

Yet Wright had only begun his reforms. The requirement that companies keep an adequate reserve, Wright explained, "made life insurance safe, but it did not make it just." Companies were still tempted to make unconscionable profits out of their reserves; and when a policyholder let his policy lapse by not paying premiums, they commonly kept the accumulated sums, or refused to return him his savings. Dishonest executives were even tempted to spread rumors of the insolvency of their company so that policyholders would let their policies lapse, enabling the executives to confiscate the sums for themselves. Until there was a "non-forfeiture" law, requiring insurance companies to return to policyholders the fair value of lapsed policies, insurance remained, in Wright's phrase, "Traps

Baited with Orphan." In 1861, for example, Wright found that of the life policies that had been terminated that year, only one tenth had been terminated by death, while all the rest had lapsed for nonpayment of premiums; yet those policyholders had been left without any legal way to recoup their savings from the company. In that year Wright pushed his "Non-Forfeiture Law" through the Massachusetts legislature.

Wright's efforts led the insurance companies to do some lobbying of their own. In 1867 they secured passage of a law reducing the number of commissioners from two to one, cleverly worded so as to leave the commission in the hands of the other commissioner, who saw his job as "helping" the companies and not policing them. Scorning an annual pension of $10,000, which some insurance executives offered him if he would keep quiet, Wright set himself up as a consulting actuary, and made a good living advising a number of reputable firms. Until his death in 1885 Wright worked for life insurance reform, an unpaid lobbyist for millions of policyholders.

These accomplishments in Massachusetts promoted similar reform in other states, since no company from another state could sell insurance in Massachusetts without conforming to the Massachusetts rules. His reforms had given life insurance companies a stability that kept them alive during the post–Civil War panic.

WRIGHT'S RARE COMBINATION of technical competence and humanitarian zeal had made large insurance enterprises honest and stable, and had protected the rights of small policyholders. But to democratize the benefits of insurance required the additional talents of salesman, promoter, advertiser, and organizer—all of which happened to be combined in the person of Henry B. Hyde.

Young Hyde at the age of sixteen had left the village of Catskill for New York City, where he worked first as a clerk in the Mutual Life Insurance Company, and by the age of twenty-five became the company cashier. Although Mutual was the largest pre–Civil War company, its sales techniques were stodgy; since the company would not insure any life for more than $10,000, policyholders were going elsewhere for additional insurance. The ambitious young Hyde conceived the idea of forming another company to pick up this business. One Saturday evening, March 12, 1859, when he asked the president of Mutual for advice on this project, he was promptly told that he was fired and must deliver his keys and settle his accounts on Monday morning. On that very Monday, Hyde rented a room on the second story of the building at 98 Broadway and equipped it with borrowed furniture. "In order to make everything agreeable and cheerful for visitors," Hyde recalled, "I purchased a box of cigars and placed them in a convenient position on the mantelpiece. On the succeeding Monday a sign, about thirty feet in length, with the inscription, 'The Equitable Life Assurance Society of the United States,' was placed directly over the smaller sign of the Mutual Life, which company, at that time, occupied the first floor of the same building." The sign gave the impression that the new company occupied all the upper floors.

Under the laws of New York, no life insurance company could be formed without depositing the sum of $100,000 with the state comptroller. Hyde quickly began to raise the money so there could be a company behind the sign. For this task Hyde was not especially well equipped by birth or by education. Insurance was "the friend of widows and orphans." And since insurance companies were not selling a commodity but building a public institution, their executives were not generally classed with dry-goods merchants, shoe manufacturers, and others who aimed to make a profit, but rather with schoolteachers, university presidents, ministers of the gospel, statesmen, and other champions of the public weal.

Henry Hyde had not gone beyond grade school, and had no impressive social standing. His father was merely an insurance agent. How was he to compete with established institutions like Mutual, whose stationery was embellished with eminent names? The halo of respectability came from the lucky coincidence of Hyde's membership in the Fifth Avenue Presbyterian Church, whose congregation included some of the city's wealthiest merchants and bankers. Hyde had become a close friend of the pastor's son—and in his quest for the required sum, this association proved invaluable. Seventeen of the fifty-two members of Equitable's first board of directors came from the Fifth Avenue Presbyterian congregation. The remunerative post of company physician was offered to young Dr. Edward W. Lambert on condition that he persuade his wealthy father to invest $25,000. A Mr. Henry Day was told he could be the company lawyer if he could raise $25,000; when he demurred, another candidate was found who was willing to meet the condition, and then Day's scruples were overcome. To hold the title of president, Hyde decided that instead of himself a more impressive choice would be William C. Alexander, brother of the pastor of the Fifth Avenue Presbyterian Church, a Princeton graduate, "a man of mature years, of long experience at the bar and in the Senate of New Jersey, and possessed of those qualities which gave to the community a high degree of confidence." Hyde, as vice-president and manager, was the operating head.

Within four months Hyde had raised the necessary $100,000 and had begun an unprecedented campaign to sell life insurance. One advantage of his religious connections, which had not escaped Hyde's notice, was the special importance given in those days to the "religious press." Each denomination had its own newspapers and periodicals; the widely circulated religious weeklies were an admirable medium for insurance publicity. When the prominent Reverend S. Irenaeus Prime made flattering remarks about Hyde's company "at a recent social gathering," Hyde saw that these remarks were printed at length in the *New York Observer,* the leading Presbyterian journal, and then extracts were reprinted in other papers. The Reverend Prime observed:

> The Equitable Life Assurance Society of the United States, has been founded with a view to meet the wants of all parts of our widely extended country. *Its founders and directors are chiefly religious and benevolent men.* They hope to enroll, in the society of the assured, good men in all the departments of business. They know that intelligence and virtue tend to prolong life, and that the most safe and profitable life insurance will be among enlightened religious communities. As they extend the range of their operations and take into their society the clergy of the whole land, they will become a most efficient, useful and blessed society for the relief of the widows and orphans and clergymen. . . . I believe your society is one of the most purely benevolent institutions in our land.

The company seal bore the motto *Aeque pauperibus prodest locupletibus aeque* ("Of benefit alike to rich and poor"). The Society's first rate book opened with a section describing "Robert Burns's Disease" (poverty) and prescribed "The Great Preventive" (insurance). Hyde distributed thousands of pamphlets stamped with the Equitable name, explaining and preaching life insurance.

Among the pious a common objection was "that life insurance implies a distrust in Providence, and is an impious attempt to prevent or control His will." One answer was that life insurance was itself a divinely ordained institution and that it providentially prolonged life by removing "corroding anxiety and uncomfortable reflection" and making men more cheerful late in life and on the sickbed. "The old feeling," a brochure of 1872 warned, "that, by taking out an insurance policy we do somehow challenge an interview with the 'King of terrors,' still reigns in full force in many circles; and the very fact that her husband has insured his life, thrills the bosom of his wife with fearful apprehensions." Hyde hired the highest religious authorities, including Henry Ward Beecher himself, to write articles explaining to prospective customers how life insurance fitted into God's plan.

Hyde's "benevolent" institution flourished beyond his wildest hopes. In 1862 the company wrote nearly $2 million in new policies. When Hyde himself was drafted into the Union Army he bought a substitute, as the law permitted, for $800; he later described this as the best investment he had ever made. The Civil War reminded men of their mortality, and in 1862 the new business of New York insurance companies was nearly double that of any earlier year. By the end of the war, life insurance in force in the nation was more than three times what it had been at the outbreak. The Equitable grew even faster than its competitors.

HYDE DEVELOPED an elaborate training program for agents, providing sales literature, prescribing sales techniques, listing the usual objections from prospects, and offering the most effective answers. By 1870 his sales conventions for exchanging sales techniques and improving morale had become a regular institution.

His national sales organization was as different from earlier salesmanship as the great American mail-order houses and department stores were different from the general store. Traveling about the country, Hyde evangelized for life insurance and he recruited agents. *The Agent's Manual,* by the Reverend Henry C. Fish, D.D., Pastor of the First Baptist Church of Newark, which Hyde circulated, explained that "life agency may fairly be called a profession," requiring certain qualities of a man:

1. He appreciates his work.
2. He is moved by high impulses.
3. His heart is enlisted.
4. He is active and industrious.
5. He is courageous and determined.
6. He has tact and discrimination.
7. He speaks the truth.
8. He has a good reputation.
9. He is agreeable in manners.
10. He is devoted to his calling.
11. His interest is in one Company.
12. He is careful in selecting risks.

Hyde inspired Equitable agents, as one of his associates remarked, "with a passionate faith in the company, and an enthusiasm for its triumphant progress which a soldier has for the flag under which he fights." When depression struck, Hyde urged, "Be not discouraged by hard times. Men will die now as formerly. Families unprovided for by an assurance will be left more destitute than before. Never was here greater need of assuring than now, in these HARD TIMES. . . . Let, then, all our agents take hold with a will." And he organized his sales force to cover the continent, hiring general agents charged with finding salesmen to cover their territory. In his letter to general agents on September 2, 1867, he noted the miracle of Equitable's assets of $4.5 million after only eight years.

His sales conventions were a combination of lecture sessions and revivalist meetings. And by 1870 Hyde's brochures were quoting the "testimony" of salesmen who had increased their earning power by what they had learned at these conventions. Hyde encouraged aggressive competition by contests and prizes; a crack salesman could be identified by his badge, "a massive and valuable gold watch and chain" with which the company had recognized his success. Bringing together all these ideas, Hyde may be said to have created the American sales convention, at the very time when expanding railroads and hotels had their own good reasons for encouraging such perennial gatherings from all over the country. Hyde himself said that he felt even more at home in a Pullman car than in a hotel.

The Great American Salesman was born. The tie to insurance created virtue by association. The aspiring American salesman, partly because of the rhetoric and the organizing energies of Henry B. Hyde and others like him, would henceforth trace his lineage not to peddlers or charlatans or showmen, not to the hawkers of patent medicine or the P. T. Barnums, but to the great preachers and reformers and philanthropists, the benefactors of mankind. The gospel of salesmanship produced its own theology and morality and folklore, its own iconography, its own "sciences," and its own philosophies. In the early decades of the twentieth century Bruce Barton, founder of a great advertising agency, would praise Jesus as the World's Greatest Salesman, and the Bible as the All-Time Best-Seller.

Hyde persuaded his sales missionaries that life "assurance" (second perhaps to the Gospel) was the one thing that *all* men needed. In 1869 he succeeded in making Equitable's tenth anniversary into a widely celebrated event; the company was already writing more than $50 million in new business annually, which was more than that of all the leading British companies combined. Within another two decades, the total value of Equitable policies in force made it the largest life insurance company in the world.

IN 1899, WHEN Henry B. Hyde died, he left his control of Equitable, in the form of the majority holding of 502 shares, to his twenty-three-year-old son, John Hazen Hyde, who then wore the mantle (in the phrase found on Equitable policies) of "protector of the widow and orphan." More than three million prospective widows and orphans were under his protection; the instrument of protection was the company's assets valued at over $400 million. While young Hyde began with the commonplace virtues and amiable vices of any other young monarch, his extravagance and irresponsibility became spectacular; a Francophile, his formal, "business-expense" dinners for French actresses sometimes cost over $10,000 apiece. Among Hyde's rivals and enemies were the Alexander family, who feared he would take from them their own smaller slice of inherited power in the company. The Alexanders themselves annually drew perquisites, commissions, and fees from Equitable totaling over $1 million. But before the public investigation of Equitable, along with other large insurance enterprises, got under way, Hyde had sold his majority shares to Thomas Fortune Ryan, a New York promoter, for $2.5 million. Legally the benefits of these shares were limited by the Equitable charter to $7 per share per year, but ownership of the majority shares conferred control over $400 million of policyholders' assets.

In 1905, when the New York State Legislature held its hearings on the abuses in insurance, a handsome and able young lawyer, Charles Evans Hughes, was in charge. His successful exposures of the extravagance, nepotism, and irresponsibility in the great insurance companies started him on his statesmanly career. And these revelations were aptly characterized by the humorous magazine *Puck* (October 1905) in its "Little Sums for Policy-holders":

> The tenth Vice-President of a big Insurance company buys one thousand shares of stock at 84. If the stock goes up ten points, how much will he win? If it goes down ten points, how much will *you* lose?

> Three directors are coming back from Europe to explain things. The first returns on a five-day steamer. The second, on a tramp steamer. The third falls overboard. Which man has the most foresight?

Puck's version of an application form for life insurance required the president of the insurance company to answer the following questions:

> What is your name, salary, and rake-off?
> Have you any predisposition, either hereditary or acquired, to any constitutional diseases, such as lying, speculatitis, grafting, grand or petit larceny?
> Have you ever had any of the following diseases:
> Paralysis of conscience?   Surplusitis? If operated upon,
> Shortness of memory?   state particulars.
> Itching palm?   Perquisitis? How many attacks?
> Acute or chronic nepotism?
> That guilty feeling?   Enlargement of the wallet?
> Have you any conscientious scruples against perjury?
> Do you know anything about the insurance business? If so, what?

It was no accident that salesmanship had a renaissance in the merchandising of insurance, the invisible commodity. For insurance was complicated and required detailed explanation to everybody, but especially to the democratic millions who in America would have the opportunity to become insurance customers. Before the mid-twentieth century, certain kinds of American insurance (for example, for airline passengers at airports), following the trend of American merchandising, would be packaged, mass-produced, and machine-vended. But the abstract and complex qualities of insurance, together with its intimate and personal aspects, continued to keep it as a last preserve for the salesman against advertising.

American enterprise, the energy and rhetoric of American Go-Getters, had helped transform insurance from speculative businesses, first cousins to gambling, into some of the nation's largest and most respectable corporations. With modern industry and its increasing risks to machine workers, the demand for insurance became universal, and before long, governments began to make insurance compulsory. In Germany, Bismarck set an example with his state system of workers' sickness insurance (1883), accident insurance (1884), and disability and old-age insurance (1889). In the United States, the Progressives pressed for a scheme of employers' liability; from the workers' point of view, this amounted to government-enforced insurance. A federal law in 1908, insuring federal employees against certain on-the-job risks, was followed by laws in most states by 1920. Beginning with the New Deal's Social Security Act in 1935, the federal government supported, enforced, and enlarged schemes of insurance covering unemployment, old age, disability, and sickness. More distinctively American were the vast privately organized insurance enterprises.

Every advance in technology produced new risks. For example, the democratizing of glass windows and their increasing use for display created costly new risks against which merchants wanted to be insured. Gas lines, electric wiring, and water pipes in houses were new hazards. And of course the locomotive, the automobile, and the airplane would multiply all sorts of risks. The widening popularity of expensive, machine-assisted sports, of skiing, boating, and snowmobiling, added still further to the opportunities and needs for insurance.

The spread of casualty insurance in the United States was itself a measure of the rising standard of living, for more and more people could afford the costly objects that brought costly risks. In earlier times the main forms of casualty insurance were against the perils of the sea and against fire. But now everyday machines in the hands of the ordinary American gave him a new power to injure his neighbor or his neighbor's property. An automobile was incomparably more lethal than a horse. And chains of automobiles moving at sixty miles an hour made any single automobile that simply stopped, into a weapon of death.

Of the new forms of insurance in the first half of the twentieth century, by far the most important related to the automobile. The first liability policy on an automobile was probably issued in 1896, when the nation held fewer than ninety automobiles, and the rates varied according to whether the insured vehicle was propelled by electricity, gasoline, or steam. When a mass-produced steam automobile still seemed probable, insurers were much concerned with the dangers of boiler explosion. In the early days the actuarial problem came from the small numbers of policyholders and from the uncertainties about their uses of the vehicles. By 1916 the differences in risks according to the numbers of automobiles and the amount of urban use in a given area were beginning to appear; then the rate for automobile liability insurance in New York City, where there were 25,000 cars insured, was twelve times that in Arizona, with only 200 cars insured. By 1965, one fourth of all premiums on property and liability insurance was in the form of automobile insurance.

The democratization of life insurance, the rise of the Equitable Life Assurance and other private insurance enterprises, had created enormous new pools of power. Like the Ford Motor Company, Equitable could not have been created except by enlisting the participation of American millions. And the great insurance companies became leviathans, which only the people as a whole had the power to create, but which the people as a whole found hard to control.

21

Statistical Expectations: What's Your Size?

THE DISTINCTIVE FACT about statistics in the United States was not their rise as a learned specialty. One by-product of democracy was an unprecedented popular diffusion of statistics, and in the twentieth century a new kind of number consciousness captured the public mind. The ballot box and the census were only two of many American ways of asking, How many? How much? How big?

In developing and reinforcing this number consciousness, nothing was more important than American industry and the American Standard of Living. Increasing pressures to make all sorts of commodities in large factories for the use of everybody led Americans to apply the techniques of statistics to everyday life in myriad ways.

A COMMONPLACE EXAMPLE was in the new democracy of clothing. We have already seen how the rise of a ready-made-clothing industry moved the center of garment making in the United States from the home to the factory. Among the many circumstances that had made this possible was the growth of a new branch of statistical science. "Anthropometry" (a word which entered English just before the mid-nineteenth century) was "the measurement of the dimensions of man" with a view to discovering those which most commonly recurred and to defining the differing proportions of the parts of the body in different ages, classes, and races. Until the mid-nineteenth century it was generally assumed, on the basis of common sense strengthened by religious notions of the uniqueness of each individual soul, that the dimensions of every man's body were quite different from those of every other man. If that was the case, then it was futile to try to manufacture large quantities of clothing that would actually fit different wearers. If a man wanted a proper fit he would have to make his own clothing or employ a tailor.

The Civil War, with its sudden demand for uniforms in great quantity, produced a fund of new information on the common dimensions of the human body. And this disclosed the crucial fact that certain sets of measurements tended to recur with predictable regularity. If a man's waist measured 38 inches and his sleeve-length was 34 inches, then in eight cases out of ten his shoulders would have a certain breadth. This simple discovery made it possible to manufacture well-fitting garments for a large population. Simple though it was, the discovery was essential to the ready-made-clothing industry, for without it no shop could be provided with a disposable stock which would fit the customers. At the end of the war, these measurements were available to guide clothing manufacturers in their efforts to supply ready-made civilian garments to an unprecedented market: hundreds of thousands of demobilized soldiers; a flood of new immigrants; prospering inhabitants of mushrooming cities like Chicago, Omaha, and Denver; and workmen in thousands of new factories. Now for the first time middle-class Americans, too, could find store-boughten clothing that was attractive and well-fitting.

Essential to all this was the increase and diffusion of information about bodily measurements. In 1880 appeared Daniel Edward Ryan's epoch-making book *Human Proportions in Growth: Being the Complete Measurements of the Human Body for Every Age and Size during the Years of Juvenile Growth*. Now at last Ryan offered a scientific guide for standardizing measurements in men's, boys', and juveniles' ready-made clothing. Ryan's system included practical charts for deriving the other bodily proportions from his statistics on body circumference and height. By 1889 Professor Franz Boas was teaching courses in anthropometry and anthropological statistics at Clark University. And these statistics on bodily growth, useful in countless other ways (for example in better design for school furniture), incidentally provided the raw material for a flourishing new science of educational psychology.

By the early twentieth century, then, for the first time in history, it was possible for a man to walk into a clothing store, indicate that he was a "42" and put on a jacket that with little or no alteration would satisfy a fastidious eye. People thus began to think of themselves as belonging to certain "sizes"—in shoes, shirts, trousers, and hats—another sign that Americans had joined statistical communities.

TO MAKE STANDARDIZED PRODUCTS that would meet the customers' expectations, it was necessary to have standardized units of measurement. We have become so accustomed to knowing what we mean by a minute, a foot, or a gallon that we forget how recently these simple terms were given clear definition. "The system of weights and measures in customary use," a leading physicist observed in 1887, "is so confusing, so unscientific, and, in some instances, apparently so contradictory that it is difficult to write of it, even briefly, without falling into error." As late as 1892 there were eight different "authoritative" values for the U. S. gallon.

These "laissez-faire standards" left the way open for any manufacturer to use whatever definition best served his advertising needs at the moment. In new industries this was especially troublesome. The president of the American Institute of Electrical Engineers complained in 1900 that because the English standard of light-measurement (which had just been adopted by the Office of Weights and Measures in the United States Coast and Geodetic Survey) was so indefinite, American scientific laboratories were using the more precise German standard. At the same time, the electric-light industry, dissatisfied with both the English and the German standards, adopted a standard of its own. As a result an electric lamp requiring 10 amperes at a pressure of 45 volts was being described in the advertising as "2,000 candlepower," when the same lamp (measured by British or German standards) actually would have been rated at only 400 to 500 candlepower.

Amidst this confusion, the construction industry found it difficult to figure costs or to meet schedules. An expert writing in *Scientific American* in 1896 reported that a prudent builder had to order about 20 percent more material than he actually needed for the job, in order to allow for uneven quality and crude standards. By 1900, when Americans had become adept at manufacturing all sorts of industrial measuring devices, it was still common to send these devices abroad, to England or more usually to Germany, to be calibrated.

Among the obvious sources of confusion were the extent and variety of the United States, the fast growth of industry, and the rapid rate of change. The federal system of government, and especially the notion that police powers and day-to-day regulation were the sacred province of the separate states, perpetuated confusion. But the Constitution (art. I, sec. 8) had given to the Congress (along with the power "to collect Taxes, Duties, Imposts and Excises" and "to coin Money, regulate the Value thereof, and of foreign Coin") the power to "fix the Standard of Weights and Measures." The establishment of nationally uniform standards of weights and measures, when it finally came, had to be justified indirectly (in deference to states' rights) as a way of satisfying the constitutional requirements concerning coinage and the requirement that "all Duties, Imposts and Excises shall be uniform throughout the United States."

For more than a century, Congress struggled with various devices for establishing a sufficient uniformity of weights and measures which would yet not infringe on the powers of the states or the independence of businessmen. Jefferson, Madison, and John Quincy Adams all made proposals, but the Congress, fearing excessive federal control, could not agree. In 1828, Congress managed to adopt the British troy pound of 1758 as the standard for American coinage. Albert Gallatin, a former Secretary of the Treasury, had, when he was minister to Great Britain in 1827, secured a brass copy of the old British troy pound which was deposited with the Director of the Mint in Philadelphia. Then copies were supplied to all the mints as the basis for the weight of a pound of gold. But when the Houses of Parliament burned in 1834, the British prototype was destroyed, and thereafter the brass pound at Philadelphia had to be defined indirectly by reference to the British avoirdupois pound. In any case, as Charles S. Peirce (the versatile and erratic philosopher who was destined to become the chief metaphysician of American pragmatism) observed in 1884 when he was head of the Office of Weights and Measures, the troy pound was quite unsuitable for precision weights. He explained that since the standard troy pound had never been weighed in a vacuum to determine its true weight, and the United States government had no apparatus capable of weighing in a vacuum, the weight of the American pound was "not known." Nevertheless, for lack of anything better, this indeterminate "pound" remained the American standard for coinage until 1911.

A federal office for weights and measures had appeared within the Department of the Treasury in response to complaints about lack of uniformity in the customs collections at different ports. The first head of the Coast Survey, Ferdinand Rudolph Hassler, a recent Swiss immigrant, found that there were no two custom houses which used the same measure for the pound or the bushel. The practical result, of course, was that customs duties were not uniform. After about 1830, Hassler made strenuous efforts to establish uniform standards, but congressional fears of federal domination forced Hassler to try to accomplish his purpose by persuading each of the states separately to adopt his proposals. This was less a scientific than a political enterprise, and his progress was slow.

Then, after the Spanish-American War of 1898, the United States plunged into world politics. In the preceding decade American exports of manufactures had nearly doubled. When the nation was a leader in world trade it was hard any longer to postpone establishing uniform American standards of measurement. Customers all over the world wanted assurance of the quality of American products. The leader of a new campaign for a national standardizing laboratory was Lyman J. Gage, a self-made Chicago businessman who had headed the board of the World's Columbian Exposition in 1893, and then as President William McKinley's Secretary of Treasury had financed the Spanish-American War. In 1900 Gage urged on Congress that the nation could no longer lean on others for the definition of its standards; American manufacturers needed a national effort to "secure the requisite degree of uniformity and accuracy" in their products. Congress enacted Secretary Gage's proposal in 1901, incidentally changing the name from Gage's more explicit "National Standardizing Bureau" to the "National Bureau of Standards." The total appropriation for 1900 for the old Office of Weights and Measures had been $9,410. In congressional debate on the bill, some congressmen had objected that the head of the new Bureau was scheduled to receive $6,000 a year, almost as high a salary as that of the Secretary of the Treasury himself. Secretary Gage knowingly replied that while "almost anybody will do for the Secretary of the Treasury . . . it takes a very high-grade man to be chief of a bureau like this."

The "high-grade man" who came to Washington to create a National Bureau of Standards fulfilled Gage's expectations. Samuel Wesley Stratton, son of an Illinois farmer, had worked his way through the University of Illinois, where he established a novel course in electrical engineering, and then he had gone on to the newly organized University of Chicago in 1892. There he worked with Albert Michelson, experimenting on the speed of light, until he joined the Navy during the Spanish-American War. At Gage's request Stratton, almost single-handed, had drawn the bill for the new Bureau. Then, one witness observed, he "mesmerized" the congressional committee with his explanations and demonstrations. As first head of the Bureau, Stratton built up its equipment and enlisted a brilliant scientific staff with a passion for research and experiment. Within twenty years he had given the Bureau a leading role in American industrial life: the transfer of the Bureau from the Department of the Treasury to the Department of Commerce in 1903 emphasized its dynamic new function.

When Stratton left the Bureau in 1923, the United States had become a world leader in techniques of testing, measuring, and standardizing. The Bureau was taking the initiative in testing all sorts of materials; it established standards for the new world of electricity, including the vast and controversial realm of public utilities, and it developed new precision techniques for measuring light and gas. The Bureau's brochures educated the consumer public on the qualities of household materials and appliances. "Usually, books on radio communication are fairly bristling with mathematics," Thomas A. Edison observed in 1919, "and I am at a loss trying to read them," but the Bureau's publication on radio was "the greatest book on this subject" he had ever read. During World War I, the Bureau experimented with substitutes for leather, paper, and textiles, and helped develop ships made of concrete. Wartime needs aided the Bureau's effort to persuade the nation's manufacturers to standardize, and after the war, the Bureau led a "Crusade for Standardization" as part of Secretary of Commerce Herbert Hoover's campaign against waste.

In the following decades and in each succeeding national crisis the Bureau of Standards played a leading, and usually a novel, role. In the Depression years the Bureau reviewed the NRA "codes" of fair competition and consumer standards. In World War II it sought ways to conserve petroleum, and joined the effort to make synthetic rubber and other substitutes for scarce materials. In the quest for nuclear power, and in the building of the atomic bomb, the Bureau provided essential research on uranium, developed a new type of fuse, and became integral to the success of the whole enormous enterprise. In the exploration of space, too, the Bureau helped in scores of ways, developing and refining instruments for testing and measuring in uncharted new ranges of dimension and in unprecedented extremes of temperature.

By 1970 the National Bureau of Standards, just outside the capital, had become a 70-acre shrine to the nation's concern with quantity, and its uses of quantity to define quality. There the high priests of measurement reinforced the nation's faith in the language of numbers.

22
Making Things No Better Than They Need to Be

THE SO-CALLED American System of Manufacturing, "the interchangeable system" which Americans had developed by the mid-nineteenth century, had sprung from a grand and simple new organizing idea which exploited American opportunities. It had been designed to produce large quantities of guns without numerous craft-skilled gunsmiths, and so made a virtue of New World limitations. A century later, the new science of statistics had provided a tool for shaping another characteristically American system of manufacturing in the mid-twentieth century. Few Americans were even aware of the revolution that had taken place, but the revolution was there, a symbol of the risks and opportunities of the quantitative approach to experience.

The earlier American system had been based on a new way of thinking about the "quality" of manufactured goods. For example, a Scottish engineer inspecting the Baldwin locomotive works in Philadelphia in the 1830's noted that "the external parts, such as the connecting rods, cranks, framing, and wheels, were left in a much coarser state than in engines of British manufacture" while "those parts of the engine, such as the cylinder, piston, valves, journals, and slides, in which good fitting and fine workmanship are indispensable to the efficient action of the machine, were very highly finished." Some of the visiting experts concluded that even the "best" American machinery was only "tolerably well finished, such as we would call second-rate machinery in our own country." What they saw confirmed their conviction that skilled hand labor really was indispensable for finishing machine-made products. They predicted, in other words, that in the long run the American interchangeable system, which aimed to make the machine do all the work, could not succeed, for its products were bound to be of poor quality.

But Americans had come to a new definition of what they meant by "quality." *Function* had come to displace *perfection*. When Americans judged a machine, a gun, a lock or a clock by its ability to do its job, all those fluted columns, ornamental arches, entablatures, curlicues and encrusted scrolls which adorned the best English-made machine were so much wasted effort. The more perceptive among overseas engineers did recognize what the Americans were doing. "In those American tools," observed James Nasmyth, the famous Manchester machine-tool manufacturer, when he visited Samuel Colt's pistol factory, "there is a common-sense way of going to the point at once, that I was quite struck with; there is great simplicity, almost a quaker-like rigidity of form given to the machinery; no ornamentation, no rubbing away of corners, or polishing; but the precise, accurate, and correct results."

In that first, early-nineteenth-century American system of manufacturing, there was already discernible the concern for economy which would distinguish the late-twentieth-century form of the American system. That first American system aimed to make products just good enough for their purpose. The aesthetic-that-was-not-functional, the ornament that was merely traditional, had no place in the American scheme. For Americans, a high-quality machine was not one that was polished and ornamented, but one that worked.

From the point of view of the foreign observer it seemed that Americans had actually made a system for building products that were "imperfect." To most English eyes, products that were "just good enough" for their job, that lacked the extra polish and ornament, fell below the highest standard. The late-twentieth-century American system went still further in outraging the Old World craftsman's ideal. For while the nineteenth-century system aimed to manufacture products that were *just good enough* for their purpose, the twentieth century actually aimed to manufacture products that were *no better than* they needed to be. Perhaps, some Americans now suggested, the interchangeable system had itself become wasteful, requiring superfluous and costly precision. The most important twentieth-century American advance in the system of manufacturing would come from this explicit American acceptance of a still newer meaning of "imperfection." And this was made possible by the rise of statistics.

THE NAME FOR this remarkable and little-celebrated American achievement was "Statistical Quality Control." By the mid-twentieth century it had entered the engineering vernacular to describe a way of applying statistics to factory organization that translated quality into quantity. Although the basic theoretical concepts were borrowed from abroad, their productive new uses were substantially American.

The man most responsible for making statistics into a tool for factory organization was Walter A. Shewhart. In 1924, while he was working as a young engineer in the new inspection engineering department of the Western Electric Company (which made apparatus for the Bell Telephone Company), Shewhart puzzled over the factory inspection records. His assignment was to find ways to use inspection data to produce a uniform product more economically. Before Shewhart's time, statistical sampling had been tried in factories abroad. But there the samples had been used to assess the quality of the *finished* product; in other words, to see how successful the production techniques had actually been. Shewhart offered the new idea that statistics could be used in production not only to discover how good the process had been but also to replan and control production while it was still going on. He transformed factory statistics from historical data into production tools, by making statistics an instrument of industrial prophecy.

Essential to Shewhart's way of thinking was an elementary new concept that had been developed abroad in the late nineteenth and early twentieth centuries. By 1909 the word "tolerance" had entered the mechanic's vocabulary with a new meaning—to describe "an allowable amount of variation in the dimensions of a machine or part." The idea behind limit gauges and the new notion of tolerance in the world of machine production was, of course, very much the same as that behind the whole interchangeable system. For while the new American system of machine production had depended on a quest for precision, on the use of calipers, limit gauges and other measuring devices, on machine-made objects shaped more accurately than any machine-made objects before, it also depended on a new mechanics of compromise. There had to be new ways of identifying the product that was just good enough. Behind it all, as the historian Eugene Ferguson observes, was the acceptance of the idea of *im*perfectibility, the idea that if *absolute* precision was actually impossible, it was, anyway, superfluous. For the only prudent industrial objective was to achieve a precision that was sufficient. The old adage about striving for "perfection" had to be revised.

To aim vaguely at a "better" product, Shewhart explained, would not necessarily lead to a more satisfactory product at a lower price. The first requirement was to set specific, mathematically defined and limited goals for each part of the product. And now statistics and the mathematics of probability could be used to reach the prescribed goal at the least cost. Essential to Shewhart's way of thinking was the idea of imperfection. He accepted the notion that "defects" were inevitable in the products of any system, and he insisted that before anything was produced, the maximum acceptable number of these defects had to be fixed in advance. Then the production could be organized so as to result in *no more* (but not necessarily less) than that number.

Shewhart's brilliantly simple notion, then, was to make a system out of imperfectibility. It was based on the common-sense fact that while "excellence" must often be a matter merely of hunches and intuition, specific defects can be counted and measured. Just as the first American System a century before had managed to make the scarcity of skilled craftsmen the incentive to an interchangeable system, so this second American System aimed to make the very imperfections of the machine the basis for more economical production. Shewhart had the courage to give up the quixotic quest for craftsman's "perfection," which American manufacturers had been criticized for not producing. Instead he tried to make a virtue of American limitations. Now for the first time a nation could economize its resources by organizing factories to produce the allowable tolerances and "imperfections," but no more. The new science of statistics had provided the techniques to make this possible.

Setting goals for production therefore first required the setting of "tolerance limits." Obviously the tolerances for a barn-door hinge were wider than those for a watch spring. And then, of course, there was the question of cost. In setting tolerance limits, Shewhart observed, "it is not only what the engineer wants, but what he can get, or at least get economically, that must be taken into account."

The pioneer treatise on quality control (apparently the first use in print of "quality control" in this sense) was by another American engineer, George S. Radford. In *The Control of Quality in Manufacturing,* Radford explained that until then, factory engineers had put "a disproportionate emphasis upon quantity of output, in the effort to effect economies." He argued that "increased output and decreased costs are more certainly attained when manufacturing problems are approached with quality, instead of quantity, as the primary guide and objective." But this paradox was only superficial, for Radford had used statistics to translate quality into quantity. His new system inspected "the flow of work in process." Improved measuring instruments in the hands of impartial inspectors would identify products outside the tolerance limits.

The object was to attain *minimum* standards at minimum cost. "Granted that the ideal standard cannot be realized in practice because quality varies continually, practical manufacturing or *working standards* must be determined. These vary from the ideal standard by certain differences or allowed errors, and by adding them to the outline design or ideal standard, a complete design is obtained." Repetition Manufacturing (in Radford's phrase) depended on "the compromise in setting tolerances." And this compromise was precisely what saved the manufacturer from costly uniformity-for-its-own-sake.

> The thought of quality as something that is continually shifting and varying, when translated into form for use in the factory, gives rise, among other things, to the whole subject of tolerances and limits. . . . no design is sufficiently complete for intelligent manufacturing purposes unless the limits for each and every governing characteristic are known.
>
> True manufacturing involves making a quantity of the same article, uniform within limits. In this respect it is the diametrical opposite of art work. The manufacturer seeks to make things alike, but the artist strives for the creation of things that are different and individualistic. The first system is far less costly; and therein lies the real value of manufacturing, because its product is thereby made more generally accessible to mankind. We make things alike because it is cheaper rather than for the sake of having them alike, although many secondary advantages accrue from this property of uniformity.

He gave the example of an inexpensive Ingersoll watch. Except for the crystal, the springs, and perhaps one or two minor parts, Radford explained, there was no special advantage, once the watch had been sold and was in use, in having any of the parts interchangeable. For it was not likely that any of the other parts would ever be replaced.

The prime purpose of an interchangeable system was "economical production." And that meant not wasting resources to produce more precision (or a narrower limit of tolerance) than was needed for a satisfactory marketable watch. If Americans failed to take this new view, Radford warned, the interchangeable system with its temptation to emphasize a theoretical ideal standard for each part of a machine could become a fetish. Machine-made uniformity, "precision" for its own sake, could then be as unproductive as the hand-finishing standards of Old World craftsmen. That would get in the way of the social object: producing masses of usable objects inexpensively. Radford warned that there was such a thing as precision over-kill. "When we generalize that it is best to make things uniform," he concluded, "we must remember always that quality varies, and that what we really mean is likeness, uniformity, or standardization of quality *within limits*. This, in a word, is why quality requires control."

OBVIOUSLY, THEN, there was a negative as well as a positive side to quality control. Since "quality" was a colloquial synonym for "excellence," then to make the "control" of quality an objective of factory planning had some disturbing implications. For quality "control" actually aimed, as engineering historians have noted, to insure that any product was not one iota "better" than it needed to be. What must we think of a civilization that aims to make its products just barely as good as they need to be, and not one bit better? "She's no better than she ought to be!" Was this the road to industrial progress, to the more democratic society, where the "quality" of objects was limited by the need to supply them to everybody?

Some engineers nostalgically lamented the rise of quality control as the decline of craftsmanship. "Much in modern design," one of them complained, "serves its purpose, but it does not preserve the grade of civilization that we are used to." Was there not a danger that products would be engineered to live down to the intentionally ambiguous claims of advertisers? Were these the perils of abandoning Old World aristocratic notions of quality to serve a New World democracy?

Quality control, shaped by Shewhart, Radford, and others, became a scheme for the more economical production of almost anything. Since quality control had to be statistical, they found ways to insure the "randomness" of samples; they designed new control charts and prescribed simplified ways of recording data. Although Shewhart had conceived his essential new ideas within a few days, he spent years elaborating and applying them. By the time his *Economic Control of Quality of Manufactured Product* appeared in 1931, the large design of his system was there, and fellow statisticians acknowledged that he had discovered momentous applications for their new science.

At the Bell Telephone Laboratories, which were responsible for improving the techniques for manufacturing telephone apparatus, Shewhart tried out his notions. Building on Shewhart's work during World War II, the armed services further developed techniques of quality control for wartime purposes. "Sequential analysis" (or acceptance sampling) used an ingeniously simple new way of keeping cumulative statistics to economize the whole process of sampling. This made it possible to arrive at reliable conclusions with the smallest possible number of samples and was especially valuable where the sampling had to destroy the object being tested.

Although the consuming public remained unaware of these developments, among statisticians and engineers statistical quality control acquired the dignity of a new science. Shewhart himself taught the first college course in the subject at Stevens Institute of Technology in 1930, and formal training spread during the war, when it reached some ten thousand specialists. In 1946, seventeen local quality control societies joined to form the American Society for Quality Control. Publications on the subject multiplied. After Shewhart's address on "The Future of Statistics in Mass Production" was published in 1939 in the *Annals of Mathematical Statistics,* numerous articles in professional journals applied Shewhart's techniques to a vast range of activities: to verifying punch-card operations, to anticipating epidemics, to checking on overtime employment, and to designing laws to protect consumers.

Even after "SQC" had entered the everyday vocabulary of American industry, and governed the mass production of nearly everything that Americans bought, its esoteric mathematical vocabulary still obscured it from public grasp.

Yet there was no better symbol of the problems and paradoxes of a democratic America. Democracy required a new lexicon, a redefinition of what was excellent, of what was good, and—most significantly—of what was good enough. The American Standard of Living had depended on new ways of making large numbers of objects which, from the point of view of the consumer, were indistinguishable from one another. But the progress in the American system of production in the twentieth century would depend on scrutinizing and measuring and defining the allowable limits of differences. Radford, Shewhart, and their fellows aimed to save Americans from the fetish of perfectionism. Their democratic and equalizing purpose was to make as many things available to as many people as possible.

In 1957 the standard textbook on quality control adopted Shewhart's motto, "The object of control is to enable us *to do what we want to do within economic limits.*" And the author opened with Montaigne's reassuringly democratic observation, "The most universal quality is diversity."

23

"The Incorruptible Cashier"

UNTIL WELL AFTER the Civil War, it was the rare merchant who knew the precise amount of his income. Few had an accurate or detailed record of sales or of receipts. Though the proprietor of a general store, hoping for scrupulous accounts, might actually instruct his clerk to record everything in the daybook "even if the house was on fire," the clerk did not like to bother. Negligence, illiteracy, and laziness made the owner's record incomplete. There were overwhelming temptations to pilfering, especially where sales were numerous, and where the salesclerk or bartender made change from his own pocket or from an open cashbox. As a result, the merchant seldom knew precisely how much he had taken in during a day, how many sales there had been at different prices, or how much leakage of merchandise he was suffering due to negligence or dishonesty. In a word, he lacked the facts he needed to figure his income or his profit.

The device which did more than any other to change all this was the "cash register," an Americanism which entered the language about 1879, and which helped define the boundaries of new statistical communities.

JAMES RITTY, son of an Alsatian immigrant druggist, was the principal inventor of the cash register. Running a café-saloon in Dayton, Ohio, he was surprised to find that though customers were plentiful, there were no profits. Ritty suspected this was due to his weak-willed bartenders, who could not keep their fingers out of the open cash drawer. Apparently Ritty was so troubled by the petty thievery which was ruining his business that he suffered a breakdown, and in hope of a cure he took a vacation trip to Europe. On shipboard one day he visited the engine room, where he noticed a machine that automatically recorded each revolution of the propeller shaft. Was it possible, he wondered, that a similar machine might somehow record each sale in a café or a bar?

Ritty cut short his European trip and returned to Dayton, where he and his brother devised a rudimentary cash register which they patented on November 4, 1879. Their first model simply showed the amount of each transaction on a dial. They soon improved this to a tablet indicator which elevated a small plate displaying the amount both to the clerk and to the customer. Ritty believed that publicly displaying the amount the clerk was expected to put in the till would reduce the temptation to pilfer. And this machine was called "Ritty's Incorruptible Cashier."

Later he added a mechanism which recorded each of the day's transactions on a paper roll so the owner could check on the amount in the cashbox and also discover the number and size of his transactions. Ritty and his brother began making cash registers in a room over the café-saloon. But they found the job too much for them. Ritty, deciding that he preferred to run a bar, sold the whole cash-register business, including the patents, for $1,000.

The new owner of Ritty's cash-register patents added a cash drawer and a bell which rang every time the drawer was opened. Now the machine displayed the amount of each sale, required the clerk to record the sale in order to have access to the cash drawer, and at the same time recorded and added all transactions for the owner. When Americans, using another new expression, spoke of "ringing up" a sale, they were bearing witness to the success of the "Incorruptible Cashier." Americans had thus found a way to give a new publicity to the shopkeeper's smallest transaction. Shopping now was a semipublic, communal activity, announced by the ringing of bells. Within a few decades, the official history of the National Cash Register Company boasted, this bell "like the historic Revolutionary shot fired at Lexington . . . would be heard around the world."

If this was only a slight exaggeration, it was because Ritty's invention had come into the hands of John Henry Patterson, whose genius for the higher strategy of salesmanship made the National Cash Register Company a model of American Go-Getting enterprise. Patterson, raised on an Ohio farm near Dayton, had answered President Lincoln's call for hundred-day enlistments in the Union Army. He graduated from Dartmouth College after the War in the class of 1867. Returning to Dayton, he started a coal business by buying coal at the nearby mines and selling it in small quantities direct to city consumers. Although he had plenty of cash customers, somehow he was losing money. Suspecting that this was due to petty pilfering from his cashbox, he installed one of the novel cash registers, and within six months he was showing a substantial profit.

One day in 1884 Patterson rashly agreed to pay $6,500 for a controlling interest in the shaky new cash-register enterprise. Other Dayton businessmen so ridiculed him for his bad judgment that the next day he offered the seller $2,000 to be released from his bargain. But his offer was refused. Patterson not only reconciled himself to his bad bargain, but brought to the prosaic world of cash registers a booster faith reminiscent of the founders of upstart cities like Chicago, Cincinnati, and Denver. And he proved an organizing talent comparable to that of Western fur traders and of the New England ice traders.

The cash register became Patterson's religion. To make a success of it at the time did require abiding faith. Businessmen had never heard of it, and when employees had the cash register explained to them, they resented it as a slur on their character. But Patterson preached his own Gospel of "Making Proper Financial Records," and he used statistics to help organize his missionaries to convert the country.

Patterson developed salesmanship itself into a new institution. On the principle that salesmen were made and not born, he opened what is sometimes called the first training school for salesmen. To an old school building near the Dayton factory he brought salesmen at company expense. He organized revival meetings in the form of regular sales conventions. Scorning the old rule-of-thumb high-pressure sales methods, Patterson taught that knowledge of his product was the salesman's best tool. At the same time he insisted on the importance of irrational factors such as the salesman's appearance; he sometimes provided a salesman with a whole wardrobe at company expense. He was adept at slogans, such as those which decried "Cash Drawer Weakness," and he composed primers of sales techniques. "There is in every store a need which, when uncovered, will lead to the sale of a National cash register." "You insure your life. Why not insure your money too! A National cash register will do it."

Patterson initiated the sales quota and the "guaranteed territory" within which a salesman received a commission on any sale, no matter by whom it was made. This motivated the salesman to develop good will for the company and also avoided a damaging rivalry among salesmen. For each guaranteed territory there was a statistically derived sales quota, based on population, bank clearings, and past sales records, which the salesman was expected to meet. The quota system, according to Patterson, would take the guesswork out of selling and put selling on a firm mathematical foundation so that production could confidently be scheduled. Quotas also were the basis for membership in Patterson's "Hundred Point Club" and his "NCR Legion of Honor."

With his slogan "It pays!" Patterson elaborated a costly program of employee welfare and entertainment. He provided company recreation rooms, he planned company banquets and picnics, he offered courses, concerts, and lectures in the company auditorium, he landscaped the factory grounds into an "industrial garden" and he exhorted employees to morality, health, and patriotism. When Patterson was instructed by his doctors to do daily calisthenics, he required the other factory executives to join him at five every morning. Active and energetic until his death at the age of seventy-eight, he was the beau ideal, if not the caricature, of the Go-Getting Salesman.

As cash-register sales increased, spreading across the country and around the world, the machine itself was improved in ways that reinforced the nation's number consciousness. Very early, Patterson himself had added a device for printing a customer's receipt. More important in the long run were improvements that automatically provided the storekeeper with multi-totals, with sales classified by individual salespersons, by kinds of transactions, and by departments. Businessmen now had reliable up-to-date statistics on their business, so they could accurately figure their profits and losses, and the sources of both. These data made possible a revolution in business accounting. More and more workers and employees began to think quantitatively about their activities, their products, and their income. They were putting themselves in countless new statistical communities.

ALONG WITH the cash register came the calculating machine. Efforts to make such machines reached back to ancient times and around the world, and centuries earlier had produced the abacus. In the early seventeenth century a Scottish mathematician, John Napier, made a rudimentary calculating device, the forerunner of the slide rule; later in the century the French philosopher-mathematician Blaise Pascal invented a device which used revolving dials to make combinations of numbers. Then in the early nineteenth century the erratic English genius Charles Babbage, who was Lucasian Professor of Mathematics at Cambridge University, became interested in calculating machines by way of statistics and astronomy. His effort to perfect an "engine of differences," which would calculate and keep a record of its work and then record the result, became notorious when it consumed £17,000 of government money.

The American calculating machines, widely used even before the end of the nineteenth century, were efforts to serve the daily needs

of bankers and merchants; and they were the work not of astronomers or mathematicians, but of mechanics. American inventors tried
to perfect a machine that would conveniently register the digits by
the depressing of keys. In 1857 a patent was issued for a key-driven
"Arithmometer" (not to be confused with Elizur Wright's calculating
machine, the "Arithmeter"), but the machine was not practical. The
quest for a practical key-driven calculator, like the quest for a typewriter, enlisted the energies of countless able mechanics and optimistic cranks. Finally a young machinist, Dorr E. Felt, while running
a ratchet-fed planing machine, was inspired to make a calculating
machine with a ratchet design. Using an old macaroni box, with meat
skewers from his butcher, staples from the hardware store, and elastic bands to serve as springs, Felt put together the first model of the
machine he patented in 1887. Called the "Comptometer," this was
the first practical key-driven multiple-order (i.e., with separate rows
for digits, tens, hundreds, etc.) calculating machine. Marketed by
Felt, it was soon in daily use at the United States Treasury and the
New York State Weather Bureau.

The need remained for a machine that not only would calculate
but would also record the items and print the result. And the solution
to this problem was the theme of one of the more spectacular industrial success stories of the age. William S. Burroughs, born in 1855 in
upstate New York, was the son of an impoverished maker of patterns
for castings and models for inventions. While spending long hours in
an Auburn bank adding up columns of figures, young Burroughs was
impressed by the drudgery of the work, by the frequency of mistakes, and by the constant need to check for errors. When his health
broke down and the doctor prescribed a more active life, Burroughs
went west to St. Louis, where he got a job in a machine shop.

At the age of twenty-six, prodded by his unhappy experience as a
human adding machine and inspired by the visionary inventors
whom he had seen in his father's shop, he determined to invent a
machine that would both add and record. In 1888 he patented a
recording-adder and persuaded several St. Louis merchants to put
up $100,000 for its manufacture. After costly experiments, Burroughs'
group had manufactured only fifty machines by 1891. But Burroughs,
according to one of his associates, "loved the machine better than he
did the dollar." Company legend records that when he found that
the machines they had made did not come up to his expectations, he
took them from the storeroom and hurled them out the window one
by one onto the pavement below. Nevertheless, he carried on his
work, and by 1892 he had patented an improved model that printed
each of the running figures as well as the final total. In 1895 Burroughs' company sold 284 machines, mostly to banks; the next year

the English patent rights were sold for $200,000. But overwork aggravated the tuberculosis which Burroughs had contracted in the bank in Auburn, and he died in 1898, before he could reap his profits. Within eight years, five thousand Burroughs adding machines were being sold annually. By 1913 the company had twenty-five hundred employees and annual sales exceeding $8 million, more than that of all its competitors together, and was sending Burroughs machines around the world.

The machine which Burroughs called his "Registering Accountant" was only a first step. Within a few years the pioneer Moon-Hopkins Billing Machine combined the typewriter with the recording-adder for speedier bookkeeping and billing. The cash register and the calculating machine had provided businessmen with their own private, accurate, up-to-the-minute statistics about their enterprises. The machines would be endlessly elaborated and refined, but the cash register and the calculating machine had already made possible an American system of merchandising and accounting as distinctive as the American system of manufacturing.

When automation became widespread and electronic computers became almost as common as the adding machine, there were new cataclysms in the jobs of Americans and in their ways of thinking. By 1967, only a half-century after the first commercially successful billing machine, the annual American production of cash registers and computing machines totaled more than $4.5 billion. When precise and up-to-date information was available about the *quantities* of everything, businessmen and consumers could not help thinking quantitatively.

24

Income Consciousness

AMERICANS WOULD FIND that classifying themselves by their income was especially congenial. But the significance of "income" brackets in the social spectrum was quite recent: a by-product of modern commerce and industry, with the new importance these gave to money and to the disposable, replaceable and attenuated forms of property. Before the nineteenth century the concept of "income" had very little importance in the Old World; it was used indirectly to measure property ownership or stake-in-the-community or as a basis for election reform. The English expression "forty shilling freehold" and similar tests of voting qualification came closer to being a test of property ownership than a test of income. In English literature in 1839, *Ten Thousand a Year* became familiar as the title of Samuel Warren's popular satirical romance; Dickens, Trollope, and other novelists of manners used income figures mainly to describe the newly wealthy whose financial worth could easily be estimated because it had been so recently acquired. "Millionaire" came into English from French (by way of Benjamin Disraeli's *Vivian Grey*, 1826) and soon appeared in American usage. But since that word referred to a person's "worth," the value of all his possessions rather than his annual income, it too was a characteristically Old World way of assessing wealth or well-being.

Among mobile Americans, a nation of recent immigrants moving from one place to another up and down the social scale, "income" was a more convenient and more universally applicable standard of measurement than wealth or property. Income was as close as one could come to quantifying the standard of living, and it provided a simple way of telling who was above or below the standard. But before Americans could be parsed into "income brackets," they had to know what their income amounted to, in numbers of dollars. In the twentieth century the American for the first time was actually required to know his income. Income consciousness, no longer merely a by-product of technology or of government statistics, became a civic obligation, under penalty of fine and imprisonment.

IN AMERICA the rudimentary notion of taxing a person's income, or his earning "faculty" (as it then was called), is found as early as 1643, when the colony of New Plymouth taxed persons "according to their estates or faculties"; three years later the colony passed a tax on the "returns and gains" of tradesmen and craftsmen. Other colonies followed. This "faculty" tax was actually rooted in the Middle Ages. It was not an income tax in the modern sense, for it did not allow taxpayers to balance losses against gains, and it was levied only on certain kinds of income. Sums received from this kind of tax remained small. Not until the mid-nineteenth century did anything substantially like a modern income tax appear. Between 1840 and 1850, six states introduced some kind of income tax. A Virginia law of 1843, for example, imposed a tax of 1 percent of salaries and professional incomes over $400 a year, and 2½ percent on interest received.

In Britain, William Pitt had imposed an income tax to finance British war efforts between 1798 and 1816, and the British later used an income tax to meet special and temporary needs. Following this example, to help finance the Civil War, Congress enacted an income tax in 1861, which would have brought in 3 percent of all incomes over $800. But Secretary of the Treasury Salmon P. Chase, complaining that the lack of statistics made it impossible to estimate what the tax might yield, never collected the tax. In 1862 an income tax was again enacted, to become the first income tax actually collected by the federal government. After an exemption of $600, the rate was 3 percent on income up to $10,000 per year, and 5 percent on income over $10,000. In addition to the basic objection that *any* income tax, "being inquisitorial," was unworthy of a free people, there were additional objections to the radical new principle of progressive taxation. The Confederacy, too, imposed an income tax, with rates exceeding 15 percent for certain classes of income over $10,000.

A special obstacle to a federal income tax was the provision in the Constitution (art. I, sec. 9, cl. 4) that no "direct" tax be imposed by Congress except in proportion to the population. To get around this objection, the first champions of the income tax had argued that it was not a direct tax at all, but rather an "indirect tax." The income tax for war purposes (reenacted with higher rates in 1864) was allowed to lapse when the legislation expired in 1872. By that time the pressure of patriotism and war needs was off, and a new campaign against the income tax had gained momentum. "The Income Tax," the New York *Tribune* declared on February 5, 1869, "is the most odious, vexatious, inquisitorial, and unequal of all our taxes. . . . a tax on honesty, and just the reverse of Protective. It tends to tax the quality out of existence." After the war, government finances improved, the national debt declined, and the need for an income tax seemed to disappear. The public appeal of the income tax, as Special Commissioner of Revenue David A. Wells observed in 1869, was largely due to the fact that only 250,000 persons in a nation of 39.5 million were paying any income tax. Still, that was an influential quarter-million, and the income-tax law lapsed on March 15, 1872.

The remaining national tax system put the whole federal tax burden on consumption. There was no federal tax on either property or income. Meanwhile, large fortunes were accumulating. By 1863, in New York City alone there were several hundred men each reputedly worth $1 million; two decades before there had not been twenty such in the whole nation. A. T. Stewart, the New York department store magnate (with a fortune valued at $50 million), reported to the federal government in 1863 an income of $1,843,000. This personal income was a larger proportion of the national income than $25 million would have been in 1929. As facts and myths about men of enormous wealth were featured in the newly popular press, as their exploits and their follies were widely advertised, public demand for an income tax increased.

These pressures, organized by William Jennings Bryan and others against "those Eastern Plutocrats," forced an income tax into the Wilson-Gorman Tariff Act of 1894. It was as the congressional champion of this tax that the young Bryan, according to himself "clad in the armour of a righteous cause," attracted national attention. A wealthy New Yorker, Ward McAllister (creator of the expression "the 400" to describe the social élite), appointed himself spokesman for those who would be taxed 2 percent on their income over $4,000. McAllister threatened to leave the country if Congress enacted the income tax. In a speech to the House, Bryan replied:

> Of all the mean men I have ever known, I have never known one so mean that I would be willing to say of him that his patriotism was less than 2 per cent deep. . . . If "some of our best people" prefer to leave the country rather than pay a tax of 2 percent, God pity the worst. . . . we can better afford to lose them and their fortunes than risk the contaminating influence of their presence. . . . let them depart, and as they leave without regret the land of their birth, let them go with the poet's curse ringing in their ears.

The income tax became law.

But the very next year the Supreme Court declared that the income tax was a "direct" tax, and so was unconstitutional because it was not apportioned among the states according to population (Pollock v. Farmers Loan and Trust Co., 1895). This decision provided Bryan his battle cry of "Judicial Usurpation!" in the presidential campaign of 1896, and so helped make the income tax a national issue.

It took a generation of muck-raking journalism, and such books as Ida Tarbell's *History of the Standard Oil Company* (1904), Lincoln Steffens' *Shame of the Cities* (1904), and Gustavus Myers' *History of Great American Fortunes* (1910), to persuade Americans that they needed an income tax. A constitutional amendment was proposed in 1909, and in 1913 the Sixteenth Amendment was adopted, empowering Congress to tax income from any source, without regard to population.

DEBATE OVER THE INCOME TAX had encouraged Americans to take an increasingly quantitative approach to their material well-being. For arguments over the justice of an income tax finally turned on statistics over the distribution of wealth and income. A study by Dr. Willford Isbell King, *The Wealth and Income of the People of the*

United States (1915), summed up the arguments for the tax and became the bible of tax reformers. The need for such a tax, he pointed out, arose from the increasing concentration of income in the hands of a few. In 1890, King observed, the richest 1.6 percent of American families received 10.8 percent of the national income, and by 1910 they were receiving 19 percent. At the same time, the 88 percent of Americans who received 65 percent of the income in 1890 received only 62 percent in 1910. According to his estimate of the money income in 1910 of different segments of the population, the poorest 65 percent of Americans received only 38.6 percent of the total national income, and had an average income of $197 per capita, while the richest 2 percent received 20.4 percent of the national income and averaged $3,386 per capita. When World War I suddenly and drastically increased the need for tax revenue, income-tax rates went up. Public debate focused more than ever on the quantity of income of different groups. The wartime Revenue Act of 1917, according to a leading economist of the day, was based on "democratic principles hitherto unrealized in fiscal history." This time the income tax had come to stay.

When all Americans were required to classify themselves in "tax brackets" in order to obey the law by paying their taxes, they became increasingly income-conscious. They were of course, putting themselves in new statistical communities. And thereafter when one American said he belonged in the same "bracket" as another, everyone understood. By 1970, American desk dictionaries included among their definitions of "bracket": "A classification or grouping; especially, one of taxpayers according to income."

As the century advanced, an increasing proportion of Americans was required to pay income tax, or at least to file tax returns. While in 1913 less than 4 percent of all Americans filed a *personal* income-tax return, by 1920 the figure exceeded 7 percent, by 1940 it reached 11 percent, and by 1945 it included 36 percent of the total population, which came to more than three quarters of the total labor force. By 1970 more than 60 percent of the total population was filing returns, which numbered some 75 million. The separate *corporate* income-tax returns, which numbered only 300,000 in 1913, exceeded 1 million by 1958 and 1.5 million by 1968. All the while, the federal income tax accounted for an increasing proportion of federal revenue. By the late 1920's income-tax receipts, individual and corporate, comprised two thirds of all federal tax receipts, and they remained the dominant item in the federal budget. The planning of government activities inevitably depended more and more on estimates of individual and corporate incomes. A slightly faulty prediction could produce an enormous deficit.

With the spread of income consciousness and the movement to

equalize incomes, the states adopted their own taxes on income. Wisconsin introduced an income tax experimentally in 1911, and in 1916 a New York State income tax displaced the general property tax as the main source of state revenue. By 1970, the District of Columbia and nearly all the states were levying their own income tax. The calculation of income required for filing the obligatory federal tax return provided a convenient basis for state taxes, and when states taxed income simply by assessing a proportion of the federal tax, they avoided the need to elaborate their own rules.

Among the oddities of American civilization in the mid-twentieth century, none seemed more remarkable to visitors from abroad than the scrupulousness of Americans in reporting their income for purposes of taxation. On the continent of Europe, in the Middle East, and elsewhere, it was a newsworthy event, and not necessarily one that improved a reputation, if a man of wealth filed a full and honest tax return. In the United States, however, even professional gamblers, confidence men, and gangsters (who were earning their income by violating state or local laws) took care to report their illegal earnings to the federal government to avoid the penalties of federal tax laws. Al Capone, the notorious gang lord and "Public Enemy No. 1," was finally brought to a legal reckoning by his failure to pay his federal income tax.

A new profession, that of Certified Public Accountant, attested the public need and desire to obey income-tax laws. In Britain in the mid-nineteenth century the first "chartered public accountants" appeared, to satisfy the requirements of the new Companies Acts of 1845 and 1868, and also to protect the public against a company's false balance sheets. Even before then there had been "public bookkeepers" in the United States, but after the Civil War, when corporations operated in a proliferating network of state and federal legislation, businessmen needed something more than a bookkeeper. Perhaps the oldest American accounting firm—Barrow, Wade, Guthrie, and Co.—was founded in New York City in 1883. New York laws in 1896 provided public examinations for candidates for the title of Certified Public Accountant. Other states followed, and a professional organization appeared in 1897, which held its first national convention in 1902. Still, the numbers of accountants and auditors remained small until the enactment of a national income tax.

The effort in 1909 to devise a corporate income tax that the Supreme Court would not declare unconstitutional produced an act that was so complicated that it created a new demand for accountants. But that act was never enforced and corporations actually were not pressed to keep accurate records of income until the Income Tax Amendment was adopted in 1913. The law passed pursuant to that amendment had been drafted with the aid of certified public accountants, who now were drawn intimately into corporate affairs but at first only to prepare tax returns. When these accountants became at home in the inner sanctums of large corporations, they not only shaped corporate accounting procedures but guided crucial decisions of policy.

The World War I excess-profits tax and the rising rates of taxation made the accountant more necessary than ever. By 1924 the Board of Tax Appeals ruled that certified public accountants (along with attorneys) would be the only representatives qualified to appear before them on behalf of taxpayers. "C.P.A." now designated the member of a potent and prestigious profession. Within the profession's first half-century, some 60,000 accountants were certified; by 1972 the figure had doubled. The total number of accountants and auditors serving American business had increased twentyfold, from some 20,000 in 1900 to nearly 400,000 by mid-century.

Even Americans in the lower brackets became the numerous clients of a national network of tax-advising services, of which the largest was H. & R. Block and Co., which by 1972 had 6,486 tax-preparation offices which prepared 7.6 million individual income-tax returns, and for these services grossed nearly $100 million. Up-to-date do-it-yourself handbooks for puzzled citizens, like J. K. Lasser's *Your Income Tax*, became best sellers.

THE NEWLY AVAILABLE STATISTICS of individual income made possible new quantitative ways of thinking about the welfare of the whole nation. Income statistics provided an arsenal for a generation of increasingly effective reformers. One of these was Isaac M. Rubinow, who had come from Russia in 1893 at the age of eighteen, then attended Columbia College and Medical School and began practicing medicine among the New York City poor. Suspecting that sickness among the poor was as much an economic as a medical problem, he turned to statistics and became a pioneer in studying the trend of real wages and the distribution of purchasing power. From detailed studies of incomes between 1914 and 1917 Rubinow concluded that while the money income and the productivity of workers had greatly increased, the purchasing power of their income had risen only slightly. Drawing on income-tax statistics, he showed that the workers were receiving an ever smaller share of the community's income. At first he saw these facts as an argument for socialism. "Things which are un-American today are very apt to become very much American tomorrow," Rubinow explained. But he gradually came to the notion that statistics could provide a new approach to all the risks of an industrial society: he argued that insurable risks ought to include not only industrial accidents but also sickness, old age, death, and unemployment. In his *Standard Accident Tables, as a Basis for Compensation Rates* (1915), he aimed to provide the foundation for wider social insurance. Rubinow urged new forms of insurance to reduce the risks of the poor and the aged, and he devised ways of incorporating these into American institutions, for events in Russia in the 1920's had disillusioned him with socialism. During the Depression of the 1930's he developed plans for state unemployment insurance, and he helped shape the Federal Social Security Act.

Within a decade after the passing of the Income Tax Amendment, a new phrase, "National Income," had entered the vocabulary of economists and was heard in the more sophisticated political speeches. The phrase and the concept were products of imaginative scholars in the new social sciences who were building institutions to gather quantitative facts and explore their meaning. What the new American law schools were to American faith in legislation as ways of shaping society (what Dean Roscoe Pound of Harvard Law School called "social engineering"), these new American institutes of economics were to the American faith in quantitative norms. In 1919 a group of brilliant practitioners of the new social "science"—economists Wesley C. Mitchell and Alvin Johnson, historians James Harvey Robinson and Charles A. Beard, and sociologist Thorstein Veblen—founded the New School for Social Research in New York. Their purpose was "that all scientific research, whatever its field of operation, should be directed not chiefly to the support of accepted ideas, but to the acquisition of new ones, and to the ways in which new knowledge may be applied to remedy existing evils and meet the ever-growing needs of mankind."

When before had a nation's pundits undertaken such explorations on a similar scale? The neutral language of numbers, using the novel vocabulary of statistics, encouraged free ways of thought. The chief statistician of the American Telephone & Telegraph Company in 1920 had led the way in founding the National Bureau of Economic Research, expressly to make quantitative studies of the public welfare. A widespread confidence in the healing powers of statistics was attested by the fact that the National Bureau's board of directors covered the whole spectrum of social philosophies, from a declared socialist to a representative of the American Bankers' Association.

Within a year of its founding the National Bureau published *Income in the United States: Its Amount and Distribution, 1909–1919,* the first comprehensive study ever made of the national income. The sober conclusion was that the wartime expansion of income had not been as large as was commonly assumed. Although per capita money income had risen from $319 in 1909 to $586 in 1918, the National

Bureau showed that the rise, in terms of 1913 prices, amounted to an increase in real income only from $333 to $372. The study pointed out that at the same time there had been a tendency toward equalization of incomes: the 5 percent who had the largest incomes in 1913–16 were receiving 33 percent of the total national income, but in 1918–19 they were receiving only about 25 percent.

The National Bureau of Economic Research was soon joined by other statistical researchers into the nation's welfare. An enterprise characteristically American in origin was the Brookings Institution, founded by a self-educated St. Louis businessman who had made a fortune in merchandising woodenware, and who then retired at the age of forty-six to spend his accumulated millions in philanthropy. Inspired by the example of his long-time friend Andrew Carnegie, Robert S. Brookings built the medical school of Washington University, which set a new standard for American medical education. Then, during World War I, when he headed President Woodrow Wilson's price-fixing committee, Brookings became interested in statistics and at the age of seventy he began studying economics. In 1928 he founded the Brookings Institution in the nation's capital "to collect, interpret, and lay before the country in clear and intelligent form the fundamental economic facts concerning which opinions need to be formed," and to supply facts to the people who shaped government policy. The Institution, independent of government support, became one of the nation's most useful and most influential interpreters of statistics.

Wartime urgencies had multiplied the government agencies that collected statistics. By the 1920's there was an enormous up-to-date fund of what Wesley Mitchell called "planning statistics." An important new source was the Bureau of Labor Statistics in the Department of Labor, which had been created in 1913. When the Depression of the 1930's came, officials in Washington were already quite familiar with the concept of "national income." A National Income Division was established in the Department of Commerce in 1932, "when bread lines were forming in the streets . . . to find out just how deep the Depression actually was." And so began the regular annual presentation of estimated national income by the federal government. In charge of these first studies was the pioneer economist Simon Kuznets, who developed the notion of "Gross National Product"; it was first published in 1946, and thereafter provided a new standard for measuring the American economy. Others, aided by Kuznets' calculations (for which he received a Nobel Prize), projected the measure back into American history to calculate trends. By the 1960's the abbreviation "GNP" had entered American dictionaries and was part of the American idiom, another everyday clue to the spread of statistical ways of thinking.

25

The Rediscovery of Poverty

THE RISE OF Protestantism and modern capitalism had some-how made a virtue of the personal qualities required to become rich, and so had begun to put poverty in a new light. Of course, there were always the "deserving poor," whose poverty, due to illness or misfortune, was no fault of their own. But the prevailing view in Britain and the United States well into the nineteenth century was that poverty properly concerned government only when a man's desperate economic condition had made him a public charge or a threat to society. The old "Poor Laws" aimed to prevent starvation and to forestall crime. Like the other rules of public sanitation, they were directed more at keeping life safe and pleasant for the well-to-do than at improving the lot of the impoverished.

Throughout the nineteenth century, as the historian Robert H. Bremner has observed, philanthropists actually directed their efforts at pauperism rather than at poverty. American, like British, programs to aid the poor were overcast by moralism and religion. Here the old-fashioned morality of self-help and hard work was reinforced by faith in New World opportunities. In America, of all places, poverty should be only a way station to comfort or even to wealth. "The best way of doing good to the poor," Benjamin Franklin had urged, "is, not making them easy *in* poverty, but leading or driving them *out* of it." It was an American axiom, then, confirmed by both fact and myth, that only a peculiarly unlucky man could not rise out of poverty if he had the will.

THIS INDIVIDUALISTIC VIEW, which explained poverty by personal failings and saw the consequences mainly for the individual, would not long survive the American condition. Such a view was alien to the rising American concern for a standard of living. And when individual well-being was assessed not in treasure but in quality of life and in opportunities for living, the poverty of the poor man became a misfortune also for his better-off neighbors. Were they not being deprived of responsible fellow citizens, of potential customers, of clients and patients? They too were losing the wholesome benefits of a contented, educated community. They too were failing fully to share the rewards of the ingenuity, industry, and fulfillment of fellow Americans. A proper American standard of living included, of course, freedom from threats of disease, violence, and crime, freedom from modern versions of "those poor who pester the streets of London" who in colonial times had driven the Georgia philanthropists to try out their philanthropy over here. In America, then, not merely pauperism (starving and destitution) but poverty (unfulfilled opportunity) was a social menace.

By the mid-nineteenth century, in Europe and elsewhere, revulsion against the old individualist view of poverty had begun to take the form of socialism and sparked a revolution against the whole economic system. While in the United States too a few revolutionary voices were heard, the more social view of poverty tended to take other forms. With some prodding and some assistance from abroad, the whole problem began to be redefined. The old problem of dependency—the social burden of those who could not feed, clothe, or shelter themselves—became the newer problem of *insufficiency*. By the beginning of the twentieth century, American concern had gradually turned from a specific worry over the public cost of keeping the impoverished from starving or stealing, to a more general worry about those who (in pioneer social worker Robert Hunter's phrase) were receiving "too little of the common necessities to keep themselves at their best." "Poverty," in Hunter's classic definition, "means lack of 'due food and lodging' and clothing."

An impulse from abroad came in the monumental study by a public-spirited English shipowner. Charles Booth's *Life and Labour of the People in London* (17 vols., 1891–1903) aimed to show "the numerical relation which poverty, misery, and depravity bear to regular earnings and comparative comfort, and to describe the general conditions under which each class lives." In England, one consequence of his work was the Old Age Pensions Act (1908). Instead of moralizing in his library, Booth had made a laborious street-by-street canvass of London districts to obtain up-to-date statistics, and he shocked complacent Londoners by his estimate that about 30 percent of the people of the metropolis were actually living in poverty. Seeking causes of poverty, he gave the lie to moralistic clichés by showing that, compared to the amount of poverty that was caused by illness and unemployment, very little was due to intemperance. In a word, Booth had demonstrated that the sentiment-ridden subject could be treated "scientifically" with statistics.

Americans followed Booth's lead. Drawing on their new wealth of statistics and the new social sciences, they sought to make a census of want in the United States. Scholars, ministers of religion, and politicians of all parties showed a new interest in those whom Lord

Brougham had called "the great Unwashed." In 1892, Congress took the unprecedented step of instructing the Commissioner of Labor (a Federal Bureau of Labor had been created in 1884) to investigate the slums of cities with populations over 200,000. What truth was there in the claims of the anti-saloon forces that alcohol was the most important cause of poverty? The new factual approach produced *Substitutes for the Saloon* (1901), a publication of a Committee of Fifty for the Investigation of the Liquor Problem, which drew on copious facts about recreational facilities in slum neighborhoods to put the liquor problem in its context.

A flood of specialized studies then collected statistics on the condition of the Negro, on the state of tenement houses, on child labor, and on the problems of working women. The movement to redefine poverty found an eloquent voice in Robert Hunter, who had served with the Chicago Board of Charities before working in the slums of New York City. His *Poverty* (1904), which H. G. Wells called "compulsory reading for every prosperous adult in the United States," was an instant success. He described the extent and the consequences of poverty in the United States by drawing on the statistics of pauperism, of charitable society caseloads, of pauper burials, and of wage rates. His shocking conclusion was that in a total population of some 80 million, there were no fewer than 10 million persons living "in poverty." Hunter's arithmetical approach was a far cry from the more traditional American view expressed, for example, by William Graham Sumner, who said that there was really no satisfactory definition of "a poor man." Sumner and other Americans feared that all easy definitions served only to cover reformist enthusiasms and "social fallacies." But Hunter's insistently statistical view—that the poor could be defined as those Americans whose income fell below an established minimum—had wide appeal. Others drew on the improved statistics of income, both individual and national, to give more precise definition to the plight of the poor.

In 1909 the Pittsburgh Survey, which scrutinized the lives of the city's workers in relentless detail, became a model for others. This new social-scientific brand of American philanthropy was supported by the fortune of a pioneer businessman. Russell Sage, born in a covered wagon going west in 1812, had almost no education. He started life in the grocery business and then was a collaborator in Jay Gould's sensational railroad manipulations. Toward the end of his life Sage became a philanthropist, and after his death his widow used his fortune to set up a foundation in his name for "the improvement of social and living conditions in the United States." A symbol of the new social approach to poverty, the Russell Sage Foundation aimed "to eradicate so far as possible the causes of poverty and ignorance,

rather than to relieve the sufferings of those who are poor and ignorant."

THE PUBLIC CONCERN for poverty, which had begun with a
few social workers, passionate reformers, and doctrinaire socialists,
broadened into a major issue of national policy by the mid-twentieth
century. After the Depression of the 1930's, no President could be
elected without a remedial program not merely for the starving and
the destitute but for all those Americans who lacked the essentials of
an American standard of living. Only a century before, the passionate
crusader Dorothea Dix had had trouble awakening a few state legislators to the predicament of "paupers" who, along with the insane,
were confined in almshouses and jails. In 1937, when President
Franklin D. Roosevelt in his second inaugural address described
"one-third of a nation ill-housed, ill-clad, ill-nourished," he sounded
a national alarm; and the nation listened.

The growth of the social sciences and the amassing of statistics gave
ever sharper definition to the statistical community of "poverty-
Americans." For example, *Social Class and Mental Illness* (1958), by
August B. Hollingshead and F. C. Redlich, showed from a detailed
statistical study of New Haven, Connecticut, that in the lowest fifth
of the population in the city there was three times as much treated
psychiatric illness as in the top two fifths. Moreover, they observed,
while in the top two fifths 65 percent of treated psychiatric illness
was for neurotic problems and only 35 percent was for the more
serious problems of psychoses, in the bottom fifth 90 percent was for
psychoses. These and other less ambiguous studies on diet, health,
and housing climaxed in the early 1960's in an organized public
concern that was without precedent.

This concern was focused in a popular book by the socialist writer
Michael Harrington, *The Other America* (1963), which used statistics
to prove that between 40 million and 50 million Americans were
living in poverty. Harrington defined the "poor" as "those who suffer
levels of life well below those that are possible, even though they live
better than medieval knights or Asian peasants. . . . those who are
denied the minimal levels of health, housing, food, and education
that our present stage of scientific knowledge specifies as necessary
for life as it is now lived in the United States." Harrington shocked
his readers with his persuasively quantitative definitions of "the
poor."

Income statistics were the raw material of these definitions. Distinctions were made according to family size, city and farm, and
region of the country. The poor, whom generations of Americans had

seen as a vaguely defined fluid mass on way stations to success, now had become a large, sharply defined statistical community which threatened to remain static. The new quantified definitions did not reduce the emotional appeal of slogans to help the poor, who became the new hyphenates; just as formerly there had been German-Americans and Italian-Americans, now there were Poverty-Americans.

"This Administration today, here and now," said President Lyndon B. Johnson in his first State of the Union message on January 8, 1967, "declares unconditional war on poverty in America." Congress established a vast antipoverty program, appropriated $1.1 billion for Appalachia alone, set up VISTA (a domestic peace corps), a Job Corps for dropouts, Operation Head Start, and a host of other projects. Cynics, recalling earlier short-lived American enthusiasms, mocked the "poverty industry." Some noted that the poor now were called the "underprivileged." Government agencies lent their authenticity to the new definitions, and gave an official reality to the statistical community of the American poor, even requiring "representation" of poverty-Americans on the boards administering antipoverty projects. But with traditional optimism, the coordinating agency, until its dissolution in 1973, was called the Office of Economic Opportunity.

In 1959 the Department of Labor surveyed twenty American cities to define a "modest but adequate" budget, below which was the poverty level. And in 1964 the Social Security Administration explicitly defined "poverty levels": based on figures provided by the Department of Agriculture's Economy Food Plan, these were designed to reflect different consumption requirements depending upon family size, age, and urban or rural residence. According to the Department of Commerce in 1968, an American was living in poverty if he had an annual income of less than $1,748 ($1,487 on farms) for a single person, less than $2,774 for a family of three members ($2,352 on farms), less than $4,706 for a family of six ($4,021 on farms). The *Statistical Abstract of the United States*, published by the Bureau of the Census, began to indicate the precise number of Americans living "below the poverty level." For 1968 this came to 12.8 percent (25.4 million persons) of the total population, down from 22.4 percent (39.5 million persons) for 1959. The Bureau's *Pocket Data Book for 1971*, along with figures on livestock production, steel output, and automobile registration, offered a chart of the "Incidence of Poverty." Income consciousness had become so prevalent that proposals to aid the poor were now sometimes stated as the need for a "negative income tax."

As the estimate of well-being became more quantitative, it did not necessarily become more vivid or more poignant. Harrington concluded his insistently statistical portrait of poverty in America by saying that even if there were ten million fewer poor than he had figured, "that would not really be important." At the same time that the United States undertook the most self-conscious and best-organized attack on poverty in all its history, some romantic and conscience-ridden young Americans, children of the comfortable middle class, were making an unprecedented effort to secede from the American Standard of Living. They hoped to share the "virtues" of poverty. And in this they were denying a dominant motif of American civilization which had been a gigantic program against poverty.

Antipoverty publicists in the 1960's, who generally defined poverty-Americans by the copious use of statistics, commonly observed that poverty in America was "invisible." This was another way of recognizing the spread of everywhere communities, new groupings of Americans held together abstractly, in common statistical categories.

26
Measuring the Mind

"INTELLIGENCE. *See* MENTAL TESTS." So learns the historian who consults the authoritative fifteen-volume *Encyclopaedia of the Social Sciences* (1930–35) to discover how American social scientists had come to think about intelligence in the early decades of the twentieth century. The new prevalence of statistics and the appetite for statistical community were nowhere more vividly expressed than in the twentieth-century American elaboration of techniques for "measuring" intelligence.

As early as the 1870's, the English geneticist Francis Galton, preoccupied with human differences, had urged the new study of "anthropometry" and the making of anthropometric records. In 1882 he opened a laboratory at the South Kensington Museum in London, where, for a fee, anyone could have certain physical measurements made, including tests of keenness of vision and hearing, and reaction time. The term "mental tests" was probably first used in 1890 by the American psychologist James McKeen Cattell to describe tests on one hundred University of Pennsylvania freshmen. These were tests on keenness of eyesight and of hearing, reaction time, after-images, color vision, perception of pitch and of weights, sensitivity to pain, perception of time, accuracy of movement, rate of perception and of movement, memory, and imagery.

Then, in 1891, Franz Boas, a young anthropologist recently arrived from Germany, under prodding from G. Stanley Hall, the psychologist-president of Clark University who was anxious to establish psychology as a useful science, took measurements of fifteen hundred Worcester schoolchildren, including tests of their memory. In the crowds at the World's Columbian Exposition in Chicago in 1893 a University of Wisconsin psychologist, Joseph Jastrow, found large numbers of subjects willing, out of curiosity, to submit themselves to psychological tests. By 1895 the American Psychological Association had set up a committee to promote cooperation of psychological laboratories throughout the country "in the collection of mental and physical statistics."

THE MENTAL TEST in the United States was a by-product, too, of two twentieth-century American institutions: mass education and the mass army. Both these expressions of a democratized society encouraged quantitative ways of thinking. The expansion of American public education and the multiplication of public high schools had created a vast new body of young Americans hopeful to enter college. While entrance to high school was automatic, or even compulsory, entrance to nearly all colleges remained selective. While the enrollment in American public high schools increased more than tenfold between 1890 and 1922 (from some 200,000 to over 2 million), enrollment in American colleges and universities increased only about fourfold (from 150,000 to about 600,000). This created a demand for new techniques of selection at the very time when a science of statistics had come on the scene.

As early as 1877, President Charles W. Eliot of Harvard, who had advocated the free public high school as a way to democratize education, foresaw the need for a new system of examinations. Only by some common system of examination could the colleges select those who would profit most from higher education. In the United States, where the subjects and standards of locally controlled public education varied beyond the wildest nightmares of European educators, the problem was quite unlike that in England or France where applicants to college came from a standardized curriculum. Since the federal government itself had no responsibility for education, only standardized tests by a private central organization could do the job.

The scheme proposed in 1890 by Nicholas Murray Butler, Professor

of Philosophy and Education at Columbia University, aimed incidentally to help shape school programs to college needs. "At that time,"
Butler recalled, "the public secondary school had just entered upon
its period of popularity and rapid growth. It was multiplying in cities
and towns throughout the United States and quite naturally found
itself everywhere in contact with the problem of admission to college. The colleges throughout the United States were going their
several ways with sublime unconcern either for the policies of other
colleges, for the needs of the secondary schools, or for the general
public interest." The recently formed College Entrance Examination Board in June 1901 gave its first examinations at sixty-seven
places in the United States and two places in Europe, to 973 candidates representing 237 schools. The curricula of the new high schools
had been inflated by courses for academic credit in art, bookkeeping,
band, stenography, journalism, printing, Red Cross, home economics, and scores of crafts, hobbies, and sports. But the Board tested
candidates in traditional academic subjects, such as English and
chemistry, and graded strictly on the academic scale of 100, requiring
a score of 60 to pass.

IN 1905 A FRENCH PSYCHOLOGIST, Alfred Binet, whom the
Minister of Public Education in Paris had appointed to a commission
on the education of retarded children, collaborated with another
French psychologist, Théodore Simon, in devising a metric intelligence scale. With his novel assumption that, up to maturity, intelligence increased with age, Binet tested numerous children to establish an average level of test performance for each age. Then, by
comparing any child's own test performance with the average, Binet
could distinguish a child's "mental age" from his chronological age.
Tests were standardized by assigning to each year-level the tests
passed by 75 percent of the children of that age, and these tests were
used for measuring variations in the intelligence of "normal" children. By 1908 the Binet-Simon tests had been translated into English
and imported to the United States. Then, in 1912 a German psychologist, William Stein, proposed dividing a subject's mental age by his
actual chronological age to produce a useful "Intelligence Quotient."
Lewis Terman and others at Stanford University revised and adapted
the Binet-Simon tests into the standard American "mental tests."
And the "I.Q." became a popular handle on the whole subject.

At American entrance into World War I in 1917, the urgent need
to classify recruits led to new techniques of testing. Two Army tests,
both suitable for administering to large groups, were designed by a
committee of the American Psychological Association to weed out

the mentally incompetent at one end of the scale and to identify the brighter "officer material" at the other. The Army Alpha Test was for men literate in English, while the Army Beta Test (with directions given in pantomime) was for illiterates and for foreigners who did not understand English. By the end of January 1919, the tests had been taken by 1,726,000 men. Although the results were not officially published until 1921, the information that leaked out during 1919 caused alarm: 47.3 percent of the white draftees and 89 percent of the Negro draftees had a "mental age" of twelve years or under. By textbook definition an adult with a "mental age" of under twelve was "feeble-minded." Was that half the American population?

The nation had only recently been aroused by respected psychologists to "the Menace of the Feeble-minded." In fact, the most vocal propagandist against that menace, Henry H. Goddard, was himself on the committee that had designed the Army Tests. It was Goddard who had translated the Binet-Simon tests; and in 1911, after testing two thousand normal children, the whole school population of a New Jersey town, he had revised the Binet-Simon scale for American use. Goddard saw the mental tests as the gateway to utopia, opening new worlds of eugenics and social reform. Attacks on his tests, he observed, "only arouse a smile and a feeling akin to that which the physician would have for one who might launch a tirade against the value of the clinical thermometer." As psychologist at the Vineland Training School, a penal institution for juveniles in New Jersey, he tested fifty-six "wayward girls," aged fourteen to twenty, who were out on parole. And he found all but four to be "feeble-minded." Then in a Newark juvenile detention home Goddard tested one hundred inmates chosen at random and found 66 percent to be "feeble-minded." He jumped to the conclusion that feeble-mindedness was the main cause of crime.

Goddard then popularized his dogma by a sensational book, *The Kallikak Family* (1912), which described the far-reaching consequences of the casual union of a Revolutionary militiaman with a "feeble-minded" tavern girl. From their illegitimate son (popularly known as "Old Horror"), Goddard traced a line of degenerates, prostitutes, epileptics, alcoholics, and assorted criminals. While the public was fascinated, Goddard protested that he had only offered a "scientific" statistical summary of the clinical record. The hereditary connection of "feeble-mindedness" and crime, Goddard himself explained, had long since been suggested but had, until his own work, lacked proper scientific support. In 1877 an amateur criminologist, Richard D. Dugdale, had also told a lurid tale of hereditary delinquency. In *The Jukes, A Study in Crime, Pauperism, Disease and Heredity*, Dugdale claimed that a single tainted family had cost the

state at least $1,308,000. In 1911 Dugdale's manuscript was acciden-
tally found, giving the real names of the pseudonymous "Jukes." A
researcher spent four years tracing their later careers and those of
their descendants: *The Jukes in 1915* concluded that half the Jukes
"were and are" feeble-minded, that the family's penchant for crime
continued, and that all the Juke criminals were feeble-minded.

To such "scientific" documents as these, Goddard added still more
statistics of his own showing the results of mental tests given to
juvenile delinquents and adult criminals. So Goddard sparked a nationwide campaign to combat crime by controlling the feeble-
minded. He received support from the Immigration Restriction
League and other nativist groups, who were using the crude statistics
found in the 45-volume congressional hearings on immigration to
favor laws to exclude all hereditary "undesirables."

Incidentally, about 1910 Goddard had invented and added the
word "moron" (from Greek *moros,* stupid) to the language. As a
result of his tests he recommended to the American Association for
the Study of the Feebleminded a classification of adult feeble-
minded into "idiots" (through two years "mental age"), "imbeciles"
(through seven years "mental age"), and "morons" (through twelve
years "mental age"). While others debated the sharpness of Goddard's definition, Goddard himself remained confident that his mental tests were measuring whatever needed to be measured, and that
if the legislatures would only act, they could accomplish wonders of
social antisepsis.

But what did it really mean, to say (as the Army tests had suggested) that half the American population was "feeble-minded"? Did
this perhaps say less about the American people than about the
usefulness of "mental tests"? Even before the Army tests, cautious
scholars had been troubled by doubts. They suspected that the Crusade against the Feeble-minded, by concentrating on criminals and
prostitutes, may have overlooked the large number of persons of
similarly limited intelligence who had become respectable citizens.
After the Army tests, as historian Mark Haller observes, a number of
the crusaders recanted. "We have really slandered the feeble-
minded," a doctor of the Massachusetts reformatory observed in 1918,
"Some of the sweetest and most beautiful characters I have ever
known have been feeble-minded people." Eventually Goddard himself wondered whether he might not have exaggerated the menace
of the low I.Q.

NEVERTHELESS, AFTER WORLD WAR I the nation showed
renewed enthusiasm for intelligence tests. Surviving the false alarm

of the Menace of the Feeble-minded and the popular prejudice aroused by the Army tests, the new brands of intelligence tests prospered as never before. And now they reached out to classify the whole community.

After World War I the College Entrance Examination Board, undaunted by the popular ridicule of mental tests, took a new tack. Noting the narrow range of attributes which the Board had tested in the past, in 1924 the Secretary of the Board pointed the future direction:

> Among the qualities in regard to which many colleges desire information and for which direct tests exist, although the Board has not yet undertaken to administer such tests, are the following—
> (1) Ethical behavior
> (2) Physical health
> (3) Powers of observation
> (4) Mental alertness
> (5) Ability to participate successfully in cooperative efforts or team work
> (6) Skill in laboratory work
> (7) Facility in conversation in foreign languages

In 1926 the Board administered its first "Scholastic Aptitude Tests," aimed at a test of "intelligence" that would be less tied to scholastic subject matters. During the next fifteen years the Board elaborated its system of examination in an effort to provide a more reliable instrument of prediction, on which applicants as well as colleges could rely. Then, in 1935, the Board revised its whole system of scaling and ceased grading on the traditional academic scale of 100. The new scale fixed the grade of the average college applicant at 500 and then distributed scores so that they ranged from about 200 to 800, in relation to the percentage of the random college-admission population above and below the average. Incidentally, these new tests had the advantage that instead of requiring costly trained readers, they could be scored mechanically.

By the outbreak of World War II the Board had developed techniques not merely for testing college-entrance subject matter, but for testing all sorts of aptitudes. On April 2, 1943, the Board administered its V-12 and A-12 tests for the armed forces to 316,000 young men at 13,000 testing centers. Experts agreed that this test of a homogeneous group was the largest and most important single exercise in the history of testing. When these tests proved successful, the Board went on to other tasks. Under a contract with the Bureau of Naval Personnel, the Board tested for 100 service jobs, which required the printing of 133 tests, answer sheets, and bulletins, to a total of 36 million pages of test materials. Then, at the end of the war, the Board administered nationwide tests for veterans returning to civilian life. Hundreds of thousands were seeking college admission under the G.I. Bill, or wanted their chance in programs sponsored by firms like Westinghouse or Pepsi-Cola, in the Foreign Service, at Annapolis or in the Coast Guard Academy.

Testing had taken on a new role that was nationwide and touched every aspect of American life. In 1947 the College Entrance Examination Board and other testing groups became part of a new Educational Testing Service. The ETS, pledged to develop "new services and new tests in areas where they are badly needed," applied its testing know-how to classifying the nation's personnel. "The vanishing continuity between school and college programs," the Secretary of the Board observed in 1950, made it more necessary than ever to rely on aptitude tests, which now by themselves seemed able to predict college success. Popular pressures to equalize educational opportunity posed a new peacetime problem of numbers. In 1951 about 525,000 of each college-age group, the Board's Secretary observed, "have an I.Q. of 110 or better and are, therefore, to be adjudged capable of doing adequate or superior college work." But of these only 210,000 actually reached college, the remaining 315,000 failing to get there apparently "because of lack of money or lack of motivation." While tests could presumably locate the qualified Americans who were not being educated up to their intellectual capacities, only a new nationwide system for financing higher education could get them to college. The twin objective was to avoid "wasted money" (from admission of students with lower than 110 I.Q.) and "wasted talent" (from failure to admit those with an I.Q. of 115 or better).

AFTER 1958, IN WHAT intelligence testers came to call the Sputnik Era, there was a new fear of academic waste, a frenetic quest for ways of finding talent and a short-lived new enthusiasm for academic excellence. Could Americans come up to the Russian standard? There were proposals for "inexpensive preliminary tests" on the Scholastic Aptitude pattern, proposals to create "a group of colleges which will be geared to student groups with ability levels from I.Q. 100 to I.Q. 115," and a new emphasis on "college guidance" (which by 1960 had become a distinct profession with its own association and its own journal). In 1960, after years of controversy, it was decided to release the test scores to the candidates. This was, of course, a significant new step in reinforcing public awareness of statistical communities of the mind. The president of the College Entrance Examination

Board, attacking the "taboo of silence," boasted now that the publicity for test scores was "a triumph of morality." He reported to an audience at Columbia Teachers College:

> There was great fear that students would have their values warped by learning their own scores, but I have learned from hearing my own children's conversation that SAT scores have now become one of the peer group measuring devices. One unfortunate may be dismissed with the phrase, "That jerk—he only made 420!" The bright, steady student is appreciated with his high 600, and the unsuspected genius with his 700 is held in awe. This is not exactly the use of College Board scores we had in mind when we decided to authorize their distribution, but it's possible to think of many worse, so perhaps we had better not complain.

As the century wore on, objective tests, and the "quotients" they provided, became raw materials for the newly specialized profession of vocational counseling and guidance, and for personnel management. And they were used increasingly in the effort to make "merit" the criterion for jobs in the Civil Service. "Intelligence tests, and the related aptitude tests," an expert observed in 1971, "have more and more become society's instrument for the selection of human resources. Not only for the military, but for schools from secondary to professional, for industry, and for civil service, objective tests have cut away the traditional grounds for selection—family, social class, and, most important, money." An increasing tendency to assimilate the nation's population (which now had been quantitatively assessed) to the nation's other matériel was expressed in a new tendency to describe people not as people but as "human resources." Textbooks on personnel management began to call themselves guides to "human resources administration."

In the late 1960's and '70's, as equalizing movements gained momentum, the quantitative approach to intelligence was attacked from another, unexpected quarter. Jefferson and his disciples had enshrined the ideal of a "natural aristocracy" in their early democratic credo. The greatness of the new nation, they said, would come from the new freedom for every man to develop his native abilities. Here, for the first time, society would have access to undeveloped "human resources" which Old World aristocracy, with its hereditary distinctions, had wasted. The new egalitarianism attacked "intelligence tests" not so much because they were culture-loaded or failed to rank people accurately according to their intelligence. The new thrust of their attack was on intelligence itself. In 1972 "The Case Against I.Q. Tests" was seriously argued by opponents of tests precisely *because* mental tests *did* measure "intelligence." They feared that any society that preferred its more intelligent citizens would lack the utopian egalitarian virtues. "Contemporary American society uses intelligence as one of the bases for ranking its members," a querulous critic objected. "We celebrate intelligence the way the Islamic Moroccans celebrate the warrior-saint." The United States Supreme Court enjoined a business firm from giving intelligence tests to its potential employees because they might be used to discriminate against Negroes. And in the temporarily fashionable enthusiasm for absolute equality, the science of mental testing became one of the most controversial of the social sciences.

27
From "Naughtiness" to "Behavior Deviation"

NOT UNTIL the late nineteenth century was it common in the United States to think of "children" as a distinct class of the nation's population, meriting and requiring special treatment. For most of modern history, the social and psychological meaning of childhood was vague; a child was, for all practical purposes, simply a small adult. The change in American thinking appeared only as "children" became a minority of the population.

As standards of health improved and longevity increased, the absolute number of Americans under twenty years of age rose from 17 million in 1860 to 47.6 million in 1930. At the same time the *proportion* of that youngest segment declined from 51 percent of the population in 1860 to 43 percent by 1900, and down to 38 percent by 1930. This decline in the proportion of "children" from over half to about one third of the population, as Robert Bremner has observed, made them "more visible and the particular needs of their condition were more easily recognized. So too youth became more self-conscious, more easily identified and more demanding of attention as a separate category in the total population."

While children as a class were beginning to claim special attention simply by becoming a new minority, other forces helped give "children" a new reality. Humanitarian movements of all sorts—to reform prisons, to improve the lot of slaves, to rehabilitate convicts (the movement of which General James Oglethorpe and the founders of Georgia had been part)—gained momentum after the American Revolution. Along with the efforts of Dorothea Dix and others in the early nineteenth century to humanize the treatment of the insane, the blind, the deaf and dumb, came efforts to remove orphan children from almshouses into institutions specifically designed for their welfare and education. Special asylums for deaf children were set up in Philadelphia and New York. A "House of Refuge," the first American institution especially for juvenile delinquents, was founded in New York in 1825 and was followed by others. By the 1840's there were institutions for needy immigrant children, and in 1855 appeared the Children's Hospital of Philadelphia, probably the first hospital in this country designed exclusively for children.

"Reform school," an American expression which implied a special attitude toward young offenders, had come into the language by 1859; and there developed a new branch of criminology, new institutions, and a new literature of "juvenile delinquency." In 1899 Illinois enacted the first "juvenile court" law (incidentally introducing another Americanism), and by 1912 twenty-two states had established juvenile courts.

In 1909 President Theodore Roosevelt convened the first White House Conference on the Care of Dependent and Neglected Children, followed in 1912 by the establishment in the Department of Commerce and Labor of a Children's Bureau, to "investigate and report upon all matters pertaining to the welfare of children and child life." Although federal legislation on child labor was declared unconstitutional (Hammer v. Dagenhart, 1918), state laws on the subject proliferated. More Americans came to see children as a special class with their own peculiar needs and interests.

WHILE THESE HUMANITARIAN MOVEMENTS focused on the children of the poor, on juvenile delinquents, and on criminals, another movement, rooted in the esoteric recesses of philosophy, bore fruit in thousands of schoolrooms and in millions of American households. The "Child Study Movement" in the United States was pioneered by G. Stanley Hall, a brilliant combination of priest, prophet, poet, and experimental scientist. Raised on a farm in western Massachusetts, he was the son of a sternly authoritarian Congregational father, who had determined to cast his son in his own image. To be prepared for the ministry, young Stanley was sent to Williams College. There he and his literary classmates formed a club for mutual uplift in which, as Stanley explained to his parents, "profanity, refreshments, smoking, drinking, impoliteness are contraband." After graduation he spent a brief period at Union Theological Seminary in New York City, where his course included mission work among "fallen" women to acquaint him with the evils of the metropolis. That missionary assignment, as Hall construed it, took him to see scandalous spectacles like "The Black Crook," a "ballet" in which one hundred scantily clad female dancers appeared for the first time on an American stage. After Hall went to see the performance again, he conscientiously reported to his parents that he "sat very near and this time was disgusted."

As Hall's interests moved from theology and philosophy to psychology, he was introduced by Henry Ward Beecher to a wealthy New York merchant who gave him $500 to study for a year in Germany. When Hall arrived in Berlin in 1869, he found German philosophy swirling with neo-Hegelian currents, but his own interests shifted toward science; he witnessed surgical demonstrations, and actually dissected a human body. After returning to the United States, he taught briefly at Antioch College, then went to Harvard, where he met William James, who had just begun to teach his course in physiological psychology. During another stint of study in Germany he was converted to the enticing new science of experimental psychology.

In 1883 Hall was appointed Professor of Psychology at the new Johns Hopkins University. There he jealously refused to make a place for either John Dewey or Charles Sanders Peirce, and he even managed to incur the enmity of the warm and tolerant William James. When Hall left Hopkins to found Clark University at Worcester, Massachusetts, in 1889, the new institution had been especially designed to explore the new frontiers of science. He resolved to make Clark the leader in the new science of psychology and in discovering its uses for education. In this he showed that he had an uncanny prophetic vision of two of the strongest currents of the American future: Psychology (a New Democratic Science of Man) and Education (a New Religion of Democracy).

Hall's experience abroad had suggested to him that reform of education might be the key to a grand spiritual reform of the United States. He saw how after the travail of the Napoleonic Wars a reformed system of education had helped build a new Germany. Perhaps education would be the new American religion, and Hall would be one of the Church Fathers. If so, the theology of this new religion would be scientific. Psychology offered both a scientific faith and a religious science qualified to reshape American institutions and to redefine American morals. The burgeoning sectarian variety—experimental psychology, physiological psychology, behaviorist psychology, psychoanalysis, to mention only a few—would provide dogmas and to spare.

There was something appealingly democratic about Hall's new

scientific faith. Christianity had relied on a ministry of the gospel, on sacred authoritative texts, and had enlisted faith in the authority and benevolence of a Fatherly God. But psychology, in Hall's vision, referred man to no Higher Authority (except perhaps the Psychologist). Its sacred text was experience and it made man a rule unto himself. Would you know what man *ought* to be? Discover, for the first time, what man *is*. In place of the "Thou shalt not's" of the Decalogue, psychology would substitute open questions: "What is man?" "How does he behave?" Psychology, the science of uniting the "is" and the "ought," was the supremely democratic science. For it referred all questions of human behavior not to any Higher Authority, nor to some traditional scripture, but to the normal behavior of men.

Psychologists, who were ministers of this new gospel, simply helped man discover what he really was, how he actually behaved. Just as Luther and the new Protestant ministry had striven to liberate men from a priesthood, from a Papal Authority on high, so the psychologists now strove to liberate men from the fears, the taboos, the inhibitions of an authoritarian Protestant morality. For moral rules and regulations, they would substitute *norms*. In this effort to democratize morality, G. Stanley Hall offered a foretaste of new opportunities and new problems to come.

"CHILD STUDY," of which Hall was the prophet, at first seemed an innocent and obvious enough subject matter. In America, were not schools the most flexible of institutions? If morals were to be democratized, were not the schools a natural place to begin? In American education within a few decades (as the historian Lawrence Cremin has shown) Hall and his followers would accomplish a new Copernican Revolution. The center of the educational universe would shift from the "subject matter" and the teacher to the child. Until his time, Hall explained, education had been *scholiocentric* (centering around the school and its demands), but now it must become *pedocentric* (centering around the child, his needs and desires). Before this revolution could take place, psychologists had to discover what the child himself thought and felt and wanted.

Hall's pioneer exploration, *The Contents of Children's Minds* (1883), attempted to discover what children knew and, also for the first time, what they did *not* know. Since the rise of cities, Hall observed, children were coming to school with an experience different and in many ways more limited than that of their farm-bred grandparents.

As novel as Hall's subject matter was his technique. He used four trained kindergarten teachers to help him draw up and administer 200 questionnaires. By 1894 Hall had devised 15 additional questionnaires, each on a different subject, such as doll playing or children's fears. At the end of that academic year he had collected 20,000 completed returns; the next year he used eight hundred workers to gather 60,000 more. The word "questionnaire" would come into the American language within the next fifteen years from child study and educational psychology, and largely as a result of Hall's work. In place of introspecting, like the great philosophers from Plato to Kant, or debating like the professors and schoolmen, Americans, following Hall, characteristically would advance their knowledge of man by finding new ways of entering into the minds of living men and women, allowing them to speak for themselves. The questionnaire was a kind of ballot, an application of the democratic suffrage to the subject matter of psychology.

Such data provided the raw materials for Hall's "child psychology," or the science of children's minds. The sheer quantity of these facts enticed him to an ever more quantitative and supposedly ever more "scientific" point of view. Hall set out to define "norms" for mental and physical growth. At Clark University he encouraged Franz Boas to gather statistics on the growth of Worcester schoolchildren, hoping in that way to set standards for "normal" growth against which subnormal or diseased children could be identified. These hopes were not quite fulfilled because Boas found such wide variation in rates of growth, but Hall's quest for norms was unabated. He went on in search of standards of performance through tests of children's sight and hearing and their ability to accomplish muscular tasks, and finally sought quantitative standards of "health" and normality. This led some of his opponents to charge that child study was a menace and was fundamentally antidemocratic because it encouraged the view that "certain children are peculiar or abnormal."

With his enthusiasm for statistics, Hall combined an extravagant romanticism. "Childhood as it comes fresh from the hand of God," he preached, "is not corrupt, but illustrates the survival of the most consummate thing in the world." The "guardians of the young," then, "should strive first of all to keep out of nature's way." In his "genetic" psychology, adapted from notions of evolution, Hall described the development of each child as a recapitulation of the development of the human race. From the Darwinian precept that ontogeny recapitulates phylogeny, Hall moved to the practical precept that psychology recapitulates history. The behavior of a "normal" child at any age had a certain sacred appropriateness. Each expression of a child's development was only a step to a higher stage, and so was neither "good" nor "bad."

In his "Children's Lies" (1890), for example, Hall objected to the traditional schoolmaster attitude toward truth telling. Lying, according to Hall, was not simply a vice but a complicated form of behavior, and its significance varied with the stage of the child's development. Most "lying" in children required not punishment but understanding. It commonly expressed the child's undervalued "mythopoetic" faculty, his quest for "easement from a rather tedious sense of the obligation of undiscriminating, universal and rigorously literal veracity." In children, lying was closely related to play, and the child's attitudes embodied the delightful naïveté of earlier stages of man's evolution. As Hall studied the child's fears and his ways of venting anger, he again concluded that they called for respect and understanding. Anger "has its place in normal development."

Hall's "stages" of child development were plainly transforming traditional morality. Parents and teachers were being prepared for a new way of thinking about "naughtiness."

Child study, as Hall prophesied, would also revise the subject matter in schools. "We must overcome the fetishism of the alphabet, of the multiplication table, of grammars, of scales, and of bibliolatry," he preached, "and must reflect that but a few generations ago the ancestors of us all were illiterate . . . that Cornelia, Ophelia, Beatrice, and even the blessed mother of our Lord knew nothing of letters." Foreshadowing the decline of grammar and the rule of the colloquial in twentieth-century America, he predicted, too, that grammar, rhetoric, and syntax would be displaced by the more democratic "language arts" and by public speaking. Language, according to Hall, should never have been taught as a formal discipline. The child should be encouraged to speak, and to speak his true feelings whatever they were, preferably in his own fresh idiom of slang. He must "live in a world of sonorous speech." He should be allowed to fight when he was attacked, as that was only natural. In a word, the child must not be confined in a strait jacket of adult morality.

BY 1902, WHEN the free public high school had begun to become a flourishing new American institution, G. Stanley Hall had gone on from child study to the study of adolescence, and he was ready with a new psychology to describe development during the high school years. In "The High School as the People's College" Hall pled for less attention to drill, discipline, skill, or accuracy, and more attention to "freedom and interest." For, he said, "the fundamentals of the soul, which are instinct and intuition, and not pure intellect, are now in season." He founded his view on a newly defined stage in human development which he called "adolescence." This notion, which was to become commonplace by the mid-twentieth century, was essentially (as the historian F. Musgrove has pointed out) a recent American development. The period of physiological change, from the onset of puberty to full maturity as man or woman, was the subject in 1904 of Hall's ponderous two-volume treatise: *Adolescence: Its Psychology and Its Relations to Physiology, Anthropology, Sociology, Sex, Crime, Religion and Education.*

This, like Hall's earlier works, was an intoxicating concoction of statistics and poetry. Using graphs and charts, drawing on countless questionnaires, measurements, and experiments, Hall defined the varying rates of growth of different parts of the mind and of different faculties at each age up to eighteen or twenty, when growth appeared to stop. "Adolescence begins with the new wave of vitality seen in growth," he rhapsodized, ". . . it is a physiological second birth. The floodgates of heredity seem opened and we hear from our remoter forebears, and receive our life dower of energy." The statistical community of adolescents, then, had to be given the respect and autonomy, the powers of self-development and self-government proper for any other community within the larger republic. "The most plastic, vernal age for seed-sowing, budding, and transplanting from the nursery to the open field . . . this requires an ever longer time during which youth is neither child nor man. . . . To prescribe for these years as if they were simply a continuation of childhood, or as if they were like the college age, minus a few years of rectilinear progress, is the fundamental mistake to which many of the great evils from which we are now suffering are due." The high school, therefore, "should primarily fit for nothing, but should exploit and develop to the uttermost all the powers, for this alone is a liberal education." It had to be a distinct entity, not dominated by the "needs" of college, but instead "the defender of this age against aggression," making its mission "how best to serve one unique age of life, and thereby do the greatest good to the community and to their pupils." Through the high school, the United States could become not merely politically but also psychologically a federal republic: each age and stage (including the neglected states of childhood and adolescence) would be properly respected and allowed to fulfill its peculiar desires.

This "invention of adolescence" in the early twentieth century was the product of American circumstances. Compulsory public education was extended up to age sixteen, for many reasons, including the fact that industry was finding child labor less profitable. Then special institutions for "juvenile delinquency" appeared. Perhaps the nation would never recover from its idealization of adolescence, its new tendency to treat "youth" as a separate right-entitled entity, a new American estate within the Union. In the late 1960's and early 1970's some adolescents themselves, encouraged by their teachers and parents, organized against the very notion of a school. They treated *any* institutionalized education, in fact any institution, as oppressive. Students themselves in unamiable hyperbole called all American schools prisons, and they wrote of "The Student as Nigger." By 1970 there appeared in Washington a bizarre new youth lobby opposing schools, publishing a biweekly newsletter, *FPS (the letters don't stand for anything)*. And at least a few solemn scholars were suggesting that such movements might be a logical expression of the United Nations Universal Declaration of Human Rights.

THE NEW STATISTICAL COMMUNITIES of the young reached beyond the school into the home and elsewhere. Child study, which was reshaping American schools, began to reshape the American family. Before the mid-twentieth century, new democratic notions of the autonomy of the child were intervening in the traditional relations of parents and children.

Arnold L. Gesell, who had become a disciple of Hall at Clark University, was the pioneer. Reaching down to the "preschool years," Gesell would transform the attitudes of parents much as Hall and others had changed the attitudes of teachers. After experience as an elementary school teacher and settlement-house worker, Gesell became interested in the problems of backward children and made a mental-test survey of New Haven elementary schools. (His title of this study, *Exceptional Children and Public School Policy* [1921], was an early American usage of the democratic euphemism "exceptional" to describe the mentally deficient.) In 1911, he founded a psychoclinic for children, the Yale Clinic of Child Development, which he directed until 1948.

Gesell focused his attention on the years when the infant could be neither tested by questionnaire nor interviewed. For the psychologists those years had been a no man's land for which there was little reliable clinical information. But Gesell developed ingenious photographic techniques, using a two-way-mirror arrangement. He and his helpers then devised a novel observation dome; shaped like an astronomical observatory, it was made of finely perforated material painted white on the inside, and it could be rotated while a narrow slot permitted lateral and vertical positions for a Pathé 35-millimeter movie camera. The child inside the dome, under the cool illumination of newly devised Cooper-Hewitt lamps, could not see that he was being observed. In this way each child's behavior could be recorded for close comparison with the behavior of other children of the same age.

Gesell's aim was to record and to analyze the "normative" progress of the infant's development. To supplement the observation dome, Gesell arranged a homelike studio for a more naturalistic photographic survey of the infant's day while the mother was present and caring for the child. Gesell now noted the infant's every move, his sleeping, waking, feeding, bathing, his play, his social behavior and all his other bodily activities. Two years' observation produced his *Atlas of Infant Behavior* (1934), with 3,200 action photographs offering for the first time norms on infant behavior at every hour and every age.

The meaning of all this for the American family began to reach the general public in 1943 when Gesell, with his assistant Frances Ilg, published *The Infant and Child in the Culture of Today: The Guidance of Development in Home and Nursery School*. The phrase "in the Culture of Today" was by no means superfluous. Written during World War II, the book was repetitiously explicit on the relation between democracy and the study of child development. The infant, like all other American citizens, should be preserved from "totalitarian" government and, at long last, should be given his autonomy. "The concept of democracy . . . ," his opening chapter on "The Family in a Democratic Culture" explained, "has far-reaching consequences in the rearing of children. Even in early life the child must be given an opportunity to develop purposes and responsibilities which will strengthen his own personality. Considerate regard for his individual characteristics is the first essential. . . . Only in a democratic climate of opinion is it possible to give full respect to the psychology of child development. Indeed the further evolution of democracy demands a much more refined understanding of infants and preschool children than our civilization has yet attained." The bulk of the book, then, was "a factual statement of the mental growth characteristics of the first five years of life." Facts collected around "age norms" and "nodal ages" (the periods of "relative equilibrium in the progressions toward maturity") from four weeks to five years provided a "Behavior Profile" and a description of a typical "Behavior Day."

Before Gesell, the American parent had no authoritative way of knowing what to expect of his infant. Of course there were rules of thumb about when the infant might be expected to crawl, to walk, to talk. There were grandparents, and there were neighbors' children to compare yours to. But now Gesell gave the parent a catalogue and a calendar of norms: all the kinds of behavior that might be expected, including the hours of waking and sleeping, patterns of crying and eating, and even the moving of fingers and toes.

Babies pass through similar stages of growth, but not on the same time table. Variations are particularly common in postural behavior. For example, we observed five healthy babies, all of whom are now intelligent school children in their teens. At 40 weeks of age, one of these babies was backward in locomotion; one was advanced. The other three were near average. Baby ONE *"swam"* on his stomach without making headway. Baby TWO *crawled.* Baby THREE *creep-crawled.* Baby FOUR *crept on hands and knees.* Baby FIVE *went on all fours.* There were special reasons why Baby ONE was behind schedule in this particular item. Her general development in language, adaptive and personal-social behavior was quite satisfactory. It would have been regrettable if the mother of Baby ONE had worried unduly over this bit of retardation. Likewise the mother of Baby FIVE had no reason to be unduly elated, since the total behavior picture was near average expectation.

From this example it is clear that age norms and normative character sketches always need critical interpretation. They are useful not only in determining whether a child's behavior is near ordinary expectations, but also whether the behavior is well-balanced in the four major fields (motor, adaptive, language, and personal-social). It is especially desirable that there be no deviations in the field of personal-social behavior. If there are extreme defects or deviations in any field of behavior, the advice of the family physician may be sought and a specialist consulted.

The thrust of Gesell's work was to provide the parent a new kind of standard, distilled from thousands of hours of scientific observation by experts, and from countless precise statistics.

THIS STANDARD IMPLIED a new attitude not only toward behavior, but also toward "misbehavior." What was proper in a child's behavior had, of course, traditionally been governed by moral rules and "Thou shalt not's." "Conceived as a growth mechanism," Gesell warned, "disequilibrium (so often associated with 'naughty' behavior) takes on a less moralistic aspect. This form of disequilibrium is a transitional phase, during which the organism is creating a new ability or achieving a reorientation of some kind. It is a phase of *innovation.*" The child whom the grandparent might have called "naughty," the mid-twentieth-century American reader of Gesell would now say was simply showing "behavior deviations." For, Gesell explained, "In a sense all children are problem children, because none can escape the universal problem of development which always presents some difficulties. On the other hand, there are few forms of malbehavior which are not in history and essence a variation or deflection of normal mechanisms."

Gesell was full of good common sense, reminding the parent, as all parents needed reminding, that his baby was not the first infant on earth. Much of what he offered in the solemn jargon of psychology was only the historian's reminder: the world had been going on for some time, and parents had always faced similar problems. But Gesell gave this banal message a new character. He set a different direction for the way parents thought of their relations with their children. Instead of looking to rules of thumb, the old saws and moral exhortations, the parent was now urged to look to scientifically established statistical norms.

Some of the problems of this new world of norms were suggested by Gesell:

> Then there is the story about the very modern boy, not much higher than a table, who wore a pair of horn-rimmed spectacles. A kindly lady leaned over and asked him tactfully, "How old are you, my little boy?" He removed his horn-rimmed spectacles, and reflectively wiped them. "My psychological age, madam, is 12 years; my social age is 8 years; my moral age is 10 years; my anatomical and physiological ages are respectively 6 and 7; but I have not been apprised of my chronological age. It is a matter of relative unimportance." Thereupon he restored his horn-rimmed spectacles.

Gesell's book was not meant for every parent. But it had a remarkable popular success, going through twelve printings in a single year. And these new ways of thinking about child rearing were soon brilliantly translated into everyday language reaching millions. In 1946 Dr. Benjamin Spock, a New Haven–born pediatrician-psychiatrist with a wide practical experience, produced the *Common Sense Book of Baby and Child Care*. In its inexpensive paperback editions it went through some thirty reprintings in ten years, and became Everybody's Guide to Raising a Family. Spock warned against old wives' remedies and urged parents to be guided by their own child's development. Generally following Gesell's notion of a "self-demand" feeding schedule, Spock urged the mother to "be flexible and adjust to the baby's needs and happiness." While the book was by no means revolutionary, reviewers agreed that it "interprets the best in modern thinking." Now every parent had an easy path into the new world of norms.

This world brought its own problems for twentieth-century American parents. Who could forget the Ten Commandments and all that one had been taught about "right" and "wrong"? But once enlightened with "norms" describing how infants or adolescents usually behaved, parents could no longer think by old-fashioned rules. A democratic society was committed to take account of what every person, from Gesell's "quasi-dormant neonate" on up, naturally and spontaneously wanted.

28

Statistical Morality

IN WESTERN EUROPE the last years of the nineteenth century and the early years of the twentieth century brought new attitudes toward sex among a vanguard few. By 1900 Sigmund Freud had published his basic works in psychoanalysis. In 1909, when G. Stanley Hall brought Freud, who was then still slightly disreputable in European scientific circles, to a conference at Clark University, he caused a stir, but he helped make Freud more respectable in America than he was in his home country. As part of his child study and his discovery of adolescence, Hall himself had described the development of sexuality, and had urged sex education in the schools.

But Hall's discussions of sex were enshrouded in a saccharine polysyllabic mist, which even his fellow psychologists called unctuous. "In the most unitary of all acts," he wrote of sexual intercourse, "which is the epitome and pleroma of life, we have the most intense of all affirmations of the will to live and realize that the only true God is love, and the center of life is worship. Every part of mind and body participates in a true pangenesis. The sacrament is the annunciation hour, with hosannas which the whole world reflects. Communion is fusion and beatitude. It is the supreme hedonic narcosis, a holy intoxication. . . ." At the same time Hall urged that the study of sex must become more objective.

THE LANDMARK ON the way to a more scientific study of sex was the work of the English man of letters Havelock Ellis, who spent much of his life trying to liberate the English-reading world from its Victorian sexual prejudices. Ellis, like Hall after him, combined science and poetry in his effort to open windows to the wonderful variety of human sexual experience. When the first volume of Ellis' *Studies in the Psychology of Sex* appeared in England in 1897 there was a prosecution for obscenity, and publication was transferred to the United States. By 1910 Ellis had published five more volumes, and a seventh was added in 1928. The work was a wide-ranging collection of examples of human sexual behavior, including numerous phenomena (eonism, undinism, kleptolagnia), the very names of which were a mystery. Ellis treated the taboo subject of autoerotism, and compared the sexual experiences of men and women. His books helped make sexual topics discussable in academic and intellectual circles. But the books themselves remained on the shelves of esoterica, and were readily accessible only to doctors and lawyers. Ellis' themes were the unsuspected variety of sexual experience, the subtle variations of sexual experience from person to person, and the wide range of sexual activity (including those generally considered erratic or taboo) among "normal" persons.

The moral, if there was a moral, to Ellis' books was that of all human activities, sex was the least amenable to moral prescriptions or to generalizations about "normality." The motives of Ellis' work remain unclear. All four of his sisters died spinsters and it has been suggested that Ellis' own interest arose from his sexual inadequacy. But the results of his work are less uncertain. He challenged traditional sexual morality by showing how unrealistic were the pious prescriptions and chaste pretensions of teachers, preachers, and doctors, and how naïve it was to be glib about what was "normal."

The contribution of the American pioneer in sexual research turned out to be quite the opposite. The effect, by no means the intention, of the work of Alfred C. Kinsey was to establish new norms of sexual behavior. Kinsey brought quantitative techniques to sexual research and so gave a new, scientifically authenticated prestige to these norms. Only gradually was he recognized as a social scientist of great stature. Like Hall, Kinsey was raised in a strict, moralistic family. Kinsey's Methodist father was so observant of the Sabbath that he would not permit the family to ride to church on Sunday, even with the minister; Sunday milk deliveries were not permitted at the house, and the whole family was required to attend Sunday School, morning services, and evening prayer meeting. After graduating from Bowdoin College in Maine, Kinsey received a Ph.D. in entomology from Harvard in 1920. For his two-volume study of the gall wasp, *Cynips* (1930, 1936), which established him as one of the leading geneticists of the day, Kinsey had gathered some four million specimens, and so had become accustomed to collecting and interpreting statistical data.

During the late 1930's, American colleges were introducing courses in sex education and marriage. This interest had been stirred by Hall's studies of adolescence, by the recently translated works of Freud, by the new profession of psychoanalysis, and by the pioneer clinical studies of Dr. Robert Latou Dickinson. While he practiced gynecology in Brooklyn and Manhattan from 1882 to 1924, Dr. Dickinson had kept careful records of more than five thousand patients, from which he published *A Thousand Marriages* (1932) and *The Single Woman* (1934). These epochal books provided valuable new information on female physiology, fertility, and sterility.

In 1938, when Indiana University decided to move with the times and to offer a noncredit course on marriage, Kinsey was put in charge. As the happily married father of four children and as an eminent biologist of unquestioned personal morality, Kinsey was the ideal choice. The only earlier evidence of Kinsey's attitudes was in 1927 when a special convocation of the male faculty considered disciplinary action against two male student editors of the literary magazine for printing the indecent phrase "phallic worship on campus." The professor of classics had to be called on to explain the meaning of the phrase, and Kinsey had unsuccessfully defended the students.

Kinsey, however, was no reformer but simply a biologist. When meetings were held to plan the course on marriage, Kinsey heard a female faculty member recall what had happened elsewhere in a course on the subject some years before. A woman doctor had given information that was "veiled and garbled, with no real value except to frighten the weak. A regular staff had to be on hand to carry out the ones who fainted each time." Kinsey's course was different. And at the end he asked students to fill out questionnaires about their own experience to guide him for the future.

As a biologist experienced with quantitative data, Kinsey had been appalled at the lack of statistical facts about human sexual behavior. He was encouraged by the pioneer work of a few biologists like Dr. Raymond Pearl of Johns Hopkins (who had made studies of the frequency of sexual intercourse and of male sexual potency), who came to lecture at Bloomington on "Man and the Animal." But the more Kinsey saw of the vast ignorance about the subject the more determined he became to try to collect a body of useful knowledge. As he turned his scientific focus from the reproductive behavior of gall wasps to the sexual behavior of men and women, he showed the same voracity for facts. "The technique we are using in this study," he insisted, "is definitely the same as the technique in the gall wasp study."

Kinsey spared no trouble in training his interviewers and teaching them to avoid "loading" their questions. His interviewer was instructed to go down an exhaustive list of all kinds of sexual activities and ask each person about all of them. "It is important to look the subject squarely in the eye," Kinsey advised, "while giving only a minimum of attention to the record that is being made. People understand each other when they look directly at each other." Since "evasive terms invite dishonest answers," Kinsey's interviewers never used euphemisms. "We always assume that everyone has engaged in every type of activity. Consequently we always begin by asking *when* they first engaged in such activity. This places a heavier burden on the individual who is inclined to deny his experience; and since it becomes apparent from the form of our question that we would not be surprised if he had had such experience, there seems to be less reason for denying it." Interviews were recorded in a code known only to Kinsey and the interviewer.

Kinsey's goal was to secure 100,000 sex histories. At the time of his death there had been a total of 17,500 interviews, of which Kinsey himself had recorded more than 7,000. That amounted, during the period of his interviewing, to an average of two per day every day in the week for ten years. During the years of his sex research, Kinsey worked more than twelve hours a day and never took a vacation. In 1956, when he was sixty-two and had had two heart attacks, his doctors warned him to rest. But they could do no more than persuade him to an eight-hour day, and he died that year of overwork.

Sexual Behavior in the Human Male, by Kinsey and his two col-laborators, was published in January 1948. A market research firm had given the publishers their "considered scientific opinion," based on an opinion poll, that the book would not sell well. Within three weeks after publication it was on the best-seller list, where it stayed for twenty-seven weeks. By March the book was in its seventh print-ing, having sold 100,000 copies. Overnight, Kinsey became a celeb-rity, his name a popular synonym for "startling revelations" about the secret places of American life.

But critics and defenders agreed that this was a pioneer effort to quantify human sexual behavior. "An accumulation of scientific fact completely divorced from questions of moral value and social cus-tom" was the book's avowed purpose. "Practicing physicians find thousands of their patients in need of such objective data. Psychia-trists and analysts find that a majority of their patients need help in resolving sexual conflicts that have arisen in their lives." Earlier scholars, such as Ellis, Freud, Stekel, and Krafft-Ebing, had provided individual sex histories to help the public toward a scientific point of view. At the outset of his book, Kinsey explained:

> But none of the authors of the older studies, in spite of their keen insight into the meanings of certain things, ever had any precise or even approximate knowledge of what average people do sexually. They ac-cumulated great bodies of sexual facts about particular people, but they did not know what people in general did sexually. They never knew what things were common and what things were rare, because their data came from the miscellaneous and usually unrepresentative persons who came to their clinics. . . . The present study is designed as a first step in the accumulation of a body of scientific fact that may provide the bases for sounder generalizations about the sexual behavior of cer-tain groups, and, some day, even of our American population as a whole.

The book showed marked differences in sexual behavior patterns between males of different social, educational, and economic levels, between groups born in different decades and those with different degrees of religious belief. Kinsey established the almost universal incidence of masturbation in young males (which pseudoscientific folklore had made the presumed cause of "masturbatory insanity"), and he found the peak of male sexual activity in the late teens. Taboo forms of sexual activity proved to be much more widespread than had been presumed. Instead of simply classifying people as either heterosexual or homosexual, Kinsey had set up a new heterosexual-homosexual rating scale as a continuum on which interviewers placed each individual.

THE COMMISSION ON Statistical Standards of the American Statistical Association reviewed Kinsey's statistical methods and reported its "overall favorable" impression. Comparing Kinsey and his collaborators with earlier sex researchers, the commission found them "superior to all others in the systematic coverage of their material, in the number of items which they covered, in the composition of their sample . . . in the number and variety of methodological checks which they employed, and in their statistical analyses. . . . their interviewing was of the best."

The public response was much as might have been expected. "It is impossible to estimate the damage this book will do," inveighed a well-known minister, "to the already deteriorating morals of America." College presidents and some gynecologists joined the attack with high emotion. But once the "guilty" facts were out, there was no way of erasing them from the American consciousness. Never again would American thinking about sexual activity be quite the same.

Five years later, in 1953, Kinsey and his staff published *Sexual Behavior in the Human Female*. Within ten days there were 185,000 copies in print, and it, too, was for many weeks on the best-seller list. The techniques in this study were the same, but Kinsey had benefited from some criticisms of his statistical method. The second book offered new facts on the frequency of various kinds of sexual activity, on male-female similarities and on differences in sexual behavior and response, and suggested a surprisingly low rate of frigidity in the female. Again, as might have been expected, Kinsey and the book were attacked, but now with unprecedented vitriol. An Indianapolis minister called Kinsey "a cheap charlatan"; a New York rabbi called the book "a libel on all womankind." With a widely reprinted article by Lionel Trilling, even the avant-garde *Partisan Review* joined the attack. The president of the liberal Union Theological Seminary saw "the current vogue" of Kinsey's work as a symptom of "a prevailing degradation in American morality approximating the worst decadence of the Roman era. The most disturbing thing is the absence of a spontaneous, ethical revulsion from the premises of the study." The Rockefeller Foundation, which had helped finance the research, was widely criticized, and dropped its support. A New York congressman demanded that the Postmaster General ban Kinsey's work from the mails because it was "the insult of the century against our mothers, wives, daughters, and sisters." Catholic publications declared that Kinsey not only was helping the Communists but was helping Americans to "act like Communists." But the president and trustees and students of Indiana University stood fast with Kinsey.

The popular result of Kinsey's work was ironic and unpredicted. His life as a biologist had been devoted to proving the importance of "individuals." According to Kinsey, "The fact of individual variation is one of the fundamentals of biologic reasoning. In its universality it is practically unique among biologic principles. The phenomenon is startling in its magnitude." But Kinsey's intentions were twisted by a public demand for simple norms.

Using the science of statistics, Kinsey had done more than anybody before him to break the taboos on the collecting of objective quantified data on human sexual activity. The next landmark, which showed how far the taboos had been dissolved, was the detailed laboratory study of more than one hundred thousand male and female orgasms. Using a variety of new laboratory devices and electronic recording machines, Dr. William H. Masters and Mrs. Virginia E. Johnson of the Reproductive Biology Research Institute in St. Louis collected statistical data on the sex act directly. They published their results in *Human Sexual Response* (1966). Within a few years, this book had sold a quarter of a million copies at $10 a copy. Masters and Johnson, by producing clinical data on such facts as heartbeat during coitus, removed the mystery from countless details surrounding sexual intercourse. In their preface they declared that their purpose, following Dr. Robert Latou Dickinson, was to help discover "the normal usages and medial standards of mankind." They hoped to join the pioneer scientists by issuing "succinct statistics and physiologic summaries of what we find to be average and believe to be normal."

THE AMERICANS' DISCOVERY of what was "normal" in sexual behavior took forms which an earlier generation would have considered not only immoral but bizarre. "Group sex"—persons having sexual relations as a couple with at least one other individual—became a publicly noted phenomenon in the mid-1960's. Kinsey's book on the male (1948) had only a single sentence on adult heterosexual group activity, and in his book on the female (1953), "wife-swapping" was dismissed in a paragraph. By the late 1960's the vulgarism "wife-swapping" was being displaced by the euphemism "swinging." By the early 1970's numerous magazines, at least one with a circulation of 50,000, were serving the interests of swingers. A network of swinging clubs reached around the country. Data on 284 swinging couples were collected by Dr. Gilbert D. Bartell, an Illinois anthropologist, and published in 1971, and a growing number of other studies made facts on group sex available to all Americans.

The new data provided convincing, vivid evidence of the widespread "normality" of many of the tendencies recounted in the antiseptic Kinsey statistics. One consequence of the rise of group sex, Dr. Bartell predicted, was "that in the future, men and women will be generally recognized as ambisexual beings, not only in the accepted psychological sense but also in the still 'embarrassing' physiological sense. . . . in swinging this is already beginning to happen, at least to some extent, even among middle-class mid-Americans."

As the new truths took the form of quantitative, scientifically authenticated norms, morality was replaced by normality. Prescriptions were displaced by descriptions. But the new statistical morality carried its own kind of latent prescription. The new knowledge of norms was as "guilty" and as unforgettable as Adam's first bite of the apple in Eden. A man who knew the norms had lost his innocence. Never again could he look on the violations of parental authority, on youthful vices, on extramarital peccadilloes, or on "unnatural" sexual satisfactions with the simple disgust of his grandfathers.

As knowledge proved the infinite variety of personal needs, even the prescription "Thou shalt not be abnormal" became meaningless. Fewer Americans were haunted by pseudoscientific fears or by moral imperatives. Instead they were thrown back on their imperfect knowledge of norms, on their lay interpretation of abstruse scientific data. How did their experience fit with that of other men and women? Americans could discover the rewards and the burdens of having to decide for themselves whether their norms were authentic, and when their deviation from the norm was itself only normal.

PART FOUR

The Urban Quest
for Place

"In founding new cities and in occupying new
lands he first devotes himself to burning the
forests, to levelling with ruthless eagerness the
hill-slopes, to inflicting upon the land, whatever its topography, the unvarying plan of his
system of straight streets and of rectangular
street crossings. In brief, he begins his new settlements by a feverish endeavor to ruin the
landscape. Now all this he does not at all because he is a mere materialist but . . . because
mere nature is, as such, vaguely unsatisfactory
to his soul, because what is merely found must
never content us. . . . Hence, the first desire is
to change, to disturb, to bring the new with
us."

JOSIAH ROYCE

MEN AND WOMEN in everywhere communities were not quite sure
where they were living. The Old World peasant, tied to his land, had
suffered fear of new places: his traditional affection was for the *land*
of his forefathers, the village where parents and grandparents were
buried in the churchyard. But merely by coming to America, an
immigrant had shown his willingness to move. Inevitably, when he
first arrived he found himself in a city, and many of the most numerous immigrant groups remained city dwellers. There, too, immigrants learned to make something new of their transatlantic customs.

And in the first stages of their immigrant urban experience they revealed a flexibility remarkable for people so long Old World–rooted. They kept old ways and yet made something American of them.

The American city, the marketing center of consumption communities, the information center of statistical communities, was the special scene of this new rooting and uprooting. Most men before had been attached to the soil, inspirited by the sunshine and sky and trees and birds of some particular corner of earth. That sense of place Americans now sought to rediscover in their corner of cemented sidewalks, on macadamed rectilinear streets, among geometric skyscrapers.

But in the twentieth century, the urban places where immigrants sought roots somehow dissolved. The wealth and organization and invention which had lifted Americans into communities of the unseen had uprooted them, too, from every particular place. As Americans became increasingly urban, their cities ceased to be units clearly bounded in geography, in economy, in government, or even in vision. As the boundaries of cities were befuzzed, each city lost much of its distinctiveness. Each citizen became less a New Yorker or a Chicagoan or a San Franciscan than a City Dweller, another Urban American. But as Americans felt more entangled with their cities, more obsessed by city problems, as they sought to cure the city's ills or to flee from them, they were bewildered over what (besides crime and pollution) they had lost, and they wondered where urban community could be rediscovered. Was the modern American city to be a twentieth-century American West, with its own special vagueness, its own mysteries, its own false promises and booster hopes?

29

An American Diaspora

THE OLD WORLD expanded across the United States in one of the great migrations of history. In the century after the close of the Napoleonic Wars in 1815 there was a mass exodus from Europe. About 50 million people emigrated and, of these, 35 million came to the United States. Had it not been so, when would this continent have been peopled? While immigration statistics are crude before 1820 when the federal government first began to record the immigrants' places of origin, only about 250,000 immigrants arrived here in the three and a half decades between the close of the American Revolution and 1819. Thereafter, although there were fluctuations, the annual influx increased spectacularly. By 1832 the annual figure exceeded 60,000; by 1850 it was more than 350,000. Not until 1858 did the annual immigration figure again fall below 200,000.

And the United States would somehow meld these miscellaneous peoples into a nation. This was the more remarkable because these peoples had come from an Old World that was overwhelmingly rural, and the great bulk of them were peasants, farmers, or villagers who had lived close to the land. When they were being drawn into American life, in the century after the Civil War, the nation every year was becoming more urban; and most of them had to find a place in an urban wilderness.

OF COURSE, MANY times before in history, population had migrated from one part of the world to another. Britain herself, as Jefferson and others reminded the British at the time of the Revolution, had been peopled by immigrants. In the long run in most countries the immigrants tended to become assimilated to the earlier residents; and so it was in America. But what was most remarkable about the American immigrant experience in the late nineteenth and early twentieth centuries was not that in a single nation American immigrants became assimilated, but that so many different peoples somehow retained their separate identities. The United States never entirely lost the flavor of Diaspora. Other nations had dissolved peoples into one. This nation became one by finding ways of allowing peoples to remain several. While the United States took for its motto the Latin cliché *E pluribus unum,* a more appropriate motto might have been *E pluribus plura.*

American national politics would remain a politics of regions and of groups of different immigrant origin. "Hyphenated Americans"— Italian-Americans, German-Americans, Irish-Americans, and so on— would include a substantial part of the population. The successful manipulation of these groups was a distinctive requirement for the successful American politician on the national stage. Immigrant groups continued to play as important a role here as did religious sects or economic or social classes in Europe. But there were important distinctions between the migrations which had peopled the United States during the colonial period and those which brought the largest numbers in the first century of national life.

In the age of *colonists,* large numbers of immigrants had been led by men with a vision who aimed to build a certain kind of community. Others had come to found a "colony" in the simple dictionary sense: "a group of people who leave their native country to form in a new land a settlement subject to, or connected with, the parent state." For the considerable number that came with visions of a City upon a Hill, an Inward Plantation, a Charity Colony, a Transplanted English Country life, or some other definable type of society, their recollections of the old were less compelling than their visions of the new. Different visions made at least thirteen different loyalties. And these made American federalism, the United States of America.

Afterward came the age of *emigrants.* This was the word first commonly used here in the era of our Revolution to describe those who *left* a foreign country to come and settle. "Emigrant" was then gradually replaced by "immigrant" (emphasizing not the leaving but the coming) or by "refugee" (emphasizing the flight and the asylum). While the American arrivals in the colonial age were dominated by those people who came with a purpose, later arrivals were dominated by those who had left for a reason and were in search of a purpose. The colonist's vision was dominated by his destination, the emigrant's by his place of departure. The colonist had been attracted, the refugee had been expelled. This is not to say that in the first age many colonists were not driven by persecution and poverty, nor that in the second age many emigrants did not have a vision of a "Golden Land." But the earlier were mainly in pursuit, the latter mainly in flight. The Pilgrim Fathers struck the keynote of the first age of peopling, the Emigrant Fathers of the second. The first era made the states, the later made the nation. The first era created an American federalism; the second created a new kind of national politics.

IN THE TWENTIETH CENTURY no other nation of comparable size had been so dominated by memories of its origins. Groups which came from Europe in the nineteenth century were held together into the twentieth by their family memories, and even by nostalgia for the places from which they had fled. And their later American experience, their place in American life and American politics were permanently shaped by the peculiar circumstances of their immigration. Although the Old World experience of each immigrant group —of the Irish, Germans, Italians, Jews, Poles, and others—had been different, the opportunities that the New World offered them were quite similar. Each group in its own way kept its identity, and by keeping its identity secured a place in the nation.

Of course no group was typical. But the Irish were the largest single group to arrive in the half-century before the Civil War. And after the war, too, their experience continued to illustrate how this New Nation would open opportunities for people to remain themselves while they somehow joined the search for nationality. Of all the millions who came to the United States in the century after 1820, about one fourth came from Ireland. Between 1820 and 1840, Irish immigrants totaled nearly three quarters of a million, an average of about 35,000 a year. This number skyrocketed in the '40's, reaching a peak in 1851 of nearly a quarter-million. Partly as a consequence of this movement to America, the total population of Ireland had decreased by about 2.5 million in the twenty years before the American Civil War.

Many found that they had changed their locale but not their fortunes. Irish paupers became American paupers. But what was remarkable was that so many of these victims of centuries of oppression actually attained power and respectability in a strange country. To those who were lucky and energetic and ambitious, America did offer a new life, first to a few leaders, then to more and more of the anonymous thousands.

When Joyce's Stephen Dedalus said, "History is a nightmare from which I am trying to awake," he summed up Irish history. And the United States was to be the place of awakening. Irish history in Ireland and Irish history in America were a set of beautifully symmetrical antitheses. While America was a land of immigration, Ireland was a land of invasions. Beginning with Henry II of England and his Norman followers in the twelfth century, efforts were made forcibly to assimilate the Irish to the ways of the invaders. Yet, however often the land was invaded, the people were never really conquered. The English came to call them "barbarians" because they held on to their own ways, refusing, for example, to become Protestant. During the seventeenth century, Irish sufferings reached a climax. On a single occasion at Drogheda, Cromwell, in what he called a "marvellous great mercy," massacred 2,800 Irish, including priests and civilians as well as soldiers. In the decade before 1652, over 600,000 Irish (one third of the population) died by pestilence, war, and famine. Cromwell redistributed most of the land to his followers, and sold thousands of Irishmen into slavery on the West Indian plantations. English rule fastened on the island.

During the eighteenth century the Irish lived not under a government so much as under a penal code. Irish Catholics, rightless in their own country, could not own a horse worth over five guineas, they could not vote or serve on a jury or carry firearms or teach school or enter the army or navy or practice law or become government officials. If they were tradesmen they could not have more than two apprentices. Catholic churches could not have spires.

In the early nineteenth century, landlords seeking to "improve" their lands and consolidate their holdings evicted tenants by the thousands. An American evangelist, Mrs. Asenath Nicholson, described a common sight in Galway in the 1840's:

> I saw a company of men assembled in a square, and supposed something new had gathered there; but drawing nearer found it was a collection of poor countrymen from distant parts, who had come hoping on the morrow to find a little work. Each man had his space, and all were standing in waiting posture, in silence, hungry and weary, for many, I was told, had walked fifteen miles without eating, nor did they expect to eat that day. Sixpence a day was all they could get, and they could not afford food on the Sabbath, when they could not work. Their dress and their desponding looks told too well the tale of their suffering.

Then came the potato rot, bringing still more evictions, famine, and starvation. Crop failures in 1845 and 1846 sent whole families wandering the countryside in futile search of food. While the weaker died along the roads, the more resigned sat by their fireside until death relieved their hunger. This Irish Famine lasted five years, during which the population of the country declined from about 8.5 million to about 6.5 million. No one knows exactly how many died of starvation, but the combined effects of malnutrition, "famine fever" (a form of typhus induced by undernourishment), dysentery (from food scavenged or eaten raw), and scurvy brought death to hundreds of thousands.

It was a scene, Captain Robert F. Forbes of Boston wrote from Cork, "to harrow up your hearts." And the Boston *Pilot* pleaded: "In God's name, give us this generation out of the mouth of the Irish grave, to feed them, that they may live and not die!" And they came. Through all ports from Boston to New Orleans, their numbers swelled American immigration from Europe to an unprecedented high in the fifteen years before the Civil War. Between May 1847, when the New York Commissioners of Emigration first kept accurate records, and the end of 1860, some 2.5 million immigrants entered the United States through the port of New York alone. More than one million of these, by far the largest single group, were natives of Ireland.

As the demand for passage to America increased, the price of passage from Ireland went up. Still, helped by American philanthropy and by the self-interest of Irish landlords, the impoverished Irish found the means to come. Some used remittances from American relatives, sent at the rate of about $1 million annually in the 1840's, firmly establishing historian Marcus Lee Hansen's principle that "Emigration begets emigration."

One recently arrived Irishman, according to the traveling French economist Michel Chevalier, showed his American employer a letter he had just written to his family back in Ireland. "But Patrick," the employer asked, "why do you say that you have meat three times a week, when you have it three times a day?" And Patrick replied, "It is because they wouldn't believe me, if I told them so." No wonder that Father John T. Roddan, editor of the Boston *Pilot,* boasted that the Irish, like the Jews, were indestructible, with "more lives than the blackest cat . . . killed so many times that her enemies are tired of killing her. . . . God made Ireland need America and he made America an asylum for Ireland." America's reward, Father Roddan prophesied, was eventual conversion to the True Faith: "a majority of Americans in the year 1950 will be Catholics."

THEIR EMIGRANT FRAME OF MIND was peculiarly open to new opportunities. The practicality of the Puritans had come from their conviction that they were on the right track. Their main problem, then, was not to discover a purpose or to develop an ideology, but to apply and fulfill their orthodoxy in America. The practicality and adaptability of the Irish came from quite opposite causes. Determined simply to escape the Old World they knew, they were anxious to discover any and all opportunities of a New World. And so they were ready to do whatever had to be done. In a word, the Puritans had been colonists, the Irish were emigrants.

Much of American vitality came from the fact that so many of the newcomers brought this emigrant frame of mind. A peculiar strength of the Irish and other nineteenth-century emigrants was their lack of a clear limiting purpose. Held together by recollections, sometimes of a past that never was, the Irish "remembered" the rural delights of their Emerald Isle, just as the Jews "remembered" the cozy community of the ghetto, as the Italians "remembered" the musical and culinary charms of their villages under Mediterranean skies.

The American nation, then, would be a confederation among past and present: a federal union of emigrant groups, memory-tied and sentiment-bound. And these groups would produce new national institutions by their very ways of remaining distinct.

30
Politics for City Immigrants

INSTITUTIONS WHICH IMMIGRANTS had developed in their Old World homelands proved providentially suited to their different needs in America. And there were no better exemplars of this than the Irish. For this new nation was rich in formal governmental organizations: constitutions, legislatures, and courts galore. The long experience of Americans in self-government was of course one of the causes of the War for Independence. And American Independence, conspicuously unlike Irish Independence, had come after only a decade or two of agitation and extralegal organization. Success in the American Revolution meant that the people now controlled their governments. Constitution making then became a national pastime, while political parties debated the proper emphasis of government under the new constitutions.

How different had been the Irish experience! While American political life took the forms of self-government, Irish political life took the forms of endless rebellion which never climaxed in revolution. While Americans were preoccupied with social compacts, rights of representation, forms of legislation, and the balance and limits of power, the Irish had been preoccupied with organized sabotage and the frustration of unjust laws. The American experience had been legalistic and formal; the Irish had been informal, extralegal, or even antilegal. But the Irish experience would not be wasted in America.

NEW YORK BECAME the first great city in history, as Daniel Patrick Moynihan has observed, to be ruled by men of the people. Other cities—Rome under the Gracchi, London under John Wilkes, Paris under the Commune—were only temporarily run by representatives of the lower classes. But in New York, from the early nineteenth century, rule by men of the people was organized into a regular and continuing system. This was doubly remarkable since that city was becoming the nation's greatest single center of wealth and power. The popular rule of New York City was an Irish achievement. For the Irish developed and perfected the big-city political machines, which brought power to representatives of the lower classes not only in New York but in other cities.

Still more remarkable, this unprecedented urban achievement was the work of a *rural* people. The political experience which the Irish brought to America was as different as possible from that of the orderly New England town meeting, the provincial legislature, or the deliberative constitutional convention. Since the regular courts in Ireland were agents of landlord oppression, the poor tenants had made their own courts and their own law. "There are in fact two codes of law in force and in antagonism," a contemporary explained, "—one the statute law enforced by judges and jurors, in which the people do not yet trust—the other a secret law, enforced by themselves—its agents the ribbonmen and the bullet." The agents of this extralegal law went by many different names: "Levellers," "Lady Clares," "Molly Maguires" (later adopted by Irish Catholic coal miners in Pennsylvania), and others. They were most generally known as "Whiteboys" from the shirts that they wore over their other clothes, the better to distinguish one another at night.

In Ireland, Whiteboyism had developed its own principles and its own techniques of enforcement. The object was to keep the actual tenant in possession of the land, to fight tithes and high rents, and generally to regulate landlord-tenant relations for the tenant's benefit. Local groups meeting secretly did their own "legislating" against particular, oppressive landlords. "Sir Francis Hopkins," went a notice pasted on an offender's door or found mysteriously at his table, "there did a Man come to look for you one Day with what you might call a boney Brace of Pistols to shoot you; and if you do not be lighter on your Tenants then what you are you shall be shurely shot, so now we give you timely Notice; and if you do not abide by this marke the Consequence." A landlord who disregarded such a notice might be murdered, and a tenant risked his life by taking land that another had been ejected from. "Strangers" (which meant Irishmen who did not live in the immediate locality and who came from other counties to compete for work in harvest time) were commonly beaten and sent back home.

This Whiteboyism was very different from the vigilantism of the American West which filled a legal vacuum. For the Irish were trying to counteract a going legal system. Secret societies, blackmail, bribery, and mayhem became everyday weapons to defend Irish peasants' rights.

At election time in Ireland in the early nineteenth century, herds of tenants were driven to the polls by their landlord not "to vote" but, as the saying went, "to be voted." All this took place, one observer remarked, with as little ceremony "as the Jamaica planter would direct his slave to the performance of menial duties." The landlords themselves, the pillars of respectability and the legal law, were paragons of corruption. Public works became their private domain. The Royal Canal, for example, was cut in the wrong direction, to enhance a certain rich man's lands. Army barracks were located to supply markets for the landlords' produce. Landlords used their tenants, compelled by high rents and a truck system, to build roads for them free, for which the landlords then received public funds. Whether rebellious or obsequious, the Irish peasant reached American shores with a political experience that was copious and vivid, but far different from that which awaited him here.

These unfortunate immigrants quickly transplanted and transformed their political institutions. Within a decade or two the downtrodden Old World Irish had become the ebullient American Irish. They now organized not against but within the government. They spoke not in the cautious whispers of midnight Whiteboy legislatures, but blatantly, floridly, raucously, in city councils, in state assemblies, and even in the United States Congress. The oppressed now could sit in seats of power. Their Irish experience, far from being irrelevant, actually provided their way of grasping power in America.

THEIR FIRST PATTERN of settlement, and even their poverty, helped make all this possible. Arriving in eastern seaboard cities, the

Irish commonly lacked the means to disperse themselves into the continent. In New York City, where the greatest number arrived, by 1850 there had accumulated some 130,000 Irish-born who comprised a quarter of the city's population; five years later more than a third of the city's voters were Irish. This story was repeated elsewhere in the northern seaport towns, notably in Boston.

Bewildered in a strange land, the Irish immigrant welcomed the familiar brogue of an earlier comer. To establish himself he needed a job, a house, food and shelter, and friends; and all these needs helped bring the big-city political machines into being. By satisfying them, the machines would thrive and would become a fixture in American politics.

Machine politics was a natural product of the emigrant frame of mind. What is the main difference between a political machine and a political party? A party is organized for a purpose larger than its own survival. A political machine exists for its own sake; its primary, in a sense its only, purpose is survival. A political party may succeed and make itself obsolete by attaining the purpose for which it was organized. This is never true of a political machine, for a political machine succeeds only by surviving.

The Irish refugee was dominated above all by the need to survive. It was no accident, then, that the first contribution of these Irish emigrants to American politics was the political machine. Machine politics, unlike party politics, needed no end outside itself. And it was this machine politics that produced the political boss and the professional politician whose business was politics. Their test was the ability to keep their business profitable for themselves and their clients.

With New York City for our example we can see how these machines, as Moynihan explains, "resulted from a merger of rural Irish custom with urban American politics." The readiness to view the going machinery of government as not wholly legitimate, the habit of enlisting the humblest citizens, the techniques of organization, the respect for hierarchy, these were all brought from the Irish countryside. With them, too, came a broad-minded willingness to use bribery, blackmail, and violence whenever they helped secure the rights of the underdog. All were reinforced by a passionate loyalty to the organization, which tolerated factionalism but never treason.

It is no wonder, then, that although the Irish were quickly and spectacularly successful in politics—and within decades of their arrival they were actually running a great city—they did not prove masters of the arts of good government. For to the emigrant, in flight from poverty and oppression, American politics had become an end in itself, a business to support himself and his fellow clansmen. When these circumstances helped make "politics" a dirty word, and "bosses" and "machines" words of reproach, the Brahmins of Boston and New York increasingly left important political jobs to these less squeamish new arrivals.

TAMMANY HALL, which the Irish would turn to such effective use, was here even before large numbers of Irish came. The Society of St. Tammany, founded in New York City in 1789, was named after a legendary chief of the Delaware Indians who was supposed to have met William Penn on his arrival in America, and who had been facetiously canonized about 1770. No one could be sure whether the name Tammany meant "affable" or "deserving," but the chief had been proverbial for his friendship to white men.

William Mooney, founder of the New York Tammany Society, was an upholsterer and wallpaper dealer who may have seen brief service in the early days of the Revolution. What Mooney and his friends first intended was a benevolent and fraternal organization aimed against both "aristocrats" like those in the Society of the Cincinnati, who shared Alexander Hamilton's Federalist principles, and "foreign adventurers." The Society's original constitution declared that only native Americans should be eligible for the office of "sachem." Mooney's own public career was far from illustrious. During his less than two years (1808–09) of public service as superintendent of the almshouse, he created a scandal by cutting provisions for the inmates in order to provide his family with rum and other luxuries. "Trifles for Mrs. Mooney," an apocryphal heading in his accounts, soon became a byword among anti-Tammany men. But none of this prevented Mooney's reelection as Grand Sachem.

During these early years the Society entertained its members by high jinks on the Indian motif and had much the character of later American service organizations. Members ranked as Hunters or Warriors, and were ruled by twelve Sachems, presided over by a Grand Sachem. Time was reckoned in "moons" and the months were given mock-Indian names. Headquarters was called The Wigwam. On the Fourth of July and on Tammany Day (May 12), Tammany braves paraded with painted faces in full Indian regalia, carrying bows and arrows, and tomahawks. The New York Society of St. Tammany chartered other, lesser wigwams.

Before the great postfamine influx from Ireland, Tammany had already become a political organization. But except when they named Patrick McKay for State Assembly in 1809, Tammany had not yet included Irish Catholics on its list of approved candidates. On the night of April 24, 1817, two hundred Irishmen marched on Tammany Hall to persuade them to nominate the talented Irish patriot refugee Thomas A. Emmet as their candidate for Congress. Despite strong arguments in the form of chair legs and brickbats, the obstinate Tammany men refused to name the Irish hero.

Then the New York State Constitutional Convention of 1821 widened the suffrage, and an amendment in 1826 removed the taxpaying qualifications. At the New York City election in the fall of 1827, the Irish played a newly conspicuous part. The national contest of the following year, expected to be between Andrew Jackson and John Quincy Adams, was in everybody's minds. The Irish, "ready-made democrats," passionately admired General Jackson, the son of poor Irish emigrants, who had trounced the English at New Orleans. Armed Irish bodyguards accompanied Jackson supporters to cast their ballots. Two hundred Irishmen in the Eighth Ward, according to a witness, "were marched to the polls by one of the Jackson candidates who walked at the head with a cocked pistol in each hand and then without leaving the polls, they voted three times apiece for the Jackson ticket." Visitors to the polls in the Fourth Ward were entertained by a five-hour-and-fifty-eight-minute fight between an Irishman and a Vermonter, which provided the Irish bodyguards their excuse for keeping out the anti-Jackson voters. Now in New York, Irishmen were following the violent pattern of the elections back home. But instead of being voted by their landlord they were voted by their fellow-emigrant bosses.

These activities understandably stirred the fears of respectable old settlers. "Everything in the shape of an Irishman was drummed to the polls and their votes made to pass . . . ," the *National Advocate* complained. "It was emphatically an Irish triumph. The foreigners have carried the day." Here, they warned, was "a foreign body in the midst of us, of alarming magnitude and overwhelming influence." These alarms in turn consolidated the Irish, who used their organs such as the New York *Truth Teller* to cement the loyalties of Irishmen to one another, and incidentally to the Democratic Party.

By the 1830's Tammany had organized a city-wide machine, with special meetings and an appropriate celebrity-leader for each immigrant group. The national election of 1832 once again stirred up Irish loyalty to the anti-English General Jackson and Irish hatred of the "Tory" Henry Clay, who, they argued, was planning to saddle the Bank of the United States on poor Americans just as the Bank of England had once been saddled on the poor Irish.

THE INCREASE AND THE CONCENTRATION of the Irish emigrant population made possible a larger role for the New York Irish in Tammany, in their city and in the politics of the nation. In the 1830's the Sixth Ward, on New York's Lower East Side, was the center of the largest Irish Catholic community in the country and (next to Ireland itself and certain communities in Lancashire and Scotland) the largest Irish community in the world. Tammany had already organized its efforts to woo emigrants. And the Irish, held together by sentiment, memory, and clan loyalty, were ready for the wooing. The Hibernian Provident Society developed political interests. The Mechanics' Benefit Society and the Brian Borihme Club (honoring Irish saints and heroes, now including St. Tammany) were already being used for political purposes by Richard B. Connolly, who came to be known as "Slippery Dick" because he was later a member and finally a betrayer of the Tweed Ring. The Irish, Tammany Hall, and the Democratic Party had already begun their long entanglement with one another, which would last into the twentieth century. Tammany's Young Men's General Committee offered political apprenticeships to the sons of Irish Catholic emigrants. John McKeon, for example, who had served on such committees and became the lawyer for Tammany clients, went to the New York Assembly in 1832 and to Congress in 1834.

One of the most effective of these new Irish political organizers was Michael Walsh. A combination of clown, demagogue, gang leader, and authentic champion of the people, Walsh had spent his boyhood learning the language and the ways of the city streets. His "Spartan Band," organized in 1840, was a gang of young Irish strong arms that followed him to meetings and forced the reluctant Tammany men to hear him out. With George Wilkes, later founder of the scandal-mongering *National Police Gazette*, he started the *Subterranean* (1843). "I know that we, the Subterranean Democracy," Walsh proclaimed, "possess the power, if we will but exercise it." Who, he asked, were those respectable shapers of public opinion? "A set of counterfeit blackguards who can write about temperance with a gallon of punch in their bellies, upon honor with their backs still smarting from the effects of a cow-skinning, and about honesty with a bribe jingling in their pockets!" Walsh prophesied that he would "ride over all this rotten opposition, like a balloon over a dunghill." And he did. With his gangs and his sharp tongue he persuaded Tammany that Walsh and his Irish constituents were worth having. In 1846 Tammany nominated him over Samuel J. Tilden, and elected him to the State Assembly; in 1850 Walsh was elected to Congress, where he served until his death nine years later.

The transformation of big-city politics in the mid-nineteenth century, in New York at least, was largely the work of the Irish. Back in 1835 Chancellor James Kent, voice of the native aristocracy, had explained that "the office of assistant alderman could be pleasant and desirable to persons of leisure, of intelligence, and of disinterested zeal for the wise and just regulation of the public concerns of the city." Only thirty years later Boss Tweed, with refreshing candor, was to call these same aldermen "The Forty Thieves." But this was not the whole story. If the introduction of an "Irish style" into American city politics had put political favors on a cash-and-carry basis, it had done something else too. It had personalized and humanized the political life of the city, making a whole new range of opportunities accessible to the people who most needed them.

The Irish politician, through his own political machine and through Tammany, which became his instrument, had made himself into a social service, or more precisely, a *personal* service agency. His clients were his fellow Irish and other emigrant newcomers. Sixth Ward aldermen in the 1830's, men like liquor dealer Dennis McCarthy, lawyer Thomas S. Brady, and grocer Felix O'Neill, did all kinds of odd jobs for their constituents. They were an employment office, providing a government job or using their influence with private employers. They brought food to the hungry, and medicine to the sick. A man who had lost his business through incompetence or bad luck had their help to start again. They organized a benefit social for an impoverished widow, or for the family of the man crippled on his job. And they performed many of the services offered by the priest in old Ireland. They dignified wakes and funerals by their presence, they guided the illiterate and the bewildered with their advice. They worked full-time and year-round.

The boss's services, private and personal, were as different as possible from what Chancellor Kent had described as "the wise and just regulation of the public concerns of the city." The boss was emphatically no Cincinnatus, temporarily serving a tour of duty in public office. He was in the politics business, classically described in George Washington Plunkitt's "very plain talks on very practical politics" at the turn of the century, when the stakes had risen and bossism was in full flower:

> No other politician in New York or elsewhere is exactly like the Tammany district leader or works as he does. As a rule, he has no business or occupation other than politics. He plays politics every day and night in the year, and his headquarters bears the inscription, "Never closed." . . .
> A philanthropist? Not at all. He is playing politics all the time.
> Brought up in Tammany Hall, he has learned how to reach the hearts of the great mass of the voters. He does not bother about reaching their heads. It is his belief that arguments and campaign literature have never gained votes. . . .

This is a record of a day's work by Plunkitt:

> 2 A.M.: Aroused from sleep by the ringing of his door-bell; went to the door and found a bartender, who asked him to go to the police station

and bail out a saloon-keeper who had been arrested for violating the excise law. Furnished bail and returned to bed at three o'clock.

6 A.M.: Awakened by fire engines passing his house. Hastened to the scene of the fire, according to the custom of the Tammany district leaders, to give assistance to the fire sufferers, if needed. Met several of his election district captains who are always under orders to look out for fires, which are considered great vote-getters. Found several tenants who had been burned out, took them to a hotel, supplied them with clothes, fed them, and arranged temporary quarters for them until they could rent and furnish new apartments. . . .

MACHINE POLITICS WAS politics without ideology. In Ireland, where loyalties had been local and personal, the ruling sentiments were not principles but interests. In the American city, too, purposes were self-defining: the needs of the individual constituent and the perpetuation of the machine. Politics for emigrants was the politics of personal need. Jobs, houses, food, friendship mattered, while the boss's position on the tariff or on foreign wars was of little consequence. Most important was the fact that in 1855, of New York City's 1,149 policemen, 431 were immigrants, and of the immigrants, 305 were Irish.

The Irish in the American cities were actually making their own kind of politics, and incidentally adding a new dimension to American political life. Just as the better-established Americans looked on their governments as service institutions, so too these newcomers had their own humbler expectations. The services they expected at first were less concerned with property than with the means of daily living. Less with validating land titles or financing a railroad than with finding a job. Just as the vast ownerless stretches of the continent were an arena where Americans assigned new services to state and national governments, so too, in the jungles of the fast-growing seaboard cities the homeless jobless immigrants expected new services. And there the needs of the oppressed Irish countrymen were rediscovered.

The decentralized American political system had incidentally helped the Irish and other immigrant groups rise to self-respect and prosperity and political power. Had there been only a single national legislature, and only a single centralized government, the immigrants' rise in politics might have been postponed until after they had been assimilated to American ways. And by that time they might have had little of their own to add. But the federal system, with its numerous governments and countless decentralized political opportunities, made easier the incorporation of the Irish and others *before* their assimilation. They were encouraged to retain their identity as the most effective way to their share of power. A newly arrived group unable to elect a member of Congress still might send one of its members to the lower house of a state legislature, or to the city council.

If the Irish were unified by no large political principles, this was no obstacle to their political success, and might even be an advantage. If a will to help the poor and the needy was no adequate program to govern a nation, it was more than enough to capture a city ward.

31
Stretching the City:
The Decline of Main Street

THE CIRCUMSTANCES of city founding, in the days before the automobile, tended to shape each American city into a clear, coherent form. Cities of the colonial age were (in the phrase of the architect Kevin Lynch) delightfully "legible." Their districts and pathways were easily identified, leaving little doubt of where to find the city center. Yet each offered its own unique visual image, reminding the visitor where he was, giving the resident a sense of being at home. The needs of defense, together with the need for access to waterways, had tended both to keep the city together and to keep it in focus.

Up and down the eastern seaboard, while Spanish, French, Dutch, and English influences had their separate ways, cities came into being with shapes that were distinctive and intelligible. St. Augustine, New Orleans, Mobile, Williamsburg, Charleston, Annapolis, New Haven, New York, Philadelphia, Boston, and others less renowned, grew in patterns that made it easy for residents and visitors to grasp in their mind's eye the city as a whole and to know at a glance where to find the headquarters of commerce and government. In the Spanish-American West, similarly, the mission, the presidio-fort, and the traditional pueblo gave form to Santa Fe, San Diego, Monterey, San Francisco, Santa Barbara, San Antonio, and scores of lesser settlements. And when the nation founded its capital city on the Potomac, it offered the world a model of visual clarity and urban focus.

THE AMERICAN OPPORTUNITY to build new towns across the continent in the late eighteenth and early nineteenth centuries offered the temptation, too, to simplify, schematize, and stereotype the visual form of a city. And just as the unmapped countryside of the West was checkerboarded into arbitrary neat rectangles for sale, so many new cities of the West were given a repetitive schematic geometry which ignored their varying landscape.

When the English astronomer Francis Baily visited Philadelphia and Baltimore in 1795–98, he was delighted by their orderly gridiron of streets—"by far the best way of laying out a city. All the modern-built towns in America are on this principle." But by the time he had reached Cincinnati and met the gridiron street plan once more, he deplored the monotony. "Oftentimes it is a sacrifice of beauty to prejudice, particularly when they persevere in making all their streets cross each other at right angles, without any regard to the situation of the ground or the face of the surrounding country. . . . For it not unfrequently happens that a hill opposes itself in the middle of a street, or that a rivulet crosses it three or four times, thereby rendering its passage very inconvenient." Still, the gridiron plan early displayed in Philadelphia and followed in the later plan for New York City had many *a priori* virtues. For example, real estate speculators found that the rectangular parcels were easy to survey and convenient to merchandise. And it fitted well with the rigid rectangular scheme for surveying public lands all across the continent.

In the long run a scheme so repetitive, which showed so little respect for varied terrain, even if it provided an orderly street plan, prevented many an American city from acquiring a distinctive visual image. Everywhere—on the prairies, in the desert, up and down the mountainside, and in the city—appeared the checkerboard.

The checkerboard pattern did not provide an obvious visual center, but in the growing cities of the West during the mid-nineteenth century and later, new forms of transportation tended to provide a focus of arrival and activity. In the age of the railroad, a few speedy lines had brought people to the city center. Partly for that reason, manufacturing and wholesaling were commonly focused there. The city's busy, impressive railway depot, a kind of inland harbor, had been a measure of its commerce and its vitality. The meeting points of railroad lines were natural city centers, and "the other side of the railroad tracks" was the natural dividing line within the city.

But within the city at first there was no public transportation at all. In the early nineteenth century, Paris set an example with its *voiture omnibus,* or "vehicle for all," which supplied the English word "omnibus," soon shortened to "bus." This was simply a large vehicle which anyone could board for a small fee, and which traveled a fixed route. Since the unpaved city streets were nearly impassable in wet weather, and paving was done with rough cobbles, a ride in a bus was slow and bumpy. An obvious improvement, then, was to lay rails, like those already used inside coal mines, and shape the wagon wheels to conform to the rails. These omnibuses on rails were still, of course, drawn by horses. "Streetcar," an Americanism, came into use about the time of the Civil War. Now it became possible for someone who could not afford a private carriage to work in the city and live outside.

The rails of streetcars, like those of the steam railroads, tended to keep the city in focus. Streetcars which ran to the center of the city, as we have seen, brought customers for department stores, visitors to museums, and audiences to theaters, and so built "downtown." And with the rise of suburbs, the rails kept the suburb, too, in focus, for the rails commonly led to a central station in each suburb; and the rail lines had determined the location of the new developments outside Philadelphia, Chicago, Los Angeles, or the areas first settled in Florida. But the steam railroad, driven by a locomotive that was cumbersome, noisy, and a fire hazard, was not well suited for shorter runs and frequent stops. Nor was it suited at all for running inside a city.

The suburb required a different kind of transportation, and some of the first suburbs were a kind of by-product of the streetcar. "Streetcar suburbs" (as historian Sam B. Warner, Jr., calls them) stretched the city. Before the coming of the streetcar, a city's natural boundaries had extended only to the distance that a man could walk from the center in about an hour. For among city dwellers, horses and carriages were mostly for the rich. The steam railroad which went to a central station had enlarged the trading area of the city but did not provide transportation for short distances, and so did not change the patterns of daily life. The streetcar was another story. While it did not take the city out of focus, it was the beginning of the end of the walking city. Boston, for example, which as late as 1850 was still a focused pedestrian city with a mere three-mile radius, had by 1900 become a suburbanized metropolis with a ten-mile radius. The instrument of this transformation was the streetcar.

An American street railway, some call it the first anywhere, was built for the New York & Harlem Railway in 1832 by an Irish immigrant, John Stephenson. His design for a huge horse-drawn omnibus mounted on four flange wheels made him the leading manufacturer of streetcars in their heyday after the mid-century.

One of the most effective of the streetcar pioneers was Stephen Dudley Field, son of a lawyer in Stockbridge, Massachusetts. Stephen's uncle, Cyrus W. Field, who had successfully laid the first Atlantic cable in 1858, installed a telegraph office in the elder Field's law chambers, and at the age of twelve Stephen became interested in the new science of telegraphy. Later, when Stephen had formed his own company to develop electrical inventions, he became especially interested in finding new uses for his improved dynamo in place of batteries, an essential step toward a feasible electric streetcar system. Importing the latest Siemens electric motors from Germany, he collaborated with Thomas A. Edison to provide an electric railway at the Chicago Railway Exposition in 1883.

Still there was the grave problem of how to transmit the electricity from a central power station to the moving streetcar without endangering the lives of people on the streets. Accidents with live rails and underground conduits led to the overhead trolley system, which, because of its safety, became the usual source of streetcar power. The overhead trolley and the carbon commutator brush which made possible an efficient streetcar motor, were the work of a Belgian immigrant, Charles J. Van Depoele, who had settled in Detroit in 1869, and whose electrical innovations eventually won him the title, "the Detroit Edison." "Trolley," displacing the English "tram," referring not to the wire but to the vehicle, was an Americanism in common use by the 1890's.

That first extensive trolley system, which appeared in Richmond, Virginia, in 1888, was a spectacular feat of organization. The man who did it was the remarkable Frank Julian Sprague. Entering the Navy after graduating from Annapolis, he invented electrical improvements for the ships in which he served. Then he resigned from the Navy to work with Thomas A. Edison. After developing a "constant-speed" motor, Sprague set up his own company, and in 1887, when he was barely thirty, "took a foolish contract to equip the Richmond, Virginia Union Passenger Railway in ninety days, with payment of $110,000, if satisfactory." To fulfill his contract he had to build eighty motors and equip forty cars, as many as were then operating on all the streetcar lines in the country. He also had to lay twelve miles of track, to erect the overhead trolley wire along the whole route, and to build and equip an adequate central power plant. All this in ninety days! The task was complicated by the steep grades and sharp curves of Richmond streets.

When Sprague fulfilled his contract and his trolley system went into operation in February 1888, Richmond citizens were amazed to see the streetcars going up the city's hills pulled by an "unseen power." "Sprague set the mule free," a citizen observed, "the long-haired mule shall no longer adorn our streets." He soon had contracts for a hundred other streetcar systems. Sprague developed the "multiple-unit" control for trains, which improved the subway and the elevated; and he incidentally found new ways of applying the electric motor to the elevator and to machine tools, printing presses, dentist drills, and many home appliances.

The electric streetcar naturally widened the reach of the city. And the spread of other services helped. By 1920 a new device, the single-residence septic tank, had come into use for houses out of reach of city sewage systems. Improved techniques of well drilling had made it easier for an unattached residence to have its own water supply. Now new techniques extended the reach of electricity. At first, under Edison's favored system of direct current, electric power could be conveniently sent out only for a mile or two. The shift to alternating current and George Westinghouse's improvements in the transformer simplified and cheapened the sending of electricity for long distances. By the early twentieth century there were practical and economical systems for distributing electricity to widely dispersed households.

Even before the opening of the new century, promoters of streetcar-suburbs proclaimed the importance of suburban life for widening home ownership and so strengthening the roots of American democracy.

Henry M. Whitney, a steamship operator who made a fortune out of his Boston street-railway monopoly, propagandized for the uniform five-cent fare by contrasting the congested, tenant-ridden cities of Europe with the new promise of suburbia. In the United States, now, he said, the city workingman could own his own home on a plot of his own. As late as 1900 only one fourth of Boston suburban dwellers owned their own homes. But this American ideal of the independent home owner, a latter-day form of the Old World sturdy independent "yeoman," helped inspire the nationwide growth of suburbs, and promised to democratize the "Old World" luxuries of country living. The very names of the new suburbs were faintly redolent of manorial establishments, while the promotional literature and the architecture of even the smallest houses conjured up for middle-class urban Americans seductive visions of "gracious living" in mini-manors and micro-palaces.

OUT FROM CITIES in all directions the new electrified street railways reached. Occasionally they went to where the people were, but more often they went where real estate developers wanted the people to come. Streetcars had become necessary for the promotion of new suburbs. Just as, a half-century earlier, railroad builders had made fortunes by attracting the people to the railroads, so now it was with the streetcar builders. Henry E. Huntington, nephew of the Collis P. Huntington who had built the Central Pacific Railroad, developed his own streetcar empire out of Los Angeles. With the fortune he had inherited on the death of his uncle and then enlarged by marrying his uncle's widow, in 1900 Henry Huntington began sending out his electric streetcar lines. By 1913 his lines had been extended thirty-five miles and touched more than forty incorporated centers. For example, at Redondo Beach, seventeen miles southeast of Los Angeles, within two months he had recouped the cost of his streetcar line by the sale of real estate. And by 1920 Huntington had helped bring into being a dozen new incorporated suburban satellites of Los Angeles.

Outside Cleveland, Ohio, the Van Sweringen brothers, without the advantage of an inherited fortune, accomplished a similar feat. Oris P. and Mantis J. Van Sweringen began as office boys in a fertilizer firm in Cleveland. When Oris was still only nineteen and Mantis was twenty-one, they envisioned a vast real estate development outside the city. While accumulating a few dollars by buying and selling real estate options within the city, they had their eye on the 1,400-acre tract east of the city which belonged to the local society of the Shakers. When the Van Sweringen brothers heard that the church was about to sell, they secured options on parcels of the land while they made efforts to raise the money to buy the whole tract. By heavy borrowing, they managed to acquire holdings in the area amounting to 4,000 acres.

But the value of the land depended on transportation, and a profitable system of transportation required the presence of a population. Since the new suburb still had no inhabitants, the only way the Van Sweringens could persuade the Cleveland Street Railways to extend their line was by offering to pay five years' interest on the cost of laying it. When they needed another line and still could not persuade the company to extend its line farther, the Van Sweringens went into the railroad business to insure the value of their real estate investment. Shaker Heights flourished. The land, which in 1900 was appraised at $240,000, by 1923 was figured at nearly $30 million, and by 1930 had reached $80 million.

The Van Sweringens managed to give Shaker Heights a special character. By deliberately avoiding the familiar grid pattern of streets, they emphasized the contrast to the central city, imitating the romantic styles of wealthy subdivisions like Frederick Law Olmsted's Brookline outside Boston. In Shaker Heights the streets curved and undulated around artificial lakes, and land was reserved for parks. The architecture of new buildings was strictly controlled within zones, and each zone reserved for houses of a different price class. In this way they kept up the prices of the superior lots. Shaker Heights set a pattern for suburbs all over the country. And restrictive covenants became an American fixture in this new era of mass romanticism and metropolitan vagueness.

Two canons of the new suburbs were: Romanticize and Stratify. Landscape architects bent their efforts to creating a rural, deliberately random, countryfied character. But to reassure settlers that their cash and their prejudices were safe, residential zoning (which the suburbs helped create) separated families according to income, race, and religion. The suburbs promised homogeneous islands, where those who could afford it and did not suffer the stigma of the wrong race or religion, could hope to live an artificial, antiseptic idyl, untroubled by any not of their own "kind."

The new suburbs would provide a ladder of consumption in housing like that which General Motors was offering in automobiles. Both provided visible, reachable goals. The newness of the suburbs and the visibility of their place in the consumption scale helped Americans who were uncomfortably but optimistically vague about their social class to locate themselves in the social scheme. One of the last legacies of the New World emptiness was this new geography of status. And while the new suburbs professed to sharpen and define, they also did much to blur the situation of Americans.

THE CHANGING PROFILE of the American city appeared in the shifting definitions used by the United States Bureau of the Census. In 1870 the census officially distinguished the nation's "urban" from its "rural" population for the first time. "Urban population" was defined as persons living in towns of 8,000 inhabitants or more. But after 1900 an "urban" person meant one living in an incorporated place having 2,500 or more inhabitants.

Then, in 1950 the Census Bureau radically changed its definition of "urban" to take account of the new vagueness of city boundaries. In addition to persons living in incorporated units of 2,500 or more, the census now included those who lived in *un*incorporated units of that size, and also all persons living in "the densely settled urban fringe, including both incorporated and unincorporated areas, around cities of 50,000 inhabitants or more." Each such new unit, conceived as "an integrated economic and social unit with a large population nucleus," was christened a "Standard Metropolitan Statistical Area" (SMSA).

Each SMSA would contain at least "(a) one central city with 50,000 inhabitants or more, or (b) two cities having contiguous boundaries and constituting, for general economic and social purpose, a single community with a combined population of at least 50,000, the smaller of which must have a population of at least 15,000." Such an area included "the county in which the central city is located, and adjacent counties that are found to be metropolitan in character and economically and socially integrated with the county of the central city." By 1970, about two thirds of the population of the United States was living in these urbanized areas, and of that figure more than half were living *outside* the central cities.

While the Census Bureau and the federal government used the SMSA (by 1969 there were 233 of them), social scientists and citizens were also using new terms to describe the elusive, vaguely defined areas reaching out from what used to be simply "towns" and "cities." A host of terms came into use: "metropolitan regions," "polynucleated population groups," "conurbations," "metropolitan clusters," "megalopolis," etc., etc. A century earlier, American city boosters had used the language of hope and hyperbole, dignifying villages as towns, towns as cities, and cities as metropolises; mid-twentieth-century Americans stretched their language with another purpose— to communicate uncertainty and penumbra.

As Jean Gottman explained in 1961 in his account of the "Megalopolis" along the Atlantic seaboard:

> Thus the old distinctions between rural and urban do not apply here any more. . . . Most of the people living in the so-called rural areas, and still classified as "rural population" by recent censuses, have very little, if anything, to do with agriculture. In terms of their interests and work they are what used to be classified as "city folks," but their way of life and the landscapes around their residences do not fit the old meaning of urban. . . . we must abandon the idea of the city as a tightly settled and organized unit in which people, activities, and riches are crowded into a very small area clearly separated from its nonurban surroundings. Every city in this region spreads out far and wide around its original nucleus; it grows amidst an irregularly colloidal mixture of rural and suburban landscapes; it melts on broad fronts with other mixtures, of somewhat similar though different texture, belonging to the suburban neighborhoods of other cities.

Inhabitants of the fringe were uncertain whether they were urban or rural, and unsure, too, about which old city they were satellites of. Along the main rail lines between New York City and Philadelphia, for example, communities might be considered satellites of either city or both, while Newark, New Brunswick, and Trenton were ambiguous units in themselves.

OF THE TWENTIETH-CENTURY TRANSFORMATION of the American city there was no more dramatic example than Los Angeles. As originally laid out by the Spanish governor of Upper California in 1781, the *pueblo* of Los Angeles surrounded a plaza "200 feet wide by 300 long, and from said plaza four main streets shall extend." Even in the mid-nineteenth century the settlement still looked like a provincial Spanish village, with a plaza and with houses for as many plots as could be irrigated nearby. Although Los Angeles grew steadily with the real estate boom that began in the 1870's, until about 1920 the city still somehow was dominated by its downtown. Los Angeles had a Main Street, which was the daytime commercial center and the nightlife center.

But by 1970, when the Los Angeles metropolitan area had spread over more than 450 square miles, included 7 million people, and had become the core of the second most populous SMSA in the United States, there was no longer a dominant downtown. Pundits competed in efforts to describe the city's vagueness. "Suburbs in search of a city," "prototype of the supercity," "autopia"—even the fertile American language was strained to suggest the nebulousness of this bizarre metropolitan entity. Whatever the other virtues of Los Angeles, it had surely become one of the least "legible" of the great settlements of the world. And it offered the visual future of American cities in caricature.

While many forces had been at work to befuzz and disperse the metropolis, the most effective was the automobile. Los Angeles' first freeway, the Arroyo Seco Parkway, was dedicated on December 30, 1940, and as freeways multiplied, the old central city declined. By 1953 the last remnants of downtown nightlife were disappearing. The closing of the Good Fellows Grotto at 341 South Main Street on December 31 of that year symbolized the diffusion of the city. A "grill and oyster house" founded in 1905, it had been a rendezvous of after-theater crowds and business lunches, which until the end advertised "The Restful Charm of the Gay Nineties in the 'Atomic Fifties.'" Now the customers were scattered into a thousand places, each an hour's drive or more from one of the others. Downtown was not only empty, but as citizens who were interviewed explained, it now seemed "alien or even menacing."

The predominant visual image of the city was no longer of an urban center but of highways. And they might lead anyplace. As Kevin Lynch reported in 1960:

> Automobile traffic and the highways system were dominant themes in the interviews. This was the daily experience, the daily battle—sometimes exciting, usually tense and exhausting. Trip details were full

of references to signal lights and signs, intersections and turning problems. On the freeways, decisions had to be made far ahead of time; there were constant lane maneuvers. It was like shooting rapids in a boat, with the same excitement and tension, the same constant effort to "keep one's head." Many subjects noted their fears on driving a new route for the first time. There were frequent references to the overpasses, the fun of the big interchanges, the kinesthetic sensations of dropping, turning, climbing. For some persons, driving was a challenging, high-speed game.

The automobile had made the citizen an outcast. While the citizen complained that he could not receive friendly, respectful service in restaurants or hotels or shops, the filling station remained an island of "good service," presumably because it was not considered degrading to serve the automobile. Parking temples preempted the best surface locations, and citizens were forced to walk underground or on platforms lifted into the air. Highways built to serve only the automobile were insulated from the landscape, from pedestrians and from people going about their business. The separated highway, on which more and more Americans would spend more and more of their waking hours, isolated citizens from one another and from their city. Even the efforts to "beautify" highways by removing billboards and commercial signs had the effects of homogenizing the landscape and deepening the driver's sense of isolation; outdoor-display companies actually argued that their billboards served a public purpose by preventing motorists from falling asleep. Yet the increasing minimum speed (on Los Angeles freeways, 50 miles per hour) and the risks of freeway travel made it difficult, and even dangerous, to look at the cityscape as you drove.

Now, when almost anybody's own high-speed-powered vehicle could go anywhere, the old city center ceased to be the natural destination of transportation from the fringes. For the automobile, unlike the railroad or the streetcar, was an anywhere-vehicle, ideally suited for the age of the everywhere community. The nation's early metropolises—Boston, Philadelphia, New York, and Baltimore in the East; Pittsburgh, St. Louis, Cincinnati, and Chicago in the West—had naturally appeared where there was access to waterways. The main roads, which commonly met in the city center, led to the principal nearby towns. In colonial Williamsburg, for example, Merchant's Square was the meeting point of Richmond Road and Jamestown Road. The canals and railroads which helped cities grow also helped them come to a focus. The streetcars and other forms of public transport, even as they diffused the population, had been built outward from the inherited cores of the old cities and so nourished the old centers.

The paving of city streets and the building of intracity, intercity, and interstate highways diffused and interfused "urban" and "rural" activities as never before. An enormous program of federal aid for highways began in 1916 when President Wilson signed the Federal Aid Road Act (the first project was the 2.55-mile "Alameda County boundary to Richmond Road"). Theoretically these roads were built to speed the mail, for the act was based on the constitutional power of Congress to establish "post roads." The real aim was a new nation-wide road network. In 1925 the Secretary of Agriculture approved a uniform system of numbering and marking highways: east–west roads were assigned even numbers, north–south roads were assigned odd numbers, and transcontinental highways were designated in multiples of 10. Under this scheme, the old north–south post road along the Atlantic seaboard became U.S. 1, and the Pacific Coast road was U.S. 101. A uniform design was adopted for the marker, the familiar shield with the state's name along the top and featuring the U.S. highway number. For their own highways the states then developed their own numbering systems.

This national network of numbered highways was a symbol of the diffused destinations of the dominant American vehicle. A highway, no longer the "highroad" to a place of importance, or to anyplace in particular, was now part of a network that took the driver anywhere and everywhere. This was the beginning of the end of the single city center to which people came in public transportation from all over.

The airplane, when it became, second to the automobile, the principal means of intercity passenger transport, diffused the city still farther. In older times the point of arrival—London Dock, Boston Harbor, the Port of New York—had been a center of city life. But now the airport was on the outskirts, only ambiguously related to the city it served. As air traffic increased, and as the construction of airports became more expensive, more and more airports appeared between cities—Norfolk–Hampton Roads, Fort Worth–Dallas and others—and they became newly ambiguous points of arrival. Improvements in the airplane, from the propeller plane to the jet to the jumbo jet to the supersonic transport, pushed big-city airports farther and farther out to the countryside so that when the visitor "arrived" on the ground he might not even see the city to which he had come.

THE NEW SPATIAL VAGUENESS of the city brought with it countless functional vaguenesses. Just as in the nineteenth century the life of a city might depend on the coming of the canal or the railroad (which had received federal and state subsidies), so, in the twentieth century, a city's prosperity might depend on federal and state aid to highways and airports. Each federal unit—national, state, county, and municipal—from the beginning expected some contribution from all the others for its everyday services like water supply, sewage disposal, firefighting, and police protection. Around Chicago, for example, there were parks (the gift of early city boosters) which were not under the jurisdiction of the city police, but which depended on the county; hence the Cook County sheriff was one of the city's principal law-enforcement officers. In a metropolitan region only an unusually well informed citizen knew which of the numerous agencies of government was responsible for each of the public services for which he was taxed or was paying fees.

The confusion was often worst in the everyday transit services which governed daily life. In the mid-twentieth century, for example, the automobile traffic in New York City was under control of the municipal government, but the state legislature governed the rest of the urban transit system, which it had divided between a New York City Transit Authority (in charge of subways) and a Triborough Bridge and Tunnel Authority, while the Port of New York Authority was still another entity. As the metropolitan citizen's taxes and tolls grew and multiplied, he was increasingly bewildered about whom his money went to, and for what.

In cities all over the nation, the need to go downtown for culture and for spectacular entertainment declined with the coming of motion pictures and the rise of the neighborhood movie houses. Then television made it possible for the citizen to see everything he wanted to see (as well as much he did not want to see) without going outside his living room.

Another institution, described in the Americanism "shopping center," came into being in the 1920's and further confused Americans about where and what their city was. The first large decentralized shopping center in the United States was the Country Club Plaza Shopping Center in Kansas City, built in 1922. It was the work of Jesse C. Nichols, who had been raised on a Kansas farm; after he graduated from the University of Kansas he went to Harvard, where he wrote a graduate thesis on the economics of land development. Having visited the English "Garden City" developments, he traveled in Spain to collect architectural ideas. He then applied what he had learned in Europe to building the Country Club District, which finally covered 6,000 acres, one tenth of the whole area of Kansas City.

The design of shopping centers became a new architectural specialty. By 1940, about one quarter of the nation's retail-trade volume in metropolitan regions was dispersed into suburban shopping centers; by 1950 the amount was about one third, and it increased with the decades. By 1955, some eighteen hundred shopping centers had been built in the outskirt business districts of metropolitan regions, and as many more were being planned.

At the same time, an increasing proportion of the population of the metropolitan regions worked at jobs outside the old central city. With the passing decades, as retailing, banking, professional centers for lawyers, doctors, and others, and factories were dispersed, a smaller proportion of the inhabitants of a metropolitan region had a clear dependent relationship to the core of the great city.

32
Booming the
Real Estate Frontier

THE TRANSFORMATION of American life in the twentieth century made it ever harder for the booster spirit to stay alive. For the booster spirit had thrived on certain simple faiths—a faith in the unpredictability of the future, a belief that the future could hold anything or everything. And especially a faith in the uniqueness of the booster's own community. Chicago or Kansas City or Omaha or Denver or Dodge City or Oleopolis, each really was "different." That was the age of the hanging comparative. Each would be bigger and better, becoming a new Athens, a new Rome, or a new London, but somehow greater than and distinct from any prototype.

During the middle and late twentieth century the facts of life taxed these hopes, and then made them untenable. The identities of urban places were dissolved by the creeping vagueness of the boundaries of cities, and by the increasing similarity of places. When anyplace became more like everyplace, it became harder to believe that anyplace was someplace special, harder to boost it and tout it to newcomers, harder to feel even that tenuous, transferable loyalty which the earlier booster town commanded. But all this happened only gradually, over the course of a century. Meanwhile, new versions of the booster spirit had their day.

"THE PURITY OF THE AIR of Los Angeles," an enthusiast wrote in 1874, "is remarkable. Vegetation dries up before it dies, and hardly ever seems to decay. Meat suspended in the sun dries up, but never rots. The air, when inhaled, gives to the individual a stimulus and vital force which only an atmosphere so pure can ever communicate." While its remoteness from civilized contagions made Los Angeles the ideal resort for the sufferer from tuberculosis, the city was eminently civilized. In a whole decade, the brochure boasted, the number of persons injured by snakes, poisonous reptiles, and other dangerous animals in southern California was less than the number killed by lightning in one year in one county in an Eastern state. "There are no dangers to travelers on the beaten track in California; there are no inconveniences which a child or a tenderly reared woman would not laugh at . . . when you have spent half a dozen weeks in the State, you will perhaps return with a notion that New York is the true frontier land, and that you have nowhere in the United States seen so complete a civilization."

Thus began the Southern California Land Boom of the 1880's. From this era came the American word "boom," meaning a sudden increase in prosperity and values. While there were similarities between the booster spirit and the booming spirit, there were also differences. The booster was a community builder, loyal for the time at least to his place, a true believer who cast his lot in advance with those whom he could persuade to join him. While some boomers were true boosters, more of them were mere speculators. The booster was a participant, taking his risks with the rest, but the boomer was a spectator. He sought his profit in the short run, on the likely possibility that the bubble would burst. If the booster deceived, he deceived himself along with others, but the boomer was interested in persuading others only long enough to separate them from their money.

The Southern California boom of the 1880's was the pattern and prototype of later American land booms. It was the classic mining hoax of the mid-nineteenth century transformed into a land hoax. The country was so big, the distances so great, the actual qualities of the land so uncertain, that it was unclear when honest optimism became swindle.

The late 1860's had already brought a small boom to Southern California. Droughts had broken up the vast ranches like the Stearn's ranchos which came to 70,000 acres and which were the heritage of Spanish-Mexican days. In their place appeared small farms practicing intensive agriculture. The extension of the Southern Pacific Railroad created a new winter-resort area and brought people to foci of growth like Los Angeles, Santa Barbara, and San Diego. By the early

'80's there was already a transportation network and a firm foundation of prosperity. When the Santa Fe Railroad came in, competition brought the rail fare from Kansas to Los Angeles down to $1.

"It has been a subject of regret ever since," lamented the novelist Charles Dudley Warner, "that I did not buy Southern California when I was there last March, and sell it out the same month. I should have made enough to pay my railway fare back . . . and had money left to negotiate for one of the little States on the Atlantic Coast." Another writer, less facetious, saw in Los Angeles "this newer and nobler life which is growing up here upon the shores of the Pacific . . . the fair promise of a civilization which had its only analogue in that Graeco-Latin race-flowering which came to the eastern shores of the Mediterranean centuries ago."

Los Angeles, which Warner christened "The Golden Hesperides," was the center of spreading, booming enthusiasms. Railroad flatcars draped in festive flags arrived with prospective buyers. Auctions, enlivened by brass bands and free lunches, stirred them to buy tracts of desert that had been marked off into 25-foot lots. Real estate agents in Los Angeles numbered more than two thousand, and in a single year sold more than $100 million of real estate. Schools, already crowded to accommodate the children of newly arrived settlers, had to offer double sessions.

The number of new subdivisions whose plans were filed in Los Angeles County during the 1886–88 boom came to 1,770. And real estate prices skyrocketed. A 25-acre tract on Seventh Street near Figueroa which found no buyers when offered in 1886 for $11,000, the next year sold for $80,000. A front foot at Sixth and Main streets which sold for $20 in 1883 went for $800 in 1887. "Los Angeles is booming," boasted the *Tribune*, "and is likely to boom for years to come."

The climax came in 1887. By then the population had increased from the 11,000 it counted before the boom, to over 80,000. In the latter half of that year, when the Los Angeles post office handled the mail of 200,000 transients, every day the real estate transfers recorded were in excess of $100,000 and they commonly reached $500,-000. During June, July, and August there were $38 million of real estate transfers in Los Angeles County.

The Los Angeles boom reached out to the shore, stretched north and south from Santa Barbara to San Diego and inland following the railroad lines. One of the most successful boom towns in the San Gabriel Valley was Monrovia, named after its founder, a railroad construction engineer who had laid out his 60-acre town in 1886. In May 1887, auctions sold inside lots (50 feet by 160 feet) for $100, corner lots for $150. In November the town (pop. 500) was incorporated, and the two inevitable hotels were built. Some of the $150 lots were now selling for $8,000. By early 1888 the city actually needed to employ a man to collect its garbage for $5 per week. Streetcar rails were laid in May of that year. By 1890 the town's population had doubled.

Imaginative advertising quickly became a substitute for whatever was lacking in the land. For example, some Los Angeles businessmen organized the Azusa Land and Water Company in December 1886, bought 4,000 acres of the old Rancho Azusa, plotted a town, and within four months started selling lots. They reserved the good agricultural land for farms, and put the town site in a spot that was sand, gravel and boulder wash. When asked why the town was put there, the promoter explained, "If it's not good for a town, it isn't good for anything." But the site proved more than good enough for a boom town. An extravagant advertising campaign attracted buyers to stand in line all night awaiting the opening of the sale the next morning. The man who stood second in line reportedly refused $1,000 from someone who wanted his place, but the man fifth in line did sell his place for $500. Nearly half the town lots were sold in the first three days, and at the end of two months the promoters had a profit of $1,175,000. They celebrated their success by erecting in the heart of the town a brick building and a hotel.

Pasadena, a more substantial boom town, had been founded by a group from Indiana in 1874, and was still a village in 1880. Soon after the Santa Fe Railroad came through in 1885, the Raymond Hotel was completed and became the main attraction, bringing more than 35,000 guests in 1886 and 1887. Two additional hotels were built, and by 1886 the town possessed fifty-three real estate agencies, boasted a population of 6,000, announced plans for a $100,000 "opera house," and recorded a rising crime rate to prove that it really was becoming a metropolis.

By the spring of 1888, for reasons not entirely clear, the Southern California boom had not actually burst, but rather, as one observer noted, "gradually shrivelled up." Boomers who had boasted that "you need not till the soil, you can look on while the earth sends forth her plenty," began to regret the lack of cultivated crops and industries. In areas like Pasadena, fertile orange groves had been neglected in the hope that they would become town lots. But population had grown so rapidly that municipal services such as water, sewerage, roads, and schools could not keep pace. The boom left its own legacy of ghost towns, along with scores of "universities," colleges, academies, and cultural centers.

The University of Southern California had been founded in 1879 with a real estate endowment, and two years later came the University of California at Los Angeles, followed by Whittier College, which

was a joint product of the religious hopes of Quakers and the commercial enterprise of the real estate firm that had successfully developed the town of Whittier.

One of the more successful of the boom colleges, Occidental College, originally called Occidental University, was incorporated in
February 1887. An evangelical Presbyterian institution, it had fixed
its tuition at $50 per year and had made Monday rather than Satur-
day the college holiday so that commuting students would not be
obliged to travel on the Sabbath. Since the college had been founded
by a gift of $50,000 worth of real estate, a campus was reserved out
of the gift, and the rest was sold to support the institution. According
to its advertising, the institution admirably combined real estate with
educational values:

UNIVERSITY HOMES
IN
OCCIDENTAL HEIGHTS TRACT

A beautiful site. Best water in the country piped to every lot. Rich soil.
Pure air. An educational center. No better place in the State for a home.
Prices $250, $300, $500. Terms to suit. Call on or write to the
President of the Occidental University

Countless other institutions, which lacked promotional talent or substantial real estate endowment, became ghost colleges, leaving no
trace on the landscape.

Whatever else the boom proved, it did dramatize the power of
advertising, and the willingness of some Americans to believe anything that was told them vividly and extravagantly and repeatedly.
Boom newspapers, in the tradition of the booster press, flourished.
When San Diego's boom population numbered 20,000, the city already possessed five newspapers. And there was hardly a boom town,
real or imaginary, that did not have at least one newspaper of its own.

The very success of Southern California in promoting its peculiar
"foreign" charm was a force that actually destroyed that charm, and
soon assimilated California to the nation. The decline of the Spanish
missions and the disintegration of the vast ranches had made possible
the first boom of the '60's and '70's, but the flavor of missions and
ranches still remained as a come-on for the boom of the '80's. By the
end of that boom much of the Spanishness of Southern California, an
inheritance of two centuries, had become nothing but an advertising
slogan. The Spanish legacy remained visible in the place-names, but
even these had been jazzed up into countless Glendoras, Venices,
Ballonas, Baronas and Englewoods. Just as the Gold Rush had

brought Northern California into the mainstream of national life, so too, as the historian Glenn S. Dumke suggests, the boom of the '80's brought in Southern California. The nation's history was being dissolved by its geography, and the continent was being suburbanized.

SOUTHERN CALIFORNIA HAD set a pattern and developed techniques which were followed even more extravagantly at the other end of the continent. If Southern California boomers could sell city "lots" in a barren desert where water was nowhere to be seen, could not Florida boomers sell city "lots" that were three feet under water? American salesmanship and advertising proved more than equal to the challenge. Florida made the California boom seem puny. During the whole boom of the '80's, real estate transactions in Southern California had totaled about $200,000,000, but in Florida, three-fourths that amount was spent on the single project of Coral Gables. Southern California was but a modest forecast of things to come.

Perhaps because so much of the state of Florida was half hidden under water, its subtropical landscape and balmy climate had made it a traditional setting for extravagant myths. Florida, the fabled location of a sixteenth-century Fountain of Youth, would become the actual location of a twentieth-century Fountain of Wealth. After the king of Spain sold Florida to the United States in 1819, two development companies, well before the Civil War, tried to sell Florida real estate, and had a modest success until hurricances, yellow fever, and hostile Seminole Indians put an end to their hopes.

How the Florida boom of the 1920's began nearly a century later remains a mystery. Apparently it was the idea of some wealthy Northern businessmen who had tried Florida as a winter resort and who were attracted by the cheapness of the vast tracts of interior wastelands, by the unspoiled seashore, and by the acres of possibly tillable soil. The Florida East Coast Railroad reached down to the remote southern tip of the peninsula in 1900, and a program then began for draining the Everglades. By 1924 the boom was under way.

The natural appeal of the state, with its exotic landscape and its faintly Spanish flavor, was endorsed by the business celebrities of the day. And if you couldn't trust the business judgment of the nation's richest men, whom could you trust? Henry M. Flagler (commemorated in Flagler Street, a main street of Miami, and headquarters of the real estate business), the close associate of John D. Rockefeller in the Standard Oil Company, built two palatial hotels (the Ponce de Leon and the Alcazar) at St. Augustine, then constructed the Florida East Coast Railroad, along which he erected numerous additional de luxe hotels. And there was Barron Collier, who had begun with a small printing business, then made a fortune pioneering in streetcar advertising, and went on to control the advertising and vending machines in New York subways. Collier bought an island off the west coast of Florida for a winter home, acquired more than a million acres of adjacent semi-swamp, built across it a road (later called the Tamiami Trail), and transformed his acres into a thriving new Collier County. A host of other business celebrities came, including J. C. Penney, John and Charles Ringling of circus fame, T. Coleman DuPont of Delaware, and others equally respectable. High-powered publicity came from Roger W. Babson, the stock-market pundit and statistician, and most conspicuously from William Jennings Bryan.

Bryan became a Florida resident and then used the eloquence that had three times secured him the Democratic nomination for President to extol Florida real estate. He proclaimed the state "a leader in education and morals" and made his own contribution to Florida education by drafting a resolution passed by the Florida legislature condemning the teaching of the doctrine of evolution in any form. His orations on Florida, delivered with religious fervor at the rallies for Coral Gables, persuaded unbelievers, while real estate agents stood by to sign up the converted. Literary enticement came from innumerable books, and especially from a widely quoted series of articles in the *Saturday Evening Post*.

The Florida boom followed the classic California pattern. Prospective customers were given free bus trips around the state by real estate promoters who had come to Florida expressly to get rich off the suckers. Big operators temporarily shifted their interests to the state from the stock market or from solid real estate dealings elsewhere, with the expectation that they would shift their investments out of Florida when they had taken their profit or when they saw the bubble about to burst. Coral Gables, promoted in a bombastic illustrated booklet by the novelist Rex Beach, promised to be a "modified Mediterranean—a new Venice, with silent pools, canals and lagoons" —but even more beautiful than the old Venice, since, from the very beginning, it would be protected by zoning. "Boca Raton will surpass in exclusiveness any resort on Florida's East Coast," prospects were assured. "But the democracy of Addison Mizner has provided large and well selected bathing beaches, golf courses, and tennis courts, aviation field, polo ground and dock rights for the use of all. No existing world resort of wealth and fashion compares with Boca Raton, and never before has there been offered such opportunity of financial reward through early participation in a Florida enterprise." When Boca Raton lots were offered in May 1925, the first day's sales reputedly exceeded $2 million, even before any of its touted glories had been transferred from paper to the landscape.

Smaller subdivisions around Miami sold out on the first day of sale.

Prospective customers were made to feel rude if they asked to see the actual sites. According to one observer, in September 1925:

> Lots were bought from blue prints. They look better that way. Then the buyer gets the promoter's vision, can see the splendid curving boulevards, the yacht basin, the parks lined with leaning cocoanut trees, the flaming hibiscus. The salesman can show the expected lines of heavy travel and help select a double (two-lot) corner for business, or a quiet water-front retreat suitable for a winter home. To go see the lot—well —it isn't done. Often it is not practicable, for most of the lots are sold "predevelopment." The boulevards are yet to be laid, the yacht basin must be pumped out, and the excavated dirt used to raise the proposed lots above water or bog level. Then they will be staked, the planning done, and the owner can find his lot.

Some conservative Eastern bankers cautioned their clients and simply asked, "When will the Florida boom collapse?" And the Florida propagandists retorted:

> Men asked the same question in George Washington's day about the Ohio country, when Cincinnati was as young as Miami is today. They doubted in Lincoln's time whether Iowa land prices were not too high. Forty years ago one could hear dire predictions of the imminent collapse of a "boom" town on Lake Michigan, called Chicago. Only recently similar forecasts were being broadcast of the ultimate fate of Los Angeles and all southern California.

Enthusiasm was beginning to abate and prices were declining by early 1926. Then, on September 19, a hurricane blew away the boom. Where "security was a certainty" there was now desolation. Undaunted optimists tried to turn away the Red Cross which came with relief for the hurricane sufferers because, they said, the publicity would damage property values.

33
Antidotes for the City:
Utopia, Renewal, Suburbia

THE VAGUENESS OF THE CITY compounded ancient problems and led Americans at first to search for remedies, then to reach for antidotes. Some tried importing Old World schemes of paternalist utopia. Others hoped that old ills could be cured by renewal, by trying to erase what was there and begin all over again. But by mid-century the future seemed to lie with refugees from the city, who were finding new ways to make suburbs into communities.

AMERICAN VERSIONS of the English or continental model industrial town were distinguished by the simplicity and coherence of their plans, by the paternalism of their government, by their initial, short-run success and by their long-run failure. In the early nineteenth century, New Englanders like Francis Cabot Lowell had built model towns to house their workers, elevate their minds, and protect their morals. Later in the century the most impressive and best advertised of such efforts was Pullman, Illinois, a model community outside Chicago, named after its founder, shaper, and ruler, George M. Pullman. By the time of the Philadelphia Centennial of 1876, "Pullman car style" was a common generic name for the products of American industrial progress. And in 1880 Pullman himself, inventor and builder of sleeping cars, decided to try to solve those city problems—crime, the slum, labor disorders—that seemed to him to be an unnecessary by-product of American industry. The "model tenement" movement in the cities, aiming at low rents and sanitary dwellings, had made little progress. Pullman, who was planning anyway to build a new factory, took the occasion to build a whole model town, where his workers would not have to live "in crowded and unhealthy tenements, in miserable streets, and subject to all the temptation and snares of a great city." Pullman hoped his workers would be "elevated and refined" by their model town, and that, incidentally, they would be discouraged from turning to drink or from pointlessly moving from job to job. And he expected, of course, that they would be less gullible to union organizers and other urban "agitators." As a company brochure explained to visitors to the

World's Columbian Exposition of 1893: "The story of Pullman naturally divides itself into three parts—the building of the car, the building of the operating system, and the building of the town."

When Pullman engaged the twenty-seven-year-old architect Solon Spenser Beman (who had recently remodeled Pullman's own Chicago mansion) to design the factory and all the other buildings on his 4,000-acre tract on the shores of Lake Calumet, the assignment itself was remarkable. For at that time it was not common for architects to be engaged to design factories. The young Beman proved equal to his novel task, and Pullman—a town where "everything fits," the nation's "first all-brick city"—became famous. Streets were planned and paved, water supply and sewage were well provided for. In the original scheme were public buildings, a shopping-center arcade, a hotel (named for Pullman's daughter), a post office, a bank, a library, a school, and a church. The "opera house," it was reported, would equal "the most elegant theaters in the country in point of architectural beauty and artistic design." The novelist Charles Dudley Warner hailed Pullman as "the only city in existence built from the foundation on scientific and sanitary principles."

But it was very much Pullman's city, designed to keep workers happy according to Pullman's own definition. He did not claim to be a philanthropist, but said again and again that it was all a "strictly business proposition." Rents were fixed to give the company a 6 percent return on investment. The long-run purpose was to provide a more stable and more docile labor force for the Pullman factory. But actually the new Pullman plant at the site was plagued by repeated strikes, culminating in the violence of 1894 which brought the National Guard with Gatling guns into the model city. Then, in 1898, the Illinois Supreme Court ruled that the company had no legal authority to build a city. By 1915 the town had fifteen saloons, the stores in the arcade were being vacated, and the original plan was abandoned. Pullman had become just another industrial suburb.

There were other company efforts elsewhere, also on the pattern of the company towns in England, France, and Germany, which aimed to cure the ills of the city while providing a contented labor force. Near Pittsburgh, for example, there were the new steel towns Homestead and Vandergrift (designed to be "a workingman's paradise"), and George Westinghouse's Wilmerding, where air brakes were made. Even when these model company towns were not the scene of violence, as in Homestead, they tended to become diversified and sordid, frustrating their creator's original purpose.

The company town became a focus for American debate over national ideals. Henry Demarest Lloyd, financial editor of the Chicago *Tribune,* who had recently become famous by his attack on Standard Oil, was commissioned in 1881 by the editor of *Harper's*

Magazine to write a piece about Pullman. Lloyd wrote the article, concluding that the "beauty and convenience" of the town were likely to fulfill the company's hopes to prevent labor trouble, since it was a place where "brains have been mixed with the mortar from the foundations to the roofs, and where the self-interest of the capitalist has been something shrewder than the selfishness of the ordinary type." But Lloyd's article was not critical enough to satisfy *Harper's* editor, and he refused it. He then turned to Richard T. Ely, a young professor of economics whose article not only satisfied *Harper's* but made Ely's public career as a social critic. Ely praised the physical plant, "the all pervading air of thrift and providence" and the absence of saloons, but he called the place undemocratic. "If free American institutions are to be preserved, we want no race reared as underlings. . . . The idea of Pullman is un-American. . . . It is benevolent, well-wishing feudalism, which desires the happiness of the people, but in such a way as shall please the authorities."

THE NOTION OF "renewing" cities and clearing slums was no American invention. Concern over the slum had grown with the rise of the industrial city. During the eighteenth century, the street commissioners of London and of Dublin had cut through their city's slums. In 1853, when Baron Haussmann began rebuilding Paris, he planned the Bois de Boulogne and cleared the avenues which gave the city its grand vistas (and presumably, too, an immunity to revolutionary barricades). After Glasgow demolished the whole of its congested ancient center in 1866, smaller slum-clearance projects followed all over Britain.

American reform movements of the late nineteenth century made slums their special target. "Slum" became the name for places where poverty, crime, prostitution, and disease festered. With the rise of photography the middle-class public could be forced to witness the conditions of slum life. Jacob A. Riis, an immigrant from Denmark, beginning in 1877 spent twenty-two years covering "the foul core of New York's slums"—places called Bandit's Roost, Bottle Alley, Kerosene Row, and Thieves' Alley—and made his reputation as a photographer and reporter of slum conditions. *How the Other Half Lives* (1890; popularizing an old phrase) was followed by *The Battle with the Slum* (1902), which reported the progress of a dozen years. Riis foreshadowed the hopes that would motivate "urban renewal" in the mid-twentieth century:

> The battle with the slum began the day civilization recognized in it her enemy. It was a losing fight until conscience joined forces with fear and self-interest against it. When common sense and the golden rule

obtain among men as a rule of practice, it will be over. . . . Justice to the individual is accepted in theory as the only safe groundwork of the commonwealth. When it is practised in dealing with the slum, there will shortly be no slum. We need not wait for the millennium, to get rid of it. We can do it now. All that is required is that it shall not be left to itself. That is justice to it and to us, since its grievous ailment is that it cannot help itself.

Since the beginning of the Civil War, the slum had three times "confronted us in New York with its challenge." One was the "treacherous mob" that led the draft riots of 1863, another was the cholera epidemic starting from "the back alleys," and a third was "the mob" led by Boss Tweed that had plundered the city's treasury. "For it is one thing or the other: either we wipe out the slum, or it wipes out us." Riis went on to warn that "when the brotherhood is denied in Mulberry Street, we shall look vainly for the virtue of good citizenship on Fifth Avenue. . . . You cannot let men live like pigs when you need their votes as freemen; it is not safe." The battle with the slum continued during the early years of the century.

A shortage of housing during World War I brought the government into the emergency effort to provide housing for war workers. Then, after 1929, the depression required a housing program in order to reduce unemployment in the building trades and to stimulate the market for construction materials; incidentally the program aimed to provide better housing. By 1933, construction of residential buildings had declined to almost nothing, annual expenditures on housing repairs had fallen from $50 million to $500,000, and home mortgages were being foreclosed at the rate of one thousand per day. Federal home loan agencies, set up to help avoid foreclosures, aided those who could afford to buy a house in the first place, but helped little in the battle against the slum. By 1934 the federal government, under the Public Works Administration, had undertaken slum-clearance projects in Atlanta, Cleveland, and Brooklyn. At first President Franklin D. Roosevelt, who felt a romantic attachment to the countryside and sought ways to draw people out of the cities, was not much interested in urban housing and slum clearance. His adviser Rexford G. Tugwell planned enticing "greenbelt towns," on the model of English garden cities, outside centers of population. Three thousand such towns were planned, and three were built.

New Deal enthusiasms finally produced the Wagner-Steagall Housing Act of 1937. Slums were torn down, and by 1941 over 160,000 dwelling units for the poor had been constructed. Their primary effect was not so much to remove as to renovate slums. Since middle-class citizens objected to having public housing nearby, new public housing was often erected in the midst of Negro districts, and to make the increase in units possible without reaching beyond the segregated areas, the public housing eventually was made taller and taller. These public-housing towers offered accommodations which were as different as possible from the preferred American housing unit, the single-family dwelling surrounded by a yard. The political liberals who had once championed large-scale public housing now attacked these towers for poor Negroes confined in Negro neighborhoods as "slums with hot running water."

"Slum clearance," which became loosely confused with "urban renewal," still remained a grand objective of hopeful reformers. The decay of houses during the Depression and the slow-down in construction during World War II worsened the shortage. The bipartisan Housing Act of 1949, sponsored by Senator Robert Taft, pushed slum clearance ahead with a program of "spot removal" which aimed to eradicate the worst slums. The first euphemism for this program was "urban redevelopment." And the enlarged act of 1954 became a program for "urban renewal." The main purpose now was to "renew" the cities—to clear away the slums, scoop out the rotten old cores of cities and replace them by a renewed city center. Now the whole city was included: not merely dilapidated residences but also commercial buildings and public services. Starting from slum clearance, this program promised "a decent home and a suitable living environment for every American family" in "well-planned, integrated residential neighborhoods."

Enthusiasm for urban renewal knew no bounds. In 1963 Congressman William S. Moorhead of Pennsylvania, quoting Isaiah on "repairing the waste cities, the desolation of many generations," extolled Pittsburgh as "the renaissance city." At the same time the president of Little Rock's First National Bank proclaimed "a vision and a goal to achieve in the rebirth of our city. We want to create a city, gentlemen, where no child will leave a slum to go to school. God willing, we shall soon have that city." Philadelphia prepared a movie reminiscent of nineteenth-century booster literature, which advertised that city as "a showcase for urban renewal." The mayor of Providence declared urban renewal "not a luxury for Providence and many other cities in this country. It is an absolute necessity if they are to remain healthy."

THE RESULTS OF the program were disappointing. There was evidence that the urban poor, supposedly the beneficiaries of the urban-renewal programs, were suffering more than ever. The demolitions resulting from slum clearance and other renewal operations (including freeways, toll roads, parking lots, airports, etc.) led to a net *loss* from the housing inventory which, during the years 1950–56, withdrew more than 200,000 units a year, increasing during the years 1957–59 to the withdrawal of 475,000 a year. In California alone, by 1960 these programs had erased 10 percent of all the housing units available in 1950, for a net loss of 359,000 units. "The emphasis on demolition and evictions," Charles Abrams, a housing specialist, observed, "has made life for many families an unending trek from one slum or furnished room to another. Building a stable life within a context of rootless living is virtually impossible. Children are uprooted from schools, parents separated from friends, and rootlessness ultimately gives way to hopelessness." The poor, and especially Negroes, Puerto Ricans, Mexicans, and other disadvantaged groups, suffered most. The new units put up in place of the old were too expensive to benefit those who were evicted. The number of new dwelling units constructed were estimated at less than one fourth of the number demolished. The median monthly rent of the private residential apartments built in 1962, which mainly replaced low-rent housing, was $195, and a considerable number rented for more than $360 per month.

The human effects of these miscalculations were disastrous. What urban renewal did to the people it was supposed to help suggested that the remedy was worse than the disease—if indeed there was a disease. To study the human problem, the sociologist Herbert Gans went to live in the West End of Boston in an area that was declared a slum in 1953. The area was to be torn down under a federal renewal program (1958–60), its inhabitants would be summarily dispersed, and within two years new tenants would be moving into the luxury apartments that had been government-financed to replace the slum. Gans discovered that the deep-rooted Italian-American "slum" community had had a flourishing community life of its own. There the food, religion, education, family life, and politics had a special character that made residents feel at home. "Redevelopment proceeded from beginning to end," Gans observed, "on the assumption that the needs of the site residents were of far less importance than the clearing and rebuilding of the site itself." The result of this urban-renewal project, then, was to destroy an existing community, and so create new problems of personal disorientation. A clinical psychologist who studied the West Enders after relocation found that nearly half the women and more than a third of the men had suffered "severe grief reaction or worse." Two years later, more than a quarter of the women were still depressed by the experience of having been evicted from their community.

By the late twentieth century the failure of efforts to renew and revive the focal "city" was itself a symptom of the attenuation of

American life, of the befogging of all distinctions, and of the desperate quest for the new. Urban renewal, like other utopian movements, was plagued by the vagueness of its definitions. What was the meaning of "slum" or "urban blight"? What housing was "substandard"? In some areas the "standard" for decent housing, fantastically high compared even to that in such countries as Sweden, was tied to the rapid pace of American technology. The growth of the American economy had created housing expectations beyond the possibilities of fulfillment. In 1967 a housing unit in the United States was not "adequate" by bureaucratic standards unless it had hot running water, a private toilet and bath, and not more than one person to a room. These definitions of "adequacy" moved ever upward in the expanding United States.

THE FAILURE OF urban renewal and the frustration of paternalistic utopias were but minor episodes in a larger epic, one of the great population movements of history. The movement to the suburbs in the early decades of the twentieth century was an internal migration which for speed was without precedent in American life. Between 1950 and 1960 the suburban population of the United States increased by about 17 million. More than 12 million of these had actually moved to a suburb, either from some central city or from a farm. The census of 1910 showed less than half as many Americans (12 percent) living in suburbs as lived in central cities (26 percent). But the census of 1960 showed almost exactly as many Americans (31 percent) living in suburbs as lived in central cities (32 percent), and the suburban proportion was leaping ahead. While the proportion of population both in central cities and on the farm steadily declined, the proportion in the suburbs grew, and by the late '60's already exceeded that in the central cities. Unless the trend changed sharply, by the end of the twentieth century most Americans would be suburbanites.

The new American habitat was described in a growing literature about the folkways, foibles, romance, and disappointments of suburbia. The focus of Sinclair Lewis' *Main Street* (1920) and *Babbitt* (1922) on the small-town hypocrisies and the follies of boosterism acquired a quaint irrelevance. By mid-century, social scientists were anatomizing suburbia as the very epitome of the American middle class. David Riesman's *Lonely Crowd* (1950), A. C. Spectorsky's *Exurbanites* (1955), William H. Whyte, Jr.'s *Organization Man* (1956), John Keats's *Crack in the Picture Window* (1957), Robert C. Wood's *Suburbia* (1958), Herbert Gans's *Levittowners* (1967), and innumerable other books used an updated social science to analyze the major community phenomenon of their day—much as their late-nineteenth-century predecessors had scrutinized the slum, immigration, and the problems of the Melting Pot. There appeared a spate of novels on love and hate, life and death in the suburbs—such as Sloan Wilson's *Man in the Gray Flannel Suit* (1955) and John Cheever's *Wapshot Chronicle* (1957)—but suburbia never became the setting for a great epic.

Folk jokes about the "city slicker" and the "farmer's daughter" were being displaced by tales of suburban wife-swapping. But there were few voices, and almost no eloquent voices, raised in defense of suburbia. The suburban transformation of American middle-class life had taken place, Americans by the millions had moved to the suburb, yet no William Allen White or Sherwood Anderson or Thornton Wilder had arisen to romanticize the new folkways.

In the early twentieth century a new American genre, the "subdivider" (the word in this sense appears to be an Americanism) or suburban "developer" came into being on the urban penumbra. An enterprising promoter would buy acreage on the edge of a promising town, "subdivide" it into lots, build streets and lay sewers, bring in electricity and water, and then advertise for buyers.

The real estate go-getter's techniques improved. From a high-pressure salesman he became a long-range planner, enlisting all the expertise of the new social scientists. After World War II, when returning veterans and expanding birth rates increased the demand for housing, speculative building enlarged real estate enterprises to a scale reminiscent of the late-eighteenth century and early-nineteenth-century Western land companies. Abraham Levitt, son of poor Russian-Jewish immigrants, pioneered in the mass production of suburban housing. Using experience acquired in building houses for the Navy during the war, Levitt and Sons began building suburban towns. The first Levittown, on Long Island, begun in 1947, was a whole new community, with houses (most appliances included) around village greens, where there were shops, a playground, and a swimming pool. The second Levittown, in Bucks County, Pennsylvania, was begun in 1951 and planned for seventeen thousand homes, including schools, churches (with land donated by the developers), and a large shopping center. Complications in this project came from the fact that the land extended over four townships and several other political units, each with its own regulations and its own governing bodies. The third Levittown, in New Jersey, planned even before the earlier project was completed, was all located in a single township, and would have twelve thousand houses by 1965. In this development, instead of all houses being built to a single design, three types in varying color schemes (from three to four bedrooms, and priced from $11,500 to $14,500) were intermixed on each street. The houses had no basement, but were built on concrete slabs with precut materials on an assembly-line system. Similar "development" cities, like Park Forest outside Chicago, or Bowie outside Washington, D.C., appeared in other parts of the country.

SUBURBS, UPSTART TOWNS in a new pattern, brought a revival of active, small-town political life. "The suburban town emerges," political scientist Robert C. Wood has observed, "equipped with a limited constituency, a homogeneity, a type of civic attitude and an amount of leisure which bid fair to put small town democracy into practice for more people and for more governments than has been possible for a hundred years." Suburbs, with their problems of creating new school systems, new recreational facilities, and new units of government, relived the conditions which accounted for many of the virtues which American historians had found in the "frontier" community. If, as historians Stanley Elkins and Eric McKitrick suggested, the special "frontier" origins of American democracy were to be traced not to the backwoods environment, but to the recurrent urgent need to build new institutions for community purposes, then the suburbs really provided a new American "frontier." The multiplication of suburbs and the trend of population to the suburb proliferated American federalism and multiplied opportunities for political participation. Just as new states and counties and upstart cities had offered new arenas for political democracy in the nineteenth century, so thousands of new suburbs with myriad local problems awakened the interests and political energies of mid-twentieth-century Americans.

In other respects, too, suburbs revived the spirit of an earlier age. Despite the rising divorce rate and other widely advertised forces which loosed the marriage bond, the suburbs, a bastion of the free-standing single-family residence, strengthened home and family. If, as was often observed, the cosmopolitan city enticed the family outside the family residence, the small town in its suburban reincarnation reinforced the home as center. The homogeneity and compatibility which characterized much small-town life in its heyday was found once again in the suburb. On the whole, suburban life was pleasant. If it lacked the cosmopolitan stimulus of the big city or the secure isolation of the farm, it provided other, blander pleasures. "Most new suburbanites," the sociologist Herbert Gans concluded after living in Levittown, New Jersey, during its formative period, "are pleased with the community that develops; they enjoy the house and outdoor living and take pleasure from the large supply of compatible people, without experiencing the boredom or malaise ascribed to suburban homogeneity."

But there was a price. In the small town, each citizen had done something in his own way to build the community. The town booster had a vision of the future which he tried to fulfill. The suburb dweller by contrast started with the future—with a shopping center for twice the population, with a school building already built, with churches constructed, with parks and playgrounds and swimming pools. These were as essential to building a suburb as the prematurely grand hotel had been to building a city in the wilderness. In large developments where the developer had a plan, and even in the smaller developments, there was a new kind of paternalism: not the quasi-feudal paternalism of the company town, nor the paternalism of the utopian ideologue. This new kind of paternalism was fostered by the American talent for organization, by the rising twentieth-century American standard of living, and by the American genius for mass production. It was the paternalism of the marketplace. The suburban developer, unlike the small-town booster, seldom intended to live in the community he was building. For him community was a commodity, a product to be sold at a profit. And the suburban home owner often moved into a whole town which had been shaped in advance by a shrewd developer's sense of the market.

The suburb was the Upstart Town, twentieth-century model, in a world where newer was better. In 1960, when about 70 percent of city dwellers were living in buildings constructed before 1940, only 42 percent of suburban dwellings were that old. The suburb was a world of brand names, of shopping centers, of franchised outlets, and of repeatable experience. Despite the increasing highway congestion, the sense of separateness from city culture was less significant than ever. For movies and radio and television, which brought urban entertainment into the suburban living room, began to make the world of distinctively urban entertainment obsolete.

The suburb was a new version, too, of the American transient community. Instead of the wagon train, where people leaned on one another as they moved across the continent, Americans in suburbs leaned on one another as they moved rapidly about the country and up the ladder of consumption. A small town was a place where a man settled. A suburb was a place to or from which a person moved. Except in a few of the most costly (and speedily disappearing) suburbs outside a few cities, suburbanites did not think of building their town for their children or their grandchildren. They expected their children to live elsewhere. And even before their children grew up, they themselves hoped to have moved to a more "exclusive" suburb. The quest to make suburbs more comfortable, more convenient, and more attractive made them more and more interchangeable.

In the late twentieth century, to move from almost any suburb to almost any other of comparable class anywhere else in the United States was like moving from one part of a neighborhood to another. With few exceptions, the products and services available, and the residence itself were only slightly different. With the addition of air conditioning to central heating as common amenities, soon to become "necessities" for middle-class Americans, even climate had less and less effect on the comfort of daily life. When they moved from the vast vague city to their very own home in the perfect suburb of their choice, they might feel that they were joining not a community of 10,000, but a community of 10 million American suburbanites living everywhere.

34
Cities within Cities:
The Urban Blues

BUT NEGRO AMERICANS, even if they had the money, were not free to join the idyllic suburb of their choice nor to enter the everywhere community of suburbanites. From their early arrival on the scene of American history, Negro Americans had an experience not shared by other Americans. Indelible immigrants, they were condemned by slavery to remain outside the mainstream of American opportunity. Even after emancipation, after a bloody civil war which purported to bring the Negro into the community of free Americans, the American Negro's experience did not cease to be distinctive. However oppressed the Negro was under slavery, that was a status plainly recognized by law, which was openly attacked by some and which many respectable Southerners openly defended. But when the Negro had become, in law, a free American, his status as an indelible immigrant became an anachronism as well as an injustice. American civilization in the twentieth century then made the position of the Negro American not simply unique, but intolerable. Nearly every novel force in the life of the nation made his situation more difficult to explain and more impossible to justify.

The Negro played a crucial and distinctive role in the changing life of the American city in the early twentieth century. In the Age of

Immigration, as we have seen—when hundreds of thousands from abroad were pouring through American ports, each group in its own way trickling into the rushing currents of American life, to be brought within a generation or two into the mainstream—the Negro remained the indelible immigrant. In the Age of the Everywhere Community, when cities had become centers of movement and mobility, when Americans were freely joining and leaving consumption communities, when they were being grouped by their interpreters and by themselves in fast-changing statistical communities, when neighborhoods had been dissolved in the vagueness of the city, when even the boundaries between city and countryside had become uncertain, the Negro found himself marked off and confined. Some called this the American Dilemma. But it was more properly the American Paradox—a contradiction that was both inexplicable and indefensible. The Negro's was an indelible community. As the century wore on, and as the nation became increasingly dissolved and diffused into looser, vaguer communities, this spectacle of one part arbitrarily kept segregated and made insoluble would trouble the nation's conscience, breeding passions that were more easily aroused than allayed, and creating problems more easily described than solved.

NOT UNTIL 1870 did the census officially list the urban population. Then, in the next half-century, the United States speedily became more and more citified. While estimates indicated that city dwellers had numbered less than one American in ten in 1830, in 1870 the urban proportion of the nation counted one American in four; increasing to one in three in 1890, to nearly one in two in 1910, to nearly two out of three in 1930, and to three out of four in the 1970's. While, as we have seen, the technical definition of an urban American shifted, the movement of population was unmistakable. This was a great internal migration, which in speed and magnitude matched the migrations from abroad which had first populated the continent.

Negro Americans joined this flow to the city, and their movement away from the countryside was even more dramatic than that of the rest of the nation. As late as 1900 only half as many Negroes as whites (in proportion to their numbers) were living in cities, but by 1960, when 68 percent of the nation's white population was classified as urban, the proportion of the nation's Negroes living in cities already came to 73 percent. Except in the old secessionist South, after the Civil War the Negro population was more urban than the white population in every decade. By 1960 the Negro population outside the South was 92.7 percent urban, and students of the census predicted that if urbanization continued at the same rate, nearly all

Negroes in the United States would be living in urban areas by 1980.

The cityward migration of Negroes was also a migration out of the South. The proportion of the nation's Negro population found in the South declined from 90 percent in 1870 to 60 percent in 1960. Negroes living in the rural South generally did not move to a Southern city on their way northward and westward. The dispersion out into the nation showed a striking uniformity. While the proportion of Negroes in the population as a whole decreased from 1870 to 1920 (from 13 percent to 10 percent), and then remained relatively stable after 1920, every section outside the South showed an increase in its Negro population.

The Negro's immigration to the city was one more American saga —as full of adventure, of hope and disappointment as any of the other migrations that had built the nation. But at this stage too, certain features sharply distinguished the Negro's experience. Other immigrant groups—the Irish, the Italians, the Jews—had generally begun their American experience in their own gathered community in a city. In the South, however, the Negro had been primarily a rural person; he had generally lived in small groups dispersed among the white population, to serve the convenience of his white master or employer. While historians disagree over the extent of residential segregation and Jim Crowism in the South just after the Civil War, the evidence suggests that the most rigid and humiliating forms of Jim Crow segregation did not come to the South until the end of the nineteenth century, and then they were actually imported from the North.

By 1900 there were seventy-two cities in the United States with a Negro population of more than 5,000. The census of 1910 showed that New York City and Washington, D.C., each had more than 90,000 Negroes, while New Orleans, Baltimore, and Philadelphia each had a Negro population exceeding 80,000.

A number of forces were bringing Negroes into Northern and Western cities. In the late nineteenth century, depression and lack of opportunity in the South sent some of the more adventurous or the more desperate on their way. Then, at the outbreak of World War I, when the flow of unskilled immigrant labor from Europe was cut off, Henry Ford and others sent their agents South and they even provided special freight cars to bring Negroes to work in their Northern factories. Negroes found employment on the Ford assembly lines, where they shared the benefits of Ford's unprecedented $5-a-day minimum wage. Because Ford was one of the first Northern industrial employers of large numbers of Negroes, the very name *Ford* conjured up visions of urban opportunities and problems, and Ford became the subject of many a blues.

> Say, I'm goin' to get me a job now, workin' in Mr. Ford's place
> Say, I'm goin' to get me a job now, workin' in Mr. Ford's place,
> Say, that woman tol' me last night, "Say, you cannot even stand
>   Mr. Ford's ways."

Others went North and West to take jobs in the steel plants of Pittsburgh or Chicago. Women found jobs as household servants. And a small number of Negro business and professional men came North (as the saying went) "to take advantage of the disadvantages."

When the Negro migrant arrived at his Promised Land outside the South, segregation ordinances, social pressures, and fear, and then inevitable choice, kept him confined in his own city within the city. Negro communities developed a life of their own with their own character, their own glamour, and their own frustrations. New York's Harlem, which was soon called "the largest Negro community in the world," was the symbol and the prototype of the metropolitan life that the Negro in his new urban congregation and segregation was building for himself.

HARLEM WAS A bizarre upstart city-within-a-city, a peculiar urban frontier, a by-product of the mobility of non-Negro Americans. It would produce its own brand of boosters and community builders and Go-Getters.

New opportunities for the Negro in the city were symbolized in the career of the talented and versatile James Weldon Johnson, a founder of the National Association for the Advancement of Colored People, a lawyer, composer and lyricist (he wrote some two hundred songs), fighter for equal opportunity, and chronicler of the New York Negro community. In 1925, in "Harlem: the Culture Capital," Johnson succinctly told the story of how, after the turn of the century, that vast and varied Negro community came into being:

> Harlem had been overbuilt with large, new-law apartment houses, but rapid transportation to that section was very inadequate—the Lenox Avenue Subway had not yet been built—and landlords were finding difficulty in keeping houses on the east side of the section filled. Residents along and near Seventh Avenue were fairly well served by the Eighth Avenue Elevated. A colored man, in the real estate business at this time, Philip A. Payton, approached several of these landlords with the proposition that he would fill their empty or partially empty house with steady colored tenants. The suggestion was accepted, and one or two houses on One Hundred and Thirty-fourth Street east of Lenox Avenue were taken over. Gradually other houses were filled. The whites paid little attention to the movement until it began to spread

west of Lenox Avenue; they then took steps to check it. They proposed through a financial organization, the Hudson Realty Company, to buy all properties occupied by colored people and evict the tenants. The Negroes countered by similar methods. . . .

The situation now resolved itself into an actual contest. Negroes not only continued to occupy available apartment houses, but began to purchase private dwellings between Lenox and Seventh Avenues. Then the whole movement, in the eyes of the whites, took on the aspect of an "invasion"; they became panic-stricken and began fleeing as from a plague. The presence of one colored family in a block, no matter how well bred and orderly, was sufficient to precipitate a flight. House after house and block after block was actually deserted. It was a great demonstration of human beings running amuck. None of them stopped to reason why they were doing it or what would happen if they didn't. The banks and lending companies holding mortgages on these deserted houses were compelled to take them over. For some time they held these houses vacant, preferring to do that and carry the charges than to rent or sell them to colored people. But values dropped and continued to drop until at the outbreak of the war in Europe property in the northern part of Harlem had reached the nadir.

In the meantime the Negro colony was becoming more stable; the churches were being moved from the lower part of the city; social and civic centers were being formed; and gradually a community was being evolved. Following the outbreak of the war in Europe Negro Harlem received a new and tremendous impetus.

As the former residents of this neighborhood—themselves immigrants or the children of immigrants from Italy, Ireland, Poland, or elsewhere—moved out to other parts of the city or to the new suburbs, their places were taken by Negro immigrants from the South.

The new settlers in Harlem came from many parts of the world, not only from the South but also from Africa and from the West Indies. Among them, as one perceptive Negro intellectual observed, were "the peasant, the student, the businessman, the professional man, artist, poet, musician, adventurer and worker, preacher and criminal, exploiter and social outcast. Each group has come with its own separate motives and for its own special ends, but their greatest experience has been the finding of one another."

As a result, according to LeRoi Jones, "The *Negro* becomes more definitely *Negroes*. . . . one essential uniformity, the provinciality of place, the geographical and social constant within the group, was erased." His metropolitan experience revealed to the Negro that he had within him wider, more varied possibilities than he had seen before. He had progressed (in historian Nathan Huggins' phrase) "from rural homogeneity to urban pluralism." But the very same circumstances which opened the wider world within him tended to develop a new kind of race consciousness. "What had defined them as a race," Huggins notes in his chronicle of the Harlem Renaissance, "was a common condition and a common problem. What was needed to make a race, however, was a common consciousness and a life in common. Life in the city, life in Harlem, would satisfy that need."

This was *The New Negro,* described in the influential book of that title edited in 1925 by Alain Locke. A Philadelphia-born Negro, Locke was one of the earliest American Rhodes Scholars to Oxford, became a professor of philosophy, and drew on his own experience of the wider world to find the Negro's new role in American life. "For generations," he said, "in the mind of America, the Negro has been more of a formula than a human being—a something to be argued about, condemned or defended, to be 'kept down,' or 'in his place,' or 'helped up,' to be worried with or worried over, harassed or patronized, a social bogey or a social burden." Now, having found himself in his own city-within-a-city, the Negro American would become "the advance-guard of the African peoples in their contact with the Twentieth Century civilization." His mission was "rehabilitating the race in world esteem." Locke drew on the traditional American belief that the nation was a City Upon a Hill: the Negro in America (reversing Kipling) would take up the "Black Man's burden."

Harlem had its Renaissance. By 1920 the Negro population of New York City, overwhelmingly concentrated in Harlem, numbered more than 150,000, making it the largest Negro community of any city in the nation. Within the next decade, the remarkable group of literary, musical, and artistic talents which flourished there had brought to that repossessed slum a world-wide reputation. The lyric poet Countée Cullen anthologized Negro verse, wrote novels, and translated Greek tragedy. Claude McKay, who had immigrated from Jamaica, wrote *Home to Harlem* (1928), the first best-selling work of fiction by a Negro American. Jake, who had deserted from the Army in World War I because they wouldn't let him fight Germans, returns to his beloved Harlem with all its problems and loves and hates, with its prostitution and narcotics and its countless confining frustrations. A McKay hero rhapsodizes, "Harlem! Where else could I have all this life but Harlem? Good old Harlem! Chocolate Harlem! Sweet Harlem! Harlem, I've got you' number down." On Harlem's stage and in the wings appeared other varied talents who merited notice not because they were Negroes, but because they were original artists or writers or creative scholars: James Weldon Johnson himself; Alain Locke; Jean Toomer, who wrote of the crosscurrents of Europe and America; Jessie Redmond Fauset, novelist of the life of middle-class Negroes; sociologists W. E. B. DuBois and E. Franklin Frazier; and publicist Walter White. One of the most widely appealing of all was Langston Hughes, a prolific man of letters who drew on the Negro's special experience to interpret the problems of all Americans. "I can never put on paper the thrill of the underground ride to Harlem," Hughes recalled of his arrival there in 1921. "I went up the steps and out into the bright September sunlight. Harlem! I stood there, dropped my bags, took a deep breath and felt happy again."

And it was not only in the familiar genres of art and letters that the newly congregated, half-liberated Negro showed his talent. While his northward cityward movement had liberated him from the traditions and shackles of plantation slavery, he was now freed only to live with himself, to discover his own community. His full liberation— into the world of the everywhere community—was yet to come. The Negroes' cities-within-cities in their segregation and immobility were oddities in American life, but they actually produced a new music which quickly spread across the nation and around the world —and at once became known as the music most characteristically American.

"THE JAZZ AGE," the decade after World War I, when the nation became predominantly urban, took its name from the rich and varied new popular music which was essentially a creation of the Negro in the city. Historians cannot agree on the origin of the word "jazz": some say it is of African or Creole origin, others that it derived from the name of a musician; many American linguists including Mencken connect it somehow with the folk-speech expression "to jazz" describing sexual intercourse. But there is no denying that this American form of music originated with Negroes in the first age of their migration to the city, and jazz flourished primarily because of the talent, energy, and imagination of Negroes in cities. In Europe, too, the years after World War I were an age of musical experiment —of Arnold Schoenberg and Béla Bartók. But jazz (as Gunther Schuller, the chronicler of its origins, observes) was a more democratic, more communal kind of experiment. For the Old World saw developing novel forms of "art music," of salon and concert-hall music, the works of composers played by performers for audiences of patrons.

Jazz, however (in the language of the musicologist), was "not the product of a handful of stylistic innovators, but a relatively unsophisticated quasi-folk music—more sociological manifestation than music . . . recently coalesced from half a dozen tributary sources into a still largely anonymous, but nevertheless distinct idiom." Early American jazz, like African native music, was not so much a distinctive art "form" as a kind of communal celebration. And again it was distinctively democratic and characteristically American in its many ways of erasing distinctions. As a music par excellence of the extemporizer and the improvisor, jazz dissolved the old distinction between composer and performer. It provided a new intimacy and interrelation between each performer and his fellows. And as a music of the dance, it was peculiarly responsive to its audience, who became somehow part of the performance.

The cheerful rhythms of "ragtime" (popularized after about 1896 and classically expressed in the performances of Scott Joplin, a Negro from Texas whose "Maple Leaf Rag" became a prototype of a new syncopation) and the melancholy liveliness of the "blues" combined with folk reminiscence and African rhythm into a free-wheeling American musical vernacular. It could be sung or played on any and every kind of implement or instrument, and spoke a musical language that almost anyone anywhere could understand.

One of the fathers of the blues was W. C. Handy, a Negro from Alabama who started in the minstrel tradition as a cornetist, and who became best known for his "St. Louis Blues" (1914). As Handy himself explained:

> The blues is a thing deeper than what you'd call a mood today. Like the spirituals, it began with the Negro, it involves our history, where we came from, and what we experienced.
>
> The blues came from the man farthest down. The blues came from nothingness, from want, from desire. And when a man sang or played the blues, a small part of the want was satisfied from the music.
>
> The blues go back to slavery, to longing. My father, who was a preacher, used to cry every time he heard someone sing *I'll See You On Judgment Day*. When I asked him why, he said, "That's the song they sang when your uncle was sold into slavery in Arkansas. He wouldn't let his masters beat him, so they got rid of him the way they would a mule."
>
> Then in the First World War, all Americans got a taste of what we had had for years—people being torn from their families and sent to faraway places, sometimes against their wishes. And blues and jazz began to have more meaning for more people. Then the depression was a new experience for many. But we had been hungry for years and had known hunger and hurt.
>
> So the blues helped to fill the longing in the hearts of all kinds of people. They took it to their hearts and felt the same thing we felt. Now when you hear a white person sing the blues, he can put as much into it as a Negro. The blues and jazz have become a part of all American music and will be developed farther and farther into infinity.

The Negro in the city was doubly uprooted: trying to begin life in America, for the second time. Uprooted against his will from Africa

to slavery in the southern United States, he had adjusted himself
somehow to the Southern life of farm and plantation; now, a voluntary exile from the land of his parents, he sought roots in the city's
hard cold pavement. His fast-paced laments from his double Diaspora provided the theme song for all the other hurried, mobile
Americans who looked in the cement for what earlier generations
had found only in the soil.

It is no wonder that the specific origins of jazz—the word, the
music, the first composers and first performers—are hard to locate.
For jazz was a democratic, vernacular music, and, as LeRoi Jones and
others have noted, it grew out of an experience that Negroes early
in this century were having in their newly formed urban congregations all over the country. It is a commonplace that jazz appeared
very early in New Orleans—where even before the Civil War,
Negroes had been somewhat freer to share the life of the metropolis.
There, after the Civil War, Negroes picked up the discarded instruments of military bands, and drawing on the African music long
heard in Congo Square, they transmuted military and funeral tunes
and rhythms into a new fraternal experience. Since jazz, and the
blues, grew out of "the general movement of the mass of black
Americans into the central culture of the country," it naturally appeared at about the same time in many cities. A product of the
everywhere communities of the Negroes' new cities-within-cities,
jazz and the blues were perhaps the first American popular music
that was not regional. New Orleans, St. Louis, Chicago, New York,
Detroit, and other meccas of the northward Negro migration were
all centers of jazz; each place (like each performer) had its own style,
but performers moved easily from one Harlem to another. Louis
Armstrong, who began in New Orleans, went on to Chicago, then to
New York and elsewhere. Jazz created a nationwide community
where players and singers knew one another.

The phonograph, too, was providentially suited to jazz and the
blues. Music that was so improvised and extemporized was not to be
captured on a frozen page of sheet music. The one-time performance, with all its spontaneity and improvisation, had a unique appeal which the record caught. Mamie Smith's "Crazy Blues," sometimes called the first best-selling disk of the blues, was recorded in
mid-February 1920 and sold for some months at the rate of eight
thousand records a week, mainly to the urban Negro market. It set
the pace and revealed the market for "race" records. Incidentally,
too, it showed the Negro in a new light: as a candidate for countless
consumption communities. "The Negro as *consumer*," observes
LeRoi Jones, "was a new and highly lucrative slant, an unexpected
addition to the strange portrait of the Negro the white American
carried around in his head. It was an unexpected addition for the

Negro as well. The big urban centers, like the new 'black cities' of Harlem, Chicago's South Side, Detroit's fast-growing Negro section, as well as the larger cities of the South were immediate witnesses to this phenomenon. Friday nights after work in those cold gray Jordans of the North, Negro workingmen lined up outside record stores to get the new blues, and as the money rolled in, the population of America, as shown on sales prognostication charts in the offices of big American industry, went up by one-tenth."

While the phonograph brought jazz out to the whole American people, and the radio created an instant musical audience of unprecedented extent, recording itself tended to change the character of jazz and the blues. A live blues song or a jazz performance was of indeterminate length. It lasted until the performers had exhausted all their spontaneous improvisations. But a phonograph record could hold only so much; and a result of these recordings, as the historian of jazz Martin Williams has observed, was to put limits where there had been none before. A singer who knew that she could manage to put only four blues stanzas on a ten-inch record would tend to offer a set "composed" piece.

White Americans like Benny Goodman took up jazz and were among its most successful and most prosperous performers. Some, like Bix Beiderbecke, made it their own kind of lament or protest against a society that they had rejected or that had rejected them. Concert halls began offering "symphonic jazz." The Original Dixieland Jazz Band, an entirely white group, was making phonograph records in 1917; and by 1920 Paul Whiteman, professing to rise above "the crude jazz of the past," was directing a full concert-hall orchestra before conventional audiences of music lovers. Now, in an appropriately ironic reversal of historical roles, white Americans were imitating their segregated Negro fellow citizens.

In a nation of everywhere communities, where standardized, nationally advertised products were rapidly flattening the flavor of the different regions, the Negroes' cities-within-cities offered colorful relief. Carl Van Vechten, a white Iowa-born journalist, found "the squalor of Negro life, the vice of Negro life . . . a wealth of novel, exotic, picturesque materials to the artist." And in his *Nigger Heaven* (1926) he offered a sympathetic but romanticized and sensationalized caricature of life in Harlem, which became an immediate best-seller. In the 1920's, slumming parties took white tourists to Harlem night clubs and hot spots to see "tantalizin' tans" and "hot chocolates" in *Blackbird Revues,* which acquired a reputation for Left Bank entertainment to rival that of Paris. For the local jet-set, Harlem was "a great playground." The Cotton Club, claiming "the hottest show in town," and other Harlem cabarets appealing exclusively to a white clientele became quite chic. The Negro, who in the South had been a symbol of peasant simplicity, in his new urban congregations was assigned the role of the uninhibited urban American. This role continued at least past the mid-century, so that when Norman Mailer sought a label for the liberated "beatnik" of the 1950's he called him "the White Negro."

THE CONCENTRATION OF Negro population into cities-within-cities made Negroes more identifiable as a group in parts of the country where they actually could vote. The Negro's movement northward and westward and cityward was a movement toward a larger role in national politics. During Reconstruction—in the thirty years after Appomattox—the South had sent two Negro senators (both from Mississippi) and some twenty Negro congressmen to Washington. But in the early twentieth century every conceivable device was used in the South to prevent qualified Negroes from voting, much less holding office. Only after his migration did the Southern Negro become a voting citizen. By 1942 there were as many Negroes voting in the United States as the total number of whites voting in all the seven States of the Deep South (Mississippi, Louisiana, Alabama, South Carolina, Arkansas, Georgia and Florida). In 1947 Democrat William Dawson, a Negro (his predecessor, the first Northern Negro in Congress, Oscar de Priest, had served three terms from 1928), was sent to the House of Representatives from the South Side of Chicago, followed two years later by Adam Clayton Powell from the Harlem district of New York City and Charles C. Diggs, Jr., from Detroit. By 1964 there were four Negroes in Congress, and by 1972 their numbers had increased to fifteen. Edward Brooke, a Republican and a Negro, was elected to the Senate from Massachusetts in 1966.

The voting power of the Negro had become so considerable (and so identifiably concentrated in Northern cities) that in 1960 for the first time in American history, Negro voters were widely assumed to have played a decisive role in a presidential election. Some knowledgeable observers credited Negro voters for the narrow popular margin of 120,000 which elected President John F. Kennedy. In 1964 the Twenty-fourth Amendment to the Constitution was adopted, outlawing the poll tax which had been widely used in the South to disfranchise the Negro. In 1967 Thurgood Marshall, a Negro, was appointed by President Lyndon B. Johnson to the United States Supreme Court. By 1970 there were forty-eight Negro mayors, three of major cities. After 1960, a series of federal laws to protect civil rights and the right to vote were beginning to insure the Negro that local discrimination, even in the South, would not deprive him of his franchise. Although the Founding Fathers had expressly reserved to each of the states the fixing of qualifications for voting, the Fifteenth Amendment to the Constitution (adopted in 1870) forbade the denial of the right to vote "on account of race, color, or previous condition of servitude." But not until the mid-twentieth century did the Negro's right to vote become a new kind of federal commodity.

The strongest and deepest currents of American life in the twentieth century were drawing the Negro—along with other Americans —into everywhere communities. Now the Negro's continuing residential segregation and the relics of his exclusion from public facilities, always anomalous, became unbearable.

But while the currents of history could be deflected, the deep channels in which the thought and feelings of large numbers of Americans had been flowing were not easily erased. The Negro had been pushed into a devious, segregated channel on his way into American life. The urban experience which began to give him his opportunity to be himself had also separated him from other Americans, had stirred his resentment and deepened his sense of indelible racial identity. This inevitably aroused fears and hostilities among his fellow Americans who did not know him but who would not have him for their neighbor. The tension between the races expressed in lynching, the illegal execution of individual Negroes, after about 1890 was exacerbated by group conflict. The age of the Negro's emergence into American life was the age when "race riot" entered the American language. Segregation and racial discrimination were reinforced by an outspoken and organized white racism. The second Ku Klux Klan, founded in Georgia in 1915, spread through the North and Middle West until it claimed a membership of four million in the 1920's. By the 1960's the slogans of "White Supremacy" which had long plagued American life, were being matched by slogans of "Black Power," and a new Negro racism became almost respectable. Shifting away from the nonviolent teachings of the Reverend Martin Luther King, Jr., a newly organized, newly proud and self-conscious Negro community experimented with every sort of technique—violent, nonviolent, and "nonviolent"—in an effort to secure their rightful place in American life.

But some of these efforts themselves threatened to postpone the day when the Negro would be undistinguished from all other Americans and so frustrated their proper purpose. Efforts to "compensate" for historical injustices by quotas, by reverse discrimination and other devices were creating a new suspiciousness and resentment in the non-Negro community; this in turn threatened to accentuate and perpetuate the Negro's indelible status, and to create problems which neither good will nor violence gave promise of solving.

Still, the strong, deep currents of American life in the Age of Everywhere Communities did justify among many the hope that equality-loving Americans could employ unpredictable New World resources to accomplish the unexpected. Could a nation which had created boundless new consumption communities and statistical communities, and which (as we shall see) could erase space and the seasons—could that nation once again fulfill the American talent for erasing barriers?

Book Two

THE DECLINE OF THE MIRACULOUS

"The place where miracles not only happen, but where they happen all the time."

THOMAS WOLFE

"Miracles happen only to those who believe in them."

PROVERB

I N AMERICA the crude intractable facts of life, without which miracles never would have been necessary, were being dissolved. The regularities of nature, by which men knew that they were alive and were only human—the boundaries of seasons, of indoors and outdoors, of space and time, and the uniqueness of each passing moment—all these were being confused. The old tricks of the miracle maker, the witch, and the magician became commonplace. Foods were preserved out of season, water poured from bottomless indoor containers, men flew up into space and landed out of the sky, past events were conjured up again, the living images and resounding voices of the dead were made audible, and the present moment was packaged for future use.

When man could accomplish miracles he began to lose his sense of the miraculous. This meant, too, a decline of common sense, and the irrelevance of the rules of thumb that had governed man since the beginning of history. Americans who could no longer expect the usual were in danger of depriving themselves of the charms of the unexpected. "Everyday miracles" added immeasurably to life, but they also subtracted something that could never be measured. Democratizing everything enlarged the daily experience of millions; but spreading also meant thinning.

Attenuation summed up the new quality of experience. Attenuated experience was thinner, more diluted, its sensations were weaker and less poignant. It was a life punctuated by commas and semicolons rather than by periods and exclamation marks.

PART FIVE

Leveling Times and Places

> "I mean to put a potato into a pillbox, a pump-
> kin into a tablespoon, the biggest sort of water-
> melon into a saucer. . . . The Turks made acres
> of roses into attar of roses. . . . I intend to make
> attar of everything!"
>
> GAIL BORDEN

THE FIRST CHARM and virgin promise of America were that it was so different a place. But the fulfillment of modern America would be its power to level times and places, to erase differences between here and there, between now and then. And finally the uniqueness of America would prove to be its ability to erase uniqueness.

Elsewhere democracy had meant forms of personal, political, economic, and social equality. In the United States, in addition, there would be a novel environmental democracy. Here, as never before, the world would witness the "equalizing" of times and places.

The flavor of life had once come from winter's cold, summer's heat, the special taste and color of each season's diet. The American Democracy of Times and Places meant making one place and one thing more like another, by bringing them under the control of man. The flavor of fresh meat would be tasted anywhere anytime, summer would have its ice, and winter would have its warmth, inside and outside would flow together, and men would live and work not only on the unlevel ground but also in the homogeneous air.

Civilization had survived man's limitations. Could it also survive his near-omnipotence? Men had been drawn together by their common weakness. Could they also find community in their new-found powers?

35

Condense!
Making Food Portable through Time

IN NOVEMBER 1846 the Donner Party of eighty-seven emigrants on their way from Sangamon County, Illinois, to California
were trapped in deep snow while camping at Truckee Lake in the
Sierra Nevada mountains. According to the familiar story, they
would all have starved to death had not the survivors sustained themselves by eating the flesh of those who had died. The rescue parties
from California managed to bring out forty-seven survivors. For
practical-minded Americans of the day this was not only an episode
in the history of morals; it also dramatized the peculiar needs of
Americans on the move.

WHEN GAIL BORDEN, a surveyor and land agent at Galveston
in the recently annexed state of Texas, heard of the starvation of the
Donner Party and the hunger of the others who were trying to cross
the continent, he was stirred to invent a way of making food more
portable. Born on a farm in central New York, he had meandered
west with his parents, first to Ohio, and then on to Kentucky and
Indiana. He personally knew the problems of westward travel. He

309

taught himself surveying, then earned his living as a schoolteacher on the borderlands of Mississippi before joining his family at Stephen A. Austin's colony in Texas in 1829. There Austin put him in charge of the official land surveys, which gave him the power to make and break fortunes. In 1835, when the colony needed a newspaper, the versatile Borden and a friend founded the weekly *Telegraph and Texas Register*. The tenth newspaper started in Texas, Borden's *Telegraph* was the first to last longer than two years. He knew the usual troubles of the backwoods booster press—scarce materials, scarce news, subscribers who could not be found or who would not pay when they were found. To make ends meet, he became the official printer to the new Republic of Texas, and the Texas Declaration of Independence was published by his press in March 1836. When the site of Houston was chosen for the capital, Borden was named official surveyor. Then he moved on again to Galveston Island, where he served as Collector of the Port, helped lay out streets, planned a water supply, sold city lots, and became a passionate booster for "The New York of Texas."

But Borden was no ordinary public servant. "He has dozens of inventions," a Galveston neighbor observed, "and he is the most wonderful of them all himself." His "Locomotive Bath House," for example, could be carried out into the Galveston surf so that ladies could bathe in modest privacy. His wedding present to his wife was his homemade revolving dining table, with a fixed rim the width of a dining plate, and a revolving center on which the dishes to be served could be rotated to each person. Noting that yellow fever was conquered by the first frost, he devised his own public-health program; by using ether, "to freeze you down to, say, 30° or 40°—I mean, to keep you for a week as if under a white frost. . . . lock up every soul in a temporary winter." Then there was his own design for a steamboat propelled not by a screw or a paddle wheel, but by a moving belt the full length of the keel mounted with paddle boards. More remarkable still was his "Terraqueous Machine"—a sail-driven prairie schooner for land and sea. When he demonstrated the machine to a crowd of his fellow townsmen at the beach, his passengers sailed into the Gulf, and so proved that his boat was really amphibious; but unfortunately the boat capsized and dumped the passengers into the water.

"I never drop an idea," boasted Borden, "except for a better one." The "better idea" to which he turned from his Terraqueous Machine would lead him to fame and fortune. When he tried to concoct a new kind of portable food for his friends who were traveling to California in July 1849, he made an "important discovery . . . an improved process of preserving the nutritious properties of meat, or animal flesh, of any kind, by obtaining the concentrated extract of it, and combining it with flour or vegetable meal, and drying or baking the mixture in an oven, in the form of a biscuit or cracker."

This was Borden's first application of the creed which would guide him in business for a lifetime. "Condense your sermons," he advised the minister of his Galveston church. "You can do almost any thing with every thing. If you plan and think, and, as fast as you drop one thing, seize upon another. . . . The world is changing. In the direction of condensing.. . . Even lovers write no poetry, nor any other stuff and nonsense, now. They condense all they have to say, I suppose, into a kiss. . . Time was when people would. . . . spend hours at a meal. Napoleon never took over twenty minutes. . . . *I* am through in fifteen. People have almost lost the faculty of fooling away their time."

Borden spent six years developing his Meat Biscuit. And in his own brochure in 1850 he listed some of those whom his biscuit would benefit: the Navy and all men at sea; travelers "on long journeys, through destitute regions" where, he pointed out, "the fire for cooking is one of the greatest dangers in Indian country, as it betrays the situation of the camp to the hostile Indians"; geologists and surveyors; explorers "in making geological and mineralogical surveys of our newly acquired territories, as well as those running the boundary"; hospitals, where "a patient can, at the shortest notice, have it prepared to any degree of nutrition, from a weak broth to the most nutritious soup"; and all families, "especially in warm weather." Elisha Kent Kane's first Arctic expedition carried several canisters of Borden's meat biscuits. Hoping to secure acceptance of the meat biscuit by physicians and by the United States Army, Borden made a partner of Dr. Ashbel Smith, a Yale graduate and surgeon-general to the Texas Republic. Smith, whose main use was in public relations, wrote an article for *De Bow's Review* explaining how the manufacture of meat biscuits would help diversify Southern industry. At the Crystal Palace Exhibition in London, in May 1851, Smith exhibited the Meat Biscuit alongside other ingenious American products, including Herring's Patent Salamander Safe (£500 to anybody who could pick the lock), Colt's revolver, and McCormick's Virginia Reaper. When it happened that Dr. Ashbel Smith was the American appointed to the international jury a consequence was that the highest award for contribution to the food industry went to Gail Borden of Texas.

"It appears to be a part of the mission of America," Dr. Smith boasted, " . . . not merely to furnish a home to refugees from the oppressions and crowded population of the old world, but also, to feed in part the poor of those countries who never taste good meat:

and to whom, even a miserable flesh is a great rarity." Borden spent six years and $60,000 in promoting his meat biscuit. But the powerful suppliers of fresh meat to the Army made it difficult for Borden's biscuit to get a fair trial. There were other problems, too. When people complained that Borden's biscuit was "unsightly" and unpalatable, Borden himself confessed that he alone really knew how to prepare his biscuit. Frederick Law Olmsted on his travels through Texas finally fed his meat biscuit to the birds, declaring that he would "decidedly undergo a very near approach to the traveler's last bourne, before having recourse to it." But even before the meat biscuit had plainly failed, Borden had turned to an even better idea which before the end of the century would make the name of Borden a synonym for milk.

ON THE ROUGH OCEAN VOYAGE back from the London exhibition in the fall of 1851, one story goes, Borden learned that the cows in the ship's hold became so seasick that they could not be milked. When he heard the hungry cries of the immigrant babies, he began to wonder whether he could not somehow use his condensing technique to provide milk for such emergencies. This was a difficult assignment, for milk was the most fragile of foods, which people all over the world had vainly tried to find ways to preserve in fresh and tasty form. To make cheese was, of course, a kind of answer to the problem. But Borden determined to find some way to condense whole milk.

Luckily, Borden did not know enough to be confused by the theories of the day, all of which had proved that it couldn't be done. So Borden simply tried his own hand with a panful of milk. In Europe there had been some success in evaporating milk for preservation, but none of the products had been marketable. And Borden probably did not know of them.

Preserving milk in some form was not too difficult. But preserving quality and taste were quite another matter. First Borden boiled milk in an open pan on a sand bath heated by charcoal, and then he added brown sugar. When the resulting liquid was sealed in glass, it would keep for months, but it had a dark color and smelled like molasses. At the Shaker Colony in New Lebanon, New York, where Borden first saw a vacuum pan, he obtained one, and with it tried condensing milk. But as the milk was heated it stuck to the side of the pan, then foamed and boiled over. Experts advised him to give up, but Borden merely greased the pan, and in that remarkably simple way perfected his technology of condensing milk. Borden's innovation was in fact so simple that he had trouble convincing the patent commissioners in Washington that he had done anything really new. But with a testimonial from the editor of the *Scientific American* and with a pile of charts and affidavits, he finally persuaded the patent officials that he had invented an essential new item: evaporating milk *in a vacuum*.

Borden's intuitive explanation, though not designed to satisfy a modern organic chemist, showed his talent for going to the heart of the matter. Milk, like blood, he said, was a "living fluid" and "as soon as drawn from the cow begins to die, change, and decompose." The vacuum would keep the milk from "dying" until it had been sealed. In 1856, Borden received both English and American patents.

Even before his condensed milk had found a market, Borden was trying to condense coffee, tea, and "other useful dietary matters." Condensing became his obsession. "I mean to put a potato into a pillbox, a pumpkin into a tablespoon, the biggest sort of watermelon into a saucer . . . The Turks made acres of roses into attar of roses. . . . I intend to make attar of everything!"

Condensed milk quickly proved to be a commercial success. Enlisting the financial support of a wealthy New York wholesale grocer whom he happened to meet on a train, Borden founded the New York Condensed Milk Company, and in 1858, in a village about a hundred miles north of the city, established his first large-scale milk-condensing plant. Neighboring farmers brought their milk to his factory, where it was condensed before being taken into the city. And in *Leslie's Illustrated Newspaper* for May 22, 1858, an advertisement, probably written by Borden himself, announced:

> BORDEN'S CONDENSED MILK, Prepared in Litchfield County, Conn., is the only Milk ever concentrated without the admixture of sugar or some other substance, and remaining easily soluble in water. It is simply Fresh Country Milk, from which the water is nearly all evaporated, and nothing added. The Committee of the Academy of Medicine recommend it as "an article that, for purity, durability and economy, is hitherto unequalled in the annals of the Milk Trade."
>
> One quart, by the addition of water, makes 2½ quarts, equal to cream —5 quarts rich milk, and 7 quarts good milk.
>
> For sale at 173 Canal Street, or delivered at dwellings in New York and Brooklyn, at 25 CENTS per quart.

It was a strategic moment to bring a superior milk product into the New York market. For at the time the city was shaken by scandals of "milk murder." The same newspaper which carried Borden's advertisement had been rousing New Yorkers by its exposure of the needlessly high infant mortality rate, caused, it said, by filthy milk. The milk then commonly distributed in the city was called "swill-milk" because it came from city cows fed on distillers' "swill" or "still-slops," the residue from the distilleries. Such milk contained almost no butterfat, and to cover up its unsavory blue, it had to be artificially colored. Manure and milk were hauled in the same wagons, and *Leslie's* told tales of how sick cows were propped up for a last milking before they expired. The city swill-dairies were a kind of "Vesuvius which belched forth intolerable and stinking stench." Swill-milk, the leading dairy authority reported, had an effect "on the system of young children . . . very destructive, causing diseases of various kinds, and, if continued, certain death."

With Borden's dairy-fresh sanitary product, the sales of the New York milk routes increased, and more routes were added. Borden set a new standard of cleanliness and quality, sending his inspectors out into the countryside where they instructed the dairy farmers. He took no milk from cows that had calved within twelve days, and he required that udders be washed in warm water before milking, that barns be clean, and that manure be kept away from the milking stalls. He demanded that the wire-cloth strainers be scalded and dried morning and night. Inspectors at the factory rejected milk that arrived with a temperature above 58 degrees. In many ways this complicated the lives of farmers, but it simplified their lives, too. For Borden had turned the dairy farmer into a milk wholesaler, who no longer had to peddle his milk around the countryside, nor did he have to churn butter or mold cheese. The farmer who had made a contract with Borden and continued to meet the Borden standards could deliver his milk to the factory dock and receive a regular check from the company.

When the Civil War broke out, then, Borden was ready to supply the Army. One of his sons, John Gail, was fighting for the Union, while his other son, Lee, had joined the Texas Cavalry on the side of the Confederacy. But the Union Army bought Borden's condensed milk as a field ration and Borden himself was committed to the Union. Even after his New York plant was turning out sixteen thousand quarts a day, he still could not keep up with the government orders, so he licensed plants in other parts of the country. By the end of 1866 the Elgin, Illinois, plant alone was purchasing from farmers nearly a third of a million gallons of milk each year.

In 1875, a year after Gail Borden's death, the Borden Company began selling fluid fresh whole milk. Although his company now was stricter than ever in its standards for dairy farmers, there were limits to what it could do. Bacterial count as a test for milk was still unknown, and the only standard of sanitation was how the milk was produced and handled. Milk was still delivered by ladling it out of large cans into the buyer's container. Until milk was bottled at the dairy and distributed in smaller units in closed containers, it was impossible to insure sanitary fresh milk in the home. By 1885 the Borden Company, under Gail's elder son, was beginning to sell milk in bottles. But it was another decade before Louis Pasteur's work made bacterial count a standard for market milk and "pasteurization" became widespread; and still another twenty years before the tuberculin testing of cattle was protecting children against tuberculosis. In one state after another, medical commissions were set up to "certify" milk.

WHILE BORDEN WAS finding ways to condense milk and put it into a can to be kept indefinitely, scores of other enterprising Americans were finding ways to bring everything to everybody year-round. The basic process of canning had been invented by a French wine maker and food supplier, Nicolas Appert, who won a prize from Napoleon in 1809 for finding a new way of supplying fresh provisions for the French navy. Appert had invented the cooking and sealing process which produced a flourishing canning industry in nineteenth-century Europe, and with a few basic improvements, continued in use into the twentieth century.

In the 1840's the American canning industry gained momentum. Corn, tomatoes, peas, and fish were canned for travelers journeying to California. Baltimore, on Chesapeake Bay, where the oysters, crabs, and fish were plentiful, became the first great American canning center. But canning techniques were still rudimentary, and when they went awry, a whole season's pack could be spoiled. Since the processing with boiling water took up to six hours for each batch, even the most efficient canners could produce no more than two or three thousand cans a day.

The outbreak of the Civil War gave the great impetus. The Union commandeered Borden's output of canned milk for the Army, but if the Army's needs were to be supplied, there would have to be a faster way to process canned goods. The maximum temperature of water boiling in an open container was 212 degrees Fahrenheit. Earlier in the century the English chemist Sir Humphry Davy had found that adding calcium chloride increased the temperature of boiling water to 240 degrees or above. In 1861, when a Baltimore canner, Isaac Solomon, made use of this discovery, he at once cut the average processing time from six hours to a half-hour. During the war many men had their first taste of canned foods, in army camps, on gunboats and in hospitals; and when the armed forces dispersed, they carried the word all over the country. While the demand for canned goods was still small, the canners had remained near the ocean, where they could put up oysters, lobsters, and other seafood for part of the year, and keep their plants at work processing small quantities of fruits and vegetables at other times. Now, with a widespread demand for all sorts of foods in cans, large-scale canneries appeared inland, in Cincinnati, Indianapolis, and elsewhere. In the decade after 1860 the number of cans of food put up annually rose from five million to thirty million.

Large-scale canning required containers by the thousands. Appert's original process for "canning" was actually a scheme for preserving food in glass containers. About the same time an Englishman had patented a technique for preserving food in tin. But cans were still fashioned by hand, and a tinsmith could make only sixty in a whole day. Then during the early nineteenth century, Americans improved tin cans and made machinery to turn them out by the thousands—machines for stamping out the tops and bottoms, for soldering the joint on the side, and for crimping and sealing the top. By 1880 a single machine worked by two men with two boys helping could turn out fifteen hundred cans in one day. Tinsmiths, who saw themselves being displaced, defended their jobs by arguing that machine-made cans were a menace to health. The solder used on the can-manufacturing machines, they said, was poisonous; and for a while some people would not eat food from a machine-made can. But by the 1920's more than a billion and a half pounds of tin plate was annually being made into cans. The tin can had begun to play its new leading role helping the American housewife—and cluttering the American landscape.

36
Meat for the Cities

BEFORE THE CIVIL WAR the fresh meat that the city dweller ate had to come into his city on the hoof. Since there was no way of preventing spoilage of meat while it was brought in from the outside, each city had its own slaughterhouses, which produced piles of offal and an offensive odor. For long-distance shipment, meat had to be preserved by salting and smoking and then be packed in barrels. When fresh meat was costly and was available only at certain seasons, the social class and income of an urban American could be gauged by the quantity and quality of fresh meat found on his table.

There is no better illustration of the American paradox—of how the very extent of the nation encouraged the finding of new ways to make life more uniform—than the story of meat. There came into being a national, even an international, market for the fresh meat raised on the Western plains.

TO EXTEND THE MARKET for fresh meat, there had to be a practical refrigerator car. Such cars would make it possible for meat packers in the West to do their own slaughtering out there for the fresh-meat market in Eastern cities. By shipping dressed beef, they would save freight on the 35 percent of the animal's weight that was unsalable. Incidentally they would save the cost of feeding live cattle in transit; they would also avoid the loss of weight, and sometimes of whole animals, from overcrowding. Naturally enough, the railroads, with their large investments in loading docks and feeding stations for shipping live cattle, feared the refrigerator car. In Eastern cities, local butchers and slaughterers spread propaganda against the "poisonous" meat that had been carried for long distances on the rails. The railroads charged an especially high rate on dressed meat so it would yield them as much profit as if the animals had been shipped on the hoof; they could hardly have been expected to take the initiative in building refrigerator cars.

The stage was set for a Go-Getter to organize railroad refrigeration and bring fresh meat to the growing Eastern cities. The leading roles were played by two Americans, a Swift and an Armour, who became household names in every corner of the continent, and in the far corners of the world. Their two careers were intertwined, not only as competitors, but as boosters and builders of Chicago.

Gustavus Franklin Swift at the age of fourteen went to work for his brother, the village butcher in Sandwich on Cape Cod. And he went into business for himself when he had saved enough money to buy a heifer, which he slaughtered and sold as dressed meat from door to door. He began dealing in cattle and gradually moved westward with the cattle market, from Cape Cod to Albany, then to Buffalo, and finally to Chicago in 1875. He began to imagine how much more beef could be sent out from Chicago if only it could be slaughtered and dressed before shipping. There had been occasional shipments of this sort, but always in winter, when cold weather kept the meat from spoiling. Swift foresaw a year-round trade.

When he first decided to ship dressed beef year-round, it seemed as risky a project as Tudor's plan, seventy-five years earlier, to send ice to the Indies. But Swift had some advantages over his well-established Chicago competitors in the business of shipping beef on the hoof, for he personally knew the meat business in New England. When none of the railroad lines that were already carrying large numbers of cattle would help, he finally turned to the Grand Trunk Railway, which agreed to carry refrigerator cars if Swift himself would provide them. Swift then boldly invested his limited capital in ten new refrigerators cars and in experiments for their improvement. By 1881 Swift had found a refrigerator car that would deliver his Chicago-dressed meat in good condition to the Eastern butchers. When the railroads realized that carrying dressed beef might actually increase their business, they began to compete for the traffic. The Eastern butchers, too, now saw their chance to sell more meat, and several actually went into partnership with Swift. Swift's shipments brought down the price of meat so that by 1882 *Harper's Weekly* in New York heralded "this era of cheap beef."

WITHIN A FEW YEARS Swift built a new giant industry, a response to peculiarly American opportunities—to vast American spaces, to the extreme contrasts of newly congested cities and still-empty Western prairies. Space and contrast offered openings for organization. Just as the annual fur-trade rendezvous meant timing the movements of men thousands of miles apart, and their coming together at an agreed-on day, so now the transporting of fresh meat from the far West to the eastern seaboard required practice and elaborate organizing

After collecting his cattle in Chicago, Swift had to devise a way to slaughter them quickly for loading into his refrigerator cars. Then, to avoid the need to transfer the meat from one car to another en route, the cars had to be sent over railroad lines of a common gauge, and that still required planning in the 1870's. To avoid spoilage when the refrigerator car arrived at its destination, in New York for instance, the car had to be brought to a halt with its doors precisely opposite those of the cold-storage building. Then the overhead rails which Swift had constructed inside each car, and on which the sides of meat were hanging, were connected to those within the building. "The meat is easily transferred to the storage room," *Harper's Weekly* marveled, "which is of the same temperature as the car, without loss of time and without being removed from the hook on which it was hung when killed."

This was only the middle step in a still more remarkable organization that reached back to the processing and slaughtering and finally to the cattle producers, as well as out from the cold-storage building to a world of consumers. Swift's knowledge of the feed business and his skill as a cattle appraiser helped him round up the animals.

But to get the most out of a carcass required a newer kind of organizing ability, and the boldness to do things in ways never tried before. To separate out all the several parts of a hog quickly and economically so that each could be sold for its own purpose required the invention (in Sigfried Giedion's phrase) of a "disassembly line." These decades of experience in disassembling hogs would prepare the way for Henry Ford's new way of assembling automobiles. What was new was working on objects while they moved, objects which were made to move so they could be better worked upon. It would no longer be possible for a man to describe his job by how long he took to do it.

The key to organizing production was, of course, to simplify. The American system of interchangeable parts had meant breaking down a product into its individual pieces and then making each separately; Swift's meat-packing house used a similar techinique. The slaughtering of the hog and the cutting of the carcass were broken down into numerous single operations. What this meant to workers on the line Upton Sinclair described in 1906 in *The Jungle:*

> The carcass hog was then again strung up by machinery and sent upon another trolley ride; this time passing between two lines of men . . . upon a raised platform, each doing a certain single thing to the carcass as it came to him. One scraped the outside of a leg; another scraped the inside of the same leg. One with a swift stroke cut the throat.. . . Another made a slit down the body; a second opened the body wider; a third with a saw cut the breastbone; a fourth loosened the entrails; a fifth pulled them out. . . . There were men to scrape each side and men to scrape the back; there were men to clean the carcass inside, to trim it and wash it. Looking down this room one saw creeping slowly a line of dangling hogs . . . and for every yard there was a man working as if a demon were after him. At the end of this hog's progress every inch of the carcass had been gone over several times.

Nearly a century after Americans had begun to apply their revolutionary technique for putting together objects of their own creation, they applied a similar simplifying, organizing technique to taking apart a complicated living organism. The most difficult single problem was how to get the live hogs into the production line, for each hog tended to go its own way. The solution was to use one live hog as a decoy: when it was penned on the moving disassembly line, the other hogs followed in good order and in a posture where they could be snagged and hoisted for the slaughter.

Swift had a genius for this kind of organizing, and an eye for detail. In the middle of the night he could be seen going down to the cold-storage rooms to check the thermometers. He organized the slaughtering so that parts that were formerly discarded could be made into marketable products, such as brushes, oleomargarine, glue, pharmaceuticals, or fertilizer. Swift spread out his production centers westward to Minnesota and Nebraska, and southward to Texas.

The increasing meat production of the Western prairies and of the packing houses far exceeded the needs of the American market, even with the rising American standard of eating. Soon after the Civil War, Chicago was processing about as much as Paris, although it had only about one-tenth the population of the European capital. Swift began selling his dressed meat in France and England, and he crossed the Atlantic twenty times to perfect these arrangements; he then added distributing branches in Tokyo, Osaka, Shanghai, Hong Kong, Manila, Singapore, and Honolulu. By 1912 Swift and Company, employing more than thirty thousand men and women, had outlets in four hundred cities on four continents.

The enterprise of Swift was matched by that of Philip Danforth Armour, who had been raised in Connecticut and also answered the lure of the West. With money he had made in the California Gold Rush, Armour entered the grocery business, first in Cincinnati, then in Milwaukee, and then he went into meat packing. Unlike Swift, he had a talent and a taste for speculation. In the last days of the Civil War, when pork was selling for $40 a barrel and going up, Armour foresaw that a Union victory would soon bring pork prices down. He went to New York to sell pork futures, and found many takers; when Union victories sent pork prices plummeting, Armour was able to buy the pork for $18 a barrel, which he had already sold for more than $30. So he was well rewarded for his patriotic confidence in the Union.

The $2 million Armour made on this deal became the foundation of his meat-packing fortune. Armour, like Swift, came to Chicago in 1875, and thereafter their careers were remarkably parallel. Armour, too, pioneered in organizing slaughterhouse disassembly lines, in finding uses for every shred of the carcass. He too was a leader in constructing refrigerator cars. His reputation, like Swift's, was not improved by the scandal of "embalmed beef," a supply of bad beef sent to troops in the Spanish-American War. Armour and Swift both became generous philanthropists. Armour's faith in education led him to found the Armour Institute of Technology. "I like to turn bristles, blood, bones, and the insides and outsides of pigs and bullocks into revenue now," he declared, "for I can turn the revenue into these boys and girls, and they will go on forever."

THE MARKET FOR FRESH MEAT which was rapidly increased by refrigeration was matched by a similar increase in the market for preserved meat. Now the most popular mode of preservation was no longer salting, spicing, or smoking, all of which had been known from ancient times, but canning. Still, ingenuity was required to adapt the can to the peculiar requirements of meat.

The market for canned meat had at first been limited by the fact that meat which was packed in ordinary cans always came out as stew. Then a new process was used for cooking the meat before it went into the can so that there would be no shrinkage. And a clever Chicagoan, J. A. Wilson, designed a can shaped like a truncated pyramid; when the housewife opened the can at the larger end, as the instructions explained, a tap on the other end "will cause the solidly packaged meat to slide out in one piece so as to be readily sliced." By 1878 a Chicago factory was turning out Wilson's cans by the thousands, and for the first time housewives could serve their canned meat in attractive slices.

"Corned meat," which English dictionaries in 1858 had described as "flesh slightly salted, intended for early use, and not for keeping for any time," took on a new American meaning. "Corned beef" was the name for the new dish which came in cans and which enriched the diet of soldiers and civilians all over the world. Meat "compressed in cans clear of all bones or gristle" weighed only one-third what the same meat weighed unboned and packed in barrels, an economy comparable to that of shipping dressed meat instead of livestock. As canned meat became more attractive, it ceased to be merely an emergency dish and was found on American tables every day.

This widening of the market for canned meat had widespread indirect effects on the American diet. Since canned meat did not require refrigeration, fewer refrigerator cars were needed to transport the output of the slaughterhouses. And the great Chicago packers who by then had invested heavily in refrigerator cars for shipping meat went desperately in search of products that could use their expensive equipment. Armour sent his agents to the South to encourage the raising of large quantities of perishable fruits and berries that would require refrigerated shipping to Northern cities. In Georgia, for example, his agents encouraged the growing of peaches.

Canning, a new source of everyday miracles, would make prose out of many an old poetic metaphor. By 1924 a historian of American canning could boast:

> Canning gives the American family—especially in cities and factory towns—a kitchen garden where all good things grow, and where it is always harvest time. There are more tomatoes in a ten-cent can than

could be bought fresh in city markets for that sum when tomatoes are at their cheapest, and this is true of most other tinned foods. A regular Arabian Nights garden, where raspberries, apricots, olives, and pineapples, always ripe, grow side by side with peas, pumpkins, spinach; a garden with baked beans, vines and spaghetti bushes, and sauerkraut beds, and great cauldrons of hot soup, and through it running a branch of the ocean in which one can catch salmon, lobsters, crabs and shrimp, and dig oysters and clams.

The canning industry of the United States was now packing more food, and more different kinds of food, than that of all other countries combined.

37
Varying the Everyday Menu

UNTIL AFTER THE CIVIL WAR, it was widely believed that all foods had the same nutritive value. There was supposed to be one "universal aliment" which helped the body grow, which kept it warm and working, and repaired the tissues. This popular notion justified the monotony of the popular diet. When men called bread "the staff of life," they were not being merely sententious. "Give us this day our daily bread," with Biblical precision went to the heart of the matter. In western Europe until about the middle of the nineteenth century the mainstays, and in some places nearly the exclusive items in the diet, were various forms of cereal, mainly bread, supplemented now and then by salted meat. Milk, fruit, and vegetables were frills, eaten for novelty by those who could afford them and when and where they could be found fresh.

Nourishment was measured by quantity: the poor suffered not because they ate mostly bread, but because they did not have enough bread. Seafarers knew that to prevent scurvy they should eat fresh fruits, but these were considered more medicinal than nutritive. Not until the beginning of the twentieth century did many people discover the meaning of "protective" foods; it was well into the century before a science of nutrition and the notion of a "well-balanced diet" of proteins and carbohydrates, vitamins, and minerals had entered the popular consciousness. Americans, showing that they believed the new "science" was real, made a business of it, and dignified the food scientist with the name "dietitian" (a combination of *diet* and *physician*), which had entered the English language through the United States by 1905. When the term "Home Economics" came into use about twenty years later, the subject was already required in some public schools and included comparison of the nutritive value of different foods, such as only a food faddist or a specialized scientist would have pursued a century before.

IN THE EIGHTEENTH CENTURY, when a monotonous diet marked the lower classes, variety of food was a delight, a dissipation, and a privilege of the wealthy. Patrick Henry accused Thomas Jefferson of an effete taste for "French Cookery." In the "Log Cabin and Hard Cider" campaign of 1840, the Whigs boasted that their candidate, William Henry Harrison, lived on wholesome "raw beef without salt," while his aristocratic opponent, President Martin Van Buren, was alleged to luxuriate in strawberries, raspberries, celery, and cauliflower. "Democratic" enthusiasm at first made a virtue of crude and tasteless food, and obsession with the delights of the palate was considered a symptom of Old World decadence. Only a few independent spirits like John Adams said that American suspicion of French Cookery was a mere relic of colonial prejudice, and so belonged to the past.

Elegant dining and imaginative cooking were given a French label: "cuisine." In the 1830's, young ladies invited out to dinner who wanted to impress their escorts would request that their vegetables be served "in the French manner," which meant each vegetable in a separate dish. They could show their sophistication by saying that it somehow took their appetite away to see all their foods jumbled together on one plate, in the familiar American manner. French influence, which at first enlarged and enriched the menus only of the well-to-do, gradually reached out. But until about the time of the Civil War, a varied, well-flavored diet was reserved for those who could afford an expensive meal in one of the few new elegant restaurants in the largest seaboard cities.

Among the best of these restaurants was Delmonico's in New York City. In 1832, at the age of nineteen, Lorenzo Delmonico arrived from the Italian-speaking Ticino in Switzerland. He opened a restaurant in downtown New York, and within a few years his name had become a synonym for elegant dining. In 1868 George Pullman named his first dining car "the Delmonico," and pretentious restaurants in Western cities called themselves "Delmonico's of the West." Delmonico imported his recipes and cooks from the best kitchens of

Europe, but he also helped Americans discover delicacies in their own backyard. Just as the colonial physicians had found natural herbs in the woods to cure American ailments, Delmonico now found unsuspected delights for the palate in the same woods. European travelers, familiar with the derogatory clichés about American food, were astonished at the specialties of fish, game, and meat which were served at Delmonico's. One of his achievements was to help Americans discover salads; and he showed how salads could be made from common New World plants. He popularized ices and green vegetables. Few did more than Delmonico to educate the nation's palate. Before his death in 1881, he was said to have served every President from Jackson to Garfield. Delmonico's restaurants had set a standard for New York gourmets which by the mid-twentieth century made that city, next to Paris, the restaurant capital of the world.

POPULAR PREJUDICES CONFIRMED the limits of the American diet. In the 1830's and 40's there was a widespread suspicion that fresh fruits and vegetables were dangerous to health, and that they were especially detrimental to children. Uncertainties about the causes of dysentery, typhoid, cholera, and other epidemic diseases made these fears more plausible. But within fifty years the United States had organized a nationwide, soon to be world-wide, trade in fresh fruits and vegetables. Diet was democratized and the diet of the common American citizen was more varied than that of many a European man of wealth.

In Europe for centuries olive groves and vineyards had been the main sources, in some places the only sources, of fruit products for export. Olive oil and wines were easy to prepare and to transport, but fresh fruits or vegetables out of season or from remote places seemed contrary to nature. "To every thing there is a season," said Ecclesiastes. From the proverb "Everything is good in its season," it was easy to conclude that "Nothing is good but in its season." The rise of canning, of course, changed the palate of the seasons, but canned goods had to be altered for their voyage through time. The miracle of freshness was something else. And many of the same forces which promoted canning were beginning to make this miracle commonplace.

Paradoxically, it was the rapid rise and growth of American cities, as much as anything else, that spread the growing and eating of fresh fruits and vegetables over the United States. If the inhabitants of large cities like London and Paris were to have fresh fruits and vegetables at all, these had to be grown in gardens on the city outskirts. And in western Europe there was a long tradition of government-controlled municipal markets, like Paris' Halles Centrales, to which farmers hauled their produce. In large American cities such as New York, the situation was much the same except that such markets were less common. Only the well-to-do could enlarge their diet beyond crops that were in season and grew in the vicinity. In late May 1833, for example, a New Yorker who wanted to eat strawberries had to pay $1.50 a quart, while a resident of Baltimore could have all he wanted for twelve cents a quart.

Railroads naturally enlarged the supply of fresh fruits and vegetables. In the 1840's the Camden & Amboy Railroad, which went through the "Pea Shore" garden region of New Jersey, ran a special train, known as the "Pea Line," to pick up farmers' produce for New York City. On a single night in June 1847, the train brought into New York City eighty thousand baskets of strawberries. The extension of railroads widened the sources for the cities. By the 1860's New Yorkers were eating produce shipped from the truck gardens around the new rail center of Norfolk, Virginia, and an enterprising commission merchant in Chicago imported green peas from New Orleans at $8 a bushel. Then the food seasons became longer, at least for prosperous Northern city dwellers. Within the three decades before 1865 the strawberry season in Northern cities had been lengthened from one month to four months, the grape season from four months to six, and the peach season from one month to six. Fresh tomatoes, which had only recently been a four-month seasonal commodity, now were available year-round.

Before about 1875 the people who lived comfortably in cities preserved their own summer perishables for winter use. Commercial canning had not yet become as important as home canning. The housewife would buy strawberries or peaches in season and make preserves or jam to use at other times of the year. Apples, potatoes, and some other fruits and vegetables, mostly of local origin, were bought in season and then stored in the family cellar.

In the last decades of the nineteenth century, two great changes in city living made it harder for each family to store its own supply of perishables for winter eating. One was central heating, for when householders put furnaces in their cellars, these became too warm for winter cold storage. The other innovation was the apartment house, a by-product of the higher land values which had come with the crowding of the cities. For example, the value of land within the corporate limits of Chicago doubled from about $500 million in 1873 to $1 billion twenty-five years later. The first apartment house (a middle-class dwelling, as distinguished from a tenement) appeared in New York City about 1870, and in Chicago soon thereafter. The apartment dweller usually had no cellar at all. As the new immigrant working class poured into the cities and increased their earnings, they had more money to spend on food, and they too enlarged the city retail market for perishables.

THESE MONEY-MAKING OPPORTUNITIES for the dealer in fresh produce brought into being more commission merchants and more wholesale buyers of fruits and vegetables. Now they could assure the farmer of a ready, regular market for all his produce, which they sold to distant consumers.

Before, the farmer, by growing early and late varieties of the same fruits, and by several plantings, might have something fresh to sell to the local market over most of the months. "Carrying-quality," not to mention such fine points as appearance, taste, and texture, did not enter much into his calculations. But the refrigerator car and the refrigerator ship changed all this. Now the farmer could devote his land to the one variety that best survived shipping and at the same time was attractive and tasty.

This led to widespread innovations in fruit and vegetable growing. While the peach industry had developed in South Carolina and Georgia between 1850 and 1870, it had almost disappeared for fifteen years until the hardy Elberta peach was introduced in the age of the refrigerator car. New strains of oranges (the navel orange from Brazil, and the Valencia orange from Europe) appeared in Florida and California in the 1870's; new varieties of lemon (the Eureka from Sicily and the Lisbon from Australia), and then the seedless Marsh grapefruit were introduced to California. A half-dozen types of potato for the first time began to be grown commercially; improved kinds of cabbage were introduced from Holland and Denmark. The development of a tomato suitable for the commercial market also dates from this period. And these are only a few examples. By 1875 Luther Burbank, a friend of Thomas A. Edison who came to be known as "the farmer's Edison," was applying his inventive genius to developing still more desirable and more marketable varieties of fruits and vegetables.

Instead of looking for streams and rocks that would yield gold or silver, enterprising Americans, in an increasingly urban America, were seeking soils and climates to grow perishable crops to ship to remote parts of the nation. Exuberant land promoters, like those who had hoaxed and victimized fortune seekers in the mid-nineteenth century, now directed their advertising to the ambitious farmer. Before World War I, pioneer fruit and vegetable growers had staked out their new orchards and truck farms all over the country. Irrigation was producing cantaloupes, watermelons, lettuce, asparagus, and tomatoes in the Imperial Valley of California and the lower Rio Grande Valley of Texas on the Mexican border; these products would be carried in refrigerator cars to markets three thousand miles away. Land that only a few years before had been scorned as desert was now supplying city dwellers in Boston and New York, in Chicago and San Francisco, with exotic fruits. A "Market News Service," begun by the United States Department of Agriculture in 1915, soon used the wires of Western Union to spread information on the shipments and prices of produce all over the country, and so helped create a fluid and responsive national market.

As the number of city dwellers increased (by 1920 it was half the nation's population) and as the urban American worked shorter hours and became more sedentary, as offices and homes were better heated, the demand for starchy, energy-producing foods declined, and Americans wanted more and more of the lighter fruits and vegetables. In addition to the greengrocer, there now appeared the fruit stand. When more women went to work and there was generally more eating at lunch counters and restaurants, there was more demand for salads that used fresh fruits, vegetables, and lettuce.

By the 1930's the average length of railroad hauls for fruits and vegetables in the United States was about fifteen hundred miles. The diet of Americans had been transformed. Fresh fruits and vegetables were no longer the food mainly of the rich, but became commonplace on American tables year-round. The discovery of vitamins in 1911 led within a few years to a spectacular increase in the use of citrus fruits and leafy vegetables. About the same time, the slim figure became fashionable for women, and insurance companies began warning against overweight; all of which reduced the demand for sweet and starchy foods, potatoes, bread, and fatty meats, and correspondingly increased the consumption of fresh fruits and vegetables. After about 1927, when the motor truck and refrigerator ships began carrying produce, perishable foods were distributed far beyond the railroad network. New Yorkers were buying fruits and vegetables from forty-two states of the Union and nineteen foreign countries, while Londoners at the Covent Garden Market could buy Washington apples, Florida grapefruit, and California pears and oranges.

ANOTHER ESSENTIAL STEP toward homogenizing the regions and seasons, toward democratizing the national diet and increasing the variety of foods of the ordinary citizen was the coming of refrigeration to every household. Enterprising New Englanders like Frederic Tudor and Nathaniel Wyeth had built a thriving ice trade well before the Civil War. But until 1830, ice was used mainly for frozen luxuries like ice cream or for cold drinks on the tables of the wealthy. By the time of the Civil War, "icebox" had entered the American language, but ice was still only beginning to affect the daily diet.

Then the ice trade grew with the growth of American cities. Ice was used in hotels, taverns, and hospitals, and by some forward-looking city dealers in fresh meat, fresh fish, and butter. The German immigration of the 1840's brought the lager-beer brewing industry, which required low temperatures and used large quantities of ice.

After the Civil War, as ice was used to refrigerate Swift's and Armour's freight cars, it also came into household use. Even before 1880, half the ice sold in New York, Philadelphia, and Baltimore, and one-third that sold in Boston and Chicago went to families for their own use. This had become possible because a new household convenience had been invented. The "icebox," or "refrigerator," was one of the first in a long series of kitchen contraptions that within a century and a half were to mechanize the American household and turn the American housewife into a household engineer.

Making an efficient icebox was not as easy as we might now suppose. In the early nineteenth century the knowledge of the physics of heat, which was essential to a science of refrigeration, was rudimentary. The common-sense notion that the best icebox was one that prevented the ice from melting was of course mistaken, for it was the melting of the ice that performed the cooling. Nevertheless, early efforts to economize ice included wrapping the ice in blankets, and all sorts of other devices which kept the ice from doing its job. Not until near the end of the nineteenth century did inventors achieve the nice balance of insulation and circulation needed for an efficient icebox.

But as early as 1803, an ingenious and enterprising Maryland farmer, Thomas Moore, had been on the right track. He owned a farm about twenty miles outside the new capital city of Washington, for which the village of Georgetown was then the market center. When he used an icebox of his own design to transport his butter to market, he found that housewives would pass up the mushy yellow stuff in the tubs of his competitors to pay a premium price for his butter, still fresh and hard in neat one-pound bricks. Moore's *Essay on the Most Eligible Construction of Ice-Houses; Also, a Description of the Newly Invented Machine called the Refrigerator* gave instructions: inside an oval cedar tub, place a tin vessel of the same shape but somewhat smaller; store the butter inside the tin vessel; then insert pieces of ice in the space between the tin vessel and the outer cedar tub; cover the whole with a hinged wooden lid lined with coarse cloth and rabbit skins hanging down to cover the joint when shut. One advantage of his refrigerator, Moore explained, was that farmers would no longer have to travel to market at night, which had been their practice to keep their produce cool. "The whole cost of this machine," he wrote, "was about four dollars: The butter always commanded from 4d. to 5½d. per lb. higher than any other butter in market; so that four times using it paid the cost."

Moore secured a patent for his refrigerator, and announced in his pamphlet that he would not charge royalty to any person who made a small refrigerator to carry his own butter to market. Permits for other sizes and other purposes could be obtained by writing to Moore and paying him a fee which varied from $2.50 to $10. But "any person in low circumstances" who offered a certificate "signed by three reputable neighbors" would be given a permit gratis, as would "any more wealthy person" certifying "that he believed the terms are hard and improper." Moore did not sell many permits. But his pamphlet helped popularize the icebox, and Frederic Tudor himself had read a copy while preparing for his first big shipment of ice to the West Indies.

By the 1840's the expression "iceman" had entered the American language, and within a few decades the iceman had acquired the vivid role which he would play for a century (Eugene O'Neill's *The Iceman Cometh* was produced in 1946) in American folklore and lovelore. In 1855 a Boston family wanting ice delivered during the season, from May to October, could receive fifteen pounds each day for $2 a month, or $8 for the whole period. By 1880 one ice company in Philadelphia was employing eight hundred men.

But while the icebox brought the sociable iceman, it had many incidental disadvantages. It required frequent deliveries, and it still left Americans at the mercy of the weather. A heavy winter meant cheap ice; the techniques of the natural-ice industry had so improved by 1883 that cutting and packing the ice might cost as little as twelve cents a ton. On the other hand, a mild winter like that of 1890 reduced the ice crop and considerably raised the price of ice.

Mechanical refrigeration developed only gradually, having been made possible by the discoveries of European chemists and physicists. The Americans discovered no new principles but again showed their talent for application. In 1834 what was probably the first United States patent for mechanical refrigeration was issued to an ingenious New Englander, Jacob Perkins, who was better known for his new methods of using steel plates for engraving bank notes. By 1839 Dr. John Gorrie, a Florida physician, was applying mechanical refrigeration to promote public health, and was on the way to patented improvements of his own. A leading citizen of Apalachicola, where he was postmaster, city treasurer, and mayor, he was intent on preventing and curing malaria. Having noticed that the disease disappeared with the coming of cold weather and that it seemed to be contracted only at night, he believed that if he could "purify" sleeping rooms by keeping them cold enough, the disease might be prevented. He suspended a bowl of ice close to the ceiling below a hole through which air was drawn down a soot-lined chimney. As the air came down the chimney, the "malaria" in it would be decomposed because of the affinity of carbon for "vapors and organic Oils," and by passing over the ice, the malarial vapors would be further condensed, thus allowing only purified air into the bedroom. An exhaust pipe near the floor helped ventilate.

Gorrie's device would not prevent malaria, but it did cool a hospital room. Obsessed by the problems of refrigeration, Gorrie studied physics, and by 1850 his machine using the expansion of air actually produced ice at a public demonstration. Gorrie was on the right track.

After Carl von Linde, a German, invented the ammonia-compression machine in 1876, the way was cleared for the commercial production of ice. By 1879 there were 35 commercial ice plants in the United States. Ten years later there were more than 200, and within another twenty years there were 2,000. For some time these ice plants remained the main source of supply for the household "refrigerator" which was still an "icebox." But by the 1920's the mechanical refrigerator was beginning to become an essential piece of furniture in the American middle-class kitchen. While in 1921 only 5,000 mechanical refrigerators were manufactured in the United States, by 1931 the annual production exceeded 1 million, and six years later the figure was nearing 3 million. By mid-century, mechanical refrigerators were found in more than 80 percent of American farm households, and in over 90 percent of urban homes.

MANY WOULD HAVE THOUGHT that when every American household had its own refrigerator this was the end of the road, that there was little more to do to equip the American for a nearly uniform year-round diet. The unpredicted next step went still further in decentralizing storage, and at the same time improved the taste and the nutritive value of storable foods.

Here the undisputed hero, Clarence Birdseye, was so successful that before his death, people assumed that "Birdseye" was the name of a product and not of a person. Birdseye was a naturalist and author of books on wildlife living in Gloucester, Massachusetts, who had been looking for better ways to preserve fish. One winter day in 1912 when the temperature was 20 degrees below zero, he was fishing through the ice in Labrador; he pulled up a fish and dropped it on the ice beside the hole, where it quickly froze solid. Birdseye took the fish home, and when he put it in a pail of water he found to his amazement that the fish started swimming. The explanation, as he later discovered, was that the cells of the fish had been frozen so quickly that there was no time for large crystals to form. It was these large crystals that usually broke the delicate cell walls and killed the fish, with the result that on defrosting, vital fluids leaked out, changing the physical character of the tissue, and incidentally its taste. Birdseye had discovered the quick-freezing of food, based on the chemical law that when solutions crystallize, the size of the crystals is in proportion to the length of time of crystallization.

Even after Birdseye had discovered the meaning of this principle for food preservation, there remained many problems before quick-frozen food could be prepared and marketed. All cell structures did not freeze or defrost in the same way or at the same rate. For each kind of food it was necessary to discover the precise temperature needed to produce the greatest number of small crystals in the shortest time. Birdseye had to invent his own machine to do the job of quick-freezing, for the familiar techniques of refrigeration were not suitable.

Until then, cold-storage and household refrigeration had generally depended on the transfer of heat by convection—a cold current of air drawing the heat out of the food to be chilled. Finding that this process was not fast enough for quick-freezing, Birdseye invented a machine which froze by conduction, that is, by pressing thin parcels of the food to be frozen directly between metal plates cooled to 25 degrees below zero. In this way, too, both the temperature and the freezing time could be more closely controlled. Birdseye's process was first applied to seafood, and it was especially well suited for that purpose: the ocean catch could be quick-frozen as soon as it was lifted aboard a trawler. Later it was found that frozen food could be precooked and sold ready to heat and serve. As frozen foods multiplied and as their popularity increased, deep-freeze compartments were included in home refrigerators, and deep-freeze refrigerators came to be developed for self-service at the corner grocery. By the 1940's in small towns, central frozen-food lockers were common where fishermen and hunters could store their season's catch to be enjoyed year-round. By 1972 one household in three had its own deep-freeze unit, separate from its refrigerator, and most American households had a place for the storage of frozen foods.

38
People's Palaces on Wheels

"WE ARE REMINDED by a prophecy which we heard some three years since," the *Illinois Journal* reported on May 30, 1865, "that the time was not far distant when a radical change would be introduced in the manner of constructing railroad cars; the public would travel upon them with as much ease as though sitting in their parlors, and sleep and eat on board of them with more ease and comfort than it would be possible to do on a first-class steamer. We believed the words of the seer at the time, but did not think they were so near fulfillment until Friday last, when we were invited to the Chicago & Alton depot in this city to examine an improved sleeping-car, manufactured by Messrs. Field & Pullman, patentees, after a design by George M. Pullman, Esq., Chicago." Pullman's railroad sleeping coach was marvelously embellished with window curtains looped in heavy folds, the richest Brussels carpeting, black walnut woodwork, French plate mirrors suspended from the walls, and beautiful chandeliers with "exquisitely ground shades" hanging from a ceiling "painted with chaste and elaborate design upon a delicately tinted azure ground." Americans had devised magical new ways to enjoy the comforts of home while on the move.

GEORGE PULLMAN (whom we have already met as the builder of a model company town), like Swift and Armour, was himself a man on the move. Born in far-western New York, he attended school until he was fourteen, then worked with his brother as a cabinetmaker in Albion, New York, a village on the Erie Canal. When the canal was to be widened, Pullman helped move the warehouses to prepare the way. Arriving in Chicago in 1855 at the age of twenty-four, he signed an unusual contract to help solve the city's problem of water-logged streets. And he was much admired for his feat of raising several blocks of brick and stone buildings, including the elegant Tremont House, to a new street level, while allowing the owners to carry on business as usual. In 1858 he made his first experiments with the railroad sleeping car; he improved two standard coaches at a cost of $1,000 each, with a generous use of cherry wood and plush. After succumbing briefly to the lure of the newly discovered Colorado gold fields, in 1863 Pullman took the earnings from the general store he had been running in one of the new mining towns and returned to Chicago. Perhaps remembering the fold-up bunks he had seen in the congested miners' cabins, he resumed his efforts to improve the sleeping car. This time he replaced his original scheme of stowing the passengers on shelves hung directly from the ceiling by devising an "upper berth" made of a hinged flap that fitted against the wall in daytime; he then improved the lower berth so that the facing seats would slide together at night to form a bed. With a new standard of luxury for furnishings, the finished car cost over $20,000. Pullman called this car the "Pioneer A"; the letter "A" suggested that there might be as many as twenty-five more.

But Pullman's bold and spacious design had produced a car higher and wider than the existing station platforms and bridges would allow. He believed that the appeal of his cars would lead the companies to widen the clearance along their lines and at the stations. The first important step in this direction came when the "Pioneer" was attached to the funeral train that carried the body of Lincoln from Chicago to Springfield in April 1865. A few years later, when the "Pioneer" was engaged to take President Grant from Detroit to his hometown of Galena, Illinois, the clearance on that way, too, was widened. Alterations were then made along other lines to accommodate "Pioneer"-sized railroad cars, until the Pullman dimensions for height and width became standard. The demand for Pullman accommodations incidentally increased the demand for a uniform railroad gauge so that a passenger could be carried from anywhere to anywhere else in parlor comfort.

The idea of a luxury sleeping car was not new. At least a hundred earlier inventors had contributed to the development. The most famous luxury car at the time was the *train impérial* which a French railroad company had built to honor Napoleon III in 1857. The product of a collaboration of the best French engineers, architects, and designers, it dazzled the world with a *wagon d'honneur*, a dining car, a sleeping car, and an open observation car. Eight years later Pullman was offering an American counterpart. But here imperial luxury was not to be reserved for emperors.

If Pullman's enterprise was to succeed he would have to democratize the luxury of comfortable travel. And he had the combination of talents to do the job. Like Henry Ford a half-century later, Pullman had the instinct "for stirring the dormant fancies of the public until they grew into demands."

Pullman became the Barnum of the railroad world as he planned tour spectaculars to dramatize the delights of "Pullman" travel. He invited a carload of prominent excursionists to take a complimentary trip on his first "Pioneer"; and in return they provided testimonials that Pullman travel was "superior to any that we have ever inspected!" They especially noted "that a daily change of linen is made in the berths of this new carriage, thereby keeping them constantly clean and comfortable, and rendering the car much more attractive than are similar carriages where this is neglected." In May 1870, only one year after the Central Pacific and the Union Pacific had joined into the first transcontinental railroad, a special Pullman excursion took the Boston Board of Trade to California on the first through train ride from coast to coast. On the sixth day out, the train's daily newspaper, *The Trans-Continental*, reported that as the train was crossing the summit of the Sierra Nevadas, a resolution was passed by the notable Bostonians meeting in the smoking car. After expressing their delight at watching the whole continent unfold out the windows of "this beautiful and commodious moving hotel," they resolved "that there will be no delay in placing the elegant and homelike carriages upon the principal routes in the New England States, and we will do all in our power to accomplish this end."

Once again, as with the first explorers, with the framers of the Constitution, with the rendezvousing fur traders, and the cattle-country trailblazers, the vastness and variety of the continent had stirred and tested the talents of great organizers. For Pullman's "beautiful and commodious moving hotel" to roll smoothly across the continent, it had been necessary for George M. Pullman to collect the capital and construct scores of luxury sleeping cars at unprecedented cost, then arrange the widening of station platforms all over the nation, and see to the replacement of scores of variant railroad gauges by a single national standard. In addition to all this, of course, he had to recruit his own army of conductors and moving-hotel attendants, ready and able to respond to travelers' whims. Pullman was motivated in all this by his faith that there was a vast American market for luxuries for everybody.

THE SLEEPING-CAR LUXURY that the French had prepared for their emperor, and that in Europe would be reserved for the rich, was destined from its American beginnings to attain a wider, more democratic reach. Pullman was eager to submit his car to the verdict of the public. Would enough Americans be willing to pay $2 a night to sleep in an expensive and luxurious moving hotel? Would the market justify building and organizing hundreds of Pullman cars to race around the continent? Pullman finally persuaded the Michigan Central to test the market by running a few of his luxury cars on the same lines where their crude sleeping cars were already familiar to the public (at $1.50 per night). The public demand for Pullmans was overwhelming, and the only complaints came from the passengers who could not get a luxury berth for their extra fifty cents. Soon the Michigan Central withdrew the older cars, and made Pullman their standard. Then one line after another found that much of their valuable passenger traffic depended on their ability to offer Pullman-luxury.

The success of the Pullman car was another sign that by the late nineteenth century, American mass production was becoming the effort to produce mass luxury. Americans were willing to pay more for the enticingly new. "Then followed a curious reversal of the usual results of competition," a railroad man of the day remarked with surprise. "Instead of levelling down to the cheaper basis on which all opposition [to Pullman] was united, there was a levelling up to the standard on which the Pullman service was planted and on which it stood out single-handed and alone."

The long-distance luxury sleeping car brought into being another democratized luxury—the dining car. As early as 1867, the Detroit *Commercial Advertiser* declared "the crowning glory of Mr. Pullman's invention" to be the "cuisine department containing a range where every variety of meats, vegetables and pastry may be cooked on the car, according to the best style of culinary art." Pullman's first separate dining car, the "Delmonico," went into operation in 1868. The inexpensive "quick-lunch" at the station counter, a characteristically American by-product of the railroads which had so annoyed European travelers, now had competition from a luxury "diner" (a new word which had entered the American language before 1890) offering meals at leisure. Pullman's improved design replaced the earliest dining-car arrangement, which had been an open baggage car with a table or counter down the center. The new dining car offered seats arranged like those in the sleeping cars at opposite sides of newly designed individual tables, which swung up from the wall of the car.

Now that there was a place for passengers to eat on board, they had to be able to walk safely back and forth from one car to another for their meals. Crossing the open vestibule of a fast-moving train on a bumpy track was risky. The answer was Pullman's improved "vestibule" train, which he patented in 1887. Elastic diaphragms on steel frames were attached to the ends of the cars, so that the faces of the diaphragms on adjacent cars were pressed firmly against each other by powerful spiral springs. And this flexible cover-way remained sealed even on sharp curves. Incidentally, in case of a wreck, it helped prevent the telescoping of cars, and also added to the passenger's comfort by reducing the oscillation of the cars at high speeds.

When George M. Pullman incorporated his sleeping-car company he christened it the Pullman *Palace* Car Company. For it was the age of the People's Palace—the American hotel. And Pullman actually called his first sleepers "hotel-cars." He had put the People's Palace on wheels, with many of the same consequences for the traveler that the hotel had for the city booster and city dweller. While the European sleeping car was from the beginning a series of closed compartments, the American Pullman sleeping car at least until the 1950's remained open in such a way that passengers could freely move about in daytime; each person had the comforting vista of his fellow passengers, and the opportunity for sociable conversation. The washrooms and smoking rooms became proverbial American mixing rooms, the locale for latter-day tall talk. The early European trains were divided into first and second class, but American carriages were orginally separated only into cars for men and cars for women.

The Pullman sleeping car democratized comfort, but did not universalize it. Pullman aimed to offer his luxury for the price of a night in a good hotel. There still remained an uncomfortable distinction between those who sat up all night in an ordinary coach, and those who could afford the price of a Pullman. But in the United States the price of a sleeper was considerably lower than in the Old World, and the comfortable places were much more numerous. In an age when European nations had not yet overcome the distinctions of the hereditary, money-inheriting aristocracy, the United States was providing its new comforts for a Democracy (and perhaps, too, an Aristocracy) of Cash.

39

Walls Become Windows

THE NEW WORLD dissolving of distinctions touched the intimacies of daily life. Of this, there is no more vivid or more neglected example than the story of glass. For glass gave a new, uncertain meaning to the wall, which now became something it had never been before; this in turn made something quite new of glass. The consequence for everyday experience was to give a new ambiguity to where people were and to confuse the boundaries of place.

The century after the Civil War vastly expanded the uses of iron and steel, and found widespread new uses for a fluid masonry, at least as old as the Romans, called concrete. These opaque materials made possible new forms that soared and reached, and so the shapes of buildings were extended and freed. But because glass was transparent it transformed the very meaning of indoors and outdoors, and the relations between them. Glass was a miracle material, which made it possible to be outdoors when you were indoors, to enjoy the flood of sun and daylight while you were sheltered. It would allow Americans to protect themselves against wind and weather, against heat and cold, while it liberated their vision.

The story of glass in the United States is all the more dramatic because glass was so ancient a material, whose meaning was so recently and so quickly transformed. In the history of technology the oldest arts are those which change most slowly. The ancient Egyptians used glass for the glazing of soapstone beads and to make imitation precious stones; glass-blown vessels were widely known in the Mediterranean before the birth of Jesus. During the Middle Ages, techniques were elaborated to make fancy containers, chandeliers, and small mirrors. By the thirteenth century, when Venice was the glassmaking center of Europe, the glassmaker's secrets were counted among the city's treasures. Venetians found a way to make a pure, colorless, and transparent glass, which was then fashioned into fragile objects to be prized in palaces. Glass, a raw material of filigreed luxury, was treated as a kind of transparent silver.

Only gradually did glass come to be used for windows. In buildings of the early Middle Ages, windows were few and small, for glass was expensive and flat glass could be made only with difficulty and in small sizes. The vivid stained-glass windows of the medieval Gothic cathedrals of France and England displayed the limitations as well as the powers of the glassmakers. It was easy to make colored glass (the color came from the quantity of different "impurities"), but hard to make perfectly clear glass. These small pieces of colored flat glass offered the architects an opportunity to use lead and to arrange them into elegant compositions. Around the sun-drenched Mediterranean, where stained-glass windows first flourished, stained glass appealed for its ability to keep out the hot sunshine while it transformed sunlight into ornamental images. Leaded windows of small panes, imitated in the twentieth century by neoromantic architects, were originally made that way not for ornamental reasons, but because larger panes were not available. Even into the nineteenth century, tax laws in the Old World found it convenient to tax household property not by square footage or the total construction cost, but by the number of its windows. The English window tax (1696 to 1851) became a model for the French door and window tax (1798 to 1917). And the connection between the number of your windows and your ability to pay was not entirely fanciful. Glass windows were not for the common people.

IN MODERN AMERICA, just as ice was changed from an item of personal luxury consumption into a commodity for everybody, so too was glass. Democratizing glass in the United States meant making it another way of removing spatial distinctions, and a means for conquering the seasons. From being the precious substance of the decorative arts, prized for its colorful, reflective brilliance, glass became a basic building material and a universal medium of vision. Again, the great theoretical discoveries and many of the basic new techniques came from abroad, mostly from Europe. But by the twentieth century the American genius for organization and diffusion had made glass into an unprecedented necessity for unprecedented numbers of people and for unprecedented purposes. Before this could happen, more economical techniques of glassmaking were required.

The commonest way of making sheet glass throughout the eighteenth century was the "crown" window-glass process, so called because the product bore a "crown," or bull's eye. This was an elaborate process commonly requiring a team of ten men and boys. The globe of glass already blown by the pipe was rolled on an iron table until it had a conical shape. Then a solid iron rod was attached to the flat base of the cone (opposite the blowpipe) and the blowpipe was removed, leaving the hot glass cone open at the small end. The most skilled member of the team then spun the cone rapidly in a reheating furnace until centrifugal force caused it to flash out into a flat disk, still adhering to the iron rod at the center (or "crown"). At that instant the glassmaker removed the disk from the furnace, and to retain its flat shape, kept whirling it until it became cooler and stiffer. An assistant then cut the glass disk free from the rod so it could be taken to a kiln for annealing. The circular sheets that could be made by this process were relatively small and became still smaller if they were cut square. And of course they always bore the tell-tale bull's-eye or "crown" in the middle. Because the glass was blown, it was uneven in thickness and thin at the edges.

Until about 1830 the bull's-eye process was the usual way to make glass for windows. It was occasionally supplemented by another, equally complicated and difficult technique, the hand-cylinder process. By this method, globes of hot glass, which had been produced by the glass blowers, were elongated into cylinders by being swung in a deep trench (sometimes reaching a depth of ten feet). The cylinder was then slit lengthwise, flattened out, and allowed to cool. This required special skill in the blower, who had to make a cylinder of uniform thickness.

Until the mid-nineteenth century, too, the glassmaker, like the alchemist or the physician, possessed a prestige and mystique. Glass-making was a world of traditional formulae and secret processes, and unlike other men who worked with their hands, the glassmaker held the status of "gentleman." While the noble and the wealthy re-mained the customers for glassware, glassmaking itself remained a monopoly, and was perhaps the most aristocratic of the crafts.

The American situation from the beginning offered opportunities for the glassmaker. A whole glass plant could be built on the personal knowledge of a single glassmaker. And the main raw materials re-quired—sand, and wood for the furnace—were abundant on the eastern seaboard. As a result, glassmaking was probably the first industry established in British America. Polish and German glass-makers were brought to Virginia in 1608, followed by Italian glass-makers a few years later, and before the mid-seventeenth century, Massachusetts Bay was offering land to attract its own glassmakers. These craftsmen made bottles, lamps, tableware, a few pieces of window glass, and incidentally provided some glass beads for the Indian trade. By 1740 a German immigrant, Caspar Wistar, was oper-ating a glassworks with four experienced Belgian glass blowers, to whom he soon added glass blowers from Germany and Portugal. His son Richard carried on the works, and in the tax-troubled year 1769 advertised in Franklin's *Pennsylvania Gazette* that "our glass is of American manufacture—and it is of interest to America to encourage her own manufactures, more especially those upon which duties have been imposed solely to raise revenue." Richard Wistar actually used the slogan "Buy American Manufactured Goods."

About the same time another German immigrant, the flamboyant Henry William Stiegel, who had imported English and German glass-makers, was producing his own elegant glassware. Drinking glasses, lenses, measures, perfume bottles, and other luxury items came from his large glass factory in Lancaster County, Pennsylvania. His grand manner of living earned him the apocryphal title of "Baron von Stiegel," and the beauty of his product made Stiegel glassware pre-cious collector's items in later centuries. But since his glassware was still made to satisfy the expensive tastes of an Old World aristocracy, Stiegel had trouble marketing his product here. He went bankrupt, languished in a debtors' prison, and finally died in poverty. In the age of the American Revolution, a new society on the edge of a continen-tal wilderness had needs more urgent than for the rich blues and purples of Stiegelware. When a prosperous American glass industry came into being, it was for a much wider and more characteristically American market.

SO LONG AS the making of sheets of glass was tied to the ancient, skilled arts of the glass blower, so long as the preparation of flat glass depended on human lung power, the reshaping of the material from a luxury-treasure into a democratic medium for transforming space was impossible. By the mid-nineteenth century some new mechanical methods of making flat glass had been developed in Europe, and these were beginning to displace the glass blower. In the twentieth century, American techniques and machines would open a new age for one of the world's most ancient crafts.

As early as the seventeenth century, a revolutionary new way of making flat glass was in use in France. A lump of molten glass was poured onto a "casting table," and while still molten, was pressed out by a roller which forced it between guides, fixed so as to insure an even surface and uniform thickness. The glass was left to anneal or cool for about ten days, then both surfaces were ground down by a smaller plate of glass, and finally polished with felt-covered boards and rollers. This technique had been imported to England before the end of the eighteenth century, but did not displace the hand-cylinder process. As a result of improvements in the hand-cylinder process, by the mid-nineteenth century it had become possible to make sheets of glass eight times the size of those known before. But the processes remained tricky and laborious, partly because of the difficulty of making durable casting tables that would not crack under extreme heat. It was still hard to conceive that glass could ever become a universal building material.

But in 1851 for the international exhibition in London, Joseph Paxton, a gardener and horticulturist, designed a structure like a greenhouse. As an observer noted at the time, it was "the first great building which was not of solid masonry construction." Paxton had become famous in 1849 when he succeeded in bringing the exotic equatorial South American water lily to bloom indoors. In the exhibition building, which he had designed following the example of earlier greenhouses in France and his own conservatories in England, Paxton gave a new prominence to glass. The whole construction was planned around the largest standard sheet of glass, then four feet long. This "Crystal Palace," as it came to be called, housed the first great international exhibit to show, in the words of Prince Albert, how modern industry was leading toward "the union of the human race." The exhibition structure itself, enclosing a ground area about four times that of St. Peter's in Rome, was by far the most extensive single building the world had seen. It foreshadowed how technology would remove the barriers of space. The whole vast building, a dazzled spectator exclaimed, "dissolves into a distant background where all materiality is blended into the atmosphere. . . . I call the spectacle incomparable and fairylike. It is a Midsummer Night's Dream seen in the clear light of midday."

Glass was now revealed on a grand scale as a medium that could erase old barriers. But before glass could shape the experience of the bulk of the American people, there had to be new mechanized techniques for making glass cheaply and in large quantities. Even before the Crystal Palace was up, Sir Henry Bessemer, later of steelmaking fame, had experimented with a revolutionary process for producing sheets of glass by passing the molten glass through rollers. The purpose was to find a continuous process, a flow technology for glass, which would avoid the need to make glass batch by batch and sheet by sheet. New tank furnaces were designed to produce a steady flow of molten glass which could be somehow flattened into long broad ribbons of uniform thickness. Sir William Siemens, the German-born inventor who emigrated to England, devised new regenerative gas-fired furnaces which reused the gases emitted by the heated glass to provide a continuous flow of large quantities of molten glass. Such gas-fired furnaces came only slowly to the United States, partly because wood was cheaper here and the glassworks had been smaller. By the 1880's, Chance Brothers, the pioneer British glass manufacturers, were passing molten glass between pairs of rollers to produce sheets, which were then ground and polished.

About the same time an ingenious method was devised to draw a flat sheet of glass direct from the furnace. A "bait," or sheet of metal, was dipped into the molten glass, and as the glass adhered to the bait, the bait was drawn upward to pull the glass out into a sheet. But as the molten glass was drawn upward the sheet tended to narrow and thicken into a thread, which made it hard to keep the withdrawing sheet of glass uniform in width or thickness. An elaborate cooling system was required to solidify the glass into the proper shape. The French were producing glass commercially in this way before World War I.

By the end of the nineteenth century, Americans were beginning to take the lead in organizing glass production and in developing new machinery. The rise of canning had increased the demand for jars, and there were numerous American improvements—for example, Mason's screw-top jar, which was patented in 1858. But the first important American contribution was in devising semi-automatic machines for making bottles. These were the most important new machines since the ancient invention of the glass-blowing iron for the making of glass containers. At the age of ten Michael J. Owens, son of a poor West Virginia miner, was shoveling coal into the furnace of a Wheeling glass factory. At the age of fifteen he was a skilled glass blower. Then, while working as manager of Edward Drummond Libbey's glass factory in Toledo, Ohio, Owens developed his pioneer bottle-blowing machine. Owens' essential idea was beautifully simple. From the surface of a pot of molten glass, a piston pump sucked a heated lump into a mold, and then the pump was reversed to blow the glass into the shape of a bottle. Owens patented this process by 1895, and within a decade had devised a completely automatic machine. On the perfected Owens machine (which was made of more than nine thousand parts), two men could produce twenty-five hundred bottles an hour. It was this machine, too, that would help light up the nation by making possible the quantity production of electric-light bulbs.

Owens, who had no business experience, had the good luck to acquire his boss as collaborator. For Libbey, a New Englander who had inherited a glassworks from his father, was a businessman of energy, imagination, and organizing ability. In 1888 he had set up a new factory in Toledo, where he was attracted both by the large quantities of natural gas for firing the furnaces, and by the good glass sand found in the neighborhood. Libbey, though no inventor, knew a revolutionary invention when he saw one. He financed Owens' efforts to perfect his machine and actually put it to work in his factories. He then made Owens his partner and organized a firm to manufacture Owens' bottle-making machines for a world market. Libbey organized the Toledo Museum of Art in 1901, used his fortune to erect its first building in 1912, and helped make it a model for the dynamic role of museums in American education.

In contrast to bottle making, the machine making of flat glass, surprisingly enough, proved to be more complicated. The earnings of Owens' new bottle machine financed a new plate-glass industry when, in 1912, Libbey bought the patents of Irving Wightman Colburn for manufacturing sheet glass and then supported him while he perfected his processes. Colburn, also a New Englander, came from a Fitchburg, Massachusetts, textile-manufacturing family and very early turned the inventive bent of his family toward the new world of electricity. At the age of twenty-two he had started the town's first agency for the sale of electrical equipment, he installed its first electric-lighting and telephone systems, and then organized his own company for manufacturing electrical equipment. Moving west to Toledo, Colburn somehow became engrossed in glass manufacture, and gave the last nineteen years of his life to solving its problems.

The Colburn Window-Glass Machine was hailed by the *Scientific American* in 1908 as "the first machine for drawing window-glass continuously in any width." Colburn had devised a way, while drawing upward a sheet of molten glass from a glass furnace, to control the width of the sheet as it was pulled. The obvious problem was still that molten glass, like all viscous substances, tended to narrow to a thread as it was elongated upward. Colburn's clever device, which he spent years perfecting, was simply a set of rotating fire-clay cylinders on the surface of the molten-glass tank, one on each side of the emerging sheet. By rotating these in opposite directions and away from the middle of the emerging sheet, Colburn could keep the glass ribbon stretched as it emerged, and at the same time produce a glass free from wavy lines and blemishes. After the sheet was drawn vertically for a few feet it was reheated enough to be bent over a horizontal roller, and then it was pulled in a continuous process through an annealing oven. "The process is remarkable," the *Scientific American* observed, "for the quality of its product. The surface of the glass has a beautiful mirror-like fire polish far superior to the blown window-glass which we see every day. Even plate glass has a surface no better. . . . the spheres in the working chamber can be adjusted to produce glass of any thickness. We have seen specimens of glass made by this machine almost as thin as fine porcelain and other specimens almost as thick as plate glass." In 1916 Colburn's machines in the vast new factory of the Libbey-Owens Sheet Glass Company at Charleston, West Virginia, were turning out hundreds of square yards of plate glass in a continuous flow. A new era had arrived for one of man's oldest materials: a new means for opening windows to the world, for giving Americans a new kind of indoor-outdoor experience.

The next stages simply improved the technology of flow. The Corning ribbon machine, for example, used the same rollers which drew out the molten glass to impress on the ribbon the shape of glass bulbs, into which puffs of compressed air were injected. Then techniques were devised for drawing the plate horizontally between water-cooled rollers. When the assembly-line production of automobiles required vast, fast quantities of glass in a continuous stream, Henry Ford built a glass-making machine at River Rouge from which a 51-inch-wide ribbon of glass for automobiles emerged uninterruptedly at the rate of three and a half miles per day for two years, to a total length of nearly two thousand miles; and the Libbey-Owens Glass Company became Libbey-Owens-Ford. The needs of the automobile for anti-glare glass, and especially for safety glass of various curved shapes, stirred glassmakers to a new range of products. The needs to soundproof and interline the automobile, and the search for simpler ways of making automobile bodies, produced fiberglass. Some even imagined that one day glass might displace steel as the basic material for cars. Meanwhile, glass did allow motorists to enjoy parlor comforts and indoor security as the landscape raced past.

BUT EVEN BEFORE glass was bringing the outdoors indoors, and changing the architecture of life on the move, it was transforming the walls of buildings. The first great school of American skyscraper construction, the "Chicago School," was marked not only by its new uses of steel, but just as much by its pioneer use of glass. Steel framing, in place of heavy masonry, provided a new open framework for windows, of which Daniel Burnham, John Root, Louis Sullivan, and others took advantage. Even while Chicago architects like William Le Baron Jenney were still using cast iron, they began to put plate glass to dramatic new uses; for example, by designing wide panels to be filled with plate-glass windows. Contemporaries hailed Jenney's Leiter Building (1889) as "a giant structure . . . healthy to look at, lightsome and airy while substantial . . . a commercial pile in a style undreamed of when Buonarroti erected the greatest temple of Christianity." Daniel Burnham's Reliance Building (1894) was described as "a glass tower fifteen stories high." Louis Sullivan's classic Carson, Pirie, Scott Building (1899–1904) was distinguished by its "Chicago windows," as regular in width as the columned exterior of a Venetian *palazzo*, in which the dominant wall feature now was flat, transparent glass.

Glass became the basis of a new international style. In Germany, Walter Gropius and Mies van der Rohe (who were both later to come to America) and Le Corbusier in France played with glass in new ways. They used it for curtain walls, they exploited its brilliance and reflectiveness. By the mid-twentieth century the rhythmic, geometric glass wall had become the most prominent feature of the American skyscraper, and it was the basic material for "enclosing" man now that he had begun living and working in the high air.

With the mass production of large sheets of transparent glass, unimagined new possibilities were found in the ancient material. For glass is nonyielding under pressure, it can be bent many times without showing the "fatigue" common in metals, it resists corrosion, and the raw materials of which glass is made are practically limitless in supply. By the mid-twentieth century the new technology had produced a vast and unprecedented array: variable transmission glass, electroluminescent glass, electrically conducting glass, microporous glass with variable resistance to air flow, solar-energy-collecting glass, malleable glass of steel-like strength, and countless other varieties.

Glass was even used to produce white "blackboards" to brighten schoolrooms. There were "variable transmittance" windows which automatically became lighter or darker as the intensity of the sun's rays varied, and "limited vision" glass especially designed for acoustical and visual privacy "without total visual isolation."

Glass became a commonplace and a key to modern home design. A symbol of the modern American spirit was this removal of the sharp visual division between indoors and outdoors, with its new peril of walking through a glass door by mistake. "Sliding glass doors," one glass manufacturer advertised, "add new dimension to living by uniting the indoor-outdoor environment. . . . Glass makes smaller homes look bigger. On exterior walls it creates the dramatic indoor-outdoor flow looked for by homemakers. As room dividers, glass creates walls that close off and yet allows an open feeling."

In America, in the twentieth century, a window was almost as much to look into as to look out of or to receive light from. Glass became a symbol of the American ambivalence about all kinds of walls. By mid-century, "picture window" meant "a large window in a house usually dominating the room or wall in which it is located, and often designed or decorated to present an attractive view as seen from inside or outside the house."

Glass, which brought together indoors and outdoors and leveled the environment, became a medium of display, to excite and titillate everybody's desires for all the objects which one's fellow citizens possessed and which comprised the American Standard of Living. As we have seen, the light cast-iron frames of the early department stores used large sheets of glass to offer ground-floor windows, making the merchandise its own vivid advertisement, and by the mid-nineteenth century "show window" had entered the language. The ambiguous expression "window dressing," the concern of specialized artists and technicians, was on its way, and "window-shopping" became a new form of consumer onanism.

In these and countless other ways, glass expressed the magic of the new technology, the democratization of things. The fragile luxury material of the Older World became a sturdy medium for erasing the distinctions between places, between indoors and outdoors, and so, too, for blurring the distinctions among people.

40

Homogenizing Space

BY THE MID-TWENTIETH CENTURY, millions of Americans were living and working high in the air. They spent whole days and nights in towers of steel and glass, and the skyscraper became a symbol of the American city. Just as nineteenth-century boosters had boasted of their hotels, their Palaces of the Public, so twentieth-century boosters boasted of their towers. Both were as much a product of hope and aspiration as of necessity. The towering skyscraper expressed a new, latter-day American boosterism, a determination to compete with Nature herself, to win over the limitations of matter and space and seasons.

The grandest went up in the largest, most congested cities. New York City's Woolworth Building (1913) and her Empire State Building (1931), and Chicago's Tribune Tower (1925), and many others responded to the real or imagined needs of the great metropolis. But in smaller cities, too, all over the nation skyscrapers shot up. For the American skyscraper was not simply a reflex response to economic need or an answer to the scarcity of land. In Tulsa, Oklahoma, for example, and in other cities of the West, mini-skyscrapers rose in the midst of endless acres of uninhabited prairie.

As Old World cities grew they had spread out. The most populous cities were inevitably the most extensive. Rome was spread over seven hills, and before the middle of the twentieth century, Greater London covered nearly 700 square miles. In European cities the tallest buildings, except for monuments, exposition towers, and occasional tours de force like the Eiffel Tower, reached up only five or six stories.

The tall structures that Americans built were not mere Eiffel Towers. They were buildings to work in and live in, for Americans had developed new ways of indoor living, ways of homogenizing space and the seasons. Americans could cease to be earthbound because they were no longer bound to the earth for their drinking water and washing water, for disposing of human wastes, for their means of keeping warm and cool, for their ways to communicate with neighbors. The skyscraper was the climactic symbol of man's ability to rise above particular places and times to satisfy his needs, to keep himself comfortable and at work, making experience for all Americans, wherever they lived, more alike.

THE FIRST LARGE American community water supplies were not motivated by the desire for household convenience, but rather for a variety of public purposes—more and better drinking water, water to flush the streets and to fight fires. The first sizable municipal waterworks in the United States, which brought the waters of the Schuylkill to Philadelphia in 1801, was a response to the city's recent yellow-fever epidemics that had decimated the population, forcing thousands to flee to the countryside. It was believed that disease could be prevented by flushing the streets daily, and especially in hot weather. The designer of the waterworks, the eminent Benjamin H. Latrobe (whom Jefferson appointed as the first surveyor of United States public buildings, and who was to build the first section of the Capitol), had encountered an assortment of fears and prejudices. Latrobe's plan for the waterworks required the use of steam engines at the pumping stations in the heart of the city. Philadelphians, who had heard about the explosions of these new-fangled engines on Western river boats, imagined that the pumping stations would bring the perils of boiling water and steam into their own neighborhoods. Latrobe finally carried the day with his declaration that "a steam engine is, at present, as tame and innocent as a clock," and his scheme was executed at a cost of about a quarter of a million dollars.

But a full year afterward Philadelphia, which with its population of 70,000 was then the largest city in the United States, had received an annual revenue of only $537 from a total of 154 water takers. A decade later, when the population of Philadelphia had reached 90,-000, the number of water takers had risen to 2,127. The idea that running water was a household necessity was at least a half-century in the future. City dwellers could still gather what water they needed free of charge from pumps or running streams. "It will be some time," one Philadelphian predicted, "before the citizens will be reconciled to *buy* their water." Paying for water to drink appeared almost as absurd as paying for air to breathe. But even that fantastic necessity seemed in the offing by the late twentieth century.

The earliest American community water supplies were brought by wooden conduits to a town or to a group of houses. During the first half of the nineteenth century such water suppliers were usually private companies authorized by state legislatures and municipal governing bodies and run for profit. Within three decades after the opening of the Philadelphia municipal waterworks in 1801, New Orleans, Pittsburgh, Richmond, and St. Louis took up the idea.

In New York it took failure by the private Manhattan Company, dominated by Aaron Burr, and a half-century of wrangling to bring the city round to providing a public water supply. Cholera epidemics in 1832 and 1834 and a scourge of fires in 1834 estimated to cost the city $1.5 million pushed the city into action. "We are at present," a

New Yorker observed, "supplied with spring water carted round in carts and brought from the upper parts and suburbs of the city. This water, although far from good, is much better than that obtained from wells in the city; for this we pay at the rate of two cents per pail, three pails per day is but a moderate quantity for a family, and three pails per day costs twenty dollars per annum." City dwellers commonly spiked their unpalatable water with spirits and incidentally added the temperance argument to all the others. "Water is one of the elements," a New Yorker found it necessary to argue, "full as necessary to existence as light and air, and its supply, therefore, ought never to be made a subject of trade or speculation." The fire of December 17, 1835, the worst in the city's history (inhabitants compared it to the conflagration of Moscow) dramatized the need.

The great Croton Aqueduct brought water thirty miles south from a reservoir dammed up from the Croton River, and on October 14, 1842, began pouring millions of gallons into New York City. "Nothing is talked of or thought of in New York but Croton water," Philip Hone noted in his diary; "fountains, acqueducts, hydrants, and hose attract our attention and impede our progress through the streets. Political spouting has given place to water spouts, and the free current of water has diverted the attention of the people from the vexed questions of the confused state of the national currency." But some New Yorkers, complaining that the water was "all full of tadpoles and animalculae," were "in dreadful apprehensions of breeding bullfrogs inwardly."

The most powerful argument for improved municipal water supplies came from London, when an English physician, John Snow, showed that the victims of that city's cholera epidemic of 1849 had all drunk water from a certain Broad Street pump. Snow proved that bad water was not simply water that did not sparkle and had an unpleasant odor, but it contained specific agents which came from feces. Even after proof that specific diseases could be traced to specific impurities in water, purifying systems came only slowly to American cities.

The notable American contribution was made by James P. Kirkwood, who had been sent to Europe by the city of St. Louis to study the purification of river water. After reading Kirkwood's report, St. Louis city officials decided not to try to filter the muddy Mississippi. But the city of Poughkeepsie then commissioned Kirkwood to build a plant to filter waters of the Hudson. It was the first large-scale water filtration plant in the United States, and became a model for the world. One of the main problems in sand-filtration plants was the accumulation of scum and impurities which were difficult to remove from the sand-filtration beds. Kirkwood's ingeniously simple proposal was that instead of scraping off the impurities from the sand, the flow of water be reversed through the filter to backwash the impurities.

In one American city after another, water began to flow in seemingly endless streams. By mid-century, running water was commonly found in upper-middle-class households in large cities. In 1860, every one of the nation's sixteen largest cities (each with a population of at least 50,000) had some sort of waterworks. All but four (New Orleans, Buffalo, San Francisco, Providence) of these were municipally owned, and many smaller cities also commonly had waterworks.

Even while running water in the household was still an upper-middle-class luxury, those Americans who could afford it were already treating the water supply as if it were inexhaustible. Planners had made the mistake of basing their predictions on the early Philadelphia experience. The Bostonians who argued against the expense of the Cochituate Aqueduct (completed in 1848) had said that it was ridiculous to imagine that the city would ever consume 7.5 million gallons a day. Yet within five years, the city's average daily consumption exceeded 8.5 million gallons. What ran up the consumption was not that there were too many families connected to the system, but that, as the Boston Water Board estimated, two thirds of the water was being wasted. In livery stables, in primitive water closets and urinals, water was left running constantly. In cold weather, when householders feared that their pipes might freeze, they kept their faucets wide open all night. During a cold spell in January 1854, daily consumption rose to 14 million gallons, the reservoirs were nearly dry, and houses in the higher parts of the city were left without water. Inspectors were sent about the city at night listening for the sound of running water so they could warn offenders that their supply might be cut off. In 1860 the Water Board complained that Boston's average of 97 gallons daily for each inhabitant was "without parallel in the civilized world," and expressed fear that the city soon would be unable to supply the citizens' demands.

These municipal waterworks, like other new resources of flow technology, were not merely new means to supply one of man's ancient necessities. They became themselves channels which brought into being inexhaustible new demands. Even before all Americans had become accustomed to the luxury of running water, the municipal waterworks had become sources of new scarcities. The story of running water would, of course, be paralleled a half-century later by the story of running electricity.

Running water made possible a host of new uses for water, and the spread of many older uses to more and more Americans. The New York water commissioners warned New Yorkers only two years after the Croton Aqueduct went into operation that they had not intended to supply fountains in all the city's parks, nor to amuse all the city's boys with water flowing from fire hydrants. At first it was generally assumed that baths would continue to be primarily a public facility. In 1849, when Philadelphia already had 15,000 houses with running water, only about 3,500 had private baths. In New York the price of general admission to a public bath was three cents, or six cents if you wanted to bathe privately in a separate room.

In other parts of the world, too, a household bathroom was still a luxury. But in the United States within a half-century it would begin to be a middle-class necessity. The nation which was world headquarters for the democratization of comfort was naturally enough the home of the democratized bath. The progress of the American bathroom was rapid and spectacular. By 1922 Sinclair Lewis' Babbitt started every day in his "altogether royal bathroom of porcelain and glazed tile and metal sleek as silver."

IN THE OLDER WORLD, the *public* facilities tended to copy the *private*. Inns were shaped like large private residences, town halls were fashioned after the palatial dwellings of rich citizens. But the urban communities which sprang up in the United States in the nineteenth century were bristling with newcomers, while there were still few rich men and, of course, no ancient palaces. Here public buildings and public facilities made their own style, which gradually influenced the way everyone lived. The large display windows to show off the wares of new-style department stores eventually were adopted as "picture windows" in apartment buildings and in private households. The history of running water and bathrooms followed a similar pattern.

The luxurious American hotels, the Palaces of the Public, were among the first and most influential American buildings to bring running water indoors. Even before Boston had installed a municipal waterworks, the Tremont House, completed in 1829, had its own water system to feed its bathtubs and its battery of eight water closets on the ground floor. The rise of running water in America was literal as well as figurative. From the ground floor it rose gradually to the upper stories, where at first there were common bathroom facilities for the residents of each floor, and then it trickled out to each room. Generally, running water was brought first to the kitchen sink, then to the wash basin, and finally to the bathtub. But as late as 1869, Catherine Beecher and Harriet Beecher Stowe's *American Woman's Home,* a popular guide to home planning, showed a kitchen sink with water drawn from a hand pump.

In the United States, hotels continued to set the pace. As early as 1853, the luxurious Mount Vernon Hotel at Cape May, New Jersey, impressed Americans and amazed travelers from Britain by equipping every room not only with running water but also with a bathtub. By 1877, one medium-priced Boston hotel offered in each of its rooms a wash basin with running hot and cold water. But it was the early twentieth century before the private bathroom became normal for every room in better American hotels. When the enterprising Ellsworth M. Statler built his new hotel in Buffalo in 1908, his advertising slogan was "A room with a bath for a dollar and a half."

RUNNING WATER WAS, first of all, a labor-saving device. In earlier times, even if there was a pump indoors at the kitchen sink, it still required muscle power to make the water flow; the wash basin or the bathtub required water to be carried by hand. When English travelers first saw plumbing fixtures in American hotels and households, they described them as simply another American response to the scarcity of menial labor. And the high cost of labor in the United States did help explain why running water and indoor plumbing so early became commonplace here.

Before there were running water and municipal sewers, the wash basin or the bathtub was moved about to wherever it was needed or wherever at the time the water could be most conveniently carried to them. There was no such thing as a "bathroom," since there was no functional reason why the bathtub and washstand should be kept in one place.

Water systems had begun as private enterprises, selling people the water they needed, but sewage-disposal systems could not start that way. This helps explain why they were so slow in coming. Running water could not become a common convenience until there were municipal systems of sewage disposal. In 1850 Lemuel Shattuck, the versatile New Englander whom we have already met as De Bow's collaborator in the census of 1850 and as a founder of American vital statistics, explained the urgent need for city sewage-disposal systems in his pioneer *Report of the Sanitary Commission of Massachusetts.* In 1860, when there were 136 city water systems in the United States, there were still only ten municipal systems for disposing of sewage. By 1880 there were more than two hundred. But at that time a sewage "system" was simply an arrangement for collecting and pouring unprocessed city sewage into nearby lakes or streams. The growth of city water systems in turn increased the urgency of the need for better systems of sewage disposal, since cities now commonly found themselves drawing their water supplies from the very streams they were polluting. Massachusetts kept the lead, by setting up a State Board of Health in 1869, and by pioneering in studies of sewage disposal at the Lawrence Experiment Station. But this was considered a nasty subject, embarrassing to discuss in mixed company. And it was only against considerable public resistance that the perils of human sewage, however diluted, for community water supplies were gradually demonstrated. At the Lawrence Station, Hiram F. Mills developed a system of slow sand filtration for sewage, contradicting the popular notions of the day that rapid flow was what purified streams, and he thus helped reduce by 80 percent the Massachusetts death rate from typhoid.

As sewage systems matched water systems, there grew up a large new market for plumbing fixtures. The "room with a private bath" in American hotels and motels, and the multiplying baths in households, required better bathtubs, easier to clean and maintain. The first two decades of the twentieth century saw a sudden increase in the production of American enamelware. In the previous decades many materials had been tried: wooden boxes lined with sheet lead or zinc or copper; cast iron, plain, painted or galvanized; sheet steel; sheet copper; porcelain crockery; and even aluminum. But all these were either too fragile, too cold to the touch, or too expensive. A durable cast-iron enameled tub had been made as early as 1870, when a manufacturer was turning out one tub per day. Until 1900, sanitary fixtures were still hand-fashioned, but production had risen to ten bathtubs per worker per day. A few cast-iron enameled tubs were used in private Pullmans before 1900. Then by 1920, the one-piece, double-shelled enameled tub, destined to remain standard for a half-century, was being machine-made and mass-produced. The castings were serially poured, cooled, and scoured, and little skill was required of the workers. Between 1915 and 1921 the annual production of enameled sanitary fixtures (wash basins, bathtubs, etc.) doubled, and then doubled again by 1925, to reach over five million pieces.

The other essential element in the American bathroom, apart from the wash basin, was of course the water closet, or flush toilet. One reason for the slow introduction of indoor water closets for the disposal of human waste was that unlike the running-water wash basin or bathtub, it was not so obviously a labor-saving device. Not until near the end of the nineteenth century was it widely believed that human waste was a dangerous source of disease infection and water pollution. Rural life and mores discouraged the making of machines to do what nature could do better. The earth was supposed to have remarkable absorbing and deodorizing powers, and the common way of disposing of human waste was on the surface of the ground. People retired to a nearby woods or to some other sheltered place;

and they tried to prevent *odors*, which were generally thought to be the real source of infection, by carefully selecting a different place each time. In villages it was found desirable to establish special private places or "privies." But privies were generally considered not so much sanitary devices as places of modest and dignified retirement. Even where there were privies, they were for use mainly by women and children, while the men still used the stable or the woods.

The first United States patents for water closets were issued in the 1830's, but it was past mid-century, after the rise of water systems and sewage systems, that the water closet began to come into general use. In 1851, when President Millard Fillmore reputedly installed the first permanent bath and water closet in the White House, he was criticized for doing something that was "both unsanitary and undemocratic." Even after there were city sewage systems, it was hard to persuade owners to go to the expense of installing plumbing and making sewer connections. Especially in the congested center of cities, where the problem of waste disposal was most pressing, it was often difficult to persuade landlords to use the sewage system. On sewered streets, thousands of persons were still using old privies and cesspools at the end of the nineteenth century.

Designing a satisfactory water closet was no easy matter, and it challenged the talents of plumbers, inventors, and hydraulic engineers. The problem was to design a bowl and apparatus that would be self-cleaning and not too noisy, and yet would not use excessive amounts of water. The modern wash-down closet that worked on the syphon principle, using suction to clean the bowl, had been invented in England by 1870 and was used by Americans who could afford it by the 1880's and 90's. The flush-valve toilet, which required less time between uses, was developed in the early twentieth century and long remained the only major improvement in toilet design. The water closet, like the bathtub, could be democratized only after the perfection of ways of mass-producing enamelware—plumbing fixtures of iron coated with enamel. By the opening of the twentieth century, American enamelware mass-produced for bathrooms had become good enough for European royalty, and the American product was installed in Buckingham Palace and in the private apartments of the king of Prussia. During the next decades, enamelware was displaced by porcelain.

In the United States a by-product of the widespread installation of water closets which required gallons of water at each flush, and another symptom of the democratization of everything, was the enormous increase in the public demand for water. As early as 1860, when it was found in Boston that the Parker House was using over

20,000 gallons a day and the Tremont House over 25,000 gallons, water meters were installed so that users could be charged for the actual amounts they consumed. Throughout the next century, novel household uses of water multiplied, with the washing machines, dishwashers, garbage-disposal machines, automatic lawn sprinklers, humidifiers, and air conditioners. Even before World War II, when the average per capita use of water in ten large European cities (including London, Paris, and Berlin) was 39 gallons per day, in ten large American cities (including New York, Philadelphia, Baltimore, Chicago, and Detroit), the per capita water use was four times as much, or 155 gallons per day. The new ways to use and to waste water seemed endless.

The new communal sources of water, and the communal outlets for sewage, became the unexpected causes for isolating individuals, incidentally changing social attitudes toward bodily functions. The old-fashioned privies, even in castles, were often designed so that their users could enjoy the company and conversation of fellow-users. The early American outhouses, too, commonly had more than one seat, to facilitate use by more than one person at a time. But the indoor toilet, partly because of its cost, was a loner. While in England, as Giedion has explained, the earliest bathrooms were large rooms, as spacious as the others in the house, in the United States the bathroom became a cell, distinguished by its compactness and insulation. This was a far cry from the bathing facilities of ancient Rome or Greece or modern Islam or Japan, where the common water source brought people together. And a far cry, too, from the sociability and gossip of the women at the well which had been proverbial ever since Rebecca's day. For Americans, the democratization of the bath meant the *private* bath.

As these mechanical devices using communal resources—water, gas, and electricity—became common in American households, they became the central unit around which buildings were planned. And as the American housewife went from the coal stove to the control panels, the engineer began to take precedence over the architect.

THE SKYSCRAPER APARTMENT or office building could hardly have become a year-round dwelling without central heating. For the problems of constructing a chimney to each of hundreds of rooms and then hoisting fuel for individual fires might have made large, high buildings impossible. And in the United States central heating, too, spread from public buildings into private households: another by-product of a fluid new world, where facilities open to the public aimed to democratize luxury. The Palaces of the Public, the luxurious

American hotels, had introduced Americans to central heating before the mid-nineteenth century. The early heating plants were hot-air systems fired by wood or coal, but before the end of the century the boilers used in steam engines were being adapted for heating. And the exhaust steam from factory engines was piped into systems that warmed factories, offices, and meeting rooms. The Chicago public schools installed a steam-heating system in 1870.

The "radiator" was an American development. And the use of the word for a fixture through which steam or hot water from a central-heating plant circulates in order to heat a room is an Americanism dating from this era. In 1874 an American, William Baldwin, devised an improved radiator consisting of short lengths of one-inch pipe screwed into a cast-iron base. The widespread introduction of central heating into American households did not come until after the mass production of cast-iron radiators was developed in the 1890's. The American Society of Heating and Ventilating Engineers, founded in 1895, built laboratories at the land-grant University of Illinois, where pioneer experiments set the pace for the nation. By 1950, some sort of central-heating plant was found in half the nation's homes, a 50 percent increase within the preceding decade. Home-heating plants were increasingly fired by fuel flowing from some central source: along with oil, the use of gas or electricity was skyrocketing. By 1960 most American homes were heated neither by coal nor by wood. New systems, including infrared radiant heating and heating by atomic power, were being tried. The latest step in the blurring of boundaries between indoors and outdoors was the increasing use of underpavement pipes to keep streets and sidewalks clear and dry in winter.

Some kind of heating was a simple necessity for living and working in most of the nation. At first air conditioning (cooling, humidifying, or dehumidifying) was a mere convenience. And just as it was far more difficult to devise a machine to keep food cold than to cook, so, too, it was far easier to devise systems for warming rooms than for cooling them. But by the 1970's new styles of architecture with fixed windows and large panes of glass were beginning to take air conditioning for granted. Even before the Civil War, as we have seen, some American efforts had been made to devise a working system of artificial refrigeration. But these were mostly aimed at cooling the air of rooms to cure and prevent fevers.

An air-conditioning system feasible for general use would be a by-product of efforts to solve certain specific problems of industry. Textile manufacturers had found that to keep their fibers soft and stretchable, to prevent the broken ends that required costly stoppage of their machines, they had to control the moisture content of the yarns. A fiber with just the right percentage of moisture was strong and pliable, and to dampen the fiber properly was called "yarn conditioning." In 1906, when an American textile engineer invented a system for accomplishing this by controlling the humidity in the air, he called it "air conditioning," and the name stuck.

For air conditioning, unlike many other innovations in indoor living, the theoretical as well as the practical advances were made in the United States. The man who developed the theory, who devised the machinery, and then envisioned the human possibilities of air conditioning, was Willis H. Carrier. In 1902, just a few months after Carrier received his engineering degree from Cornell, he noticed that the plant in Brooklyn where the humorous magazine *Judge* was printed could not line up their paper properly during the summer. The magazine covers were printed in color, and as the humidity varied during the summer, the paper stretched and shrank so that the successive colors applied by the machines did not "register" precisely one on top of the other.

With a flash of insight and ingenuity that would make him the founder of a great new industry, Carrier focused on the crucial relations between temperature and humidity. And he devised a machine to control both temperature and humidity to solve the plant's problem. In his "Rational Psychrometric Formulae; Their Relation to the Problems of Meteorology and of Air Conditioning," a paper he read to the American Society of Mechanical Engineers in 1911, he provided the theoretical basis for twentieth-century air conditioning. He then developed the devices needed to make air conditioning feasible in tall buildings and in individual residences. His new centrifugal compressor for refrigeration in 1923 reduced the number of moving parts, cut down noise and maintenance costs, provided a more compact machine, and finally extended the reach of air conditioning to the tallest skyscrapers. But as buildings grew larger, new problems appeared: it was impossible to provide enough ceiling space between the floors to accommodate all the ducts. Carrier solved this problem, too, by an ingenious new system of small high-velocity ducts which sped the air to room units which cooled or heated the air as required and diffused it around the room. For feasible home units the next requirement was a safe, noninflammable refrigerant, which the Du-Pont Company developed in 1931 in the form of "Freon 12."

Chocolate factories, which formerly had to close down during hot, humid periods, now, when air-conditioned, could operate regardless of the weather. Bakeries and chewing-gum factories, tobacco factories and ceramic factories, printing plants and munitions factories—all of which had been menaced by changes in the weather—were now free to make their own weather and so keep their production lines moving. The New York Stock Exchange installed a rudimentary air-conditioning system in 1904, followed three years later by New York's Metropolitan Museum of Art. A theater in Montgomery, Alabama, installed a system in 1917. In 1922, Grauman's Chinese Theatre in Hollywood installed a new-style system by which the conditioned air was poured in at the ceiling and the stale air was removed in ducts under the seats. Air-conditioned railroad cars came next. The comforts of the movie theater in the 1930's awakened Americans to their "need" for air conditioning in their offices, factories, shops, and homes.

Once again machines and techniques were spreading from the public commercial world into the private personal world. Room air conditioners, produced in small quantities in the 1930's, had become big business by the 1950's. In the 1960's more than three million such units were being produced annually, three-fourths for use in homes. By the mid-twentieth century, central residential air conditioning had become the industry's biggest market, and before 1970, $1 billion worth of central residential air conditioning was being installed every year. Even in automobiles, air conditioning was beginning to become standard equipment.

"Every day a *good* day" had been Carrier's motto in 1919 when he advertised that a visit to an air-conditioned movie theater "imparts the same splendid physical Exhilaration you would feel after a two-hour vacation in the naturally pure air of the Mountains." He described hotel dining rooms "where even the Air is Appetizing." And he predicted that "*you* will see the day when Manufactured Weather is making 'Every day a *good* day' all over the land, in every type of building from the modest bungalow to the spreading industrial plant enclosing millions of square feet of space. Mark my words."

Carrier's booster optimism was more than justified. Americans, in the 1960's and 70's, became accustomed to air conditioning in their schools and working places and homes, and they began to expect it wherever they went. Vast shopping centers, like Rochester's Midtown Plaza, Savannah's Oglethorpe Plaza and Dallas' North Park Mall, each of which enclosed nearly 1.5 million square feet, were air-conditioned. Imaginative planners like Walt Disney and his colleagues explored the possibility of city centers entirely enclosed and air-conditioned.

A climax of the new stage of indoor-outdoor confusion came appropriately enough in 1965 with the building of the Houston Sports Astrodome which aimed to bring an entire 650-foot span, large enough to enclose a baseball diamond or a football field, under air conditioning. For this purpose there was an elaborate set of testing instruments: outdoors, a pyroheliometer on the roof to measure the angle and intensity of the sunlight, and an anemometer to record the velocity and direction of the wind; indoors, an ultraviolet sensor to register the density of smoke and dust in the air, and to note variations of visibility, humidity, and temperature in all parts of the arena. The clear plastic shell, admitting sunlight to the ground inside, actually allowed real grass to grow on the playing field, but this produced a blinding glare for the baseball player who looked up to catch a high fly. When the plastic was painted over to keep out the sun glare, the grass died. To preserve an outdoor effect, this stubble was at first painted green. Then plastics technicians devised a new kind of artificial grass, "Astroturf," which had the appearance of grass from a distance, and for playing purposes had resilience and the other qualities required. For sports purposes, Astroturf soon proved in many ways superior to the real thing, and was then installed on some outdoor football fields and outdoor "lawn" tennis courts; it even began to appear in some city lawns.

There was less difference than ever before between what man could do indoors and what he had to go outdoors and brave the weather for. There were all sorts of new indoor ways of getting water to drink, of disposing of human waste, of enjoying sports. Americans began to carry their indoors with them when they listened to stereo music and radio news in their air-conditioned auto capsule or on the beach. The common-sense distinction between outdoors and in, between the world Nature's God had made and man's little artificial world was blurred as never before, leaving Americans more disoriented than they commonly realized.

PART SIX

Mass-Producing the Moment

> "O mamma, come into the drawing-room; there is a man in there playing the piano with his hands!"
>
> Quoted by John Philip Sousa in "The Menace of Mechanical Music"

AMONG THE NEWER FORMS of leveling in America, none was more remarkable than the changed meaning of the moment. The "fleeting moment" was the poet's cliché because nothing was more obvious than that the instant now was never to be recaptured. Or, as John Donne put it:

> Go, and catch a falling star,
>   Get with child a mandrake root,
> Tell me where all past years are,
>   Or who cleft the Devil's foot.
> Teach me to hear mermaids singing.

The unrepeatability of the moment was the very meaning of life— and of death. It was another name for man's mortality. For only God was omnipresent. He could be everywhere and anywhere at once, He was not confined by space or by times, nor was He restrained by weather or the seasons. Only God could see all events as if they still happened, or happened all at one time. Only God could see the moving forms and hear the voices of the dead. Now man could do all these things.

In earlier times man had discovered himself by what he could not do. "Art," said Goethe, "lies in limitation." What new meanings could Americans discover in life when they had broken ancient bounds? History had been man's effort to accommodate himself to what he could *not* do. American history in the twentieth century would, more than ever before, test man's ability to accommodate himself to all the new things he *could* do.

41

Time Becomes Fungible: Packaging the Unit of Work

"LOST TIME," said *Poor Richard's Almanac,* "is never found again." The work ethic was based on the notion that each working moment was unique and irrecoverable. There were morning hours and evening hours, and there was something different about the labor of each man. Each brought his own shovel to the coal yard, and shoveled in his own peculiar way, and any one man's shoveling was apt to be very different from another's. And somehow it seemed that this was not only right and proper, but inevitable. Man was the only measure of man. Life was a series of unrelivable, unrepeatable episodes. Time was a procession of unique moments—each was now and never again. The past was what had gone beyond recall.

In twentieth-century America even this old truism would cease to be true. For time became "fungible," a series of closely measured, interchangeable units. Time was no longer a stream and had become a production line.

CLOCKS AND WATCHES were scarce in the United States until the mid-nineteenth century. If every unit of time was vague and imprecise, then, of course, a unit of work could not be measured by the time it required. The contours of the work unit were necessarily uncertain so long as work hours were bounded by daylight and darkness.

Punctuality was not one of the virtues which Benjamin Franklin listed for his self-perfection. And this was not surprising, since in his day, watches were carried only by the wealthy few. Others could not know the exact time unless they were near a clock. Travelers could not leave or depart on a precise, preannounced schedule. Washington or Jefferson or Adams judged whether a guest was late simply by whether he arrived after he was expected. The delightful clocks with sonorous chimes in the plazas of European towns (which wristwatched Americans now find quaint and charming) in their day were built to be a public utility. They were symptoms, too, of the fact that a common citizen could not afford his personal timepiece. Well into the nineteenth century a watch was an heirloom, to be worn pompously at the end of a heavy gold chain. The watch which Mrs. Abraham Lincoln wore on her wrist at her husband's inauguration was considered a curious piece of jewelry. The expression "wristwatch" did not enter English until nearly 1900. Widespread use of the wristwatch, and the universal awareness of horological time, did not come until after such watches had been worn by servicemen in the Boer War (1899–1902) to synchronize the movements of their army units. Only when Americans could afford to buy watches and clocks and had found ways to make them in unprecedented numbers did they begin to wear wristwatches and to measure their lives in minutes.

"Efficiency," an American gospel in the twentieth century, meant packaging work into units of time. In a nation where labor was often scarce and always costly, efficiency was measured less by "quality" or "competency" than by the speed with which an acceptable job was accomplished. Time entered into every calculation. An effective America was a speedy America. Time became a series of homogeneous—precisely measured and precisely repeatable—units. The working day was no longer measured by daylight, and electric lights kept factories going "round the clock." Refrigeration and central heating and air conditioning had begun to abolish nature's seasons. One unit of work time became more like another.

And there were special American incentives to mark off and record standard work-time units. Mass production was standardized production. Patterns for making parts of uniform shape and size were only a beginning. The American System of Manufacturing had required progress in the measurement of all kinds of units and in the making of units to a standard. Henry Ford added the techniques of flowing production. And after Ford, mass production also meant assembly-line production, which required removing all uncertainty about the duration of each task. Now the job was brought to the man. In order to keep up production it was essential that each man's task be timed so that the line could be kept flowing and not a moment would be wasted. The speed of the assembly line, which now meant the speed of production, depended on the speed with which the slowest task could be done. All this meant timing.

FREDERICK W. TAYLOR, the Apostle of the American Gospel of Efficiency, was the first man to proclaim these truths with dogmatic clarity. His life and character embodied the dilemmas of modern America. On the one hand he preached an almost inhuman obsession with things, a single-minded concern for efficiency—for producing more and better and cheaper things. "In the past," Taylor wrote in *The Principles of Scientific Management* in 1911, "the man has been first; in the future the system must be first." Yet, on the other hand, he preached a sentimental, sometimes passionate concern for the fulfillment of each individual man and for a loving harmony among men. He was troubled to see men stunted by what William James called "the habit of inferiority to your full self." To Taylor, an inefficient man was like "a bird that can sing and won't sing." Taylor therefore showed a tireless experimental patience in finding a more economic way to make ball bearings for bicycles, but he expressed irritable impatience with the individual man who felt sentimentally attached to the particular shovel that he had handled for years. Was there, somehow, a necessary contradiction between the fulfillment of a man's individuality and the fulfillment of his productive possibilities? In America, where man's productive energies were unleashed as never before, the question would be tested.

Taylor's mother and father were birthright Quakers. His mother, a passionate abolitionist, had accompanied Lucretia Mott to London in 1842 as a delegate to the International Anti-Slavery Convention. Until the end of his life Taylor dressed plainly, in the Quaker tradition. An enthusiastic English admirer compared him to Jesus. "He went up to men—hundreds of men a day, that he saw humdrumming along, despising themselves and despising their work and expecting nothing of themselves and nothing of anyone else and asked them to put their lives in His hands and let Him show what could be done with them. This is Frederick Taylor's profession." Yet when the young Upton Sinclair objected to his system, Taylor did not shrink from describing the ideal pig-iron handler as "merely a man more or less of the type of the ox, heavy both mentally and physically."

Taylor seemed untroubled by these contradictions of purpose and feelings, for he possessed an evangelical belief in the healing, harmonizing power of efficiency. His panacea was the greater production and diffusion of things. "The one element more than any other," Taylor observed, "which differentiates civilized from uncivilized countries—prosperous from poverty-stricken peoples—is that the average man in the one is five or six times as productive as the other." This was his gospel:

> Scientific management involves a complete mental revolution on the part of the workingman. . . . And it involves the equally complete mental revolution on the part of those on the management's side. . . . in the past a great part of the thought and interest . . . has been centered on what may be called the proper division of the surplus resulting from their joint efforts. . . . The great revolution that takes place . . . under scientific management is that both sides take their eyes off the division of the surplus as the all-important matter, and together turn their attention toward increasing the size of the surplus until this surplus becomes so large that it is unnecessary to quarrel over how it shall be divided.

Taylor therefore opposed labor unions. Had they not been made superfluous by his God, a harmonious and efficient God, the God of Productivity?

In his own daily life, Taylor was very early obsessed by efficiency. He measured his stride and counted his steps to find the most economical way to walk to his job. He invented his own spoon-handled tennis racket and then proved its efficiency in 1881 when he and his partner won the national doubles championship. Later in life, after he had turned to golf, he designed his own putter and tried to grow a better grass for fairways and greens. In an age of high-button shoes, he regularly wore slip-on's with elastic sides, to save the time wasted on buttons. He loved sports, and did not use tea or coffee or tobacco because they interfered with his athletic efficiency.

His parents sent him to Phillips Exeter Academy to prepare for Harvard Law School. He did graduate at the top of his Exeter class, but only at the cost of a physical breakdown which led him to give up a legal career. When his doctor prescribed manual labor, he became an apprentice machinist, starting as a common laborer in the Midvale Steel Company in Philadelphia. At the same time he studied mechanical engineering at night and passed the examinations for a degree from Stevens Institute of Technology in 1883. He had discovered his vocation as an engineer: before he was thirty he had been made chief engineer of the plant and had already begun the career of invention that eventually secured him a hundred patents. These included the design for the largest steam hammer ever built in the United States. If he had accomplished nothing else, he would be remembered for his discovery of an alloy and heat treatment that resulted in "high-speed steel." When made of this steel, cutting tools in lathes would not soften at red heat, they lasted longer and cut metal twice as fast as before, and doubled the productive capacity of machine shops all over the world.

But Taylor's most important (and unpatentable) invention was a new system for organizing *all* factories. What Taylor called the principles of scientific management in 1911 aimed to reshape the very concept of work. Taylor's essential idea was to do for the work unit what Eli Whitney, and his predecessors and successors, had done for the material unit in the American system of manufacturing. Taylor broke down every operation in a factory into the simplest tasks, then timed each to find the most economical way of performing it.

Time was Taylor's ruling dimension, the stopwatch his essential tool. When Taylor went to work for the Bethlehem Steel Company in 1898, he undertook a series of experiments "to find out how quickly the various kinds of work that went into the shop ought to be done." Taylor's prescription for a proper time study was:

> First. Find, say 10 to 15 different men (preferably in as many separate establishments and different parts of the country) who are especially skillful in doing the particular work to be analyzed.
>
> Second. Study the exact series of elementary operations or motions which each of these men uses in doing the work which is being investigated, as well as the implements each man uses.
>
> Third. Study with a stop watch the time required to make each of these elementary movements and then select the quickest way of doing each element of work.
>
> Fourth. Eliminate all false movements, slow movements, and useless movements.
>
> Fifth. After doing away with all unnecessary movements, collect into one series the quickest and best movements, as well as the best implements.
>
> This new method, involving that series of motions which can be made quickest and best, is then substituted in place of the 10 or 15 inferior series which were formerly in use.

Taylor and his staff spent five months gathering this kind of data at Bethlehem on the best way of shoveling.

The "science of shoveling" (the butt of his opponents' jokes), which was the result of Taylor's research, became his classic example of the promise of scientific management. In 1912, before a special committee of the House of Representatives, he suggested that if he actually could make a science of shoveling, there was nothing in the world he could not make a science of. Taylor recounted his experience at the Bethlehem Steel plant. On his arrival there he had found that each laborer brought his own shovel to the yard and used the same shovel to move all sorts of material. "We would see a first-class shoveler go from shoveling rice coal with a load of 3½ pounds to the shovel to handling ore from the Messaba Range, with 38 pounds to the shovel. Now, is 3½ pounds the proper shovel load or is 38 pounds the proper shovel load? They cannot both be right. Under scientific management the answer to this question is not a matter of anyone's opinion; it is a question for accurate, careful, scientific investigation."

After gathering data on the tonnage of each kind of material handled at Bethlehem by each man each day, Taylor had designed his own shovels and supplied them to the men. He then noted the result as he changed the length of the handle. He found, for example, that by cutting off the handle so that the shoveler picked up 34 (instead of 38) pounds in each shovel-load of ore, he could increase the shoveler's daily handling from a total of 25 to 35 tons. Taylor continued to cut off the shovel handle until he found that at 21½ pounds per load, the men were doing their largest day's work. By pursuing this kind of study, he found that the best results in the plant as a whole were obtained when there were fifteen different kinds of shovels, each one for moving a different kind of material—ranging from small flat shovels for handling ore up to immense scoops for handling rice coal, and forks for handling coke. And he had also defined the proper technique for the use of each of these tools:

> There is one right way of forcing the shovel into material of this sort, and many wrong ways. Now, the way to shovel refractory stuff is to press the forearm hard against the upper part of the right leg just below the thigh, like this [indicating], take the end of the shovel in your right hand and when you push the shovel into the pile, instead of using the muscular effort of the arms, which is tiresome, throw the weight of your body on the shovel like this [indicating]; that pushes your shovel in the pile with hardly any exertion and without tiring the arms in the least. Nine out of ten workmen who try to push a shovel in a pile of that sort will use the strength of their arms, which involves more than twice the necessary exertion.

Taylor sent his team about the plant instructing the laborers in the science of shoveling.

After three and a half years, as a result of Taylor's new science, 140 men were doing the work formerly done by 600. The cost of handling material was cut in half, and the shovelers still employed were receiving a 60 percent increase in wages.

WHAT TAYLOR DID for shoveling, he and his disciples were soon attempting to accomplish for all the other operations in hundreds of factories over the nation. Under the name of "scientific management," time-study men were breaking down jobs into their components, timing each component, and designing the best way to do each one. Factory work had been atomized into precisely separated and precisely timed tasks. "The work of every workman is fully planned out by the management at least one day in advance, and each man receives in most cases complete written instructions, describing in detail the task which he is to accomplish, as well as the means to be used in doing the work." Taylor's disciples went still further in atomizing the factory's operation, in describing elementary human movements, and in measuring split seconds. At Bethlehem, H. L. Gantt invented new tools to help the worker do the task precisely as instructed, and developed new techniques for instructing the worker on the job how to do it the one right way.

One of the most energetic of those who joined in Taylor's work was Frank Gilbreth, whose elaborate efforts to organize an efficient household with his numerous children made him the hero of the best-selling book and the popular movie *Cheaper by the Dozen* (1948). Gilbreth, who had worked as a bricklayer, collaborated with his wife in a three-year time-and-motion study of bricklaying. Gilbreth then reported to Taylor his shocking discoveries of waste: "My God . . . that is nothing short of barbarous. Think of it! Here I am a man weighing over 250 pounds, and every time I stoop down to pick up a brick I lower 250 pounds of weight down two feet so as to pick up a brick weighing 4 pounds, and then raise my 250 pounds of weight up again, and all of this to lift up a brick weighing 4 pounds. Think of this waste of effort. It is monstrous." Gilbreth and his wife spent a year and a half trying to cut out that motion. When they had finished they had perfected a method for laying bricks which required only five motions per brick, in place of the previous eighteen motions. Out of this the Gilbreths developed their own new science of "motion economy." It included, among others, the principle that two hands should not be idle at the same instant except during rest periods, that motions of the arms should be in opposite and symmetrical directions. Each elementary motion they called a *therblig* (Gilbreth spelled backwards). After Frank Gilbreth's death, Lillian Gilbreth wrote several books showing how these notions could be applied to running a household.

"Scientific management" became a synonym for good housekeeping in the industrial world. The unlikely popularizer of the phrase and of the idea was "the people's lawyer" and champion of labor, Louis D. Brandeis. In late 1910, when the Interstate Commerce Commission held public hearings on the application by the Eastern railroads for an increase in their freight rates, Brandeis appeared for the shippers to oppose the increase. He had read Taylor's *Shop Management,* which had been published in 1903, and he had met Taylor, whom he found to be "a really great man—great not only in mental capacity, but in character." Brandeis won his case against the rate increase by showing that the railroads were poorly managed and that simply by a more efficient, a more "scientific" management, they could actually profit more than by their requested raise in rates. Brandeis supported his case by a dramatic procession of the managers and owners of companies that were already using Taylor's system. Newspaper accounts of the hearings became advertisements for what Brandeis repeatedly praised as the system of "scientific management." Until this time Taylor himself had been undecided on the best name for his system; he had thought of calling it "functional management" or "task management." It was Brandeis' rhetorical flair and the success of Brandeis' argument that decided Taylor when he published his *Principles* in 1911, to adopt "scientific management" —not merely a name but a slogan!

Taylor's concept of time study and his notion of the elementary task were soon incorporated in the calculations both of manufacturers and of labor unions. By mid-century, General Motors, in its contracts with its workers, had divided the hour into six-minute periods, had fragmented the work to fit the periods, and the worker was being paid by the number of tenths of an hour that he worked. The United States Steel Corporation contract with the C.I.O. on May 8, 1946, defined a "fair day's work" as "that amount of work that can be produced by a qualified employee when working at a normal pace . . . a normal pace is equivalent to a man walking, without load, on smooth, level ground at a rate of three miles per hour." In their wage-rationalization program the next year, they described 1,150 jobs within 152 classifications. The Aluminum Company of America spent three and a half years and a half-million dollars developing a formula to rationalize and classify 56,000 jobs.

IN THE NINETEENTH CENTURY, European visitors had noted the initiative and intelligence and freedom from routine which they said helped explain the higher American standard of living. But now Taylor warned American workers against the old-fashioned virtue of "initiative." The workman who was required to do his job in the one "right" way, he said, was no more being inhibited than was the surgeon who was instructed in the one best way to perform an appendectomy. Most of what passed for "initiative," Taylor insisted, was really nothing but waste: the futile rule-of-thumb efforts of the ignorant to reinvent old ways. If the worker was paid by the tenth of an hour for performing his task precisely as prescribed, then he would have no need and little opportunity for initiative. And the fractioning of work by the new calculus of scientific management would make the meaning and the value of the factory-worker's exertions harder than ever for the worker himself to understand.

Those rule-of-thumb ways of doing things which were anathema to Taylor had at least given a man on the job the feeling that he was doing what he should. To abolish the rule of thumb in factory work would excise a part of every worker's emotional investment and personal satisfaction. Could a worker now fail to feel that he was doing somebody else's job, or a job dictated by the machine? Rule of thumb was personal rule. Scientific management, which made the worker into a labor unit and judged his effectiveness by his ability to keep the technology flowing, had made the worker himself into an interchangeable part.

Scientific management had its effect, too, not only on *how* anything was produced but also on *what*. Items to be manufactured were designed and selected for production according to how quickly and economically they could be produced. In place of the naïve consumer, the "scientific" system now made its own demands. Was this a price for the limitless productivity which the American system of manufacturing promised? Was this the end of America's brilliant new techniques for "conserving" human resources?

The full pathos and the subtle contradictions in the new American effort to make the most of men could not long remain hidden. It was revealed in a famous experiment by Elton Mayo at the Hawthorne Works of the Western Electric Company in Chicago in the 1930's. For thirteen weeks six girls employed in assembling telephones were studied. Every possible variable was noted and calculated: the heat and the light in the workroom, the amount of sleep they had the night before, or two nights before. For the purposes of the study, one variable at a time was changed and the results noted, but no individual variable proved to be the controlling factor. Regardless of what the experimenters changed in the work situation, the productivity of these six girls rose and continued to rise. Mayo's shrewd conclusion was that the real explanation was the experiment itself—the show of concern for the particular workers, together with the esprit it gave them as a working team. A moral of Mayo's study, of course, was that no physical improvement in scientific management could overwhelm the feelings that living men and women had about their work and their relation to it.

Before long this discovery itself became the basis of another new doctrine in the quest for greater productivity. If workers produced more when they felt that the employer was interested in them as individuals, then the most efficient means must be found for giving workers the impression that the employer was interested. And here was another step in what the sociologist Daniel Bell calls the movement "from authority to manipulation as a means of exercising dominion." Scientific management brought in its wake as a catalyst, or perhaps even as an antidote, a "science of human relations," with the novel profession of personnel management. But this science, too, while ostensibly designed to take fuller account of man's humanity, was destined (in Elton Mayo's phrase) to become "a new method of human control."

42
Making Experience Repeatable

"HERE THEY ARE," Decca Records advertised in December 1934, "your favorite stars of radio, screen, and stage—in their greatest performances of instrument and voice! . . . Hear them *when* you want—as *often* as you want—right in your own home." Before the mid-twentieth century, Americans had perfected many new techniques for repeating sights and sounds at their own convenience. Uniqueness had once been the hallmark of experience. Each moment of life was supposed to be unrepeatable; the visible body and gestures, and the voice of a man, lasted during the brief span of his life and then dissolved with his death. Images of the past required the artistry of painter or sculptor; bygone actions could be recaptured only by the mimicry of the actor. The most vivid accounts of the dead were the work of men of letters.

Now without anyone having so intended it, a host of inventions and innovations, large and small, were beginning to add up to a whole new grasp on past experience. The terminus of human life was, of course, still there, but the content of the years of life was transformed. And the range of sights and sounds that any man could enjoy in a single lifetime was vastly widened.

THE DECISIVE INNOVATION was photography. The story of the rise and perfection and simplification of photography has often been told, but photography as a transformer of experience has not been given its due. Such repeatable experience as was possible in Old World cultures had been mainly through the aristocratic arts of literature, painting, sculpture, and music, or through the popular but limited arts of minstrelsy, folklore, folk art, and folk music. Only language itself, or the ritual and liturgy of church and state, had tied people to the past by repetitions of word and gesture.

Photography took the first giant step toward democratizing the repeatable experience. This it did by transcending language and literature so that anybody, without even needing to be literate, could preserve at will the moments of experience for future repetition. Again the basic theoretical discoveries that would make this possible came from the Old World, and once again Americans were ingenious and resourceful in finding ways to apply these discoveries, in organizing, democratizing, and diffusing their uses.

For a full half-century after the Frenchman L. J. M. Daguerre made public his daguerrotype process in 1839, and even after the Englishman W. H. Fox Talbot had devised a way to make many positives from a single negative, photography remained an esoteric technique. On seeing Daguerre's photographs, the French artist Paul Delaroche exclaimed, "From today painting is dead!" Photography was already beginning to take over and transform some of the traditional roles of the artist, but photography in America would reach out far beyond the former domain of the artist.

By the time of the Civil War, many Americans had begun to feel the impact of photography. Even before the war, Mathew Brady's photographic portrait studios in New York and Washington were doing a thriving business. Then, during the Civil War, and soon thereafter, photographs by Brady and Alexander Gardner and others were exhibited in galleries, sold in books, and reproduced in newspapers. They brought to Americans a more vivid and more realistic view of that war than of any that had happened before. While action photography was not yet possible, photographs with startling and novel authenticity did portray the war's architectural and human debris.

But photography was still cumbersome and complicated. Traveling across the battlefields, Brady needed a special wagon to carry his equipment. Until about 1880, the photographer's equipment included (in addition to the camera, several lenses, and a tripod) bottles of different solutions for coating, sensitizing, developing, and fixing his negatives, besides glass plates, dishes, measures, funnels, a pail to carry rinsing water, and sometimes even a supply of water, and (so that he could perform the essential chemical operations on the spot) a portable dark-tent. The equipment even for a single day commonly weighed more than a hundred pounds, which the photographer who did not have a photographic wagon had to push around in a special wheelbarrow, or "photographic perambulator."

"Wet plates" made all this necessary. As long as the complicated wet-plate collodion process was the best and fastest way of making photographs, the photographer had to make his own photographic plates on the spot, and had to develop them instantly after they were exposed. The key to this system was a solution of collodion (guncotton dissolved in ether) containing potassium iodide, which, just before the picture taking, was poured onto a glass plate that was tilted back and forth until the solution formed an even, sticky coat. The sticky glass plate was then made sensitive to light by immersion in a silver nitrate solution. The picture had to be taken while the plate was still wet, because as the collodion dried its light-sensitivity was progressively lost; for this reason, too, the picture actually had to be developed before the glass plate had dried. This meant, of course, that the photographer had to carry his whole laboratory with him. And also that you could not be a photographer unless you were something of a photographic chemist adept at preparing as well as developing your photographic plates. Since the papers for making prints were not very sensitive, photographs were seldom enlarged, and therefore serious photographers had to use large plates (12 by 16 inches was not unusual), which were heavy to carry and required a bulky camera. Despite ingenious devices, no way was found for the photographer to manage without his dark-tent.

Photography could not become universal until there was some simpler method of taking a picture. By about 1880, English chemists had found a way to coat a glass plate with light-sensitive chemicals that would not lose their sensitivity when dry. Soon commercially produced glass plates were on the market. These "dry plates" could be used in a camera without any special chemical preparation on the spot by the photographer. But the glass plates still required were heavy, fragile, and hard to ship.

CENTURIES OF CHEMICAL PROGRESS in the Old World had been required to make photography possible at all, but the transformation of photography into a popular, universal medium had to await one extremely practical, and apparently trivial, improvement. The missing link in the chain of progress toward democratizing photography was the invention of a new artificial substance, to be called "celluloid."

John Wesley Hyatt, an unsung American hero, was the son of a blacksmith in rural New York. In 1853, at the age of sixteen, he went west to Illinois, where he started life as a printer, and at twenty-four he had begun his inventing career with a new way of making solid emery wheels to sharpen kitchen knives. Then he heard of a $10,000 prize offered by a New York manufacturer for some new material which would be a satisfactory substitute for ivory in the making of billiard balls. Hyatt spent his nights and Sundays trying to solve the problem, and he finally succeeded by combining paper flock, shellac, and collodion, and won the prize. When he noticed that a removable "artificial skin" was left when the collodion dried, he began to look for still other new materials. Since he was not a chemist, he did not realize that he might easily have blown himself up by heating gun-cotton (nitrocellulose) under pressure, and he had not been discouraged by the earlier failures of English plastics chemists, because he did not even know of them. Another incentive for his experiments was the interest of dentists (plagued by the high price charged by the "rubber monopoly") in finding a cheaper substitute for rubber in molding dentures.

In 1873 Hyatt invented and registered the name "celluloid." What he had invented was actually not a new combination of chemicals but a new way of molding the plastic and making it stay hard. For some years Hyatt used celluloid only for making solid objects.

Hyatt went on to a versatile career of invention. By 1882 he and his brother had perfected a new system of water filtration. The previous systems had brought the water to a tank where coagulants were added to remove the impurities, which after twelve hours would settle to the bottom. Hyatt's ingenious scheme added the coagulants to the water while it was on the way to the filter, and thus removed the need for the large tanks and the long settling time. He invented a new kind of sugar-cane mill, which was cheaper to run and which produced a cane dry enough to serve as fuel. Besides an improved sewing machine which could make fifty lock stitches at once, a new way of making school slates, and a method of solidifying wood for bowling balls and golf-club heads, he devised a roller bearing which General Motors eventually made the basis for many of its improvements in the automobile.

The opportunity for Hyatt's celluloid to help transform the American consciousness came from the collaborating talents of another upstate New Yorker who combined a bent for invention with a talent for organization and for marketing. George Eastman, the son of a penmanship teacher who started the first commercial college in Rochester, began clerking in a bank and became so interested in photography that in 1877, when he was making only $1,500 a year, he spent $94 on a photographic outfit. Seeing that the new "dry plates" would make possible a whole new market for photographic equipment, within two years Eastman had invented and patented a new machine for coating the glass plates. He saw, too, that the perfection of dry-plate photography would be more than merely a convenience for professional photographers, because now, for the first time, the taking of a picture could be separated from the making and the developing of the plate. But he also saw that a popular market for photography would have to await a substitute for the heavy, breakable, hard-to-ship glass plates. Until the 1880's, of course (because photographs were commonly made on emulsion-coated glass), photography was not especially associated with the word "film." What Eastman needed was some flexible, light, and unbreakable substance that could be coated with the photographic emulsion. In 1884 Eastman patented a way of coating strips of paper so that they would work in a camera, and from this starting point he initiated the popular revolution in photography.

To dramatize the novelty of his kind of camera, he decided to make up a word that would be short, distinctive, and (looking toward a world market) pronounceable in any language. It is said that he started with "K," the first letter of his mother's maiden name, and finally came up with "Kodak." Eastman registered the trademark "Kodak" in 1888 and put his new camera on the market. A marvel of compactness and simplicity, his little black box was about the size of the later familiar "Brownie" box camera. "The Kodak," Eastman's first advertisement read, "is the smallest, lightest and simplest of all Detective Cameras—for the ten operations necessary with most Cameras to make one exposure, we have only *3 simple* movements. No focusing. No finder required. Size 3½ by 3¾ by 6½ in. Makes 100 Exposures. Weight 35 oz."

The camera had no focusing apparatus and only a single speed on the shutter. Of course, since the camera also had no finder, the photographer might not be able to include precisely what he wanted in the picture, but on the other hand, he did not have to worry about adjusting or focusing his apparatus. Eastman had made everybody into a photographer. And his Kodak flourished on the slogan "You press the button—we do the rest."

Eastman shrewdly had made an additional selling point of the smallness of his Kodak by calling it a "detective camera." Other manufacturers had already put on the market an assortment of smaller cameras camouflaged in the shape of opera glasses, paper parcels, luggage, books, and watches; some were made to be hidden in hats or behind neckties. These were called "detective" cameras because, in contrast to the old large boxes, they were supposed to be able to take a picture surreptitiously, as a detective would. There was something intriguing about this idea, but actually these other products were little more than toys.

Eastman's was a "detective camera," too. But unlike the others, his was inexpensive for its day, and it really worked! What he offered Americans was a photographic system as remarkable in its own way as the organizing achievements of nineteenth-century fur traders or of twentieth-century assembly-line builders. The $25 which Eastman charged for one of his simple black boxes included the first roll of film, together with the processing of all its one hundred pictures. When the owner had used up the roll, he sent the whole camera to the factory. Then the factory sent back his camera (loaded with a new roll of film, for $10) and the mounted prints of all his successful pictures. George Eastman's system, like Eli Whitney's interchangeable system, was a substitute for skill. To any American with $25 (however ignorant of chemistry or photography) Eastman now offered the power to make pictures.

The weak link in Eastman's system was the film itself. At the Kodak factory, the emulsion bearing the image had to be stripped from the paper, then pressed into a sheet of clear gelatin, and dried. To avoid this delicate operation there was need for a better film material, preferably one that was both flexible and transparent. Celluloid, which had been on the market for fifteen years, would prove to be the solution to the problem. While Eastman was one of the first to discover this fact, others too grasped the possibility and entered the race for a practical film. Until this time Hyatt's celluloid had been used only for solid objects. Then, in 1888 a Philadelphia photographic-plate manufacturer asked Hyatt to produce sheets of clear celluloid with a uniform thickness of 1/100 inch, which he then coated with the photographic emulsion. This celluloid was still too thick and inflexible for roll film.

The first application for a patent on transparent roll film made of celluloid came from the Reverend Hannibal W. Goodwin, a sixty-five-year-old Episcopal minister of Newark, New Jersey, who had been trying to find some material that was better than glass for the photographic illustrations of Scriptural stories he was making for Sunday Schools. After ten years' labor, on May 2, 1887, he applied for a patent for a "Photographic Pellicule." Meanwhile Eastman had set one of his researchers to work, and two years later Eastman received his own patent for the "manufacture of flexible photographic films." There followed the familiar lengthy litigation over patent rights. And it was fifteen years (just before Goodwin's death) before Goodwin actually received his patent. During this time the energetic Eastman had been manufacturing celluloid film on a vast scale. He was now producing nearly 90 percent of all roll film, and he had monopolized the world market.

With his new celluloid roll film, easily loaded and easily developed (no need any more for the delicate stripping operation), Eastman opened up the world of amateur photography. The novel features of the Kodak, as an English historian observed, "enabled the camera, like the bicycle, to enrich the leisure hours of the many." Soon millions of Americans were snapping pictures, and camera clubs sprang up all over the world. While the earlier photography had flourished on the making of studio portraits and the occasional outdoor photographing of significant scenes by professionals, the new popular photography found new subjects. What had once been advertised as the "Royal Road to Drawing" now became the democratic highway to art. Everyman could be his own artist. Years before, when Oliver Wendell Holmes saw Brady's realistic "stereographs" of Civil War battlefields, he had called the camera "the mirror with a memory." Now anyone could provide himself with such a mirror, so that his everyday experience could be captured for visual repetition at any time in the future. Now, instead of merely photographing persons or scenes that were especially memorable or historic, Americans would photograph at random and then remember the scenes *because* they had been photographed. Photography became a device for making experience worth remembering.

ON OCTOBER 8, 1888, A statement was filed with the Patent Office by Thomas A. Edison:

> I am experimenting upon an instrument which does for the eye what the phonograph does for the ear, which is the recording and reproduction of things in motion, and in such a form as to be both cheap, practical and convenient. This apparatus I call a Kinetoscope, "moving view." . . . The invention consists in photographing continuously a series of pictures occurring at intervals . . . and photographing these series of pictures in a continuous spiral on a cylinder or plate in the same manner as sound is recorded on a phonograph.

Soon after beginning work on his Kinetoscope, Edison made certain basic discoveries. He found, for example, that while his recording phonograph had to run continuously to provide a record of continuous sound, a camera record of pictures of motion would have to run intermittently so that the phenomenon of persistence of vision would give the viewer the illusion of motion. It had to be possible, therefore, to take pictures at rapid intervals, and then show them successively without a blur. But at first Edison had been dominated by the analogy with his rudimentary phonograph, which then worked by recording sound on a cylinder. Tiny pictures arranged in series on a cylinder were viewed directly through a magnifying lens.

Edison very early sensed the importance of celluloid. The perfection of a feasible camera and projector that would show moving pictures of considerable duration depended on finding a suitably flexible substance for the film. It is hard to imagine how Edison could have made his movie camera without celluloid, or something like it. When he first saw the emulsion-coated sheets of celluloid, which were still too rigid to be handled in rolls, he wrapped some sheets around the big cylinder of his Kinetoscope machine. But with celluloid of suitable characteristics he hoped to be able to abandon his cylinder design and (as had been impossible with glass plates) somehow run continuous strips of film directly through his machine.

Edison was no longer working on a "phonograph arrangement" (as Eastman had called Edison's earlier efforts, because they were so closely modeled on the phonograph), but on an entirely new type of camera for taking and projecting moving pictures. When he heard of Eastman's improved roll film, he urged Eastman to help him make a motion-picture camera by producing the flexible film in long strips. And when Edison's assistant, in late 1889, brought him the first fifty-foot strip, Edison, with a "seraphic smile," shouted, "That's it—we've got it—now work like hell!"

With the new strip film Edison made his first working Kinetoscope, which was the grandfather of all later motion-picture machines. Positive prints on strip film were rolled from one spool to another inside a cabinet while the spectator looked directly at the illuminated film through a magnifying lens in a fixed eyepiece in a hole in the cabinet. This was a peep show for only one person at a time. The screen was yet to come, but the basic ideas were there. When Edison applied for a patent on an "Apparatus for Exhibiting Photographs of Moving Objects" in August 1891, he still made no mention of a projecting apparatus or a white screen. In any case, the photographs he had been using were so crude that they would not bear magnifying and projecting. Edison still assumed that the whole entertainment future of moving pictures would be like that of the phonograph, which was then used by individuals who inserted a coin in a machine to hear their favorite tune. Edison, "The Man of a Thousand Ideas," was still so casual about this peep-show toy that when his lawyers advised him to take out European patents at a cost of $150, he refused because, he said, "It isn't worth it."

While Edison sometimes misjudged the commercial promise of his ideas, he did have the inventor's genius for recognizing the essence of a problem and so seeing the simple solution. He showed this in his approach to moving pictures by intuitively avoiding the blind alleys which had already brought modest fame to others. English and French inventors, whose work Edison knew, had tried to record motion by placing numerous cameras along the line of movement, each photographing a successive scene. Eadweard Muybridge, an English-born photographer working in California, had created a world-wide sensation in 1878 with his series of pictures published as "The Horse in Motion." He had first taken these in order to satisfy a whim of former Governor Leland Stanford of California, who wanted to advertise his prize trotter, Occident, and he incidentally answered an old question by proving that a galloping horse actually had all his feet off the ground at certain moments. Muybridge's work had stimulated a French professor of physiology who was interested in animal locomotion to invent a camera which would take a series of exposures on a single glass plate and so photograph the motion from a single point of view. Edison made his crucial simplifying decision when he determined not to follow the path of Muybridge. Instead of making a series of motion photographs from different points of view, he decided, following the French professor's hint, to devise a machine that would photograph motion from a single point of view.

Edison's other elementary insight (which now seems so obvious as hardly to be an insight at all) was to imagine a simple unified system; that is, an arrangement which would somehow make use of the very same film on which the moving pictures were recorded as the moving pictures to be viewed. Could a series of photographs that had been taken on a single film somehow provide the pictures to be viewed in motion? For a feasible motion-picture system this idea was as crucial as Eastman's idea of separating picture taking from picture developing had been in popularizing still photography. In Edison's scheme, then, what a single camera saw and recorded was precisely what the spectator would see.

Edison boldly adopted celluloid film in a standard width for both cameras and projectors. Then he added another marvelously simple idea, never before used on photographic film: he perforated the edge of the film. The two tiny rectangular perforations which he punched on each side of each picture solved many problems at once. By using two toothed wheels, one on each side of the film to be exposed or to be projected, Edison could now produce the controlled intermittent motion of the film which his predecessors had been unable to provide and which was required to give the viewer the illusion of motion. The Edison-designed film became the standard. While railroad gauges varied throughout the world, while some nations used Fahrenheit and others Centigrade, while mankind could not all agree on a system of measuring land or of weighing potatoes, Edison's 35-millime-

ter film would rule the world. In this there was a poetic appropriateness, for movies were the American invention which, more than any
other before, focused the vision of the world. And motion pictures
became the great democratic art, which, naturally enough, was the
characteristically American art.

THE TECHNOLOGY OF repeatable experience was self-propa-
gating. Each step taken toward capturing, recording, and making
replayable another aspect of experience opened the way and created
a demand for still another improvement and still newer techniques.
Edison's own interest in motion pictures had been awakened by his
determination to use photography, along with the phonograph, to
make talking pictures. And the phonograph, even more than the
camera, would be a product of American energy and ingenuity.
Perhaps this was because sound was a simpler phenomenon than
sight. The problem of recording sound was essentially mechanical. It
required very little new theory, and very little chemistry.

There are few modern inventions of comparable importance
which in their first making owed as much to a single man as did the
phonograph. Others abroad were conceiving the possibility of a machine to record and replay sounds, but it was Edison who made the
first practical talking machine. He had been led toward the phonograph by his work on an instrument to record and repeat telegraph
dots and dashes. Then, in 1877, after he had invented a transmitter
for Alexander Graham Bell's telephone, Edison became worried that
the high cost of telephones might limit their use. He thought that
many more people would benefit from the telephone if there could
be what he called a "telephone repeater." Edison's notion was that
if somehow a person could record his spoken message, then the
record could be taken to a central station where it could be replayed
and transmitted to the addressee over a telephone. In this way even
a person who could not afford a telephone might still send a message
in his own voice. When Edison had his inspiration for the shape of
the machine, he made a model. It was a rotating, grooved metal
cylinder around which a piece of tin foil was wrapped to record the
sounds. Into the machine Edison shouted the verses of "Mary Had
a Little Lamb"; then the machine played back Edison's voice to
Edison and his assistants. "I was never so taken aback in all my life,"
he recalled. "Everybody was astonished. I was always afraid of things
that worked the first time." Edison applied for his patent in December 1877, and received it within two months—an unusually brief
time, because the patent officials could find in their files nothing
remotely resembling this device.

The news of this latest example of Edison's wizardry created a sensation. Around the country in public halls the machine was demonstrated as a novelty. A single "exhibition" phonograph brought in more than $1,800 in one week in Boston, where people gladly paid admission to hear a machine that could talk in any language, that could bark like a dog, crow like a cock, and cough "so believably that physicians in the audience could instinctively begin to write prescriptions." In the *North American Review* for June 1878, Edison forecast ten uses for his phonograph:

1. Letter writing, and all kinds of dictation without the aid of a stenographer.
2. Phonographic books, which will speak to blind people without effort on their part.
3. The teaching of elocution.
4. Music.—The phonograph will undoubtedly be liberally devoted to music.
5. The family record; preserving the sayings, the voices, and the last words of the dying members of the family, as of great men.
6. Music boxes, toys, etc.—A doll which may speak, sing, cry or laugh may be promised our children for the Christmas holidays ensuing.
7. Clocks, that should announce in speech the hour of the day, call you to lunch, send your lover home at ten, etc.
8. The preservation of language by reproduction of our Washingtons, our Lincolns, our Gladstones.
9. Educational purposes; such as preserving the instructions of a teacher so that the pupil can refer to them at any moment; or learn spelling lessons.
10. The perfection or advancement of the telephone's art by the phonograph, making that instrument an auxiliary in the transmission of permanent records.

For more than fifteen years Edison insisted that his Number 1 use—for dictating letters—was the only one likely to find a wide market. With scant musical knowledge or sensitivity himself (Edison was partially deaf), at first he found it hard to believe it would be profitable to mass-produce the recordings of musical performances. Nevertheless, by 1894 Edison had decided to try to promote the phonograph for entertainment, and he had begun designing an inexpensive machine to sell to everybody. In 1897 he made a machine that sold for $20. But for some time, the most popular use of the phonograph was in public places for machines that played a record for a nickel.

Edison's phonograph cylinders were inconvenient and expensive to reproduce. They were to the phonograph what the glass plate was to the camera. The popularizing of the phonograph and a mass market for recordings would await the invention of a new design and new materials.

This problem was not solved by Edison himself, but by Emile Berliner, the music-loving son of a Talmudic scholar in Hanover, Germany, who emigrated to the United States at the age of eighteen. Although he had only a grade-school education, he found work in a scientific laboratory where he began studying acoustics and electricity. Before Berliner was twenty-six he had invented a telephone transmitter which was superior to the one that Alexander Graham Bell had exhibited at the Philadelphia Centennial Exhibition in 1876, based on a new principle that later made possible the microphone. In 1878 Berliner sold his telephone invention to the Bell Company for a large sum; then, turning his attention to the phonograph, he developed a new way of recording.

Edison's original phonograph operated on the "hill-and-dale" method. The sound caused the recording needle to vibrate up and down and made vertical grooves of varying depths; these were the movements which, when replayed, reproduced the sound for the listener. As the wax phonograph cylinder was rotated, the needle followed this groove. In order to keep the needle and sound box moving along the length of the cylinder to follow the groove of Edison's rotating wax cylinder, a special screw mechanism was required.

Berliner simplified both the recording and the reproducing machines, and incidentally made easier the mass production of records. Instead of a cylinder, Berliner used a flat disk. And instead of the up-and-down movement of the needle in Edison's "hill-and-dale" system, Berliner recorded his sound with a needle's sideways zigzag. This scheme, which Berliner had working successfully by 1888, proved to have many advantages. The need for a special screw mechanism was removed, since the spiral groove on the revolving platter automatically kept the needle moving along at the proper speed. Disks, compared with cylinders, were simpler and easier to reproduce, and more convenient to store.

None of these advances could have democratized the phonograph without some inexpensive way of duplicating the disks. And Berliner soon supplied this, too. Instead of making the master record on an all-wax plate, he used a disk of zinc covered with wax. After the music was recorded on this wax surface, acid was applied to etch the characteristic zigzags into the zinc. And this provided the "master" from which duplicates could be made. A metal casting (or negative matrix) was made of the original record, and then stamped into a suitable material, leaving the impression of the original. In this way thousands of duplicates could be made from a single original recording. It was still necessary to find a suitable material for the duplicates, but after six years of experiment, Berliner succeeded in that too. He used hard rubber, and then made a new durable material from shellac. At first

these were called "plates," but by 1896 they were known by the new
name of "record." On Berliner's inventions, and on his simplification
of the phonograph and its records, the vast American record industry
would be founded. This was not the end of Berliner's ingenuity or
imagination. In 1919 when he was nearly seventy, this remarkable
man helped design a helicopter that actually flew.

Berliner's "Gramophone" (the trademark for his invention) awakened the imagination of the twenty-nine-year-old owner of a small
machine shop in Camden, New Jersey, to whom Berliner had taken
his primitive machine to improve its motor. "It sounded like a partially educated parrot with a sore throat and a cold in the head,"
Eldridge Johnson recalled, "but the little wheezy instrument caught
my attention and held it fast and hard." It was Johnson's craftsmanship and production know-how which, by 1897, had transformed the
expensive "partially educated parrot" into the mass-produced "Improved Gramophone." Before long "His Master's Voice" made the
irrelevant image of a black-and-white fox terrier listening to Johnson's machine one of the leading images in American iconography.
Johnson founded the Victor Talking Machine Company, which
helped create, and then for a while dominated, this new market. An
unpredicted advantage of the disk appeared in 1904, when an enterprising New Yorker started a German company with the novel idea
of stamping a record with grooves on *both* sides.

"THE MENACE OF MECHANICAL MUSIC," in *Appleton's Magazine* for September 1906, was a blast against the newly repeatable
experience by one of the nation's most popular composers. John
Philip Sousa, son of a Portuguese immigrant, had composed the International Fantasy for Offenbach's orchestra at the Philadelphia
Centennial Exhibition in 1876, and as conductor of the United States
Marine Band from 1880 to 1892 was to the march (some said) what
Johann Strauss was to the waltz. Financed by a musical impresario,
he formed Sousa's Band, performed at the Chicago Columbian Exposition of 1893, and became rich and famous by regular tours around
the United States. Sales of the sheet music for his most famous composition, "Stars and Stripes Forever" (composed in 1897), brought
him about $300,000. "I foresee a marked deterioration in American
music and musical taste," Sousa warned, "an interruption in the
musical development of the country, and a host of other injuries to
music in its artistic manifestations, by virtue—or rather by vice—of
the multiplication of the various music-reproducing machines."

Exercising his considerable imagination, Sousa conjured up the
future horrors of "musical automatics." Going on from the menace

of the player piano, he heard "the exclamation of the little boy who rushed into his mother's room with the appeal: 'O mamma, come into the drawing-room; there is a man in there playing the piano with his hands!' "

> There was a time when the pine woods of the north were sacred to summer simplicity. . . . But even now the invasion of the north has begun, and the ingenious purveyor of canned music is urging the sportsman, on his way to the silent places with gun and rod, tent and canoe, to take with him some disks, cranks, and cogs to sing to him as he sits by the firelight, a thought as unhappy and incongruous as canned salmon by a trout brook.
>
> In the prospective scheme of mechanical music, we shall see man and maiden in a light canoe under the summer moon upon an Adirondack lake with a gramophone caroling love songs from amidships. The Spanish cavalier must abandon his guitar and serenade his beloved with a phonograph under his arm. . . . Never again will the soldier hear the defiant call of the bugle to battle, and the historical lines must be changed to:
> "Gentlemen of the French guards, turn on your phonographs first."
> And the future d'Auteroches will reply:
> "Sir, we will never turn on our phonographs first; please to turn yours first."

Sousa was outraged by the prospect that the authentic, spontaneous voice of man's soul should be hampered by "a machine that tells the story day by day, without variation, without soul, barren of the joy, the passion, the ardor that is the inheritance of man alone." And he asked, "When a mother can turn on the phonograph with the same ease that she applies to the electric light, will she croon her baby to slumber with sweet lullabys, or will the infant be put to sleep by machinery? Children are naturally imitative, and if, in their infancy, they hear only phonographs, will they not sing, if they sing at all, in imitation and finally become simply human phonographs— without soul or expression?" Sousa finally observed that, in 1906, the copyright laws appeared to give no protection to the composer when his work was sold on records. And if these new machines should deprive composers of their reward, would musicians still go on composing?

The 1909 copyright law provided protection for composers, and pressure by the American Society of Composers, Authors, and Publishers (founded in 1914) succeeded in procuring royalties. Before the third decade of the twentieth century, the nation was flooded with "musical automatics." By 1914 more than 500,000 phonographs were being produced each year, and five years later the figure reached 2¼ million. In 1921 the annual production of records exceeded 100 million; in the post–World War II year of 1947, over 400 million records were sold. Improvements in the technique of recording (with an electrical in place of a mechanical or "acoustic" method, by 1925) and reproducing, and improvements in the fidelity of the sound, increased the demand and before long produced an exacting and sophisticated new audience for *recorded* sound.

The new techniques which the British Coastal Command had required in World War II for the training records they made to illustrate the difference between the sounds of German and of British submarines eventually produced "full frequency range reproduction" (ffrr), and set a new standard of fidelity for reproduced music. Then in 1948 came the long-playing microgroove disk, which slowed down the speed from 78 to 33⅓ revolutions per minute and increased the playing time from four to twenty-three minutes.

Just as the Kodak made every man his own artist, now with the phonograph every man became his own musician. And so the vaudeville joke: "Do you play on the piano?" "No, but I do play on the phonograph." The phonograph was used, of course, to spread the pleasures of the classical-music repertoire. But it gave a new incentive to the makers of popular music. Formerly the famed music makers had been those who composed or performed ceremonial or symphonic or operatic or chamber-music works under the patronage of wealthy aristocrats. Now the great American public could become the patron. Music was being democratized, not only because the nation's millions could now enjoy music once reserved for a few, but also because the millions now commanded the most profitable musical market, had a new power to shape musical taste, a way of making it worth a composer's or performer's while to give the millions what *they* wanted.

Without the phonograph, it is difficult to imagine how American popular music, before the era of radio, could have sent its sounds around the world. In May 1917 Victor turned out their first "jass" record—"the latest thing in the development of music"—a blues and a one-step played by the Original Dixieland Jazz Band. The fat profits of the record companies in the early 1920's, as we have seen, were explained mainly by the annual sales of millions of jazz records. Never before had a form of music so permeated a vast nation, or become so universal an influence in the daily life of a whole society. "Does Jazz Put the Sin in Syncopation?" was being asked by an August 1921 article in the *Ladies' Home Journal.* And the National Music Chairman of the General Federation of Women's Clubs denounced jazz—

> that expression of protest against law and order, that bolshevik element of license striving for expression in music. . . . Dancing to Mozart minu-

ets, Strauss waltzes and Sousa two-steps certainly never led to the corset check-room, which holds sway in hotels, clubs, and dance halls. Nor would the girl who wore corsets in those days have been dubbed "old ironsides" and left a disconsolate wallflower in a corner of the ballroom. . . . Such music has become an influence for evil.

The phonograph now made popular fashions in music possible on a new scale. By the mid-1950's the test of a musical celebrity was how many "golden records" of at least one-million circulation he had turned out. The phonograph was making a commonplace of musical classics. While the fortunes of the "top ten" popular records themselves became news as the ratings changed every week, it was now finally possible in everybody's living room to revive the best music of earlier centuries. "This mechanical civilization of ours," Jacques Barzun observed in 1954, "has performed a miracle . . . it has, by mechanical means, brought back to life the whole repertory of Western music. . . . Formerly, a fashion would bury the whole musical past except a few dozen works arbitrarily selected. . . . the whole literature of one of the arts has sprung into being—it is like the Renaissance rediscovering the ancient classics and holding them fast by means of the printing press."

The paradoxes of repeatable experience were nowhere more dramatic. A record that was in the top ten one week might become unsalable a few weeks later. Yet in 1954 Americans could find in their record stores five unabridged versions of Bach's *St. Matthew Passion,* ten of Mozart's *D Minor Piano Concerto,* twenty-one versions of Tchaikovsky's *Romeo and Juliet* or of Beethoven's *Eroica.* The machines that brought a vast new stock of repeatable experience into everyone's living room or automobile had the power both to enrich musical experience and to trivialize it.

Which force was running stronger? In scores of new ways, the record makers enlivened the common experience with new categories of musical experience and actually brought novel forms of music into being. In 1956 the Broadway production of *My Fair Lady* was entirely financed by the Columbia Broadcasting System with a view to the exclusive rights to sell the records. Their investment proved fully justified by the unprecedented sales of five million of the original-cast albums. After that it was common for Broadway musicals to be financed by record companies which hoped to recoup their investment by selling the repeated experience on records.

When music became only another, universally accessible form of repeatable experience, it lost much of its distinctiveness as an experience. Music then was only another element in the atmosphere and the environment, like the temperature, the humidity, or the illumination. By 1960 the new techniques were being used to make music of any and every kind ubiquitous. "We don't sell music," a spokesman for Muzak, the most prosperous seller of piped-in sound, declared, "we sell programing. We believe that the best results are attained when you consider the factors of time, environment and activity." Before the 1950's were out, Muzak sound conditioning could be heard in (among other places) the Yankee Stadium, Fenway Park, Slenderella Reducing Salons, cemeteries in Los Angeles and San Angelo, Texas, a Kansas City puppet factory, a Chicago sausage plant, pet hospitals, the vaults of the Federal Reserve banks, an olive-stuffing plant in Cincinnati, a uranium company in Denver, and under water in the swimming pool at Eaton's Motel in Hamilton, Ohio. When "music" was everywhere, was it music any more? Were listeners really listening? Did Americans really know whether or not they were listening?

THE CAPACITY OF the camera and the phonograph to make experience repeatable was still limited by the time required to develop the film or to manufacture the record that could be replayed. The coming of "instant replay"—techniques for recording experience in a form that was immediately replayable—was another decisive step in dissolving the uniqueness of an experience.

The crucial new idea was magnetic recording. If sound could be transformed into magnetic impulses and a wire could be magnetized a little piece at a time, then the wire would record the sound, which could immediately be played back simply by transforming the magnetic impulses into sound again. A device to accomplish this was the invention of Valdemar Poulsen, a young Danish engineer who patented it first in Denmark in 1898, then in the United States two years later. The whole idea seemed to contradict the current experience with magnets. For example, it was common knowledge that when a bar magnet was broken into little magnets, all the little magnets would be equally magnetized, each with its two poles; and if they were stuck back together again, the result would be only one magnet. Could it be possible, then, to magnetize not a whole bar, but just one spot on a wire? Perhaps this could be done by drawing the wire rapidly past the electromagnet so that different spots would be magnetized to a different degree. If this could somehow be managed there would be obvious advantages over all the other known kinds of recording: a magnetic recording could be used countless times without a loss in acoustical quality, and the recording material could be used again and again simply by demagnetizing. Poulsen called his device the "telegraphone," and with it won the Grand Prix at the Paris Exposition of 1900, where it was as sensational as the telephone had been in Philadelphia in 1876.

When the American Telegraphone Company proved a financial failure, the idea of magnetic recording seemed to be dead, and it was not resurrected for two decades. In Poulsen's original design the recording wire had to travel so fast that enormous quantities of wire were required, and rewinding it took so long that it caused a delay in playback; and also the playback level was too low for practical use. But the United States Naval Research Laboratory continued its researches with the result that tape began to replace wire in the 1930's. During World War II, magnetic recording was revived and exploited for its obvious advantages under extremes of heat, cold, and vibration when disk recording was not feasible. Wire-recording devices were soon compacted into pocket size. By the end of the war, magnetic recording had been proven superior to disk recording for many purposes. A steel tape, it was found, could be replayed a hundred thousand times without measurable deterioration; improvements in amplification and in recording materials such as homogeneous paper and plastic tape with magnetic coating promised a new versatility.

The magnetic recording of visual images was more complicated, but it came soon enough, hastened by the rise of television. Immediate video playback would not only provide the viewer with instant images of what had just happened; it meant that the producer of a program could monitor pictures while he was taking them. But the earliest video-tape recorders posed problems similar to those of sound tape: they ran at excessive speeds and used too much tape. By 1956 a video recorder was developed that ran at the same speed as sound recorders. The next year the first practical video-tape recorder was manufactured by RCA and Ampex, and came into general use; although it gave a sharp image, the recording apparatus was cumbersome. By the mid-1960's the improved "helical scan recorder" offered a less sharp image, but used a light and portable recording machine that could be taken anywhere.

By the 1960's, "instant replay" had become commonplace. Americans watching a boxing match, a horse race, or a baseball or football game could, at the pleasure of the producer, see any moment replayed any number of times. But tragedy and melodrama could also be replayed. On November 24, 1963, video tape showing Jack Ruby shooting Lee Harvey Oswald, the assassin of President Kennedy, was reshown within hours across the nation.

Ever since the advent of radio, Americans had listened in on the excitement at Times Square as the old year ebbed. The American's new sense of time was symbolized on New Year's Eve, December 31, 1971, and reported nostalgically in *The New Yorker*'s Talk of the Town:

The holy moment came: Lombardo counted backward "Nine, eight, seven, six, five. . . ," the glowing ball atop the Allied Chemical Building fell, the faithful little miracle had occurred. Horns, shouting, television patterns and spirals, "Auld Lang Syne." Then, incredibly, the whole half-minute was replayed in instant replay. "Seven, six, five, four . . ." and the same horns silently blew and the same spirals wildly flickered, and we seemed to be being asked to inspect some nuance in the event. Had it been a quarterback sneak? A double reverse? Had something replayable indeed occurred? If not, was the second time less real than the first? Were we insane? Or was the replayer? Pondering such bottomless questions, we curled up in our small fever and fell numbly into 1972.

Home tape recorders soon gave the American consumer his opportunity to relive at will any of his personally experienced moments. Families gathering at birthdays, Thanksgiving, or Christmas were no longer driven to reminisce in order to compare impressions of earlier occasions. On went the tape recorder to make reminiscence superfluous.

One of the charms of photography was the suspense as to whether and, if so, how your picture "came out." And of course this led to the taking of repeated photographs just to be sure that there would be one satisfactory result. In 1947 an ingenious, Go-Getting New Englander, Edwin H. Land, invented what he described as a "camera that delivers a finished photograph immediately after exposure is made." Photographic historians and critics, and Land himself, first hailed the new achievement as important mainly for the *art* of photography. In the early days, they recalled, the man who made a daguerrotype or a tintype could see a finished positive within a few minutes after he had taken the picture. But the later negative-positive system postponed the opportunity for such comparisons by dividing the process of *taking* from the process of *making* a photograph.

Land's Polaroid camera provided a new version of the one-step technique. Now the Polaroid photographer, like any other artist, could observe the subject and see his likeness of it at the same time. As Land himself explained:

By making it possible for the photographer to observe his work and his subject matter simultaneously, and by removing most of the manipulative barriers between the photographer and the photograph, it is hoped that many of the satisfactions of working in the early arts can be brought to a new group of photographers. . . . The process must be concealed from—non-existent for—the photographer, who by definition need think of the art in the *taking* and not in *making* photographs. . . . In short, all that should be necessary to get a good picture is to *take* a good picture, and our task is to make that possible.

The ordinary citizen, impatient for a replica of the moment, found in Polaroid the convenience of seeing a copy of his experience (a "double take") only a minute after. In May 1972 Polaroid announced a camera that produced a positive print instantaneously, just as it came out of the camera, within two seconds after exposure.

IN THEIR BEGINNING the new techniques of repeatable experience had added a dimension to life, making experience richer and subtler. "You cannot say you have thoroughly seen anything," the French novelist Émile Zola observed in 1900, "until you have got a photograph of it, revealing a lot of points which otherwise would be unnoticed, and which in most cases could not be distinguished." Everybody's new power to take pictures and, after the tape recorder, to make sound recordings, was more than another source of spare-time pleasure. This new technology was reshaping human consciousness.

In the democratic booster-enthusiasm for life enrichment through art and hobby-fun, the wider meaning of these techniques was easily overlooked. It was easy to see that the camera and the phonograph instantly increased knowledge or widened experience. But it was hard to foresee that in the longer run, these and other machines that made experience repeatable could actually dilute experience, dull consciousness, and flatten sensations. Originally, many of the charms of the photograph and of the phonograph record came from their novelty—and from the very difficulty of securing a good photograph or a good recording. But within a few decades, when these techniques had become instamatic, cheap and easy and universal, what was their meaning in the American's experience?

Did the very perfection of techniques for widening experience, and especially those for creating and diffusing the repeatable experience—did all this, somehow, impoverish experience in the very process of democratizing it? Was it inevitable that a democratized experience, however rich and technologically sophisticated, should be impoverished? Was there an inherent contradiction between the aim of democracy—to enrich the citizen's everyday life—and its modern means? Did the very instruments of life enrichment, once available to all, somehow make life blander and less poignant? Could it possibly be true that while *democratizing* (the process) enriched, *democracy* (the product) diluted? These were some novel, tantalizing questions which would haunt American democracy in the twentieth century.

All this suggested still another question, a clue perhaps to the hidden rationale of the American booster spirit. Was the brighter, richer, more open life that America promised a product, then, not of a *high* standard of living, but only of an always *rising* standard of living? Did the human richness of American democracy come not from the attainment of wealth, but from the reaching for it? Perhaps, then, the mission and the doom of American technology were the continual discovery of new techniques. Perhaps the best things in democracy came not from having but from seeking, not from being well off but from becoming better off. Would a high standard of living, no matter how high, always open vistas that would become flat and stale? And was it necessary to keep the standard of living ever rising if the vistas were to remain wide and open and fresh?

43
Extending Experience:
The New Segregation

ÉMILE ZOLA'S OBSERVATION that "you cannot say you have thoroughly seen anything until you have got a photograph of it," now applied a hundredfold in the world of television. By the late twentieth century the man on the spot, the viewer of the experience where it actually happened, began to feel confined and limited. The full flavor of the experience seemed to come only to the "viewer," the man in the television audience. Suddenly, from feeling remote and away the televiewer was painlessly and instantaneously transported *into* the experience. Television cameras made him a ubiquitous viewer. The man there in person was spacebound, crowd-confined, while the TV viewer was free to see from all points of view, above the heads of others, and behind the scenes. Was it he who was *really* there?

Making copies of experience, sights and sounds, for *later* use was one thing. Conquering space and time for instantaneous viewing was quite another, and even more revolutionary.

BEFORE THE CIVIL WAR, Morse's telegraph had hastened the pace of business and was speeding news to the papers within a day after it happened. When Bell's telephone was displayed at the Philadelphia Centennial Exposition in 1876, in the very year that Alexander Graham Bell had received his first telephone patent, it was still a great curiosity. Only two years later the first telephone appeared in the White House, under President Rutherford B. Hayes. Scores of inventors, including Thomas A. Edison and Emile Berliner, improved the telephone. By the early twentieth century the telephone had become an everyday convenience, and Bell's company, overtaking U.S. Steel, had grown to be the largest corporation in the United States. On remote farms and ranches, medical care by telephone saved the life of many a child—and incidentally saved the doctor a long ride, in the days when doctors still commonly made house calls. New businesses were started by Go-Getters who sold their goods exclusively by telephone, having discovered that customers who had formed the habit of throwing away their "junk mail" would still answer every ring. The telephone (like the typewriter, which was perfected at about the same time) provided a whole new category of jobs for women.

By the time the fifty-millionth American telephone was ceremoniously placed on President Dwight D. Eisenhower's desk, it was unusual for any American family to be out of reach of the telephone. The business of government was conducted by phone. The United States possessed more than half the telephones in the world, and by 1972 nearly a half-billion separate phone conversations were being carried on in the United States each day. Still, the telephone was only a convenience, permitting Americans to do more casually and with less effort what they had already been doing before. People found it easier to get their message to other individuals whom they wanted to reach.

Television was a revolution, or more precisely, a cataclysm. For nobody "wanted" television, and it would create its own market as it transformed everyday life. It extended simultaneous experience, created anonymous audiences even vaster and more universal than those of radio, and incidentally created a new segregation.

Back in the 1920's, as we have seen, young David Sarnoff had had difficulty persuading his RCA colleagues that radio had an all-American future. Earlier commercial forms of communication had routed a message to a specific addressee. He believed that this novelty could prove to be radio's special virtue. And Sarnoff imagined a democratized world of anonymous addressees. His own experience must have impressed on him the advantages of this way of communicating. In April 1912, when Sarnoff was manning the wireless station which Wanamaker's in New York had installed as a publicity stunt to keep in touch with their store in Philadelphia, by chance he had caught the wireless message: "S.S. *Titanic* ran into iceberg. Sinking fast." He quickly established communication with another steamer, which reported that the *Titanic* had sunk and that some survivors had been picked up. While President William Howard Taft ordered all other stations to remain silent, the twenty-year-old Sarnoff stayed at his post for seventy-two hours, taking the names of survivors which, along with the name of Sarnoff, became front-page news.

Five years later, when working for the American Marconi Company, Sarnoff urged the marketing of "a simple 'Radio Music Box.' " His plan, he noted, "would make radio a 'household utility' in the same sense as the piano or phonograph." In 1920 he proposed a plan for manufacturing these radio music boxes for $75 apiece, and prophesied that at least one million families would buy them within three years. He proposed that money would be made from selling advertising in *Wireless Age* (a magazine that RCA had bought), which would carry an advance monthly schedule of the programs to be broadcast. Sarnoff's optimistic production schedule for the one million sets proved conservative. Radio was launched on a career that transformed the American entertainment world, as well as the world of advertising and news reporting.

By 1930, advertisers were spending $60 million annually on the radio, a figure that was to be multiplied tenfold in the next ten years. Thirty years after the granting of the first commercial broadcasting license to KDKA (Pittsburgh) in 1920, there were more than two thousand stations and more than 75 million receiving sets. Before World War II, the annual production of radio sets numbered 10 million. By 1960 the national average showed three radio sets per household.

Radio had remained primarily an "entertainment" and "news" medium, allowing people to enjoy the melodrama of "soap serials," the jokes of Jack Benny, Fred Allen, and Bob Hope, the songs of Bing Crosby, the breathless sportscasting of Grantland Rice. The newscaster himself—H. V. Kaltenborn or Lowell Thomas—was a kind of "performer" who told the radio listener in solemn or lively tones what it was really like to be there.

TELEVISION OPENED another world. It did not simply multiply the sources of news and entertainment, it actually multiplied experience. At the TV set the viewer could see and hear what was going on with a rounded immediacy. Simultaneity was of the essence. When you took a picture you had to wait to have it developed; when you bought a phonograph record you knew in advance how it would sound. But now on TV you could share the suspense of the event itself. This new category of experience-at-a-distance would transform

American life more radically than any other modern invention except the automobile.

On the surface, television seemed simply to combine the techniques of the motion picture and the phonograph with those of the radio, but it added up to something more. Here was a new way of mass-producing the moment for instant consumption by a "broadcast" (i.e., undefinable and potentially universal) community of witnesses. Just as the printing press five centuries before had begun to democratize learning, now the television set would democratize experience, incidentally changing the very nature of what was newly shared.

Before, the desire to share experience had brought people out of their homes gathering them together (physically as well as spiritually), but television would somehow separate them in the very act of sharing. While TV-democratized experience would be more equal than ever before, it would also be more separate. TV segregation confined Americans by the same means that widened their experience. Here was a kind of segregation that no Supreme Court ruling could correct, nor could it be policed by any federal commission. For it was built into the TV set.

This was again the familiar consequence of having a centralized and enlarged source, now not merely for running water or running electricity. Just as Rebecca no longer needed to go to the village well to gather her water (and her gossip), so now, too, in her eighth-floor kitchenette she received the current of hot and cold running images. Before 1970, more than 95 percent of American households had television sets. Now the normal way to enjoy a community experience was at home in your living room at your TV set.

In earlier times, to see a performance was to become part of a visible audience. At a concert, in a church, at a ball game or a political rally, the audience was half the fun. What and whom you saw in the audience was at least as interesting as and often humanly more important than what you saw on the stage. While she watched her TV set, the lonely Rebecca was thrust back on herself. She could exclaim or applaud or hiss, but nobody heard her except the children in the kitchen or the family in the living room, who probably already knew her sentiments too well. The others at the performance took the invisible form of "canned" laughter and applause. The mystery of the listening audience which had already enshrouded radio now became the mystery of the viewing audience. The once warmly enveloping community of those physically present was displaced by a world of unseen fellow TV watchers. Who else was there? Who else was watching? And even if they had their sets turned on, were they *really* watching?

Each of the millions of watching Americans was now newly segregated from those who put on the program and who, presumably, were aiming to please him. Television was a one-way window. The viewer could see whatever *they* offered, but nobody except the family in the living room could know for sure how the viewer reacted to what he saw. Tiny island audiences gathered nightly around their twinkling sets, much as cave-dwelling ancestors had clustered around their fires for warmth and safety, and for a feeling of togetherness. In these new tribal groups, each child's television tastes were as intimate a part of family lore as whether he preferred ketchup or mustard on his hamburger. With more and more two-TV families (even before 1970 these were one third of all American households) it became common for a member of the family to withdraw and watch in lonely privacy. Of course, broadcasters made valiant and ingenious efforts to fathom these secrets, to find out what each watcher really watched, what he really liked and what he really wanted. But the broadcasters' knowledge was necessarily based on samples, on the extrapolation of a relatively few cases, on estimates and guesses—all merely circumstantial evidence.

There was a new penumbra between watching and not-watching. "Attending" a ball game, a symphony concert, a theatrical performance or a motion picture became so casual that children did it while they wrote out their homework, adults while they played cards or read a magazine, or worked in the kitchen or in the basement. The TV watcher himself became unsure whether he was really watching, or only had the set on. Experience was newly befogged. The most elaborate and costly performances ceased to be special occasions that required planning and tickets; they became part of the air conditioning. Radio, too, had become something heard but not necessarily listened to, and its programing was directed to people assumed to be doing something else: driving the car, working at a hobby, washing the dishes. Car radios, which numbered 15 million in 1950, exceeded 40 million by 1960. With the rise of the transistor, miniaturized radio sets were carried about on the person like a fountain pen or a purse, to assuage loneliness wherever the wearer might be.

Newly isolated from his government, from those who collected his taxes, who provided public services, and who made the crucial decisions of peace or war, the citizen felt a frustrating new disproportion between how often and how vividly political leaders could get their messages to him and how often and how vividly he could get *his* message to them. Except indirectly, through the opinion polls, Americans were offered no new avenue comparable to television by which they could get their message back. Private telegrams began to become obsolete. The citizen was left to rely on the telephone (which might respond to his call with a "recorded message") or on a venerable nineteenth-century institution, the post office.

By enabling him to be anywhere instantly, by filling his present moment with experiences engrossing and overwhelming, television dulled the American's sense of his past, and even somehow separated him from the longer past. If Americans had not been able to accompany the astronauts to the moon they would have had to read about it the next morning in some printed account that was engrossing in retrospect. But on television, Americans witnessed historic events as vivid items of the present. In these ways, then, television created a time myopia, focusing interest on the exciting, disturbing, inspiring, or catastrophic instantaneous *now*.

The high cost of network time and the need to offer something for everybody produced a discontinuity of programing, a constant shifting from one sort of thing to another. Experience became staccato and motley. And every act of dissent acquired new dramatic appeal, especially if it was violent or disruptive. For this lost feeling of continuity with the past, the ineffective TV antidote was Old Movies.

TELEVISION, THEN, BROUGHT a new vagueness to everyday experience: the TV watcher became accustomed to seeing something-or-other happening somewhere-or-other at sometime-or-other, but all in Living Color. The common-sense hallmarks of authentic firsthand experience (those ordinary facts which a jury expected from a witness to prove that he had actually experienced what he said) now began to be absent, or only ambiguously present, in television experience. For his TV experience, the American did not need to go out to see anything in particular: he just turned the knob, and then wondered while he watched. Was this program live or was it taped? Was it merely an animation or a simulation? Was it a rerun? Where did it originate? When, if ever, did it really occur? Was it happening to actors or to real people? Was that a commercial? —a spoof of a commercial?—a documentary?—or pure fiction?

Almost never did the viewer see a TV event from a single individual's point of view. For TV was many-eyed, alert to avoid the monotony of any one person's limited vision. While each camera gave an image bigger and clearer than life, nobody got in the way. As the close-up dominated the screen, the middle distance dissolved. The living-room watcher saw the player in left field, the batter at the plate, or rowdies in a remote bleacher more sharply than did the man wearing sunglasses in the stands. Any casual kook or momentary celebrity filled the screen, just like Humphrey Bogart or President Nixon. All TV experience had become theater, in which any actor, or even a spectator, might hold center stage. The new TV perspective made the American understandably reluctant to go back to his seat on the side and in the rear. Shakespeare's metaphors became grim reality when the whole world had become a TV stage.

In this supermarket of surrogate experience, the old compartments were dissolved. Going to a church or to a lecture was no different from going to a play or a movie or a ball game, from going to a political rally or stopping to hear a patent-medicine salesman's pitch. Almost anything could be watched in shirt sleeves, with beer can in hand. The experience which flowed through the television channels was a mix of entertainment, instruction, news, uplift, exhortation and guess what. Successful programing offered entertainment (under the guise of instruction), instruction (under the guise of entertainment), political persuasion (with the appeal of advertising) and advertising (with the charm of drama). The new miasma, which no machine before could emit, and which enshrouded the TV world, reached out to befog the "real" world. Americans began to be so accustomed to the fog, so at home and solaced and comforted by the blur, that reality itself became slightly irritating because of its sharp edges and its clear distinctions of person, place, time, and weather.

As broadcasting techniques improved, they tended to make the viewer's experience more indirect, more controlled by unseen producers and technicians. Before, the spectator attending a national political convention would, simply by turning his head, decide for himself *where* he would look, but the TV watcher in the living room lacked the power to decide. Cameramen, directors, and commentators decided for him, focusing on this view of a brutal policeman or that view of a pretty delegate. As these conventions became guided tours by TV camera, the commentators themselves acquired a new power over the citizen's political experience, which was most vividly demonstrated at the Democratic National Convention in Chicago in 1968. Even as the American's secondhand experience came to seem more real and more authentic, it was more than ever shaped by invisible hands and by guides who themselves upstaged the leading performers and became celebrities.

Television watching became an addiction comparable only to life itself. If the set was not on, Americans began to feel that they had missed what was "really happening." And just as it was axiomatic that it was better to be alive than to be dead, so it became axiomatic that it was better to be watching *something* than to be watching nothing at all. When there was "nothing on TV tonight," there was a painful void. No wonder, then, that Americans revised their criteria for experience. Even if a firsthand experience was not worth having, putting it on TV might make it so.

Of all the wonders of TV, none was more remarkable than the

speed with which it came. Television conquered America in less than
a generation, leaving the nation more bewildered than it dared admit. Five hundred years were required for the printing press to
democratize learning. And when the people could know as much as
their "betters," they demanded the power to govern themselves. As
late as 1671, the governor of Virginia, Sir William Berkeley, thanked
God that the printing press (breeder of heresy and disobedience!)
had not yet arrived in his colony, and he prayed that printing would
never come to Virginia. By the early nineteenth century, aristocrats
and men of letters could record, with Thomas Carlyle, that movable
type had disbanded hired armies and cashiered kings, and somehow
created "a whole new democratic world." Now with dizzying speed,
television had democratized experience. It was no wonder that like
the printing press before it, television met a cool reception from
intellectuals and academics and the other custodians of traditional
avenues of experience.

44
The Decline of the
Unique and the Secret

"WHY ARE SO MANY government secrets now leaking to the
press?" the knowledgeable James Reston of the *New York Times*
asked in January 1972. To this question, which had been troubling the
nation since the unauthorized publication of the Pentagon Papers,
the voluminous background material on the Vietnam war, Reston
offered an explanation which was neither political nor philosophical
nor moral, but purely scientific and technical. "The real source of the
leaks," he proposed, "is Chester Carlson, who invented the electrostatic copying or Xerox system, which now dominates the federal
government and influences the flow of information in every other big
institution in the country." With the Xerox machine, anybody could
instantly make a copy of any document. According to Reston, this
machine, which had been devised in order "to expand information
and truth," had produced the ironic result of making government
officials wary of expressing their honest opinions in writing.

For all practical purposes, it was no longer possible to be sure that any document was unique. Photo-offsetting and other similar techniques had imperilled the uniqueness of precious literary manuscripts and first editions; by 1965 a photo-offset copy of a First Folio Shakespeare (an original sold for $30,000) could be bought for only $15. It had become so easy and so inexpensive to make copies of books and parts of books that the law of copyright was becoming obsolete.

Xerox and other forms of electrostatic copying would add new dimensions to the repeatability of experience, enabling anyone who had access to a simple machine to destroy the uniqueness or confidentiality of any document. Now, too, the Polaroid camera, the tape recorder, magnetic tape, video tape and other devices provided instantaneously replayable copies, making daily life into a world of mass-produced moments. Now almost anything that was seen or heard by anyone could also be seen or heard by countless unidentifiable others.

THE PROBLEM OF making multiple copies was as ancient as writing. The rise of the printing press and of movable type had, of course, begun to democratize learning. But the cost of setting type could not be justified except by making numerous copies, and the more copies that were made, the lower the cost of each one; the printing press was obviously most useful when the copies desired ran into the hundreds or thousands. Just as Edison's problem in democratizing electric light would be how to fragment light into smaller sources, there was a similar problem in the technology of copying. For centuries after the printing press had come into general use, the lack of any other way to make single copies of handwriting sustained the profession of the "copyist," who reproduced the original in his own handwriting. The ingenious "polygraph," an eighteenth-century invention, attached a device to the writer's pen to reproduce its movements on another sheet of paper, and so made a copy of the letter as it was being written. Thomas Jefferson was intrigued by the machine and made some improvements of his own. Still, the common way of making a single copy was by the letterpress: after a letter had been written, it was rolled between sheets of blotting paper, to transfer some of the ink to another sheet. Carbon paper, unknown in Jefferson's time, would be a great convenience because it required no mechanical apparatus, it was inexpensive, and it provided the copies at the same time as the original.

The machine which made it easier to make legible copies in small numbers was, of course, the typewriter. Even before the nineteenth century some progress toward a writing machine had been made by English inventors. By 1845, two decades before there was a practicable manual typewriter, Samuel F. B. Morse and his partner were sending machine writing long distances electromagnetically, using a keyboard much like that of the typewriter. C. Latham Sholes, a Wisconsin pioneer who made his living as a Milwaukee printer and editor, had been working on an automatic numbering machine when a friend proposed that he develop a letter-printing machine. His crucial typewriter patents were issued in 1868 and "Type-Writer" entered the language as an Americanism. But it was early twentieth century before the typewriter in its modern form appeared, with upper and lower case letters on a single keyboard, and producing fully "visible writing" (i.e., on a carriage which the operator could see as he wrote).

The earliest commercially successful mass-produced typewriters were made by the Remington Arms Company, which turned them out in its sewing-machine department in the 1870's. Ornamented with floral designs, these machines sat on a sewing-machine stand, and with the treadle arranged so it would operate the carriage return. The first market for typewriters was among authors, editors, and ministers, and it was assumed that the machine would be mainly a tool for the world of letters. Mark Twain boasted of his willingness to use this curious new machine, and *The Adventures of Tom Sawyer* is reputed to be the first typewritten manuscript to be set into a book. (By 1930, union printers were refusing to set books from any other kind of manuscript.) Originally there were doubts, however, that the typewriter could ever serve the business world, since its product was so impersonal and so standardized. And, as we have seen, when farmers objected to receiving "machine-made" letters from Sears, Roebuck, the company had to go to the trouble of hiring secretaries who would write the business letters by hand.

The typewriter was destined, of course, to become an important force in American life. By providing a socially acceptable employment for women in the commercial world, it opened new office careers, and (with the telephone) helped bring women out of the kitchen into the world of affairs. But machine writing had other, subtler effects on everyday experience. As the typewritten letter became the norm for business correspondence, handwriting declined and that meant the decline of a visibly distinctive character in what anyone wrote. Throughout the nineteenth century, a clear and elegant handwriting remained a useful skill for the ambitious young man. Colleges of penmanship, in their day, were as important as commercial colleges would become, with their teaching of shorthand and typing.

In widening the reach of the typewriter and in multiplying its effect, few inventions were as important as carbon paper. The idea behind carbon paper was simply to coat a sheet of paper with a special composition of wax and dye which would be transferred to a page when rubbed by a pen or struck by type. What was perhaps the earliest patent for carbon paper (issued in 1869) described this "Improvement in the Preparation of Copying Paper" to be "used with particular advantage in making copies of letters while the same are being written." But this copying paper was still designed as a simpler alternative to the polygraph which was a cumbersome machine and could copy only handwriting. In 1872, in the early days of the typewriter, there was a patent for "Carbon Paper" specially designed for use with the machine. This new expression entered the American language, bringing unprecedented temptations to fill endless filing cabinets. In the long run, the special advantage of carbon paper (that it made the copy along with the original) proved its limitation.

Convenient techniques for making a small number of multiple copies from a completed original would come from applications of the stencil process. One of the most successful of these was the "mimeograph," a word coined (from *mime,* "to imitate," and *graphein,* "to write,") in 1890 by Alfred Blake Dick, who had started in the lumber business in Chicago before going into sale of labor-saving devices for offices. The perfected "mimeograph" combined the process that Dick had patented a few years before with processes that Thomas A. Edison had patented earlier, and with another inventor's patent for a rotary-drum duplicating machine. Dick marketed a device which inexpensively reproduced copies in ways helpful not only to businesses but to churches, political and reform groups, and many others.

To make a facsimile of a letter that had already been written required photography, which was time-consuming and costly. What was needed was some new technique for inexpensive, speedy, and reliable copying. Microfilming, the histrionically celebrated tool of espionage, had come into use by scholars, archivists, and banking and real estate enterprises before the mid-twentieth century; but it remained too complicated for everyday office use in making single copies.

A REMARKABLE FEATURE of the next step was that it was actually taken by Go-Getting businessmen in search of a new product. In 1946 a small firm in Rochester, New York, called the Haloid Company, was worried about its future. It had produced photocopying equipment to a volume of about $7 million that year, but its profit had fallen to $150,000. The company leaders, Joseph C. Wilson and

Dr. John H. Dessauer, decided that the firm needed a new product, although they were not sure what. Dessauer, the director of research, happened on an article in an old issue of *Radio News* (July 1944) describing a new technique called "electrophotography." The author of the article and the inventor of the process was Chester F. Carlson, a native of Seattle who had worked his way through the California Institute of Technology and had then been employed in the Bell Laboratories. Carlson's experience with patents and his interest in the problems of patent lawyers (he was attending New York Law School in the evenings) persuaded him that there was a need for some inexpensive office device to make copies of all sorts. He suspected that this future could not lie with photography (the use of chemicals to record images), since the large research budgets of the big companies had probably pushed photographic research to its limits.

Long evenings in the New York Public Library led Carlson to the comparatively unexplored field of photoconductivity. Was it possible that somehow electricity, instead of light, might be used to make an image? On October 22, 1938, in Astoria, Queens, with the aid of a German refugee physicist, he produced his first electrophotographic image. A 2-inch by 3-inch zinc plate was coated with sulfur, then charged electrostatically by being rubbed with a handkerchief and exposed for ten seconds to a glass slide showing the inscription "10-22-38 Astoria." The plate was dusted with lycopodium powder, which made the latent image visible, and then a piece of wax paper was pressed against the powdered image, and so imprinted with the image. To distinguish it from photography, this was called "xerography" (from the Greek *xeros*, "dry," and *graphein*, "to write").

Carlson's first efforts to secure financial support failed. He tried twenty companies, he went to the National Inventors Council and to the Army Signal Corps, but none was interested. Then in 1944 he finally awakened interest at the Battelle Memorial Institute, a research foundation in Columbus, Ohio, which agreed to develop his process in exchange for a major share of the royalties. But the institute was willing to invest only a few thousand dollars, and when this money was used up, Carlson needed additional support to keep the project alive. It was at that time, in 1946, that Wilson and Dessauer of Haloid went to Battelle; they saw the experiments, decided that this would be their firm's new product, and invested $10,000. Within the next six years, Haloid raised more than $3.5 million to develop the process, and under the new company name of Xerox became the industrial phenomenon of the mid-century. The Xerox stock paid to Battelle in return for its royalty share in the process had a market value in 1965 of more than $355 million.

The first production-line automatic copier, the Xerox 914 (it made copies up to 9 inches by 14 inches) was delivered in 1960. This Xerox machine, offering inexpensive high-volume copying in a central location in an office, had the advantage over competitors that its copies were made directly onto ordinary paper without need for stencils or any intermediate step. The machines were rented out by Xerox and the unit charge for their use decreased as larger numbers of copies were made. Whole new office systems were developed: the Food and Drug Administration used Xerox to copy labels without taking them off bottles; police officers quickly recorded the contents of a suspect's pockets. People had to be shown that the novel machine really worked. But since a 650-pound copier could not be carried about by a salesman for demonstration, Xerox turned to television. The company relied heavily on television advertising and pioneered in sponsoring an impressive series of serious, sometimes controversial, programs ("The Kremlin," "The Making of the President—1960," "Cuban Missile Crisis," "The Louvre," etc.).

When Haloid adopted Xerox as its name, the firm explained that "The ability to process information in quantity; to present it in a form to be read; to print things rapidly and cheaply; to copy things inexpensively; these are capacities that may spell the difference between a society that is growing fast enough commercially and one which is not." Having developed and perfected its technique for copying, which satisfied all these requirements, Xerox, soon followed by collaborators and competitors, went in search of anything and everything to be copied.

45

In Search of the Spontaneous

WAS IT ANY WONDER, then, that modern Americans were eagerly, sometimes desperately, looking for unique, spontaneous, and exciting episodes with which to spice their lives of increasingly repeatable packaged experience? The "sensationalism" of the twentieth century, while more flamboyant than that of any earlier era in American history, was not the product merely of the greed of newspaper publishers or the morbidity of public taste. Like other institutionalized vices it was a response to a human need—in this case a generalized need for sensation. This need was satisfied in several ways. The rise of popular journalism brought a new flood of interest in crime and in sports. These two staples of the democratized newspaper might look incongruous to a moralist, who would see in one the dramatic violations of the community's laws, in the other dramatic exhibitions of obedience to rules for their own sake.

IN AMERICAN JOURNALISM a new style emphasizing the unique and the sensational had been set by the Hungarian immigrant Joseph Pulitzer, who took over the New York *World* in 1883. "There is room in this great and growing city," Pulitzer announced to his readers, "for a journal that is not only cheap but bright, not only bright but large, not only large but truly democratic—dedicated to the cause of the people rather than to that of the purse potentates —devoted more to the news of the New than the Old World—that will expose all fraud and sham, fight all public evils and abuses—that will battle for the people with earnest sincerity." Pulitzer's *World,* commonly considered the nation's first modern mass-circulation daily, sold for two cents a copy and in fifteen years increased its circulation from 15,000 to 1.5 million.

Sensationalism meant a new prominence and vividness for crime, disaster, sex, scandal, and monstrosities. The journalistic approach of the old *World* before Pulitzer took it over was illustrated by a lead story in its last issue headlined "ELECTION OF AN EXECUTIVE COMMITTEE OF THE AMERICAN COCKER SPANIEL CLUB." Pulitzer's first issue, by contrast, dominated the front page with "THE DEADLY LIGHTNING," a story of a fire in New Jersey that took six lives and destroyed a hundred thousand barrels of crude oil; another lead story described the last hours of a condemned killer, detailed his protestations of innocence, his rattling of the cell door, his refusal to see a priest, and finally his response to the reading of the death warrant. The front page also carried a companion story on an execution in Pittsburgh, with the caption "WARD M'CONKEY HANGED. SHOUTING FROM UNDER THE BLACK CAP THAT HIS EXECUTIONERS ARE MURDERERS." In the following years Pulitzer spiced his columns— or rather filled them—with tales of abortion, sexual molestation, mayhem, and quintuple murder. He commonly added illustrations and made a map of the murder scene ("X marks the spot") an essential part of the story.

To awaken interest and keep up circulation, Pulitzer planned stunts and crusades and sought out (or invented) public scandals. In 1885 the *World,* "the people's paper," by appealing for nickels and dimes to build a pedestal for the Statue of Liberty, raised $100,000 from 120,000 contributions. Pulitzer's reporter Nellie Bly (whose real name was Elizabeth Cochran) feigned insanity to get into the asylum at Blackwell's Island and then wrote a shocking newspaper exposé (later published in her book, *Ten Days in a Madhouse*). Pulitzer then assigned her to beat the round-the-world record of Jules Verne's Phineas Fogg. And when the *World* offered a free trip to Europe to the person whose guess came closest to the actual time it took Nellie Bly to circle the globe, they received nearly a million replies. Pulitzer brought her by special train from San Francisco to New York, to complete the trip in 72 days, 6 hours, 11 minutes, and 14 seconds.

ALONG WITH CRIME and stunts, Pulitzer gave a new prominence to sports. Sporting events had, of course, long been a staple of the press, but Pulitzer set up a whole sports department. Formerly, horse racing was reported along with the cattle news. Pulitzer proclaimed his new emphasis when he named a leading authority on horse racing as head of his sports department. Before the end of the century other dailies followed with extensive and specialized sports sections.

People who could not watch the games, much less play them, could follow sporting "news," enjoying a suspense and elaborating a cultic lore missing elsewhere in their lives. News of horse racing, bicycle racing, walking races, roller-skating races, and boxing helped swell the *World*'s circulation. After the Civil War the new sport of baseball overshadowed all others and seemed providentially suited to be reported in the newspapers. Statistics accumulated in the news provided fans and reporters with a nearly inexhaustible source for "firsts" in the playing (and not merely in the outcome) of any game. The origins of baseball are clouded in myth—the most venerable legend being that the game was invented in 1839 by Abner Doubleday in Cooperstown, New York, which was to become the site of the National Baseball Hall of Fame. By the 1840's baseball was being played by gentlemen of leisure around New York City. But it was designed to be a democratic sport, since, unlike horse racing or polo or tennis, it could be played by amateurs with little equipment and without a specially prepared field. During the Civil War, baseball became popular behind the lines with the troops (at least with those of the North), who spread the game when they returned home. In 1865, baseball was not quite the game we know, since pitchers still used an underhand delivery, catchers caught the ball on the first bounce, and fielders did not wear gloves.

The Cincinnati Red Stockings, the first professional baseball team, toured the nation and managed to remain undefeated after fifty-six contests which took them over eleven thousand miles. Teams from eight cities formed the National League of Professional Baseball Clubs in 1876, which codified the rules, planned regular schedules, and for a while dominated the baseball scene. When minor leagues were formed, they were approved under rules set by the National League. Then, over the initial opposition of the National League, the American League was formed in 1901. The two leagues made their truce and gave the national sport its twentieth-century form when they played the first World Series in 1903.

Professional baseball became one of the most highly organized national sports in history. After the Chicago "Black Sox" scandal, when eight members of the Chicago White Sox took bribes to throw the World Series of 1919, the leagues hired their own commissioner, a federal district judge, Kenesaw Mountain Landis. He barred the offending players and established a high standard of honesty in the game.

The transformation of the game which came in 1920 made it a greater source of statistical and spectator excitement than ever before. Popular excitement had been aroused when Babe Ruth, who was raised in a Baltimore orphanage, broke all records by hitting twenty-nine home runs for the Boston Red Sox in 1919. Discovering the dramatic appeal of the home run, the leagues then redesigned the ball to make the ball livelier, thus making it easier for a good hitter to become a home-run hitter. This new "Home-Run Game" enlarged the baseball crowds, changed the style of playing and increased the dramatic appeal. The Babe hit fifty-four home-runs in 1920, fifty-nine in 1921, and sixty in 1927. Every year the game seemed to have a wider reach. When President Herbert Hoover appeared at the 1931 World Series, he was booed, but a Cardinal rookie named Pepper Martin was cheered for his .500 Series batting average. The loyalty of citizens to their local baseball team had no parallel in earlier American sporting history. City people gathered regularly by the thousands to find excitement and suspense in a game whose sportsmanship they believed in.

Technology soon gave the game an even larger national role. In the late 1940's, major-league games were televised. Until the 1950's, train travel had limited the major-league teams to the eastern seaboard and to a few cities on the eastern fringe of the Middle West. It was air travel that made possible the spread of major-league baseball over the country. In 1953 the Boston Braves moved to Milwaukee, the Brooklyn Dodgers and the New York Giants had moved to California by 1958, and by 1969 both major leagues had increased their clubs to twelve, making it possible for cities all over the nation to take part. A Montreal team joined the National League, and the annual Japanese All-Star Game was being broadcast live to the United States via satellite.

Other sports competed with baseball, but at least until the late twentieth century no other team game seemed to have comparable appeal. Basketball, perhaps the only major popular sport undisputably invented in the United States, was thought up in 1891 by a Springfield, Massachusetts, YMCA athletic director as a bad-weather team sport to be played indoors. Football, a derivative of an English game, was first played in the Ivy League colleges in the 1870's. It was given something like its late twentieth-century form by the Intercollegiate Football Association in 1880, and by the 1890's crowds of fifty thousand spectators, who were loyally following the teams of Harvard, Yale, or Princeton. During the early decades of the twentieth century, when football came to dominate the American college scene, it was not unheard of for the college football coach to be paid more than the college president. Football "scholarships" were more remunerative (and sometimes carried more kudos) than others.

But professional football had an independent history, developing about 1910 in the industrial and mining towns of Ohio and western Pennsylvania, including players who had begun the game on their college teams. The professional association founded in 1920 soon gave the game a federal organization and a monopolistic discipline like those of baseball. What the home run did to enliven baseball was accomplished for football by the forward pass. Football lore traces the transformation of the game from a sheer pushing match between linemen to the use of a forward pass by a Wesleyan University team against Yale in 1906. By 1970, when professional football had developed a strategy far more intricate than that of baseball, television was giving living-room spectators all over the country an intimate (and replayable) view of the game. The annual number of paid admissions at professional football matches had reached some ten million. Football became a national ritual symbolized when the Thanksgiving religious services and the meal were topped off and overshadowed by—"the Game."

Could Americans in the twentieth century really succeed in finding in sports some relief from their increasingly packaged and repeatable experience? Even in the world of sports it was hard to keep alive the sense of spontaneity and dramatic suspense.

Baseball itself became a solemn, statistical science. *The Baseball Encyclopedia*, published in 1969, offered 2,335 pages of carefully tabulated statistics of nineteen thousand games, on everything from batting averages to a detailed statistical career analysis of every player who had played in the major leagues at least a hundred times, and causes of interruption of play, to pinch hits at bat, and new indices like the HR% (the number of home runs per hundred times at bat). This work was the product of Information Concepts Incorporated, which used a computerized system to build a baseball data bank. Television revenues and the growing popularity of the game had displaced the old sportsman owner by a diffused corporate ownership.

THERE WERE a few other areas, too, where Americans hoped to find a residual stock of the unrepeatable and the unpredictable. One of them was a new and widespread interest in weather and weather prediction. In a nation that every year held a smaller proportion of farmers, where fewer livelihoods depended on rainfall or frosts, where the principal form of daily transportation, the automobile, was remarkably weatherproof, where people were increasingly accustomed to central heating, air conditioning, humidifying and dehumidifying, this awakened interest in the weather-to-come was hard to account for. Was it perhaps another clue to the American's quest for the spontaneous?

The special importance of weather forecasting for air travel did not explain the new upsurge of interest in weather data and weather prediction by city-dwelling Americans. After World War II, six hundred commercial broadcasting stations were giving regular daily (sometimes hourly and half-hourly) weather information. With television, the weather became a regular evening feature illustrated by weather maps and enlivened by the patter of performers who now made careers of their one-man vaudeville acts about the weather. In 1950, automatic telephone forecasts (Dial-the-Weather) were introduced in Cleveland and Philadelphia, and spread to other cities.

There had been many causes for the growth of an efficient national weather service. Meteorology progressed in the nineteenth century, along with other branches of the natural and physical sciences. But since meteorology depended on the collecting of simultaneous information in distant places, little could be done to develop the science and make it useful in daily life before the invention of the telegraph. In 1849 the first meteorological observations to be communicated by telegraph reached Joseph Henry, Secretary of the newly founded Smithsonian Institution, who organized a network of observers. By 1854 these Smithsonian observers were at work in thirty-one states, Canada, Nova Scotia, and Paraguay; and by the outbreak of the Civil War there were five hundred weather stations. During the war, weather observations were collected for military purposes, and when

Congress created a national weather service in 1870, it was placed within the signal corps of the Army. Forecasts were sent by telegraph to weather stations, railroad stations, and the Associated Press, and copies were made and distributed to post offices, where they were received five hours after the making of the midnight predictions.

Forecasts were obviously most important for the farmer. In the early 1880's a thirty-six-hour advance frost warning was sent to Madison, Wisconsin, which would have allowed some time to protect the ripened tobacco crop, but because a negligent telegraph operator failed to relay the information speedily, the crop was lost. In 1891 the Weather Bureau was put under civilian control in the recently established Department of Agriculture, where it improved and expanded its services. Three-day forecasts came in 1901, along with improved cold-wave and frost warnings. Enlarged services included hurricane and flood warnings, a new system to inform the public of dangers of forest fire, and warnings of severe storms to protect the operators of pleasure craft. In 1940, with the increased importance of aviation, the Weather Bureau was moved to the Department of Commerce. Then, on April 1, 1960, as a by-product of the space program, the "Tiros" weather satellite was launched into orbit, and its two TV cameras gave meteorologists for the first time a view of large-scale weather patterns.

In a world of prefabricated, packaged, predictable, repeatable experience, the fickleness and mystery of the weather had taken on a new piquancy. Efforts to make and control outdoor weather were still rudimentary. Despite the new predictive vistas opened to meteorologists, the citizen still found an element of surprise in the shining of the sun, the coming of rain or snow. Pundits had said that "Change of weather is the discourse of fools." But now an interest in the weather was itself a tie to the past, a wistful reminder of the limits of man's powers to make and repeat whatever experience he wished, and so a refuge of mystery and spontaneity.

Book Three

A POPULAR CULTURE

"An American may do with impunity . . . what a European could only do in the spirit of the most reckless gambler or in the confidence of inspired genius. Freedom, and the newness and breadth of the land, explain this favored condition of the American."

CHARLES W. ELIOT

"Pi Omega Ro asked whether it would be correct to assume that Americans were free to say what they think, because they did not think what they were not free to say."

LEO SZILARD, *The Voice of the Dolphins*

"All the ills of democracy can be cured by more democracy."

AL SMITH

T H E R E was no mystery about what gave Old World civilizations their aristocratic character. Culture and wealth were in the hands of a few: and just as earlier revolutions had aimed to open the vehicles and instruments of knowledge to large numbers, revolutions there since the nineteenth century aimed to disperse property more widely to accomplish justice or equality. American civilization, in the course of fulfilling its democratic mission, would diffuse property widely and give it novel forms. The liberal movements of early modern times had brought knowledge out of the dusty recesses of Greek and Latin, Hebrew and Arabic, into the fresh air of the vernacular. In the United States the democratizing of language and knowledge went one bold step further. The colloquial language and what passed for knowledge in the marketplace became the arbiters of the classroom and the academy. Knowledge and the arts were redefined to make them accessible and appealing. And the sophistication supposed to come from a familiarity with faraway places—once reserved for the rich and the powerful—was now within reach of the common citizenry.

PART SEVEN

The Thinner
Life of Things

"Property is desirable, is a positive good in the
world. Let not him who is homeless pull down
the house of another, but let him work dili-
gently and build one for himself, thus by example assuring that his own shall be safe from
violence when built."

ABRAHAM LINCOLN

"A corporation is just like any natural person,
except that it has no pants to kick or soul to
damn, and, by God, it ought to have both!"

A WESTERN JUDGE

IN THE UNITED STATES in the century after the Civil War, ownership
was enjoyed by unprecedented numbers. What they owned was not
only land and houses and cattle and the tools of their trade, the
traditional "property" of recorded history. This new nation produced new kinds of property. The automobile was only one of innumerable objects that were manufactured in such large numbers and
so widely desired that their ownership came to seem a standard of
subsistence. Men who did not possess these new objects were said to
be deprived, yet those who possessed them were not necessarily
thought to be well off.

Subtle consequences followed from the proliferation and the
democratization of property. The most potent form of property and

the most potent creator of property, the corporation, was both the most legalistic and the most ambiguous. New devices like the automobile stimulated novel forms of paying, of lending and borrowing. When more men "owned," it became oddly uncertain in precisely what sense they owned.

America, where priority rule had governed the mines and the unoccupied Western plains, was where the law of property had been brought back to its fundamentals. But it was also where property became more elaborate, more metaphysical, more attenuated. Speedy change transformed the objects of experience. Advertising gave a new meaning to outer shapes; the package became the thing.

46

Endless Streams of Ownership

IN AMERICA the corporation would have a fertile new life. Since corporations, the creatures of government, could be made immortal and could be given whatever powers the lawmakers wished for them, popular leaders had long feared the corporation. Sir Edward Coke, seventeenth-century champion of common-law rights against a tyrant-king, warned that corporations "cannot commit treason, nor be outlawed nor excommunicated, for they have no souls." While Americans never succeeded in giving corporations a soul, they did see the corporation magically transformed in other ways. Corporations here would multiply as never before, they would spread over the land, and finally permeate every citizen's daily life. While the American corporation, a new species of an old genus, was not without its own menacing features, it became (what Coke could never have imagined) the democratizer of property.

The states themselves had their roots in corporations: the Virginia Company of London, the Massachusetts Bay Company, and other colonies had been established as trading corporations under authority of a royal charter. Throughout history, corporations had been units of self-government, with the power to make bylaws, and to do many of the things which a more remote central government had neither the means nor the knowledge nor the will to do. Our colonial

413

history was a catalogue of what corporations were learning to do in America. In a sense, then, American federalism was a by-product of the corporation—of the novelty and variety of its creations.

WHAT HAD BEEN feeble seventeenth-century corporations would become a community of varied sovereign states. In the nineteenth and twentieth centuries, these in turn would make possible tens of thousands of new-style corporations, diffusing their ownership among tens of millions of citizens.

But the same uncertainties of law and constitution which occasioned the American Revolution had befogged the early American law of corporations. Although the government of each of the thirteen colonies was "sovereign" in some sense or other, its power to create "corporations" was uncertain and ill-defined. This vagueness gave American colleges and universities—Harvard, William & Mary, Yale, and Dartmouth, among others—an opportunity to blossom into something unheard of in the Old World. And a striking proportion of the epoch-making decisions of the Supreme Court before the Civil War (including, for example, the Dartmouth College Case, McCulloch v. Maryland, and Charles River Bridge v. Warren Bridge) were efforts to clarify the role of the corporation in this new federal world.

The Revolution made it clear that a sovereign power to create corporations resided on this side of the Atlantic. The Continental Congress chartered the Bank of North America in 1781. Under the new Constitution the Congress chartered a national bank, and before 1800 the new state governments had chartered more than three hundred corporations, mostly for banking and insurance, and for building canals and roads. Each of these corporations had been custom-made by a special act of some state legislature. Nevertheless, in the early years of the nineteenth century, such corporations were being created in ever increasing numbers. By 1830, in New England alone, there were some two thousand corporations.

Even before the Civil War, the American states had begun to devise new legal machinery in the form of "general incorporation laws." With these procedures, it was no longer necessary to have a friend at court, to bribe a king or his advisers, or to reward legislators for their help in securing a special act of incorporation. The corporation was democratized by being made a standardized product, available to anyone who followed the simple steps prescribed and paid a small registration fee.

The Old World situation was reversed, and instead of businessmen anxiously seeking the special privilege of incorporation, the states competed for the favors of businessmen. The enticements offered by land speculators, city boosters, and railroad promoters to natural persons and their families were matched by enticements to these artificial persons. Businessmen were urged to domicile their newly created legal entities in Delaware rather than in Massachusetts, in New Jersey rather than in Pennsylvania, in Nevada rather than in New York. The less populous states, such as Delaware, New Jersey, and Nevada, were especially eager and ingenious in the competition. We have seen in some detail how Go-Getters in Nevada, for example, exploited this, along with other "federal commodities."

There were two publicly declared motives for these general incorporation laws. One was to protect the public from the special privileges that corporations had devised for themselves when each could draw up its own act of incorporation for adoption by a friendly legislature. The other was to encourage commerce and industry.

After the general incorporation laws were adopted, it was not much more difficult for legally qualified persons to procure a state charter for a new corporation than it was to secure a marriage license. New York had led the way in 1811, followed by Connecticut in 1817 and Massachusetts in 1830. With the passing of the anticorporation bias of the Jacksonian era, similar laws appeared in Maryland, New Jersey, Pennsylvania, Indiana, and Virginia. Before 1861, a dozen states had written into their constitutions provisions that in the future, corporations could not be created by special acts of the legislature, but only under general incorporation laws. From state to state the rules varied, as did the privileges extended to the new corporate entities. In the two decades before the Civil War, banks and factories and hotels, canals and railroads and telegraph lines were built by these artificial persons who had been mass-produced by state legislatures.

The corporation had many advantages over the enterprising individual. A creature of the law, it was immortal, and therefore its contracts and leases had a longevity which no natural person could provide. For vast and risky undertakings it had other obvious advantages. Pieces of ownership, in the form of shares of stock, could be offered to thousands of small investors, who (as "limited liability" became common) could be confident that they would not be liable for the debts of the company, and so could lose no more than the amount paid for the stock. These investment units could be divided and multiplied according to the needs of the enterprise and the extent of public interest. The state laws of incorporation, together with the bylaws which each corporation was empowered to make for its own government, could delegate the running of the enterprise to a few managers. Stockholders could share windfall profits; yet, by "limited liability," they were protected from unpredictable losses.

"Property," multiplied in these ways, in this new form which separated ownership from management, acquired a new meaning, a new mystery, a new unintelligibility. Of course, the common citizen never was at home with the ways of the wealthy. But the counters of the wealthy—land, houses, gold, furs, precious stones—were no mystery. Now there was a new metaphysic of property. And the very counters in the prosperous gambles of the powerful became entities as abstract and nearly as baffling to the uninitiate as the Plotinian quintessences of the Neoplatonists or the theological emanations of the Holy Ghost would have been to a medieval serf. Yet at the same time the ordinary citizen was invited to acquire these entities, and by the twentieth century he had entered the market for corporate securities.

The high priests of this new metaphysic of property were the lawyers. Just as the lawyers held the clues to the obscure nuances of patents which made a fortune for one inventor or another, so now lawyers presided over the mysteries of corporation law. No layman could imagine all the new ways of building, combining, and controlling corporate wealth which lawyers might concoct. They made the subtleties of Duns Scotus and Aquinas look like child's play. Property became a new realm of the occult.

THE CLASSIC PRODUCT of this new metaphysic was the Standard Oil Trust. The general incorporation laws in the years just after the Civil War had not offered any legal way in which corporations could combine to form larger corporations. Obviously this was inconvenient for giant Go-Getters like John D. Rockefeller who lived by the axiom that the most economical, and hence the most profitable, enterprise was the largest. Rockefeller and his collaborators needed a method for forming a "corporation of corporations." They were looking for some legal way to combine the resources of several corporations so they could swallow their competitors. Pursuing this purpose, in 1879 under a secret agreement the stockholders of the Standard Oil Company of Ohio transferred their shares to nine trustees, and in return received "trust certificates." The trustees had the power and the duty to administer the Company, while the stockholders received the profits. This Standard Oil Trust, then, by making similar arrangements with the stockholders of other corporations, became, for all practical purposes, a "corporation of corporations."

The "trust" concept itself was an ancient English legal device, commonly used in the law of estates to look after the interests of widows and minor children, and for charitable purposes. Since that idea had been elaborated by "equity" (a supplementary branch of

English law) instead of by the common law, the "trust" had been left more loosely defined, more flexible, and more informal than other legal entities.

The rudimentary document of 1879 (elaborated in the Trust Agreement of 1882) which first accomplished this purpose was devised by Rockefeller's ingenious lawyer, Samuel C. T. Dodd, whose life was itself an allegory of the American lawyer. Son of a carpenter in western Pennsylvania, Dodd had worked his way through Jefferson College and then studied law as an apprentice in a small-town law office. He was admitted to the bar in 1859, the year of Drake's first oil strike, which happened to be nearby. Foreseeing that fortunes would be made in oil, and that the oil magnates would require advice on how to organize their enterprises, Dodd studied the intricacies of the laws of corporations and of equity. At first he fought for the consumers and the small producers. As a delegate to the Pennsylvania Constitutional Convention of 1872–73, he had written into the constitution a clause forbidding rebates, a device which Rockefeller had been using to suppress competition. Then in 1881 he became a lawyer for the Standard Oil Company and moved to New York. In order to give his client Rockefeller the most detached and reliable legal advice, he actually refused to accept stock in the company, and he only received what, for the time, was a moderate salary. But he became one of the most ingenious legal metaphysicians of the age. His widely copied innovations eventually provided much of the essential legal framework for the growth of big business between the Civil War and the opening of the twentieth century.

These potent new legal devices made it possible to conduct the largest transactions in the deepest secrecy. And the very subtlety of the legal essences which lawyers were concocting actually allowed the powerful Go-Getters to keep their arrangements informal. For years John D. Rockefeller had been adept at hiding his consolidating activities. The men who were negotiating with the Standard Oil Company had been writing their letters under assumed names, and Rockefeller had cautioned them "not to tell their wives." The entities conjured up by Dodd and other lawyers were intended to emanate an aura of legality over all sorts of necessary transactions.

This wonderful combination of deviousness and informality was dramatized in the testimony of one of Rockefeller's closest associates before an investigating committee of the New York State Legislature in 1879. H. H. Rogers, who had pioneered in the oil industry by inventing a way of separating naphtha from crude oil and had become a leader in the affairs of the Standard Oil Trust, was on the stand.

Q. You said that substantially 95 percent. of the refiners were in the Standard Oil arrangement?

A. I said 90 to 95 per cent. I thought were in harmony.

Q. When you speak of their being in harmony with the Standard, what do you mean by that? . . .

A. If I am in harmony with my wife, I presume I am at peace with her, and am working with her.

Q. You are married to her, and you have a contract with her?

A. Yes, sir.

Q. Is that what you mean?

A. Well, some people live in harmony without being married.

Q. Without having a contract?

A. Yes; I have heard so.

Q. Now, which do you mean? Do you mean the people who are in the Standard arrangement, and are in harmony with it, are married to the Standard or in a state of freedom—celibacy?

A. Not necessarily, so long as they are happy.

Q. Is it the harmony that arises from a marriage contract? . . .

A. Well, not going too far into detail, I would say that the relations are very pleasant.

Q. But we want the detail; we want precisely what that harmony is, what it consists of, and what produces it.

A. Well, is it a railroad abuse, or is it an abuse to be in harmony with people?

Q. No; it is not an abuse to be in harmony; there are some kinds of harmony that the law considers conspiracy.

A. Well, I have heard so. . . . but it is a question in my mind whether it is a proper thing for me, even if there is no harm done by it, to divulge my business secrets.

It is not surprising that Rogers became the friend and financial counselor of Mark Twain.

For six years the Standard Oil Trust Agreement of 1882 was kept secret. But meanwhile other Go-Getters were following Dodd's example—forming an American Cotton Oil Trust (1884), a National Linseed Oil Trust (1885), and a Distillers and Cattle Feeders Trust (1887). When consumers and politicians became alarmed at the growth of monopolies, they passed the Sherman Antitrust Act in 1890 against "every contract, combination . . . or conspiracy in restraint of trade or commerce among the several states." But the Go-Getting builders of big enterprise, aided by their legal metaphysicians, were not to be stopped. Legislating against them was like passing a law against the wind. The decision of the Supreme Court of Ohio in 1892 that the Standard Oil Trust was an illegal combination, and that by entering the trust the Standard Oil Company of Ohio had exceeded its corporate powers, proved to be merely a challenge to lawyerly ingenuity.

When the trust was outlawed, Dodd devised the "holding company." This was a new kind of corporation whose corporate powers implicitly included the power to hold the shares of other companies. Finding that such a device was not outlawed by New Jersey's new General Incorporation Act, Dodd set up the Standard Oil Company of New Jersey in 1899 as a holding company. Others followed. The United States Steel Corporation, founded in 1901 under the guidance of an enterprising Illinois lawyer, Elbert H. Gary, on Dodd's holding company pattern, was the nation's first billion-dollar corporation.

Until the early years of the twentieth century the trend toward combination continued. By 1904 it was estimated that nearly half the nation's manufacturing capital was controlled by some three hundred trusts, or trustlike legal entities. Despite the multiplying laws against combination (notably the Sherman Antitrust Law of 1890 and the Clayton Act of 1914), and despite occasional epidemics of law enforcement, big business grew bigger and bigger. Louis D. Brandeis, the Boston lawyer who had made "scientific management" a national slogan by his attacks on the inefficient northeastern railroads, became the public's champion. And in 1913, in his exposé of the legal manipulations which gave enormous new power to a secretive few, he coined a powerful self-explanatory slogan: "Other people's money."

The investment trusts, Brandeis explained, not only dealt in the corporate securities of already existing corporations but actually manufactured stocks and shares out of thin air, to suit their own purposes. "Thus it was that J. P. Morgan & Company formed the Steel Trust, the Harvester Trust, and the Shipping Trust. And, adding the duties of undertaker to those of midwife, the investment bankers became, in times of corporate disaster, members of security holders' 'Protective Committees': then they participated as 'Reorganization managers' in the reincarnation of the unsuccessful corporation and ultimately became directors." Brandeis became the eloquent voice of a crusade against "the Curse of Bigness." Woodrow Wilson's New Freedom, shaped on Brandeis' pattern, was to be a freedom from trusts, which meant, too, a freedom from bigness.

The debate on trusts and on bigness continued through the twentieth century. In 1911 the Supreme Court of the United States declared that only "unreasonable" restraints of trade which did not serve the public interest were outlawed. Many economists and public-spirited lawyers gradually came around to the view that bigness itself was not a curse, or that in any event industrial America could not flourish except by vast and growing enterprises. Reformist efforts, instead, went mostly into devices to protect small investors and small businessmen. "Blue-sky laws" spread from Kansas, where they were enacted in 1911, to nearly all the other states—another American legal invention, this time to protect innocent citizens against unscrupulous promoters. These latter-day counterparts of the nineteenth-century Diamond Hoaxers located their El Dorados deep in the Dark Continent of Corporation Law where they had lured victims by promising them everything in the Great Blue Sky. After the stock-market crash of October 1929, popular demand grew for laws to control the securities market and so prevent frauds. In 1934, following a series of federal and state laws, the Securities Exchange Act created the Securities and Exchange Commission to oversee the stock market and to require stock promoters to publish verifiable facts. But no amount of government supervision could dispel the miasma of incomprehension which enshrouded the nation's great and crucial corporate enterprises from the view of the common citizen.

AFTER THE CIVIL WAR the corporation became the normal business entity in the United States, and not only for large enterprises. Even before 1900, two thirds of all manufactured products in the United States were made by corporations; by 1930 the figure was well over 90 percent, and corporations employed more than 90 percent of all persons employed in manufacture. And the trend continued toward the concentration of productive wealth and production in the largest corporations. The hundred largest manufacturing corporations, whose proportion of the nation's total manufacturing corporation assets was 40 percent in 1929, had increased their share to nearly 50 percent in 1962. The corporation form was reaching into all corners of American life, not only into manufacturing, merchandising, and construction but more and more even into personal services.

And the corporation had created a whole new world of property ownership. Nor merely for a few "capitalists" or financiers or bankers but for increasing millions of citizens. By 1929, shares of common stock were owned by about 1 million Americans, by 1959 the figure was 12.5 million, and by 1970 the total reached about 31 million. The United States was becoming a nation of citizen-stockholders. Owners of corporate stock were found among Americans of all occupations, all levels of education, in the city and on the countryside, and in all regions. More than ever before, "owners" were no longer managers. Even in 1929, the stockholder lists of the largest railroad (the Pennsylvania Railroad: 196,119 stockholders), the largest public utility (the American Telephone & Telegraph Company: 469,801 stockholders), and the largest industrial corporation (United States Steel: 182,585 stockholders) showed that the principal stockholder in each case owned less than 1 percent of the stock.

After A. A. Berle and Gardiner C. Means published their *Modern Corporation and Private Property* in 1932, it was a commonplace that in modern America the very experience of owning property had become something new—in one sense plainly more democratic, but at the same time more occult. In this "people's capitalism," more and more millions of citizens "owned" the means of production. But what did they own?

For most of these millions, their powers of ownership were clouded with ambiguity. And the very forms of "democracy" in the communities of stockholders made their ownership experience only more puzzling. Many stockholders, of course, considered their shares of stock simply a more speculative form of money in the bank. But control over the nation's biggest enterprises rested legally in the hands of the stockholders, and the voting power of stock ultimately controlled the destiny of American industry. On March 8, 1929, John D. Rockefeller, Jr., wrested control of the Standard Oil Company of Indiana from Colonel Stewart by rounding up the votes of 5,519,210 shares against Stewart's 2,954,986 shares. In 1955 at a dramatic meeting of Montgomery Ward stockholders in the Shriners' Temple in Chicago, Sewell Avery, after three decades, was deposed from management, and Ward's was given a new direction. Again and again proxy fights of corporate democracy made front-page news or were featured on television, while they baffled the millions. These Americans had acquired a share in a vast new institution, in what Berle and Means called "passive property."

But this was only half the story, and perhaps not the most characteristically American half. The American nation had thrived on ambiguity—the ambiguity of the landscape, the ambiguity of what it meant to be an American, the booster-vagueness of the line between present and future. When American stockholders owned powers of which they were uncertain or ignorant, property itself, once the most reassuringly concrete of man's possessions, had become a new source of ambiguity. By the late twentieth century the possibilities were only partly fathomed; the future of these invented entities was endless and unpredictable.

"Private" property was less private than ever before. So long as a company was owned by a few men, the responsibilities and the locale of ownership were apt to be discoverable. But when such a company went "public," conjuring itself into a corporation with millions of shares, its ownership was dispersed and diffused. Going "public" therefore could mean going "private." For size and numbers—the dimensions of democracy—had themselves become a resource of uncertainty and of secrecy.

47

New Penumbras of Property

WHEN HENRY FORD'S assembly line began turning out automobiles by the thousands, it was not hard to awaken the American's desire to own a car. But democratizing the automobile was not merely a question of engineering or of automotive and production design. The first Model T, produced in October 1909, could not be bought for less than $900. Even after improved production techniques and widening demand reduced the 1916 Model T Runabout to $345, the price strained the budget of the American millions. For the first time there was a mass-produced consumer's item that cost between 10 and 20 percent of a family's annual income.

To put the automobile in the hands of the American people required other social inventions no less novel than the assembly line. After the mid-1920's (except for the World War II years), the birth rate of new passenger cars generally exceeded that of persons, and before 1960 there were some sixty million passenger cars registered. This had been made possible by new institutions for selling and buying and financing which had developed even more rapidly than the techniques of automobile production. These would give a new ambiguity to ownership.

EVEN WHILE FORD was willing to try all sorts of new ways to produce automobiles by the millions, he stuck by his old-fashioned morality. He thought people should be thrifty and prudent, buying what they could pay for. From the beginning Ford opposed all sorts of time-payment plans. The only kind of consumer-financing arrangement he supported was not really a credit plan at all but, like the Christmas Clubs, was a scheme to encourage people to save up their money until they could pay for their Ford with cash. In 1923 he announced the Ford Weekly Purchasing Plan, under which the customer registered with a Ford dealer, paid at least $5 into a bank, and made weekly payments until he had accumulated the price of a Ford. Meanwhile he received interest, and could withdraw his money if he wished. As soon as he had saved the full price, the customer handed over the money and the dealer gave him his car. In the first year and a half of this plan, about 400,000 persons enrolled, of whom 131,000 (fewer than the number of Fords then regularly sold in one month) finally completed their payments and acquired their cars. Dealers, looking for quick turnover, lost interest in the scheme, and salesmen did not like to wait for their commissions. From the buyer's point of view the fatal flaw was that he had to wait until he had saved the full price before he could have his car.

What was needed was some scheme allowing people to "own" cars before they really owned them. The millions who could not "afford" to buy a car wanted cars anyway. If a costly new product like the automobile was speedily to become a common possession, Ford's old-fashioned morality, with its calculus of abstention, thrift, and foresight, would not do.

The "installment plan"—an Americanism that had first come into use for purchasing land—was the answer, and with the spread of the automobile it became a major American institution. Henry Ford himself clung to his ethic of thrift. But other enterprising Americans risked fortunes on schemes which revised the old notions of saving and owning; and they helped sell Fords by the millions. In 1923, more than three and a half million passenger cars were sold, nearly 80 percent on some kind of time-payment plan. The essence of these plans was that they enabled the buyer to possess and use a car as his own before he had saved the price.

A similar arrangement had long been familiar in the mortgage of land. But in all western European legal systems, the law of mortgages was extremely technical. It was hedged around with all sorts of safeguards for the lender's security against irresponsible borrowers, and with protections for borrowers against unreasonable lenders. But land was, of course, indestructible and immovable. The creditor always knew where to find his security, and the debtor could not abscond with the property. Real estate was a peculiar commodity. And until automobiles came off the assembly lines by the millions there was no other object of universal use so costly as to require a scheme for time payments.

After the mid-nineteenth century there had been some American experiments with installment plans in selling sewing machines and a few other expensive mass-produced consumers' items like stoves and pianos. These, however, were simply manufacturers' sales schemes which did not spread through the economy. But even before the automobile there were clearly new forces already at work which would prepare the way for a nation of installment buyers. Industry was using newly improved metals (especially iron and steel) to turn out millions of durable objects which nearly every citizen could imagine owning. Since a sewing machine could usually be reconditioned for the secondhand market, it did not seem imprudent for the retailer to allow a customer to use the machine while he paid for it. Moreover, with the rise of industry, the rhythm of wages was changed. The farmer's or farm laborer's flow of income was seasonal. But the factory worker, who was becoming a larger proportion of the population, received a regular flow of wages, and he was therefore in a better position year-round to keep up the weekly payments on an installment purchase.

Still, the transformation of installment buying into a dominant American institution did not come until the age of the automobile, and it was essentially the story of the automobile. The American expression "installment plan" was both more ambiguous and more optimistic than the English term "hire-purchase." The automobile was too costly an item for the dealer himself to subsidize credit purchases by his customers. In 1915, when the annual sales of passenger cars had reached nearly one million, some businessmen in Toledo, Ohio, organized a corporation, the Guaranty Securities Company, to finance the installment purchase of Willys-Overland cars. When the company was overwhelmed by the demand from the dealers in other makes, the company moved to New York, and announced to both car buyers and dealers that in the future Guaranty Securities would finance the installment purchase of twenty-one listed makes. Calling themselves "The First Organized National Service to Help Dealers Sell Automobiles," their advertisement in the *Saturday Evening Post* promised: "You Can Now Get Your Favorite Car on Time Payments." By 1917 there were 40 sizable automobile-sales-finance companies; in 1922 they numbered 1,000, and by 1925 the number of such companies exceeded 1,700. Automobile manufacturing now ranked first among the nation's industries.

The major car manufacturers began to set up their own financing firms. General Motors, seeing the success of the new Guaranty Securities Company, pioneered the field in 1919. Ford finally changed its policy in 1928 with its Universal Credit Corporation, which had the dual purpose of financing dealers in the stocking of Fords and Lincolns, and of helping customers to buy cars. The corporation required a dealer to advance only one tenth of the price of each car he stocked; and then financing by the corporation enabled the customer to take delivery of his car for a payment of only one third the purchase price, with a full year to pay the rest. Fire and theft insurance was included at no additional charge. Ford now began to include the cost of installment financing in their production figures, explaining that "this cost of credit is just as vital as the cost of any of the material that goes into the building of the automobile. It is in every sense a commodity."

The shift in point of view was dramatized by the fact that the old established institutions lagged behind. The commercial banks, which might have seemed the normal agencies for financing installment sales, resisted and even opposed this new style in owning. "The bankers," Alfred P. Sloan, Jr., of General Motors noted, ". . . must have had their minds on Barney Oldfield and Sunday outings in landaus along the boulevards then in existence; that is, they thought of the automobile as a sport and a pleasure, and not as the greatest revolution in transportation since the railway. They believed that the extension of consumer credit to the average man was too great a risk. Furthermore, they had a moral objection to financing a luxury, believing apparently that whatever fostered consumption must discourage thrift." In 1926 the American Bankers Association, still believing that automobiles ought to be bought for cash, advised its members not to finance installment purchases by their customers. But by the early 1930's the banks themselves had gone into the installment credit business, and before World War II they were energetically seeking customers for installment loans. The expression "down payment" entered the American language about this time. The new "credit unions" (also an Americanism) were cooperatives formed to make installment buying easier, and by the mid-1950's they had outstanding more than $1 billion of installment credit.

THE CONCENTRATION OF automobile manufacturing into a few firms encouraged the growth of installment credit. For in the early years of the century, new makes of automobiles had come and gone with the seasons. Up until 1950 about two thousand different makes of automobiles had been manufactured in the United States. In a market so uncertain, there was a good chance that by the time a particular car was paid for, the manufacturer might have gone out of business, making it impossible to secure parts and keep the car in running order. When the market had come to be dominated by General Motors, Ford, and Chrysler, as it was by the 1950's, the customer was buying an established brand, and this reduced the lender's risk.

Installment buying then became as reliable and as respectable as any other form of credit. During World War II, bankers feared that the millions of buyers who had entered the service would take advantage of the Soldiers' and Sailors' Civil Relief Act, which freed persons in the armed forces from the need to make installment payments in wartime. But actually few servicemen interrupted their payments or turned in their installment-purchased cars. And this remarkable fact established installment buying even more firmly after the war. Within less than a half-century (1919–63) General Motors' Time Payment Plan had financed nearly fifty million car buyers.

While the automobile provided the opportunity for the biggest pool of installment credit in the nation, installment buying became a more common way of acquiring the increasing number and variety of durable consumers goods. It was hardly an exaggeration to say that the American Standard of Living was bought on the installment plan. At the outbreak of World War II, the major appliances sold on the installment plan included radios and phonographs, refrigerators, gas and electric stoves, food mixers, water heaters, washing machines, ironing machines, and vacuum cleaners. Twenty-five years later the list for the general market had expanded to include air conditioners, dehumidifiers, power lawn mowers, food freezers, waste disposers, dishwashers, FM radios, television sets, wall ovens, counter cooking units, dryers, floor polishers, automatic coffee makers, blenders, hair dryers, saunas, exercising and reducing equipment, and electric knives. Easy installment plans were enlarging the market, too, for costly leisure items such as motor boats, vacation trailers, and European holidays. By the mid-'60's, the volume of installment credit was three times that of any other kind of consumer credit. More than one quarter of all American families were buying their automobiles on installment. Small down payments and easy terms made it possible for Americans to climb up the ladder of consumption, each year buying a higher-priced car. By 1970, two thirds of all new passenger cars and half of all used cars were being bought on the installment plan.

As installment buying became the normal way, the personal qualifications for securing installment credit became lower, or virtually disappeared. Almost anyone could buy a car on time. The down payment on a new car was often only one fifth or less of the purchase price, and it was not uncommon for the buyer to be given three years to pay the balance. As annual and semiannual model changes were featured, and as advertising campaigns touted the indispensable virtues of the latest model—by implication advertising the inadequacy of last year's model—the emotional attachment of many buyers to their last-year's or year-before-last's model meant less and less. But the lenders' risks were being justified by hidden high interest rates, by the accumulation of voluminous statistics on the resale value of cars of all makes and ages, and by information available from consumers-credit-rating agencies.

The American's fickle love affair with his late-model automobile was fraught by attenuated feelings. When he took delivery of his new car, usually he was by no means the owner, and he was tied to it by only a small investment. By the time he had paid for it, it was obsolete (or at least so he was told by the automobile manufacturers themselves). "Once in my life," Willy Loman, the hero of Arthur Miller's *Death of a Salesman* (1949), complained, "I would like to own something outright before it's broken! I'm always in a race with the junkyard! I just finished paying for the car and it's on its last legs. The refrigerator consumes belts like a goddam maniac. They time those things. They time them so when you finally paid for them, they're used up."

When installment credit became universal, the old thrift ethic had less meaning than ever. For the American Standard of Living had come to mean a habit of enjoying things before they were paid for. And that habit was becoming an industrial necessity.

BY THE MID-TWENTIETH CENTURY, the needs of the automobile had given birth to still another piece of business machinery which threatened to transform the very function of money. As the automobile had spread over the nation, competing gasoline companies had tried to attract motorists to their brands by offering credit. But gas-station credit had to be as mobile as the automobile. As a result, gasoline companies issued to their customers identifying cards which were valid in thousands of outlets throughout the country. This was the beginning of the "credit card"—an Americanism which proliferated into an institution and became a symbol of the American Standard of Living.

The gasoline credit card was then transformed into an all-purpose credit device. Beginning in 1950 with Diners' Club, followed by Carte Blanche and American Express, supplying credit cards and assuming the risk of credit-card accounts became a profitable new business. Incidentally exploiting the federal income-tax laws which required records and receipts of business expenses to justify deductions, these firms supplied a single itemized bill for a businessman's deductible expenses. The retailer was enticed into the scheme by the card-issuing firm's commitment to pay him promptly in cash, less a service fee varying from 2 to 5 percent, for all accounts charged against cards. And customers were induced to pay their annual membership fees (from $6 up) for the convenience of a ubiquitous charge account. Banks soon began issuing their own charge cards. By 1967 there were more than two million holders of the BankAmericard (issued by the Bank of America), and their annual billings amounted to $250 million.

The credit card in still another way democratized the world of business. Now the owner of even a single filling station or of a small restaurant could benefit from the advertising done by a vast national organization, and in addition have the advantages of its nationwide credit network. Credit cards became so universal a form of currency that thieves preferred credit cards to dollar bills. And the extreme in attenuating the personality of the consumer came when it was possible to steal and use another person's credit without his knowledge. Credit, once closely tied to the character, honor, and reputation of a particular person, one of a man's most precious possessions, was becoming a flimsy, plasticized, universal gadget. By 1971 the *Wall Street Journal* was facetiously recounting the troubles of a customer who insisted on paying cash. The structure of retailing was now planned around the charge account, and the cash customer had become the Vanishing American.

48

The Semi-Independent Businessman

"AND SO—TO THE FIRST STEP," instructed a businessman's handbook in 1966. "You don't write a letter or call the bank, or even add up your financial assets. The first step is reflective. . . . are *you* cut out for independent enterprise?" Just as the corporation offered new ways of owning the enormous machinery of production, and the millions of citizen-stockholders in America made European clichés of capitalism and socialism obsolete, so, too, there emerged a newly flourishing American institution—in a new way of "owning" the smaller units of business. This was the "franchise."

The franchise offered an opportunity to own, and yet not to own, to risk and yet to be cautious. It democratized business enterprise by offering a man with small capital and no experience access to the benefits of large capital, large-scale experiment, national advertising, and established reputations. It also democratized and leveled consumption by offering the same foods and drinks and services in all sorts of neighborhoods, across the country. It created new forms of dependence and new kinds of independence. It lessened the differences between times and places, between ways of selling and buying anything and anything else. It added new ambiguities to the relations among buyer and seller and maker. It attenuated the experience of things, and created another frontier of vagueness.

IN THE NINETEENTH CENTURY the spread of enterprises had generally required the risking of large capital by some organization at the center. The great retailing chains (for example, A & P and Woolworth) had owned their networks of stores. But in the twentieth century an American standard of living, which depended on national advertising, on national distribution, and on unending streams of novelty, also required new techniques of distribution and new modes of ownership.

The "franchise" was admirably suited to these needs. A franchise was the right granted by a manufacturer to a dealer to sell his product, or by the owner of a brand name, trademark, or business technique to someone to use it in his business. It covered a vast range of activities. It was the right of a Ford dealer to sell Fords, of a Pepsi-Cola bottler to make Pepsi, of a corner stand to make Dunkin' Donuts, or Colonel Sanders' Kentucky Fried Chicken, of a Midas Muffler Shop to install Midas mufflers. It included special techniques for washing cars, for providing secretaries, for collecting charge accounts, for rustproofing machinery, or for installing saunas. It covered almost all the products and services in the American Standard of Living, and in the 1970's it was reaching into more and more areas of life. By 1965 there were some 1,200 different companies granting franchise, with about 350,000 franchised outlets, totaling (among other items) more than one third of all retail sales in the United States.

While the franchise would be given a new, expansive form in the United States, it was, of course, an old idea. "Franchise" came from a Middle English word derived from the Old French word meaning "free," for the franchise gave freedom to do what would not otherwise have been permitted. In the Middle Ages a franchise usually was some monopoly or special privilege, such as the right to hold a fair or freedom from a tax or from the jurisdiction of a particular court, but in early modern times it came to mean "the suffrage," or the right to vote. The notion of granting a commercial benefit in return for a fee was ancient; and then, the patent granted to an inventor came to imply his right to grant franchises.

In twentieth-century America, "franchise" acquired a new meaning. Like so many other distinctively American institutions of mid-century, this, too, had come with the automobile. In order to market a mass-produced consumer item as expensive as the automobile, there had to be numerous far-flung outlets. Each dealer had to make a large investment; there had to be close cooperation between dealer and manufacturer. The automobile dealer's franchise, although created by a contract, was not merely a contract but was the framework for a continuing relationship. For example, the Chrysler Corporation would agree to supply a dealer with automobiles and gave him the exclusive right to sell new Chryslers in his area. In return the dealer agreed to market these automobiles, to service old and new Chryslers, and to keep a stock of parts. While the agreement could be canceled after due notice on either side, there were strong incentives on both sides to preserve the relationship. If the dealer was successful he had a large and increasing investment in good will, in the brand name, and in the know-how of selling and servicing a particular make. The manufacturer on his side had a desire to keep uninterrupted the flow of his cars to buyers in that area.

As the institution of the annual model developed, the need for the franchise became greater than ever. This year's cars were best sold by dealers well acquainted with last year's model; the make was not likely to be bought unless a buyer could continue to count on a local dealer for parts, even for older models. The enormous sale of trade-in used cars (a by-product of the annual model) made a stable dealer arrangement more than ever desired by both manufacturer and dealer. Better than any other known arrangement, the franchise could provide and maintain a national network of qualified, well-stocked, and profitable sales outlets for automobiles.

By 1911 the franchise had become the industry's standard system of distribution. And within a decade the automobile franchise had become a novel network of shared management and semi-management. In mid-century the leading automobile manufacturers were requiring their dealers to start with a capital of about $100,000. Both manufacturer and dealer depended on the realities and images of national advertising, both depended on the continuous flow of the product off the assembly lines. And the community of their relationship became so intimate, so complicated, and so subtle that by the 1960's General Motors, influenced by the Automobile Dealers Day in Court Act (1956), had established a special administrative board of review to insure full and fair consideration of issues arising out of franchise contracts. The automobile had created a whole new world of semi-independent businessmen.

Automobiles needed "filling stations" (an Americanism first recorded about 1921) and oil companies wanted to sell their product to the millions of car owners. To provide numerous outlets on the highways for their brand of gasoline, the oil companies used the franchise.

The filling station quickly became an American institution. Buying a franchise for a station to sell Standard Oil, Gulf, Shell, Mobil, or some other brand required only a small capital, yet instantly provided the benefits of national advertising, at the same time that it put a man "in business for himself." By 1970 there were more than two hundred thousand gasoline service stations in the nation (more than the total number of motor vehicles in 1910), and they averaged fewer than three paid employees in each. When a young man asked Sinclair Lewis how he could gather the experience to become a great American novelist, Lewis advised him to run a filling station.

THE FRANCHISING INSTITUTION soon reached out to all kinds of activities everywhere, spawning endless novelties, speedy innovations, and ambiguous proprietorships. The multiplication of cosmetics, patent medicines, and countless new national-brand health needs brought into being the Rexall-franchised stores. The rise of national-brand soft drinks—Coca-Cola, Seven Up, and others—produced hundreds of local bottling franchises.

A classic success story was the franchising career of "Mister Donut." When Harry Winokur, an accountant, suffered an eye accident which forced him to seek a new occupation, he opened a little doughnut store in Revere, Massachusetts. In addition to the old standard doughnut, he offered forty other varieties of every conceivable flavor. When that store flourished, within a year he added four more stores, and then he set out to build a chain. Not having the needed capital, he turned to franchising, hoping to make his money by selling the ingredients and the know-how to franchisees. Winokur would bring a prospective franchisee to one of his original stores in Massachusetts where he trained him in doughnut making and store management. He then went to great lengths to find a good location for each franchised store, arranged the lease, and supervised the building of a Mister Donut shop of standard design. He aimed to make it possible for the franchisee to pay off Winokur's own investment from the operating profits within three years, and that became the pattern. By 1968 there were over two hundred franchised Mister Donut shops in forty States, and the company was planning for fifty new franchises each year. Franchisees included a miscellany of mobile Americans—a former scrap-metal dealer, a bakery-route salesman, a coffee grower who had lived in Guatemala, a retired Marine Corps Air Force officer who had suffered a heart attack which prevented him from flying.

The range of the franchising business was an index to the explosive novelty of American life. When an unemployed paperhanger in Hammond, Indiana, invented a continuous intermittent freezer (a machine that could both freeze and dispense ice cream), he sold the rights in 1939 to a manufacturer of ice-cream mixes who opened a drive-in in Moline, Illinois, called "Dairy Queen"; a Moline business-man bought franchising rights for five states, and by 1969 the nation was sprinkled with 3,750 "Dairy Queens." In 1949 a New Yorker who was annoyed by dry-cleaning delays developed a process by which clothes could be dry-cleaned in an hour; within twenty years there were 2,500 "One Hour Martinizing" shops in forty-eight states.

During the postwar automobile boom a bright young Chicagoan observed in 1950 that there was no pleasant or convenient way of replacing auto parts: repair garages were grimy, slow, and unreliable. He designed and organized franchised shops where a car owner could sit in an attractively decorated interior and watch his children play in a playpen while the parts of his car were promptly replaced. He started with the muffler, and within twelve years there were 460 franchised shops for Midas Mufflers. The new gold-colored mufflers were installed while-you-wait in fifteen minutes. "We took this lowly being, the muffler," Gordon Sherman explained, "and elevated it with romantic flair into an almost religious object." "Can a Nice Guy Succeed in Business?" read his advertisement in the *Saturday Review of Literature.* "Or How to Overcome the Inverse Relationship between Amount of Education and Yearly Income." Soon Midas Muffler franchises were being operated by ex-rabbis, former teach-ers, retired Army officers, and many ex-academics.

A spectacular franchising success was McDonald's Hamburgers, which by 1972 ranked second of all food-service operations in the United States, with more than one thousand franchisees and a gross annual business of over $300 million. McDonald's exploited the ap-peal of the large consumption community at each outlet by advertis-ing how many billions of hamburgers they had sold. The gargantuan enterprise had begun only in 1954 when Ray Kroc, who was selling milk-shake mixers to a chain of seven drive-ins owned by the McDon-ald brothers, bought their franchise rights.

The franchise provided the speediest means ever devised for the inventor, the manufacturer, the promoter, the man with know-how to diffuse his product or his service over a continent-nation. The Go-Getter at the center needed a good idea and considerable organ-izing ability, but he required relatively little capital. After the intro-duction of the business corporation, the franchise was the most im-portant invention for collecting the resources of many small investors into a large enterprise. In the mid-twentieth century this newly democratized form of nationwide business widened and has-tened the stream of novelty pouring into daily life.

For the citizen with little or no capital who wanted to be his own boss it offered a new opportunity for quasi-independence. "The franchisee is his own boss," a handbook explained, "but he looks to the parent company, the franchisor, for every form of assistance imaginable, from cash loans or credit to designing, building, staffing, promoting, and publicizing the business. He looks for research and new-product ideas or new ways to make old products more profitable. Most of all, he looks for training to learn the business and to operate profitably after the business is established." A man with little education and no business experience could quickly secure specialized training along with the benefits of national advertising and the fruits of the experience of thousands. Franchising was promoted by the United States Department of Commerce (1966) as a ladder of opportunity and a means for "equal opportunity in business."

In a world of franchisees, the American consumer's buying opportunities and buying experience were transformed. Neighborhood shops, "Mom and Pop" enterprises (in the jargon of the trade), were displaced by outlets of national franchises. The distinctive local hangout was displaced by an Orange Julius or McDonald's Hamburgers; where the corner garage had stood, there was now a Western Auto Supply or a Midas Muffler Parlor. Instead of haphazard personal enterprise, the American consumer found standardized, market-tested, nationally advertised brands of all products and services. He became the beneficiary, as he was the target, of the most sophisticated market research, product research, and sales know-how. His neighborhood world was flattened into the national consuming landscape. He patronized the highway outlet of a Dunkin' Donut or Colonel Sanders' Kentucky Fried Chicken because he could be sure of what he would get. Wherever he traveled across the continent, he felt a new assurance that he would be at home, and somehow in the same place. By using the guide to a chain of franchised motels—the Holiday Inns, Quality Courts, Howard Johnsons, Ramada Inns, or any of a dozen others—when he stopped for the night he would know where to find the ice maker, the luggage rack, the TV set, he would recognize the cellophane wrapping on the drinking glass, the paper festoon on the toilet seat, whether he was in Bangor, Maine, in Peoria, Illinois, or in Corvallis, Oregon. Nationwide franchises made consuming, anywhere in the U.S.A., into a new kind of repeatable experience.

The American landscape became a world of product clichés. Consuming itself began to have some of the handy but unsurprising quality of the cliché in language. Everything sold for a purpose served its purpose well, and sometimes in a surprising new way. But when the surprise itself became standardized that, too, lost much of its charm. Consuming, like the common discourse of package words, became a perfunctory, flavorless act and lost its nuances.

The slogan of franchise-filled America could have been: Does he or doesn't he? Is he or isn't he? More and more products and services were offered by semi-independent businessmen. While consumers could be more confident than ever of the standard quality of what they bought, they were haunted by a new puzzlement about *whose* product it was. Who, if anyone, was really responsible in case what they bought wasn't what it was supposed to be? "Are you the owner or the manager?"

49
From Packing to Packaging: The New Strategy of Desire

IN THE UNITED STATES by the early twentieth century, all sorts of objects were being offered in newly attractive garb—creating a democracy of things. In the Old World, even after the industrial age had arrived, only expensive items were housed in their own box or elegantly wrapped. A watch or a jewel would be presented in a carefully crafted container, but the notion that a pound of sugar or a dozen crackers should be encased and offered for purchase in specially designed, attractive materials seemed outlandish. Essential to the American Standard of Living were new techniques for clothing objects to make them appealing advertisements for themselves. Industries spent fortunes improving the sales garb of inexpensive objects of daily consumption—a pack of cigarettes or a can of soup.

Just as the rise of factory-made clothing and the new American democracy of clothing leveled people and made it increasingly difficult to distinguish a man's occupation, his bank account, or the status of his family by what he wore, so it was with packaging. Here was a new way of democratizing objects, of leveling and assimilating their appearance. By looking at a newly designed machine-made package, it was hard to tell the quality of the inside object, and sometimes hard to tell even what the object was.

Packaging, which by the mid-twentieth century dominated the consciousness of the American consumer, had entered the lives of Americans unheralded and unchronicled for the very reasons which made it distinctive. The rise of packaging was a parable of the unno-

ticed, multiplex, anonymous sources of innovation. Packaging overcast experience with yet another pall of ambiguity and became the
dominant new fact of everyday epistemology. Packaging fuzzied the
edges of things, making it hard to know where the desired physical
object ended and where its environment began.

PACKING WAS, of course, as old as the making and moving of
things. "To pack" meant "to put into a receptacle for transporting or
storing." And the purpose of packing was to keep a thing safe and
secure, to make it portable or preservable. The better a thing was
packed, the less apt it was to be damaged, the farther it could travel,
the longer it could be stored. Packing served transportation. It is not
surprising, then, that in the nineteenth century the United States
pioneered in techniques and materials of packing. The American
factories that aimed to serve a national or international market, the
department stores that drew their merchandise from all over, and
the mail-order houses that shipped their goods to remote parts—all
these required secure and durable ways of shipping.

The American distances, whether served by wagons, railways, automobiles, or airplanes, posed problems of preparing and encasing
goods which were never faced by makers for a local market. Refrigerator cars and canning were, of course, ways of packing goods for
markets distant in time or space. Americans also developed other
materials and machinery for moving their products safely around the
world. Before the Civil War, flour was shipped in cotton sacks (which
found many other uses on the farm), for no one had yet made a paper
bag that could do the job. But when the war stopped the supply of
cotton for flour millers, a papermaker in upstate New York produced
a paper bag sturdy enough to carry fifty pounds of flour. By 1875,
American machinery for making metal boxes was being exported to
Britain. But during these years, the design of a parcel was still dominated by the needs of shipping and storage. Containers were large
and protective, suitable for the rural housewife's larder or for the
floor of the country store.

Packaging (as it displaced *packing*) created whole new vistas for
the consumer. For while packing was designed to transport and to
preserve, packaging was designed to *sell*. Early in the twentieth
century, "to package" had entered the American language as a verb.
The story of packaging is the story of all the new things that Americans produced for sale. Packaging was a by-product of new American
ways of selling, and the package itself became a new, and distinctively American, kind of salesman.

The wrapping of objects, naturally enough, had begun with the making of objects for sale. Gourds and banana leaves and baskets are still used in primitive markets. In western Europe in the days before mass production, wrapping itself was mostly a form of packing, designed to help the individual buyer carry home something he had bought. The package had not yet become part of the product for sale. There were a few exceptions. In the sixteenth century, German papermakers made wrappers for their own products. In the seventeenth century, quack medicines were sold in London in paper wrappers embellished with the signature of the inventor and an impressive coat of arms, and some tobacconists were using printed wrappers. Occasionally a wine bottle would bear the initialed seal of the tavern owner. But it was common in those days for a tea merchant's advertisement to remind customers to "bring a convenient Box." During the eighteenth century there was more packing of groceries, drugs, and cosmetics in forms convenient for the consumer. But still wrapping and labeling were less for sales appeal than for identification.

One reason for the slow progress of packaging was the scarcity of paper. In the seventeenth century the misjudgments of book publishers helped supply the lack. In those days it was not uncommon for a London bookseller to stock his books in the form of the unfolded, unbound printed sheets. When a customer wanted a book, the sheets would be put together, folded, and bound to his taste. The London bookseller's stock of sheets that remained unsold as books could then readily be sold for papers to grocers and apothecaries; a theological tract that could not elevate the mind would at least serve to wrap potatoes. In the early nineteenth century these indignities became less common with the invention of papermaking machinery. Until then, paper had been made by hand, sheet by sheet, but in 1807 the Fourdrinier brothers in London patented a machine for making paper in continuous rolls. Within ten years Thomas Gilpin, using his own secret invention, produced in Delaware the first American machine-made paper, and others followed. Soon there were American machines that could turn out paper at the rate of forty-five feet per minute. New quick-drying machines made production independent of the weather, and every stage was speeded up. By 1830 the United States had become the greatest paper-producing and the greatest paper-consuming country in the world, and remained so.

With better machinery and increasing demand, there was a renewed search for raw materials to make paper cheaper and in larger quantity. The traditional European way of making paper required rags, and in colonial America the supply of rags had been especially scarce. After the middle of the seventeenth century, when people began papering their walls for decoration, the supply of rags became more inadequate than ever. Not until the early nineteenth century was paper made either from straw or wood pulp; by 1890 nearly all paper was being made from wood pulp. Then the paper supply was further increased by new ways of de-inking printed paper so that it could be re-pulped. This use of wood pulp for paper had the effect of denuding large tracts of the continent, transforming the beauties of primitive forests into tundras of unread newspapers. By 1934 a single machine operated by four men could turn out twenty tons of wood pulp a day. About this time a Georgia chemist discovered a new sulfate process by which Southern pine could be used for paper, and when this process was applied to other timbers it drastically reduced the cost of paper, besides providing a profitable use for Southern wastelands.

In the twentieth century the simplest and quickest form of packaging for the American shopper was, of course, the paper bag. But not until the mid-nineteenth century had ready-made paper bags come onto the market; an enterprising Englishman began to travel the English countryside peddling his handmade bags to grocers. In 1852 a primitive paper-bag-making machine was operating in Bethlehem, Pennsylvania. By 1860 an ingenious mechanic, Charles Hill Morgan, had designed a machine for making bags which finally showed commercial possibilities and which he used in his paper-bag factory in Philadelphia. By the 1870's Americans were in the business of selling bag-making machines.

American careers once again were to be made from commodities that had not even existed a half-century before. Luther Childs Crowell, the inventive son of a New England sea captain, was led somehow by his experiments with "aerial machines" (that never flew) to design a superior machine to make paper bags, for which he received a patent in 1867. A few years later he invented the square-bottomed paper bag (still used in the late twentieth century) and a machine for its manufacture. Following the pattern of other major innovations, his paper-bag patent was the subject of long and bitter litigation.

While paper bags were mostly for the customer's convenience, the new large-scale merchandisers were looking for new ways to speed their sales. A salesman could be making a second sale in the time it took to wrap a parcel in paper and twine. To cover their high overhead and make a profit, department stores needed to make volume sales to the big-city crowds who were in a hurry. It is not surprising, then, that soon after the Civil War, New York bag makers were beginning to prosper by selling their product to Macy's, Lord & Taylor, and other department stores. The bags themselves, when imprinted with the store's name, became advertisements. In 1889 the economist David Ames Wells, an enthusiast for American efficiency and himself the inventor of a device for folding paper on power presses, observed quite seriously that the cheap paper bag had been the most effective innovation during the preceding decade in speeding up American retail sales, especially the sale of groceries. By Wells's time, American factories each week were turning out millions of paper bags, which had begun to become standard equipment for the American retailer.

BUT EVEN the improved paper bag was not versatile enough for all the tasks of packaging required by the novel mass-produced products of American factories. There was a need, too, for boxes of all shapes and sizes. And these would have to be machine-made, easy to store, easy to ship, and sturdy in use.

In England the early box makers were more akin to luggage manufacturers than to packagers. They made boxes to sell empty, for any use the buyer wished. The boxes were made by hand, mostly from wood, heavy paper, or cardboard. Since there was no easy way to make clean creases or sharp corners, many boxes were made round or oval, hand-shaped around a wooden form. But these products could not satisfy modern factory needs, because the containers, when empty, consumed so much space. The most important packaging inventions in the nineteenth century, after the flat-bottomed paper bag, were to be a more compact kind of box and the machine for its manufacture. If a way could only be found of making a box that would remain flat until it was filled with the product, factories could buy boxes in large numbers and stack them in a small space until needed. But to make folding boxes inexpensively there had to be a machine that would cut and crease cardboard.

By mid-century a Boston firm which had been making jewelers' boxes developed a machine that would crease and cut wood for boxes. The Dennisons had already been making "set-up" boxes, which the jeweler could unfold to display his merchandise on the counter or in a show window. But paper cartons were still made in the same laborious way, shaped one at a time by hand around wooden forms.

The crucial invention was made by Robert Gair, a clever Scotsman who had immigrated to New York City at the age of fourteen. After a tour in the Union Army, Gair set up a factory for paper bags, selling his product to department stores and other big-city shops. He enlisted in his firm the man who during the war had devised a sturdy paper bag for flour. Gair's catalogue soon offered a variety of bags for flour and buckwheat, grocers' bags, seed bags, and other bags imprinted with the merchant's name. But in his factory, bags were still made by hand in the laborious old way.

Gair saw that if cardboard cartons could be made quickly and cheaply in a form easy to store and easy to use, they would vastly enlarge the market for packaging. Then, in April 1879, one of Gair's workers who was tending a printing press for seed bags had carelessly allowed a metal rule on the press to slip up so that the paper was not only printed but actually cut. This gave Gair the clue that he needed. He designed a multiple die which used a sharp metal rule set high to cut the cardboard while it used blunt rules set lower to do the creasing. From this simple invention came the machine-made folding box. On a secondhand press which Gair bought for $30, he fitted the cutting and creasing rules; this paper-box machine could cut and crease 750 sheets an hour, each sheet providing ten carton blanks, amounting to an hourly production of 7,500 cartons.

Before the end of the nineteenth century there were nearly a thousand patents related to folding boxes and their machines. American machines to make cartons helped popularize the folding box in England. In 1898, Wills' Three Castles cigarettes were being packed in machine-made folding cartons (three million a week) from a machine that was made in Philadelphia. Folding cartons, run off the presses by the millions, provided a versatile new form of packaging. By the second decade of the twentieth century these cartons were being made for candles, candy, oats, breakfast foods, cookies, and almost every other machine-made product. And the packagers had already begun to play a role in manufacturing and advertising. When someone from the National Biscuit Company in New York came to Robert Gair's son and told him that they were planning a new, nationally advertised product, he said, "You need a name." Uneeda Biscuits were the result. These words also spelled the end of the cracker barrel.

The rise of American packaging produced a host of packages of new and ingenious design. Until 1841 such collapsible packaging as there was had been made from animal bladders. Then an American artist patented a collapsible metal tube for artists' colors, and in 1870 there appeared the first American tube-making machinery. By 1892 a Connecticut dentist was putting up toothpaste in tubes, and soon afterward, Colgate's pioneered in the large-scale marketing of toothpaste in this form. By 1912 Mennen's took the lead with tubes to market shaving cream, and this new convenience—the death of the shaving mug!—must have had something to do with the changing fashion of men's faces in the following years. The very first Mennen shaving-cream tube showed a man with a clean-shaven chin.

Packages themselves became an important new commodity, and the packaging industry grew. Manufacturers designed closures specially adapted to powder, paste, or liquid, and they designed easy-dispensing caps, measuring caps, and containers in all shapes and sizes. These were accompanied by improvements in lithography, which reduced the cost of reproducing pictures on boxes and labels, and by new ways of printing on wood, glass, steel, tin, and aluminum. Cellophane, invented by a Swiss chemist in 1912, was developed and first manufactured by a French firm that had been making rayon, and then was commercially produced in the United States by DuPont in 1924.

The endless possibilities of packaging were symbolized in the mid-twentieth century by "aerosol." This Americanism, made up from "aero" + "solution," which appeared in dictionaries in the late 1960's, described a push-button package. Although available before World War II, at first these packages were heavy and costly and were used mainly for insect repellents. It took a decade to perfect this can into a safe, inexpensive, light-weight device that properly combined the propellant which forced the product out of the pack, with the product itself. By 1955, about 240 million aerosols were produced annually for non-food purposes alone; by 1956 the figure was 320 million. The use of aerosols was spreading, and soon left an indelible public mark in the form of graffiti applied with aerosol paint cans. By the 1960's, packaging in the United States, valued at more than $20 billion a year, had become a major American industry.

BUT PACKAGING WAS more than merely another industry. It pervaded American life and transformed the American's experience of nearly all the objects which he bought or wanted to buy or thought he wanted. It brought one of the most manifold and least noticed revolutions in the common experience.

At first many of the consequences of packaging were of a familiar sort: cleanliness, convenience, and economy. As late as 1925 the American Sugar Refining Company was urging on its wholesale dealers the advantages of packaged, as against bulk, sugar:

> Do you know that it takes a man about an hour and three-quarters to weigh out a 350-pound barrel of granulated sugar in five-pound paper bags; that a man averages only about 69 five-pound bags when he weighs out a 350-pound barrel; that the five pounds lost by spillage and down-weight represent 1.4 per cent of the cost price of the sugar; that, in addition to sugar wasted, bags, twine and labor amount to about forty cents added to the cost per cwt. of the sugar; and—that 350 pounds of Domino Package Sugars mean 350 pounds sold with a profit on every pound; that no time is lost and no material or sugar wasted; that, therefore, a retailer makes more money per pound when he sells Domino Package Sugars; and that he will appreciate your pointing out these facts to him, thereby enabling him to make more money on sugar. . . .

Now, if the grocer must scoop his sugar, weigh it, wrap it, tie it, give downweight, lose some by spillage—then we acknowledge that the margin of profit is not worth the trouble. And that is why for years we have been urging the grocery trade to handle Domino Package Sugars. With this line you eliminate all handling costs, all expense, all losses. On that basis, 200 per cent profit is practically clear. Why not try it out?

But this was still a novel idea for the grocer. And in 1928 only 10 percent of household sugar was sold in package form.

Salt became a new, more profitable, item for the grocer. Before the age of packaging, salt was packed in cotton bags, retailing at from two to five cents each. The producer's profit margin was so narrow that it actually depended on the fluctuation in the price of cotton. Since the cotton bag gave no more protection against moisture than an ordinary salt shaker, much of the contents of a bag of salt might be unusable in humid weather or by the time the housewife needed it. When producers began marketing salt in convenient square wax-wrapped cartons or in round cartons with aluminum spouts, they found that housewives were willing to pay three or four times the price for the same quantity. When the Morton Salt Company made "When it rains it pours" into a household phrase, they were really selling a new kind of package.

But packaging was not merely a new way for the more profitable retailing of old products. Packaging created new uses, and opened wider markets, with the result that products themselves were transformed. Before 1900, tea was sold in bulk by the grocer, and perfume was ladled out by the druggist for each customer from his large bottle into smaller, plain bottles. Within two decades the tea bag had made it possible to make tea where there was no teapot, and luxury packaging transformed perfume into a gift parcel and a bedroom ornament. Matches, which formerly were items for the kitchen or the fireplace, or which had to be carried about the person in a matchsafe, were now packaged into compact books of matches and became a new advertising medium. Ice cream, too, became a newly portable commodity when it was put up in an edible package, like the ice-cream cone (an Americanism first recorded in 1909) or the Eskimo Pie (an American trade name introduced in 1921).

The growth of American mass-merchandising, along with the rise of national advertising and national branding, offered new opportunities for the ubiquitous selling of small quantities of all sorts of things. Packaging opened a new market for candy. Early in the twentieth century candy had been sold only at confectioners' and in few other stores, by the half-pound, pound, two-pound or five-pound box, or in bulk. It was messy and inconvenient to carry about just a few pieces. Then, in the 1920's, small packages of candy began to be displayed in drugstores, cigar stores, newsstands, grocery stores, and scores of other even more unlikely places, tempting people to pick up a nickel "candy bar" (an American expression, first recorded in print in 1943) for their pocket or desk drawer. One result was that even while the number of confectionary stores in the United States declined quite steadily, from some 63,000 in 1929 to fewer than 14,000 forty years later, during these years the opportunities for buying and consuming candy were becoming more widespread than ever. "Hershey," "Baby Ruth," "Oh Henry!," and "Mars" became colloquial expressions for units of candy—the products of small-unit packaging. The same story could be told of the spreading consumption of potato chips, nuts, and scores of other foods, newly distributed in small packages.

Some things could not have had a wide market at all without speedier, more attractive and more functional packaging. When two young businessmen bought the Mint Products company that produced Life Savers, the little round mints with the hole were packed in sturdy cardboard cartons that were held together by paste. After a few weeks on the dealer's shelf these Life Savers would lose their mint flavor and they absorbed the flavor of the paste. The new management at Life Savers discarded the old boxes and instead used tin foil, which did not absorb the flavor, which was easily sealed again after one mint was removed, and which looked attractive on the counter. Cigarettes and chewing gum too could hardly have found their universal market without machine-made packages. By the mid-1920's a single automatic wrapping machine could turn out 50 cigarette packages a minute. A single chewing-gum packaging machine wrapped gum in foil at the rate of 400 sticks a minute, 200 boxes (twenty packages per box) each hour, or 1,800 packages a day.

The new packaging machinery helped modify retailing in still another way, by providing contents to fill the newly perfected vending machines. Before the mid-twentieth century, in American everyday parlance the word "vendor" no longer meant a *person* who sold but "a machine that dispenses goods upon the deposit of a coin or coins." These new ways of merchandising gave a new importance to packaging and made new demands of the package. Packaging became an art of selling-without-salesmen. And after the rise of advertising itself, nothing did more to contribute to the decline of salesmanship than the improved technology of packaging.

By the 1950's, "packaging engineering" had become a new American occupation: larger firms had their own specialized staffs and smaller firms consulted packaging engineers. By the late 1960's, consumer products accounted for 70 percent of all packaging materials. Without anyone having intended it, and when few even noticed, everyone had become increasingly dependent on packaging. Businessmen could well say, "No packaging, no brands—no brands, no business."

THE PACKAGING REVOLUTION, like other transformations of American experience, came rapidly—within a third of a century. As late as 1920, few of the housewife's purchases were packaged. Of common household groceries, packaged goods then included only a small proportion of sugar, salt, rice, flour, tea, or coffee. The unpackaged products were seldom sold under brand names. But the growth of national advertising and national brands (which had been both a cause and an effect of department stores, five-and-tens, chain stores, and the earliest self-service stores) produced still another new American institution: the supermarket. Dictionaries defined this new Americanism as "a large retail market that sells food and other household goods and that is usually operated on a self-service, cash-and-carry basis." But by mid-century, merchandising specialists were defining a supermarket as a store that did at least $1 million of business annually.

While the self-service grocery store, as we have seen, had been pioneered before World War I by Piggly Wiggly and others, the supermarket became increasingly important only after World War II. Giving a smaller role than ever to the salesman, it was preeminently a place of self-service. The widening spectacle of competing items and competing brands displayed to the customer on open shelves gave the package a newly seductive power.

During World War I, when labor was scarce, the large grocery markets had turned to self-service, and the customer was provided a basket to carry the purchases he selected off the shelves. One of the first supermarkets, San Francisco's Crystal Palace, opened in 1923 in a large steel-frame building on the site of a former baseball diamond and circus ground with 68,000 square feet of selling area and parking for 4,350 cars (one hour free). Offering food, drugs, tobacco, liquor (after 1934), jewelry, a barber shop, a beauty parlor, and a cleaning establishment, the store by 1937 had set sales records of 51,000 pounds of sugar in one hour, 5 carloads of eggs in a month; in a single year it sold 200 tons of lemons, 250 tons of oranges, and 300 tons of apples. By this time other supermarkets were beginning to show comparable sales.

An important accessory of the supermarket, which increased sales by making it easier for the customer to give in to his purchasing temptations, was the shopping cart. An employee of a Houston grocery store in the early 1920's removed the handle from a toy express wagon, fastened a shopping basket on the wagon, and then made the front wheels stationary so that the customer could guide the cart by the basket handle. By the later 1930's, similar carts were being manufactured for sale to grocery-store owners. In the 1950's, shopping carts came into use in self-service hardware stores, appliance stores, and discount department stores.

Department stores and supermarkets brought together many kinds of merchandise under one roof. During World War II the scarcity of certain goods had increased this tendency toward "scrambled" merchandising. When drugstores could not get some of their usual items, they stocked small appliances, food, luggage, and toys, while supermarkets carried clothing, kitchenware, hardware, drugs, and cosmetics, and department stores branched out into food, liquor and a variety of new services. The parking problem, more acute every year, made customers eager for "one-stop" or "one-parking" shopping.

While the differences between one kind of shop and another were dissolved, so too were the distinctions between shopping and non-shopping hours. As early as 1931, a Long Island supermarket was advertising, "Come in your Lincoln, Come in your Ford, Come with the Baby Carriage. Come with any old thing but come, come, come! Fri. 9 P.M., Sat. 10 P.M." Supermarkets, and then self-service hardware and department stores, and discount stores began to stay open nightly, including Sundays.

The increasing size of the stores, the increasing number of items, the increasing competition for the buyer's attention by items arrayed so the buyer could reach them for himself, made packaging into a newly sophisticated and self-conscious industry. The salesman was nowhere to be seen. The housewife-customer, equipped with a shopping cart, wandered without guidance and often without clear purpose through a wilderness of packages. Not unless she had trouble finding some particular item did she get advice or assistance (except from a fellow customer) until she reached the check-out counter. She had to make decisions for herself, based on her preferences for certain brands or on the appearance and appeal of the packages on the shelf. Once again, the American lived the public-private paradox. The flood of goods into these enormous channels of merchandising pushed the citizen-consumer back on himself. The decision to buy or not to buy had become more private than ever before.

The overwhelming new power of packaging, then, came from self-service. In 1928 the pioneer book, *Packages That Sell*, by Richard B. Franken and Carroll B. Larrabee, foreshadowed the new emphasis. "The package," they said, "should be merchandised . . . in the same way that the product is merchandised." This was the final stage in the attenuation of things. For while every object had a different purpose—to brush teeth, to comb hair, to please the palate, or whatever else—all packaging shared one purpose, namely *to sell*. Whatever the content of the package, whatever its other purposes, every package was shaped somehow toward that same end. And the new merchandising tended to put every package in competition with every other.

However well any package might protect or preserve its content, it failed if it did not sell. Therefore the important, the substantial and essential qualities of a package were the qualities that forced the reluctant or indifferent buyer to buy. From this new point of view, color, size, shape, material, and function had but one test for all packages: What impression did the package make on the prospective customer?

The important size of a package, for example, was its *apparent* size. Using the so-called Order-of-Merit Method, which an American psychologist, James McKeen Cattell, had used in 1902 to measure the relative brightness of two hundred shades of gray, Franken and Larrabee proposed a way to "obtain a quantitative measurement of a qualitative or subjective thing. In packaging this method will tell us beforehand which of a series of packages will help stimulate the sale of the product to the greatest extent, and will thus enable us to formulate principles upon which to build the future packages." As an illustration they showed, from the results of tests of consumer preference, why a certain shape of 10-ounce can was the best package for codfish cakes. "The apparent size of objects," they explained, "depends somewhat on their shape. . . . the flat 10-ounce can . . . was selected for Gorton-Pew's Ready-to-Fry Codfish Cakes because it looked larger than the tall can . . . although both cans had the same cubic capacity."

NOW THE PACKAGE—as well as, or instead of, the product—was what was advertised. From a sampling study of large-circulation general magazines, Franken and Larrabee observed that while in 1900 only 7 percent of the advertisements of packaged products showed a picture of the package, by 1925 the proportion had reached 35 percent and was going up. "The primary function of advertising is to create a desire in the consumer's mind to buy a product. This desire, once created, must be carried to the point of sale. . . . Best of all . . . is to picture the package in the advertisement. Even if only a favorable impression has been created, without the desire to buy, the sight of the actual package may turn this impression into active desire on the part of the consumer." In stores, then, it was more important to display the distinctive brand-named carton than the usable object itself. The "dummy carton" began to play a leading role in store windows and on counters.

The supermarket offered new opportunities for "impulse buying"; and impulse buying was essentially the buying of packages. With the rise in the American Standard of Living, the increase of disposable income, and the multiplication of novel objects, more and more people went to the supermarket hoping to be seduced into buying something they "really wanted." In England and elsewhere in the Old World, it was still true in the late twentieth century that middle-class shoppers went to market to buy what they wanted, while Americans went increasingly to *see* what they wanted.

A series of studies by the DuPont Company, begun in 1949, showed that "impulse buying" was on the increase. As a large producer of packaging materials, the DuPont Company, of course, had a special interest in proving the growing importance of impulse buying, and so of packaging. But their conclusions were widely substantiated. By 1959 more than half the housewife's purchases in a supermarket were "unplanned"—that is, they were purchases that she had not intended to make before she entered the store; and less than a third of her purchases had been specifically planned before coming to the store. In the five years from 1954 to 1959, the DuPont study showed, the number of supermarkets in the United States had increased by nearly 40 percent (to some 30,000 stores), and the number of different items stocked in supermarkets had increased nearly 30 percent (to an average of 6,000 items and a high of 8,000 items in larger supermarkets). "The shopper is depending on the supermarket for more and more items she needs . . . she is spending 50% more time in the supermarket (27 minutes per trip against 18 minutes five years ago) and has increased the number of items purchased. . . . the supermarket has become her 'shopping center' rather than just a food store."

What did it mean, then, to speak of the "demand" for *products* when so large a proportion of what consumers bought was determined by the appeal of the packages? What was the meaning of "desire" when the housewife in the supermarket averaged fourteen (13.7) buying-decisions in twenty-seven minutes? Packaging, which at the end of the nineteenth century was still only a means to protect a product, had become a thing-in-itself. Now where did the package end and the product begin? Who could say?

Shrewd manufacturers and merchandisers could not fail to become adept at what Dr. Ernest Dichter, a psychoanalytic marketing consultant, called "the Strategy of Desire." A good *product* was not enough; success required a *package* that would stimulate desire. From one point of view, as Dr. Dichter explained in 1961, this was a result of the uniform and high quality of American products.

When people buy soap, they know that they are going to get soap. They know they do not any more have to worry about getting a piece of chalk. But because our technological development has been so good and so fast, the fact is that almost all our products are uniformly good, so that there is in reality very little difference, in the same price category, between a product with one brand name and a product with another. What people actually spend their money on are the psychological differences, brand images permitting them to express their individuality.... We have reached ... a psychoeconomic era. It is because of the improved quality and reliability of our merchandise that we can allow ourselves the luxury of making our decisions on the basis of more purely psychological factors.

To say that products were more and more standardized was to say that the consumer's world, like the world of the photograph and the phonograph, had also become a world of repeatable experience. Packaging and brand-naming had helped make the experience more reliably repeatable. The packaging of convenience foods, as a study by Arthur D. Little & Co. argued, plays "an important role in reducing the risks of non-repeatability in the preparation of food products. The ability of a housewife to repeat the quality of a given meal is increased." The familiar package justified the hope that it would be the same this time, too.

While the American consumer now had an unprecedented guarantee that the experience of a particular product was repeatable, other aspects of his experience were overcast by new penumbras. The package or the object? Form or content? Did he really want it, or had he been persuaded to buy it on impulse? Would he have bought it if it had been offered to him in a package of different size, shape, or color, or if it had been displayed on a different shelf or beside something else more attractive? Or if he had not had his shopping cart so handy? The anonymous product—the product without a brand name, which had dominated the stores a half-century before—had by the mid-twentieth century become slightly disreputable. Everything had a name, and packages were commonly bought because the name on the package had become familiar in print or on the television screen. Inevitably, then, the packaged world with its new strategy of desire brought a vagueness and uncertainty of desire. Had packaging, like clothing, become a badge of man's lost innocence?

PART EIGHT

Language, Knowledge, and the Arts

"Knowledge is no longer an immobile solid; it has been liquefied. It is actively moving in all the currents of society itself."

JOHN DEWEY

"When we Americans are done with the English language it will look as if it had been run over by a musical comedy."

FINLEY PETER DUNNE

"It is not easy to know what you like. Most people fool themselves their entire lives through about this."

ROBERT HENRI

NEVER BEFORE HAD democracy been tried on such a large scale, nor allowed to shape the academic standards of a whole nation's language, to redefine its higher learning and reconstruct its notions of art. Out of this remarkable opportunity came pervasive new ambiguities and uncertainties about the standards by which all culture was to be measured. Was your language "right" or "wrong"? Were you speaking eloquently or crudely? Were you acquiring knowledge or falsehood, were you being educated, propagandized, entertained, or actually deceived? What were the proper boundaries of your profession? What were the roles of teacher or of pupil? What was knowledge and what was ignorance? What knowledge was "useless" and what was "useful"? Did art have to be "beautiful"? And if not, what was art anyway?

Underlying the democratic transformations of the ways of judging and measuring was a faith in "the people," in their inherent spontaneous wisdom, when unguided by authority or by tradition. *Vox populi, vox Dei* (the voice of the people is the voice of God) became the ruling maxim of more and more of American life. Even if this democratic faith was never quite universal, and only a few dared make it explicit, in America it had become a nation's orthodoxy. And democracy had made society into a mirror where people saw the way things were, and made that the measure of the way things ought to be.

50

The Decline of Grammar:
The Colloquial Conquers the Classroom

IN THE EARLY TWENTIETH CENTURY, American technology blurred the proverbial distinctions between speech and writing. After the telephone came into common use, it was of course no longer true that the reach of the spoken word was limited by the power of the speaker's lungs. After the phonograph, future generations could not only read a man's written words, they could actually hear the sound of his voice. The new technologies of repeatable experience made speech, for all practical purposes, as durable and as easily diffused as writing.

At the same time a new science of language, which aimed to dissolve pedantic and aristocratic ways of thinking, gave a new dominance to speech as against writing and made new problems for the naïve citizen. Americans, since the colonial period, had assuaged their insecurities of social status by the reassuring certainties of grammar and spelling. While the spoken language in America was more classless and more uniform than the spoken language of England, while the American vernacular was free and lively and inventive, bursting with anticipation and exaggeration, language teaching aimed to instill the rules of "correct" speech and writing. The American language championed by Noah Webster and others was conceived to be a "purified" English language with rules all its own. One virtue of democracy, according to Webster, was that it offered people a "standard"—in "the rules of the language itself"—more uniform than the language of aristocracies.

BY THE MID-TWENTIETH CENTURY, new democratic criteria had come into the classroom, changing the notion of what standards, if any, a democratic society could apply to its language. These were the product of a new science of linguistics. Until about the mid-nineteenth century, studies of the origin and development of language had been tangled with theology, philosophy, rhetoric, and logic. Then, when a modern descriptive science of language began, in Europe it focused on the relationship among the so-called Indo-European languages, and their derivation from hypothetical original forms. Effort to make this study more "scientific" had tied it to specific new theories of psychology. By the early twentieth century, European scholars had begun to survey the way language really worked. The monumental *New English Dictionary on Historical Principles* (commonly called the *Oxford English Dictionary*, 12 vols., 1888–1928), together with the works of continental scholars, provided raw materials for a new era of generalizing.

A new American school of linguistics used distinctive American opportunities. The two founders, Edward Sapir and Leonard Bloomfield, both discovered their point of departure in the languages of the American Indian. Sapir, son of an immigrant German Jewish cantor, had come to America at the age of five and won the scholarship competition for "the brightest boy in New York City." As a young man he became interested in the nature of language, went to the state of Washington to study the language of the Wishram Indians, and then in 1921 produced his basic work, *Language: An Introduction to the Study of Speech*. Bloomfield had studied the language of the Menominee and the Plains Cree Indians before he produced his influential *Language* in 1933.

Earlier scholars in Europe had focused on Indo-European languages which were recorded in abundant documents, and which were essentially similar to one another in structure. By taking off from the American Indian languages, Sapir and Bloomfield found a new linguistic perspective. For in American Indian communities the dominant and in some cases the only form of language was *spoken;* most of their languages had no written form, and when they had, often there were no grammars and no available texts. To study these languages, then, inevitably meant reconstructing patterns of meaning from the actual sounds of speech. Such studies of "primitive" spoken languages revealed that contrary to the snobbish clichés which insisted that peoples without an elaborate literature had no more than a few hundred words in their vocabulary, each of these languages was found to contain upwards of 20,000 words. The anthropologist A. L. Kroeber found 27,000 words, for example, in the spoken vocabulary of the Aztec Nahuatl. Spoken languages, then, proved to have an unsuspected copiousness and flexibility.

Primarily from study of these exotic, nonwritten languages grew the new science of structural linguistics. During World War II, structural linguists proved the validity of their approach by making it the basis of speedy new ways to teach non-European languages in training programs for interrogating officers and occupation forces.

Although only a small number of Americans had even heard of the new linguistic science, within two decades it would become the dominant influence on the teaching of the American language in schools. The effect, the linguist Mario Pei explained, was "an excessive reverence for the spoken tongue and a corresponding disregard of, not to say contempt for, written versions, even where these exist and are of value in tracing a language's nature, history and affiliations; and excessive regard for the phonetic portion of the language and a corresponding neglect of its semantic role; and a tendency to accept as the standard form of a tongue that which is common to the bulk of uneducated native speakers, rather than that which is consecrated by tradition as 'good usage.'" If the science of structural linguistics was new and remained esoteric, its dogmas were at one with the folk wisdom of democracy.

About the same time that scholars were elaborating their solemn new science a powerful voice spoke with the biting self-assurance of a prophet. H. L. Mencken, a Baltimore-born journalist, reached a wide audience from the pages of the *American Mercury* (1924–33), where he attacked the American "Boobocracy." Setting a vigorous example with his own richly colloquial style, Mencken had become a pioneer scholar of the American language. By 1910 he was collecting examples of the differences between the British and the American language. With the coming of World War I, when Mencken dared to doubt whether defeating Germany and hanging the Kaiser would make the World Safe for Democracy, he took refuge in his studies of the language, which became a monumental work, *The American Language* (3 vols., 1919–48). There Mencken provided a storehouse of information that gave courage to champions of popular American speech, and he pleaded for the full-bodied colloquial language against the skimmed milk of the schoolmarms. The American language, Mencken's first volume prophesied, was diverging so rapidly from the English language that the speakers of either one would soon be unintelligible to the speakers of the other. Twenty years afterward he observed that the language of England was becoming nothing more than a dialect of American. Mencken's work, contradicting the dogma of the stupidity of the masses which he had preached in the *American Mercury,* celebrated the peculiar democratic grandeur of the language. An American Rabelais, he pilloried obscurantism and pomposity as energetically and as wittily as he championed learning. His *American Language,* widely bought but not widely enough read, was a vivid if cumbersome American saga: the hero was the whole motley churning American people using words as their weapons in perpetual battle with a novel reality.

Mencken himself became a one-man Institute for the Study of American. He enticed American scholars of "English" to abandon the clichés of English literature for the study of their own spoken language. He helped plan the Linguistic Atlas of the United States, was a founder of the Linguistic Society of America, and joined in establishing a lively new journal called *American Speech.* Following Mencken's lead, others built monuments of scholarship such as *A Dictionary of American English on Historical Principles* (W. A. Craigie and James Root Hulbert, eds., 4 vols., 1938–44) and *A Dictionary of Americanisms on Historical Principles* (Mitford M. Mathews, 2 vols., 1951), proving beyond pedantic doubts the delightfully special character of the language of Americans.

THESE NEW VIEWS of language in general and of the American language in particular were developing at a time when the task of the American language teacher, especially in the high schools, was being transformed. In 1900, of Americans in the age group 14 to 17, only about one in ten was attending high school, and of those aged 18 to 21, only one in twenty-five was attending college. By 1920 the enrollments of high schools had quadrupled; by 1930 more than half the children aged 14 to 17 were in high school. The proportion of Americans aged 18 to 21 going to college had become one in ten, and was going up. The democratizing of the high school, an easily forgotten American achievement of the twentieth century, brought into the classroom more and more students whose parents had had only a scanty formal education. As a result, the linguist Raven I. McDavid, Jr., explains, "ever larger proportions of those in the classroom have come from homes where the traditional values of humanistic education are of little importance, where even the standard language is a foreign idiom. To cope with the new situation created by the new clientele, especially in high school and college, new theories of language analysis have been introduced; old theories of grammar and usage . . . have been continually reexamined in the light of new evidence and of insights provided by other disciplines." As the schoolroom was expected to perform a remedial function, the temptations were increased for insecure, upward-mobile teachers to impose "Rules of Good English" on their insecure, upward-mobile students.

But there was also the Democratic Temptation—to flatter the people by assuring them that whatever they were already doing was right and best. Teachers sought to relieve their new students of feelings of inferiority by suggesting that perhaps the language they heard at home was not actually "incorrect" after all. This temptation became increasingly potent as the century wore on. Before the century was out, some who still called themselves "teachers" of language thought they could bolster the egos and reduce the aggressions of their underprivileged Negro students by validating "Black Language" and so relieving them of the need to learn Standard English.

The democratic argument was summarized by an official of the Modern Language Association writing in 1968:

> It is no exaggeration to say that linguistic naiveté on the part of the teacher of English in the urban school contributes to rioting in the streets and a hostility between community and school which the United States cannot afford in the next decade. Teachers must begin by dispossessing themselves of linguistic myths: Southerners have lazy speech habits; Boston English is "purer" than Bronx English; "ain't" is a mark of linguistic inferiority. The English teacher must admit that a student's ability to spell or punctuate, to write or recognize a compound-complex sentence or a 200-word paragraph which has unity and coherence is less important than his learning to speak openly and honestly, to listen well, to read many kinds of books and magazines and newspapers, and to write what he believes and thinks and feels.

These streams—the new science of linguistics, the new data of American language habits, and the currents of democratic feeling—became a flood which overwhelmed the schoolmarms.

The structural linguists, appalled by the pomposities and pedantries of the pedagogues, were determined to be more than the detached classifiers of language habits. In their vocabulary, "grammar" became a synonym for obscurantism. Although one of their manifestoes, by Robert A. Hall, Jr., in 1950, was entitled *Leave Your Language Alone!*, they would not leave the grammarians alone. In fact, they launched a crusade against the grammarians which was probably more widespread and more effective than any comparable movement outside the totalitarian countries in changing popular attitudes to institutions.

The brilliant Charles Carpenter Fries, a professor at the University of Michigan, pointed the morals of linguistic science for schoolteachers of English. His two influential books aimed to discover the "structure" of the American language, not from the grammarians' rules, but from how ordinary Americans actually wrote and spoke. *American English Grammar* (1940), nearly twenty years in preparation, was the product of Fries's study of three thousand letters written by families of servicemen to a branch of the War Department during World War I. Having finally secured official permission to use these letters (provided he omitted all names of persons and places), he made them the raw source of his new terminology for "the grammatical structure of present-day American English with special reference to social differences or class dialects." To identify the social class of each writer, Fries used the sworn biographical statements in the War Department files.

Financed by the National Council of Teachers of English, this study by Fries aimed to tell schoolteachers how to improve their instruction in English. His book insisted on a "scientific" point of view. "Instead of having to deal with a mass of diverse forms which can be easily separated into the two groups of *mistakes* and *correct language*," Fries explained, "the language scholar finds himself confronted by a complex range of differing practices which must be sorted into an indefinite number of groups according to a set of somewhat indistinct criteria called 'general usage.' " Fries therefore banished such terms as "mistake," "correct," and "error" from his vocabulary, and he urged all English teachers to do the same. After offering his own scheme to describe the structure of actual usage, he concluded that the "study of the real grammar of Present-day English" had actually never been found in the schools. He urged English teachers to change their methods in order to teach students the everyday practices of their community, aiming finally "to stimulate among our pupils observation of actual usage and to go as far as possible in giving them a practical equipment for this purpose."

Fries's next book, *The Structure of English* (1952), was based, significantly, not on written but on spoken usage. To be sure that the language he was studying would not be stilted or self-conscious, Fries secretly recorded fifty hours of the ordinary conversations that went over the two telephones in his house. The recordings, made before the law that required a warning beep on tapped phones, were taken without the knowledge of the speakers. In this book he discarded the whole old-fashioned vocabulary of "nouns," "verbs," etc., displacing them with a novel antiseptic system of his own: Class I, Class II, Class III, and Class IV, and "Function Word" for leftovers. His scheme was constructed simply by classifying the word structures that he had heard actually spoken on the telephone.

This system, according to Fries and his allies, at long last made it possible to modernize the language classroom, and so take schoolchildren out of what they called "the pre-scientific age." They prepared new textbooks and teachers' guides: "English Grammar" now became "Patterns of English." The new textbooks abandoned the old idea of grammar as a set of commandments for the well-educated. As the teacher's guide to one of the most successful of the new textbooks explained in 1956, Paul Roberts' *Patterns of English* "does not dwell on sentence errors as such. It is, or tries to be, purely descriptive, and descriptive of good writing rather than poor writing." Roberts began by reminding the student that the language he spoke was in some ways "the most important language in the world," since it was spoken by some three hundred million people spread around the world; but he quickly added that "among all these speakers of English there are no two people who speak it exactly alike. We have all noticed how we can recognize our friends' voices on the telephone, even before they tell us who is speaking."

The new point of view was illustrated by Roberts' approach to one troublesome problem of usage:

> Probably some educated speakers of English live long and happy lives without ever letting the word ["whom"] pass their lips. *Whom* is strongest, of course, in Choice Written English, where it is used regularly according to handbook precepts. It is used more sparingly in Choice Spoken English; many radio announcers, for example, avoid it altogether; possibly they feel that the average radio audience would find it too hoity-toity. In General Written English it is avoided more often than not, and it is seldom heard in General Spoken English.
>
> Those who avoid definite *whom* do so in two ways. First, they may use the nominative form, even though the pronoun is an object:
> > a fellow who we used to know
> > a girl who I used to go with
> Or, and this is more common, they simply omit the relative:
> > a fellow we used to know
> > a girl I used to go with.

This new attitude toward language carried contempt for the grammarians' knowledge, which was now labeled superstition. "The methods and philosophy of grammar teachers are of as little moment to linguists," declared a leader of the new movement, "as the horoscope-casting methods of astrologers are to astronomers."

While the new linguists took a ruthlessly descriptive view of the language, they knew, of course, that educated Americans had been indoctrinated at school with the canons of traditional linguistic respectability. When the new linguists were told that "bad grammar" might prevent a person from getting ahead in the world, they did not disagree. But they insisted that this was very different from making the rules for getting ahead into a linguistic ethic. "It is not correct," they argued, ". . . to tell a boy who says 'I didn't see no dog' that he has stated he did see a dog. His statement is clear and unequivocal. What we can tell him is that he has made a gross social *faux pas*, that he has said something that will definitely declass him. . . . If you say *it ain't me* instead of *it is not I*, or *I seen him* instead of *I saw him*, you will not be invited to tea again, or will not make a favorable impression on your department head and get the promotion you want . . . [But] in itself, and apart from all considerations of social favor, one form of speech is just as good as another." Speaking too "correctly," they warned, might also have its penalties, for example in leading to overcharges "from such relatively uneducated but highly practical citizens as plumbers and garagemen."

Still, the new linguists took the classroom by storm. The decline of the teaching of Latin had made the victory easier. *Patterns of English* and similar iconoclastic texts began to displace the traditional *English Grammar*. Parents who had learned "a noun is the name for a person, place, or thing," and who could never forget the drudgery of diagraming sentences, found their children saying "a noun is a word that patterns like apple, beauty, or desk" and thinking more about the way people actually spoke.

THE UNCOMPROMISING DESCRIPTIVE point of view was reflected more slowly in the dictionaries. For while the dictionary makers themselves, in contrast to grammarians, had tended to be more realistic in their approach to language, the dictionary users had a sanctimonious reverence for dictionaries such as they had never felt for grammars. Throughout life, people were accustomed to "look it up in the dictionary" to see what a word "really meant" and to find out whether they were "right" or "wrong." Besides this, compiling or even revising a large dictionary was enormously expensive, and required years of work. No prudent publisher was apt to invest several millions of dollars on a book that was faddish or that would not command continuing respect from the learned world.

In 1961, both the power and the novelty of the new point of view were dramatized by the appearance of an unabridged dictionary which was ruthlessly descriptive and speech-oriented. Perhaps never before had a product of the green-eyeshaded lexicographers been so explosive. On September 27, 1961, the G. & C. Merriam Company of Springfield, Massachusetts, published *Webster's Third New International Dictionary*. The 2,720-page volume weighed thirteen and a half pounds and sold for $47.50. It was the first completely new Merriam-Webster unabridged dictionary in twenty-seven years. Of course there were many other dictionaries, but the Springfield publishers had managed to hold on to the kudos of the famous Noah Webster, who had died in 1843. When people said, "Look it up in Webster," they usually meant "look it up in the latest unabridged Merriam-Webster." This new edition, according to the publishers, was the product of a permanent staff of more than a hundred specialists and hundreds of consultants, and had cost more than $3.5 million. The main vocabulary section, based on a file of 10 million citations, offered 450,000 entries, including 100,000 new words or new meanings never before found in the unabridged Merriam-Webster.

In the language of public relations, this was definitely a Publishing Event. Publication date was preceded by numerous teaser news stories for background. The book was launched, the publishers boasted, with "the greatest concentration of advertising ever used by any publisher to promote any single book." It was greeted by front-page stories and leading editorials in daily newpapers, followed by articles in general-circulation weeklies and literary reviews. With few exceptions these were a barrage attack. "WEBSTER'S LAYS AN EGG," announced the Richmond *News Leader*. "NEW DICTIONARY, CHEAP, CORRUPT," declared the Rt. Rev. Richard S. Emrich in the Detroit *News*, in a review that explained how the new *Webster's* expressed "the bolshevik spirit." The assistant managing editor of the *New York Times* circulated a memorandum to his staff informing them that the editors of the news, Sunday, and editorial departments "have decided without dissent to continue to follow Webster's [earlier] *Second Edition* for spelling and usage." And a Washington *Post* editorial exhorted readers: "KEEP YOUR OLD WEBSTER'S."

The prim *Atlantic Monthly* reviewer labeled the new Webster's "a fighting document. And what the enemy is out to destroy is every obstinate vestige of linguistic punctilio, every surviving influence that makes for the upholding of standards, every criterion for distinguishing between better usages and worse." This, the most important event in American linguistic history in the mid-twentieth century (as many called it) was declared to be "a very great calamity."

These expressions of outrage from respectable journalists and editors of literary reviews were a measure of the unnoticed revolution in the thinking of the scientific linguists who had already dominated the American classroom. Most of these reviewers, of course, had been raised on the old "right-or-wrong" school of grammar and themselves knew little or nothing about the new linguistic science. While the influential journalists, preachers, and popular reviewers deplored the product of the new linguists, they had hardly noticed that their own children were being raised on *Patterns of English*. The new linguistics had conquered the classroom in a secret victory.

But most linguistic scientists enthusiastically approved the new *Webster's*. For few critics could deny that the new *Webster's* was an accurate, up-to-date, and comprehensive *description* of American usage. What disturbed most of the lay critics was that this "authoritative" work deliberately failed to provide the guide to "right" and "wrong" usage of their language. Wasn't that what they had always wanted from *Webster's?* Even in a democracy, these educated Americans still believed, they ought to be able to use their dictionary, their sacred *Webster's*, as an authority. And even if the community had become confused on all other subjects, in language at least there ought to remain some agreement on "right" and "wrong."

The new *Webster's* was so heavily colloquial in point of view that it had actually abolished the distinguishing label "colloquial." And it made little use of the familiar stigmata—slang, cant, facetious and substandard—which the earlier *Webster's* had applied to words not in the standard written usage of educated Americans. The new *Webster's* not only defined 100,000 words which were not found in the earlier edition but was extremely permissive in admitting to its list, without marks of reproach or disparagement, such words as "ain't" (which it said was "used orally in most parts of the United States by cultivated speakers"), "wise up," "get hep," "ants in one's pants," "hugeous," and "passel" (for "parcel"). The illustrative quotations, culled from the ten million in their file, came not only from statesmen and famous authors but from movie stars, night-club entertainers, baseball players, and boxing promoters; not only from Winston Churchill, Dwight D. Eisenhower, Edith Sitwell, Jacques Maritain, and Albert Schweitzer but also from James Cagney, Ethel Merman, Burl Ives, Willie Mays, Mickey Spillane, Jimmy Durante, Billy Rose, and Ted Williams.

Within a few years other American dictionaries came on the market which took some account of the new linguistics but still offered readers a semblance of the "authority" they were looking for. In 1966 appeared *The Random House Dictionary of the English Language,* a 2,096-page volume, the product of eight years of work by 150 editors and 200 outside consultants. It was intended to compete with the new *Webster's* but it sold for only $25, and so aimed at a wider market. This work, the publishers explained, had been shaped by extensive surveys of teachers, professors, librarians, and journalists, the very groups that had cried "Murder!" to the new *Webster's*. Avoiding the New Linguists' temptation to be "so antiseptically free of comment that it may defeat the user by providing him with no guidance at all," this dictionary preserved tradition at least to the extent of informing its readers of "long-established strictures in usage." For example, "ain't" was stigmatized as "nonstandard" and the reader was warned that "it should be shunned by all who prefer to avoid being considered illiterate." At the same time, "to have ants in one's pants" was labeled "slang," and then illustrated by "She had ants in her pants ever since she won that ticket to Bermuda." Instead of drawing illustrative quotations from athletes, entertainers, and other not-necessarily-educated celebrities, and so offending the literati—or from highbrow authors and scholars, and so proving they were out of tune with the new linguistics—the quotations offered had been made up by the editors themselves. Here was a compromise, the editor explained, "a linguistically sound middle course" between the antiquated "authoritarian" point of view and the futuristic "descriptive" approach. But this dictionary, too, was permissive, plainly dominated by the living, spoken language. When "usage" was prescribed, it was only in order to make the book *"fully* descriptive." *The Random House Dictionary*, partly because of its differences from the new *Webster's*, was an enormous commercial success.

Soon another, smaller dictionary succeeded by taking still another step backward toward the traditional "right-or-wrong" approach to language. In 1969 the editor of the new *American Heritage Dictionary of the English Language* announced that the publishers, with a "deep sense of responsibility as custodians of the American tradition in language as well as history. . . . would faithfully record our language, the duty of any lexicographer, but it would not, like so many others in these permissive times, rest there. On the contrary, it would add the essential dimension of guidance, that sensible guidance toward grace and precision which intelligent people seek in a dictionary." The editors were freer than their predecessors in applying the stigmas of "slang" or "vulgar," but they too sought to avoid the stigma of pretending to be authoritative. In an ingenious device of democratic acquiescence they made their "Usage Notes" the product of a kind of opinion poll. In these Notes, a "Usage Panel" of about a hundred members, which happened to include many of those very people who had been so uncharitable in their judgments of the new *Webster's*, reported their opinions of dubious words. After "ain't" (labeled "nonstandard") the entry noted that the word was "with few exceptions . . . strongly condemned by the Usage Panel. . . . *ain't I* is unacceptable in writing other than that which is deliberately colloquial, according to 99 per cent of the Panel, and unacceptable in speech to 84 per cent."

THE SHREWDEST HISTORICAL JUDGMENT on the development of the American language was probably the one reported in *Business Week:* the new *Webster's* "was right" but had appeared some thirty years too soon. For the spoken language had long been establishing its sway. The new linguistic scientists were not bolsheviks or anarchists, nor were they conscious opponents of the good, the true, and the beautiful. Neither were they bad scientists. What the new *Webster's* had revealed was a long-accelerating revolution, far wider and deeper even than the linguistic conservatives had imagined. In linguistic science, as in countless other surprising ways, Americans were using their new techniques simply to describe the way the world really was. A world so visibly speedy, so obviously kaleidoscopic, was newly interesting to describe, and newly difficult to prescribe for.

Everywhere one looked in the United States in the twentieth century, today's hastening world seemed to make irrelevant the traditional standards of how the world ought to be. The triumph of science and democracy was not yet total—at least in the world of language. People remained nostalgic for the language ways of the "best" speakers. But the attempt of prudent dictionary makers to keep alive an authoritarianism, however mild and enlightened, was only a rear-guard action. The self-consciousness with which they aimed to "preserve" the language (while they bowed low to the new descriptive linguistics) hinted where the currents of history were running. When Americans looked for standards in so simple an everyday matter as their words, they no longer found an unambiguous authority.

51

From Oratory to Public Speaking: Fireside Politics

"ORATORY IS THE PARENT OF LIBERTY," explained a popular American handbook in 1896. "By the constitution of things it was ordained that eloquence should be the last stay and support of liberty, and that with her she is ever destined to live, flourish, and to die. It is to the interest of tyrants to cripple and debilitate every species of eloquence. They have no other safety. It is, then, the duty of free states to foster oratory." Before the Civil War, when this was an axiom of American public life, the nation had produced a peculiarly American declamatory literature, and it was taken for granted that there were standards of eloquence. A patriotic citizen knew the Great American Orations; and Great Statesmen, while they championed the People, steadily increased the world's stock of Oratorical Classics.

Within a half-century this view of oratory was as obsolete as high-button shoes. Many of the very same democratic tendencies which had nourished oratory were to be the death of it. As the spoken word found new vehicles and a new reach, it became less a creature of rules, and it relaxed. The public was transformed, along with the public style of American politics. Even while the uttered word reached out magically and brought everybody into the audience, even as the audience became larger, in strange new ways it also became more intimate. In the post-oratorical era, the citizen would feel both closer to and farther from his democratic leaders.

THE McGUFFEY *READERS*, the work of a professor of moral philosophy which dominated the schoolbook market for nearly a half-century after their appearance in 1836, have been noted for making clichés of certain American classics while they popularized morality. But the 122 million copies of McGuffey which reached the classrooms, while they gave Americans their declamatory literature, also democratized the arts of the spoken word. It is sometimes forgotten that these books, out of which generations of American schoolchildren learned to read, aimed to teach boys and girls how to read *aloud*. McGuffey's *Fifth Eclectic Reader* (1879 ed.) began by describing the purpose of "reading as a rhetorical exercise," and went on with Twelve Rules and examples of "correct" and "incorrect" Articulation, Inflection, Accent, Emphasis, Modulation, and Poetic Pauses.

> Rule IX.—The different members of a sentence expressing comparison, or contrast, or negation and affirmation or where the parts are united by *or* used disjunctively, require different inflections; generally the *rising* inflection in the *first* member, and the *falling* inflection in the *second* member. This order is, however, sometimes inverted.

But McGuffey recommended "uniformity of tone . . . to express solemnity or sublimity of idea, and sometimes intensity of feeling." The opening exercise for students was a threnody: "Death of Franklin (To be read in a solemn tone)."

During the nineteenth century, children in the primary grades were promoted according to their ability "to read aloud deliberately and correctly." In secondary schools, ceremonies of Public Reading and Recitation, with "declamation and exercises of a forensic kind," were common. William Jennings Bryan, one of the last paragons of the old-fashioned oratory, recalled how his high school training in a literary society and a debating club had taken him "a step forward in the art of declamation."

In the multiplying American colleges of the nineteenth century, rhetoric, elocution, and oratory were essential subjects. Henry Adams, who had been a student at Harvard College in the 1850's and who knew the cultivated European, remarked that to the American "nothing seemed stranger" than "the paroxysms of terror before the public which often overcame the graduates of European Universities." After his college experience, Adams was "ready to stand up before any audience in America or Europe, with nerves rather steadier for the excitement." "Whether he should ever have anything to say," he added, "remained to be proved." But the question of content did not unduly trouble young American orators. By the early years of the twentieth century, intercollegiate debating, a predecessor of intercollegiate football, had become one of the most organized activities of higher education, with a specialized apparatus of coaches, textbooks, schedules, and intercollegiate "leagues."

This prominence of oratory in higher education came from a number of peculiarly American circumstances. The scores of new colleges and universities had recruited their part-time faculties from the ministers in neighboring pulpits. And the ambitious American undergraduate was preparing himself for a seat in one of the numerous legislative bodies which were multiplying with the growth of the nation. As oratory flourished and as Americans learned their history through the public utterances (real or supposed) of patriots and statesmen, it became an axiom of American democracy that there really were great models and correct standards for the public word. Educated persons, it was assumed, would agree on the meaning of "eloquence" and would have little difficulty deciding which works belonged in a collection of "The World's Great Orations." And these were profitably marketed in ten-volume buckram-bound sets to become the parlor furnishings of households that possessed few other books besides the Bible and a mail-order catalogue.

Thousands of young William Jennings Bryans came to believe that oratorical standards were a kind of test of their qualifications for statesmanlike greatness. The study of Greek and Latin, still widespread in high schools and colleges, was supposed to provide classic models for the student who tried to decipher the phrases of Demosthenes or Cicero. And the custom of memorizing and declaiming the famous orations of patriot-orators—Patrick Henry's "Give me liberty or give me death," James Otis' "Against the writs of assistance," Daniel Webster's "Against Hayne," Henry Grady's "New South," and others—gave generations of schoolchildren a further vested interest in believing that a "great oration" was something very special.

Students were taught the rules by which these models of greatness had been created. Rhetoric remained a basic subject in American secondary schools and colleges, where the classical curriculum included Cicero's *De Oratore*, Horace's *Ars Poetica*, and Longinus' *On the Sublime*. And instruction in the proper modes of public speech penetrated all the studies of language and literature. *Lectures on Rhetoric and Belles Lettres* (1783) by Hugh Blair (a Scots minister who "would stop hounds by his eloquence"), was long a textbook at Yale and Harvard, and in its Philadelphia edition went through thirty-seven printings before the mid-nineteenth century. Works like John Quincy Adams' *Lectures on Rhetoric and Oratory* (2 vols., 1810; his lectures as Boylston Professor of Rhetoric and Oratory at Harvard) adapted classical models and British textbook principles to American circumstances.

Competing "schools" of rhetoric offered their own dogmas, with specialized vocabularies and systems of instruction, to help professors dignify their subject. Dr. James Rush (the seventh of Dr. Benjamin Rush's thirteen children), aiming to give "physiological data to Rhetoricians," dominated the late nineteenth century with his *Philosophy of the Human Voice* (1827; six editions by 1867) and its elaborate terminology. His distinctions between the "radical" and the "vanish," and his classification of "tonics," "subtonics," and "atonics," became the foundation of numerous other textbooks which tried to explain ancient rhetoric by the modern sciences of physiology and psychology. One school was based on "Vocal Gymnastics." Another (the Delsarte System of Expression, founded by a Paris singing teacher) expounded the Holy Trinity in The Three Forms of Movement: "normal," or movement about a center, expressing Life; "eccentric," or movement away from a center, expressing Mind; and "concentric," or movement toward a center, expressing Soul. All elocutionary gestures and attitudes were then classified into nine derivative forms, from "normo-normal" through "eccentro-concentric" to "concentro-concentric." To compete with Rush's textbook and with Vocal Gymnastics, American disciples of Delsarte offered "Harmonic Gymnastics," which remained popular until the opening years of the twentieth century.

Still, there were a few ominous signs of skepticism about the usefulness of this apparatus. As early as 1835, when Jonathan Barbour, Harvard's first "scientific" teacher of elocution, whom the orator Wendell Phillips acknowledged as his master, required his students to fit themselves into a bamboo-slatted sphere so they could better acquire the gradations of gesture through a full 360 degrees, the students rebelled, actually forcing the ingenious professor to resign. His successor at Harvard, the brilliant Edward T. Channing, who trained many of the famous New England orators of the pre–Civil War era, warned students against slavishly following classic models: the orator should not be a "leader of the multitude" but instead should consider himself "one of the multitude, deliberating with them upon common interests." Yet the reverence for "Great Orations" lasted.

When the youthful William Jennings Bryan's "Cross of Gold" oration won him the presidential nomination at the Democratic National Convention in Chicago in 1896, the popular awe for great orations in the bombastic style was confirmed. Meanwhile the prominence in public life of potent "orators" in the traditional mode—Senator Albert J. Beveridge of Indiana, Senator Robert M. La Follette of Wisconsin, Senator William E. Borah of Idaho, Senator Hiram W. Johnson of California—kept the tradition alive. And the special role in American life of lawyers like Rufus Choate, Elihu Root, Charles Evans Hughes, Louis D. Brandeis, and Clarence Darrow, seemed to reassure young men that advocacy and the forensic arts were a road to fame and fortune. When Woodrow Wilson, a master orator in the old style, revived the practice of delivering the President's annual message in person as a speech to Congress, he again reminded the nation of the orator's power.

In the early twentieth century, American schools and colleges were still teaching the techniques of declamation. The vogue of the subject increased with the founding of new national associations of teachers of speech. By 1930 a course on speech or public speaking was in the regular curriculum of the larger high schools, not because of any revived interest in classical models, but because American education was drawing subjects into the curriculum "in proportion to their relative importance for useful and successful living." The sophisticated revival of rhetoric in the form of a "New Criticism," stirred by the writings of Ezra Pound and T. S. Eliot, and shaped by the critical writings of I. A. Richards and Kenneth Burke, was confined to literary reviews and scholarly studies.

THIS WIDENING TWENTIETH-CENTURY INTEREST in public speech could hardly have been called the "New Rhetoric," for it had very little to do with the traditional study of classical models and revered principles. The focus had shifted to the practical problems of personality and "making a good impression." Now teachers aimed to help students learn to "relax" before an audience, and tried to give them a better understanding of the audience's point of view. The

popular new textbooks aimed to cultivate "the conversational manner." The self-consciously democratic emphasis defined the objective
(requiring a good heart more than a trained mind) as "learning to
speak openly and honestly," because "the real skill in communication
comes when a pupil has learned to find the proper voice, the best
tone for a particular audience, and when he has something to say and
is deeply committed to saying it."

The advancing knowledge of the physiology and psychology of
speech was applied to correcting speech defects such as stuttering
and stammering, and to speech therapy for patients of all ages. By
1920 there were remedial speech programs in the public schools of
Chicago, New York, Cleveland, and elsewhere, and specialized clin-
ics in several universities.

The shift in focus was dramatic: from the models and standards of
"eloquence" and "oratory" to the person and his problems, from
"elocution" and "declamation" to self-improvement and personal
success. The popular symbol of this new view of the public word was
Dale Carnegie. While he was ignored by academic teachers of rhetoric (his name does not appear in the ponderous academic histories of
"speech education" in America), his books had a spectacular popular
success and his name became a household word.

Dale Carnegie's life was itself a classic American success story.
Born in 1888 on a Missouri farm, he attended State Teachers College
at Warrensburg. Lacking the money to pay for a dormitory room, he
continued to live on the farm, where he helped with the chores, and
rode horseback six miles to class every day. Since he was not heavy
enough for the college football team, he joined the debating team
instead. After graduation he tried his luck as a salesman. Then at a
"social evening" in New York in 1912 he impressed the manager of
the Y.M.C.A. on 125th Street by his recitation (to piano accompani-
ment) of James Whitcomb Riley's "Knee Deep in June" and "Gid-
dyap Napoleon, It Looks Like Rain." Carnegie wanted to teach a
course in public speaking at the Y.M.C.A. While the manager was not
willing to risk the $2-per-evening fee he usually paid his teachers, he
did let Carnegie offer classes on a profit-sharing basis. His students,
Carnegie recalled, "wanted to be able to stand up on their feet and
say a few words at a business meeting without fainting from fright.
Salesmen wanted to be able to call on a tough customer without
having to walk around the block three times to get up courage. They
wanted to develop poise and self-confidence. They wanted to get
ahead in business. . . . I had to be practical if I wanted to eat."
Developing his own techniques for teaching these men how to "conquer fear," he opened night classes in Philadelphia, Baltimore, and
Wilmington, and he wrote his own textbook.

To meet the growing demand for his "Dale Carnegie Course in Effective Speaking and Human Relations," he organized centers in other cities, he trained instructors, and then he franchised the right to use his system all over the United States and abroad. By 1970 the Carnegie courses (tuition $135 to $185, depending on locality) counted a current enrollment of more than 1.5 million. *How to Win Friends and Influence People*, the text that Carnegie had written for his courses, was a booksellers' phenomenon. For the first two years after its publication in 1936 by Simon and Schuster (whose general manager had taken a Carnegie course for executives), it sold five thousand copies a day at $1.98 a copy. It remained on the best-seller lists for a decade, and by 1970 had sold nine million copies.

Carnegie's book, despite the sneers of the literati, was squarely in the classical tradition of self-help literature. The essays of Francis Bacon and Montaigne, Castiglione's *Courtier*, and Lord Chesterfield's *Letters to His Son* gave advice to the ambitious young man who aimed to improve himself. In England, Samuel Smiles, with his *Lives of the Engineers*, and his cheery essays on Self-Help, Thrift, and Duty, had begun to adapt this literature to the wider audience and the sterner demands of an industrial age. The most popular and most frequently quoted passage of Benjamin Franklin's *Poor Richard's Almanac* was Father Abraham's Speech, entitled "The Way to Wealth." For most Americans who heard Ralph Waldo Emerson lecture and who read his books, Emerson was no transcendentalist, but the man who showed them the path to "Self-Reliance," and so to successful living. A bizarre latter-day American prophet of self-improvement was the pseudo-Bohemian Elbert Hubbard, whose leaflet *A Message to Garcia* (1899), a parable of the resourcefulness and self-reliance of an American lieutenant in the Spanish-American War, sold over forty million copies, mostly to industrial firms for circulation to their employees. While Dale Carnegie's work showed no literary distinction, it was written in the plain style and had the virtues of the most effective advertising copy. Brilliant in its psychological insights and in its practicality, it long remained the most successful adaptation of the moralistic tradition of self-improvement to the special circumstances of twentieth-century America.

How to Win Friends and Influence People had appeared in a time of depression and unemployment when Americans grasped for some new success formula. "The only thing we have to fear is fear itself," the best-remembered utterance of President Franklin D. Roosevelt's first inaugural address, in 1933, expressed the central notion on which Dale Carnegie was building his program. But literary reviewers and academic intellectuals were contemptuous. After Sinclair Lewis read Carnegie's "six ways of making people like you" (including Rule 2:

Smile), he admitted that they might help the student make money, "though there is the slight trouble that they may make it . . . impossible for his wife to live with him." James Thurber declared the "disingenuities" in Carnegie's case histories to be transparent and conspicuous, "like ghosts at a banquet." One clever young man, a short time before he committed suicide, wrote a book-length burlesque, *How to Lose Friends and Alienate People.*

When a prominent person or high executive enrolled in the early days of the Carnegie courses, it was often under an assumed name. But by the 1950's the Carnegie courses had the public confidence of American men of affairs. The alumni included a United States commissioner of education, a governor of Kentucky, a governor of Maryland, ambassadors and admirals, as well as the board chairman of B. F. Goodrich Rubber Company, the president of the National Biscuit Company, the president of the Regal Shoe Company, and the president of Dun & Bradstreet. Many large enterprises, such as Westinghouse, the McGraw-Hill Book Company, the American Institute of Electrical Engineers, and the New York Telephone Company, presented the Carnegie courses in their own offices to their employees and executives. Dale Carnegie was obviously offering a useful commodity that Americans were willing to pay for.

In a nation with a Go-Getting tradition, Dale Carnegie became the Go-Getter's Go-Getter. He achieved fame and fortune by selling salesmanship. The Carnegie enterprise used organization, advertising, and the optimistic booster spirit, appealing to every American whose success "had not yet gone through the formality of taking place." And the Carnegie Courses, along with the Carnegie books, reached out to forty-five countries. Premier U Nu of Burma translated Carnegie's *How to Win Friends* (along with Karl Marx's *Das Kapital*) into Burmese. When he visited the United States he reported that, in Burma at least, Carnegie was outselling Marx, and the person he himself most wanted to meet here was Dale Carnegie.

Earlier American programs of self-help had tended to be programs of self-improvement, developing the character while showing "The Way to Wealth." Carnegie's emphasis was not on character but on personality: "Smile" because it is "A Simple Way to make a Good First Impression." Unlike most of his predecessors in the self-help tradition, he focused on speech and the spoken word. And democracy in technologically ingenious twentieth-century America fulfilled the prophecies of ancient philosophic antidemocrats like Plato and gave overwhelming new power to the spoken word. American democracy would increasingly depend on the spoken word and the impressions made by it.

BY 1900 THE UNITED STATES had nearly 1.5 million telephones, by 1932 there were 17.5 million. Until the coming of the telephone, the main means of communication between people at a distance had been the written or printed word. But in the new era of oral communication, it would become possible for almost anybody to *talk* to almost anybody else about almost anything, or nothing. Communication became more informal. The telephone became the means for conducting business. Social invitations, formerly by letter, now came by telephone. The love letter was displaced by long-distance sweet-talk.

When the radio first became workable in the early 1920's, people naturally thought of it at first as a kind of "wireless telephone." As we have seen, it was the fact that this wireless telephone failed to offer the privacy needed for person-to-person communication that led many to believe that it could never be commercially feasible. Who would pay to talk on a telephone to which anyone could listen? Only a few visionaries, like David Sarnoff, imagined otherwise—and only because they envisaged radio as a means of entertainment. In 1922, nevertheless, fearful that the growth of radio might somehow bring down the value of telephone stock, the American Telephone & Telegraph Company decided to enter the field which they then called "public radio telephone broadcasting." "We, the telephone company," an executive recalled, "were to provide no programs. The public was to come in. Anyone who had a message for the world or wished to entertain was to come in and pay their money as they would upon coming into a telephone booth, address the world, and go out." They called this "toll broadcasting" from a "phone booth of the air." The future of broadcasting, of course, did not lie in this particular direction, but rather in exploiting the novel features of the new technique which now made it possible for messages or music to be sent out to an indeterminate, unseen, uncountable audience.

And the public word would be transformed. When the only way to address thousands was from a platform, the formal, oratorical mode had been inevitable: the speaker had to stand up, shout loudly, and make broad gestures in order to be understood in the far corners. Before the days of the public address system, William Jennings Bryan's success with his "Cross of Gold" speech at the Democratic convention of 1896 had depended on his powerful, resonant voice.

Radio changed all this, and so altered the style of American politics. Both speaker and listener found themselves in a new locale, which made possible a new relationship. Oddly enough, radio did remain a one-to-one communication, and in a sense became more private than ever. No matter how many people were being addressed, there could be a new intimacy. And it was a seldom noted paradox that the enormous increase in the audience actually informalized the situation. Radio, like television more emphatically afterward, was creating a new segregation: the listener sitting before his receiver in his living room, his kitchen, his workshop, or his automobile felt alone, and could be alone, with the broadcasting voice. Between listener and speaker a new feeling arose. "Public speaking" became just talking.

In the early days of motion pictures, producers had kept the real names of their star performers secret, fearing that if the identity of the "Biograph Girl" were known, she would demand impossible fees and her celebrity would overshadow that of the company. Similarly, before 1925, radio broadcasting stations generally tried to keep their announcers anonymous, although some stations allowed an announcer to sign off with his cryptic code initials. When a fan wrote to station WHAS in Louisville, he received a form letter: "It is against the rules of this radio station to divulge the name of our announcer." But as the new relationship between speaker and listener emerged, fan mail increased, and listeners insisted on knowing more about the speaker. In 1922, as Erik Barnouw, the historian of broadcasting, notes, performers still thought of themselves in a great hall, but by 1925 there was a "cozier" image. "Many artists like to imagine the audience as 'a single person.' Letters encouraged this; no other medium had ever afforded an audience this illusion of intimacy shielded by privacy." Fan letters became more and more intimate and even passionate. "Would you like to thrill a lady in person?" read a letter to announcer Ted Husing at WJZ. In this new world of the radio "personality," any owner of a receiving set could enjoy a secret long-distance rendezvous.

After Graham McNamee announced the 1925 World Series for WEAF, he received fifty thousand letters. Norman Brokenshire, son of a revivalist minister who traveled for the Salvation Army, set a pattern for later radio personalities with his talent for microphone stealing. On his pioneer program of advice to housewives he would introduce his featured guest by giving an anecdote about himself ("I have a confession to make: this morning I wiped my razor on one of my landlady's best towels"), which brought fan mail to him instead of to the featured performer. When he went to Washington to broadcast the inauguration of President Calvin Coolidge, he ad-libbed for two hours, repeating his own name at every opportunity. "For the nice listeners I think I even spelled it several times." Late-night programs gave the opportunity for still more intimacy between speaker and listener, and the late-night radio personalities were in great demand for "personal appearances."

Now it really was possible for one man to converse with millions.

Now for each listener the public message could be a one-to-one experience, no matter how many others were listening. With radio it could not be otherwise, for the listener had no way of knowing who else was listening, or where. At the season of one of the first radio Christmases, on December 20, 1922, a Westinghouse executive announced: "Fellow patrons of KDKA: Now that we are assembled again in KDKA's unlimited theater, where rear seats are hundreds of miles from the stage and where the audience, all occupying private boxes, can come late or leave early without embarrassing the speaker, or annoying the rest of the audience. . . ."

But this was one-way communication. Even in a large hall, any member of the audience had been able to shout a protest, to cheer or applaud or hiss, all in the hearing of the speaker. Now the listener could hear the speaker, but could not reply. Of course he could write a letter, and he sometimes did. As we have seen, the effort to discover who the listeners were, and how they felt, would bring into being a sophisticated technology for studying "audience reaction."

An unpredicted new twist was given to the ancient clichés about democracy. To be sure, more people than ever could now hear the voice of their leader. But the people were no longer a "mob," no longer *"The Crowd"* of the European sociological classics, of Gustave Le Bon and Gabriel Tarde and Graham Wallas, and the others. No longer were listening Americans the sociologist's "more or less dense aggregation of people in the same locality" nor were they "face-to-face groups." For the first time, each member of the listening multitude had the opportunity and the burden of shaping his own reaction, without visible guidance from the rest. "Canned" laughter and studio-audience applause tended to supply the missing clues. But despite these, "people" had become more privatized and in one sense at least more individualized, for the "audience" had suddenly become a sum of individuals who were listening separately. What would this mean for the axioms of democracy, for the proverbial weaknesses and strengths of "the people" as a self-governing mass?

SINCE RADIO ADDRESSED an undifferentiated audience—an audience newly fluid and unpredictable—broadcasters had to provide something for everybody. Recognizing that the radio listener could walk out on any program simply by turning a knob, and seeing how easily the listener might find something that pleased him more, the broadcasters desperately tried to keep their invisible listeners from turning their knobs. So they offered a potpourri. In the early 1920's the radio programs were mainly musical, interrupted by occasional talk shows, lectures, and in the proper season, by political speeches or the President's inaugural address. The most important thing was the mix. The 1923 programs of WJZ, New York, included the Rheingold Quartet, Schrafft's Tea Room Orchestra, the Wanamaker Organ Concert, book reviews, and talks on fashion and sports. To this sort of fare, WGY players, among others, soon added fulllength performances of popular Broadway plays *(The Garden of Allah, Get Rich Quick Wallingford, A Fool There Was, Seven Keys to Baldpate, The Wild Duck)*, and then of plays written for radio. The networks (National Broadcasting Company, 1926; Columbia Broadcasting System, 1927) developed serials like *Great Moments in History, Biblical Dramas,* and *True Story.* One of the most successful of these was *Amos 'n' Andy*, which some said did more than anything else (except for the Democratic National Convention of 1924) to make radio into a national medium. The broadcasting stream was the most motley current of sounds that had ever reached a citizenry.

Radio blurred the distinction between entertainment and everything else and between the paid advertisement and the public service. From the very beginning, as we have seen, there was some confusion about who would or could or should pay for sending words and music "broadcast." David Sarnoff's notion in January 1920 was that "Every Purchaser of a 'Radio Music Box' would be encouraged to become a subscriber of the *Wireless Age* which would announce in its columns an advance monthly schedule of all lectures, recitals, etc." Just as with the movie magazines that were already enjoying a wide circulation, the profits would come from selling the space to advertisers on the printed page. At first the broadcasters tried to solve their problem by keeping their costs down; they did not pay the performers, who, they maintained, were compensated enough by the publicity. In 1925 WEAF offered, "in the case of a lady, a nice bouquet of flowers together with a nice automobile to pick her up at her residence and bring her to 195 Broadway." Some companies thought the money they spent on broadcasting would be regained by their increased sales of radio receivers.

At the Washington Radio Conference, summoned by President Warren G. Harding and chaired by Secretary of Commerce Herbert Hoover in 1922, Hoover had vaguely mentioned the possibilities of "ether advertising." But Hoover added reassuringly, "It is inconceivable that we should allow so great a possibility for service to be drowned in advertising chatter." On the analogy of Andrew Carnegie's endowment of libraries (his gift was to be matched in each town by local funds), it was proposed that radio should be supported by philanthropists' endowing stations all over the country. All sorts of possibilities were proposed, on the assumption that the undesirable last resort would be "direct advertising," the hiring of time for straight commercials.

By 1925, stations were beginning to thrive on "indirect" commercials, which meant the sponsorship of a program or a series. This produced the Cliquot Club Eskimos, the Gold Dust Twins, the Lucky Strike Orchestra, the Ipana Troubadours, and the A & P Gypsies. But for some time the misgivings about handing over radio to the mercies of "direct" advertising led to various evasions. On the air, WFAA Dallas, for example, tactfully described its sponsors as "chaperones." Even in the late twentieth century, when "direct" advertising had lost some of its stigma, the aura of ambiguity remained. Reflective citizens who heard "sponsored" programs "in the public interest" remained confused (as perhaps the advertisers intended) over the sponsors' motives.

IN AMERICAN POLITICS a new conversational style appeared, taking its cue not from Demosthenes and Cicero or Patrick Henry and Daniel Webster, but from the more successful radio announcers. For the first time it was possible in that style to reach the millions. Despite a few successful surviving practitioners like Senator Everett Dirksen of Illinois, the platform orator, the gesticulating spellbinder played a smaller role than ever. The first president to become a radio personality was Calvin Coolidge. On December 4, 1923, four months after he succeeded to the presidency, his opening message to Congress (the first of these to be broadcast by radio) established the new style of public utterance, and incidentally made President Coolidge a distinctive human figure. His flat conversational delivery in his characteristic nasal twang was punctuated by the turning of his manuscript pages, clearly audible through the microphone. During the next decade Americans became accustomed to hearing the once hidden sounds of their political life, and political figures worked toward a new intimacy.

The national political conventions of 1924 were reported on-the-spot to a nation that heard the actual proceedings at the moment they occurred. There was an ironic appropriateness in the character and style of the leading new reporters—Graham McNamee, who had already made a reputation as a sports reporter and Major J. Andrew White, who had reported the Dempsey-Carpentier fight—announcing the 103 ballots at the Democratic convention. Eighteen stations linked by telephone cables received broadcast descriptions from WEAF which they relayed to their listeners.

By the time Franklin Delano Roosevelt was inaugurated, in March 1933, the nation was emotionally as well as technologically ready for a friendly radio voice. And just as the talents of Caruso had played a providential role in popularizing the phonograph for music, so FDR turned radio into a vehicle of politics. The radio and FDR were made for each other. Even his infirmity, which led him to deliver his radio talks while seated, proved an asset. Before FDR, it was customary for public figures to deliver their "addresses" from a formal standing posture, but now the President of the United States sat relaxed in his parlor and spoke to citizens individually in their parlors. It did not seem so strange then for him to address the 150 million citizens as "my friends." The President was no longer Delivering a Public Address; he was joining other Americans for a "Fireside Chat."

And radio, in turn, had an effect on how both the President and the people felt about each other, as it was described by FDR's Secretary of Labor, Frances Perkins:

> When he talked on the radio, he saw them gathered in the little parlor, listening with their neighbors. He was conscious of their faces and hands, their clothes and homes.
>
> His voice and his facial expression as he spoke were those of an intimate friend. After he became President, I often was at the White House when he broadcast, and I realized how unconscious he was of the twenty or thirty of us in that room and how clearly his mind was focused on the people listening at the other end. As he talked his head would nod and his hands would move in simple, natural, comfortable gestures. His face would smile and light up as though he were actually sitting on the front porch or in the parlor with them. People felt this, and it bound them to him in affection.
>
> I have sat in those little parlors and on those porches myself during some of the speeches, and I have seen men and women gathered around the radio, even those who didn't like him or were opposed to him politically, listening with a pleasant, happy feeling of association and friendship. The exchange between them and him through the medium of the radio was very real. I have seen tears come to their eyes as he told them of some tragic episode, of the sufferings of the persecuted people in Europe, of the poverty during unemployment, of the sufferings of the homeless, of the sufferings of people whose sons had been killed in the war, and they were tears of sincerity and recognition and sympathy.
>
> I have also seen them laugh. When he told how Fala, his little dog, had been kicked around, he spoke with naturalness and simplicity. He was so himself in his relation to the dog, based on the average man's experience of the place of a pet in the home, that the laughter of those gathered around radios of the country was a natural, sincere, and affectionate reaching out to this man. . . .

The people whom he had reached individually responded individually. FDR's first inaugural brought to the White House a half-million letters. The sudden and enormous expansion of the White House mail became a measure of the new personal politics. And a new dimension was added to the measure of every public man. Commentators praised FDR's radio technique and called him "a real pro"— much as Americans a century earlier might have called Daniel Webster a great orator.

While radio created the friendly national politician, it could also become a tool for demagogues. But it was significant that both Hitler and Mussolini (even in the Age of Radio) built their movements with huge face-to-face rallies where the hysteria of the whole crowd and storm-troop discipline could enforce the dictated enthusiasm. In the totalitarian countries the individual citizen's radio receiver, because it was so private a medium, was regarded with suspicion as a potential vehicle of treason. Efforts to suppress or restrict use of the private radio were never entirely successful. Radio Free Europe (an American venture in the Cold War) and other broadcast intrusions reached secretly into the homes of oppressed citizens. In the United States, on the other hand, the privacy of radio reception was an aid to petty would-be dictators, merchants of hate, and demagogues who secured living-room audiences of Americans who might have hesitated to attend one of their public rallies.

As early as 1927 the "Radio Priest," Father Charles E. Coughlin, at his Shrine of the Little Flower outside Detroit, was receiving 4,000 fan letters a week attesting to his far-flung audience of the air. After his speech of February 14, 1932, attacking President Hoover as "the Holy Ghost of the rich, the protective angel of Wall Street," he received over 1,200,000 letters from radio listeners. The priest then had to employ ninety-six clerks to handle the 80,000 letters he received weekly. Listeners described him as "a voice made for promises"—"a voice of such mellow richness, such manly, heart-warming, confidential intimacy, such emotional and ingratiating charm, that anyone turning past it almost automatically returned to hear it again. . . . one of the great speaking voices of the twentieth century." At first he was one of FDR's most effective and most enthusiastic supporters, but in 1934 when the President and Secretary of the Treasury Henry Morgenthau opposed his scheme for inflation through free silver, he became an outspoken anti-Semite and made his own political organization, the National Union for Social Justice, an American voice for Hitler.

Huey Long, another early supporter of FDR who eventually turned against the President, made himself a national political figure by his own intimate and vulgar radio style. When he christened himself "the Kingfish" (after the chief of the lodge in the *Amos 'n' Andy* radio series), he proclaimed himself a product of the radio age. In Louisiana his uninhibited radio personality was driven home to listeners on late-night programs that sometimes lasted four hours. Then, in mid-March 1933, after introducing into the Senate his Long Plan for the Redistribution of Wealth (a scheme for capital levies on all fortunes over $1 million), he actually purchased time from the National Broadcasting Company to speak for his bills and so became the first American politician to buy radio time to reach a national audience. He began: "Hello friends, this is Huey Long speaking. And I have some important things to tell you. Before I begin I want you to do me a favor. I am going to talk along for four or five minutes, just to keep things going. While I'm doing it I want you to go to the telephone and call up five of your friends, and tell them Huey is on the air."

Others—the demagogue Rev. Gerald L. K. Smith, who served on Long's staff; Dr. Francis E. Townsend of the old-age pension—developed their own styles for radio. In the bitter presidential campaign of 1936 the Republicans tried to counter FDR's radio appeal by ingenious adaptations of soap operas called "Liberty at the Crossroads," which dramatized the horrors of the New Deal, and by radio "debates," in which Senator Arthur Vandenberg spoke against recorded excerpts of FDR's speeches. By this time radio had become firmly established as a tool of national politics.

American democracy was no longer a nation of crowds. Physical presence meant less than ever before. For now a man in his living room seated before a radio was part of a larger, and in a sense more public, audience than had ever before been possible in the largest assembly hall. The crowd had become the "public": everywhere-communities held together simply because they were all responding to the same distant stimuli. While listeners a century earlier had wondered whether Daniel Webster could really be as noble as he sounded, now they might ask themselves whether Franklin D. Roosevelt or Father Coughlin or Huey Long could really be as friendly as they sounded.

When Americans abandoned traditional standards of rhetoric and eloquence, they once again had made the world as it was their only measure of the world as it should be. "Nothing succeeds like success," the old French proverb, might help the novelist tell his story, but was a dubious guide for everyman. Among the charms of American civilization none was greater than its capacity to transform once outrageous witticisms into clichés. It had been simply amusing for Oscar Wilde to say "Being natural is a pose," but New World fortunes would be made by teaching people how to "relax" and "be themselves." Naturalness itself was becoming a rare commodity which individual citizens were willing to pay for, while being (or at least seeming) natural became a special political talent, handsomely rewarded by public office. "Hesitate about doing the natural thing, the impulsive thing," Dale Carnegie had warned, "That is usually wrong. Instead, turn to these pages. . . ."

52

A Higher Learning for All

ALONG WITH THEIR prematurely grand hotels, nineteenth-century town-boosters built their own colleges and universities, ostensibly institutions of higher learning, each for his new Athens, his new Rome, or his new Oxford. The grandeur of these institutions lay in the future, and as often as not that future never came. The apparatus of American education tended to grow in an anticipatory, upside-down fashion. The mark of this curiously inverted order of development would remain, creating unforeseen opportunities and unprecedented problems which incidentally would change the very concepts of knowledge and of education in a ruthlessly democratic America.

If there was to be a new American religion of education, the universities were its cathedrals, just as the high schools later would become its parish churches. It was no accident that American universities adopted the architecture of the great age of European cathedral building. "Collegiate Gothic" naturally became standard for institutions that could afford it. Just as the great cathedrals overshadowed the parish churches, so too the universities would overshadow the high schools. And in this American Church, cathedrals of learning were actually built before the parish churches. American education had a hierarchy before it had a qualified congregation.

In the United States, unlike the more settled countries of western Europe, education became a curiously inverted pyramid. Institutions of "higher learning," presuming to offer the whole citizenry access to the most elevated and most difficult branches of learning, multiplied in numbers without precedent—even before the nation had a suitably extensive and democratic apparatus of preparation. Higher learning spread over the land, in ambitious and pretentious institutions generously supported by public treasure, even before the courts of the land had removed doubts about whether it was legally permissible to collect taxes to support a public high school.

There is no entirely rational explanation of why American institutions developed in this way. The order of events had not been planned. And to insure these new universities a sufficiently numerous student body, the enthusiastic American champions of higher-learning-for-all had to redefine the subject matter of higher learning.

How else could a "university" be brought within the intellectual and physical capacities of every citizen male or female? If an "opera house" in an upstart Western town would somehow bring into being the performances to justify its name, would not a "university" also create its own constituency?

The community booster colleges of the early nineteenth century were born by the hundreds, and they died by the hundreds; four fifths of those founded before the Civil War had ceased to exist by the mid-twentieth century. But that fate befell fewer of the colleges and universities born after the Civil War. More of these were richly supported by public funds, which it was somebody's political death to withdraw; and those that had been founded and sustained by large private endowments and individual gifts commanded pious loyalties, which made them immortal. Nearly all resisted reform, even while they became increasingly responsive to popular fads and fancies, to the "democratic" demands of students and others.

In the late twentieth century, the American "system" of education, insofar as there was any system, would still be upside down. American colleges and universities had reached standards of excellence in nearly all fields of learning which exceeded those in other advanced nations; and on the whole they had more resources than they knew what to do with. At the same time, elementary schools and high schools, which supplied the lifeblood of the colleges and universities, were weak in resources, and had begun to be corrupted (as the universities had been a half-century earlier) by the very institutions of local control which had once been their strength.

THERE WAS NOTHING anywhere else quite like the array of American colleges or universities, or the speed with which they grew. In 1870 the United States had 563 institutions of higher learning. By 1910, when these institutions numbered nearly 1,000, their enrolled students totaled one third of a million. At that time the 16 universities of France enrolled altogether about forty thousand students, a number nearly equalled by the faculty members of the American institutions. By 1935, American institutions numbered some 1,500, with over one million students; by 1960 the institutions numbered 2,000 with over three million students. And by 1970 the institutions numbered nearly 2,500 with over seven million students.

The United States, then, unlike England or France, was not merely providing higher education to prepare certain citizens to become a professional élite. "European universities," James Bryant Conant noted in 1959, "are essentially a collection of faculties concerned with the education of future members of the learned professions. The general or liberal education of the doctor, lawyer, theologian, engineer, scientist, or professional scholar is provided by special secondary schools, admission to which is determined by a highly selective procedure at age ten or eleven. Not more than 20 percent of an age group are selected from the elementary school and enrolled in the preuniversity schools. . . . The other 80 to 85 percent stop their formal education at age fourteen and go to work."

To compare the proportions of American youth attending college with those in other countries was therefore quite misleading. "It is true," Conant added, "that something like a third of our young people are 'going to college,' and only about a fifteenth or twentieth of the boys and girls in a European country are university students. But the vast majority of the Americans are *not* university students in the European sense of the term—that is, students preparing for a profession." It was not correct, then, either to praise American higher learning for spreading to vast numbers what in Europe was confined to a few, or to disparage American universities for not providing the commodity offered by their counterparts in Europe. European universities, even in the mid-twentieth century, remained primarily places of instruction where skills and subject matters were imparted to those who would need them in their occupations.

The characteristic American college was less a place of instruction than a place of worship—worship of the growing individual. If subject matters were vague, if options were numerous, and if the boundaries between athletics and academics, between curricular and extracurricular activities were uncertain, none of this was surprising. For "growth" was hard to define, and was of course different for each American. By the mid-twentieth century, increasing numbers of Americans agreed that any citizen who had not been sent to some institution of higher education had been cheated of his opportunity for maximum growth. Agreement on any other definition of higher education seemed both impossible and unnecessary.

The stereotype of "conformity" with which foreign critics indicted Americans, and to which naïve and ill-informed Americans pleaded guilty, had nothing to do with the case. There was, to be sure, an orthodoxy: this belief in growth, in the fulfillment of the individual. It was not widely enough admitted that, generally speaking, American colleges and universities were meant to be Hotels of the Mind, providing for each American community's mental and cultural activities many of the democratic conveniences which its hotel provided for their social and commercial activities. American universities tended to be public, popular, and democratic. But the common faith, far from producing any uniformity of standards, produced a fantastic, disorderly diversity, in the frenetic effort to find something uniquely suited for everybody.

The tradition the Americans inherited from Europe assumed that universities were repositories of the Higher Learning, which meant, of course, the most advanced and difficult and recondite subject matters. They were the topmost rungs on the Ladder of Learning, but Americans found the very idea of a Ladder of Learning uncongenial. Democracy had little patience with hierarchies, and certainly not in education. If the prime aim of education was growth, then each man was a ladder unto himself. John Dewey's new Democracy of Facts meant also a new Democracy of Subjects. The old collegiate choice between a Bachelor of Science and a Bachelor of Arts was not enough. There must be courses to suit every taste, and a degree for anybody. By the mid-twentieth century, American colleges were offering a host of new degrees, including among others: B.Did., B.L.S., B.F., B.N., B.P.S.M., B.S.H.E., B.S.L.A., B.N.S., B.Phil., B.B.S., B.C.S., A.B. in L.S., A.B. in Ed., A.B. in Soc. W., B.S. in P.A.L., B.Voc.E., B.R.Ed., B.V.A., B.S. in H.Ec., and B.O. (Bachelor of Oratory). It was not helpful to define the Higher Learning simply as what was taught in universities—when anything and everything was taught there. Democracy in higher education meant a new blurring of the boundaries between lower and higher, practice and theory, liberal and vocational.

THIS NEW HIGHER EDUCATION was a product of many American circumstances. Curiously enough, it had been made possible by the very emptiness of the continent, which unexpectedly proved to be a main resource for building and supporting the new institutions. The lands owned by the federal government and held for all the American people were what made possible the land-grant colleges. While these would be only one kind of American institution of higher learning, they were a decisively new influence. It was appropriate, too, that the gospel of the new higher education should not come from the great Eastern cities, which lay in the shadow of Old World learning, but from the West.

Jonathan Baldwin Turner, son of a Massachusetts farmer, was expected to stay home and run the family place because his elder brother Asa had gone to Yale to train to be a missionary. In 1827 Asa walked the 240 miles home from New Haven to persuade his father to allow Jonathan, even at the advanced age of twenty-four, to go to Yale. Jonathan's reading at Yale was mainly in the Greek and Latin classics, garnished with current textbooks on ancient subjects. In New Haven he was converted to the temperance movement and acquired a reputation for piety. Meanwhile, brother Asa had gone West in the "Yale Band" of seven pledged to promote "religion and learning" in the American wilderness. When Asa returned East in

1833 to recruit for the work of "colonizing and civilizing," he enlisted Jonathan, whom the president of Yale excused from final examinations so that Jonathan could immediately join the mission at Illinois College in Jacksonville.

Arriving in Jacksonville, Illinois, in May 1833, Jonathan Turner found the college with its faculty of five housed in a forty-foot square "spacious brick edifice." Turner accepted permanent appointment as professor of rhetoric and belles lettres, but in 1847 his outspoken antislavery views and his dissent from the orthodox doctrine of predestination finally forced his resignation from the college.

"Colonizing and civilizing" Illinois meant attracting farmers. But the absence of trees on those Western prairies meant lack of timber for fencing, and without fences there could not be prosperous farmers. Barbed wire (Glidden did not obtain his patent until 1874) was still far in the future. Turner took it for granted that the fencing material for Illinois pioneers, whatever it might turn out to be, would have to be something grown in the soil of Illinois. The ideal fence he imagined would be some sort of hardy, thick-growing, prickly hedge which the farmer could plant wherever he wished, which required no repair or replacement, and which would be "horse-high, bull-strong, and pig-tight." Seeking a plant to meet these specifications, Turner experimented with barberry, box, hawthorn, and other familiar trees and shrubs, and even sent abroad for some exotic plants.

Then one day in 1835 Turner heard from an itinerant preacher about a thorny plant, the Osage Orange, that grew on the banks of the Osage River in Arkansas. He secured a few plants and seeds, and so found the solution to the Illinois farmers' fencing problem. The Osage Orange was described (1847) in Turner's advertising brochure:

> It is a native of Arkansas and Texas, and will grow on any soil where common prairie grass will grow. Overflowing the land does not harm it. It will live for weeks, even months, entirely under water. It endures all climates, from Boston to New Orleans, perfectly well. Prairie fires will not destroy it or often injure it. It is armed with a very stout thorn under every leaf. Its dense iron branches soon become so interlocked that no domestic animal, not even a common bird, can pass through it. Both its thorns and its bitter acrid juice prevent all animals and insects from browsing or feeding on its branches. Its seed is like the orange seed and its root like the hickory. Consequently it can never spread into the field. One hedge around a farm secures orchards, fruit-yards, stables, sheepfolds, and pasture-grounds, from all thieves, rogues, dogs, wolves, etc. One good gate, well locked, makes the whole farm secure against all intruders. It may be trained so high as to afford shelter to stock and break the rough prairie winds.

Some called the professor's fantastic fence "Turner's Folly," but his business prospered. Turner imported Osage Orange balls from Arkansas, and after the Civil War encouraged Illinois farmers to grow trees for seed, for which he paid $5 a bushel. "In the Mississippi Valley," a neighbor noted before the end of the century, "he made forty-acre and quarter-section farms possible, where otherwise there would have been broad plantations, or still larger baronial estates."

Turner's success with the Osage Orange persuaded him that future generations of farmers needed a new kind of "higher learning." Turning his missionary passion to the democratizing of education, he helped organize the Illinois State Teachers Association, then campaigned around the state for tax-supported public schools. By 1851 he had proclaimed his gospel of "A State University for the Industrial Classes." All civilized society was "necessarily divided into two distinct cooperative, not antagonistic, classes"; the "professional" class (doctors, lawyers, men of letters, and preachers) comprised only about 5 percent of the people, while the "industrial" class included all the rest.

Since the common schools, which offered reading and writing, were not providing education itself, but merely the tools for securing an education, the substance of education—knowledge and skills— had to be provided in the higher institutions, which until then had remained a monopoly of the professional 5 percent:

> But where are the universities, the apparatus, the professors, and the literature specifically adapted to any one of the industrial classes? Echo answers, Where? . . .
>
> Nor am I unmindful of the efforts of the monarchs and aristocrats of the Old World in founding schools for the "fifteenth cousins" of their order, in hopes of training them into a sort of *genteel farmers,* or rather *overseers* of farmers; nor yet of the several "back fires" . . . set by some of our older professional institutions to keep the rising and blazing thought of the industrial masses from burning too furiously. They have hauled a canoe alongside of their huge professional steamships and invited all the farmers and mechanics of the State to jump on board and sail with them; but the difficulty is, they will not embark. We thank them for even this courtesy.

To build a true democracy, Turner proclaimed, the industrial classes must also have their universities, at least one in each state. He noted with satisfaction that the recently founded Smithsonian Institution had begun to cultivate learning that was useful for the people, but it was only a beginning. The new universities would teach agriculture, manufacturing processes, and bookkeeping; they would provide experimental farms and orchards and herds of stock; and they would be "open to all classes of students above a fixed age, and for any length of time." Commencement ceremonies would be marked not by a Latin oration, but by an *annual fair,* exhibiting the products of the experimental farms in competition with similar products gathered from the whole state.

The effect on the society as a whole, preached Turner, would be as great as that of any earlier religious reformation. A people educated in this way would show new respect for "the law of nature, instead of the law of rakes and dandies." The industrial class would become *"thinking laborers,"* while the professional class would be transformed into *"laborious thinkers."* Work—fruitful, democratic work—would be glorified as never before. "If every farmer's and mechanic's son in this State could now visit such an institution but for a single day in the year, it would do him more good in arousing and directing the dormant energies of mind than all the cost incurred, and far more good than many a six months of professed study of things he will never need and never want to know."

Turner staged a series of educational revivalist meetings throughout the state to persuade the Illinois legislature to petition Congress for grants of federal lands to establish an industrial university in each state. In 1853 the Illinois legislature sent its request to Washington.

AT THE TIME of the Civil War, the federal government still possessed a vast treasure of public land, which it was free to give, and which required no authorizing taxation. After the American Revolution, lands had been given to veterans, and during the first half of the century, tracts had been offered for sale at low prices to populate the West. Millions of acres were granted through the states to the railroads to encourage construction and to help attract settlers who would make the railroads profitable. A homestead movement to give parcels of this land free to all settlers had been growing.

Among those concerned with the use, and the waste, of the public lands was a storekeeper from Vermont who had been elected to Congress on the Whig ticket in 1854, but who soon joined the new Republican Party. Justin S. Morrill hoped to use the public lands "to do something for the farmer," and incidentally, too, for the Republican Party, by proving that party to be the friend of the common man. In 1857 Morrill wrote a bill incorporating Turner's grandiloquent language, to encourage the establishment of an industrial university in each state by granting each state a tract of the public lands. The sums from sale of the lands were to be spent by each state for at least one college where, without excluding other subjects, and including military tactics, instruction would be offered in "agriculture and the mechanic arts . . . in order to promote the liberal and practical education of the industrial classes."

After President Buchanan vetoed the bill in 1859, Morrill tried again, and in July 1862, President Lincoln signed the Morrill Act. And so an American scheme for land-grant colleges and universities came into being in wartime. Public lands owned by the federal government were to be granted to each state: 30,000 acres for each of its senators and representatives in Congress. The states that did not have federal public lands within their borders would be granted scrip which could be used for public lands elsewhere. To receive the benefits of the law, a state had to accept within two years. The total grants to the states under this first Morrill Act totaled 16,000 square miles.

At first there was a wild scramble for land-grant funds by the colleges and universities that were already operating in 1862. Private institutions like the Massachusetts Institute of Technology, Rutgers, Brown, Sheffield Scientific College (at Yale), and Vermont College, and the state universities in Georgia, Tennessee, Delaware, Missouri, Wisconsin, Minnesota, Florida, and Louisiana, and the existing agricultural colleges in Michigan, Pennsylvania, Maryland, and Iowa —all these (some of which barely existed yet) were invigorated by the land grants. Before 1880, land grants had helped build another great private institution, Cornell University, in New York, and had helped found state colleges or universities in eleven additional states, eight new agricultural and mechanical colleges, and six separate colleges for Negroes. These early statistics are misleading, however, for many early land-grant institutions were hardly more than a few experienced farmers or mechanics talking to the neighborhood boys.

The *American Agriculturalist,* in 1867, gave these simple do-it-yourself instructions for building a land-grant college:

> Set a number of earnest men, capable of teaching agriculture, down upon a good farm, with a good large house and barns upon it, and the cooperation of a good farmer; put up a few temporary buildings, if need be, for lecture rooms now, and perhaps for stables by and by; give the Faculty a little money to spend upon books, apparatus and fitting up; let them know that they shall have more as fast as they can show results; let all permanent improvements be made with a view to the future and leave the Faculty as unhampered in regard to matters of instruction and discipline as possible, and success of the most gratifying character will be almost certain in any State of the Union.

Most of the subjects taught, for example, at Kansas State in 1875, lent themselves to these unpretentious beginnings. Among courses listed in their catalogue were: The Farm, The Nursery, Carpentry, Cabinet Making, Turning, Wagon-Making, Painting, Blacksmithing, Dress-Making, Scroll-Sawing, and Carving. A few others, like Telegraphy, Engraving, and Photography, required more elaborate equipment.

The influence of the Land-Grant Movement on American higher education could not be measured merely by the number of new "Agricultural and Mechanical Colleges" that were founded under the Morrill Act. For in order to meet the competition of these new institutions and in order to qualify for continuing federal grants, many other colleges and universities leavened their curricula with appealingly "democratic" offerings.

In 1882 the total land-grant enrollment was only 2,243, but by 1895 enrollment reached nearly 25,000—twice the total American higher-education enrollment in 1870. By 1916, land-grant colleges had enrolled some 135,000, one third of all the nation's students in higher education. Ten years later land-grant enrollment reached nearly 400,000. When President Buchanan vetoed Morrill's first land-grant college bill in 1859, he had objected that if the federal government made this grant, the states would constantly be coming back to the federal government for financial support for their educational enterprises. And he was correct, for the Act of 1862 was only the first of a long series. The Second Morrill Act (1890) provided annual federal appropriations to support land-grant colleges, and that support increased in the twentieth century.

The federal grants stirred the states to a more generous support of the New Higher Education. By 1910, land-grant institutions were receiving only one third of their income from federal sources, and by 1932 this proportion had dropped to one tenth. Optimists for American federalism could find cheer in the fact that few American institutions had proved more regional in their flavor or more responsive to local needs than those land-grant institutions which had been founded with federal funds.

The regional feelings, the desire to improve the local community, which had inspired American college foundings since the colonial beginnings of Harvard and William & Mary and Yale, were expressed once again in the "A & M" colleges. Now the aim of course was not to provide a learned ministry, but to help farmers and mechanics do their jobs better wherever they were. In a new sense, higher education would now be dominated by the needs of the local community. "It was an old idea," Liberty Hyde Bailey, the pioneer of "nature study" in schools explained in 1907, "that education in some way should be 'adapted to' the needs of life. We now have taken a somewhat different point of view, feeling that education should develop out of the needs of life and be fundamentally native and indigenous." The A & M colleges became centers for studying local crops and for improving the neighborhood breeds of cattle. Out of them came scores of farm experiment stations, Farm Bureaus with local agents to help farmers with daily problems, and Farmers Cooperatives to aid farmers in buying and selling.

Along with emphasis on the practical and the useful there came a growing suspicion of the traditional subjects. "Of what good is it," they asked, "when a man can say 'I am hungry' in six or seven languages, but cannot earn his own bread and butter?" The land-grant-college spirit, the demand for regional usefulness and contemporary relevance, expressed democracy in a realm where Old World traditions of monasticism, clericalism, and aristocracy were still very much alive. While Jonathan Turner had accurately called the new Colleges for the People "a distinctively American system of education," the idea intoxicated him with visions of what he called The Millennium of Labor. "Almighty God was not mistaken," Turner preached, "when he put the first man in the garden instead of the academy, and made his own son a carpenter instead of a rabbi." In 1861 Senator Stephen A. Douglas had prophesied that Turner's land-grant plan would be "the most democratic scheme of education ever proposed to the mind of man!"

"COEDUCATION," AN AMERICAN WORD which first came into common use in the era of the land-grant colleges, was largely a by-product of the New Education. When Oberlin College (founded in 1833) opened its doors to women, along with men, in 1837, the public was scandalized, and it was some years before others followed. A few state universities in the West (Utah, Iowa, and Washington) had begun admitting women students even before the federal bounty was handed out. But it was Morrill's land-grant act that decisively encouraged coeducation. The new land-grant institutions, with their emphasis on service to all the people, their openness to new and practical subject matters and their freedom from the snobbish and segregated social traditions of the older colleges, could hardly deny a place to women. Until then, higher education for women was offered only in special women's colleges like Vassar (1861), Wellesley (1875), or Bryn Mawr (1880), or in Barnard or Radcliffe, which were coordinate to men's colleges. But some Western land-grant colleges were open to women as well as men from the start, and during the 1870's, Eastern institutions began to follow their lead.

The most potent of the myths that had prevented coeducation was that woman, "the weaker vessel," could not survive the rigors of academic discipline. It was expected that women might faint from the strain, and that while losing "the delicate bloom of womanhood," they would inevitably lower the academic standards for men. Traditional fears—the dangers of "enforced familiarity" of the sexes, the corruption of morals, the destruction of the romantic relation between the sexes with a predicted decline in the marriage rate and "race suicide"—all these slowed the attendance of women. But it was found that the female physique could survive, and even thrive, in a college atmosphere.

The old objection that while higher education was needed to train men for the professions, it could be of little use to women, no longer applied. These new institutions invented new subjects that would be useful to housewives. For the first time "Home Economics" (the expression was an Americanism, first recorded in the 1920's) became an academic subject. As early as 1871, Iowa State College listed "Domestic Economy" in its "Ladies Course," with the wife of the first president offering lectures on cooking. Kansas and Illinois followed, with courses on sewing and on the application of chemistry to foods. By 1905, eighteen land-grant colleges, mostly in the West, had their regularly organized departments of home economics. Coeducation had become so established an American institution by 1920 that women were already receiving one third of all university degrees, most of them from coeducational institutions.

The Southern pattern of segregation found expression in separate land-grant colleges for Negroes, since white Southerners had found these less objectionable than assimilating Negroes into a single democratic system of higher education. After 1938 the Supreme Court, by a series of decisions, began to uphold the right of Negro citizens to share in the common bounty of higher education.

Not merely education but a higher education was now believed to be every American's right. After the American Revolution, veterans had been rewarded by grants of land; the new American patrimony was education. When veterans returned from World War II, the "G.I. Bill of Rights" provided federal grants (up to $500 a year for tuition and books) and a monthly allowance of $50 (later $65) to allow any veteran to secure four years of college education. Similar rights were legislated for the veterans of the Korean War (Public Law 550, 1952). When that program ended in 1956, it had sent several million Americans to college.

THE AGE OF THE LAND-GRANT COLLEGE saw other acts of faith in the new religion of education. The years between the end of the Civil War and the beginning of World War I were an era of great private philanthropies. The earliest American private colleges—Harvard, Yale, Princeton, Dartmouth, Amherst—had been founded with relatively small capital sums, aided later by generous public grants and by the modest philanthropy of their loyal sons. Then the booster colleges before the Civil War had depended on the meager resources of the denominations or on piecemeal support from local communities.

The late years of the nineteenth century saw educational philanthropy on a new scale. In 1873 Johns Hopkins, from the fortune he had made as a commission merchant, banker, shipowner, and as the largest individual stockholder in the Baltimore & Ohio Railroad, bequeathed $7 million to found the Johns Hopkins University and the Johns Hopkins Hospital. With this he set a new standard for educational munificence in the United States, and an impressive number of his wealthiest fellow Americans would follow. Andrew Carnegie, from his steel millions, founded the Carnegie Institution (1902) to promote research, the Carnegie Foundation for the Advancement of Teaching (1905), and the Carnegie Corporation (1911) for science and the humanities, and he helped build scores of public libraries throughout the nation. Leland Stanford, out of the fortune he made in Western railroads, founded Leland Stanford, Jr. University in memory of his son, and left it an additional $2.5 million at his death. John D. Rockefeller, from his Standard Oil profits, gave $10 million in 1891 to found the University of Chicago, and he supported it generously thereafter. James B. Duke, who built the American Tobacco Company, in 1924 created a trust, valued at some $100 million, to establish Duke University. And there were many others.

With a few exceptions—Rockefeller was a high school graduate and Leland Stanford had attended an academy—these cathedrals of learning were founded by self-made men who had little or no formal education themselves. Their munificence must have been rooted in faith. And their gifts to universities were their own way of revolting against the European idea of a "university." Matthew Vassar had expressed his democratic desire to prove that intellectual pursuits would not damage the health of women and so to support the cause of woman suffrage. Stanford founded his institution to "qualify students for personal success and direct usefulness in life." At the inauguration of Drexel Institute in 1891 Chauncey Depew, president of the New York Central Railroad, complained that the culture of the classical college had become "the veneer of the quack, and finally the decoration of the dude." The times required "not culture, either in its lofty significance or in its degraded use. . . . The old education simply trained the mind. The new trains the mind, the muscles, and the sense. The old education gave the intellectual a vast mass of information useful in the library and useless in the shop."

This remarkable pattern—the makers of large fortunes generously supporting institutions of higher learning—attested an American orthodoxy. If the new millionaires had second thoughts about their techniques of amassing their fortunes, if they were troubled by the accusations of the Muckrakers and Populists and Progressives, perhaps here was their way to salvation. Just as Henry VIII devoted his takings from the confiscated monasteries to the founding of Trinity

College, now, too, men of great wealth who wanted admission to the democratic heaven, or at least hoped for an honorary degree as absolution from their industrial sins, made munificent gifts for educational cathedrals.

53

Educating "the Great Army of Incapables"

IT WAS NOT hard to see that to prepare student minds (as well as student bodies) for a truly "higher" education, there would have to be preparatory institutions above the elementary grade open to all citizens. The obvious answer to this need was the "high school." The expression itself was an Americanism which had appeared earlier in the nineteenth century to describe any school beyond the elementary level where students were taught "all those branches which fit a young man for college."

To complete a democratic apparatus of education, these high schools would have to become universal, free, and public. Never before in any modern nation had there been such a need, simply because the opportunity to enter institutions of higher learning had never been so widespread. Now, about 1900, when the American people found themselves possessed of a vast array of colleges and universities for the benefit of everybody, they began to wonder how "everybody" was going to be prepared.

The free public high school, which would prove one of the nation's most significant, most distinctive, and least celebrated institutions, was an American invention. For all practical purposes, it was to be a creature of the twentieth century. As late as 1890, the high school had touched only a tiny minority of the American people; of the nation's children aged 14 to 17 years, the number enrolled in all high schools and private secondary schools amounted to less than 7 percent. Of that number, only an insignificant percentage went on to college. In 1897, when President Charles W. Eliot of Harvard described "the function of education in a democratic society," he was announcing a hope and not recording a fact. "Democratic education being a very new thing in the world," he explained, "its attainable objects are not yet fully perceived."

ELIOT'S HOPE WAS to emancipate every American by putting him on a path of schooling which might conceivably lead him to the most learned professions. There would still be a traditional ladder of learning: each student, having chosen his ladder, would advance from the simpler to the more complex, always climbing up. For the democratic mission was to open all careers to all men of talent. A newer version of Thomas Jefferson's system for Virginia in the late eighteenth century, Eliot's plan, too, aimed to sift out the ablest, regardless of wealth or class, so they might advance in learning.

The struggle for the high school and the debate over its proper role in American democracy would focus once again a question that had recurred throughout American history and that would bedevil the nation in the twentieth century. It was in some ways the central problem of modern democracy, for it was nothing less than the question of the meaning of human "equality." Was the good society one which allowed all citizens to develop their natural differences, including their natural *in*equalities? Or was it a society which tried to *make* men equal? Did "equality" mean the maximum fulfillment of each, or did it mean the leveling of all?

This question was nowhere more sharply posed than in education, and especially in the high school. For the elementary schools, offering only the rudiments of reading, writing, and arithmetic, presumably offered something which could be profitably consumed by all citizens, except only those few retarded or defective. But the "high" school was something else. If it was to be the road to a "higher" learning, then perhaps all citizens might not be equally qualified to go up the road. Should the high school, then, be a sieve, to select out those who could from those who could not profitably go on to a college or university? And then what should be done for each of these groups? Should a comparable share of the public tuition be expended on those unable to take the college path?

From the beginning, two different views with quite different emphases battled for control of the new American high school. In the tradition of Thomas Jefferson, Eliot held that the duty of democratic education, in addition to preparing a whole literate populace, was to cultivate the natural aristocracy, so that the whole community could benefit from the fulfillment of its ablest citizens. And so that educational resources would not be wasted on those unable to employ them profitably. This view required rigorous standards, the same for all.

Opponents of this view, who also were enthusiasts for the free public high school, were led by G. Stanley Hall, whom we have already met as a founder of child study and the discoverer of adolescence, and by John Dewey, a disciple of Hall, who was destined to be the most influential exponent of the New Education. Fearful of a "natural aristocracy," these new philosophies of democratized education espoused the cause of those whom Hall called "the great army of incapables." Hall agreed that President Eliot's scheme for a uniform high school, where subjects would be taught in the same manner to all students, would open the way for more poor boys of superior talent to go on to college. But, Hall asked, what of those vast numbers "for whose mental development heredity decrees a slow pace and early arrest"? They needed special treatment. While Eliot did not deny that there were hereditary incompetents, he insisted that these were only an "insignificant proportion" of schoolchildren. "Any school superintendent or principal," said Eliot, "who should construct his program with the incapables chiefly in mind would be a person professionally demented." It was precisely these "incapables" about whom Hall was primarily concerned.

The distance between Eliot on the one hand and Hall and Dewey on the other was a measure of how far the new American religion of education would move beyond the Old World institutions of schooling. For while Eliot, reformer though he was, still thought and talked about "subjects" of study, Hall, Dewey, and their followers thought and talked about the pupil. While Eliot aimed to emancipate the student from narrow, antiquated subject matters, giving him a freedom to "elect" the subjects of greatest interest, the others aimed to liberate the student *from* subject matter, to emancipate him to be himself. While Eliot's changes meant a radical reform, the Hall and Dewey proposals implied a revolution. And this revolutionary new view of education would transform the secondary school in America from an institution providing specialized learning for a few (as it was and still remains in most of the world) into something else much harder to define, an expression of a new American religion.

CHARLES W. ELIOT himself was an apostle of one of the less radical sects of this new American religion of education. Born in 1834, the only son of a wealthy Boston civic leader, he graduated from Boston Latin School and Harvard College (1853) where he remained as instructor in mathematics and chemistry. In 1863, when Harvard would not promote him, he resigned, traveled abroad, and then returned to a professorship of chemistry at M.I.T. Early in 1869 Eliot's two articles on "The New Education: Its Organization" in the *Atlan-*

tic Monthly attracted wide attention. Later that year Harvard, which only recently had refused to name him an associate professor, elected him president of the university. The election was not without controversy, but was finally approved by a divided vote of the Harvard Overseers. Throughout his forty years as Harvard's president, and until his death in 1926 in his ninety-second year, Eliot remained a figure of intellectual adventure and of controversy. But because he spoke from Harvard, the most venerable American institution of higher learning and the inner sanctum of New England Brahminism, he was doubly persuasive as a spokesman for his version of democracy in American education. More than any other American educator, he was qualified to give an aura of respectability to the tendencies of the New Education.

"Conditions of business and ways of living in America," Eliot wrote in 1869, "are fundamentally different from European habits and conditions. An average American does not eat, drink, sleep, work, or amuse himself like an average European. . . . The spirit of a European school cannot but be foreign in many respects to American habits. . . . We have inherited civil liberty, social mobility, and immense native resources. The advantages we thus hold over the European nations are inestimable. The question is, not how much our freedom can do for us unaided, but how much we can help freedom by judicious education." If democracy, the freedom to move up and to be oneself, distinguished America, then, Eliot argued, it must also distinguish American education. He therefore championed new ways to bring democracy into education: by giving every American the opportunity to choose what he wanted to learn, by opening the paths for growth, by liberating all from the artificial barriers of wealth and of class.

Eliot began at Harvard. There he opposed the traditional aristocracy of subjects, which still ranked Latin, Greek, and mathematics above modern subjects like English, French, German, history, economics, or the natural sciences. He believed every student should have the opportunity to grow in his own way, to make his own choices, to be stirred by his own interests. Over strong faculty opposition he introduced his system of "free electives," which meant a new equality of subjects and a new freedom for students to study whatever they wished. By 1894 a Harvard undergraduate could earn a Bachelor of Arts degree by taking (in addition to English and a modern foreign language) the required number of courses in *any* subjects of his choice.

The same democratic motives which led Eliot to open up choices for Harvard students made him a reformer in the secondary schools. There the besetting evil was to force an early choice on the pupils and their parents. Bcause there were two kinds of secondary schools, one preparing for college and the other preparing for "work," children were irrevocably classified at the age of ten or eleven. Eliot declared that he refused

> to believe that the American public intends to have its children sorted before their teens into clerks, watchmakers, lithographers, telegraph operators, masons, teamsters, farm laborers, and so forth, and treated differently in their schools according to these prophecies of their appropriate careers. Who are to make these prophecies? Can parents? Can teachers? . . . I have watched many hundreds of successful careers which no one . . . could have prophesied of the runners at twelve years of age; and I have always believed that the individual child in a democratic society had a right to do his own prophesying about his own career, guided by his own ambitions and his own capacities. . . .

To liberate the American child, then, to emancipate him from his poverty and his ancestry, to allow him to fulfill himself, required a single kind of secondary school, the same for all.

Eliot wished to make this possible, first by changing college-entrance requirements to give admission credit for "modern subjects" and then by changing the standard high school courses to include subjects equally useful to all. When Eliot became president of Harvard in 1869, the only subjects counting for admission to the college were Latin, Greek, elementary mathematics, ancient history, and geography. Thirty years later, under Eliot's influence, all sorts of modern subjects—including the English, French, and German languages; English, European, and American history; physics, chemistry, and physiology—were accepted.

The report on American secondary education which Eliot prepared as chairman of the National Education Association's Committee of Ten (1892), urged higher standards and greater uniformity in the high schools: more "modern" subjects should be taught to all, and all subjects should be taught in the same way to all students. This was a wide departure not only from the venerated European traditions of the French *lycée* and the German *Gymnasium* but from the established American practice which still took for granted that all girls, and the boys who did not intend to go on to college, needed no more than an "elementary" education. "Secondary" education, following the European tradition, was needed only to "prepare" the young man for the university, which meant giving him more Greek and Latin, more ancient history and mathematics so that he could meet the university requirements. A secondary education and a college preparatory education had been the same.

It was this rigid, academic emphasis that had led Benjamin Franklin back in 1743 to propose another kind of post-primary school, to be called an "academy," which would offer mathematics (not then taught in "Latin Schools"), modern languages, science, modern history, and geography. Franklin, too, had aimed to widen the knowledge of all young Americans, including those who did not intend to be teachers, clergymen, doctors, or lawyers. Between the Revolution and the Civil War some 1,300 "academies" had been founded all over the country; they were generally private institutions, aiming to provide a better post-primary education for children who were not going on to college. Phillips Andover Academy (chartered in 1780) and Phillips Exeter Academy (1781), Erasmus Hall (1787), and others which later became eminent as college-preparatory schools had been established not only to teach young men academic subjects "but more especially to learn them the great and real business of living." Before the mid-nineteenth century, however, a new kind of public secondary school had begun to appear in the United States.

The first public high school in the American pattern was opened in Boston in 1821. This "English High School" for boys aged 12 to 15, whom it admitted by examination, aimed to prepare them for "mercantile and mechanical employments." A separate high school for girls was opened in 1826, but it was so popular that within two years its operating costs exceeded the city's budget, and it was closed. A Massachusetts law of 1827 required, under heavy penalty, that every community of 500 families provide some such school offering classes for ten months a year. Philadelphia Central High School, which opened in 1837, was "imposing in appearance, convenient in its location, and equipped with all the devices [including an astronomical observatory] that an acute and interested Board could secure."

Now there was a High School Movement, hoping to provide some post-elementary education for all citizens, and as a result more than three hundred high schools were in existence in the United States before the Civil War. The development, however, was not without opposition from taxpayers. The legislature of Pennsylvania received more than thirty thousand petitions against its education law of 1834, from citizens who objected because they believed the public high school to be an unconstitutional burden on the taxpayers and an undemocratic interference with the rights of parents to control the education of their own children. But the state supreme courts one by one upheld the laws establishing public high schools, on the grounds that the state constitutions did justify the provision of an educational minimum at public cost. Not until 1874 did the classic statement by Chief Justice Thomas M. Cooley of the Michigan Supreme Court (30 *Michigan Reports*, 69) finally dissolve doubts of the legality of the tax-supported public high school.

FOR THE SHAPE AND DIRECTION of the public high school, the doctrines and preachings of G. Stanley Hall had decisive implications. We have seen how he developed new attitudes toward the morality of children, how child study led him to belief in a child-centered curriculum, and how his discovery of adolescence led him to espouse a high school where the adolescent himself was the only important subject matter.

His teachings were reinforced, popularized, and given practical effect by his more prosaic and even more prolific disciple. John Dewey, a Vermonter who had studied under Hall at Johns Hopkins, was to be the most influential American educationist and the most representative American philosopher of the twentieth century. Dewey lived to be ninety-three and he influenced American life until the very end. He left scores of books on every subject, from art and logic and language and morals to manual training, politics, and foreign policy. His writings are colloquial and pedantic, lucid and obscure, easy and unintelligible. Although few would deny that he was America's leading philosopher, many philosophers, with good reason, called him an anti-philosopher. While he was the nation's leading apostle of education, some respected educators called him the leading American enemy of education.

Dewey made his most interesting suggestions on the frontiers between traditional man-made boundaries: between ideas, between activities, between professions, and between ideas and action. And Dewey spent his life breaking down barriers, trying to let experience flow. He spoke for the future, an America where old landmarks were to be dissolved, so that men would be more free, though perhaps more lost, than ever before. He pushed the American promise to its extreme. He made an America of the mind. And he brought men new promise, new hope, and new bewilderment.

At his seventieth-birthday celebration in 1929, Dewey described himself as "a man who was somewhat sensitive to the movements of things about him. He had a certain appreciation of what things were passing away and dying and of what things were being born and growing. And on the strength of that response he foretold some of the things that were going to happen in the future. When he was seventy years old the people gave him a birthday party and they gave him credit for bringing to pass the things he had foreseen might come to pass." He foresaw the mystery of America being transferred from the continent out there inwardly into the experience of Americans.

In Burlington, Vermont, where Dewey was raised, he had seen a burgeoning citified America surrounded by families on farms. And he was impressed by how the distinction between "schooling" and "education" seemed to tyrannize and narrow experience. The school that he saw was a world of individual recitation, where children learned reading, writing, and arithmetic, all of which had very little to do with their later life on the farm. The family farm, the world of sharing, of learning-by-doing, was where the boy or girl received his real "education," his preparation for the tasks of life. Dewey's New Education could have been described as his effort to make the school as much as possible like the old family farm, where children learned by doing, and enjoyed joining in common tasks.

In *School and Society* (1899), Dewey told how the transformation of society was requiring the transformation of schools:

> Back of the factory system lies the household and neighborhood sys-
> tem. . . . The clothing worn was for the most part not only made in the
> house, but the members of the household were usually familiar with the
> shearing of the sheep, the carding and spinning of the wool, and the
> plying of the loom. Instead of pressing a button and flooding the house
> with electric light, the whole process of getting illumination was fol-
> lowed in its toilsome length, from the killing of the animal and the
> trying of fat, to the making of wicks and dipping of candles. The supply
> of flour, of lumber, of foods, of building materials, of household furni-
> ture; even of metal ware, of nails, hinges, hammers, etc., was in the
> immediate neighborhood, in shops which were constantly open to in-
> spection and often centers of neighborhood congregation. The entire
> industrial process stood revealed, from the production on the farm of
> the raw materials, till the finished article was actually put to use. Not
> only this, but practically every member of the household had his own
> share in the work. The children, as they gained in strength and capacity,
> were gradually initiated into the mysteries of the several processes.
>
> We cannot overlook the factors of discipline and of character-building
> involved in this: training of habits of order and of industry, and in the
> idea of responsibility, of obligation to do something, to produce some-
> thing, in the world. There was always something which needed to be
> done, and a real necessity that each member of the household should
> do his own part faithfully and in cooperation with others.

As the old family farm disappeared, Dewey argued, the school had to be reshaped into an effective substitute.

He assumed that preparation for life was a preparation for an *intelligible* world. But would this assumption be old-fashioned in late-twentieth-century America? Could an educational system be "progressive" if it aimed to recapture life on a Vermont farm?

The first reform of education was to make "school" and "society" into one. "Education," Dewey preached, "is a process of living and not a preparation for future living." The school was not a place where boys and girls acquired knowledge and skills for adult use, but was itself a living community. The ideal community, then, was a vast school in which all shared the processes of learning-by-doing; the ideal school was a whole community. "The school, as an institution, should simplify existing social life; should reduce it, as it were, to an embryonic form. Existing life is so complex that the child cannot be brought into contact with it without either confusion or distraction."

Dewey and his wife showed what all this meant in the Laboratory School that they set up at the University of Chicago. There the emphasis was on "activity" rather than on discipline, on doing rather than on learning. Instead of reciting their lessons, the children examined stones and insects, made things with hammer and saw, conversed and discussed and conferred. "There is a certain disorder in any busy workshop; there is not silence; persons are not engaged in maintaining certain fixed physical postures; their arms are not folded; they are not holding their books thus and so. . . . Our whole conception of school discipline changes when we get this point of view." While dissolving old notions of discipline, Dewey also dissolved subject matter and even curriculum. All subjects merged in a community of action.

Incidentally, as Dewey idealized activity he erased many of the old distinctions in philosophy. Philosophers had ranked entities by putting the concrete individual fact or experience at the bottom, and giving the place of honor to the abstract, generalizing absolute. In Dewey's new world there was no place for such hierarchies.

Dewey's grand encompassing aim was "growth"—growth for every citizen, and growth for the society. And this became the elusive aim of the New Education. Growth, a *mysterium tremendum*, a promise of salvation, was the heart of the new religion.

Everybody knew what growth meant, yet nobody knew its limits. Knowledge could be *acquired*, learning could be *possessed*, but growth was a *process*. As Dewey explained:

> If we go back a few centuries, we find a practical monopoly of learning. The term *possession* of learning was, indeed, a happy one. Learning was a class matter. This was a necessary result of social conditions. There were not in existence any means by which the multitude could possibly have access to intellectual resources. These were stored up and hidden away in manuscripts. Of these there were at best only a few, and it required long and toilsome preparation to be able to do anything with them. A high priesthood of learning, which guarded the treasury of truth and which doled it out to the masses under severe restrictions, was the inevitable expression of these conditions. But as a direct result of the industrial revolution . . . this has been changed. Printing was invented; it was made commercial. Books, magazines, papers were multiplied and cheapened. As a result of the locomotive and telegraph, frequent, rapid,

and cheap intercommunication by mails and electricity was called into being. Travel has been rendered easy; freedom of movement, with its accompanying exchange of ideas, indefinitely facilitated. The result has been an intellectual revolution. Learning has been put into circulation . . . a distinctively learned class is henceforth out of the question. It is an anachronism. Knowledge is no longer an immobile solid; it has been liquefied. It is actively moving in all the currents of society itself.

Dewey might have gone further. Knowledge was not only liquefied, it was rarefied, dispersed into the atmosphere, where it could not be confined or defined.

WHEN DEWEY HAD MADE Growth the sacred end and Activity the sacred means, education was not only modernized but thoroughly Americanized. Knowledge would become a kind of motion picture of the mind, which offered its meaning only in movement. Since youth was the period of greatest growth, it was inevitable that Americans should idealize youth as the period of most vivid knowing. And the problems which the New Education bequeathed to modern America were akin to the problems which came from the idealizing of change and expansion in many other areas of life.

Growth for what? Activity toward what end? "The objection," Dewey noted, "is that growth might take many different directions: a man, for example, who starts out on a career of burglary may grow in that direction, and by practice may grow into a highly expert burglar. Hence it is argued that 'growth' is not enough; we must also specify the direction in which growth takes place, the end toward which it tends." Dewey's answer was that there was a test, there was an end: more growth. The burglar's growth was not what it should be because his growth as a burglar did not promote his "growth in general."

Dewey protested when his disciples tried to circumscribe the New Education (which they dogmatized into "Progressive Education"). "Growth as education and education as growth" meant that only by growing could one discover how and in what direction one could grow. "Learning is a method of growth and . . . the educative process does not consist in acquiring a kit of tools but is a process of learning means and methods of human growth which can never be fixed but must be constantly developed." He was appalled at the "conversion —or perversion—of means and methods into a fixed, self-sufficient subject-matter."

As the New Education prevailed, Americans became increasingly puzzled over the meaning of education. This puzzlement itself somehow made it all the easier for Americans to invest education with a religious aura. Because Americans could never be confident of what education really was, they could, for that very reason, be the more persuaded that it should and could be given to everybody. In a democracy, was it not everybody's *right* to grow? And to receive from his community all the necessary means of growing?

The new American institution in which the faith of the New Education became embodied and most widely diffused was the American high school. After 1890 the high school grew at a fantastic pace. While, as we have seen, in 1890 less than 7 percent of the nation's population aged 14 to 17 were in high school, by 1920 the figure had reached one third, by 1950 the figure was three quarters, and every year going up, until by 1970 the number was near 90 percent. The new American religion of education was becoming universal, and the high school was every citizen's place of worship.

At an earlier stage of American history, too, the public school had been where children of immigrants were taught to speak American, a place for "Americanizing." But these aspirations and subject matters of the American public schools, while intimately expressive of main currents of national history, had not been radically new. Horace Mann, in his classic *Report of the Massachusetts Board of Education* (1847), had declared that American education would be "the great equalizer of the conditions of men—the balance-wheel of the social machinery" and what he called "intellectual education" was to be the means of removing poverty and securing abundance. Mann was arguing that a valuable ancient commodity, once reserved to the privileged few, should now be diffused to all. The American public school, though organized in newly communal ways, still taught Old World subject matters.

But the New Education transformed the very meaning of the school and of school-taught "knowledge." Its creature was the American high school; and even more plainly than the elementary schools, the high school bore the American mark. "Of all the departments of education," the editor of the *School Bulletin* noted in 1899, "the high school is the most firmly entrenched. The stone which the builders at one time seemed likely to reject has become the head of the corner. The high school is the people's college. Its principal should be an educational bishop for the community. The building should be in the best location, and the handsomest in town." When the National Education Association reported and adopted its Seven Cardinal Principles of Secondary Education in 1918, it declared the credo of the new American high school. The "Main Objectives" which they listed, without regard to priority, were: "1. Health. 2. Command of fundamental processes. 3. Worthy home-membership. 4. Vocation. 5. Citizenship. 6. Worthy uses of leisure. 7. Ethical character." High school principals made these their commandments. The National Congress of Parents and Teachers (whch had originated in 1897 as the National Congress of Mothers) adopted the Seven Cardinal Principles as their national platform, and made the theme of their 1928 convention how to apply these "to 'The Whole Child' from babyhood through his high school years."

After the Russians launched their sputnik into orbit in 1957, some Americans, suspecting that the Russian success was a product of a more solid school curriculum, began to wonder whether American education had dissolved into a vague and purposeless national mystique. In 1959 when James Bryant Conant, then recently retired as president of Harvard University, looked back over the preceding half-century, he recalled, in the tradition of his predecessor President Eliot a half-century before, "how enormous was the power of the twin ideals of equality of opportunity and equality of status ... the American people had come to believe that more education provided the means by which these ideals were to be realized." The great symbol was the American public high school, "an institution which has no counterpart in any other country," and Conant viewed the high school as the crux of the problem of increasing knowledge in a democratic America. While he urged improvements in curriculum and a minimum size for an effective high school, he reaffirmed the democratic faith in "a high school accommodating all the youth of a community." While this faith was national, its hallmark was diversity and local control. "When one tells a foreign visitor that we have tens of thousands of local school boards with vast powers over the elementary schools and the high schools, he is apt to say, 'This is not a system but a chaos.' To which I always reply, 'But it works; most of us like it; and it appears to be as permanent a feature of our society as most of our political institutions.' "

54

Art Becomes Enigma

ALONG WITH LANGUAGE and the higher learning, art too took on a remarkably popular character. And what had been a domain of patrons, of men of wealth and family, became Something for Everybody. At the same time that art became more accessible than ever to the common citizen, and aimed more and more to appeal to him, he became less certain than ever whether what he saw really was art, and if that wasn't art, what really was. Art, and especially painting, once the realm of definite rules and categories, the abode of unquestioned beauty, where the real thing was certified and authenticated by Academies and by the generations, in modern America became a world of novelties and puzzles.

DURING THE EARLY COLONIAL PERIOD, in America, as in England, "artist" had meant a person skilled in any "art"—whether one of the *liberal* arts presided over by the Muses (i.e., history, poetry, comedy, tragedy, music, dancing, or astronomy) or, more usually, one of the *manual* arts. Thus a colonist could complain of the lack of "artists of all classes, especially smiths, carpenters and joiners, brick masons and layers, painters and glaziers." Beginning in the eighteenth century, "artist" came to mean primarily one who practiced the arts of design, "one who seeks to express the beautiful in visible form," and soon the word designated more specifically a person who cultivated the art of painting as a profession. When the American Republic was founded, and for nearly a century thereafter, an "artist" was commonly someone pursuing and embodying the community's traditional notions of beauty.

The rise of the painter from craftsman to artist was marked by the creation of Academies which were citadels of tradition and which guaranteed the respectability of the most successful painters. In 1768 the Royal Academy of Arts was founded in London under the patronage of King George III, with a limited membership of forty. "I would chiefly recommend," Sir Joshua Reynolds, the Academy's first president, urged in his inaugural address, "that an implicit obedience to the Rules of Art, as established by the practice of the great Masters, should be exacted from the young Students. That those models, which have passed through the approbation of ages, should be considered by them as perfect and infallible guides; as subjects for their imitation, not their criticism."

This traditional character of painting and the tradition-perpetuating role of the painter were widely accepted. Reynolds himself assigned the highest rank to History Painting. When the colonial American painter Benjamin West arrived in London and was made a charter member of the Royal Academy, George III's accolade took the form of appointing him Historical Painter to the King, and West then succeeded Reynolds as president of the Royal Academy. Gilbert Stuart, an American pupil of West's, exhibited his early works at the Royal Academy in 1781. The most prosperous and widely praised artists on both sides of the Atlantic painted the portraits of aristocrats and famous personages, and depicted grand historical scenes.

During most of the nineteenth century, painting in America, with a few exceptions, played this role which had been created for it in the Old World. Here, too, portrait painting and history painting were the most respectable. And to these were added some characteristically American subjects: nature in America by Mark Catesby, William Bartram, Alexander Wilson, John James Audubon, and others; the grandeur of the American continent, by Albert Bierstadt and Thomas Moran; Indian life by George Catlin; campaigning, voting, and the scenes of great congressional debates by Samuel F. B. Morse, George P. A. Healy, Currier and Ives, and others. The currents of European romanticism and neoclassicism ran strong on this side of the water, appearing in the canvases of Washington Allston, Thomas Cole, Asher Durand, and their fellows of the Hudson River School.

ON THE WHOLE, the fine arts in the United States had been the least American of the expressions of this transatlantic civilization. Wealthy American collectors and the patrons of American painting knew the European academies and museums; their notions of art, and of beauty in the fine arts, were shaped by the Old Masters whom Sir Joshua Reynolds and his followers had worshiped. It was in a studio in Florence that Horatio Greenough (sometimes called the first American professional sculptor) spent eight years chiseling the statue of George Washington which had been commissioned by the Congress and was finally placed in the Capitol in 1843, and he depicted the nation's hero in the undress of a Greek god. At the end of the nineteenth century the leading American painter of the rich and the famous, John Singer Sargent, who had been born in Florence, had studied in Italy, France, and Germany, then made his headquarters in London, and was admitted to the Royal Academy in

1897. Between the 1880's and the early decades of the twentieth century, an American, J. P. Morgan, was a leading patron of artists in England. Wealthy Americans, from Newport, Rhode Island, to San Marino, California, were building replicas of English manor houses, French châteaux, and Rhineland castles, and then stuffing them with antiques and Old Masters. Observers from abroad, like the Irish poet Mary Colum, described that as "intellectually America's most colonial period." But in the era of Mark Twain and William James, she would have been more accurate if she had limited her strictures to the fine arts.

Against the flamboyant and extravagant cultural colonialism which American Croesuses could afford to indulge, some American movements in art were beginning to take form. "America has yet morally and artistically originated nothing," Walt Whitman lamented in *Democratic Vistas* (1871). "She seems singularly unaware that the models of persons, books, manners, etc., appropriate for former conditions and for European lands are but exiles and exotics here." The Centennial Exposition in Philadelphia in 1876 proudly displayed American industrial achievement, but reminded some Americans of how far the nation still had to go. In 1884 the young Henry Cabot Lodge, in his "Colonialism in the United States," observed that the increasing American wealth had not yet stifled that sterile "colonial" spirit:

> The luxurious fancies which were born of increased wealth, and the intellectual tastes which were developed by the advance of higher education, and to which an old civilization offers peculiar advantages and attractions, combined to breed in many persons a love of foreign life and foreign manners. These tendencies and opportunities have revived the dying spirit of colonialism. We see it most strongly in the leisure class, which is gradually increasing in this country. . . . men and women of talent going abroad to study art and remaining there. . . . a wilderness of over-educated and denationalized Americans who are painting pictures and carving statues and writing music in Europe or in the United States, in the spirit of colonists, and bowed down by a wretched dependence. . . . Sometimes these people become tolerably successful French artists, but their nationality and individuality have departed, and with them originality and force.

Lodge summoned his countrymen to fulfill Herbert Spencer's prophecy that "the Americans may reasonably look forward to a time when they will have produced a civilization grander than any the world has known."

THE APOSTLE OF anticolonialism in art was the eloquent Robert Henri. Born in Cincinnati, in the year of Appomattox, Henri had his fill of academy art by studying first at the Pennsylvania Academy of the Fine Arts, then in Paris at Bouguereau's Academy and at the École des Beaux Arts. Returning to the United States, he became spokesman and organizer of an assertive new independence among American artists:

> Art is not in pictures alone. Its place is in everything, as much in one thing as another. It is up to the community as a whole, in conduct, business, government and play. We will never have an art in America until this is understood, and when this idea is really understood it will bring us about as near the millennium as we can hope to get. . . .
>
> In this country we have no need of art as a culture, no need of art as a refined and elegant performance; no need of art for poetry's sake, or any of these things for their own sake. What we do need is art that expresses the spirit of the people of today. What we want is to meet young people who are expressing this spirit and listen to what they have to tell us.

When Henri was named a judge for the 1907 spring exhibition of the eminently respectable National Academy of Design in New York, he was unable to persuade the jury to accept the paintings of his talented young friends George Luks, John Sloan, William Glackens, Rockwell Kent, and Carl Sprinchorn; and the jury slighted two of Henri's own paintings. He then withdrew all his canvases from the Academy, and organized a show of works by three of the rejected painters and other independents.

In February 1908 the exhibition of "The Eight" opened at Macbeth's Gallery, then the only New York gallery that showed the works of contemporary American artists. Whatever the academicians thought, The Eight did meet Henri's prescription to express the life of their time. Four of them were magazine or newspaper illustrators, and they were not a "school," for they had no common style; but they shared a willingness to paint whatever the artist saw, even if the subject was not "artistic." Among their conspicuously un-Academic subjects were John Sloan's "Hairdresser's Window," William Glackens' "The Shoppers," Everett Shinn's "Sixth Avenue Elevated After Midnight" and his scenes of the Music Hall stage. Critics objected that their canvases showed a "clashing dissonance" and that the subjects were unpretty. Technically these painters could have been classified simply as "realists," but the hostile connoisseurs preferred to call them "the Ashcan School." The connoisseurs had unwittingly gone to the heart of the matter, for in twentieth-century America the artist was to be liberated from traditional expectations: he no longer had to make his work follow the styles of others, nor would he have to offer what was generally recognized as "beauty."

AMERICAN PAINTERS who had studied in Paris carried back the inspiration of the great European independents. A group of American artists outside the Academies, led by the prosperous Arthur B. Davies, formed a loose organization to bring the gospel of the independent artist to a larger American public. The epoch-making show which they planned on a shoestring and for which they rented the vast 69th Regiment Armory at Lexington Avenue and Twenty-fifth Street in New York City was to be as different as possible from shows seen in the prim salons of the Academies. While this show purported to be international, the non-American works were mostly French, and there many Americans would see for the first time the brilliant canvases of Cézanne, Gauguin, and Van Gogh.

When the Armory Show opened on February 17, 1913, it offered Americans a novel democratic experience of painting. The catalogue listed 1,112 works by 307 American artists, but more paintings were added after the show opened, and the number exhibited finally came to about 1,600. Since the show aimed to exhibit canvases by the young, the unknown, and the unconventional who would have been ignored or rejected by the Academies, it obviously could not apply usual standards. "It was bedlam," one of the planners recalled, "but we liked it." The watchword of the show, borrowed from Henri, was "Independence," the motto was "The New Spirit," and the official emblem was the pine-tree flag used by Massachusetts during the American Revolution.

"Art is a sign of life," the catalogue explained, "There can be no life without change, as there can be no development without change. To be afraid of what is different or unfamiliar, is to be afraid of life. . . . This exhibition is an indication that the Association of American Painters and Sculptors is against cowardice even when it takes the form of amiable self satisfaction." Walt Kuhn, a painter who had gone to Europe to collect works for the show, bristled when someone praised him as a better painter than Cézanne; such praise, he said, expressed "the same damned provincial loyalty which has hurt us so long."

Public attention was snatched by the most novel and unintelligible of the French painters, and especially by the Cubists. The bombshell of the show was Marcel Duchamp's "Nude Descending a Staircase," which was a sitting duck for old-fashioned critics. "This is not a movement and a principle," one of them wrote. "It is unadulterated cheek." The *American Art News* sponsored a contest to find the nude in the painting, and the winner explained, "It isn't a lady but only a man." The cliché joke was that it was "A Staircase Descending a Nude," while others called it "an explosion in a shingle factory." But to get to see the picture people had to stand in line.

"The lunatic fringe," Theodore Roosevelt's picturesque phrase for the Cubists and Futurists, was repeated with gusto by the critics of the time and by later historians of American art. But Roosevelt himself, in his "Layman's View" of the Armory Show, had actually praised the New Spirit:

> In some ways it is the work of the American painters and sculptors which is of most interest in this collection, and a glance at this work must convince anyone of the real good that is coming out of the new movements, fantastic though many of the developments of these new movements are. There was one note entirely absent from the exhibition, and that was the note of the commonplace. There was not a touch of simpering, self-satisfied conventionality anywhere in the exhibition. Any sculptor or painter who had in him something to express and the power of expressing it found the field open to him.

After a hundred thousand visitors saw the show in New York, it went to Chicago, where outraged students of the Art Institute who could not share Roosevelt's sympathy for the adventurous spirit burned Matisse in effigy; and then on to Boston. About a quarter-million Americans saw the show.

A symbolic victory for the champions of modern art was won by John Quinn, a prominent lawyer and a member of the Democratic National Committee who had helped the Armory Show. Until then, paintings less than twenty years old, and hence presumably not genuine art, were subject to United States customs duty when they were brought into this country. Quinn testified before the Senate hearings on the tariff that this law was undemocratic because it favored the rich, who alone could afford the high-priced Old Masters. Others, too, he argued, should be allowed to enjoy painting without having to pay a penalty. The Congress agreed and so endorsed the "artistic" quality of the most recent painting.

BUT THE ARTISTS' new independence of the stuffy Academies would before long lead to a new bafflement and new burdens of judgment for the layman. "There is a state of unrest all over the world in art as in all other things," declared Sir Caspar Purdon Clarke, J. P. Morgan's handpicked director of New York's Metropolitan Museum of Art, when "The Eight" opened their show. "It is the same in literature, as in music, in painting and in sculpture. And I dislike unrest."

Some of this unrest was a by-product of the revolutionary and already popular technique of photography. Soon after the Civil War, photographers on both sides of the Atlantic had seen some promise for photography as art, although it was still unclear precisely what that promise might be. The posed studio portraits by Mathew Brady and his followers had brought photography into one of the domains formerly monopolized by painters. Still, the technical limits of wet-plate photography and the long exposure time required had strictly limited the photographers' subjects. Action photography was out of the question, and spontaneity seemed impossible.

But as early as 1887 a pioneer American photographer, the young Alfred Stieglitz, foresaw that photography, more than any earlier art, somehow might be able to capture the moment. Stieglitz, the Hobo-ken-born son of a German immigrant wool merchant, had gone to the Berlin Polytechnic in 1881 to become a chemical engineer, but he acquired there a passion for photography that shaped his life. Before he was thirty, by taking advantage of technical improve-ments, including the new dry plate, he demonstrated in a series of photographs how the camera could transcend the old limits. "A Good Joke" showed Italian children surrounding their mother at her household chores; "Sun-Rays" showed a young lady at her sewing; others showed a peasant girl asleep on a pile of kindling wood, villag-ers at the pump. Stieglitz had joined the new English movement of "Pictorial Photography," which had seceded from the Royal Photo-graphic Society to establish their own annual salon where they aimed to set an aesthetic standard for photographic artists.

Returning to the United States, Stieglitz became an apostle of Pictorial Photography. His own works included a cabdriver in the snow on Fifth Avenue, a horse trolley preparing to leave from an uptown terminal, and a street scene of immigrants milling outside "Five Points Clothing House: Cheapest Place in the City." While the photographic technicians still wanted to keep photography techni-cal, simply a device for making the "precise" likenesses needed by newsmen, scientists, and salesmen, Stieglitz championed photogra-phy as an art medium that was free to do all sorts of things.

Stieglitz and his friends withdrew from the conservative Camera Club, and at the National Arts Club in New York in 1902 they offered their own exhibition, which they called "Photo-Secession." From this small beginning Stieglitz became the apostle of liberation in all American art. By the mid-twentieth century, when the United States had become the innovating center of painting in the Western world, Alfred Stieglitz would have played a leading role. While Stieglitz made photography his point of departure, he insisted that all art was emphatically an individual vision. If the photographer could actually make something individual and fresh out of the automatically correct image, then people might see all painting with refreshed eyes, and be ready for individuality there too.

In 1905, when Stieglitz rented three small rooms at 291 Fifth Avenue and christened them "The Little Galleries of the Photo-Secession," at first he showed only photographs. Later, when he began to show drawings and paintings, photographers objected. "The Secession Idea is neither the servant nor the product of a medium," Stieglitz replied, "it is a spirit. Let us say it is the Spirit of the Lamp; the old and discolored, the too frequently despised, the too often disregarded lamp of honesty; honesty of aim, honesty of self-expression, honesty of revolt against the autocracy of convention." In 1908 he shocked the New York art world with a show of Rodin watercolors, followed by the first American exhibitions of Matisse (1908), Toulouse-Lautrec (1909), Rousseau (1910), Cézanne (1911), Picabia (1913), Braque (1914), and Severini (1917); he offered an extensive show of Picasso (1911), and gave Brancusi his first one-man show (1914). "291" became famous—"the largest small room in the world."

In other ways, too, Stieglitz set free the artistic imagination of the American audience. He exhibited the works of untaught children; and he offered the first American show (1914–15) of African sculpture exhibited not as anthropology but as art. Stieglitz was not only showing how photography could help liberate the American's vision of all art. He was also beginning to say—what would become an American cliché in the late twentieth century—that art might be anything that anybody anywhere produced in his quest for self-expression.

Even before the end of the nineteenth century, photography had begun to deprive painters of their staple, the portrait. Photoengraving was displacing wood engraving, while machine production and countless techniques for making repeatable objects brought chaos to the whole world of handicrafts. Many of the craftsman's traditional opportunities were disappearing. One result, as the art historian Edgar P. Richardson explains, was that painting became "diluted with talents that did not belong to it. . . . overwhelmed by a flood of displaced talents." Painting was now the métier of the "untrained professional." At first, Americans who could afford to buy original works of art were puzzled that "artists" were no longer painting dead fish and cows beside purling brooks. But they gradually began to think of the artist as simply another American pursuing his own kind of novelty, not so different from the inventor in his laboratory or the Go-Getter in merchandising.

The series of "One-Man Shows" at "291" helped set a new style in the exhibition world and provided Stieglitz his way of offering conspicuous hospitality to the individual with a private vision. As the One-Man Show, in contrast to the Academy Exhibit of a "school" of painting, became the dominant form for introducing works of painters to the public, it helped authenticate the new role of the artist.

Stieglitz—and after him numerous other owners of private galleries —found their stock in trade to be not craftsmanship but originality, not tradition but idiosyncrasy.

Of course the idea of a One-Man Show was not new in twentieth-century America, nor was it an American invention. A patron who visited an artist's studio anywhere would view a private one-man-show of that artist's work. And in the United States, even a half-century before Stieglitz, there had been a few public showings of the works of only one artist, but it appears that planned public showings of the works of only one artist were rare. When they occurred, as with an exposition of the works of John G. Chapman in 1848, or of the works of J. F. Cropsey in 1856, they merely exhibited conventional academic works, and aimed to show how the particular artist's work fit into the accepted tradition. Commercial art galleries had dealt almost exclusively in older works, in Old Masters or their imitators, while the Academy salons at any one time customarily showed the works (approved in advance by an eminent jury) of numerous artists in the dominant style. By the early twentieth century, however, the One-Man Show had become the usual format for commercial galleries and was familiar in public museums.

The One-Man Show, by putting the spotlight on the individual artist, aimed to display the range of his originality. While from the artist's point of view the art world was newly atomized, for the layman the world of art was a new set of puzzles. The gallery visitor, like the supermarket shopper, was thrust back on his own judgment, to decide whether this was good art, or indeed whether it was art at all. But while the consumer in a wilderness of packages was bewildered by the similarities of things, the layman in the world of democratic art was tantalized by the spectacle of unintelligible originality.

THE LAYMAN BEGAN to believe that he was supposed to be puzzled. The sophisticate in art was no longer the connoisseur (of whom Bernard Berenson was the American prototype) who knew all about the schools and traditions and techniques of the Old Masters. The democratized sophisticate was a person who was open to shock but still remained unshockable. He was a man who admired novelty. By the late twentieth century, the alert American was flooded by "art" from new galleries, from new museums of modern art, using novel materials and innovative techniques. Whatever other satisfactions he was securing, he could no longer look to art as his refuge from the flux of experience. Art, the *par excellence* arena of novelty, taxed the individual judgment. Where could the American find his objects of tradition-guaranteed beauty?

The stage was set for a struggle between older and newer meanings of democracy in art. The champions of novelty were saying that the layman, for the first time, should be allowed to decide for himself without the intervention of Academies, what he liked, and even what was art. "It is not easy to know what you like," Robert Henri observed. "Most people fool themselves their entire lives through about this." But the new traditionalists insisted that a truly democratic art was one which the people could understand, and which anybody could recognize as art.

The few strong talents who united in revolt against the new dogma of novelty themselves became a popular school of American painting, and they produced some of the best traditional painting that had yet come from this country. They celebrated the American landscape and everything else that they found characteristically American. Forced home from the Paris Left Bank by the Depression, they were inspired by the New Deal and supported by the Works Progress Administration (W.P.A.). And their regional painting, unlike much of the earlier American genre and landscape painting, was not bland and genteel. It was a vigorous search for roots, an outspoken and even vituperative reaction against the New Spirit of Novelty.

The leaders were Thomas Hart Benton (1889–), Grant Wood (1892–1942), and John Steuart Curry (1897–1946). They had all been to Paris, and came back to live in their American hometowns, spiritually as well as physically. Benton made Missouri his base for painting murals of American history, Wood painted Iowa people and places, Curry depicted Kansas. And there were scores of others, less vigorous and less original, who were encouraged by these three and who also painted, in traditional ways the layman could understand, the scenes of all America.

Thomas Hart Benton was the voice of their protest, which resounded louder than their affirmation. In his *Artist in America* (1968), he explained:

> . . . We were all in revolt against the unhappy effects which the armory show of 1913 had had on American painting. We objected to the new Parisian aesthetics which was more and more turning art away from the living world of active men and women into an academic world of empty pattern. We wanted an American art which was not empty, and we believed that only by turning the formative process of art back again to meaningful subject matter, in our cases specifically American subject matter, could we expect to get one . . . The coteries of highbrows, of critics, college art professors and museum boys, the tastes of which had been thoroughly conditioned by the new aesthetics of twentieth-century Paris, had sustained themselves in various subsidized ivory towers and kept their grip on the journals of aesthetic opinion.

... They had, as a matter of fact, a vested interest in aesthetic obscurity, in highfalutin symbolisms and devious and indistinct meanings. The entertainment of these obscurities, giving an appearance of superior discernment and extraordinary understanding, enabled them to milk the wealthy ladies who went in for art and the college and museum trustees of the country for the means of support. . . . Wood, Curry and I were bringing American art out into a field where its meanings had to be socially intelligible to justify themselves . . .

Benton blamed "this anarchic idiocy of the current American art scene" partly on the uncritical importation of foreign ideas of art, but also on "over-intellectualization," and especially on "the 'public be damned' individualism of the last century." He begged artists to seek "American life as known and felt by ordinary Americans."

Despite the wide appeal of their individual paintings, these regionalists were fighting a losing battle. More and more "ordinary Americans" could now be reached by the "highfalutin" priests and arbiters of artistic taste. Laymen, increasingly puzzled by what was really meant by art, could feel less uncertain of what they meant by novelty. And they relished its habit-forming delights. Americans had shallower roots; the nation was becoming less a landscape of regions. The local scenes which the Regionalists celebrated were each year becoming less characteristic than ever. A democratic nation of everywhere communities was now measuring its success by its power to erase differences.

Wood and Curry both died discouraged. In 1946, in his last talk with Curry, Benton tried to bolster his friend's spirits by telling him that he would have a lasting place in American art. "I don't know about that," Curry replied, "maybe I'd have done better to stay on the farm. No one seems interested in my pictures. Nobody thinks I can paint. If I *am* any good, I lived at the wrong time."

In the struggle between the old Americanism which celebrated the place, and the newer Americanism which celebrated man's ungovernable reach for novel visions and juxtapositions, the result was not in doubt. The next stage in American painting was as far as possible from a patriotic regionalism.

PERHAPS THE MOST IMPORTANT FIGURE was Jackson Pollock (1912–56), whose career was itself a parable of the new dilemmas of art in American democracy. Born in Wyoming and raised in Arizona and California, Pollock lived through many of the vital movements in the painting of his day. He studied with Thomas Hart Benton and worked on Federal Arts Projects before coming to his own version of "Abstract Expressionism," which, as christened by Harold Rosenberg, came to be called "Action Painting." Pollock had unwittingly translated John Dewey's idealization of growth and action into a philosophy of painting. Pollock himself explained:

> My painting does not come from the easel. I hardly ever stretch my canvas before painting. I prefer to tack the outstretched canvas to the hard wall or the floor. I need the resistance of a hard surface. On the floor I am more at ease. I feel nearer, more a part of the painting, since this way I can walk around it, work from the four sides and literally be *in* the painting. This is akin to the method of the Indian sand painters of the West.
>
> I continue to get further away from the usual painter's tools such as easel, palette, brushes, etc. I prefer sticks, trowels, knives and dripping fluid paint or a heavy impasto with sand, broken glass and other foreign matter added.
>
> When I am *in* my painting, I am not aware of what I'm doing. It is only after a sort of "get acquainted" period that I see what I have been about. I have no fears about making changes, destroying the image, etc., because the painting has a life of its own. I try to let it come through. It is only when I lose contact with the painting that the result is a mess. Otherwise there is pure harmony, an easy give and take, and the painting comes out well.

Along with Pollock came other originals—Adolph Gottlieb, Franz Kline, Willem de Kooning, Morris Graves, and others—each with his own notion of what a painting might be.

In the artists' world, the world of Academies and "schools" and movements, as the art historian James S. Ackerman has explained, this quest for novelty led to "the Demise of the Avant Garde." The concept of an avant garde, ahead of and in advance of the culture of its time, was rooted in French romanticism, although it would reach a climax in twentieth-century America. Originally the idea had meant the artist's freedom to work without worrying about his audience. Then the rise in the United States of a new class of "professional manufacturers of opinion" in the art world, together with the increase in the business of selling paintings (from private galleries to department stores and Sears, Roebuck, which opened a traveling show in the 1960's), made change a value in itself. The opinion manufacturers, by multiplying museums, by reducing the cost of color reproductions and increasing circulation of "serious" cultural media, turned art into a kaleidoscope.

The innovating painter found his works snapped up by critics, exhibitors, and collectors, who were always in search of the next shocker. "Minimal Art" (which consists of doing little or nothing to an object, but simply considering an object as art) and "Pop Art" (the determination to treat a common object as art) showed the desperation of the late-twentieth-century quest for novelty. Innovation became the condition of survival. The last stage in democratizing the art-flavored experience, as Ackerman observes, was that "there is almost no territory left to conquer on the extreme borderline between art and non-art."

What did this mean for the naïve layman, for whom art was still a synonym for beauty? With Jackson Pollock and action painting, with the certification of sheer novelty as art, Benton's "ordinary American" felt puzzled, troubled, and perhaps even deprived.

55

The Exotic Becomes Commonplace

ONE OF THE BEAUTIFUL IRONIES of modern American history was that the children of refugees from the Old World had the wealth, the leisure, and the technical means to return for a holiday to the scenes of their parents' poverty and oppression. There were few more vivid symbols of American democracy, or of the special relation of Americans to the world, than this reverse Odyssey of American tourists in the mid-twentieth century. The man whose ancestor had fled penniless and in desperation from Sicily or Ireland or Germany returned in air-conditioned comfort to rediscover the "romance" of the Old World.

UNTIL THE 1920'S, American travelers abroad were almost exclusively the rich and the privileged. In 1895, for example, about two thirds of the hundred thousand Americans and Canadians who sailed to Europe were traveling first class; and the servants accompanying these rich travelers accounted for some passengers in the other classes. The Black Ball Line had opened the first scheduled transatlantic passenger service in 1818 with regular sailings between New York and Liverpool, followed by the Red Star Line, the Swallow Tail Line, the Dramatic Line (ships named *Shakespeare, Sheridan, Garrick,* and *Siddons*), and the French Line, which sailed to Le Havre. While an increasing number of Americans traveled to Europe even before the Civil War, a trip abroad remained a major undertaking, requiring both the time and the money that few Americans could afford. *Ninety Days' Worth of Europe* were described by the popular writer Edward Everett Hale as "a happy little dash." Not until the early years of the twentieth century did second-class accommodations become more comfortable and less expensive. Before World War I, the Americans who could afford it found a trip to Europe full of delights. The gala sailing from New York was celebrated by bon voyage boxes, flowers, and champagne. First-class life on shipboard, embellished by clothing from numerous "steamer trunks" and "wardrobe trunks" (both Americanisms dating from about 1890), was a round of parties beside swimming pools, in ladies' parlors, grand ballrooms, and picturesque cafés. The North German Lloyd advertised their new second-class facilities as "comfort without luxury." Passports were still not required.

American travelers to the European continent who believed (in the words of one of them) that the Old World "ought to look old" were not disappointed. And they were sometimes titillated by what they saw. "I placed my hands before my face for very shame," Mark Twain reported of his first sight of the cancan in Paris, "but I looked through my fingers." This was much the same reaction that Abigail Adams, in Paris about a century before, had described on seeing her first ballet. "I felt my delicacy wounded," she wrote to her sister back home in Massachusetts, "and I was ashamed to be seen to look at them. Girls, clothed in the thinnest silk and gauze, with their petticoats short, springing two feet from the floor, poising themselves in the air, with their feet flying, and as perfectly showing their garters and drawers as though no petticoats had been worn, was a sight altogether new to me." But, she confessed, "repeatedly seeing these dances has worn off that disgust which I at first felt, and. . . . I see them now with pleasure."

But even late in the nineteenth century, all Americans were not so open to new impressions. In 1907 William Jennings Bryan reassured his countrymen that they would return from a trip abroad "more widely informed, but more intensely American." What he saw had simply confirmed his faith that "in all that goes to make a nation great materially, commercially, politically and morally, our country has no peer." But since few of Bryan's constituents could yet afford to confirm their patriotism by going abroad, the impact of foreign travel on American life as a whole was still indirect. It had come through the lectures and writings of literary men like Ralph Waldo Emerson, Washington Irving, and Henry James, through the painting and sculpture of Horatio Greenough and Hiram Powers, and others.

The daughters of American families of wealth and distinction who traveled abroad were apt to succumb to the charm of European titles. In 1874 the beautiful Jennie Jerome of New York married Lord Randolph Churchill (their son was Winston Churchill); President Grant's granddaughter married a Russian prince, Michael Cantacuzene; and Vice-President Levi P. Morton's daughter married the Duc de Valençay et de Sagan. An article in *McCall's* in 1903 enumerated fifty-seven such recent marriages of American women "dowered with loveliness and dollars." A muckraking historian complained that as a result of five hundred of these social-climbing marriages, the United States had lost some $200 million into the pockets of scheming Europeans.

But the traveling rich also brought treasure home with them. In the last decades of the nineteenth century, several ambitious American women of wealth sent back to the United States millions of dollars' worth of painting and sculpture. Mrs. Potter Palmer, who had one of the largest fortunes (as well as, reputedly, one of the smallest waists) in Chicago, used the fortune which her husband had made in the Marshall Field Department Store and in the Palmer House Hotel to buy works of art. In Paris her mentor was the remarkable Mary Cassatt, wealthy daughter of a Pennsylvania banking family who, as a girl, had traveled the continent with her family and finally emigrated to Paris in 1874. After studying the Old Masters, Mary Cassatt became the friend and disciple of Degas, who considered her one of the great painters of the day. It was Mary Cassatt's taste and her personal acquaintance with the French impressionists (on one occasion she arranged the purchase of four Renoirs for $5,000) that enabled Mrs. Palmer to build the collection which, after her death, enriched the Art Institute of Chicago. Mrs. Isabella Stewart Gardner, the eccentric Boston socialite daughter of a wealthy New York importer, spent her fortune buying a wide assortment of works by the European painters from Bellini to Zorn. With the advice of the young Bernard Berenson, who was just building his reputation as a judge of Italian painting, she put together a spectacular collection, then built Fenway Court "as a museum for the education and enjoyment of the public forever."

The Metropolitan Museum of Art in New York City became the chief beneficiary of the energetic and discriminating collecting of J. P. Morgan, who traveled abroad frequently and was always scouting for artworks to bring home. He paid $200,000 for a Cellini cup, and $484,000 for a Raphael altarpiece. A contrast to Morgan's discrimination was the magpie collection of William Randolph Hearst; he squandered his fortune on a miscellany whose only use was extravagantly to document (for example, in René Clair's *The Ghost Goes West*) European prejudices about Americans of wealth.

IN THE 1920'S, foreign travel by Americans began to be demo-cratized. Before World War I, as William Allen White observed, "any Emporian's trip to Europe was a matter of townwide concern." But the rising American standard of living, and improvements in the less expensive steamship facilities, allowed an increasing number of Americans to go abroad. In 1929, more than a half-million Americans traveled overseas.

The next great increase was to come with the rise of the airplane which reduced the time and the cost of transoceanic travel beyond earlier imaginings. The dramatic catalyst, of course, was Charles A. Lindbergh's solo flight from New York to Paris on May 20, 1927, which brought him the most enthusiastic popular welcome ever given to an American citizen on arrival abroad. Lindbergh's warm reception by the French was doubly remarkable since he had not gone there to spend money.

Only a dozen years later, on June 28, 1939, Pan American Airways opened its first commercial flight to Europe. The "Dixie Clipper," a four-engine Boeing flying boat, which carried twenty-two passengers drawn from a waiting list of five hundred, stopped for refueling in the Azores, landed in Lisbon where the passengers spent the night, and went on to its destination, Marseilles. After the interruption of World War II, and facilitated by wartime improvements in aircraft design, tourist air travel became routine. By 1950, when Americans going abroad numbered 676,000, the air passengers outnumbered those who traveled by sea; in 1955, when the total going overseas exceeded one million, twice as many went by air. And by 1970, when the Americans going abroad each year numbered nearly five million, the travelers by sea accounted for only 3 percent. The issuing of passports became a bureaucratic problem of major proportions: in 1950 there were three hundred thousand passports issued, and twenty years later the annual figure approached two million.

The United States was the first nation in history so many of whose citizens could go so far simply in quest of fun and culture. The size of this phenomenon made international travel, for the first time, a major element in world trade, a new problem for the American economy and for American balance of payments, and a new oppor-tunity for the destination countries. In 1970 the Department of Com-merce estimated that the expenditures of American travelers over-seas had reached $2 billion each year. In the United States, economists began to count foreign travel as a major import, and other countries began to plan for tourism by Americans as a principal export.

The democratizing of foreign travel had required extensive and energetic efforts of salesmanship, advertising, and organization. It took two full centuries (from the eighteenth to the twentieth) to bring fifty million people to the United States from overseas. In the late twentieth century, every year one-tenth that number of Americans would fly across the ocean in the opposite direction. Democracy had reduced a transoceanic adventure to a two-week holiday. The travelers went, usually, for no life-shaking purpose, but only for vacation, for the instruction and delight of new places, for new sights and new sensations.

Vacation travel became a mass-produced, packaged commodity. Not until the 1960's did the threat of air piracy, promoted by the irresponsible sensationalism of the press, radio, and television, add an unpleasant new fillip of adventure to a trip abroad.

The pioneer in packaging travel for mass consumption was not an American, but the Englishman Thomas Cook. In the 1840's, Cook's first planned tour took nearly six hundred people the eleven miles from Leicester to Loughborough for a temperance convention, at a reduced round-trip third-class fare of one shilling a head. Cook was soon sending hundreds to Scotland (1846) and Ireland (1848), and then he brought thousands to the Crystal Palace Exposition in London in 1851. In that year, too, Cook offered Britons his first "grand circular tour of the continent," and by 1869 he advertised the first middle-class Conducted Crusade to the Holy Land. Cook's sophisticated countrymen called his tours a "new and growing evil," vulgarizing the sights that had been properly reserved for the aristocratic, the knowledgeable, and the wealthy. "The Cities of Italy," the British consul in Florence complained in *Blackwood's Magazine* in February 1865, were now "deluged with droves of these creatures, for they never separate, and you see them forty in number pouring along a street with their director—now in front, now at the rear, circling round them like a sheepdog—and really the process is as like herding as may be. I have already met three flocks, and anything so uncouth I never saw before."

But Thomas Cook defended his tours as "agencies for the advancement of Human Progress." How foolish to "think that places of rare interest should be excluded from the gaze of the common people, and be kept only for the interest of the 'select' of society. But it is too late in this day of progress to talk such exclusive nonsense, God's earth with all its fullness and beauty, is for the people; and railways and steamboats are the result of the common light of science, and are for the people also. . . . The best of men, and the noblest minds, rejoice to see the people follow in their foretrod routes of pleasure." But the democratic spirit that Cook praised had not yet entirely prevailed even in America, where daughters of wealth lusted after foreign titles. A few rich scions like James Hazen Hyde (inheritor of

New York Life Insurance millions) and William Waldorf Astor (heir to the $100 million Astor fortune) who began by mimicking European aristocrats finally became expatriates.

In the United States in the last decades of the nineteenth century, when the promoters of transatlantic travel still found it more profitable to deal in immigrants than in tourists, Americans who wanted a planned European tour still relied on Thomas Cook & Son. President Grant used Cook's. And Mark Twain, in a published testimonial in which he disavowed knowing Cook personally, informed all Americans that "Cook has made travel easy and a pleasure." Not until the twentieth century did Cook's have a serious American competitor.

Wells, Fargo and the other companies which became the American Express Company had been organized in the mid-nineteenth century to forward goods and money across the continental spaces of the growing nation. Later in the century these same companies did a flourishing business arranging remittances from successful, recently arrived Americans to their needy families back in Europe. In 1895 American Express opened its first European office, which offered traveling Americans a mail-forwarding service, assistance in securing railroad tickets and in making hotel reservations, and help in finding lost baggage. President James C. Fargo, who was in charge until 1914, insisted that there was no money in the tourist business: the company had begun in freight and express and should stay there. But when World War I forced the consolidation of the different express companies, American Express branched out into new services. Before the end of the war the company had begun developing a foreign travel service, which grew spectacularly at the war's end. By 1970 American Express had about a thousand offices throughout the world, and was serving tourists everywhere.

American Express sent the first postwar escorted tour to Europe in October 1919, and three years later dispatched the first all-water round-the-world pleasure cruise. With its packaged tours, American Express abolished tourist worries and made the knowledge or the previous experience of the traveler unnecessary. Specializing in people going places for the first time, they made it possible for middle-class Americans to take a trip abroad at a precisely predictable cost, going to the cities and staying in the hotels which American Express had already expertly tested on a mass market.

In the old days, carrying money to distant places had been a problem solved only by the complicated apparatus of bank drafts and letters of credit. The ordinary citizen who spoke no foreign language and had no connections abroad was bound to be troubled. In 1891 American Express copyrighted the first Travelers Cheque which ingeniously provided transfer of small sums of money for people who were unknown where the money was to be spent. This was, of course, another step toward democratizing foreign travel. When Americans were stranded in Europe in 1914 at the outbreak of the war, the American Express Travelers Cheque was one of the few forms of financial paper honored by European banks. By 1960, about $2 billion worth of these American Express Travelers Cheques were being sold annually. The insurance feature of the Travelers Cheque made it a new kind of "unlosable money," and by relieving the traveler of still another worry, further enlarged the market for distant travel.

OF THE EVERYDAY American institutions that helped popularize foreign travel, none was more pervasive than the postal card. The earliest known postal card is the one for which John P. Charlton of Philadelphia secured a copyright in 1861. It was a plain card to which the sender affixed a postage stamp, blank on the reverse where the message was to be written. Under the Postal Act of that year, the required postage was one cent. A law of 1872, which directed the Postmaster General to "issue with postage-stamps impressed upon them, 'postal cards,' manufactured of good stiff paper," brought another Americanism into the language. For advertising foreign places and the delights of foreign travel, an event of major importance was the First International Postal Treaty (1875), in which the member countries agreed that postcards could be sent between the member countries at half the letter rate.

In the 1890's pictorial-view postal cards were being widely sold in Europe, and were beginning to reach American hometowns with enticing views of the scenic beauties of the Old World. The pioneers in printing these cards were the Germans, who by 1895 had popularized the *"Gruss aus"* (Greetings from) card, with appropriate local pictures from all over the world. This was an ingenious new form of packaged, mass-produced tourist greetings, ready-made for the lucky members of the new packaged tours. The card that showed a European castle or palace, a scene along the Rhine, the Seine, or the Thames, or a picturesque glimpse of an Old World city street with a standardized message and the words "Greetings from" elaborately printed, offered the special advantage that it left only a tiny blank space for the hurried traveler's "Having a wonderful time!" along with his signature. These were forerunners of the still further improved American cards of the next century which required the tourist only to check off his message from a ready-made list. At first, presumably to protect the sale of the official, ready-stamped post-office cards, the United States Post Office prohibited the private printing of postcards. Meanwhile the postcard industry flourished in

Germany, and colored picture postcards of scenes from everywhere were printed in Berlin. An increasing number of Americans traveling abroad used these to greet, and to impress, their friends back home.

Incidentally the cards, with romanticized versions of foreign sights and continental hotels, advertised overseas travel and awakened the envy and the desire of hometown folks. In Germany during 1899, eighty-eight million postcards of all kinds were mailed; and in 1902, when a half-billion were mailed in England, the German figure exceeded one billion. By the turn of the century the United States Post Office was already troubled by the problem of what were then called "naughty or suggestive" postcards emanating from the arcades of the Rue de Rivoli in Paris. And an imperial decree of the Ottoman Empire in 1900 forbade some of their most interesting postcards when, applying the Muslim prohibition of images, it outlawed those of religious ceremonies, mosques, or Turkish women.

The camera, which began to be popularized by Eastman's Kodak in 1888, would before long transform the traveler's experience. Even before every tourist carried a camera, photography was shaping the American view of the travel world, but new techniques were required to reproduce photographs in large numbers. At first the only way to make a photographic postcard was to affix each photograph separately to the back of a card. It was 1900 before the half-tone photoengraving process, which had already created the illustrated newspaper, produced inexpensive photographic postcards.

The traveler's sense of adventure, which once came from encountering the risky and the unpredictable, began to be dulled as the Grand Tour became the Packaged Tour. The traveler became the "tourist" consuming a mass-produced, guaranteed product. When the travel agent arranged facilities which were as much as possible like those back home, casual encounters with "natives" became fewer and more bland. The room was already reserved, the menu prearranged, the check had been paid in advance. Covered by ingenious new forms of insurance against all risks (including inclement weather and loss of baggage), secure in possession of his unstealable money, the tourist returned home with fewer memories but with more photographs. His satisfaction or his grievances were aimed less at the people in the country he had visited than at the hometown travel agent who had sold him the package.

Most important in diluting the novelty of the travel experience were those accessories and appliances in the American home which began to make actual trips to faraway places seem superfluous, and even perhaps inferior to what he could get with little trouble and almost no expense. The "stereopticon" (an Americanism which came into use after the Civil War) first allowed Americans in their own parlors to see realistic, three-dimensional views of the Holy Land, the Sphinx, and other exotic sights. Later, more and more Americans brought back their own photographic record, displacing the old traveler's diary. Then movies at the neighborhood theater showed travelogues with sights (after the 1920's in full color) and sounds of London, Paris, Istanbul, and New Delhi at all seasons of the year, at negligible cost, and without travel risks. For many Americans it was these movie trips even more than those in person that created their authentic image of places. By the early 1930's Americans were visiting the Houses of Parliament to see where George Arliss had been Disraeli in the famous movie of that name, as later they visited the Trevi Fountain in Rome to see whether it was really the way it had looked in *Three Coins in the Fountain*. By late-century, television was bringing these and other exotic places with sound and in full color into American living rooms, bedrooms, and kitchens. If the faraway places still interested Americans, the interest could be conveniently satisfied in their own homes—at the flip of a switch.

Book Four

THE FUTURE
ON SCHEDULE

"The American journey has not ended. America is never accomplished, America is always still to build. . . . West is a country in the mind, and so eternal."

ARCHIBALD MACLEISH

A M E R I C A N civilization, from its beginnings, had combined a dogmatic confidence in the future with a naïve puzzlement over what the future might bring. The Puritans believed in a Divine Providence who would keep the world in order, and their belief was all the deeper because they firmly doubted that they really could know what Providence had planned. When later Americans affirmed the nation's Destiny, even when they sometimes called it "manifest," their faith once again was firmer because the reach of the American destiny could never be sharply defined.

Twentieth-century America saw a future fuller of novelty than any nation's future had ever seemed before. Yet the novelty itself was becoming a planned product, predictable and familiar.

PART NINE

Search for Novelty

"Make it new."

EZRA POUND

"A fever of newness has been everywhere confused with the spirit of progress."

HENRY FORD

"One of the fundamental purposes of research is to foster a healthy dissatisfaction."

CHARLES F. KETTERING AND ALLAN ORTH

AMERICANS ORGANIZED in search of novelty, they democratized novelty, until they would finally make it commonplace. All the resources which had been used to lay tracks across the continent, to develop an American System of Manufacturing in its several versions, now went into American Systems of Inventing. In modern America everything became an incentive for invention.

The Social Inventor, the Inventor-for-the-Market, saw a need and tried to satisfy it. And then there were Communities of Inventors, whose incentive was not the market but the autonomous needs of invention itself. They lived by the internal logic of novelty. For them each new thing required another. Finding the use or the market was somebody else's problem. Working in islands freed from everyday necessities, they had the power to require society to recast its needs to make their discoveries useful. They delighted in making silk purses out of sows' ears, for they were free to think of the neglected obvious and the feasible that still seemed outlandish.

Then the momentum of production itself became an unexpected force toward innovation. The American System of Manufacturing, the production of millions of similar objects, the democratized consumption of costly novelties, produced a need for slightly *dis*similar objects. This path to innovation, the Path of the Annual Model, came not from the needs of society, nor from innovation-for-its-own-sake, but from the need to keep people buying. Next year's model had to be just different enough. Flow technology, an assembly-line society, implied in itself the need, with a scheduled regularity, to change, however slightly, the product that was flowing. But how different was different enough?

56

The Social Inventor:
Inventing for the Market

IN THE SPRING of 1876 the young Thomas A. Edison, not yet thirty years old, moved fifteen of his workers to the isolated village of Menlo Park, New Jersey. To his 30 feet by 100 feet white clapboard building, horse-drawn trucks brought rolls of wire, boxes of chemicals, books, a brown steam engine, and a gasoline converter to supply gaslight. From this miscellany it was impossible to guess what Edison aimed to concoct, for he had decided to go into the "invention business."

"Discovery is not invention," said Edison, "and I dislike to see the two words confounded. A discovery is more or less in the nature of an accident." Did Americans want new products? Then they could not wait for "discoveries." They would have to go in search, organizing for this as they would have organized for anything else. Inventions, according to Edison, were not strokes of luck by minds exploring at random; they were the products of purpose. And Edison believed that the right men, properly organized, could turn out inventions just as regularly and as intentionally as a factory could turn out any other product.

AT MENLO PARK, Edison intended to turn out "a minor invention every ten days and a big thing every six months or so." By an "invention" Edison meant a social, or more precisely, a marketable product. And this gave his very idea of "invention" a distinctively American cast.

Edison was a *social* inventor. He had focused his first inventive efforts on telegraphy, which until then had been electricity's most important practical application. His first encounter with telegraphy had come by a lucky accident. When Edison was only fifteen, selling newspapers on the Grand Trunk Railway, he had rescued the three-year-old son of the Mount Clemens, Michigan, stationmaster from the path of a moving train. The father showed his gratitude by inviting young Edison to come and live with his family, and he trained the boy as a telegraph operator. This was what brought Edison into the mysterious new world of electricity.

Before he was twenty-one, Edison was granted his first patent—for a telegraphic vote-recording machine. He had developed this machine while he was reporting the votes of Congress over the press wires, and he noticed the time lost in polling the members for their voice votes. With his invention, at every roll call each congressman would simply press a button at his seat, immediately registering his vote at the Speaker's desk, where the votes were counted automatically. But Edison's instant vote recorder would have abolished one of the traditionally cherished opportunities to filibuster. "Young man," declared the chairman of the congressional committee to whom Edison had just given a demonstration, "that is just what we do *not* want. Your invention would destroy the only hope that the minority would have of influencing legislation. . . . And as the ruling majority knows that some day they may become a minority, they will be as much averse to change as their opponents." This taught Edison a lesson that he never forgot; thereafter, as Edison himself noted, he would aim at a "commercial demand."

The decade after the Civil War was the heyday of speculation. When Edison came to New York City in 1869, the telegraph was already serving the Gold Exchange with a new "gold indicator" that transmitted numerals as electrical impulses and instantaneously sent information of market fluctuations to distant places. At the height of the speculative mania, when the gold indicators broke down, Edison quickly found the trouble, fixed the machines, and was engaged by the Gold Indicator Company at the then handsome salary of $300 a month. He made a series of inventions serving the gold market. Then Edison and a few friends set themselves up as "electrical engineers" to devise further improvements in telegraph apparatus. When the powerful Western Union discovered his talents, he was added to the company's team of inventors and given a half-million-dollar order to manufacture twelve hundred stock tickers of his new design. In 1871 Edison could report to his mother that at only twenty-four years of age he had become a "Bloated Eastern Manufacturer."

In telegraph technology at that stage, the urgent need was for some way to send more than one message at a time over a telegraph wire. By 1869 Edison had already made progress toward a "duplex" machine that would simultaneously send a message on a single wire in both directions. By 1874 he had developed his even more remarkable "quadruplex" machine (he also invented the word), which made it possible to send *two* messages in both directions at the same time. This one device had the effect of doubling the Western Union facilities and resulted in savings of millions of dollars. Jay Gould bought Edison's interest in the quadruplex by a transaction so complicated that it supported lawyers for a decade; in the resulting litigation Edison heard lawyers in the courtroom call him a "Professor of Duplicity and Quadruplicity."

By the time that the young Edison opened his Menlo Park Laboratory, then, he had already well established himself as an inventor. Besides these improvements in the telegraph, his inventions had included an "electric pen," a mimeograph, and other lesser items.

Edison's invention factory was emphatically a *factory*, where he intended to turn invention into large-scale business, meeting the needs of the market. Although off in a village, it was not intended to be a research institute or a place of withdrawal for scientific speculation. Just as stove factories were bringing together workmen who could make the different parts of a stove, so Edison intended to assemble men who would be able to make the different parts of an invention. He had his own toolmakers, and before long he added a mathematical physicist. Edison believed that the best way to invent was to collect a sufficient number of competent men with the best possible equipment, and then organize them for the dogged pursuit of their object. The businesslike Edison actually put little store by "inspiration" or the idea of inventive "genius." He was, as his biographer observed, "a genius who held that there was no such thing as a genius."

In the United States after the Civil War the successful inventor was seldom the lone visionary. Although people called Edison "The Wizard of Menlo Park," the folklore of the alchemist in his secret chamber was beginning to be out of date—and Edison would help make it so. Yet somehow the lone inventor would never become entirely obsolete. A study of seventy case histories of major twentieth-century inventions in Europe and America would show that some of these did come from the lonely inventor with meager resources, struggling to perfect his device against the indifference of the established enterprises. Their inventions would include the jet engine, the gyrocompass, the process of hardening liquid fats to make soap and margarine, power steering, magnetic tape-recording, Bakelite, the helicopter, the Kodachrome process, the zipper, and the self-winding wristwatch.

But there is nothing new about the way of the lonely inventor. There *was* something new in the organized quest for inventions. In modern America the most substantial, most calculating citizens, the largest, most respectable enterprises would be the mainstay of this organized quest. The American inventor would pursue a respectable profession.

For Edison himself, inventing would be a passion. He sometimes complained that every young applicant for a job at Menlo Park wanted to know only how much was the pay and how long were the hours. And he would tell them, "Well, we don't pay anything, and we work all the time!" But many young men shared his passion and joined him on the job.

THE INVENTION FACTORY was incorporated into the American economy with the forming of the Edison Electric Light Company in 1878. The system of electric lighting which transformed daily life in the twentieth century was a calculated product of Edison's new institution.

A decade before Edison moved to Menlo Park, others had made a start on electric lighting. In England in the 1860's arc lights were used for coastal lighthouses, and at the Philadelphia Centennial Exposition of 1876, three arc lights burning in the open air gave off a dazzling white glow. The general counsel to Western Union was so impressed by the brilliant electric arc lighting at the Paris Exposition of 1878 that when he returned to the United States, he persuaded Edison to explore its commercial possibilities. Earlier Edison had experimented briefly with electric lighting, but he had temporarily given it up to experiment with the phonograph.

Arc lighting was, of course, the light made by an electric arc. An electric current flowing between the points of two pencil-like rods of carbon produced a brilliant white light as it burned off the points. At the first public demonstration back in 1808, Sir Humphrey Davy had lit his arcs with a battery of two thousand cells. And the arc light did not become practical for general use until the invention of the dynamo, which in the 1880's displaced the batteries.

In the growing cities, where some kind of lighting had become essential to public safety, the main competition for arc lighting came from gaslighting. By 1835, gas companies in Baltimore, Boston, New

York, Brooklyn, and New Orleans were lighting some streets, a few factories, and a small number of wealthy private residences. Forty years later there were more than four hundred gas companies. But the lighting of streets by gas was still confined to the big cities, where it was profitable to run a central station. Remote factories that wanted gaslight had to install their own gas plants. In small towns and on the farm, Americans relied on candles and oil lamps. It still seemed that when artificial lighting came into more general use, it would be produced by gas.

When the Edison Electric Light Company was formed in 1878, arc lighting gave no promise of lighting homes, offices, or small shops. The arc light, like gas, produced light by burning, and hence could be used only where an open flame was not dangerous; and the carbon rods had to be replaced frequently. But its special limitation was that the arc gave a dazzling light which could not be reduced. Hence even the smallest workable arc lights were not suitable for small-space indoor lighting. In addition, arc lights operated on a "series circuit," which meant that they all had to be turned on or off at the same time. And if even a single arc short-circuited, the whole system was in peril. By contrast, then, gaslighting had many advantages, and over 90 percent of the revenues of gas companies still came from lighting offices and homes.

Edison's grasp of the problem of electric lighting proved to be as far as possible from the intuitions of simple "Yankee ingenuity" or of the naïvely inventive gadgeteer. For him this was a *social* problem, which meant, of course, a problem of the market. In September 1878 he witnessed an exhibition display of eight brilliant 500-candlepower arc lights, presented as the latest thing in arc lights.

> I saw that what had been done had never been made practically useful. The intense light had not been subdivided so that it could be brought into private houses. In all electric lights theretofore obtained the intensity of light was very great, and the quantity (of units) very low. I came home and made experiments two nights in succession. I discovered the necessary secret, so simple that a bootblack might understand it. It suddenly came to me, like the secret of the speaking phonograph. It was real and no phantom. . . . The subdivision of light is all right. . . .

To a reporter for the New York *Sun,* he revealed his vision of a total *system:* a central station would send out electric power through a wire network to every household, where the current would illuminate thousands of small household lights. He rashly predicted there would soon be a half-million in downtown New York alone. And his flamboyant predictions, even at this early stage, enlisted the financing of Vanderbilt and of Drexel, Morgan & Company.

Edison still had only the vaguest notion of how this could be done.

But he had confidence in the ability of his invention factory to devise almost anything, once the need had been specifically defined. Within two weeks Edison cabled his European agent: "HAVE STRUCK A BONANZA ON ELECTRIC LIGHT—INDEFINITE SUBDIVISION OF LIGHT." American boosters were in the business of making dreams come true, and Edison too was simply describing events "which had not yet gone through the formality of taking place."

He had, however, drawn his dreams with commercial precision. Knowing that by 1878 only about 10 percent of the vast gaslighting industry was in street lamps, he was convinced that no more than that small segment of the lighting market could ever be displaced by arc lighting, whose characteristics limited it essentially to the outdoors. This meant that 90 percent of the gas-illumination business remained open to some new kind of competition. Edison wrote in his notebook:

> *Electricity versus Gas as General Illuminant*
> Object: E. to effect exact imitation of all done by gas, to replace lighting by gas by lighting by electricity. To improve the illumination to such an extent as to meet all requirements of natural, artificial and commercial conditions. Previous inventions failed—necessities for commercial success and accomplishment by Edison. Edison's great effort—not to make a large light or a blinding light, but a small light having the mildness of gas.

If gaslights, even with all their inconvenience (Edison noted: "So unpleasant . . . that in the new Madison Square theater every gas jet is ventilated by small tubes to carry away the products of combustion"), were so much in demand, what might be the profits in a lighting system which had all the advantages of gas, but without its unpleasantness or its risks? Out of the back numbers of gas-industry journals, Edison dug up the facts about gaslighting during the previous fifty years. And he thought of these as outlining for him the market he hoped to capture for electricity.

Edison imagined, then, a universal network of electric power lines. He figured the cost of obtaining gas from coal (as in the systems then in use) against the cost of converting coal and steam power into electrical power. He observed that in the urban areas, where shops and small factories required the most electricity to run their motors, there might be less demand for individual electric lights, "while in the better residential areas, where less electric power would be required for running motors, more would be needed for individual electric lights." And he concluded: "Poorest district for light best for power—thus evening up whole city." To "subdivide" light and so bring it into every home required, first of all, a new kind of individual electric light; then a new kind of circuit so that each light could be turned on or off separately; and finally, of course, a central power station actually wired to thousands of outlets. Edison began working on all these at the same time.

The obvious first step would have been to try to subdivide the arc light, but from the very beginning Edison chose another path. He set out to develop an electric light that would make a *small* illuminating glow in an *enclosed* lamp. This meant an "incandescent" light, using electricity not to produce a flame (like that of gaslighting or like the fire that consumed the carbon rod in the arc light), but rather to bring some sort of filament to a glowing white heat. The earlier work on the arc light would be of little help here.

For at least a half-century, inventors had been trying to perfect a "glow lamp." They had used conducting filaments of metal or carbon in a glass vessel from which air had been removed, but none of these had glowed for more than a few minutes. The experts had come to the firm conclusion that incandescent lighting was both theoretically and practically impossible. These earlier unsuccessful efforts had used carbon or platinum burners incandesced by a current to which the filaments offered *low* resistance. In such a system the filament used a relatively large amount of current (say, 10 amperes of current at 10 volts, with a resistance of 1 ohm), and the circuit required enormous amounts of expensive copper wire. It was this high cost of the copper wiring, as much as anything else, which had persuaded the experts that a system of this type was uneconomic.

INSTEAD OF FOLLOWING the path of his predecessors, and then worrying about the character of the filament or the price of copper wire, Edison took a fresh look at the problem as a whole. In fact, he suddenly turned the problem around. Suppose the filament in the lamp became incandescent by offering a *high* resistance to the current; then each lamp would use only a small amount of current (say, 1 ampere of current at 100 volts in lights of 100 ohms resistance). This system, because it used a current of high voltage, would require only one hundredth the amount of copper wire in its circuit, and such a saving would itself help make the whole scheme feasible.

By rethinking the problem in this fashion, Edison had incidentally prescribed the qualities of the incandescent burner he had to find. After disappointing experiments with platinum wire, Edison began trying all sorts of other materials. Finally, in October 1879, his trial bulb with a carbonized cotton filament showed promise of success, and it actually glowed for forty hours. This was due, also, to the improved vacuum which Edison had managed to obtain in his bulbs.

On November 1, 1879, Edison applied for a patent on a carbon filament lamp. At the same time he designed a parallel circuit whose
thousands of outlets could be independently turned on or off. And he
developed an improved dynamo. Edison thus was not simply "inventing" a new incandescent bulb, he was organizing a new electric
lighting system for whole communities.

Like the pioneer organizers of the fur-traders' rendezvous a half-
century before or like the blazers of cattle trails, he, too, was thinking
of times and places and people. He had to push ahead on all fronts
at once, to provide a source of power, a network of wires, to serve
his new-style electric "candles." But Edison was building on proven
ground: the gaslighting industry, which had prospered by providing
"subdivided" light for offices and homes, had already tested his market. If only he could provide a cheaper, better substitute for gaslight,
he could be reasonably confident that his business would prosper.

Since the object was to produce a total working system, Edison
knew that he could not reap the benefits of solving any one of his
problems unless he could solve them all. But Edison also knew that
some evidence of his progress would encourage New York investors
to stake him in his researches. He therefore set about using his flair
for the dramatic to advertise the grandeur of his quest, along with
his successes (real or imaginary). A front-page story in the New York
Herald on December 21, 1879, proclaimed:

EDISON'S LIGHT THE GREAT INVENTOR'S TRIUMPH
IN ELECTRICAL ILLUMINATION
A SCRAP OF PAPER
IT MAKES A LIGHT WITHOUT GAS OR FLAME, CHEAPER THAN OIL
SUCCESS IN A COTTON THREAD

The well-briefed reporter told the suspenseful melodrama of Edison's magic: applying an electrical current to "a tiny strip of paper
that a breath would blow away" produced "a bright, beautiful light,
like the mellow sunset of an Italian autumn." With no intention of
hiding his light under a bushel, Edison announced that Menlo Park
would be illuminated by the magical new lighting on New Year's
Eve, 1880. In the week between Christmas and New Year's, crowds
flocked to Menlo Park to see Edison's miraculous "light of the future." Forty incandescent bulbs, all lit from a single dynamo, amazed
the visitors. What impressed them was not merely the lights themselves, but even more the fact that they could instantly be turned on
and off.

The next summer Edison announced that he was sending agents
all over the world to find the perfect vegetable fiber for his incandescent filaments. Since, only a few years before, Jules Verne had pub-

lished *Around the World in Eighty Days,* which was still at the peak
of its popularity, Edison had a ready-made foil for his research stunt
to keep alive the interest of investors and to awaken the interest of
future customers. He sent one agent to Japan and China, another to
the West Indies and Central America, and a third to the upper
Amazon. It was not quite the kind of publicity Edison had bargained
for when his agent in Cuba died of yellow fever. But his Amazon
agent sent back columns of exciting copy for the sensational dailies;
then, after returning to New York, being paid off, and enjoying a
festive meal at the city's most elegant restaurant, the agent mysteriously walked out into the darkness, never to be seen again. The
papers dubbed Edison's agents the "dauntless knights of civilization." In the search for "a material so precious that jealous nature had
hidden it in her most secret fastness," they were risking Cuban fevers, the poison of Amazonian arrows, and death itself, to help Edison
illuminate American homes.

Meanwhile a railroad promoter who had recently gone into the
shipping business gave Edison his first chance to install a complete
lighting plant. In May 1880, when the S. S. *Columbia,* a steel ship of
3,200 tons, left the yards at Chester, Pennsylvania, for its maiden
voyage around the Horn to California, it was the first electrically lit
ship in history. At the end of her two months' voyage the *Columbia*
arrived in San Francisco with all her 115 incandescent lamps still
aglow after 415 shipboard lighting hours. The next year at Holborn
Viaduct in London, Edison was operating the first urban incandes-
cent-lighting system. Two jumbo generators, designed by Edison and
sent from New York, provided power to some two thousand lamps
in the neighborhood, including those of the Central British Post
Office Building.

DRAWING ON THIS EXPERIENCE, Edison planned his first
American central power station, to be built on lower Manhattan
Island. "It is my intention," Edison had promised, back in 1878,
"never to show or offer the electric light until it is so perfected in
economical and all other aspects that I can feel sure of its instantaneous victory over gas." At the Paris Exposition of 1881, Edison displayed a model of his system which, a German expert reported, "was
as beautifully conceived down to the very last details, and as
thoroughly worked out as if it had been tested for decades in various
towns. Neither sockets, switches, fuses, lamp-holders, or any of other
accessories were wanting." Samuel Insull, a twenty-one-year-old
Englishman who had worked with the British Edison Company, had
taken on the job of combating the gas companies; and he helped

Edison secure the money and the franchises for the projected Pearl Street station. Edison and Insull had found a site 50 feet by 100 feet where they aimed to build a plant to supply electricity to an area about a half-mile square.

The Pearl Street neighborhood was shrewdly chosen to include much of the Wall Street financial section. For there the success of Edison's electric lights could immediately win over the men whose support could then make electric lighting possible all over the country. The plant was located in the center of the district, which also included tenements and small factories. Over the protests of city officials and of his financial backers, Edison decided not to string wires overhead, but to go to the expense of burying them underground. In order to do this he developed new tubing, and he set new standards of insulation which were then incorporated in the earliest New York laws on electric power.

When Edison met an unexpected problem, he would make it the occasion to issue another cheery statement. "I kept promising through the newspapers that the large central station in New York would be started at such and such a time. These promises were made more with a view to keeping up the courage of my stockholders, who naturally wanted to get rich faster than the nature of things permitted." About $600,000 had been spent on the Pearl Street operation. "The biggest and most responsible thing I had ever undertaken," Edison recalled. "There was no parallel in the world. . . . All our apparatus, devices and parts were home-devised and home-made. Our men were completely new and without central-station experience. What might happen on turning a big current into the conductors under the streets of New York no one could say. . . . The gas companies were our bitter enemies in those days, keenly watching our every move and ready to pounce upon us at the slightest failure."

At 3 P.M. on September 4, 1882, Edison's chief electrician threw the switch. The lights went on—four hundred of them in the service of eighty-five customers. "It was not until about 7 o'clock, when it began to be dark," remarked the *New York Times* (whose offices now glowed with fifty-two Edison lamps), "that the electric light really made itself known and showed how bright and steady it was." In the *Times* office "it seemed almost like writing by daylight." The nation had its first glimpse of city lights.

Edison was still only thirty-five. Enticed by his opportunity to transform night into day for millions of Americans, he declared that he had definitively become a businessman, and would "take a long vacation in the matter of inventions." Edison's plants, organized by the Go-Getting Samuel Insull, spread over the country. And the flamboyant publicity paid off in a flood of books and articles about the young Tom Edison, the "King of Inventors," the "Modern Magician."

In 1883 the ultimate popular accolade came when Niblo's Garden, the famous New York Music Hall, offered "a great Mimical Dramatic Ballet" celebrating Edison's victory over darkness. An electrically lit model of the new Brooklyn Bridge provided background for a dance in which each ballet girl waved a wand tipped with an Edison lamp. In the final preparations a journalist saw the versatile young Edison (who had just wired a whole city neighborhood) wiring the costumes of ballet girls. "Moving about among the girls and adjusting their corsets" so the wires would work, he inserted a little battery in the bosom of each dancer, so that lights would actually glow from their foreheads. The program proudly announced "novel lighting effects by the Edison Electric Light Company under the personal direction of Mr. Thos. Edison."

57

Communities of Inventors: Solutions in Search of Problems

RESEARCH AND DEVELOPMENT (R&D) did not become a focus of national interest until long after it had become a national institution. When the nation in the mid-twentieth-century became concerned about its institutions of learning and its ability to advance the frontiers of scientific knowledge, people worried over schools and universities, and sometimes over government research, but the nation as a whole seemed barely aware of the decisive and growing role of the industrial research laboratory. Not until the Depression of the 1930's had stirred awareness of the connection between scientific progress, employment, and prosperity had statistics on such research become available. By 1956 the total national annual expenditure for Research and Development in the natural sciences alone came to nearly $8.5 billion, more than twice the total national expenditure in that year for all institutions of higher education. By the 1960's R&D had entered dictionaries as another Americanism. Despite the dramatic increase of national expenditures on higher education (from some $7 billion in 1960 to $13 billion in 1965 and $23 billion in 1970), the growing annual expenditures on R&D remained steadily ahead, totaling $27 billion by 1970. While federal funds for this purpose were an ever increasing proportion, the expenditures by private industrial firms, at least until the mid-twentieth century, accounted for fully half the totals.

THE INDUSTRIAL RESEARCH LABORATORY was not invented in the United States. Since ancient times, philosophers and visionaries had imagined ideal communities in which men of science collaborated. In the early seventeenth century, Francis Bacon's *New Atlantis* described "Solomon's House," where sages pooled their knowledge and searched for its uses. The actual societies of learned men, like the French Academy, founded in 1635, and the Royal Society in London, founded in 1662, were primarily literary and honorific; they never produced that active scientific collaboration which Bacon had desired. The first modern industrial research on a large scale occurred in Germany, where, before the end of the nineteenth century, chemical and optical firms had shown how profitable it was to apply science to industry. Germany, too, had many of the negative advantages found in the United States. Since industry developed there later than in England, Germany lacked the petrifying traditions which had kept science separated from technology. And the new synthetic-dye industry in Germany depended heavily on laboratory discoveries, especially in synthesizing indigo and other products. The new German optical industry, led by Carl Zeiss, also successfully dominated the world market in its field, and so discouraged the growth of industrial research elsewhere. The Kaiser Wilhelm Institute, founded in 1911, flourished at first under the joint sponsorship of government and industry, but the Nazis proved its ruin.

In the United States the modern industrial research laboratory would eventually find the habitat where it could flourish without precedent. Here too it was to be a phenomenon of the twentieth century, quite distinct both in scale and in purpose from earlier American efforts.

We have already seen how individual scientific adventurers had set up laboratories for a variety of purposes. The pioneer oil men had employed Benjamin Silliman, Jr., to analyze their oil samples. Charles T. Jackson, who had introduced Samuel F. B. Morse to the principles of the electric telegraph, opened a chemical laboratory in Boston in 1836, where he experimented with guncotton and sorghum, and proposed the application of ether in surgery. At about the same time, a Philadelphia chemist, James C. Booth, set up a chemical laboratory for researches on sugar, molasses, and iron, and there he provided instruction to ambitious young chemists.

During the nineteenth century, ingenious individual inventors struggled and sacrificed and braved public ridicule. Eli Whitney, Oliver Evans, Elias Howe, Gail Borden, Samuel F. B. Morse, Alexander Graham Bell, George Eastman, John Wesley Hyatt, and scores of others spent their own lives, and plagued their families, to make some particular novelty into a marketable commodity. They were inventor-businessmen. Having imagined a sewing machine, they had to fashion it with their own hands, demonstrate it, show how it could be manufactured, and finally persuade someone to do the manufacturing, unless they decided also to do that themselves. Then, too, there were the businessmen-inventors, who had a nose for the new, and were willing to risk their energy and their capital. They were the host that included Frederic Tudor, Edwin Drake, Isaac Singer, Gustavus Swift, and John Henry Patterson; each had something of the inventor in him, but they were mainly organizers and promoters. What characterized all of them was single-minded persistence, what the American catalogue of schoolboy virtues called "stick-to-it-iveness." They pursued a fixed idea despite sickness, poverty, or public ridicule. Like the prospector who knew what he was seeking, they were uncertain only of where to find it.

But the industrial research laboratory was organized to seek in a new spirit. New institutions and new men would arise, with a new attitude toward their purpose, toward time and cost and "need." They spoke a new idiom of "feasibility" and "pilot plants." The men who searched in these laboratories were a new breed. It would be hard to make them popular heroes, because they were working on frontiers that most Americans did not even know were there. They were no longer amateurs, nor rule-of-thumb men. They were no longer workers-in-attics, but scientist-statesmen with advanced training, using an esoteric language in the highest councils of the nation. No longer looking for some particular thing, they were going as much to seek as to find. The community emphasis, the vague hopes and booster optimisms of the earlier movers across physical America, they were now reliving in the mysterious wilderness of science.

"ELECTRICITY," wrote Charles W. Eliot on his inscription for the Union Depot in Washington, is "carrier of light and power; devourer of time and space; bearer of human speech over land and sea; greatest servant of man—yet itself unknown." To explore this unknown and discover its treasure was the self-appointed mission of the pioneer American industrial research laboratory founded by General Electric in 1900.

The prophet and the pioneer organizer of the new institution was Willis R. Whitney. As the son of a chair manufacturer in Jamestown in far-western New York, Whitney had been expected to learn a trade. But in high school he was inspired at the evening classes run by a local businessman who had made a hobby of science. There he looked through a microscope for the first time, and then he persuaded his parents to buy one for him. Whitney went on to the Massachusetts Institute of Technology (a land-grant institution), where he graduated in chemistry in 1890, and then on to two years more and a doctorate at the University of Leipzig in Germany, followed by six months at the Sorbonne. Returning to M.I.T., he taught chemistry, explored the boundaries between electricity and chemistry, and developed an electrochemical theory of corrosion. When the General Electric Company decided to organize a research laboratory, they turned to the thirty-two-year-old Whitney. His first response, as they all later recalled, was "I would rather teach than be President!"

Whitney's reluctance to leave the university for General Electric was understandable. For in the United States until then, scientific research as well as teaching had, except for a few government-sponsored enterprises like the Smithsonian Institution, been centered in colleges and universities. The General Electric Company that had grown out of Edison's company needed the talents of a Whitney, since Edison himself had become a businessman. The brilliant German immigrant Charles P. Steinmetz, as the company's consulting engineer, had made advances in the theory of alternating currents, but he was a loner, and by temperament not qualified to organize anything. The original Edison lamp patent had expired in 1894, and other early patents had either expired or had lost their value because of later advances. General Electric still controlled most of the incandescent lamp sales in the United States, but gaslighting and arc-lighting continued to be competitors. German firms had developed filaments far superior to the original carbon filament, now made of osmium, tantalum, and other new materials. General Electric also needed new ideas, new materials, and new products. As Whitney recalled:

> The time, the year 1900, was most propitious. . . . The panic and depression of 1893–96 had shaken things down. The prejudices of the pioneer days had largely passed away. We had learned that there was a field for all the various applications of electricity, whether of alternating current

or of direct current, such as the arc lamp, incandescent lamp and the electric street railway, and we were busy welding these together. The opinion seemed to have been generally held that no radically new developments could arise. Copper was the best conductor of electricity; iron the best for magnetism; carbon the best for electrodes for arc lamps and lamp filaments and for brushes for commutators. As far as we could see it was likely that these materials would always remain the best for their respective purposes. Such at least was the opinion of most engineers. However there were a few who thought differently. . . .

At first when Whitney went to the General Electric plant at Schenectady, he worked in a barn at the back of Steinmetz's house. Then, as he organized the laboratory, he secured a new building and gathered a galaxy of scientists with whose help he gradually defined his enterprise.

William D. Coolidge—a poor farm boy from Massachusetts, who also had gone through M.I.T. on scholarships, then on to a Leipzig degree, and back to M.I.T.—was one of Whitney's most brilliant early collaborators. In 1908, within three years after joining Whitney, Coolidge invented a process for making tungsten filaments which (combined with other improvements) produced lamps two and a half times as efficient as those used before. Coolidge went on to develop a cathode tube which opened a new era in X-rays and gave General Electric the lead in that young science. Irving Langmuir, who also came with a German doctor's degree in physical chemistry, found that the tungsten filament functioned much more efficiently when set in a bulb filled with inert gas. Then, as Langmuir moved on from light bulbs to vacuum tubes for radio, he incidentally developed a new atomic theory which proved essential for the exploitation of atomic energy. No one had intended, or even imagined, these particular directions. Like the Spanish and Portuguese navigators four hundred years before who sought a short path to the Orient and found a New World in their way, these science explorers were touching the edges of unknown continents. But supporting such explorers as these became normal in the plans and budgets of American enterprise, and came to be taken for granted by the man in the street.

The proper job of American engineers, Whitney argued, was to produce obsolescence. A large enterprise like General Electric, he explained, could not stay alive merely by producing the best of old products.

> Our research laboratory was a development of the idea that large industrial organizations have both an opportunity and a responsibility for their own life insurance. New discovery can provide it. Moreover the need for such insurance and the opportunity it presents rise faster

than in direct proportion to the size of the organization. Manufacturing groups could thus develop their continuity beyond that of the originator because the accumulated values of knowledge and experience became generally recognized. No one yet knows the possible longevity of a properly engineered manufacturing system.

Out of the vagrant researches in Whitney's laboratory came products as diverse as the "calrod" (a new insulated wire that made possible the electric cooking range), underwater stethoscopes for detecting enemy submarines, improvements in public-address systems, and high-frequency dielectric heating to induce artificial fevers for the treatment of syphilis, arthritis, boils, and bursitis.

WHITNEY, THEN, BECAME an American Heraclitus, preaching and teaching that only change is real. Into his world of science he carried the faith of William James and John Dewey that all old categories of knowledge, of need, and even the familiar definitions of invention and of novelty were the enemies of life and progress. As "director" of the laboratory he said he did not want to direct. "A director merely points, like some wooden arrow along the highway. Research directing is following the openings of acceptable new ideas. It is watching the growth of thought in the minds and hands of careful investigators. Even the lonely mental pioneer, being grubstaked, so to speak, advances so far into the generally unknown that a so-called director merely happily follows the new ways provided. All new paths both multiply and divide as they proceed." A research laboratory was not where men fulfilled assignments, but where (in Langmuir's phrase) men exercised "the art of profiting from unexpected occurrences." Habits, procedures, "science" itself, were somehow an obstacle in the pursuit of the still unknown.

Whitney was fond of quoting the physiologist Claude Bernard's words, "The goal of all life is death." For Whitney this meant that "the interesting processes of life will still go on and forever change." "The grand goal of good gadgets is gradual obsolescence, or, expressed differently, we may get better every day." Recalling the dogmatic prophecies of his own time—the expectation that electric streetcars would one day reach into every alley of every town, that electric lighting was the final improvement in street lighting—he wondered whether one could ever predict the next form of transportation; or whether there might not be some way of putting "phosphors" into the cement of the roadways to collect and store cheap daylight and feed it back at night, thus making all earlier forms of street lighting obsolete.

INDUSTRIAL RESEARCH LABORATORIES grew and flourished on the borders of all the newly discovered worlds—of electricity and electronics, and of photography, of petroleum, of rubber and glass, and of synthetics. DuPont laboratories appeared in 1911, and in 1912 George Eastman founded the Kodak Research Laboratories, followed by laboratories in the United States Rubber Company in 1913, in the Standard Oil of New Jersey in 1919, and in the Bell Telephone Company in 1925. By mid-century the nation had two hundred large industrial research laboratories and two thousand others. From the Kodak laboratories, besides innovations in photography, there came apparently irrelevant, incidental discoveries, such as the finding that concentrated Vitamin A could be distilled from fish-liver oil. From the United States Rubber laboratories, in addition to advances in rubber technology, there came latex threads, latex textiles, latex insulated wire, new paper, and new adhesives.

These laboratories were as varied in sponsorship and support as the hundreds of American institutions of higher learning. Besides the laboratories of industrial firms, there were government laboratories pioneered by the Department of Agriculture and those in the Department of Commerce established by the Bureau of Standards. In 1930, although scientific research expenditures by the federal governnent already exceeded those of universities for all scientific research, the federal figure reached only $23 million. During World War II, federal research expenditures rocketed to $750 million. And after the war these figures kept rising, with continuing research on atomic energy, aircraft development, space exploration, and countless other projects. Meanwhile, technological research institutes were founded and supported by large industrial firms. The Mellon Institute, founded in 1913 at the University of Pittsburgh, offered an arrangement whereby an industrial firm that supported a researcher would acquire his discoveries as the property of the firm. The Battelle Memorial Institute (1929), founded from an iron-and-steel fortune "for the purpose of education and creative and research work and the making of discoveries and inventions for industry," financed Xerox in its early stages, as we have seen, and established a reputation for supporting adventurous research.

The trade associations opened their own laboratories, led by the National Canners in 1913 and followed by the successful laboratories of the National Paint, Varnish, and Lacquer Association, the Institute of Paper Chemistry, the Textile Research Institute, the American Petroleum Institute, and others. Some of these aimed mainly to improve public relations, but by mid-century there was hardly a major labor union or a trade association that was not somewhere supporting authentic industrial research.

Second only to Willis Whitney as an apostle of the new research was the pioneer of the private consulting laboratory, Arthur D. Little. Born into an old Massachusetts family, Little studied chemistry at M.I.T., and incidentally acquired a lively interest in literature. In 1886 he and another young chemist announced "the Chemical Laboratory which we have established at No. 103 Milk Street, Boston. . . . Mr. Griffin and Mr. Little have had several years' experience in the development of new chemical processes on the commercial scale and are prepared to undertake, either in their own laboratory, or upon the spot, investigations for the improvement of processes and the perfection of products." After his partner was killed in a laboratory accident in 1893, Little carried on alone.

At the Paris Exhibition of 1889, when Little saw "artificial silk" made from nitrocellulose, he was enticed by the possibilities of artificial fibers. He secured the American license to use a new viscose process to solubilize cellulose. Few businessmen were willing to invest in so dubious an enterprise, but in 1900 Little finally found backers for his Cellulose Products Company. Although the firm was a financial failure, before the company was dissolved it had succeeded in opening up the new world of cellulose products. Eastman Kodak bought the firm's patent for the first noninflammable motion picture film, and the Lustron Company bought the "artificial silk" patents which enabled them to pioneer in the American manufacture of acetate silk. After Little co-authored a textbook on paper manufacturing, he was drawn into the chemistry of cellulose. And in 1911, when the United Fruit Company engaged him to find a way to make paper from bagasse (the waste-fiber by-product of making sugar from Cuban cane), Little devised an experimental paper machine. This became one of the earliest "pilot plants" (a new American expression) in the United States. These and other Little experiments incidentally helped establish the practice of building factories expressly to test new techniques before risking large-scale production; and pilot plants in turn stimulated the search for novelty.

In 1916 Little moved his operations into a grand new Cambridge edifice, one of the first buildings in the United States specifically designed for industrial research, which soon became known as Little's Research Palace. There he and his research team explored a wide miscellany: petrochemicals; odors and flavors, how to produce them and how to classify them; glass containers for perfume, toothpaste, and other purposes; stencil paper; and improved materials for battery boxes. During World War I the Little laboratories improved airplane glue and devised better gas-mask filters.

The unexplored territory where Little worked—like the American West in the nineteenth century—was, of course, a natural habitat of hoaxers. And Little enjoyed exposing them. One Little client had invested a half-million dollars in a scheme to generate electricity directly by the oxidation of carbon electrodes, but Little showed that the "inventor" was only a clever charlatan who had secretly attached the bushings of his generator to the regular power lines.

In his will, Little bequeathed ownership of his firm to M.I.T., and after his death in 1935 the work of his laboratories went on. In 1942 the company helped the government of Puerto Rico devise its "Operation Bootstrap" to promote industrialization: its wide-ranging recommendations included ways to improve the culture of sugar and the distillation of rum, changes in the island's tax structure, and a program to promote tourism. During World War II the firm's researchers developed the Kleinschmidt vapor compression method, still used for making drinking water from sea water. They developed new techniques for liquefying oxygen and other gases, and advanced the new science of "cryogenics" for the study of phenomena at low temperatures. They collaborated on support equipment for the first hydrogen bomb in 1952, they helped devise liquid-fuel loading systems for use in space missiles, and they improved the design of space suits. And they developed new uses of radioactive tracers in medicine and in manufacturing. In 1966, under the Model Cities Program, when A. D. Little, Inc., devised a plan for East Cleveland, the scheme touched everything from city government, transportation, schools, and shop-front architecture to child day care, garbage removal, and the colors of lampposts.

"Research," Little had preached, "is the mother of industry." In a world where, as Kipling said, "any horror is credible," Little argued that unlimited progress was also credible. "The United States," he declared, "is an aggregation of undeveloped empires, sparsely occupied by the most wasteful people in the world."

AS THE PROPHETS of novelty were changing the meaning of the new, the possible, and the necessary, common sense was understandably losing its persuasive power. "You can't make a silk purse out of a sow's ear"—this bit of folk wisdom had irritated Arthur D. Little. So, in order to prove that in modern America *any*thing was possible, Little set out in 1921 to do the proverbially impossible. From Wilson & Co., the Chicago meat packers, he secured ten pounds of gelatine "manufactured [according to an accompanying affidavit] wholly from sows' ears." From this he spun an artificial silk thread, he wove the thread into a fabric, and actually produced an elegant purse "of the sort which ladies of great estate carried in medieval days—their gold coin in one end and their silver coin in the other.

It is one of which both Her Serene and Royal Highness the Queen of the Burgundians in her palace, and the lowly Sukie in her sty, might well have been proud." Little offered the purse for public display, and then described the process in a pamphlet which was subtitled "A Contribution to Philosophy." He might have called it "A Caution against Philosophy," and against all modes of thought that fence men in from the future.

Little's kind of exploring carried its price. When novelty ceased to be astonishing and unusual and became normal and expected, the boundary between the usual and the unusual, between the commonplace and the surprising, was blurred. "New impressions so crowd upon us," wrote Little, "that the miracle of yesterday is the commonplace of today." When the unexpected and the miraculous were expected, what comfort or security was there in expectation? When invention became the mother of industry, invention soon became the mother of necessity. Americans would have to look about them at the state of technology, and read the advertisements in their paper or watch the commercials on television to discover their "needs."

And Americans were finding solutions for which they had not yet discovered the problems. Americans had turned on the tap of novelty. Would they, or could they, turn it off?

58

Flow Technology: The Road to the Annual Model

ANOTHER FORCE IN twentieth-century America that stimulated and multiplied novelty—or what passed for novelty—was an institution that was not originally devised for that purpose at all. Quite the contrary. The assembly-line system of production, which would flood the nation with automobiles and nearly everything else, was developed in the first place to produce most economically the maximum number of precisely similar copies of the same object.

But there was an ironic and paradoxical feature of the assembly line that did not at first appear. Assembly-line production was production by flow. To keep the line moving at a constant and continuous rate required the breaking down and the splitting of tasks which called for an unprecedented precision in the definition, management, and timing of each of the little jobs that kept the production line in motion. This, of course, required extensive planning, and an enormous expenditure on the machinery that made each of the separate parts. It required, too, an unprecedented investment in "machine tools," the machines that made the intricate machines of a smoothly flowing production. In earlier days, when a carriage maker wanted to vary the design of the carriage he was making, or to introduce an attractive new feature on one particular carriage, that had been easy enough. He simply handled his tool differently, or spent more time on the wheel, the seat, the springs, or whatever had awakened his inventive interest. With flow technology, this was no longer possible. The production line would not flow, and the waste would have been intolerable if any workman on the line could delay the whole process just in order to satisfy his own taste or his inventive imagination. And the individual assembly-line workman who had in his hands nothing but a wrench, or who commanded a lathe or a press that was preset to perform one operation in only one specific way, had no power to vary the final product. He could fail to put in his part, he might neglect to tighten the screw or to trim off the excess material; that would make the final product shoddy, dangerous, or unusable, but it would not turn it into something desirably new.

Now, as assembly-line production triumphed, it began to shape profoundly the American's need for novelty and his notions of novelty. The costliness and intricacy of this machinery of flow technology had the effect, oddly enough, of making production more rigid than ever before. The conservatism of an Old World guild craftsman was flexibility itself compared to the frozen modes of a factory once tooled up to produce one particular model of automobile. To change even the slightest detail of the product might require a year of planning and six months of machine tooling. The understandable temptation of the manufacturer, therefore, and the one to which Henry Ford fatally succumbed, was remarkably similar to the temptations of Old World guilds—to go on forever producing the same old thing.

And it did not take long, with production going full speed, before this inherent conservatism of assembly-line technology had resulted in a monotony of production which would incite far-reaching reactions, and in turn create a new institution. The result (the career of the automobile once again became a parable) was quite another temptation: to make regularly scheduled innovations, minor variations on the original theme, which were now motivated not by the need for some particular improvement, nor by the irresistible appeal of some new discovery. The annual model appeared, as much as for any other reason, simply to relieve the monotony itself, and so keep the consumers' saliva flowing regularly and continually for more products of the assembly line.

For this purpose, too, flow technology would be providentially suited. Now it would be possible, by skillful planning, to change a doorknob or a windshield wiper on next year's model, yet leave all the rest of the product's design intact. Since flow technology was a technique of producing anything at all, the technology itself was always just as well suited for next year's model. Instead of the demand for innovation arising from the object itself, whose actual functions somehow made their own demands, the design of the object became nothing more than a basic theme on which it became the duty of designers to invent annual variations. The extent and the character of these variations—which, to be marketable, had to be advertisable as innovations—were dictated by the pace and framework of production, inhibited and controlled by the tastes (real or supposed) of the consumers.

HENRY FORD'S DREAM was to make a new and better kind of family horse—a car which everybody could afford and which would last forever. Essential to the plan, of course, was the perfecting of his Model T. He was experimental in developing his car, but he believed that once the design was fixed, the object would be simply to find ways to make it by the millions.

It was essential, then, that all the cars should be alike. Mass production, what Henry Ford called "the democratization of the automobile," required standardization. "The way to make automobiles," Ford explained in 1903, "is to make one automobile like another automobile, to make them all alike, to make them come through the factory just alike; just as one pin is like another pin when it comes from a pin factory, or one match is like another when it comes from a match factory." To Ford this meant finding ways to turn out millions of Model T's. And he was confident that he could succeed. In 1909 a friend warned Ford that the automobile would create a "social problem" by frightening all the horses on the highway. "No, my friend," Ford replied, "you're mistaken. I'm not creating a social problem at all. I am going to democratize the automobile. When I'm through everybody will be able to afford one, and about everyone will have one. The horse will have disappeared from our highways, the automobile will be taken for granted, and there won't be any problem."

To this end Ford focused his efforts on making his car as cheap as possible, making repairs inexpensive and easy. He continued to believe it was his mission simply to turn out copies of the same durable product. In 1922 he still insisted:

> We cannot conceive how to serve the consumer unless we make for him something that, as far as we can provide, will last forever. We want to construct some kind of a machine that will last forever. It does not please us to have a buyer's car wear out or become obsolete. The parts of a specific model are not only interchangeable with all other cars of that model, but they are interchangeable with similar parts on all the cars that we have turned out.

Henry Ford's unique achievement was less in designing a durable automobile than in organizing newer, cheaper ways to make millions of one kind of automobile. He transformed the making of automobiles from a jerky, halting process to a smooth-flowing stream. His ideal (which he never quite achieved) was a continuous, nonstop flow from raw material to finished product, with no pauses even for warehousing or storage. If Ford had succeeded perfectly, a piece of iron would never have stopped moving, from the moment it was mined until it appeared in the dealer's showroom as part of a completed car.

The watchword, then, was "Flow!" Ford sought and found ways to keep the raw materials flowing in and to keep the growing vehicle moving along. The factory was no longer a place where a skilled worker put together the many parts of a machine. Now it was where a machine grew on assembly lines that were tended by strategically located men.

Under the old arrangement, each part of the automobile had been put together by a single workman. One worker, for example, would assemble a single magneto (which would provide the car's ignition), in about 20 minutes. In 1913, at his Highland Park factory, Ford began dividing the magneto-making operation among twenty-nine men spaced along a moving belt which carried the magneto as it took shape. The average time to make a magneto was reduced to 13 minutes, 10 seconds. A year later, when the moving belt was raised to a more convenient height, this time was reduced to 7 minutes; closer study then brought the time down to 5 minutes. The moving-line technique of production was applied first to the motor, then to the transmission; to apply it to the bulky chassis required elaborate and neatly timed systems of hooks and hoists. But within less than a year, the assembling of a chassis too was reduced from 12½ hours to 1½ hours.

The assembly line, as we have seen, was not Ford's invention. "The idea," he said, "came in a general way from the overhead trolley that the Chicago packers use in dressing beef." The bold Frederick W.

Taylor, the atomizing scientist of the new science of management, had been ingenious at breaking each task down into the tiniest units of matter and motion. Ford's new emphasis was on flow, on devising production that was continuous. To do this, he had to keep his eye on the process as a whole. The automobile, in his mind's eye, grew by a gestation process all its own. The men simply tended and fed the assembly lines, to keep the process continuous. The problem was to keep all the materials moving at a speed best suited to the growth of the automobile.

The new "mass production" was not merely "quantity production," but, Ford himself explained, it was "the focussing upon a manufacturing project of the principles of power, accuracy, economy, system, continuity, speed, and repetition." Once Ford had transformed production from groups of disconnected operations into a flowing stream, it would not fit into the old machine shops which had been designed for the individual craftsman. Flow technology required a new architecture to fit, confine, channel, and hasten the flow—and so brought into being a new science of factory design.

The pioneer was Albert Kahn, a German immigrant who, as a boy of twelve, had come to the United States, where he became an architect specializing in concrete construction. In 1903, when there were still only eight hundred automobiles on the streets of Detroit, Kahn had provided a revolutionary design for the new Packard Company works. Although Packards were not yet being produced on a moving assembly line, Kahn arranged the building so that the materials which entered at one end were moved forward, with a minimum of carrying and hauling, to each of the operations needed to produce a finished automobile. Then in 1909 Kahn helped Ford solve his problem of railroad-freight charges by designing a new kind of branch assembly factory adjacent to the railroad yards in Kansas City, Missouri. This made it possible to ship Fords in a knocked-down form, which economized space and required no special freight cars, and then reassemble them at their destinations. In that same year, well before the assembly line was perfected, Kahn began building the new Highland Park Ford plant. It was a wonderfully airy structure, with sunlight streaming through its 50,000 square feet of glass; four stories high, 865 feet long and 75 feet wide, it was the largest building in Michigan under a single roof. When Ford's River Rouge plant went up in 1917, the buildings were actually designed to accommodate the flowing streams of production. Ford himself watched over every step of the construction, and so helped shape a new industrial architecture.

In an age of great architects like Louis Sullivan and Frank Lloyd Wright, Kahn and his associates created a new genre of architectural greatness. Their factory buildings, fashioned for the new logic of production, brought a new man-made grandeur to the American landscape. The mystery in Thomas Moran's vast canvases of Yellowstone and of the Grand Canyon was rivaled by the man-made brilliance of Charles Sheeler's paintings of Ford's plant at River Rouge.

TO KEEP THE PRODUCTION STREAM flowing, more and more Americans had to buy Fords. In January 1914, when Ford startled the nation with his $5-a-day wage, he explained that "this is neither charity nor wages, but profit sharing and efficiency engineering." And better-paid workers would buy more Model T's.

Ford had begun producing his Model T in 1908. The next year he announced that thereafter he would build *only* Model T's, and that the same chassis would be used for the runabout, the touring car, the town car, and the delivery car. Three years later he made the famous pronouncement which became the conundrum describing the American consumer's dubious new freedoms: "Any customer can have a car painted any color he wants so long as it is black." Despite temptations to "improve" his car, Ford stuck to his guns. On May 26, 1927, the fifteen millionth Model T was produced. In that year the number of Model T's still being licensed (and therefore still presumably on the road) came to 11,325,521. But the Model T was in trouble.

By 1920, Henry Ford's success in democratizing the automobile, in building an inexpensive car that would last almost forever, had produced a vast secondhand car market. Dealers faced a new kind of competition, no longer from the horse but from the millions of still usable used Fords. At the same time, the American buying public was stirred by a rising standard of living, by rising expectations (encouraged, of course, by Ford's $5-a-day wage), and by a love of speed and a love of newness. Americans demanded something different.

But Henry Ford's spectacular success had been in a static model. He had hardly thought of style or of consumer taste. His genius at producing new things was a genius at producing millions of the same thing, the Model T. Ironically, Henry Ford's faith in the Model T was an Old World faith: a belief in the perfectible product rather than the novel product. And it was his old-fashioned insistence on craftsmanship and function rather than on consumer appeal that eventually left him behind. Without intending it, he had heralded and organized a new age beyond his imaginings, and not at all to his taste.

The spirit of this new age was expressed in 1932 by what Charles F. Kettering and Allan Orth, speaking from the vantage point of General Motors research, called the New Necessity. "We cannot reasonably expect to continue to make the same thing over and over," they predicted. "The simplest way to assure safe production is to keep changing the product—the market for new things is infinitely elastic. . . . One of the fundamental purposes of research is to foster a healthy dissatisfaction." Alfred P. Sloan, Jr., then led Americans toward this new ideal by shifting the manufacturer's focus to the buyer. After Sloan went to General Motors, he developed a new and characteristically American institution, which by mid-century had become so familiar that Americans assumed it was part of the order of nature, as inevitable as the changing of the seasons.

This was the annual model. The spirit and the purpose of the annual model were, of course, quite opposite to those of Ford and his Model T. "The great problem of the future," Sloan wrote to Lawrence P. Fisher, maker of the Fisher Bodies, on September 9, 1927, "is to have our cars different from each other and different from year to year." The annual model, then, was part of a purposeful, planned program. And it was based on creating expectations of marvelous, if usually vague, novelties-always-to-come.

Sloan and his able collaborators at General Motors set up a styling department (which by 1963 would employ more than fourteen hundred workers). They showed a concern for color, they "invented" new colors, and gave aphrodisiac names to old colors. Now for the first time their automobile designers included women. "It is not too much to say," Sloan explained, "that the 'laws' of the Paris dressmakers have come to be a factor in the automobile industry—and woe to the company which ignores them."

The invention of the annual model widened the appeal and enlivened the drama of each year's offerings. But it also created new problems for planning and production. The buyer demanded novelty, but how much novelty would he tolerate? How titillate and attract the buyer without frightening him by too much novelty too soon? The bulgy Buick of 1929 (nicknamed "the pregnant Buick") was an admirably functioning car but a disaster on the market. Yet it was the result, according to Sloan, of a design mistake of not over 1¾ inches in excess body curve.

THE ANNUAL MODEL was an answer not only to the growing American demand for newness. While it institutionalized novelty, it responded to other distinctively American needs. In a democracy of cash, how were people to prove that they really were climbing the social ladder? The annual model, as Sloan elaborated it, provided a visible and easily understood symbol of personal progress, and so produced what we could call a "ladder of consumption." When the Model T became cheap and reliable and almost universal, cheapness and reliability were no longer enough. Universality and uniformity actually became drawbacks. As the Model T helped more and more Americans move around the country, it became less useful than ever in helping Americans show that they were moving up in the world. While Sloan, in order to keep the automobile industry and General Motors flourishing, elaborated the idea of the annual model, he incidentally gave the automobile a new and wider symbolic role in American life.

When Alfred P. Sloan, Jr., went to General Motors, the company was manufacturing numerous makes of cars with confused and overlapping markets. Sloan decided to clarify the appeal of each General Motors make so that, for example, the Buick would plainly be a more desired car than a Chevrolet. He aimed to design a car for every purse, and to create a noticeable price gap between different makes. The gap, however, was not to be so great that many Chevrolet owners might not hope someday to be in the Buick class, or so that many Buick owners might not hope someday to move up to a Cadillac.

This ladder of consumption began to dominate General Motors production plans. Sloan started with a price schedule of six separate price ranges from $450–$600 up to $2,500–$3,500, and then he had automobiles designed to fit the prices. "Price lining," which F. W. Woolworth had made the basis of his five-and-ten empire, was thus being extended to the most expensive American consumption items, and would become a framework for status in a democracy of cash. "We proposed in general that General Motors should place its cars at the top of each price range and make them of such a quality that they would attract sales from below that price, selling to those customers who might be willing to pay a little more for the additional quality, and attract sales also from above that price, selling to those customers who would see the price advantage in a car of close to the quality of the higher-priced competition. This amounted to quality competition against cars below a given price tag, and price competition against cars above that price tag." Toward this end Sloan developed a new form of industrial organization in which a giant corporation was split into semi-autonomous divisions that at times competed with one another (e.g., Chevrolet and Pontiac competed at the borders of their price ranges).

In his objective, Sloan was just as clear as Ford had been. But Sloan had set himself a production problem even more complex than Ford's, and requiring still another vast and unprecedented feat of coordination. Sloan now aimed at what he called the "mass-class" market. He saw that the future of the American economy lay not merely in providing machines to do things never done before. For Americans would always be reaching for a slightly better, slightly more appealing, slightly newer machine to do what was already being done. The American economy, then, would have to grow *by displacing objects that were still usable.* This need was rooted in the matrix of American life, in the expanding wealth, the personal uncertainties, and the vague social classes. Americans would climb the ladder of consumption by abandoning the new for the newer.

It was actually Ford's unprecedented success at satisfying the need for inexpensive, durable, reliable automobiles that had forced Sloan, as he himself explained, to imagine this new kind of demand.

> In 1921 Ford had about 60 per cent of the total car and truck market in units, and Chevrolet had about 4 per cent. With Ford in almost complete possession of the low-price field, it would have been suicidal to compete with him head on. No conceivable amount of capital short of the United States Treasury could have sustained the losses required to take volume away from him at his own game. The strategy we devised was to take a bite from the top of his position, conceived as a price class, and in this way build up Chevrolet volume on a profitable basis. In later years, as the consumer upgraded his preference, the new General Motors policy was to become critically attuned to the course of American history.

Sloan's annual model, and the accompanying ladder of consumption, came closer than any earlier American institution to creating a visible and universal scheme of class distinction in the democratic United States of America.

But in the long run the annual model, as it spread through the American economy, actually became the enemy of novelty. No other institution would do so much to make Americans begin to doubt the newness of the new. By the late twentieth century the newness of new models had begun to consist of trivial minutiae such as concealed headlights and high-speed windshield wipers. To devise every year a full line of automobiles dramatically different from their predecessors defied the ingenuity of style-conscious designers and of imaginative production engineers.

Wracking their brains, they began to make nonsense of the ladder of consumption, as they offered some Chevrolets that looked more impressive than some Cadillacs. The economy luxury car and the luxurious economy car were beginning to be confused. The few manufacturers, mostly foreign-car makers like Volkswagen and Mercedes-Benz, who did not visibly change their annual product, discovered that this refusal to change itself became a valued "special feature" with a sales appeal that was itself quite novel. By the 1960's the desperate competition for novelty had led some American manufacturers to offer half-yearly new models, even though the gigantic machinery of production had made it slower, more complicated, and more expensive to change any detail. A new model now required two years of planning and retooling. As tastes became more volatile, and as buyers became more open to novelty and more hungry for the unfamiliar, it was more difficult than ever to produce a car that really satisfied the buyer's latest whim. Each large manufacturer began to set his design destination at least five years ahead so that he could move toward it by measured steps. In this way newness became a commodity to be measured out sparingly and cautiously.

The deepest effect of the annual model, when it had become an American institution, was on the American's attitude to all newness. The stories of the designing and marketing and testing often became more interesting to prospective purchasers, and hence more widely advertised, than the usable qualities of the final result. When novelty was no longer spontaneous, the future became more and more assimilated to the present. Next year's model would be nothing but the next stage in somebody's planned strategy of marketing. Then nothing was more predictable than the new.

Ford, in his fear of novelty, had been wiser than he realized. "Change is not always progress . . .," he complained in 1926. "A fever of newness has been everywhere confused with the spirit of progress." But even he had not imagined that the frenetic quest for novelty might make novelty itself pall. The success of the static Model T had itself created the demand for an annual model. And now the annual model was being dissolved by success. What next?

PART TEN

Mission and Momentum

"Destiny is not a matter of chance, it is a matter of choice; it is not a thing to be waited for, it is a thing to be achieved."

WILLIAM JENNINGS BRYAN

"All life is an experiment. Every year if not every day we have to wager our salvation upon some prophecy based upon imperfect knowledge."

OLIVER WENDELL HOLMES, JR.

THE NATION'S VIEW of its future and of its relations to the world never lost the mark of its earliest past. The Puritans were sent on their "Errand into the Wilderness" not by a British sovereign or by London businessmen, but by God Himself. Whatever names later Americans used to describe the direction of their history—whether they spoke of "Providence" or of "Destiny"—they still kept alive the sense of mission. "We shall nobly save or meanly lose," Lincoln warned, "the last best hope of earth."

A *mission* (from Latin, *mittere*, to send), whether assigned by Providence or Destiny or by the Promising Land itself, was an errand which the individual American remained free to refuse. But democracy in twentieth-century America had succeeded in making every man part of the social matrix. No longer a mere responder to calls from without, every man had been brought into the womb of society, where he was part of its mysterious creative power.

The sense of mission, then, the voluntary sense, was being over-whelmed by an involuntary sense: a sense of momentum. In physics, *momentum* meant the product of a body's *mass* and its *linear velocity*. Translated into social terms, this was the sense not of mov-ing but of being moved, not of pushing but of being pushed. Momen-tum kept things going the way they were already going.

In a society, too, the force of momentum depended on *size* and *speed*. And these, of course, were precisely the dimensions which had distinguished American history. The American boast, and the butt of Old World ridicule, was how big everything was here and how fast everything moved. The United States was a large and speedy nation; Americans knew it, and for the most part, they loved it. Land Promoters, Tall Talkers, Land Hoaxers, and Go-Getters all bragged about the bigger and the faster. You might be a laggard or you might refuse to be a booster, but you still couldn't stop the nation from growing and moving.

Now the American assignment seemed to come no longer from the conscious choices of individual citizens, but from the scale and velocity of the national projects themselves. Growth, ever more and faster, seemed to have become the nation's whole purpose.

Man's problem of self-determination was more baffling than ever. For the very power of the most democratized nation on earth had led its citizens to feel inconsequential before the forces they had unleashed.

59
Prologue to Foreign Aid

THE ENLISTMENT OF the missionary spirit in the service of American patriotism was dramatized in 1899 at a memorial service in Boston when Mrs. Julia Ward Howe, who had been an abolitionist and was now a leader in the woman suffrage movement, rode in the same carriage with the former Confederate General Joseph Wheeler, who had volunteered to serve in the Spanish-American War. They both sang Mrs. Howe's "Battle Hymn of the Republic" for the "crusade" against Spanish tyranny. A half-century later, General Eisenhower entitled his account of World War II *Crusade in Europe*.

From the beginning, Americans had been unwilling to believe that their emigration, their expansion, their diplomacy, and their wars had no high purpose—and they commonly defined that purpose as a "mission." In North America, several of the British colonies had been founded with the explicit missionary purpose of converting the pagan natives, but this was by no means universal elsewhere in the British Empire. The English East India Company, for example, was hostile to the missionaries, who they feared might antagonize the natives and get in the way of profits. What was probably the oldest Protestant foreign missionary society anywhere was founded in 1649 by John Eliot, the Apostle to the Indians, to propagate the Gospel in New England. Both in England and America the religious revivals of the eighteenth century, which were stirred by John Wesley, George Whitefield, and others, created a new missionary movement. Unlike earlier missions, Catholic or Protestant, this movement would be supported by millions of small voluntary contributions in the country from which the missionaries were drawn.

The latter-day Protestant missionary movement would be as different from earlier missions, both in source of support and in mode of operating, as the vast democratized modern joint-stock corporations differed from their closely held predecessors. The roots of foreign aid, of the Peace Corps, and of numerous other American institutions of diplomacy and foreign relations lay deep in the American missionary tradition which thrived in the nineteenth century.

SAMUEL JOHN MILLS, founding father of American foreign missions, was born in Connecticut in 1783, the very year of peace with England. Like some other great evangelists and expansionists, he was not a man of deep thought or sharp intellect. Even his friends described him as having "an awkward figure and ungainly manners and an unelastic and croaking sort of voice." But he had an intensity of purpose, a grandeur of vision, and a restless energy that made him an American prodigy in his brief thirty-five years of life. As son of a country pastor, he was raised to believe in predestination, in the essential evil of man, and in the unpredictability and power of grace. When at the age of fifteen he still had not been overwhelmed by a converting experience, he lapsed into melancholy: "Sorry that God ever made me"; he saw "to the very bottom of hell." Then one day at the age of eighteen, according to Mills's own account, while walking through the woods, he suddenly felt conversion, saw God's glory, submitted his will to God, lost concern for himself, and became "willing to be damned for the glory of God." Determined to give his life to "communicate the Gospel of salvation to the poor heathen," he entered Williams College, where he led his first religious revival. On an August day in 1806 during his freshman year, he gathered four collegemates for prayer in a nearby grove which, according to missionary legend, was the miraculous birthplace of the far-flung American mission movement. When a thunderstorm drove the five to take shelter under a haystack they heard Mills, inspired by a recent geography lesson about Asia, propose that they set up missions in India. "We can do it," he said, "if we will." From these, who came to be known as "the Haystack Group," Mills went on in his senior year to organize the Society of Brethren. Like many another college fraternity, this was a secret society, its constitution was written in cipher, and even its existence was supposed to be kept concealed. The theory was that such secrecy would prevent the missionary movement from being brought into disrepute if the Haystack Group should fail.

The Brethren took their movement to other colleges. Mills studied theology for a few months at Yale, where he met a young Hawaiian, Henry Obookiah. Then only seventeen years old, Obookiah had been orphaned during one of the civil wars in Hawaii, and had actually begun training there for the priesthood in a pagan Hawaiian cult. But he became a cabin boy on a ship which had come out from New Haven, where he finally arrived and was befriended by his young Yale tutor. Mills took Obookiah under his wing, sent him to Litchfield Academy, then brought him to Andover Theological Seminary in Massachusetts, which had become headquarters for Mills and his Brethren. In 1810 the young Mills, impatient for action, addressed the Assembly of the Congregational Churches of Massachusetts and beseeched them to organize missions to the whole world. The result that very year was the American Board of Commissioners for Foreign Missions. In 1812 the American Board sent ten missionaries to Calcutta and others to Ceylon, and so became the nucleus of an American missionary movement which would be without precedent in the extent and numbers of its voluntary supporters. By 1820 the American Board had sent out eighty-one missionaries. And out of Mills's secret society of Brethren grew the Student Volunteer Movement for Foreign Missions later in the century, which recruited thousands of young missionaries and became a prototype for the Peace Corps and other youth movements.

Mills himself was not among the first missionaries to be sent abroad, since he was said to be needed as a recruiter back home. But when he graduated from Theological Seminary in 1812, he was dispatched by the home missionary societies on a survey of religion in the American West. After two extensive tours, which took him on foot and on horseback through trackless wilderness, he reported that he had seen a shocking "religious destitution." A result of his report was the founding of the American Bible Society. And he helped organize missions to the Indians and to the peoples of Mexico and South America. Mills then surveyed religion in the new urban slums, especially in New York City. Long an antislavery man, in 1816 he helped found the American Colonization Society (supported by Thomas Jefferson, Henry Clay, and Andrew Jackson, among others), which, besides promoting the emancipation of Negroes in the United States, aimed to settle colonies of American Negroes in Africa, and so "transfer to Africa the blessing of religion and civilization." He went to Africa, helped select an area for the settlement, and actually negotiated with African chiefs for that territory which became Liberia. On his way home, in 1818, Mills died of a fever on shipboard and was buried at sea.

Mills's legacy was the effective organization of American missions, and a vision of what was possible. He was to the foreign-mission movement what John Jacob Astor was to the fur trade: promoter and organizer *par excellence*.

The American foreign missions, which would reach all continents and win the support of millions at home, enlisted other impressive talents. Among these was the brilliant and attractive Adoniram Judson, who had joined Mills's Brethren at Andover. One of the members of that first group sent to Calcutta by the American Board in 1812, Judson spent time on shipboard reading theology on the question of baptism in preparation for meeting the English Baptist missionary William Carey. Judson and his wife were converted to the Baptist doctrine; he resigned his assignment from the American Board (which was Congregational) and urged the founding of a Baptist Foreign Mission Society, of which he became the first missionary. The Judsons went to Burma, which all along had been their favorite missionary field; there Judson studied the Burmese language and began a career noted more for its physical hardships and scholarly achievement than for its works of conversion. When war broke out between Britain and Burma, Judson, already weakened by malaria, was imprisoned in Burmese jails, where he was tortured, beaten, and for over a year laden with five pairs of heavy fetters. Judson's wife and two infant daughters died during these persecutions, but he carried on his Burmese missionary efforts until his death in 1850. During his twenty years of work there, Judson preached in Burmese, translated the whole Bible into Burmese, prepared a scholarly grammar, and nearly completed a monumental Burmese-English dictionary. Although it had taken Judson five years in Burma to make his first convert, before his death he was supervising 163 Burmese missionaries, and the Burmese church had attained a membership of seven thousand.

Almost everywhere the work of conversion was slow. One missionary worked in Africa for eleven years to make a single convert. During twenty-one years at the Marathi mission in west India, the number of missionaries who died exceeded the number of Indian converts.

BUT RELIGIOUS CONVERSION pure and simple was no adequate measure of the meaning of American missionary effort abroad. Missions became a way of hallowing American democracy and the American Standard of Living; and in the course of the nineteenth century, the foreign-missionary effort actually helped give a religious authenticity to the ways of Americans at home. Education, which was becoming a secular religion within the United States, became an agency of missions abroad. American missionaries carried this gospel of education to the farthest corners of the world. They established schools of every kind with American money, which they collected in millions of dollars and in millions of pennies. For example, John Franklin Goucher, a Methodist minister from Pennsylvania who married into the wealth of an old Maryland family, helped build the Woman's College of Baltimore (later called Goucher), and then carried his educational mission to the Far East. In the 1880's he supported 120 vernacular primary schools in India; he founded the first Christian school in Korea; and he helped found missionary colleges in China and Japan. By 1904 he had spent a quarter of a million dollars on these projects.

One of the most remarkable and most sophisticated of the American educational missionaries was Cyrus Hamlin, son of a Maine farmer, who began life as an apprentice silversmith. After studying for the ministry by himself, he attended Bowdoin College and then spent three years at Bangor Theological Seminary preparing to be a missionary. The American Board sent him out to Turkey to open a school. In 1840, at Bebek, a suburb of Constantinople, he opened a school which he directed for twenty years. "Almost everything is out of joint," Hamlin observed, in the far-off cultures where the missionary worked. Therefore, he argued, the missionary's secular and religious purposes were inseparable. Where *everything* needed to be "straightened out," only the American Christian missionary could do the job. He brought the gospel of a whole new way of life, aiming not merely to convert individuals but to introduce the "heathen" peoples to the spade and the plow, to the use of bills of exchange, and to "the whole organization of civilized life" in order to hasten the "transition from heathenism to civilization; from utter and hopeless indolence to industry; from a beastly life to a Christian manhood."

Despite the ridicule of fellow missionaries, Hamlin trained his Armenian students on the Bosporus to make sheet-iron stoves and "right smart American rat-traps." In 1847, when an Armenian professor who had come to Turkey to help the government set up a school of mines tried to construct a telegraph line, Hamlin made parts for the telegraph apparatus in his seminary workshop. And he helped arrange a demonstration before the sultan (one station was set up in the throne room, another in a far corner of the palace). The delighted sultan exclaimed, *"Mashallah! Mashallah!"* (Allah be praised!) and then, to show his gratitude, he sent to Samuel F. B. Morse an imperial diploma and a diamond-encrusted decoration, the first that Morse ever received. Six years later, to serve the needs of the Crimean War, the Turks installed their first telegraph, linking their country to the world. During the Crimean War, when Hamlin saw the piles of

English soldiers' vermin-infested uniforms, he used empty beer casks to make crude washing machines, thereby providing employment for Turkish women and cleaner clothing for the soldiers.

Hoping to make his students self-supporting, Hamlin started a bakery, which soon prospered by making "Protestant bread." Over the opposition of his missionary colleagues, who feared that Hamlin's bakery would "secularize the missionary work," Hamlin introduced the Turks for the first time to bread made with good hop yeast, and incidentally set a new standard in the marketplace because each loaf actually weighed a little more than its legally required weight. One day in 1856, when Christopher Rhinelander Robert, a wealthy New York merchant and railroad magnate, visited in Constantinople, a boat along the shores of the Bosporus attracted his attention by the delicious aroma of its cargo. Learning that this was some of Hamlin's "Protestant bread," Robert looked up Hamlin, and so began the collaboration which eventually produced Robert College. That new missionary college opened in 1863 at Bebek; in 1871 its students moved into a grand new site overlooking the Bosporus, where the school flourished into the late twentieth century.

Robert College, as organized by Hamlin and initially financed by Robert, trained leaders for the whole Middle East, pursuant to Hamlin's prophetic prescription for reform of the Ottoman Empire: "Peace, Time, and Education!" When Hamlin returned to the United States to ask rich Americans to contribute to the college, he secured numerous small subscriptions of $100 and less, but somehow he failed to get the large donations he needed. "They [the rich]," he wrote, "do not like to *unload*. They are prosperous, and they feel *savage* when asked to give. How can a man who has an income of $40,000 give anything when he has been accustomed to spend $45,000 to live? He is already economizing $5,000."

Americans founded other missions—schools, colleges, hospitals, and churches—on all continents. Many of the benefactors were, in a euphemism of the time, "noted more for distribution of their wealth than for their activities in attaining it." Before the Civil War one New York merchant provided free passage to China for fifty missionaries, and then contributed a ship so they could distribute eighteen thousand volumes of Christian literature. A Quaker businessman left $10,000 for an Episcopal mission in Liberia. A former Confederate chaplain who had made a fortune in Sunday School literature gave more than $100,000 for religious works, including a girls' school in Coahuila, Mexico. The Dodges, a wealthy New York family, endowed the American University in Beirut. A New London banker gave a substantial sum in 1889 for a graduate scientific department at Doshisha University in Kyoto, Japan. And there were many others.

AT THE CENTENARY of the American Board of Commissioners for Foreign Missions in 1910, the president of the Board, Samuel Billings Capen, himself symbolized the new American missionary spirit. Born in Boston of a poor family, he had begun as an office boy in a carpet firm at $75 a year, then finally became a partner and made his fortune. Although he himself never went beyond high school, he was an enthusiast for education and he worked hard to introduce "business" methods into education and philanthropy. He made the Sunday School publishing firm of the Congregational Church into a profitable enterprise; on the Boston School Committee (1888–93) he introduced manual training, he helped streamline the administration, and he developed a building program; he became president of the board of trustees of Wellesley College. Good business and sound religion, Capen preached, were complementary and inseparable. The first condition of success in both was "fidelity"—"that kind of conscientiousness which performs the smallest details well; that faithfulness which sweeps under the mat and into the corners; that which lays a poor carpet ten miles out of Boston as thoroughly as a better carpet on Beacon Street; that which tries as earnestly to sell an oil covering in the basement, as a Wilton on the main floor."

The menace to American civilization, according to Capen, was materialism. "Commerce is going everywhere, and commerce without Christ is a curse. It means firearms and the slave trade and rum." He noted that the United States exported more than a million gallons of rum, valued at $1.5 million, and nearly all of it went to Africa.

But, far from being an enemy of commerce, the successful Christian missionary, said Capen, inevitably made customers. "When our missionaries arrived in Hawaii, in 1820, the people were only one stage above the brute. Under the teachings of the missionary, and the influence of Christianity, they were so far developed that at the end of twenty years their business with the United States, as shown by the tables which I studied recently in the Boston Chamber of Commerce, was as follows: Imports, $227,000; exports, $67,000; total trade with the Islands, $294,000." In Turkey he noted the sale of ten cotton gins in one locality, one hundred grain-winnowing machines in another. He told of a pastor who had trouble persuading his parishioner, who was a rich manufacturer of plows, to support foreign missions— until the parishioner visited a distant country where missionaries were opening the market for Christianity and for plows. The manufacturer opened up so much business there that he ended by supporting four missionaries; and yet the market for plows proved so great that the salaries of these missionaries were only a fraction of his added profits.

To the Board for Foreign Missions, Capen observed in 1910:

The business interests of the world are with us; they are recognizing more and more the benefit to themselves which is coming everywhere with the opening of the world to Christianity. When a heathen man becomes a child of God and is changed within he wants his external life and surroundings to correspond; he wants the Christian dress and the Christian home and the Christian plow and all the other things which distinguish Christian civilization from the narrow and degraded life of the heathen. The merchant knows how the business of the world has been increased by the progress already made by Christianity, and he knows that with the further spread of the Gospel, business will be largely increased.

Of course Capen was attacked as a vulgar materialist; but most of his missionary colleagues joined in Capen's paean to so profitable a Providence. In the long run, he urged, the Christian mission was the only real antidote for materialism, because only Christianity could make material prosperity virtuous. "It is no part of the business of the missionary to develop foreign commerce. He is not interested in selling modern machinery; his one thought is to help and save men. But from his work of Christianizing and educating men and planting Christian homes these other results follow as inevitably as the mist disappears before the rising sun." Capen recalled that in a century of missions, Americans had given more than $40 million for the work, and that in the preceding year alone, the native missionized Christians in foreign lands had given the equivalent of $3 million.

As American technology, and especially American medicine, advanced, the missionary effort increasingly took the form of hospitals and medical missionaries. This new effort produced a pantheon of heroic figures, from Mary Reed, the Methodist missionary who contracted leprosy in India in 1884 and then survived to a ripe age superintending a leper asylum in the foothills of the Himalayas, to "the Burma Surgeon" of the mid-twentieth century, Dr. Gordon S. Seagrave, who came from a family of American Baptist missionaries and gave forty years to his "hospital in the hills." By the early twentieth century, a Go-Getting energy suffused the whole American missionary enterprise.

THE LARGEST SINGLE benefactor of American foreign missions at the opening of the century was John D. Rockefeller. A devout Baptist, he had given large sums to Baptist missions, but by 1905 he had not yet aided other denominations. Early that year, when the secretary of the Congregational Board wrote Rockefeller asking for $160,000 to support their missions, Rockefeller responded by giving $100,000. He followed his usual practice, of never himself announcing his gifts publicly. When the gift was reported in *The Congregational-ist* in March 1905, thirty Church members, mostly ministers, met in Boston and signed a formal protest demanding that the money be returned. They argued that since Rockefeller was "under repeated and recent formidable indictment in specific terms for methods that are morally iniquitous and socially destructive," to accept his gift would subject the Board "to the charge of ignoring the moral issues involved." Congregational ministers vied with one another in fulminating against Rockefeller. Most violent was Dr. Washington Gladden, moderator of the Church's National Council, who preached a jeremiad against Rockefeller in Columbus, Ohio, on March 26. "The money proffered to our board of missions comes out of a colossal estate whose foundations were laid in the most relentless rapacity known to modern commercial history. The success of the business from the beginning to now has been largely due to the unlawful manipulation of railway rates." In a phrase that would stick, he called the gift "tainted money."

The nation suddenly overflowed with moralists. Cynics suggested that what was wrong with Rockefeller's gift was not its source but its size. Champions of Rockefeller remarked that it was un-Christian to disparage a man's good deeds because of the evil he might have done, and that anyway, according to the American creed loudly professed by Dr. Gladden and his associates, a man should be assumed innocent until proven guilty; Rockefeller had not yet been found guilty in any court. But Gladden was joined in his attack by such powerful voices as William Jennings Bryan and Robert M. La Follette. "He gives with two hands, but he robs with many," La Follette inveighed to a Chautauqua audience. "If he should live a thousand years he could not expiate the crimes he has committed. . . . He is the greatest criminal of the age." One of the more instructive spectacles of pastoral morality was the Congregational Board itself. Discovering the unpopularity of its action, the Board at first remained silent; then the secretary, the Reverend James L. Barton, who actually had solicited Rockefeller for the money, took cover by telling the *New York Times* that Rockefeller's gift had not been requested but was "unsolicited and spontaneous." When Rockefeller's representative, the Reverend Frederick T. Gates, threatened to give the full correspondence to the Associated Press, the Reverend Barton retreated to the truth and secured a statement from the Congregational Board admitting that the gift had in fact been solicited. In this fog of competing hypocrisies, Dr. Gladden himself shifted his position, and the Board gratefully accepted the Rockefeller gift.

When it was announced, on June 28, that Rockefeller had given $1

million to Yale, and two days later that he had given $10 million to
the General Education Board, the voices of protest which only three
months before had called Rockefeller's $100,000 gift "tainted money"
were dramatically still. "Gifts of ten millions," the New York *Sun*
observed, "deodorize themselves."

60

Samaritan Diplomacy

FOR MOST OF the nation's history, the United States remained
uncomfortable, inept, and on the whole unsuccessful in diplomacy.
The problems of the American statesman in foreign policy were
especially complicated by the vagaries of American domestic politics. The United States was itself a United Nations, with a kind of veto
power in the hands of its numerous ethnic and national groups. The
sympathies of German-Americans, Irish-Americans, Italian-Americans, and others, tended to involve the United States willy-nilly in the
problems of the world.

But while American demography—a nation of immigrants—had
drawn the nation into the world, American geography had kept the
world at a distance. Two oceans and the accident of weak or friendly
neighbors had preserved the nation from the peril of foreign invasion. The international diplomacy of the United States thus showed
a curious combination of involvement and detachment unlike that of
any other great power.

If Americans were not at home in the dark corridors of diplomacy,
then they had bright visions and philanthropic hopes of what nations
could do together. A part of nearly every other nation was within
America. The United States had been born out of colonialism; and
(with some conspicuous exceptions) the nation's foreign policies did
not exhibit the worst features of European colonialism, of imperialism, or of the "White Man's Burden." Never having had a foreign
empire, the United States had less to lose from championing self-
government abroad.

The naïveté of colonial Americans lived on in the hopes of Woodrow Wilson. If President Wilson had been more at home in the real
world, where Lloyd George, Clemenceau, and Orlando had been

reared, then after World War I he might have secured a better treaty to serve American interests. But he would hardly have created a League of Nations. In the long run, American "successes" in diplomacy—from the Louisiana Purchase to the League of Nations and the United Nations—would, as often as not, prove to be the by-product of American innocence and of the nation's geographic remoteness from the world.

IN THE MID-TWENTIETH CENTURY, when air power had transformed a two-ocean nation into a one-sky country, the United States developed a new and characteristically American way of dealing with the nations of the world. This was as distinctive a product of American circumstances as were the other American political institutions. It was rooted not only in the missionary tradition which had helped found the nation and had continued to inspire many Americans, but also in some peculiarities of the role of the American government in expanding the nation from ocean to ocean. In the nineteenth century the notion of government as a service institution had dominated many an American's view of what he could expect from his government. That notion had grown out of the bounty of this continent: where there was so much virgin land, and where so much of it had been public domain in the gift of the government, everyone felt it his right to have his piece. And what the government had the power to give, it had the duty to make useful and productive. The expectations of immigrants, of would-be homesteaders, farmers, ranchers, and canal and railroad builders in the nineteenth century, became the expectations of truckers, highway builders, airline promoters, and others in the twentieth century. Depression and crisis made it easy for Americans to move on from belief that government was obliged to make land accessible and profitable to belief that government was somehow obliged to keep the whole economy functioning and prospering.

If the nation had created a Democracy of Cash, why not also a Diplomacy of Cash? In foreign affairs, the most important new American institution of the twentieth century was also a product of the fabled wealth and proverbial optimism of the New World.

"Foreign aid" expressed a belief that abroad, too, the American government would be a service institution, enabling other peoples to make the most of their land and their resources. This notion while a novelty in the world of diplomacy, had roots, as we have seen, in the missionary hope that the American Standard of Living could (in the phrase of Capen the missionary leader) "turn Heathen*dom* into Christen*dom.*" By mid-century a new sort of missionary spirit had come to dominate American foreign policy and the American budget for government expenditures abroad. With a new specialized meaning, "foreign aid" entered the American vocabulary in the late 1940's, it soon was contracted to "aid," and quickly found a place in dictionaries of the American language.

Americans were inclined to treat this remarkable innovation as simply a matter of "foreign policy," without noting how dramatic was the institutional novelty, how traditional was the spirit, or how great was its significance.

From earliest times the political relations among nations had been dominated by certain familiar customs and practices: wars, alliances, confederations, treaties, and secret understandings. And their economic relations had comprised exports and imports, controlled and influenced by tariffs, bounties, credits, and loans. Then, occasionally, when a stronger nation could impose its will on a weaker, it might demand blackmail or tribute, in payments, goods, or privileges exacted from the weak for the strong. Occasionally, of course, there were acts of international charity: money, food, medical assistance, or clothing sent from one people to another to relieve famine, to cure plagues, to mitigate suffering from fire, earthquake, volcanic eruption, or other disasters. And a new era was opened when the Geneva Convention in 1864 gave international immunity in time of war to Henri Dunant's Red Cross League. But gifts of charity were only occasional, and small, and they played a minor role in international politics or world trade.

The rise of world empires from the fifteenth to the twentieth centuries had confused these relationships and mixed up the categories. Colonialism was a way of giving to the relations among peoples at a distance some features of the relations within nations. Laws took the place of treaties, "international" trade became trade within an empire. The money that the British government spent in India in the nineteenth century was not precisely an import or an export, not exactly an act of charity or simply a fact of economics. The political fortunes and the welfare of imperial and colonial peoples were involved with strong forces of industrial progress, exploitation, development, and benefaction.

FOREIGN AID—grants of government money to aid misery or distress, to relieve catastrophe, and to promote welfare abroad—was no part of American foreign policy in the nineteenth century. In fact, it was generally agreed that such a use of the funds of the United States government would be unconstitutional. Repeatedly when Congress was put under pressure to appropriate funds for such purposes, the objection prevailed that such expenditure was prohibited by the Constitution. In 1847, for example, Congress was pressed to appropriate money for the relief of Irish famine sufferers; the potato famine of 1845 and the years after had, as we have seen, made Ireland a charnel house. Americans, especially those of Irish descent, were moved when they read eyewitness accounts of the starvation that killed more than one million Irish men, women, and children. This catastrophe shocked the country into its first nationwide money-raising effort for charity abroad. Petitions to appropriate federal money to feed starving Ireland poured into Congress. Few congressmen needed to be reminded of the high political stakes—the votes of the growing numbers of Irish-Americans.

These requests came when the nation, led by the Democratic President James K. Polk, was still fighting the Mexican War, which was unpopular in many quarters. Horace Greeley, a leading Whig opponent of the war, noted bitterly that while the United States government somehow had the power to send troops to dash out the brains of Mexican children, yet it lacked the power to feed the starving. But even he refused to sign a petition asking Congress to appropriate money for such "unconstitutional" purposes. "Our sympathy with her [Ireland's] noble and suffering people," agreed the Washington *Daily Union*, from the Democratic side of the political fence, "should not mislead us into any violation of our constitution." One congressman explained his constitutional scruples by observing that the proposed appropriation was really "designed to afford food for party vultures to feed upon, rather than bread for the starving people of Ireland." President Polk himself announced to his Cabinet that even if Congress passed the appropriation, he would veto it, since the Constitution did not permit the use of public funds for charity. He added that, of course, he was not lacking in sympathy for the suffering Irish, and to prove it he personally contributed $50 to the relief fund.

When famine struck Russia in 1891, Congress again was pressed to give aid. Once again the constitutional objection (together with others) prevailed, and even the proposal to appropriate $100,000 to ship donated food to Russia was defeated. In the debates on aid to Russia, Congressman Constantine B. Kilgore of Texas recalled that a few years before, when the people of his state had suffered a disastrous drought and he appealed to Congress for $10,000 to buy seed, the President had quite properly turned down their request for lack of constitutional authority. At that time President Cleveland had vetoed the measure "to indulge a benevolent and charitable sentiment" because, Cleveland explained, he could "find no warrant for such an appropriation in the Constitution." Congressman William

Jennings Bryan of Nebraska recalled that a similar request in the summer of 1890 from the drought-stricken people of his state had been rightly refused on constitutional grounds. These precedents were presumed to add up to a conclusive objection against sending congressionally financed charity to the Russians.

During the nineteenth century there had actually been a few exceptions to this general ban on government aid. But the exceptions were rare, the amounts involved were small, and each instance could be explained by unique political pressures. The earthquake in Venezuela in March 1812, at a time when Latin-American revolutions were enlisting the republican sympathies of the American people, drew from Congress, strongly urged by Congressman John C. Calhoun, an appropriation for relief amounting to $50,000. And in 1880, when the Irish were again suffering from famine, Congress passed a joint resolution which appropriated no funds but authorized the Secretary of the Navy to use a naval vessel to carry voluntary relief gifts to the Irish. But in the 1890's and thereafter, in debates over other requests for foreign charity, the Venezuelan example was generally ignored as inapplicable and the Irish case was regarded as a regrettable stretching of the Constitution to catch the Irish-American vote.

American aid to foreign peoples in distress, throughout the nineteenth century, then, had generally taken the form of voluntary gifts by private citizens and their organizations. The government played a minor role, and even that role was widely believed to be of dubious legality. The amount of American charitable contributions to distressed peoples abroad is hard to measure because the sums were gathered by so many agencies and were transmitted in so many different forms. The private donations to the Irish alone, between December 1846 and mid-July 1847, probably came to about $1 million. The grain, corn, and flour in a single gift ship for the famine-stricken Russians in 1892 amounted to $200,000. Because of the international origins of the American people, there was hardly a gift that was not greeted with disapproval from some national group within the United States. Anglo-Americans said that the aid sent to the Irish was really an insult to the English, and many American Jews, horrified at the Russian pogroms, opposed the gifts to Russia in the 1890's as an endorsement of anti-Semitism. Nevertheless, by the early twentieth century, sizable privately donated American gifts to peoples in distress had encircled the globe. Clothing had been sent to the Greeks, bread to the Irish, money to needy Lancashire textile workers, clothing and provisions to the Cretan refugees from Turkish oppression, food and clothing to the Armenians and others in the Near East, wheat to Calcutta and Bombay, food to Cuba and China.

THE PEOPLE OF THE UNITED STATES had taken on a role as Samaritans to the world. Still, the effort rigorously to separate charity from government policy lasted well into the twentieth century. The aid that Americans sent to Belgium after the Germans had occcupied that country in 1914, and which Herbert Hoover administered under the Commission for Belgian Relief, was a collection of private gifts. In response to a suspicious German official who asked Hoover, "What do you Americans get out of this?," Hoover retorted, "It is absolutely impossible for you Germans to understand that one does anything from pure humanitarian, disinterested motives, so I shall not attempt to explain it to you."

When famine struck Russia in 1921 in the wake of the war and the Bolshevik Revolution, and soon after Attorney General A. Mitchell Palmer's reckless arrests and deportations of communists and alleged communists, the efforts to keep charity separate from policy were strained. Herbert Hoover again took the lead in organizing relief. This time Congress, departing from the constitutional tradition, allocated $4 million of surplus Army medical supplies to the Red Cross for relief to the Russians. But again the great bulk of the $80 million of relief came from private sources. In 1922 Hoover's organizing talent brought medicine, food, and clothing to some ten and a half million destitute Russians at eighteen thousand stations. Making the most of his resources, for example by persuading the Russians to change their eating habits so they would use American corn and other foods unfamiliar to them, he accomplished the most extensive American charitable work until that time. "The generosity of the American people," Maxim Gorky, an exile from Russia, wrote Hoover in 1922, "resuscitates the dream of fraternity among people at a time when humanity greatly needs charity and compassion." At an official banquet in Moscow, the President of the Council of People's Commissars, whose government was still not recognized by the United States, presented Hoover with a scroll of thanks "in the name of the millions of people who have been saved."

In sharp contrast to the apolitical generosity of private relief abroad was the official government policy of the United States. The notorious controversy over "reparations" and "war debts" dominated American debates on international economic relations for more than a decade after the Armistice. After World War I, the sums owed to the United States, for war loans and for relief loans to the Allies and to the new countries created by the peace settlement, totaled more than $10 billion. And the United States government under Presidents Harding and Coolidge insisted on treating these as strictly financial transactions. President Coolidge's succinct and often quoted "They hired the money, didn't they?" summed up the official American position. The reluctance of the United States to cancel or reduce the Allied debts controlled the nation's economic relations to Europe, and remained an obstacle to a more realistic approach to German reparations, which the Allies hoped to use to repay their debts to the United States. At home, the issue befuddled American politics and accentuated the postwar desire to withdraw from Europe and the world. But the controversy itself showed how far American thinking still was from the era of foreign aid.

It was the isolationist effort to remain "neutral" in European conflicts that first brought the United States government into legal supervision of foreign charitable efforts. Under pressure from Americans who feared that large-scale charity to Spain or other countries that were erupting in civil war might somehow involve the nation as a belligerent in Europe, the Department of State began its official supervision of overseas relief.

The much publicized hearings from 1934 to 1936 of the Senate Munitions Investigating Committee under Senator Gerald P. Nye of North Dakota seemed to show that the United States had been enticed into World War I by greedy bankers and munitions makers. Then came a series of "neutrality" acts aimed to keep the United States out of the next war by restricting American loans and by supervising American gifts. By the time that World War II broke out in Europe, the federal government had been given the statutory duty to supervise and scrutinize all forms of American aid to countries at war. The Neutrality Act of November 4, 1937, allowed only the "cash-and-carry" export of arms and munitions. As late as the Lend-Lease Act of March 11, 1941, Americans were trying to preserve the traditional distinction between the voluntary gifts of citizens for charitable or ideological motives and the acts of government which were matters of international finance and foreign policy.

THE AMERICAN INSTITUTION of foreign aid was a by-product of World War II. It marked a new stage in American foreign policy, in which charitable, fiscal, political, ideological, and military motives would be more confused than ever before. Incidentally, too, foreign aid would newly confuse the techniques, attitudes, and institutions of peace with those of war, and so would help open an era in American foreign relations when the American people were neither at war nor at peace.

Although the hostilities of World War II had ended in 1945, the United States did not finally approve a definitive treaty of peace with either Japan or Germany until 1951. Meanwhile President Truman, with bipartisan support, had brought into being a new kind of diplomacy, perhaps the first distinctively American mode of dealing with nations at a distance. It was characteristically American in that it was less the product of a new philosophy of foreign affairs than a set of new enterprises elaborately organized for current needs. For the first time it aimed to apply American ingenuity, enterprise, know-how, and wealth to the problems of the whole world. In 1943, while the war was still on, the United Nations Relief and Rehabilitation Administration (UNRRA) had been set up to help the liberated peoples. Although forty-four nations joined UNRRA, the United States paid 72 percent of the operating expenses. Through UNRRA the United States government gave $2.7 billion. But even this sum would soon seem insignificant as the United States was pushed toward its new era of Samaritan Diplomacy.

By the early spring of 1947 President Truman, who had never shared President Franklin D. Roosevelt's optimism about long-term cooperation with Soviet Russia, was persuaded that he could wait no longer to show American determination to prevent the Soviets from dominating the world. One sign after another, culminating in Soviet demands that Turkey cede territory for new Russian naval bases in the Bosporus and in efforts to create a communist regime in Turkey, unmasked Stalin's determination to use the Allied victory to surround and subvert nations that were not yet communist. The next American policy was sketched by George F. Kennan, counselor of the United States embassy in Moscow, who knew Russia and the Russians as did few American diplomats before him. The survival of the United States and the free world, he urged, would depend on "a long-term, patient but firm and vigilant containment of Russian expansive tendencies."

On March 12, 1947, President Truman, before a joint session of Congress, made his momentous statement of American intentions toward the world. The Truman Doctrine, as a departure in American foreign policy, would rank with President Monroe's statement more than a century earlier and with President Wilson's utterances before World War I, and in some ways it combined their purposes. The Monroe Doctrine—that the United States would not tolerate outside interference in the internal affairs of the nations of the New World —was now to be made world-wide; American power and American wealth were offered to keep the world safe for democracy. "It must be the policy of the United States," the President declared, "to support free peoples who are resisting attempted subjugation by armed minorities or by outside pressure. . . . our help should be primarily through economic and financial aid which is essential to economic stability and orderly political processes." His request for $400 million for aid to Greece and Turkey in order to give them the strength to resist a Communist takeover was approved by Congress.

In June, Secretary of State George C. Marshall asked European governments to work out their plans for reconstruction and to give the United States their requests for assistance. In July, representatives of non-Communist European countries met in Paris, and in September they submitted a long-term European recovery plan requiring $22.4 billion in loans and grants from the United States. In the following spring, Congress appropriated $5.3 billion for the first twelve months of the new aid program. Seldom had there been such widely based support for so costly a "peacetime" program. The Marshall Plan, as this was called, had bipartisan support (with Senator Arthur Vandenberg leading the Republicans), as well as support from farm groups, organized labor, and the National Association of Manufacturers. Yet it was only a beginning. The plan, which commanded $22 billion of United States resources in the next three years, was generally agreed to have been responsible for the remarkable economic recovery of western Europe, and for the resistance of western European countries to communism. Figures showed that by 1950, Marshall Plan countries had increased their gross national product by 25 percent.

THIS SUCCESS OF foreign aid in Europe encouraged the belief that it could work equally well anywhere else—in Asia or Africa or Latin America. In his inaugural address of January 20, 1949, President Truman offered a supplementary program especially adapted to countries outside Europe. "Point Four," it came to be called, because it was the fourth point, a "major course of action," in his Program for Peace and Freedom:

> We must embark on a bold new program for making the benefits of our scientific advances and industrial progress available for the improvement and growth of underdeveloped areas. More than half the people of the world are living in conditions approaching misery. Their food is inadequate. They are victims of disease. Their economic life is primitive and stagnant. Their poverty is a handicap and a threat both to them and to more prosperous areas.
>
> For the first time in history, humanity possesses the knowledge and the skill to relieve the suffering of these people. . . .
>
> Only by helping the least fortunate of its members to help themselves can the human family achieve the decent, satisfying life that is the right of all people.
>
> Democracy alone can supply the vitalizing force to stir the peoples of the world into triumphant action, not only against their human oppressors, but also against their ancient enemies—hunger, misery, and despair. . . .

Therefore President Truman asked the Congress to provide funds for a program to supply the "underdeveloped areas" with "technical, scientific, and managerial knowledge" and also "production goods and financial assistance in the creation of productive enterprises." He concluded, "Before the peoples of these areas we hold out the promise of a better future through the democratic way of life. It is vital that we move quickly to bring the meaning of that promise home to them in their daily lives."

Congress was stirred to action by the communist takeover of Czechoslovakia in early 1948 and by news that the Soviets had set off an atomic bomb in the summer of 1949. Point Four provided a new rationale for extending foreign aid beyond those allies of western Europe who had suffered devastation during World War II. It reached beyond "recovery" and "relief" to the world-wide construction of a new way of life and a higher standard of living for those peoples who had the *least* resources. As a consequence, by 1966, of the total $122 billion which the United States had spent on foreign aid, nearly two thirds had gone to nations *outside* Europe. A considerable amount (the precise sum was not made public) of all foreign aid went for military purposes, to strengthen the armed forces of the receiving countries. But military aid to allies or prospective allies was, of course, an old story. What was new was the additional effort to save the world for democracy by the purposeful sharing of American know-how, American education, American resources, and American dollars, with the remote and underdeveloped parts of the world.

The Marshall Plan after World War II was, of course, a dramatic departure from earlier American policy: a leap from the war-debt psychology to the psychology of foreign aid, from the vocabulary of the banker to that of the missionary, the humanitarian, and the social scientist. After World War I politicians had talked of reparations and "honest debtors," of interest rates and the capacity of countries to pay back what they had borrowed. Now, after World War II, they were talking about standards of living, they were comparing the health and prosperity and literacy of different nations, and they were examining the opportunities for personal freedom and the decency of political institutions everywhere. The Marshall Plan expressed a profound and sudden change in official American thinking and feeling about the relation between the New World and the Old: not only in the focus on recovery and prosperity rather than on principal and interest, but also in the call for initiative, collaboration, and planning by the benefiting countries. Its focus was not so much on individual nations as on Europe as a whole.

The Marshall Plan, because it was directed to former allies, was still a kind of war relief. If it succeeded, it would help once prosperous countries with high standards of living to put their houses back in order. But there was momentum in this enormous new enterprise of foreign aid. Like the gargantuan new undertakings in atomic research and in the exploration of space, foreign aid had a mass and a velocity which combined into a nearly irresistible accelerating force. When the American program moved from war relief to former allies whose language, religion, customs, and history were familiar and reached out to others who not only had not been allies but who were remote and hardly known, the United States had embarked on a boundless sea of hope.

Except in the religious missions, the nation had no substantial precedent for a world-wide program of foreign aid. And however similar the missionary efforts may have been in spirit, they were dramatically different in scale. Whether offered as United Nations Relief and Rehabilitation, or under Point Four, or through the score of other programs, foreign aid now expressed faith that American wealth could raise the standard of living of people anywhere. A people with a higher, more nearly American standard of living, it was assumed, would be more apt to be democratic, and hence more apt to be peace-loving and friendly to the United States. Implied, also, was the complementary assumption that poverty, misery, and industrial backwardness would make any people less peaceful and less democratic, hence more prone to communism, and therefore more inclined to join the enemies of the United States. This chain of reasoning, which implied some bold generalizations about history, was not always explicit. But, spoken or not, it lay beneath the quasi-religious faith in democracy, and expressed a traditional American confusion of the "ought" and the "is."

Some of the more obvious and more painful facts of foreign policy in the twentieth century should have given Americans pause. For as Russia had become more industrialized, and as she produced more goods for her people, she did not become more friendly to the United States. Russian industrialization was neither the product of democracy, not did it prove to be a source for more democracy in the Soviet Union. As that country became stronger it did not become more peaceable. In the course of World War II the United States gave $11 billion of Lend-Lease aid to the Russians, but the government of Russia had never before been so hostile to the United States as in the years of the Cold War which followed. As the Soviet Union became stronger it became more bellicose, and in the little wars which it fostered and sponsored in Asia, it found allies in countries which had also been large beneficiaries of American foreign aid.

The story of American foreign relations in Asia in the postwar years showed the folly of American hopes that foreign aid would necessarily propagate democracy or promote peace. In 1945–48 the Nationalist Chinese received $2 billion in aid (in addition to war matériel), but mainland China became Communist and the American ally on Formosa, Chiang Kai-shek, was hardly democratic. A by-product of the Communist Revolution in China was the Korean War. Korea, too, for some years the recipient of the largest quantity of foreign aid, remained far from the democratic ideal. And the other recipient of major foreign aid in Asia (apart from India and Pakistan) was South Vietnam.

By 1966, when the foreign aid program had disbursed more than $122 billion altogether, while Europe's share was $47 billion, East Asia had received $27.6 billion, the Near East and South Asia $25.4 billion, Latin America $11 billion, and Africa $3.6 billion. About two thirds of this whole amount was for economic rather than military purposes, and about two thirds of the economic aid was in the form not of loans, but of outright grants.

As the foreign aid program grew and became a fixture in American foreign policy and in the annual budget, it brought new confusions into other traditional ways of thinking, and especially into the ancient distinctions between peace and war. The Prussian military theorist Karl von Clausewitz had observed that war was merely the continuation of politics by other means. And now the same could be said of foreign aid. The new foreign aid philosophy, which saw the whole world as a field for missions and a battleground between democratic and antidemocratic forces, had made peace itself into the continuation of war by other means.

61

Not Whether but When: The New Momentum

IN MID-CENTURY the largest government-supported national projects which the United States had set itself took on some of the familiar character of a mission. These gargantuan enterprises, which dwarfed the expenditures even of foreign aid, were the first occasions, other than military ventures, when the nation as a whole focused its public resources on such costly achievement. The two grandest triumphs of American technology were produced by such efforts. One was success in splitting the unsplittable: fissioning the atom and producing a self-sustaining nuclear chain reaction. The other was in reaching the unreachable: conquering interplanetary space and landing on the moon. Both were American conquests of the impossible. And they would symbolize even more than other successes of New World civilization what democratic man was sacrificing for his successes. For, oddly enough, their national triumphs would give individual Americans a new sense of powerlessness.

These two American spectaculars showed certain conspicuously common characteristics. Both were incited and accelerated by pressures from outside the nation: one by the wartime fears of earlier success by Nazi Germany; the other by "peacetime" fears of being overshadowed by the success of Soviet Russia. Both were facilitated by the brains, the imagination, and the energy of immigrants: one by refugees from the rise of the Nazis; the other by refugees from the fall of the Nazis. Both pursued objectives which, though never before attained, were still quite specific. Both operated on a definite time schedule set long in advance. To accomplish their purposes both of these far-flung efforts had to reach their predicted goals within a specified time.

In some respects, too, these triumphs of American democracy offered extreme contrasts. One was undertaken in wartime, the other in "peacetime." And while the one was perhaps the most closely guarded secret ever kept about so enormous an enterprise spread so widely and employing so many people, the other was probably the most widely publicized and most widely witnessed of all enterprises in human history.

Whatever the obvious differences between these two enterprises —the exploration of the inconceivably minuscule world inside the atom and the exploration of the inconceivably vast universe of outer space—they both had the effect of deepening man's sense of momentum and accentuating his feeling of the new unfreedom of omnipotence.

EVEN IN AMERICAN HISTORY there had been no close precedent. Perhaps the most nearly comparable American achievement was the building of the first railroad across the North American continent. Before the Civil War, publicists were characterizing the railroad as "that work of art which agitates and drives mad the whole people; as music, sculpture, and pictures have done in their great days respectively." Thoreau warned in *Walden* (1854): "We do not ride on the railroad; it rides upon us."

While the transcontinental railroad itself was more novel in its dimensions than in any other way, many viewed it with the same awe and alarm that would accompany the first explosion of an atomic bomb three quarters of a century later. When the Central Pacific and the Union Pacific were nearing the link-up which would complete the tracks across the continent, Charles Francis Adams, Jr., the New England railroad magnate, in the passage already quoted at the opening of this volume, observed that "from a period long before the Christian Era down to 1829 there had been no essential change in the system of internal communication." Now he saw suddenly let loose "an enormous, an incalculable force . . . exercising all sorts of influences, social, moral, and political; precipitating upon us novel problems which demand immediate solution; banishing the old before the new is half matured to replace it; bringing the nations into close contact before yet the antipathies of race have begun to be eradicated; giving us a history full of changing fortunes and rich in dramatic episodes." The railroad, he thought, might be "the most tremendous and far-reaching engine of social change which has ever either blessed or cursed mankind." At the time, the railroad men's conquest of the continent was a spectacle without rival anywhere in the world. The Trans-Siberian Railway was not begun until 1891, and the Berlin-to-Baghdad Railway was a product of the same era. The transcontinental railroad, like the most impressive achievements of American technology in the twentieth century, had succeeded in reaching a definite goal within a specified time.

The greatest works of cooperative exploration before the twentieth century—the discovery of America in the fifteenth, sixteenth, and seventeenth centuries, the exploration of Oceania in the eighteenth century and the Nile in the nineteenth century, exploration of the Arctic and Antarctica in the twentieth century—all these had reached toward goals that were more or less vague. From the nature of those older enterprises, it long remained uncertain whether, much less when, their goals had been attained. By contrast, Americans in the mid-twentieth century discovered that the more vast and the more centralized and more far-reaching their national enterprises became, the more definite became the objective and the more rigid the time schedule.

There was another remarkable and unprecedented feature to this new kind of race for empire—for the empire of the atom and the empire of outer space. When the microcosm (the atom, the invisible within) and the macrocosm (the universe, the invisible without) had both become worlds for exploration on schedule, the stakes were unimaginable, failure was inconceivable, and success would be apocalyptic. These new empires, like the old, became scenes of frantic racing to get there first. But in the old race for land and territory, one nation's gain was another's loss. The dividing line which Pope Alexander VI drew in 1493 one hundred leagues west of the Azores and Cape Verde Islands (apportioning the newly discovered lands between Spain and Portugal) expressed the spirit of the old colonialism. That was a race for place, for lands to be occupied and exploited, people and territories to be ruled. When the world opened up to seafaring explorers in the fifteenth and sixteenth centuries, peoples and places at a distance became the subject of fable, folklore, and optimistic advertising. Only a few people at home even knew that America existed.

But the New Worlds of the twentieth century were everywhere. Everything was atoms and everyplace was an avenue to the heavens. If one nation was there, that did not mean another nation could not also be there. To match the everywhere communities, there were now to be everywhere colonies.

IN THE EARLY YEARS of World War II, the great nuclear scientists who arrived in England as refugees from Hitler were for security reasons not allowed to do military research. Excluded from "practical" work like that on radar, they were given ample time to speculate on what would prove to be the most explosive practical issue of modern technology, the feasibility of an atomic bomb.

To the notion of an atom bomb there were several dimensions of impossibility. "Splitting" the *atom* (from Greek *atomos* meaning "indivisible") was, of course, a contradiction in terms. Such indivisible units had been the foundation of modern physics. After the nineteenth century had elaborated a theory of the atom, it was generally believed that each "element" was truly elementary, that the atom was the lowest common denominator of matter and that an atom of one element could never be transformed into an atom of another element.

Then late in 1938 two German physicists, at the Kaiser Wilhelm Institute in Berlin, Otto Hahn and Fritz Strassmann, discovered that when they bombarded the heavy element uranium with neutrons, they produced some quantities of a different, lighter element, barium. This process of apparently transforming one "element" into another was the first public hint that the "indivisible" atom might not be indivisible after all, that an atom of one element might conceivably be "split" into atoms of other elements. Two Austrian physicists, Lise Meitner, a collaborator of Hahn, and her nephew Otto Frisch, who had been expelled from their country because they were Jews, were then refugees in Sweden. They boldly accepted this new possibility that the atom was not indivisible; and they called it "fission" (from Latin *findere*, "to split") by analogy to the biological process of bacteria, which reproduce by splitting.

Over the centuries, of course, alchemists and charlatans had dreamed of transmuting "base" elements like lead or iron into gold or silver. But now that their dream was coming true, it had a quite unexpected result. For the twentieth century had become less interested in matter, and in the precious elements like gold and silver, than in energy. If fission could actually be accomplished, then, according to Einstein's formula ($E = mc^2$) a fantastic amount of energy would be released. Even though the mass of any one atom was small, the energy released would be multiplied by "c^2" (the speed of light squared), an enormous multiple evolving upwards of 100 million electron volts.

About the same time that Hahn and Strassmann were doing their work in Berlin, a French physicist Frédéric Joliot-Curie in Paris, and the Italian Enrico Fermi and the Hungarian Leo Szilard (both of whom were now in the United States as refugees from Mussolini and Hitler) discovered that the fission of uranium would free more neutrons. The conclusion seemed clear, then, that by allowing these neutrons to split more uranium, it would be possible to produce still more neutrons to split still more uranium, setting up a "chain reaction," in which each split in its turn would produce enormous quantities of energy. This energy might be used either for a new source of industrial power or as a new kind of explosive.

The community of scientists, and especially of theoretical scientists, was international. Hitler and the millions of German Nazis had enriched the rest of the world community of scientists by driving out of Germany and German-occupied Europe those brillant physicists who, according to the Nazis, were not "racially pure." These were to be the very same men and women who played a crucial role in conceiving and planning the atomic bomb. By 1939, when Hitler had begun his march across Europe, science and technology in the United States had already been remarkably strengthened by these refugee physicists who were committed to the Allies.

On August 11 of that year, a letter from Albert Einstein (who had come to the United States in 1933, whom the Nazis deprived of German citizenship in 1934, and who promptly became an American citizen) was delivered to President Roosevelt. Einstein's letter informed the President of the possibility "that the element uranium may be turned into a new and important source of energy in the immediate future," and therefore called for "watchfulness and, if necessary, quick action on the part of the Administration." Forecasting the magnitude of an atom bomb, Einstein reminded the President that while the United States had only meager ores of uranium, the most important world sources were in the former Czechoslovakia and in the Belgian Congo, both readily accessible to Germany. He therefore uged that the government try to secure and stockpile uranium, that experimental work be supported, and that the government be alert to any evidence that Germany was proceeding to make a bomb. On receiving Einstein's letter, the President appointed a committee on uranium, and on November 1 he let a year's research contract for $6,000. Meanwhile in several universities the European refugee physicists were working with American physicists to learn more about fission.

By this time, experimental physics had become a lively subject in the graduate schools of American universities. While Americans were not leading the world in theoretical speculation, they had shown remarkable success in devising apparatus to test the theories. By 1931 Ernest O. Lawrence at the University of California in Berkeley had made the first cyclotron, which had greatly facilitated research into the atom and experiments with radioactivity; and Robert Van de Graaff at Princeton had devised a high-voltage electrostatic generator for creating beams of subatomic particles. American experimental equipment was inferior to none.

Large-scale government support of atomic research did not come until after Pearl Harbor on December 7, 1941, but then it came promptly. By mid-January 1942, Arthur H. Compton, a member of a new planning committee who had been surveying the implications of the most recent research for the making of a bomb, announced to his physicist colleagues a definite schedule: (a) to determine whether a chain reaction was possible, by July 1, 1942; (b) to achieve the first chain reaction, by January 1943; (c) to have a bomb, by January 1945. "Research and Development," another name for this vast effort, would require an enormous national investment which was dispersed over the continent.

FROM THE DAY of commitment, the question at each stage was not *whether* but *when*. The theoretical and practical uncertainties did not dilute the faith that a bomb would be made. But the pressure of war, which made the job urgent, required an especially costly mode of procedure. By mid-1942 it was still uncertain which of the five conceivable ways of producing fissionable materials would be most effective. Under other circumstances each would have been tried in turn, starting with the procedure that seemed most promising, until the best one was found. Against this approach, Compton observed, "The Germans are at present probably far ahead of us. They started their program vigorously in 1939, but ours was not undertaken with similar vigor until 1941." It appeared that even a few months' delay might give the Germans the deciding advantage. The planning committee of scientists therefore determined to explore all five methods at the same time, even though this meant building a costly plant for each of them, and with the expectation that in the long run all the plants except one would prove unnecessary. By December 1942, the committee was able to reduce the possibilities. The four plants that they recommended building would cost about $400 million.

Planning and construction of these, along with administrative responsibility for the whole bomb project, was put under the direction of Brigadier General Leslie R. Groves, who had been the Army's Deputy Chief of Constructions and supervised the building of the Pentagon, the world's largest office building. Groves, the son of an Army chaplain, had been raised in army posts, and had spent a year and a half at M.I.T. before going to West Point, where he graduated fourth in his class in 1918. He had no special knowledge of physics or the atom. But as the Army's Deputy Chief of Constructions he had a responsibility for spending some $600 million each month, and he had a reputation for getting things done.

When the original schedule (along with the decision to spend the hundreds of millions) was made, it still had not even been demonstrated that there could be such a thing as a nuclear chain reaction. Experiments had shown that an atom of uranium might be split into atoms of another element. It had not yet been shown that the neutrons liberated on fission of a uranium atom could be harnessed to split still more uranium atoms to liberate still more neutrons to liberate still more neutrons, and so on. If the neutrons were inevitably lost in the process, the splitting of the atom, however interesting to the physicist, would be of little practical significance; but if a self-sustaining chain reaction could be produced, an immeasurable new source of energy would have been discovered. On December 2, 1942, in a secret laboratory which had been improvised from a squash court under the grandstands at Stagg Field of the University of Chicago, Enrico Fermi performed the first nuclear fission and proved that the reaction would be self-sustaining. The planners had shown confidence in their calculations (and in Fermi's prediction that he could prevent a runaway reaction and explosion) by performing this risky experiment in the heart of a densely populated city instead of in a remote country laboratory.

But even before Fermi had given his decisive proof, enormous sums had been committed, and new cities were being built at Oak Ridge, Tennessee, at Hanford, Washington, and at Los Alamos, New Mexico. These secret "cities in the wilderness" were twentieth-century "cities upon a hill": cities for production and experiment full of threat and promise for all mankind. The most far-flung and most costly technological effort in history aimed to accomplish man's control over the smallest dimension in his reach.

The program remained substantially on schedule. All the different steps necessary to provide any of the conceivably feasible raw materials for a bomb were taken simultaneously, while at the same time scientists and technicians were already designing the bomb itself. It proved to be an enormous industrial task to produce enough fissionable material. While, on the whole, judgments, guesses, and predictions proved correct, the riskiest forecast was that it would be possible to produce a bomb at all. On July 16, 1945, within six months of the time that had been indicated by Compton back in January 1942, the first atomic device was exploded at Alamogordo in the New Mexico desert. "It was like the grand finale of a mighty symphony of the elements," wrote William L. Laurence of the *New York Times*, who witnessed the explosion from the observation post twenty miles away, "fascinating and terrifying, uplifting and crushing, ominous, devastating, full of great promise and great foreboding. . . . On that moment hung eternity. Time stood still. Space contracted to a pinpoint. It was as though the earth had opened and the skies split. One felt as though he had been privileged to witness the birth of the world—to be present at the moment of Creation when the Lord said: 'Let there be light.' "

Just three weeks later, on August 6, 1945, an atomic bomb was dropped on Hiroshima, destroying four miles of the heart of the city and bringing death or injury to more than 160,000. Three days later a second bomb was dropped, on Nagasaki. On the following day, August 10, the Japanese offered to surrender. As for the Germans, against whom the American physicists had been racing, they had surrendered three months before.

THE NEW WORLD of the divisible atom brought new dimensions of catastrophe as well as of knowledge. The destructive power of the atomic bomb, made in the U.S.A. and first used by Americans, gave Americans a new sense of the community of man. But many Americans were haunted by fear that in the mushroom cloud over Hiroshima they had conjured a fifth rider of the Apocalypse. Along with Pestilence and War and Famine and Death, was there now a horse reserved for Science? Bewilderment at the magnitude of the new power began to be overshadowed by a sense of common worldwide doom. If Americans could make an atomic bomb, why could it not be made by others? If a uranium bomb was destructive, why not a hydrogen bomb, or some future model still more potent?

Nothing before, not even the great immigrations or two "world" wars, had made Americans feel so immersed in the world. This apocalyptic terror of the late 1940's also brought scientists who had made the bomb into the political arena. With their Federation of Atomic Scientists (later expanded into the Federation of American Scientists) they aimed to save mankind from the consequences of their success. In the United States they secured civilian control of atomic evergy and they organized a movement for international control of the atom.

Oddly enough, the new instruments and evidences of American omnipotence brought a new sense of powerlessness about the future. Fate and Providence and Destiny were being displaced or at least overshadowed by a growing sense of Momentum: a deepening belief in the inevitability of continued movement in whatever direction the movement was already going. "Momentum" described the new sense in many ways. By contrast with the notion of God's Will or the Economy of Nature or Progress or Destiny, it was neutral. It suggested a recognition of the force, a sense of powerlessness before it, and an uncertainty about whether it was good or evil. Perhaps never before in modern history had man been so horrified and bewildered by the threat of his own handiwork. His sense of where things were going was no less clear, perhaps it was even clearer than ever, but his sense of his freedom to change the direction and of his power and his duty to judge the direction had dwindled.

A hint of the new way of thinking had been the theme of Anne Morrow Lindbergh's much publicized *Wave of the Future* (1940): "The wave of the future is coming and there is no fighting it." The view that the future was governed by forces man could see but could not shape or deflect was long since beginning to be felt by Americans who had lost their sense of the miraculous, who saw fewer and fewer limits to the power of organized man, and who were suddenly confronted by the immeasurably explosive power of their gargantuan technology.

Of all this, the history of atomic weapons had been a classic example. Albert Einstein, Leo Szilard, and the others who had prodded President Roosevelt in 1939 to hasten to make an atomic bomb, had been impelled then by their fear that Nazi Germany might already be on its way to making such a bomb. Before August 1942 some of the physicists (as later recalled by Alice Kimball Smith, who was personally acquainted with them) "found comfort in the hope that some insuperable obstacle might demonstrate the impossibility of an atomic weapon." But already by 1943, when the large staff of scientists was recruited for the project, it appeared unlikely that the weapon would prove impossible. "People were saying rather that if a bomb could be made the fact should be settled once and for all."

During this period, few scientists seemed troubled by the consequences of their work. "Almost everyone," Robert Oppenheimer recalled in 1954, "realized that this was a great undertaking. . . . an unparalleled opportunity to bring to bear the basic knowledge and art of science for the benefit of his country. Almost everyone knew that this job, if it were achieved, would be a part of history. This sense of excitement, of devotion and of patriotism in the end prevailed." Or, as one of them recalled, "I worked on the bomb because everybody I knew was doing it."

By late spring of 1945, some of the leading physicists were persuaded that their organized efforts had succeeded and that a usable atomic bomb was about to be produced. A number of them, including several who had been the most energetic in initiating the project six years before, were appalled. Faced with the product of their work, some of these prime movers of the bomb worked frenetically to prevent its use in the war. The brilliant Leo Szilard prepared memoranda and petitions, and circulated them among his colleagues. He then tried desperately to convey his apprehensions directly to President Roosevelt and Mrs. Roosevelt, and later to President Truman. He proposed, for example (as some of the physicists had originally envisaged), that the bomb be used only for a demonstration in some uninhabited place; there it presumably would be so destructive that it would persuade the enemy to surrender. On one occasion he even suggested that to avoid a postwar nuclear arms race against Russia, the United States should not use the bomb against Japan at all, and so should try to convince the Russians that American efforts to make a bomb had failed. But these products of Szilard's fertile imagination simply gave him a reputation for being erratic; the more he proposed, the less he persuaded. When Szilard, with two other atomic scientists, called on James F. Byrnes (President Truman's personal adviser, and about to become his Secretary of State) to urge restraint in using the bomb, Byrnes saw the bomb mainly as something to impress the Russians with, and worried only about how to justify to Congress the $2 billion that the bomb had cost.

James Franck, one of the most famous of the German refugee physicists, had joined the project in 1942 with the express understanding that if the United States was the first to build a bomb, he would have an opportunity to offer his views about its use to the highest American officials. On June 11, 1945, Franck presented a report, signed by six of his eminent colleagues, including Szilard, to the President's committee:

> Thus, from the "optimistic" point of view—looking forward to an international agreement on the prevention of nuclear warfare—the

military advantages and the saving of American lives achieved by the sudden use of atomic bombs against Japan may be outweighed by the ensuing loss of confidence and by a wave of horror and repulsion sweeping over the rest of the world and perhaps even dividing public opinion at home.

From this point of view, a demonstration of the new weapon might best be made, before the eyes of representatives of all the United Nations, on the desert or a barren island. The best possible atmosphere for the achievement of an international agreement could be achieved if America could say to the world, "You see what sort of a weapon we had but did not use. We are ready to renounce its use in the future if other nations join us in this renunciation and agree to the establishment of an efficient international control."

After such a demonstration the weapon might perhaps be used against Japan if the sanction of the United Nations (and of public opinion at home) were obtained, perhaps after a preliminary ultimatum to Japan to surrender or at least to evacuate certain regions as an alternative to their total destruction. This may sound fantastic, but in nuclear weapons we have something entirely new in order of magnitude of destructive power, and if we want to capitalize fully on the advantage their possession gives us, we must use new and imaginative methods.

Dissent among other atomic scientists in the laboratory at Chicago was so deep and so frequently expressed that Compton, who was in charge of atomic research, directed that they be polled on the use of the bomb. A hasty poll appeared to show that only 15 percent of the atomic scientists favored full military use against Japan, 46 percent favored a limited military demonstration first, and the rest favored other forms of limitation on its use. The sampling of scientists' opinion on the use of the bomb which General Groves gave to the Secretary of War before the final decision was made showed only a small minority in favor of using the bomb without warning.

The most obvious example of momentum was the simple fact that although the bomb was initiated by men with a passionate hatred of the Nazis and a fear of Nazi domination of the world, it was not used against the Nazis at all, but against the Japanese. As the historian Donald Fleming has observed, the Japanese had to take Hitler's medicine. Several months before the Nazi surrender on May 8, 1945, Americans no longer feared that the Nazis could have perfected an atomic bomb. While United States forces were closing in, it was still generally assumed that to end the war in the Pacific, the United States would actually have to invade the home islands of Japan.Shortening the war against Japan, even with its saving of perhaps millions of lives, still was a different objective from preventing Nazi domination of the world. But an atomic bomb had been made, and at enormous cost. In the end, all the voices urging caution and second thoughts about long-term consequences were barely audible above the roaring, crunching momentum of the gargantuan organized effort.

President Truman took full responsibility for introducing the world to the atomic bomb. "But," Alice Kimball Smith observed, "his decision was not so much a positive act as a choice not to halt the enormous, multifaceted effort which he had found well advanced three months earlier. To have called such a halt, contrary to the advice of his most trusted associates, would have required an almost inconceivable exercise of individual initiative." The President's decision, General Groves later recalled, "was one of non-interference—basically, a decision not to upset the existing plans."

The next stage in atomic weapons research, the quest for a "super" (or hydrogen) atomic bomb, was prodded by the revelation in 1949 that the Soviets possessed the bomb, and further dramatized the overwhelming force of this New Momentum. The moral uncertainty which briefly delayed decision to proceed with the bigger bomb was dissolved as soon as the uncertainty over the possibility of building the new bomb was dissipated. But as building a thermonuclear bomb —one based on fusion rather then fission—came to appear possible, there was widening agreement that the effort actually to build it was necessary. The "can" had smothered the "ought."

LIKE THE ATOMIC BOMB, the American space enterprise was a by-product of World War II, and of the challenge of German technology. The full story of American exploration of space would, of course, reach back to the beginnings of the airplane, back to Robert Goddard's experiments in New Mexico, to the Wright brothers at Kitty Hawk and beyond. But in the latest stage, the American effort was stimulated and made possible because the German V-2 had shown the usefulness of rocketry in warfare. In January 1945, as the Russian armies approached the launching station of Peenemünde, the German rocket scientists decided to flee to the West. This crucial decision brought the most advanced rocket scientists themselves, along with the technical documents recording the successes and, most important, also the failures, of earlier German efforts in rocketry. Then, during 1945, under the code name "Operation Paperclip," the U.S. Army transported to military bases in the United States the men and the documents which comprised the world's best resources for the new sciences of rocketry and space exploration. Foreign scientists, now fleeing not from Hitler's victory but from his defeat, were newly enlisted in the American space enterprise, where they played as large a role as they had in the atom.

The steps in the American space venture are familiar enough. From the improvement of launching rockets to the first American satellite (Explorer I) in 1958, to the first American in orbit (Project Mercury) and the first American communications satellite (Telstar I) in 1962, to American two-man spacecrafts (Project Gemini) in 1965, and on to the program (Apollo) for landing Americans on the moon. The dramatic details of this story have been told and will be retold by others. What concerns us here is less the exploits than the enterprise, what it showed about American ways of doing whatever was desired or required, and what it meant for the American's sense of control over his present and his future—in a word, what it tells us of the growing sense of momentum.

The most stirring event in the beginnings of American space enterprise was not anything accomplished on American soil or by American technicians. On the morning of October 5, 1957, the world was startled to see in the sky an artificial satellite launched by the Russians. "Sputnik" (meaning, in Russian, fellow traveler of the earth) was an aluminum alloy sphere less than 2 feet in diameter and weighing 184 pounds. Never before had so small and so harmless an object created such consternation. The world stage was set. Four years of preparation had alerted nations to the International Geophysical Year (IGY), to be held in 1957–58 as a symbol of peaceful exploration of outer space. In 1955, when the Russians announced their intention to launch a satellite within two years, the three armed services in the United States were still competing for control of the space effort. But Americans assumed that this could not affect the outcome of the space race, since Soviet technology was so far behind and was destined to remain behind because of the axiomatic inferiority of its political system. It was an article of faith that "communism" could not beat "democracy" in the arena of science and technology where the free competition of ideas spelled progress. It is not surprising, then, that Sputnik shocked and confused Americans, and bewildered American friends abroad.

Another reason for American alarm was less complicated. For Sputnik had been launched by an intercontinental missile which, as Nikita Khrushchev explained over the Moscow radio on August 26, 1957, could be accurately directed from the Soviet Union "to any part of the world." Experts quickly saw that Soviet technology could now deliver an atomic or hydrogen warhead to a target in the United States. But the official American reaction generally followed political party lines.

"A silly bauble in the sky" was how Sputnik was described by the usually prescient Clarence Randall, then a special assistant to President Eisenhower. He contrasted it disparagingly with the basic

American strength shown in a display of American supermarkets in Zagreb, Yugoslavia. President Eisenhower's Director of the Budget, Percival Brundage, was reported to have told a dinner partner that within six months Sputnik would be forgotten—to which Perle Mesta replied, "and in six months we may all be dead." President Eisenhower himself tried to brush off Sputnik as a stunt that had no bearing on military capability, and in his press conference declared, "Now, so far as the satellite itself is concerned, that does not raise my apprehension one iota."

The widespread feeling in the nation was better expressed by Democratic Senator Richard Russell of Georgia. "Sputnik," he said, "confronts America with a new and terrifying military danger and a disastrous blow to our prestige." However unloved by those it aimed to please, the United States had been respected and feared for its technological superiority. Now even this was in doubt. Sputnik II, a second Soviet satellite carrying the dog Laika and weighing 1,120 pounds, was launched only one month after Sputnik, on November 3. Then, on December 6, the Vanguard missile, designed to send up the first American satellite, upon starting up from its launching pad quickly collapsed in flame. The world press outdid itself in headlining snide epithets like "Kaputnik" (London *Daily Express*) or "A Pearl Harbor for American Science" (Tokyo *Yomiuri*).

These accumulating evidences of Soviet superiority in space technology triggered a concern bordering on hysteria, for the quality of American education, especially in mathematics and the sciences. And the Soviet challenge did influence the curriculum of some schools. But within another decade, the worry over "excellence" in American public education was to be displaced by a similarly hysterical anxiety to lower academic standards in order to provide "open" college admission.

Despite pressures, President Eisenhower remained generally cool toward the space enterprise, and especially toward programs for landing a man on the moon. But after the National Aeronautics and Space Administration (NASA) was established by Congress in 1958 as a way out of interservice rivalries, the momentum of space activities gathered force. In August 1960, when NASA sent to the Bureau of the Budget a request for $1.25 billion for the fiscal year 1962 in order to move ahead with its manned space flights, the President requested a special study by a panel of scientists. At a White House meeting in December 1960, the committee reported that "the first really big achievement of the man-in-space program would be the lunar landing." And they estimated the costs: $350 million to complete Project Mercury; $8 billion for an Apollo circumlunar voyage; $26 billion to $38 billion for a lunar landing. In justifying this expenditure, the obvious comparison was made to Columbus' voyage of discovery to America, which had been financed by Queen Isabella, who, according to legend, had to pawn her jewels to secure the funds. President Eisenhower retorted that he was "not about to hock his jewels" to send men to the moon. The mood of this decisive meeting, one participant reported, was "almost sheer bewilderment—or certainly amusement—that anybody would consider such an undertaking. Somebody said, 'This won't satisfy everybody. When they finish this, they'll want to go to the planets.' There was a lot of laughter at that thought."

President Eisenhower did not see the military or the scientific need for such a space program, and he thought it imprudent to spend so huge a sum for international public relations. Nevertheless, the NASA budget was increased from $494 million in its first full year of operation to $923 million in the second year, and in November 1960 NASA actually increased its budget request by another $100 million from its August figure of $1.25 billion to $1.35 billion. Nearing the end of his presidency, Eisenhower was more than ever conscious of his figure in history, and of his need somehow to embody his belief that the role of government in American life should be reduced. This meant cutting the budget and keeping speculative expenditures (and what was more speculative than a voyage to the moon?) at the lowest level. Reinforcing this was President Eisenhower's Cincinnatus-complex. Haunted by his military background, the President was determined to keep American life civilian-oriented and peace-minded. In December 1960, only a few weeks before his farewell address to the nation, President Eisenhower refused to approve funds to continue the space program toward a moon landing. In the farewell address on January 17, 1961, he warned the nation to "guard against the acquisition of unwarranted influence, whether sought or unsought, by the military-industrial complex. The potential for the disastrous rise of misplaced power exists and will persist. . . . We must also be alert to the . . . danger that public policy could itself become the captive of a scientific-technological élite."

WHEN JOHN F. KENNEDY became President on January 20, 1961, he had no special knowledge of space matters, and no particular interest in space policy. His overriding world-concern came from his sense of rivalry between the West and the Communists and from his obsessive determination that the United States should not be out-shone by the Soviets. Just as President Eisenhower, a man of military experience, demanded that a costly space program be justified by clear military uses and distrusted public-relations pretexts, so President Kennedy by contrast was preoccupied with prestige, with how to make the American reputation prevail over that of the Soviets. In retrospect we can see that the space enterprise, and especially a moon landing, was tailor-made for improving United States public relations and for raising prestige abroad. For while space exploration had a military significance, this was by no means obvious, and the enterprise could therefore appear as a symbol of the American love of peace and of the pursuit of knowledge for its own sake. At the same time, the act itself—putting a Man on the Moon—was so easy to grasp that it was bound to be a show stopper on the world stage. A moon landing, properly planned and scheduled, would fill television screens everywhere.

President Kennedy withheld his directive for the moon landing until he could be briefed by his own advisers, until the American lag behind the Soviets in space technology appeared indisputable, and until the prestige competition with the Soviets had reached a crisis. These impelling conditions accumulated in rapid succession within four months of his coming to the White House. The Space Science Board of the National Academy of Sciences, with a new head who was a devotee of space exploration, persuasively urged the scientific benefits, and Vice-President Lyndon B. Johnson was a space enthusiast. James Webb, whom President Kennedy appointed as the head of NASA, was a man of vision, with extraordinary powers of organization and leadership. Having quickly assimilated the complex technical problems of the enterprise, Webb proved effective in convincing reluctant congressmen and the vacillating President.

Meanwhile the Soviets had pushed ahead with dramatic success. On April 12, 1961, Moscow announced:

> The world's first space ship *Vostok* with a man on board, has been launched on April 12 in the Soviet Union on a round-the-earth orbit. The first navigator is Soviet citizen pilot Major Yuri Alekseyevich Gagarin.

Phoning Gagarin his congratulations, Khrushchev crowed, "Let the capitalist countries catch up with our country!"

On the evening of April 14, President Kennedy held a meeting in the Cabinet Room with his principal advisers, significantly combined with an interview with Time-Life correspondent Hugh Sidey. The stated purpose of the meeting was "to explore with his principal advisers the significance of the Gagarin flight and the alternatives for U. S. action." According to Sidey's report (which the President himself had checked for accuracy):

> "Now let's look at this," said Kennedy impatiently. "Is there any place we can catch them? What can we do? Can we go around the moon

before them? Can we put a man on the moon before them? What about Nova and Rover? When will Saturn be ready? Can we leapfrog?"

The one hope, explained [NASA official] Dryden, lay in this country's launching a crash program similar to the Manhattan Project. But such an effort might cost $40 billion, and even so there was only an even chance of beating the Soviets.

James Webb spoke up, "We are doing everything we possibly can, Mr. President. And thanks to your leadership we are moving ahead now more rapidly than ever. . . ."

"The cost," he pondered. "That's what gets me." He turned to Budget Director Bell questioningly. The cost of space science went up in geometric progression, explained Bell. . . . "Now is not the time to make mistakes," cautioned [Science Adviser] Wiesner. . . .

Kennedy turned back to the men around him. He thought for a second. Then he spoke. "When we know more, I can decide if it's worth it or not. If somebody can just tell me how to catch up. . . ."

Kennedy stopped again a moment and glanced from face to face. Then he said quietly, "There's nothing more important."

On April 15, three days after the Gagarin triumph, Cuban exiles trained by the CIA began their attempted coup with air strikes against Castro's planes, followed forty-eight hours later by an invasion at the Bay of Pigs. Within two days it was clear to the world that the Bay of Pigs was a disaster for the United States. Never was American self-esteem or the American reputation abroad more in need of a lift. Now the President felt under special pressure, as the President's Science Adviser explained, "to get something else in the foreground." The President could use a "space spectacular."

Within the week, at a press conference on April 21, President Kennedy announced that he had asked a committee, headed by the Vice-President, to recommend the national investment in space, and to report "any program now, regardless of cost" which could give the United States a good chance to beat the Soviets in space. Wernher von Braun told the Vice-President on April 29 that "we have a sporting chance of sending a 3-man crew around the moon ahead of the Soviets." and "an excellent chance of beating the Soviets to the first landing of a crew on the moon (including return capability, of course)." Other experts had agreed that a lunar landing was the first space spectacular in which the United States might beat the Soviets. On May 5 the first public success of Project Mercury sent Astronaut Alan Shepard into a manned space flight. In a memorandum to the Vice-President, James Webb and Defense Secretary Robert McNamara urged:

It is man, not merely machines, in space that captures the imagination of the world. All large-scale projects require the mobilization of resources on a national scale. They require the development and successful application of the most advanced technologies. Dramatic achievements in space therefore symbolize the technological power and organizing capability of a nation. It is for reasons such as these that major achievements in space contribute to national prestige. . . .

Major successes, such as orbiting a man as the Soviets have just done, lend national prestige even though the scientific, commercial or military value of the undertaking may by ordinary standards be marginal or economically unjustified. . . . Our attainments are a major element in the international competition between the Soviet system and our own. The non-military, non-commercial, non-scientific but "civilian" projects such as lunar and planetary exploration are, in this sense, part of the battle along the fluid front of the cold war.

This same memorandum was delivered to President Kennedy on the afternoon of May 8, and by the next day word had been leaked to the press that the President was approving a program to put an American on the moon. The Webb-McNamara memorandum became the President's program. This required an increase of $549 million (61 percent over President Eisenhower's figure) in the space budget for the following fiscal year, and billions more over the next five years.

President Kennedy's speech to Congress on May 25, 1961, on "Urgent National Needs" laid out his space program: "that this Nation should commit itself to achieving the goal, before this decade is out, of landing a man on the moon and returning him safely to earth." With very little debate, Congress approved President Kennedy's space program, which, Senator Robert S. Kerr explained, "will enable Americans to meet their destiny."

Less than ten years later, on July 20, 1969, at 4:17 P.M. Eastern daylight time, an American did land on the moon. The most ambitious goal of human technology had been achieved by Americans, and on time. At the launching of Apollo II, a member of President Kennedy's family, R. Sargent Shriver, poignantly recalled that in 1961 at the time of announcing the national commitment to go to the moon, President Kennedy had remarked, "I firmly expect this commitment to be kept. And if I die before it is, all you here now just remember when it happens I will be sitting up there in heaven in a rocking chair just like this one, and I'll have a better view of it than anybody."

MOMENTUM, AN EVER more prominent feature of the American's relation to his future, had of course dominated the space venture. Despite President Eisenhower's grave doubts about the wisdom of increased expenditures on space exploration and his lack of imagination about its possibilities, he still found himself approving a NASA budget of over $1 billion. In retrospect, President Kennedy's decision to proceed toward landing an American on the moon had many of the features of President Truman's decision to use the atomic bomb. The wartime momentum was no longer there, but there were other momentums: the force of competition with the Soviets, and most of all the increasing mass and velocity of the space enterprise itself. While President Kennedy claimed personal responsibility and must be given personal credit for making the timely decision to go to the moon, in the perspective of history that decision, too, appears less a positive act than a decision not to halt another enormous, multifaceted effort.

As American civilization became increasingly permeated by its technology, it lay increasingly at the mercy of the internal logic of advancing knowledge. Science and technology had a momentum of their own: each next step was commanded by its predecessor. To fail to take that next step was to waste all the earlier efforts. Once the nation had embarked on the brightly illuminated path of science, it had somehow ventured into a world of mystery where the direction and the speed would be dictated by the instruments that cut the path and by the vehicles that carried man ahead. The autonomy of science, the freedom of the scientist to go where knowledge and discovery led him, spelled the unfreedom of the society to choose its way for other reasons. People felt they might conceivably slow the pace of change—they might delay the supersonic transport (SST) for a year or two—but they wondered whether they were in a position to stop it.

Precisely because the United States had been so democratized, the Old World barriers between "science" and "technology," the institutions which traditionally separated the men who *thought* from the men who *did*, were broken down. In fact, the very distinction between the "theoretical" and the "practical" acquired a shocking new irrelevance. While the atomic enterprise, which had been urged by that Patron Saint of the Abstract, Albert Einstein, let theoretical physics prove itself practical, the moon enterprise led toward an objective that was ultimately abstract. The most costly scientific venture in history (which by 1972 had reached many times the cost of the atomic bomb) was undertaken by a nation that was only vaguely aware of what "practical" purpose, if any, it might serve.

The sense of momentum which overwhelmed Presidents burdened the ordinary citizen. The pace of Research and Development, of advertising, of ingenious, pervasive, and inescapable new ways for making and marketing nearly everything to nearly everybody, made it seem that the future of American civilization and the shape of everyday life could not fail to be determined by the mass and velocity of the enterprises already in being. This pervaded the public feelings about all sorts of industrial developments: the elaboration of packaging (from the paper bag and the folding box to cellophane to double-wrapped in cellophane to who-could-tell-what); the automobile (from the Model T to the "annual" model to semiannual models to who-could-tell-what); and countless other momentums big and little.

Fewer decisions of social policy seemed to be Whether-or-Not as more became decisions of How-Fast-and-When. Was it possible even to slow the pace, to hold back the momentum—of packaging, of automobile production, of communications, of image-making, of university expansion, of highway construction, of population growth?

This new climate of negative decision, this new unfreedom of omnipotence was confirmed by forces outside the industrial machinery. For the atomic bomb along with the space adventure and a thousand lesser daily demonstrations—the automobile and the airplane, radio and television, computer technology and automation, and the myriad products of Research and Development—were showing that the "advance" of science and technology, whether guided or vagrant, would control the daily lives of Americans. Not legislation or the wisdom of statesmen but something else determined the future. And of all things on earth, the growth of knowledge remained still the most spontaneous and unpredictable.

EPILOGUE:

Unknown Coasts

Three and a half centuries before Americans were debating their voyage to the moon, William Bradford reported how the Pilgrims, having taken temporary refuge in Holland, debated their voyage to America.

". . . it raised many variable opinions amongst men, and caused many fears and doubts amongst them selves. Some, from their reasons and hops conceived, laboured to stirr up and incourage the rest to undertake and prosecute the same; others, againe, out of their fears, objected against it, and sought to diverte from it, aledging many things, and those neither unreasonable nor unprobable.

"As that it was a great designe, and subjecte to many unconceivable perills and dangers; as, besids the casulties of the seas (which none can be freed from) the length of the vioage was such, as the weake bodies of women and other persons worne out with age and traville (as many of them were) could never be able to endure. And yet if they should, the miseries of the land which they should be exposed unto, would be hard to be borne; and lickly, some, or all of them togeither, to consume and utterly to ruinate them. For ther they should be liable to famine, and nakednes, and the wante, in a maner, of all things.

"The chang of aire, diate, and drinking of water, would infecte their bodies with sore sickneses, and greevous diseases. And also those which should escape or overcome these difficulties, should yett be in continuall danger of the salvage people, who are cruell, barbarous, and most trecherous, being most furious in their rage, and merciles wher they overcome; not being contente only to kill, and take away life, but delight to tormente men in the most bloodie manner that may be; fleaing some alive with the shells of fishes, cutting of the members and joynts of others by peesmeale, and broiling on the coles, eate the collops of their flesh in their sight whilst they live; with other cruelties horrible to be related.

"And surely it could not be thought but the very hearing of these things could not but move the very bowels of men to grate within them, and make the weake to quake and tremble. It was furder objected, that it would require greater summes of money to furnish such a voiage, and to fitt them with necessaries, then their consumed estats would amounte too; and yett they must as well looke to be seconded with supplies, as presently to be transported. Also many presidents of ill success, and lamentable misseries befalne others in the like designes, were easie to be found, and not forgotten to be aledged . . .

"It was answered, that all great, and honourable actions are accompanied with great difficulties, and must be both enterprised and overcome with answerable courages. It was granted the dangers were great, but not desperate; the difficulties were many, but not invincible. For though their were many of them likly, yet they were not cartaine; it might be sundrie of the things feared might never befale; others by providente care and the use of good means, might in a great measure be prevented; and all of them, through the help of God, by fortitude and patience, might either be borne, or overcome.

"True it was, that such atempts were not to be made and undertaken without good ground and reason; not rashly or lightly as many have done for curiositie or hope of gaine, etc. But their condition was not ordinarie; their ends were good and honourable; their calling lawfull, and urgente; and therfore they might expecte the blessing of God in their proceding. Yea, though they should loose their lives in this action, yet might they have comforte in the same, and their endeavors would be honourable. . . ."

The American journeys—to America, by Americans, in America, and from America—never ceased. Ever since those Pilgrim landings, people of this nation of New Beginnings had lived on the dangerous fertile verge between the wild and the familiar. The large outlines of a new civilization were being drawn. Even after centuries the continent had never become "settled." Would it ever be?

ACKNOWLEDGMENTS

MY DEBTS FOR this, the third and final volume of a trilogy which I began to plan a quarter-century ago, must include the acknowledgments in *The Americans: The Colonial Experience* and *The Americans: The National Experience,* for those volumes provide the background for *The Americans: The Democratic Experience.*

To the University of Chicago I am grateful for having provided me the freedom, the opportunity, the resources, and the stimulus for planning the work as a whole; there much of the earlier part of this volume was prepared.

To the Smithsonian Institution of Washington, D.C., where I have been the Director of The National Museum of History and Technology since 1969, I owe a similar debt for having offered an atmosphere congenial to my scholarly and research needs in the exhilarating setting of the nation's capital.

To the Relm Foundation of Ann Arbor, Michigan, and to its Secretary, Richard A. Ware, I am especially indebted for their continuing assistance; in a bureaucratic age they have somehow managed to keep their faith in the individual scholar.

The staff of the University of Chicago Library, particularly the Law School Library, the Library of the Department of Education, the Department of Special Collections, and the Inter-Library Loan Department, have been continually helpful.

The staff of the Library of the Smithsonian Institution, and especially of The National Museum of History and Technology, has contributed to this work in countless ways. The rich resources and the cooperative staff of the Library of Congress have been indispensable.

Other libraries which have provided resources include: the Library of the Chicago Historical Society, the Chicago Public Library, the John Crerar library and the Newberry Library of Chicago; the Public Library of Washington, D.C.; the Huntington Library of San Marino, California, which hosted me as a fellow for six months in 1969; and the Library of Cambridge University, England.

Crucial to this work has been the help of my research assistants, each of whom in turn has shown patience, imagination, and resource-fulness in tracking down facts, has stirred me with ideas, and has helped make this book a stage in my own education. Professor Stanley K. Schultz of the University of Wisconsin and Professor Perry Duis of the University of Illinois in Chicago aided me generously while they were graduate students at the University of Chicago. Dr. Peter C. Marzio, now associate curator of prints in The National Museum of History and Technology, has offered essential assistance in collecting raw materials and in giving astute scholarly counsel both in Chicago and in Washington. In the last stages of the book I have been ably assisted by Louis Gorr, whose remarkable instinct for knowing where to find the undiscoverable fact, and whose unstinting industry and counsel, have been of great help.

I am grateful to my students at the University of Chicago and elsewhere and to my colleagues at the University of Chicago and at The National Museum of History and Technology for their stimulating suggestions and criticisms over the years.

A number of my friends and colleagues throughout the country have shared their insights with me, have given me suggestions, or have read all or part of the manuscript. For their acute comments, their generosity, and their frankness, it is a pleasure to thank them all. They include Professor M. Barbara Akin of Grove City College, Dr. Oscar E. Anderson of NASA, Professor Erik Barnouw of Columbia University, Professor James P. Baughman of the Harvard Business School, Mr. Silvio A. Bedini of The National Museum of History and Technology, Dr. Ray A. Billington of the Huntington Library, Professor Nelson M. Blake of Syracuse University, Mr. David West Boorstin, Mr. Jonathan Boorstin, Mr. Paul Boorstin, Mrs. Adelyn D. Breeskin of the National Collection of Fine Arts, Professor Robert H. Bremner of The Ohio State University, Professor Carl W. Condit of Northwestern University, Mr. Fairfax Cone, Dr. Eugene M. Emme of NASA, Dr. Eugene S. Ferguson of the Hagley Museum, Professor Wayne E. Fuller of the University of Texas at El Paso, Professor Joe B. Frantz of the University of Texas at Austin, Professor Nathan Glazer of Harvard University, Professor Norman Graebner of the University of Virginia, Professor John E. Jeuck of the University of Chicago, Professor Harry W. Jones of Columbia University, Professor Morton Keller of Brandeis University, Professor Melvin Kranzberg of the Georgia Institute of Technology, Professor Philip B. Kurland of the University of Chicago, Professor Raven I. McDavid, Jr., of the University of Chicago, Dr. Frank J. Malina, Professor Hans J. Morgenthau of the City University of New York, Professor Norval Morris of the University of Chicago, Professor Gilman M. Ostrander of the University of Waterloo, Professor John B. Rae of Harvey Mudd College, Professor Dorothy Ross of Princeton University, Susan Skramstad, Dr. Harold K. Skramstad, Jr., of The National Museum of History and Technology, Dean Alice Kimball Smith of the Radcliffe Institute, Mr. William Sweetland, Professor Laurence Veysey of the University of California at Santa Cruz, Professor Sam Bass Warner, Jr., of Boston University, Professor Harold F. Williamson of the Eleutherian Mills-Hagley Foundation. They have saved me from many errors; but I have sometimes differed with them on facts or on interpretations, so that I alone am responsible for the emphases and the errors which remain.

At every state in the preparation of the manuscript, the assistance, devotion, and discrimination of Miss Genevieve Gremillion have been essential. Her interest in the enterprise, her intelligence and scrupulous accuracy, have been a rare good fortune for me and for this book. I also wish to thank Miss Alice Gergely, who helped type the manuscript.

My special thanks go to my friend Mr. Jess Stein, Vice-President of Random House, who brought the book and the publisher together in the first place and whose continuing faith in the trilogy has encouraged me to carry the work to completion.

The manuscript has profited immeasurably from the advice and criticism of my editor at Random House, Mr. Robert Loomis. His intuitive gasp of the enterprise and his acute observations and ready counsel have helped shape this book. Mrs. Barbara Willson has been a superb copyeditor. Mr. Philip Lockwood has prepared the index.

My companion and intimate collaborator in the planning, researching, writing, and rewriting of this book has been my wife, Ruth F. Boorstin. She has been my principal editor for all three volumes of *The Americans,* and has played an especially crucial creative role in this volume. My debt to her is beyond words. She has been my co-explorer of the Unknown Coasts which have become this book. At the end of this effort to rediscover America, I must confess that the most delightful of all the discoveries has been our collaboration.

BIBLIOGRAPHICAL NOTES

FOLLOWING IS A LIST of works useful for studying the period covered in this volume. It is meant to help the reader who may wish to pursue further some of the topics I discuss, to suggest the kinds of material on which I have relied in my research, and to indicate my heavy debt to other scholars. I hope that it may also point to some unexplored territory for future historians. But it is not a complete bibliography of any aspect of the subject, nor does it include all the works I have used. After a General section, the bibliography is arranged into ten Parts, corresponding with the grouping of topics in my chapters. In each Part, I have begun by mentioning works of general interest and easiest accessibility, and I have then proceeded toward the more "primary" and more esoteric materials. For books on topics which reach back into the years before the Civil War, the reader is also referred to the Bibliographical Notes for *The Americans: The Colonial Experience* and *The Americans: The National Experience.*

GENERAL

SINCE THIS IS A BOOK about modern America, the reader himself is a source more "primary" than any book. At the same time he is embarrassed by printed matter in unprecedented abundance. The twentieth-century printing-press overwhelms us. What can help us understand American Civilization in our time? The simple answer, of course, is "Everything!" The problem of guiding a reader, then, is bizarre and, strictly speaking, insoluble. For while on many subjects there are vast libraries of books and journals, on others (including some of the most characteristic and most interesting topics) which have not yet seemed to become "history" and which do not fit into the academic pigeonholes, the sources are scrappy or nonexistent.

Everyman is an authority on his own age, and is *the* authority on his own experience. Contemporary history therefore is the easiest—but also the most treacherous—kind of history. Everything we say or think about ourselves (including, of course, any misconception) is an authentic part of our history. The temptations to overgeneralize are irresistible. While each of us, better than any future historian, ought to know how confusing is the experience of our time, each of us is specially tempted to solace himself with simplifications. In this way we learn to sympathize with the oversimplifying historians of other ages, but we do not necessarily help the uninitiated to grasp the fullness and peculiarity of being alive in our time.

One such peculiarity in the late twentieth century is a strangely unhistorical, or even anti-historical bias. While the historical profession proliferates, the historical sense declines. The brevity of our past, the belief in a New World, the speedy transformations of American life, all have made latter-day Americans readier with complaints and critiques of any and every custom and institution than with epics of American achievement. At the same time, Americans have tended to lose their sense of the story. The American considers every moment a new climax, and he is so often told that every event is "historic" that he loses his appetite for history. The reader who looks for contemporary historical writing comparable to the works of Bancroft, Parkman, or Henry Adams will be disappointed; but he does have the benefit of an abundant and miscellaneous harvest.

Events which have not yet become "history" have not yet become the property of historians. Where ruts have not yet been worn, it requires less effort to stay out of them. Our problem here is not so much to correct the oversimplifications of others as to find some meaning for ourselves in the myriad facts that crowd on us, all the while resisting the temptation to be Polyannas or Cassandras. The problem for us is less to discover the way it really is (which each of us inevitably senses) than to see the meaning of the way it is, to see what our civilization promises, and what unsuspected possibilities in man it may reveal.

A beautiful starting point for rediscovering America is *The National Atlas of the United States of America* (1970), which provides an attractive sample of the best in American printing, and puts the events of the nation graphically in context. A few hours spent with this book will reward and entice. The American will be startled by facts about his land which he has never imagined. He will see the variation—topographic, climatic, demographic, economic—in the parts of the nation. He will note similarities and differences in income, in resources, in products made and consumed, in modes and vehicles of communication and transportation, which are the setting for the present volume.

Unfortunately the *National Atlas* is too costly for most pocketbooks and will have to be consulted in a library. And there is no adequate substitute for its large maps in many colors. But it does not entirely supersede Charles O. Paullin, *Atlas of the Historical Geography of the United States* (1932) for historical maps or Ralph H. Brown, *Historical Geography of the United States* (1948) for interpretation.

A handy guide to the statistics of modern American life is the *Pocket Data Book* ($2), published biennially since 1967 by the United States Bureau of the Census. This admirable little volume is a selection from the several annual volumes of the *Statistical Abstract of the United States* (published since 1878 by the U.S. Department of Commerce, reissued by Simon & Schuster under the title *The U.S. Book of Facts, Statistics, & Information*), which is the essential starting point for quantitative information. Census and other data are conveniently arranged in historical series in *Historical Statistics of the United States: Colonial Times to 1957* (U.S. Dept. of Commerce), ingeniously updated in *Statistical History of the United States* (Horizon Press, 1965). A useful reference book for chronology is *The Encyclopedia of American Facts and Dates* (ed. Gorton Carruth and others, 4th ed., 1966).

A copious bibliography, useful for special topics, is *A Guide for the Study of the United States of America* (Library of Congress, 1960). A valuable selected bibliography is *The Readers' Adviser* (ed. Winifred F. Courtney, 11th ed., 1969), Vol. I. And see *The Harvard*

Guide to American History (ed. Oscar Handlin and others, 1954; Atheneum Paperback, 1967).

For countless facts—trivia, and not-so-trivia—about recent American life, the inexpensive and handy annual reference books are indispensable. One of the best of these is *The World Almanac* (continuously published under several auspices since 1868, when it was first published by the New York *World*). Others are: *Information Please Almanac* (since 1947), and more specialized yearbooks such as *The American Jewish Yearbook* (since 1899). An avenue into the facts recorded in the *New York Times* is *The New York Times Index* (available for all years since the establishment of the paper in 1851). A handy interpretive compendium for those unaccustomed to using Census or Statistical Abstract data is Ben J. Wattenberg and Richard M. Scammon, *This U.S.A.* (1965), a survey of the nation based largely on the 1960 census, and its successor volume on the 1970 census.

BIOGRAPHIES OF SOME of the most remarkable Americans are inaccessible. The *Dictionary of American Biography* (ed. Allen Johnson and Dumas Malone; 20 vols., 1928–37; with two supplements to include prominent Americans deceased before 1941) is the basic reference work; abridged in *The Concise Dictionary of American Biography* (1964). This work provides admirable critical biographies of the leading figures in American political and literary history and of a selection of other shapers of the American experience. But the emphasis is very much that of academic departments of history, omitting many of the men and women who have decisively shaped some of our intimate everyday experience. The omitted include inventors, businessmen, organizers, merchants, lawyers, and a host of ingenious Americans who have actually earned a place in history by creating new categories of experience.

The lives of many of these must be dug out of miscellaneous local publications, company advertising brochures, newspapers, ephemeral magazines, and unpublished memoirs. Many of the figures who play a role in this book offer enticing opportunities for the imaginative and energetic historian-biographer. A useful source of rudimentary facts is *Who's Who in America* (since 1897), together with *Who Was Who in America* (4 vols.) and the Historical Volume (*Who Was Who in America, 1607–1896* [1963]), and the regional *Who's Who's.*

The efforts of biographers have always been focused on the rich, the famous, and the notorious. But some of the most readable biographers of these prominent figures, by painting in the background for their hero, have incidentally provided us some of our richest, most accessible, and most vivid accounts of everyday life. For example, for earlier periods, Douglas Freeman's *Washington,* Carl Van Doren's *Franklin,* and Albert Beveridge's *Lincoln* have supplied useful sketches of the daily experience of ordinary citizens. For the most recent period, biographies of traditionally prominent figures give us less than we might wish of the background of everyday life out of which the hero arose. Some readable exceptions are Ray A. Billington, *Frederick Jackson Turner* (1973); Joseph Dorfman, *Thorstein Veblen and His America* (1934); Allan Nevins and Frank Hill, *Henry Ford* (3 vols., 1954–62); Allan Nevins, *Rockefeller* (2 vols., 1940; and revisions); and Joseph F. Wall, *Andrew Carnegie* (1970).

An unorthodox selection of major documents illustrating American civilization is *An American Primer* (ed. Daniel J. Boorstin; 2 vols., 1966; New American Library Paperback, 1968) with detailed index and concordance.

During the years covered in this volume, the American novel has flourished, and has become increasingly preoccupied with the relation of the hero (or anti-hero) to his society. Many of these works are autobiographical or semi-autobiographical. Few other novels are as successful in grasping the times or as wide in sweep as John Dos Passos, *U.S.A.* (3 vols., 1930, 1932, 1936), but others with a narrower focus are Edward Eggleston, *The Hoosier Schoolmaster* (1871); Frank Norris, *The Octopus: A Story of California* (1901); Willa Cather, *O Pioneers!* (1913); Sinclair Lewis, *Main Street* (1920); Theodore Dreiser, *An American Tragedy* (1925); James T. Farrell, *Studs Lonigan* (1932–35); John Steinbeck, *The Grapes of Wrath* (1939); James Jones, *From Here to Eternity* (1951); Herman Wouk, *The Caine Mutiny* (1951); Ralph Ellison, *Invisible Man* (1952); Saul Bellow, *The Adventures of Augie March* (1953); and Allen Drury, *Advise and Consent* (1959). The best novels, and those which endure longest, are not necessarily those which tell us most about the problems, sensations, and dilemmas peculiar to a particular time and place. The great novelist must have an obsessive interest in some special kind of hero or experience, which may enrich our understanding of man in the long run but does not necessarily help us grasp the peculiar transformations of an epoch. With the rise of the social novel, the novel has taken the place of the tract or the pamphlet as a form of polemical literature. As a result the reader must be aware that novels from Harriet Beecher Stowe's *Uncle Tom's Cabin* (1852) through Upton Sinclair's *Jungle* (1906), Richard Wright's *Native Son* (1940), Frederic Wakeman's *Hucksters* (1946), and Sloan Wilson's *Man in the Gray Flannel Suit* (1955), while valuable as an expression of the ideals, reformist passions, and preoccupations of writers and readers, do not tell us what we want to know about the tenor of daily life. Fiction—in the novel and the short story, on film, and on television—has taken over much of the polemical role once performed by sermons and pamphlets. This kind of polemics, perhaps an inevitable part of the apparatus of a literate, technologically advanced democracy, has often tended to fire the social passions instead of allaying them, and has too often been the end rather than the beginning of popular reflection and national action on the subject.

Social history, in an age when more and more citizens are self-consciously aware that they are making social history, has appeared in valuable and vivid new forms. Some of our ablest journalists (of the pre-TV age), accustomed to reporting rather than attacking or defending, have drawn together their observations into a new genre of contemporary history. Mark Sullivan's *Our Times: The United States 1900–1925* (6 vols., 1926–36) has few equals as an illustrated contemporary compendium of the objects, events, fads, notions, and sensations that gave a special flavor to those years. Other works, less rich in detail but with a wider focus, are Frederick Lewis Allen, *Only Yesterday: An Informal History of the Nineteen-Twenties* (1931), *Since Yesterday* (1940), and *The Big Change: America Transforms Itself, 1900–1950* (1952). All writings by journalists are, of course, autobiographical, but the explicit autobiographies of these professional observers are among our best introductions to the age. *The Autobiography of Lincoln Steffens* (1931) is deservedly a classic, the vivid observations and astute reflections of a journalistic picaro. Others are Mark Sullivan's *The Education of an American* (1938) and *The Autobiography of William Allen White* (1946), with memoirs of a Kansas boyhood in the 1870's and '80's.

Some of the most perceptive reporting on the U.S.A. in the mid-twentieth century is found in the brilliant and witty trilogy by Cleveland Amory, *The Proper Bostonians* (1947), *The Last Resorts* (1952), and *Who Killed Society?* (1960), and in the luminous poetic essays of Tom Wolfe, *The Kandy-Kolored Tangerine-Flake Streamline Baby* (1965), *The Electric Kool-Aid Acid Test* (1968), *The Pump House Gang* (1968), and *Radical Chic and Mau-Mauing the Flak Catchers* (1970). Taken with a proper antidote, the acrid and egocentric reporting of Norman Mailer, who came to fame with his potent realistic novel of World War II, *The Naked and the Dead* (1948), can tell us something not otherwise accessible in print, especially in *The Armies of the Night* (1968) on the October 1967 antiwar march to the Pentagon, *Miami and the Siege of Chicago* (1968) on the national political conventions of 1968, and *Of a Fire on the Moon* (1971), an impressionistic account of the launching of Apollo 11.

Halfway between journalistic survey and traveler's guide is John Gunther's *Inside U.S.A.* (1947), which reports many facts not elsewhere noted and also gives us a view of what a leading journalist thought worth noting. In a similar genre is John Steinbeck's delightful *Travels With Charley* (1962), an account of his automobile journey across country. An interesting collection of miscellaneous observations by travelers, journalists, and others is Neil Harris (ed.), *Land of Contrasts, 1880–1901* (1970).

Much useful information in guidebook form is found in the W.P.A. Federal Writers' Project, *American Guide Series* (1937–52), offering volumes on the several states, a project of the New Deal. These books, while uneven in quality, had the special virtue of surveying the landscape, buildings, artifacts, and events associated with a particular place. There is no more speedy introduction (apart from the *National Atlas*, above) to the varieties of American regions than a few hours spent browsing through the guide to Arizona or to Oklahoma alongside that to New York or to California. In some instances these volumes offer us the best accounts of the conditions and events which shaped the futures of cities and states.

THE BRILLIANT INSIGHTS of free-wheeling social scientists are found in the writings of Thorstein Veblen, such as his *Theory of the Leisure Class* (1899), and in *The Lonely Crowd* (1950; Anchor Paperback), by David Riesman (with Nathan Glazer and Reuel Denney), which introduced such useful terms as "inner-directed" and "other-directed," among others. Information collected in the categories of social science is found in the products of presidential commissions, sometimes supported by foundation grants. These include: W. F. Ogburn (ed.), *Recent Social Changes* (1929); President's Conference on Unemployment, *Recent Economic Changes* (2 vols., 1929); President's Research Committee on Social Trends, *Recent Social Trends* (2 vols., 1933). Examples of what energetic and imaginative sociologists could gather in the field are Robert S. and Helen M. Lynd, *Middletown: A Study in Contemporary American Culture* (1929) and *Middletown in Transition* (1937), pioneer sequential studies of Muncie, Indiana. A later study, also based in fieldwork and intensive research, but more focused on the implications of social variation for political life is Neal R. Peirce's ingenious trilogy on "people, politics, and power": *The Megastates of America* (1972), *The Mountain States of America* (1972), and *The Pacific States of America* (1972).

A new kind of contemporary history has come from the tape recorder, which Studs Terkel has used to report interviews with a variety of unfamous Chicagoans in *Division Street: America* (1967) and *Hard Times: An Oral History of the Great Depression* (1970). But the show of objectivity in such reports as these is often misleading. The extensive Oral History Project of Columbia University recording the lives of the great and famous does incidentally provide insights into the currents of daily life in the past. A readable and readily available example is *Felix Frankfurter Reminisces* (1960), recorded in talks with Harlan B. Phillips.

While "Intellectual" History has

flourished as an academic discipline, and while since the late nineteenth century "Social" History has produced an extensive literature, both popular and academic, many of the intimate, vivid, and characteristic features of American experience have been left to the periphery and have been treated as curiosa—or not at all. The objects and pictures which happen to remain from the past refuse to fit into academic categories, and they tell us willy-nilly what historians have not told. Lively and accessible compendia are Roger Butterfield, *The American Past* (1947), and Mary Cable, *American Manners and Morals: A Picture of how we Behaved and Misbehaved* (1969).

Photography and the motion picture have, of course, provided a new source of unparalleled vividness and authenticity. But they have not quite yet attained respectability in the historical profession. At this writing they are generally relegated to the technology of "audio-visual" *aids,* as if they somehow were less authentic than the printed word. A student of any period of the recent American past could do much worse than begin with a collection of the photographs or films or newsreels of the age. One copiously illustrated book on recent America is *American Civilization* (1972), in which, as editor, I have brought together visually documented essays by historians and critics. Valuable collections of motion pictures from the earliest period are found in the Library of Congress (a product of work by the American Film Institute), in the Ford Collection of the National Archives, in the Museum of Modern Art in New York City, and elsewhere. An unequaled guide to the film sources of our history (and also to film history) is the *American Film Institute Catalog of Motion Pictures Produced in the United States* (executive editor, Kenneth W. Munden; under general direction of Sam Kula; 1971–) of which the first two volumes have appeared and which will eventually give essential facts on fea-

ture films, short films, and newsreels. The volumes are chronologically arranged, and offer for each period from the beginning a copious subject index which will make it possible to find films depicting every American interest from Abalones to the Ziegfeld Follies.

The unprecedented historical record, since the advent of television, of films and videotapes of current events made by the newsreporters of the networks is still inaccessible, and remains in chaos. These sources are daily disintegrating, the tapes are being erased, and the essential steps to preserve them are still to be taken. Our national irresponsibility about these essential and characteristic records of our time is comparable to the burning of the library in Alexandria.

In the conventional divisions of history, the historical literature for recent America is abundant and of high competence. It is so vast that here I can do no more than suggest a few of the more accessible, more readable, and more insightful works. The recent scholarly and reliable one-volume works of reference include: *Concise Dictionary of American History* (ed. Thomas C. Cochran, 1962); *Encyclopedia of American History* (ed. Richard B. Morris and Henry Steele Commager; rev. ed., 1970); *The Oxford Companion to American History* (ed. Thomas H. Johnson, 1966); *The Encyclopedia of American Facts and Dates* (ed. Gorton Carruth and others; 4th ed., 1966), especially useful for its four-column arrangement, which reminds us that many things were happening at the same time, and shows us what.

For the history of technology, a good short introduction is Roger Burlingame, *Machines That Built America* (Signet Paperback, 1955), which can be complemented by Burlingame's *March of the Iron Men* (1938) for the period before the Civil War, and his *Engines of Democracy* (1940), for the period since. For the earlier period covered by this volume there is still no competitor to

Waldemar B. Kaempffert, *A Popular History of American Invention* (2 vols., 1924), which also lets us share the delighted amazement of Americans when Horatio Alger was still alive and before miracles had become commonplace. A valuable, if pedestrian, work of reference is John W. Oliver, *History of American Technology* (1956). And see Ernest V. Heyn, *A Century of Wonders: 100 Years of Popular Science* (1972), a résumé of what the interested lay public was seeing in one of the more widely circulated magazines. The saga of American technology still calls for its Samuel Eliot Morison.

To put the American story in the world context, two useful works are Abbott P. Usher, *A History of Mechanical Inventions* (1929) and T. K. Derry and Trevor I. Williams, *A Short History of Technology from Earliest Times to 1900* (1960), an abridgement of the admirable five-volume *History of Technology* (ed. Charles Singer and others, 1954-58), which includes specialized articles by experts and which should be referred to for specific topics. A stimulating pioneer interpretation of the relation of technology to experience is found in the works of the Swiss historian Sigfried Giedion: *Mechanization Takes Command: A Contribution to Anonymous History* (1948) and *Space, Time and Architecture: The Growth of a New Tradition* (1949). A readable introduction which relates inventions to the cultures from which they sprang and which they transformed is: *Technology in Western Civilization* (ed. Melvin Kranzberg and Carroll W. Pursell, Jr.; 2 vols., 1967), to which I am much indebted. And see the *Cowles Encyclopedia of Science, Industry and Technology* (1969). The layman who needs elementary explanations is lucky to have *The Way Things Work* (2 vols., 1967-71), in nontechnical language with simplified charts and plans. An indispensable reference tool is Eugene S. Ferguson, *Bibliography of the History of Technology* (1968).

On scientific thought and its role in transforming experience there is still no better introduction than *The Education of Henry Adams* (1907), which, despite its dense and cryptic style, recounts the revolution which came to literate and thoughtful men when the preoccupation of American science shifted from the "natural history" emphasis, described in the earlier volumes of this work, to a concern with physics and the inorganic material world. To illuminate Adams himself, we are now fortunate to have Ernest Samuels' definitive *Henry Adams* (3 vols., 1948-64). The travail of the pioneers in this movement toward the physical sciences is described by Muriel Rukeyser in her *Willard Gibbs* (1942), and some of its adventures are recounted in the life of Henry Adams' hero, the brilliant American geologist, *Clarence King* (1958), by Thurman Wilkins. A newly intimate view of one of the American pioneers of physical science will come from Nathan Reingold's edition, in preparation, of the papers of Joseph Henry (1797-1878), the first secretary of the Smithsonian Institution, whose very name became part of the electrical vocabulary, and who was a founder of the national system of weather reporting. For the wider story, see *The Golden Age of American Science* (ed. Bessie Z. Jones, 1966), which offers biographies of some of the great figures in nineteenth-century science from the pens of their contemporaries and scientific colleagues. A useful introduction with a selected bibliography is *Science and Society in the United States* (ed. David D. Van Tassel and Michael G. Hall, 1966).

AN INTERESTING AVENUE into the economic history of the period is *Men in Business: Essays in the History of Entrepreneurship* (ed. William Miller, 1952), which raises questions that can be surveyed more systematically in: *The Growth of the American Economy* (ed. Harold F. Williamson, 1951); Edward C. Kirkland, *A History of*

American Economic Life (1939); Chester Wright, *Economic History of the United States* (1941); *American Economic History* (ed. Seymour E. Harris, 1961), a collection of essays by twenty-two experts dealing with the influence of ideas in American history, problems of economic policy, determinants of income, and regional growth. Two readable works which, from diverse points of view emphasize the force of economics in American life are George Soule, *Economic Forces in American History* (1952), and Louis M. Hacker, *The Triumph of American Capitalism* (1950), which comes up only to 1900. The closest approach to a full-length interpretation of American economic history is the multivolume *Economic History of the United States* (ed. Henry David and others) which sets a high standard of scholarly precision and which ranges widely, but does not come through mid-century. The relevant volumes are: Fred A. Shannon, *The Farmer's Last Frontier: Agriculture, 1860–1897* (1945); Edward C. Kirkland, *Industry Comes of Age: Business, Labor, and Public Policy, 1860–1897* (1961); Harold U. Faulkner, *The Decline of Laissez-Faire, 1897–1917* (1951); George Soule, *Prosperity Decade: From War to Depression, 1917–1929* (1947); and Broadus Mitchell, *Depression Decade: From New Era through New Deal, 1929–1941* (1947). Joseph Dorfman's *Thorstein Veblen and His America* (1934) is unexcelled as an introduction to the myriad interconnections of the axioms of economic thought with American thinking about everything else; a comprehensive treatment of the subject is his *Economic Mind in American Civilization* (5 vols., 1946–59), the last three volumes of which bring his interpretation down to 1933.

Perhaps the most important new orientation of the academic study of American history in the mid-twentieth century—a counterpart to the "invention" of American Intellectual History in the early years of the century—is quantitative history, sometimes called "cliometrics." It is an application to historical research of the statistical approach described in Part Three of this volume, and it has progressed with the elaboration of mathematical techniques in economic theory. For an effort to place this development in the history of American historical writing and to explain the resistance of traditional historians to this new approach, see "Enlarging the Historian's Vocabulary," my introductory essay to *The Reinterpretation of American Economic History* (ed. Robert W. Fogel and Stanley L. Engerman, 1971). That volume offers a valuable sampling of some of the most interesting contributions of the quantitative approach to a variety of topics. A perceptive critique of these essays and of emerging cliometrics is Harold D. Woodman, "Economic History and Economic Theory: The New Economic History in America," *Journal of Interdisciplinary History*, III (1972), 323–50.

The best full-scale survey of American intellectual history is Merle Curti, *The Growth of American Thought* (3d ed., 1964). A perceptive, more selective work focusing on schools of thought is Stow Persons, *American Minds* (1958). Other readable interpretations touching on the period of this volume are: Morris R. Cohen, *American Thought: A Critical Sketch* (ed. Felix S. Cohen, 1954); Henry Steele Commager, *The American Mind* (1950), on the period since 1880; Howard Mumford Jones, *Age of Energy: Varieties of American Experience, 1865–1915* (1971). An example of the techniques of intellectual history at their best is Richard Hofstadter, *Social Darwinism in American Thought, 1860–1915* (1944).

Literary history is one of the most widely and most easily cultivated of the academic fields of American history. Since its subject is printed matter, usually quite accessible, it tempts its authors into facile subjective generalizations and aesthetic polemics. The best concise work of reference is James D.

Hart, *The Oxford Companion to American Literature* (4th ed., 1965). Readable introductions to the leading authors, genres, and styles of American literature in this period will be found in *Literary History of the United States* (ed. Robert E. Spiller and others; 3 vols., 1948); the third volume offers an indispensable critical bibliography of leading authors. For insights into the role of publishers and the rise of the "best seller," see: James D. Hart, *The Popular Book: A History of America's Literary Taste* (1950); Frank Luther Mott, *Golden Multitudes: The Story of Best Sellers in the United States* (1947); Donald Sheehan, *This Was Publishing: A Chronicle of the Book Trade in the Gilded Age* (1952). On the technical side, see Hellmut Lehmann-Haupt and others, *The Book in America: A History of the Making and Selling of Books in the United States* (2d ed., 1952). An American classic of the social interpretation of literature is the unfinished third volume of Vernon L. Parrington's *Main Currents in American Thought*, published as *The Beginnings of Critical Realism in America, 1860–1920* (1930), which offers a miscellany of helpful insights. The essential guide to the periodicals of the age is Frank Luther Mott, *A History of American Magazines* (5 vols., 1957–68). Other works on the literature of the period which I have found of special interest include: Granville Hicks, *The Great Tradition: An Interpretation of American Literature Since the Civil War* (1933; rev. ed., 1935), a Marxist view; Edmund Wilson, *Patriotic Gore* (1962), a lively, fact-packed and opinionated survey of the literature leading up to and out of the Civil War; Van Wyck Brooks, *New England: Indian Summer, 1865–1915* (1940), a chatty, armchair introduction to the leading figures; Bernard De Voto, *Mark Twain's America* (1932); Henry Nash Smith, *Virgin Land: The American West as Symbol and Myth* (1950); Richard W. B. Lewis, *The American Adam* (1955) and "Written Words; The Making of American Literature" in *American Civilization* (ed. Daniel J. Boorstin, 1972); Richard Chase, *The American Novel and its Tradition* (1957); Leo Marx, *The Machine in the Garden: Technology and the Pastoral Ideal in America* (1964); Justin Kaplan, *Mr. Clemens and Mark Twain*, (1966).

TRAVELERS' IMPRESSIONS and the view of America from the outside can be discovered in an increasing number of books (of declining quality) in the years after the Civil War. As travel to and from the United States grew easier, the travelers who came, and those who published, generally had fewer special qualifications for their judgments than had been the case in the eighteenth and early nineteenth centuries. A valuable view of what European travelers looked for and expected to find in the United States in the late nineteenth century is *Baedeker's United States* (1893), the first of Baedeker's efforts to survey the United States, happily now available in a reprint (1972) with a new introduction by Henry Steele Commager. This volume contains numerous facts about daily life in America, illuminated by contemporary essays by experts on many aspects of American life.

The best travelers' book of this age and one of the best interpretations of American civilization in this epoch is *The American Commonwealth* (2 vols., 1888; supplemented and revised, 1910), by James Bryce, an English historian and diplomat who wrote his work after five visits to the United States; Bryce was ambassador to the United States 1907–13. Every student of American life, and especially students of politics, should read his work, which focuses on American political institutions, habits, and folkways, but which incidentally tells volumes about all other aspects of American civilization. Bryce had an eye for paradox and a feeling for the human foibles which give the study of history much of its charm. Readers who give themselves the pleasure of reading such of his chapters as Chapter 8, "Why Great Men Are Not Chosen Presidents"; Ch. 78, "How Public Opinion Rules in America"; Ch. 85, "The Fatalism of the Multitude"; and Ch. 110, "The Influence of Democracy on Thought," will go on to the rest.

Numerous series of readable volumes on this period are directed to the general reader or the beginning scholar. One of them is The Chicago History of American Civilization (published by the University of Chicago Press), which I have edited, and which provides brief volumes by experts on periods and topics in American history, including chronologies and brief selected bibliographies. Of special relevance to this book are the chronological volumes: John Hope Franklin, *Reconstruction: After the Civil War;* Samuel P. Hays, *The Response to Industrialism: 1885–1914;* William E. Leuchtenburg, *The Perils of Prosperity: 1914–32;* Dexter Perkins, *The New Age of Franklin Roosevelt: 1932–45.* And topical volumes: John Tracy Ellis, *American Catholicism;* Nathan Glazer, *American Judaism;* Winthrop S. Hudson, *American Protestantism;* Richard M. Dorson, *American Folklore;* Henry Pelling, *American Labor;* Robert H. Bremner, *American Philanthropy;* Maldwyn Allen Jones, *American Immigration;* Robert G. McCloskey, *The American Supreme Court;* William T. Hagan, *American Indians;* John F. Stover, *American Railroads;* Bernard A. Weisberger, *The American Newspaperman;* Irving L. Sablosky, *American Music;* John B. Rae, *The American Automobile;* Wayne Fuller, *The American Mail.* An excellent, more detailed work (also supplying selected bibliographies) is the New American Nation Series, edited by Henry Steele Commager and Richard B. Morris, which focuses the learning of the best professional historians on brief periods and on sharply defined aspects of American history. A new kind of series, made possible by photo-offset and other copying processes, is that offered by the Arno Press, which reissues sets of basic works which are out of print, selected by scholars, to make more accessible essential books on many aspects of American civilization, including education, immigration, foreign policy, journalism, labor, the Negro, technology, broadcasting, the movies, police, poverty, religion, the city, women's rights, and utopias. I have selected one such series of reprints under the title "Technology and Society" (53 vols., 1972).

Periodical literature on this period is enormous, and specialized journals will be listed for the Parts below. Journals ebb and flow with the tides of opinion, with reform enthusiasms, and changing fads. For the layman, an excellent periodic stimulant to an appetite for American history is the bimonthly *American Heritage,* published since 1949 for the Society of American Historians. Of the learned journals, among the most accessible and the most helpful to the layman or the beginning student are the *Journal of American History* (published 1914–64 under the title *Mississippi Valley Historical Review*) of the Organization of American Historians, the *Journal of Southern History,* the *New England Quarterly, Western Historical Quarterly, Western History, American Quarterly,* and *Technology and Culture,* each of which is the official journal of a specialized society of professionals. The *American Historical Review,* while concerned with all history, does offer regular (but much delayed) reviews of current books on American history. A boon to all is the *Journal of Interdisciplinary History* (quarterly since 1969), which opens vistas with its readable and scholarly reviews and articles. Articles putting current facts in their historical context are found in the *Wall Street Journal,* whose stories range from the cash register and cellophane wrapping to motels—subjects which academic historians have sometimes considered beneath their dignity.

Political history, which the historical profession generally treats as the main stream but which this volume treats as simply one part of the social context, produces the largest number of works that generally hold the public spotlight. The improvement of means of reproduction—from the typewriter and carbon paper to mimeograph and Xerox— has multiplied the pieces of paper that attest to the proliferation of government activities, while the increasing use of the telephone has made these documentary records less revealing than ever of how, when, and where crucial decisions were really made. The expansion of the National Archives into presidential libraries throughout the country has been impelled by this multiplication of words on paper. The quantity of "manuscript" materials for a single administration (for example, the 31 million pages in the Lyndon B. Johnson Library at Austin, Texas) approaches the quantity (35 million pages) of the whole manuscript collection of the Library of Congress on all subjects.

Political history inevitably has been written as if the national capital monopolized the governmental activities of the nation, and the politics of counties, cities, and states has been given short shrift, or too often left to local genealogists or antiquarians. Correctives to this misplaced emphasis are these interesting points of departure: James Michael Curley, *I'd Do it Again* (1957) on Boston big-city politics in the early years of the century; Arthur Mann, *La Guardia* (2 vols., 1959, 1965); and T. Harry Williams, *Huey Long* (1969). Of the many novels around these themes, the reader might begin with Robert Penn Warren, *All the King's Men* (1946), a political novel based on the career of Huey Long, and Edwin O'Connor, *The Last Hurrah* (1956), about Mayor Curley.

The autobiographies of Presidents tend to be stilted and defensive. Some exceptions are: Ulysses S. Grant, *Personal Memoirs* (2 vols., 1885–86); Theo-dore Roosevelt, *Autobiography* (1913); Calvin Coolidge, *Autobiography* (1929); Herbert Hoover, *Memoirs* (3 vols., 1951–52); Harry S. Truman, *Memoirs* (2 vols., 1955–56). The most readable and accessible works on Presidents and their administrations include: Allan Nevins, *Grover Cleveland: A Study in Courage* (1932); H. C. F. Bell, *Woodrow Wilson and the People* (1945); Arthur Link, *Woodrow Wilson* (5 vols., 1947–65); Robert Sherwood, *Roosevelt and Hopkins* (1948); Frank Freidel, *Franklin D. Roosevelt* (3 vols., 1952–56); Arthur M. Schlesinger, Jr., *The Age of Roosevelt* (3 vols., 1957–60); Margaret Truman, *Harry S. Truman* (1973). Books which transcend political history to show the connections between the politics and the civilization of the age include: Matthew Josephson, *The Politicos, 1865–1896* (1938); Richard Hofstadter, *The Age of Reform: from Bryan to F.D.R.* (1955); Eric F. Goldman, *Rendezvous with Destiny: A History of Modern American Reform* (1952) and *Crucial Decade: America, 1945–1955* (1956). A brilliant scholar-journalist, Theodore H. White, has invented a new literary genre for putting American presidential elections in their context, and incidentally he has performed the remarkable feat of giving the most recent political events the perspective of history: *The Making of the President, 1960* (1961); *The Making of the President, 1964* (1965); *The Making of the President, 1968* (1969); *The Making of the President, 1972* (1973). A valuable source of facts on recent and current legislative activity are the publications of the Congressional Quarterly Service (1945–), which include a weekly report, an index every ninety days, and an annual almanac. Statistics on presidential elections are available in *History of American Presidential Elections, 1789–1968* (ed. Arthur M. Schlesinger, Jr., and Fred L. Israel; 4 vols., 1971) and in the publications of the Election Research Center, Richard M. Scammon, director, especially in *America Votes* (biennially since 1954). For presidential papers, there are the numerous volumes issued by the Government Printing Office since 1945, *The Public Papers of the Presidents of the United States.*

BOOK ONE

EVERYWHERE COMMUNITIES

PART ONE

THE GO-GETTERS

WHILE AMERICAN FICTION, folklore and drama abound with Success Stories, while the doings and misdoings of the Men Who Made Good have been the staple of popular magazines and the daily press, historians have given short shrift to American enterprise and the careers of enterprising Americans. Perhaps because, even in the United States, moneymaking is more envied than celebrated, and because academic historians themselves have a vested interest in assuming the inverse ratio of effort to financial reward, the stories of business success have been left to the self-serving literature (a barely disguised form of advertising) issued by the companies themselves or to the exploitation of sensation mongers, muckrakers, and debunkers. In this unequal competition, the muckrakers have easily won. As a result, "Robber Barons" and similar phrases have entered the vernacular of students of American history, who treat the crimes and outrages of Big Business as self-evident dominant features of the nation's history, while they hardly notice the feats of energy, imagination, and organization which built the American economy and made possible the American Standard of Living.

In the mid-twentieth century, a number of large firms have begun to take their histories seriously, have established company archives, and have engaged competent professional historians to set their records in order and to write their story. Even in the late twentieth century, however, it remains true that the chronicle of American business is generally seen either through the jaundiced eyes of debunkers or through the roseate spectacles of "authorized" histories. There are still relatively few works written neither to indict nor to praise, but to assess the role of enterprise in American civilization. For an earlier stage in the evolution of the American Go-Getter, see *The Americans: The National Experience*, Parts One, Two, Three, and Five, and Bibliographical Notes.

In contrast to the countless histories of the United States that hang the whole story of American civilization on the slender thread of politics—most often only federal politics, and then often on presidential federal politics—few works have made American enterprise and industry the framework for the story. A happy exception, and a lively introduction, is *The History of American Business and Industry* (1972), by Alex Groner and the editors of *American Heritage* and *Business Week*, copiously illustrated and with biographical vignettes of crucial figures who have not elsewhere had their due. Other readable works that describe the businessman's role include: James Truslow Adams, *Our Business Civilization* (1929); Thomas C. Cochran, *The American Business System: A Historical Perspective, 1900–1955* (1957), *Basic History of American Business* (1959), and

American Business in the Twentieth Century (1972); Miriam Beard, *A History of Business: From Babylon to the Monopolists* (1938; 2 vols., Ann Arbor Paperbacks, 1962); William H. Whyte, Jr., *The Organization Man* (1956). The articles and reviews in *Fortune* (monthly since 1930) provide a rich and readable source of information on men, industries, their adventures, hopes, and problems. While the growth of American law schools has done little to sharpen the historical consciousness of Americans and has even discouraged a humanistic view of the law, the growth of business schools has begun to make business history academically respectable, helping to bring it into the mainstream of history. A sample of the kind of approach to business history which has developed in our best graduate schools of business is Norman S. B. Gras and Henrietta M. Larson, *Casebook in American Business History* (1939). Especially valuable are the Harvard Studies in Business History and articles in the *Business History Review* (1930–), the *Journal of Economic History* (1940–), and *Business History* (1958–).

FOR AMERICANS the West has been shrouded in romance, legend, folklore, and fiction. The West is generally believed to be the most American part of the nation, and yet popular knowledge about the West is much less specific than about those routine topics of political and constitutional history that fit into Old World categories. But there has been a good deal of fact in the fiction, and the upshot of Western novels, movies, and TV shows has probably been to give most twentieth-century Americans a more intimate feel for daily life in the post–Civil War–American West than for the tenor of life in most other sectors of the American past. The essential problem is that fiction and romance focus on crises and explosive events, while of course their life, like ours, actually was a flowing cur-

rent. For some of the characteristic American institutions of the earlier West, see *The Americans: The National Experience*, Parts Two, Five, and Six, and Bibliographical Notes.

A view of Western cattle raising and of the cattle trade is one way to sense the perfunctory daily tenor of that West. The cattleman's West has engaged some of the most vivid writers of our history. Two enticing points of departure are Walter Prescott Webb, *The Great Plains* (1931), on the cattleman's land, its peculiar opportunities and problems; and Joe B. Frantz and Julian Ernest Choate, Jr., *The American Cowboy: The Myth and the Reality* (1955). A valuable elementary description of cowboy ways, costumes, tools, and activities for which all dudes will be grateful is Philip A. Rollins, *The Cowboy* (rev. ed., 1936). A useful introductory anthology is *The Cowboy Reader* (ed. Lon Tinkel and Allen Maxwell, 1959).

A galaxy of writers have provided us with a delightful and varied library on the West of this era. Among them are Theodore Roosevelt, who, having "retired" to a Dakota ranch after the nomination of his opponent James G. Blaine for the presidency, acquired a romantic admiration of Western men and ways—expressed not only in his *Winning of the West* (4 vols., 1889–96), which covers the earlier period, but in numerous volumes including *Hunting Trips of a Ranchman* (1885) and *Ranch Life and the Hunting-Trail* (1888). Some of the most attractive volumes on this era remain those by Emerson Hough (1857–1923) an Iowa-born lawyer-turned-writer who began his career in Whiteoaks, New Mexico (a town which he called "half cow town and half mining camp"). He spent much of his life among these people he wrote about in *The Story of the Cowboy* (1897), *The Story of the Outlaw* (1907), and *The Passing of the Frontier* (1918). Of his numerous historical romances the most influential was *The Covered Wagon* (1922), which shaped American folklore through the deservedly popular movie which it became. As a devotee of Yellowstone National Park and the national-park movement he became one of the most persuasive spokesmen for the conservation movement and for the efforts to preserve what remained of the American wilds. For the look, the men, and the costume of the cowboy, one should see the collections of drawings and sculpture by Frederic Remington (1861–1909) and Charles M. Russell (1865–1926), for example in the C. M. Russell Gallery in Great Falls, Montana, in the Remington Memorial Museum in Ogdensburg, N.Y., in the Amon Carter Museum of Western Art in Fort Worth, Texas, and the Thomas Gilcrease Institute of American History and Art in Tulsa, Oklahoma.

No one interested in the West will want to miss the exciting novels of Andy Adams (1859–1935), who left Indiana for the Southwest, where he collected materials "from the hurricane deck of a Texas horse" for his classic *Log of a Cowboy* (1903). See also: *The Outlet* (1905), his account of the tangle of railroads, politicians, and cattlemen; *Reed Anthony, Cowman* (1907), about a Texas rancher; and *Cattle Brands* (1906), short stories. J. Frank Dobie (1888–1964) has combined historical scholarship with a crisp and vivid style to produce some of the best books on the West. Begin with *The Longhorns* (1941). Of his numerous other works, especially interesting are: *A Vaquero of the Brush Country* (1929); *Coronado's Children: Tales of Lost Mines and Buried Treasures of the Southwest* (1930); *The Voice of the Coyote* (1949). He has also provided a *Guide to Life and Literature of the Southwest* (rev. ed., 1952). In another genre is the work of the Texas writer-artist Tom Lea: *The Brave Bulls* (1949); *The King Ranch* (2 vols., 1957), a chronicle of one of the biggest ranches, published in appropriately rich and copious format.

The Western Frontier Library, published by the University of Oklahoma Press, provides numerous handsome but inexpensive reprints of sources and classics of Western life and history.

A readable introduction to the Western cattle trade is found in Ernest S. Osgood, *The Day of the Cattleman* (1929), and Edward E. Dale, *The Range Cattle Industry: Ranching on the Great Plains from 1865 to 1925* (new ed., 1960). One of the most valuable (and now accessible) sources is *Historic Sketches of the Cattle Trade of the West and Southwest* (1874; reprinted 1951) by Joseph G. McCoy, a pioneer cattleman who helped open the Chisholm Trail and helped found the railroad terminus for cattle at Abilene, Kansas.

On the Western landscape there are a number of books more readable than is usual in geographic monographs. Interesting points of departure are W. Eugene Hollon, *The Great American Desert* (1966) and William H. Goetzmann, *Exploration and Empire: The Explorer and the Scientist in the Winning of the American West* (1966). A heroic and attractive figure in Western exploration after the Civil War is John Wesley Powell (1834–1902), who came from a remarkable Illinois family. His brother, William Bramwell Powell (1836–1904), was an urban pioneer who did much to liberate the high school curriculum, became superintendent of the Washington, D.C., schools, where he founded what was reputedly the first business high school, and wrote textbooks under such unpedantic titles as *How to Talk; or Primary Lessons in the English Language* (1882) and *How to Write; or, Secondary Lessons in the English Language* (1882). John Wesley Powell, who did his pioneering in the West, had studied natural history and made extensive boat trips by himself observing and collecting specimens on the Mississippi and Ohio rivers, enlisted in the Union Army, and lost his right arm at the Battle of Shiloh. His physical disability did not prevent him from leading the perilous 900-mile boat trip (financed by the Smithsonian Institution) through the

Grand Canyon on the turbulent Colorado River (May 24–August 29, 1869) which produced one of the most vivid books on geology, his *Explorations of the Colorado River of the West and Its Tributaries* (1875; rev. as *Canyons of the Colorado*, 1895; ed. Wallace Stegner, 1957). His epochal *Report on the Lands of the Arid Region of the United States* (1878; 2d ed., 1879) contained much prophetic (but long-unheeded) wisdom about land use in the West. For a delightful account of Powell's explorations and his scientific contributions, see Wallace Stegner, *Beyond the Hundredth Meridian: John Wesley Powell and the Second Opening of the West* (intro. Bernard Dé Voto, 1954; Sentinel Paperback). Powell moved on from geology to anthropology and was the energetic founding-director (1879–1902) of the Bureau of Ethnology of the Smithsonian Institution. See *The Americans: The National Experience*, Ch. 29, and Bibliographical Notes.

Other books of special interest include: Leonard J. Arrington, *Great Basin Kingdom: An Economic History of the Latter Day Saints, 1830–1900* (1958); Mark H. Brown and William R. Felton, *Before Barbed Wire: L. A. Huffman, Photographer on Horseback* (1956), for a photographic record; Angie Debo (ed.), *The Cowman's Southwest* (1953); Everett Dick, *The Sod-House Frontier* (1954); Maurice Frink and others, *When Grass Was King* (1956); Mary Wilma Hargreaves, *Dry Farming in the Northern Great Plains, 1900–1925* (1957); Paul Horgan, *Great River: The Rio Grande in North American History* (rev. ed., 1960); Carl F. Kraenzel, *The Great Plains in Transition* (1955); James C. Malin, *The Grassland of North America* (1967); E. V. Smalley, "The Isolation of Life on Prairie Farms," *Atlantic Monthly*, LXXII (1893), 378–82; Henry D. McCallum and Francis T. McCallum, *The Wire That Fenced the West* (1965), on barbed wire.

For details of cattle raising and the cattle trade, in addition to the above, see especially: Lewis F. Allen, *American Cattle* (1875); Robert G. Athearn, *High Country Empire* (1960); James S. Brisbin, *The Beef Bonanza* (1885; Western Frontier Library, 1959); James Cox, *Historical and Biographical Record of the Cattle Industry* (reprint, 1959); Edward Everett Dale, *Cow Country* (1942); Clarence Gordon, "Report on Cattle, Sheep, and Swine," in U.S. Dept. of Interior, Tenth Census, *Report on the Productions of Agriculture* (1880); Paul C. Henlein, *Cattle Kingdom in the Ohio Valley, 1783–1860* (1959); Ora B. Peake, *The Colorado Range Cattle Industry* (1937), especially for stock associations and the law of the industry; Louis Pelzer, *The Cattlemen's Frontier* (1936); Lewis Nordyke, *Cattle Empire* (1949); James W. Thompson, *A History of Livestock in the United States, 1607–1860* (1942); Charles W. Towne and Edward N. Wentworth, *Cattle & Men* (1955); G. Weis, *Stock Raising in the Northwest, 1884* (1951); Alvin H. Sanders, *Red, White, and Roan* (1936); Walter Baron von Richthofen, *Cattle-Raising on the Plains of North America* (1964), an autobiographical account by an immigrant who helped create the cattle boom of the 1880's and so made his fortune. While the successful cattlemen and cowboys were not necessarily men of letters, they had a way with words, which can be sampled in James W. Freeman (ed.), *Prose and Poetry of the Livestock Industry of the U.S.* (reprint, 1959), and Ramon F. Adams, *Western Words: A Dictionary of the American West* (rev. ed., 1968).

Life on the cattle trail is copiously recorded in works of varying reliability and readability. Unique in its detail and its sweep is J. Evetts Haley, *Charles Goodnight: Cowman & Plainsman* (1949). Some of the more valuable include: Andy Adams, *The Log of a Cowboy* (1903); Wayne Gard, *The Chisholm Trail* (1954); Lewis Nordyke, *The Great Roundup* (1955); (Col.) Jack Potter, *Cattle Trails of the Old West* (1939); Mari

Sandoz, *The Cattlemen* (1958); "Range and Ranch Cattle Traffic," 48th Cong., 2d Sess., 1884–85, *House Exec. Doc.* (1885). The cattle barons and the great ranches have a literature all their own, an American counterpart to the chronicles of Old World feudal barons and châteaux. Some of the more interesting include: C. L. Douglas, *Cattle Kings of Texas* (1939); Codia S. Duke and Joe B. Frantz, *6,000 Miles of Fence: Life on the XIT Ranch of Texas* (1961); Maurice Frink, *Cow Country Cavalcade: Eighty Years of the Wyoming Growers Association* (1954); Will Hale, *Twenty-four Years a Cowboy and Ranchman* (Western Frontier Library, 1959); J. Evetts Haley, *The XIT Ranch of Texas* (1929) and *George Littlefield, Texan* (1943); Frank S. Hastings, *A Ranchman's Recollections* (1921); C. L. Sonnichsen, *Cowboys and Cattle Kings* (1950). Robert R. Dykstra's *The Cattle Towns* (1968) is an admirable introduction to life in the cow towns which can be supplemented by the works listed in the bibliography, and especially by: Stanley Vestal, *Queen of Cowtowns* (1952); Robert M. Wright, "Personal Reminiscences of Frontier Life in Southwest Kansas," *Trans. Kansas Hist. Soc.*, VII (1901–02), 47–83, and *Dodge City, The Cowboy Capital* (1913).

For material on the relation between Western cattlemen and Eastern bankers, and other matters, I have leaned heavily on Gene M. Gressley, *Bankers and Cattlemen* (1966), a model of readability and scholarship.

For the stockmen's associations, the wars of the range, and the careers of lawmen and outlaws, the literature is as unreliable as it is copious. Sifting the literature is like trying to sift molasses: fact and myth, inseparably mixed, flow together to fit the receptacle of prejudice or loyalty. A good introduction to the spirit of those times and places is the work of the sheriff who was Billy the Kid's friend and assassin, Patrick F. Garrett, *The Authentic Life of Billy the Kid, the Noted Desperado of the South-* *west, whose Deeds of Daring and Blood made his Name a Terror in New Mexico, Arizona, and Northern Mexico* (Western Frontier Library, 1954), to be read with J. C. Dykes, "Billy the Kid: The Bibliography of a Legend," *U. of New Mexico Pub. in Language and Literature*, VII (1952). Some of the more useful works include: Ramon F. Adams, *Six-Guns and Saddle Leather* (1954), an extensive bibliography; G. B. Anderson, *History of New Mexico* (2 vols., 1907); Chris Emmett, *Shanghai Pierce* (1953); Erna Ferguson, *New Mexico: A Pageant of Three Peoples* (1955); Robert H. Fletcher, *Free Grass to Fences* (1960): Maurice G. Fulton, *History of the Lincoln County War* (1968), a detailed chronicle, reprinting many documents, which the author made his lifework and which was published posthumously; Wayne Gard, *Frontier Justice* (1949); Emerson Hough, *The Story of the Outlaw: A Study of the Western Desperado* (1907); David Lavender, *The Big Divide* (1948); A. S. Mercer, *The Banditti of the Plains; or, The Cattlemen's Invasion of Wyoming in 1892: The Crowning Infamy of the Ages* (Western Frontier Library, 1954); Frederick W. Nolan, *The Life & Death of John Henry Tunstall* (1965), including letters and diaries of the unlucky young Englishman who was murdered in the Lincoln County War; Frank R. Prassel, *The Western Peace Officer: A Legacy of Law and Order* (1972); Rupert N. Richardson and Carl C. Rister, *The Great Southwest* (1934), an economic, social, and cultural survey; C. L. Sonnichsen, *Roy Bean: Law West of the Pecos* (1943); Agnes Wright Spring, *Seventy Years* (1942), a publication of the Wyoming Stock Growers' Association; Walter Prescott Webb, *The Texas Rangers* (1965). A knowledgeable bibliography is Stanley Vestal, *The Book Lover's Southwest* (1955).

To put these chapters in context, consult the illuminating writings of Ray A. Billington, especially *Westward Expansion* (3d ed., 1967); and *America's Fron-*

tier *Heritage* (1966), a volume in the valuable series projected for eighteen volumes, Histories of the American Frontier (1966–), which he has edited and which touches many aspects of Western history. For a succinct summary of the classic controversy about the influence of the West in American civilization, see Billington's *The American Frontier Thesis: Attack and Defense* (Am. Hist. Assn. Teacher's Service Center; rev. ed. 1971), and for a lively biography of the father of "the frontier thesis," see his *Frederick Jackson Turner* (1973). Other works which, from different points of view, put the Western Go-Getters in perspective are: Gilbert Fite, *The Farmer's Frontier, 1865–1900* (1966); Horace Greeley, *An Overland Journey: From New York to San Francisco in the Summer of 1859* (1964); Emerson Hough, *The Covered Wagon* (1922); Robert E. Riegel, *The Story of the Western Railroads* (1926); Frederick Jackson Turner, *The Frontier in American History* (1920); Oscar O. Winther, *The Transportation Frontier: Trans-Mississippi West, 1865–1890* (1964).

For special topics, the reader should consult the local historical publications such as *Montana History, Nebraska History, The Southwestern Historical Quarterly, Western Historical Quarterly,* and *Western History.*

THE STORY OF OIL is peculiarly American, not only because petroleum was one of the hidden treasures of the continent but also because of its novelty as an item of commerce, because of the speed with which it became significant in the national economy and became the object of some of the most remarkable American organization. The basic work on the subject is *The American Petroleum Industry,* a scholarly and readable two-volume work by Harold F. Williamson and collaborators: *The Age of Illumination* (1959) and *The Age of Industry* (1963). A brief general account is J. Stanley Clark, *The Oil Century: From the Drake Well to the Conservation Era* (1958). The problems of disentangling fact from myth in these petroleum suburbs of El Dorado are suggested by Mody C. Boatright's lively volumes: *Folklore of the Oil Industry* (1963) and (with William A. Owens) *Tales from the Derrick Floor: A People's History of the Oil Industry* (1970). For the early years, see: J. Leander Bishop, *A History of Manufacturers* (3 vols.; 3d ed., 1869), especially Vol. II, pp. 462 ff.; *The Derrick's Hand-Book of Petroleum* (1898), an oilman's handbook; Leonard M. Fanning, *The Rise of American Oil* (1936); John J. Flaherty, *Flowing Gold: The Romance of the Oil Industry* (1945); Paul H. Giddens, *The Birth of the Oil Industry* (1938), *The Beginnings of the Petroleum Industry, Sources and Bibliography* (1941), and *Pennsylvania Petroleum 1750–1872: A Documentary History* (1947); J. T. Henry, *The Early and Later History of Petroleum, with Authentic Facts in Regard to Its Development in Western Pennsylvania* (1873); John J. McLaurin, *Sketches in Crude Oil: Some Accidents and Incidents of the Petroleum Development in All Parts of the Globe* (1896); Ernest C. Miller, *John Wilkes Booth, Oilman* (1947), an account of a less-noted venture of the assassin of Lincoln; Ernest C. Miller, *Tintypes in Oil* (1961), biographies of early oilmen; Sir S. Morton Peto, *The Resources and Prospects of America* (1866), the observations of an acute English railroad promoter who visited America, observed the booming oil towns, and prophesied that the Americans would somehow "show the way to the profitable application of rock-oil."

On the discovery of oil, see: Charles C. Leonard, *The History of Pithole* (1867), one of the earliest accounts; Hildegarde Dolson, *The Great Oildorado: The Gaudy and Turbulent Years of the First Oil Rush* (1959). For the sale of oil as patent medicine, see James H. Young, *Toadstool Millionaires* (1961).

Life in the early oil fields is described in: Herbert Asbury, *The Golden Flood: An Informal History of America's First Oil Field* (1942); Andrew Cone and Walter R. Johns, *Petrolia: A Brief History of the Pennsylvania Petroleum Region . . . from 1859 to 1869* (1870); Rev. S. J. M. Eaton, *Petroleum: A History of the Oil Region of Venango County, Pennsylvania* (1866); Boyce House, *Oil Boom: The Story of Spindletop, Burkburnett, Mexia, Smackover, Desdemona, and Ranger* (1941); Frank F. Latta, *Black Gold in the Joaquin* (1949); Ernest C. Miller, *Oil Mania: Sketches from the Early Pennsylvania Oil Fields* (1941); Edmund Morris, *Derrick and Drill, or an Insight into the Discovery, Development, and Present Condition and Future Prospects of Petroleum in New York, Pennsylvania, Ohio, West Virginia, etc.* (1865); J. H. Newton (ed.), *History of Venango County, Pennsylvania* (1879); W. E. Youle, *Sixty-three Years in the Oil Fields* (1926). For a dramatic account of a later episode in the discovery of oil, see James A. Clark and Michael T. Halbouty, *The Last Boom* (1972), which recounts the excitement of the oil boom in the East Texas field in the years of the Great Depression.

On the transportation of oil, see: William Beard, *Regulation of Pipelines as Common Carriers* (1941); J. D. Henry, *Thirty-Five Years of Oil Transport: The Evolution of the Tank Steamer* (1907); Arthur M. Johnson, *The Development of American Petroleum Pipelines: A Study in Private Enterprise and Public Policy, 1862–1906* (1956), the best study of the ramifying legal and social problems of oil transport in a federal continent-nation; U.S. Federal Trade Commission, *Report on Pipe-line Transportation of Petroleum*, February 28, 1916; U.S. House Report No. 2192, 72d Cong., 2d Sess., *Report on Pipe Lines* (1933). For the chemistry of the oil industry, these are especially useful: American Petroleum Institute, *Glossary of Terms Used in Petroleum Refining* (1953); J. H. A. Bone, *Petroleum and Petroleum Wells* (1865); Abraham Gesner, *A Practical Treatise on Coal, Petroleum, and other Distilled Oils* (1865), an essential early study; George T. Walker, *Petroleum: Its History, Occurrence, Production, Uses, & Tests* (1915).

Some clues to the easily forgotten importance of petroleum for illumination in daily life are found in: Catharine F. Beecher and Harriet Beecher Stowe, *The American Woman's Home; or Principles of Domestic Science* (1869), on the oil and kerosene lamps; Hamlin Garland, *Boy Life on the Prairie* (1899), for kerosene lamps; S. F. Peckham, "Report on the Production, Technology, and Uses of Petroleum and its Products," 47th Cong., 1st Sess., House Misc. Doc. 42, Part 10, Dept. of Census (1884); People's Petroleum Company, *Prospectus* (1865).

The literature about the growing oil industry is vast and tends to be either in attack or in defense. Two interesting starting points are John D. Rockefeller, *Random Reminiscences of Men and Events* (1909); and Upton Sinclair, *Oil!* (1927), a sensational muckraking novel (based on the oil scandals of the Harding Administration), in which the hero is led by his disgust with capitalist machinations to embrace socialism. And for an introduction to the story, see Allan Nevins' readable *John D. Rockefeller* (1959), abridged from his two earlier works: *John D. Rockefeller: The Heroic Age of American Enterprise* (2 vols., 1940) and its revision, *A Study in Power: John D. Rockefeller, Industrialist and Philanthropist* (2 vols., 1953). A sampling of the various points of view would include, among others: Chester McA. Destler, *Roger Sherman and the Independent Oil Men* (1967); John T. Flynn, *God's Gold: The Story of Rockefeller and His Times* (1932); Raymond B. Fosdick, *The Story of the Rockefeller Foundation* (1952), a sympathetic account; Paul H. Giddens, *Standard Oil Company (Indiana), Oil Pioneer of the Middle West* (1955); Ralph W. and

Muriel E. Hidy, *Pioneering in Big Business, 1882–1911* (2 vols., 1955), and *History of the Standard Oil Company (New Jersey)* (2 vols., 1955–56), a massive work based on unrestricted access to company documents, providing a sympathetic account of the organizing feats of the company from 1882 to 1927; Gilbert Holland, *The Rise and Progress of the Standard Oil Company* (1904); William H. Hutchinson, *Oil, Land, and Politics: The California Career of Thomas Robert Bard* (2 vols., 1965), a comprehensive and friendly account of a founder of the Union Oil Company of California; Gustavus Myers, *The History of Great American Fortunes* (1910), a muckraking work of special interest; Ida M. Tarbell, *The History of the Standard Oil Company* (3 vols., 1904), a still more readable muckraking account, considered sensational at the time, which did much to focus public attention on Rockefeller and his company.

FOR BOOKS ON the legal profession in the United States and for some peculiarly American legal problems and opportunities, see the Bibliographical Notes for *The Americans: The Colonial Experience* (Parts Six and Seven) and *The National Experience* (Parts One, Two, Four, and Eight). A valuable modern survey of the vague and diverse activities of American lawyers in the mid-twentieth century is Martin Mayer, *The Lawyers* (1967), an anecdotal, statistical account all the more valuable because it is by an experienced reporter who is not a lawyer. A valuable work on the earliest age of the American legal profession is Anton-Hermann Chroust, *The Rise of the Legal Profession in America* (2 vols., 1965), a massive compilation of facts about the profession and its practitioners until 1820. American legal history, to the shame of the well-paid and luxuriously equipped American legal profession, remains one of the worst-chronicled of important American institutions. Much of the material in my chapter has been culled from local histories, dictionaries of biography, company histories, and sources other than full-length specialized monographs on the roles of lawyers. For the relations of Western lawyers to Eastern businessmen and bankers, I have again drawn on Gene M. Gressley's excellent *Bankers and Cattlemen* (1966). On the history of Dun & Bradstreet, see Edward N. Vose, *Seventy-five Years of the Mercantile Agency, R. G. Dun & Co., 1841–1916* (1916). For the career of James Frederick Joy, I have followed Richard C. Overton's pathbreaking and indispensable works of railroad history, *Burlington West: A Colonization History of the Burlington Railroad* (1941) and *Burlington Route: A History of the Burlington* (1965). For the career of Samuel C. T. Dodd, the best source (in addition to those noted above on Rockefeller and Standard Oil) is his *Memoirs, Written for His Children* (1907).

For the patent litigations which characterized American industrial life in this era, references will be found in the Bibliographical Notes to those parts of this book specially concerned with the particular inventions. For George B. Selden and his battle with Henry Ford, see William Greenleaf's thorough monograph, *Monopoly on Wheels: Henry Ford and the Selden Automobile Patent* (1961), and for the context consult Allan Nevins and Frank E. Hill, *Ford* (3 vols., 1954–63), and the references to Part Nine below. Other works of special relevance here include: Association of American Law Schools, *Law Schools in the United States and Canada* (1972); Esther Lucile Brown, *Lawyers and the Promotion of Justice* (1938); Jerome E. Carlin, *Lawyers on Their Own: A Study of Industrial Practitioners in Chicago* (1962); John R. Dos Passos, *The American Lawyer, as He was—as He is—as He Can Be* (1907); Joseph Goulden, *The Superlawyers* (1972); Erwin N. Griswold, *Law and Lawyers in the United States: The Common Law Under Stress* (1964); Marlise James, *The People's Lawyers* (1973); Philip C. Jessup, *Elihu Root* (2 vols., 1938); W. Draper Lewis (ed.), *Great American Lawyers* (8 vols., 1907–9); Edward S. Martin, *The Life of Joseph Hodges Choate* (1920); Merlo J. Pusey, *Charles Evans Hughes* (2 vols., 1951); Alfred Z. Reed, *Training for the Public Profession of the Law* (1921); Erwin O. Smigel, *Wall Street Lawyer* (rev. ed., 1970); Arthur E. Sutherland, *The Law at Harvard: A History of Ideas and Men, 1817–1967* (1967), including an account of the evolution of the case method of instruction; American Bar Foundation, *The Legal Profession in the United States* (1965); Floyd L. Vaughan, *The United States Patent System: Legal and Economic Conflicts in American Patent History* (1956); Bruce W. Bugbee, *The Genesis of American Patent and Copyright Law* (1967), on the beginnings. Especially valuable on the relation between law and lawyers and American civilization are the articles in *Law and Contemporary Problems* (1937–), a quarterly published by the Duke University School of Law. See also the *American Journal of Legal History* (1956–).

WHILE NUMEROUS BOOKS have been written on almost every other aspect of the American federal system—on political theory, constitutional law, on the separation of powers and the centralization and decentralization of governmental activities—few have focused on what I here call "the federal commodity," which is the benefit that accrues to a community or to an individual as a by-product of American federalism. The federal commodity has been unpredictable and diverse, ranging from the benefits derived by the citizens of Nevada and some other states from the federal diversity of laws of divorce and gambling to the benefits derived by some citizens disenfran-

chised by local laws who eventually secured their civil and political rights by federal pressures. The so-called Civil Rights Movement might almost have been called a Federal Rights Movement, for it became a movement to bring the pressure of forces in the federal system (other states in Congress and the federal government itself) on particular states which were denying citizens their political and civil rights.

A lively and scholarly introduction to the Nevada story is Gilman M. Ostrander, *Nevada, the Great Rotten Borough* (1966), on which I have leaned heavily. To put this story in its setting of climate, geology, and topography, we have the delightful *Desert Challenge: An Interpretation of Nevada* (1942), by Richard G. Lillard, who knew the state intimately from inside. Other works which I have found especially useful include: Sam P. Davis (ed.), *The History of Nevada* (2 vols., 1913); James W. Hulse, *The Nevada Adventure* (1965); W. Turrentine Jackson, *Treasure Hill, Portrait of a Silver Mining Camp* (1963); Effie Mona Mack, *Nevada* (1936); Grant Smith, *The History of the Comstock Lode, 1850–1920* (1943); Mary Frances Stewart, *Adolph Sutro* (1962); A. J. Wells, *The New Nevada: The Era of Irrigation and Opportunity* (1908), a brochure of the Southern Pacific Company; Thomas Wren, *A History of the State of Nevada* (1904). And for special topics consult Helen J. Poulton, *Index to the History of Nevada* (1966).

For some time we have had better histories of divorce than of marriage or the family in the United States. Arthur W. Calhoun, *A Social History of the American Family* (3 vols., 1945–46; University Paperback, 1960), of which Vol. III deals with 1865–1919, is a valuable and copious compendium and an avenue to the sources, but offers few organizing ideas. A boon to social historians is the massive *Children & Youth in America: A Documentary History* (ed. Robert H. Bremner and associates; 2 vols., 1970–71; Vol. II: 1866–1932), which provides an intelligently selected and discreetly edited body of documents on the experience, hopes, and problems of young people in the United States. This material is, of course, quite relevant to the problem of divorce in America. There is no similar collection, to my knowledge, on the institution of marriage in the United States. We are fortunate to have an excellent, carefully documented and readable monograph in Nelson M. Blake's *The Road to Reno: A History of Divorce in the United States* (1962). Other useful items include: Henry S. Cohn, "Connecticut's Divorce Mechanism: 1636–1969," *American Journal of Legal History*, XIV (1970), 35–54; J. P. Lichtenberger, *Divorce: A Social Interpretation* (1931); Anne F. Scott, *The Southern Lady: From Pedestal to Politics 1830–1930* (1970); Andrew Sinclair, *The Better Half: The Emancipation of the American Woman* (1965), solid and lively; Bernhard J. Stern (ed.), *The Family Past and Present* (1938), a handy compendium of essays on the family in different cultures.

On gambling in Nevada, see: Katharine Best and Katharine Hillyer, *Las Vegas* (1955); Oscar Lewis, *Sagebrush Casinos* (1953); Keith Monroe, "The New Gambling King and the Social Scientists," *Harper's Magazine*, CXXIV (Jan. 1962), 35–41; Harold S. Smith, Sr., with John W. Noble, *I Want to Quit Winners* (1961), a flavorful account by one of the principals. For background, see John S. Ezell, *Fortune's Merry Wheel, The Lottery in America* (1960).

JUST AS WE have better works on divorce than on marriage, so too we have better books on crime than on law obedience or law enforcement. The seminal article on the subject which has shaped my thinking is Walter Lippmann's "The Underworld as Servant" (1931), reprinted in Gus Tyler (ed.), *Organized Crime in America: A Book of Readings* (1962), at pp. 58–69. A bril-

liant survey of the problem of crime in the 1960's from a similar point of view is Norval Morris and Gordon Hawkins, *The Honest Politician's Guide to Crime Control* (1969), which, despite its flippant title, offers a fact-packed and closely reasoned case against what the authors call the "overreach" of the criminal law.

The best introduction to Prohibition, its causes and its consequences, is Andrew Sinclair, *Prohibition* (1962). A delightful account of the battle ax of the crusade is Robert Lewis Taylor, *Vessel of Wrath: The Life and Times of Carry Nation* (1966). Prohibition was almost as great a boon to the publishers who sold books about it as it was to the gangsters who sold the booze. And the library which it produced was incendiary, flip, ponderous, self-righteous, indignant— almost everything but illuminating. The least illuminating works were often the most prestigious, for example the five-volume Report of the National [Wickersham] Commission on Law Observance and Enforcement, "Enforcement of Prohibition Laws," 71st Cong. 3d Sess. . . . , *Sen.Doc.*, No. 307 (1931). A sampling of the literature would include such works as: Kenneth Allsop, *The Bootleggers and Their Era* (1961); Harry Elmer Barnes, *Prohibition versus Civilization* (1932); Stanley Baron, *Brewed in America: A History of Beer and Ale in the United States* (1962); Ernest H. Cherrington, *The Evolution of Prohibition in the United States* (1920); Norman H. Clark, *The Dry Years* (1965); D. Leigh Colvin, *Prohibition in the United States* (1926); W. C. Durant (ed.), *Law Observance* (1929); Irving Fisher, *Prohibition at its Worst* (1926), and *The Noble Experiment* (1930); Fabian Franklin, *What Prohibition Has Done to America* (1922), and *The A.B.C. of Prohibition* (1927); Ernest Gordon, *The Wrecking of the Eighteenth Amendment* (1943); Roy A. Haynes, *Prohibition Inside Out* (1923); Henry Lee, *How Dry We Were* (1963); John H. Lyle, *The Dry and Lawless Years* (1960); Arthur

Newsholme, *Prohibition in America* (1921); C. C. Pearson and J. Edwin Hendricks, *Liquor and Anti-Liquor in Virginia, 1619–1919* (1967), a documented story for one state; Laurence F. Schmeckebier, *The Bureau of Prohibition* (1929); Clark Warburton, *The Economic Results of Prohibition* (1932).

On crime in Chicago, a vivid introduction is the section (Part III) of the Illinois Crime Survey of 1929, reprinted as *Organized Crime in Chicago* (1968), by John Landesco, which collects documents, sworn testimony, and other items toward an engrossing if terrifying picture. See also: Herbert Asbury, *Gem of the Prairie, An Informal History of the Chicago Underworld* (1940); Walter N. Burns, *The One-Way Ride: The Red Trail of Chicago Gangland from Prohibition to Jake Lingle* (1931); The Vice Commission of Chicago, *The Social Evil in Chicago* (1911); *Report of the City Council of the City of Chicago* (1915); Jack Lait and Lee Mortimer, *Chicago Confidential* (1950); Walter C. Reckless, *Vice in Chicago* (1933).

"Organized" crime can be surveyed in the pages of Gus Tyler (ed.), *Organized Crime in America* (1962), a handy and well-selected anthology. Some of the most suggestive ideas on the subject will be found in Daniel Bell, *The End of Ideology* (1960), especially chs. 7–12. See also: Fred C. Cook, *Secret Rulers: Criminal Syndicates and How they Control the U.S. Underworld* (1966); Martin Mooney, *Crime Incorporated* (1935); Roger Touhy, *The Stolen Years* (1959); U.S. Congress, Senate Special Committee, *Investigation of Organized Crime in Interstate Commerce* (1959–62); *Investigation of So-called "Rackets," Hearings before a Subcommittee of the Committee on Commerce,* U.S. Senate, 73rd Cong., 2d Sess. (2 vols., Washington, 1933–34); *The Attorney General's Program to Curb Organized Crime and Racketeering, Hearings before the Committee on the Judiciary,* U.S. Senate, 87th Cong., 1st Sess. . . . (Washington, 1961). On the "Mafia" and

on the relation of Italian immigration to organized crime, begin with Daniel Bell, "Crime as an American Way of Life," Ch. 7 in *The End of Ideology* (1960). Other items which can help us grasp this myth-filled subject are: Irwin L. Child, *Italian or American?* (1943); "The Black Hand Scourge," in *Cosmopolitan Magazine* (June 1909); Robert F. Foerster, *The Italian Emigration of Our Times* (1919); Norman Lewis, *The Honored Society* (1964), on the Mafia; Eliot Lord, *The Italian in America* (1905); John H. Mariano, *The Italian Immigrant in Our Courts* (1925); Raymond V. Martin, *Revolt in the Mafia* (1963); Michael A. Musmanno, *The Story of the Italians in America* (1965); Lawrence F. Pisani, *The Italian in America* (1957); Philip M. Ross, *The Italians in America* (1922); Enrico C. Sartario, *Social and Religious Life of Italians in America* (1918); Tommaso Sassone, "Italy's Criminals in the United States," *Current History,* VII (Oct. 1921); Giovanni Schiavo, *Four Centuries of Italian-American History* (1958), *The Truth about the Mafia* (1962); Frederick Sondern, Jr., *Brotherhood of Evil* (1959); "Immigration and Crime," *Reports of the Immigration Commission* (1911); Phyllis H. Williams, *South Italian Folkways in Europe and America* (1938); William Foote Whyte, *Street Corner Society* (1943). The motion picture *The Godfather,* starring Marlon Brando, made from Mario Puzo's novel, was a box-office success in 1972; it did much to perpetuate old myths about the Mafia and to create some new ones.

For the drug traffic, see *Organized Crime and Illicit Traffic in Narcotics, Hearings before Permanent Subcommittee on Investigations of the Committee on Government Operations.* U.S. Senate, 89th Cong., 1963–65, 1st Sess. & 2d Sess. (6 vols.), see especially testimony of Joseph Valachi; Edwin Schur, *Crimes without Violence . . . Abortion, Homosexuality, Drug Addiction* (1965). And on prostitution: Roy Lubove, "The Progressives and the Prostitute," *The*

Historian, XXIV (May 1962); Jean Turner-Zimmermann, *Chicago's Black Traffic in White Girls* (n.d.), issued by the Department of Purity and Heredity of the Cook County W.C.T.U.; Howard B. Woolston, *Prostitution in the United States* (1921), Vol. I, "Prior to the Entrance of the United States into the World War."

The traditional view of law enforcement and the causes of crime is expressed in: J. Edgar Hoover, *Crime in the United States* (1965); Estes Kefauver, *Crime in America* (1951); Don Whitehead, *The FBI Story: A Report to the People* (1956). Another vantage point for surveying the history of American attitudes to crime is Gerhard O. W. Mueller, *Crime, Law and the Scholars: A History of Scholarship in American Criminal Law* (1969).

The heyday of organized crime also produced a peculiarly American hero who made it his business to champion the individual against society. Clarence Darrow (1857–1938) became a myth. His remarkable career, which was almost precisely contemporary with that of Al Capone, was recorded in his own autobiography (1932), and related in other readable volumes: *Darrow, Attorney for the Damned* (ed. Arthur Weinberg, 1957); Alan Hynd, *Defenders of the Damned* (1960); Irving Stone, *Clarence Darrow for the Defense* (1941). His social philosophy was dramatized in the novel *Compulsion* (1956), by Meyer Levin, which was based on the Leopold-Loeb kidnap case (1924) and which also was made into a successful motion picture.

A remarkable, and too-little-celebrated American institution, a by-product of alcoholism, is Alcoholics Anonymous, which can be discovered in *Alcoholics Anonymous: The Story of How Many Thousands of Men and Women Have Recovered from Alcoholism* (new ed., 1955) and *Alcoholics Anonymous Comes of Age: A Brief History of A.A.* (1957).

PART TWO

CONSUMPTION COMMUNITIES

THE PRODUCTION AND the distribution of goods have been chronicled as "economic" history, as part of the history of labor, of technology, and of transportation. But there have been remarkably few efforts to describe what these add up to for the consumer—the person at whom all these economic efforts are directed. "Standard of Living" is a characteristically American name for what this means, and I have tried to sketch the notion in "Welcome to the Consumption Community," *Fortune*, LXXVI (September 1967), 118.

While quantitative assessments of the quality of experience are misleading and incomplete, statistics on what people made, what services they rendered, and what they bought are valuable clues. For the years since 1878, we have the advantage of the annual *Statistical Abstract of the United States*. Few historians have tried to give a rounded description of the standard of living in a particular period. A helpful exception which provides bench marks is Edgar W. Martin, *The Standard of Living in 1860: American Consumption Levels on the Eve of the Civil War* (1942).

To discover those prominent features of daily life which are so obvious and universal that natives and residents seldom mention them, we can use the writing of travelers. References for travelers' literature of the earlier period will be found in the Bibliographical Notes to *The Americans: The Colonial Experience* (General Section) and *The National Experience* (Parts Two and Four). As travel becomes democratized in this later period, travel literature declines in quality and becomes more indiscriminate. But, luckily for the historian, this is also the period of the more self-conscious immigrant, who often records in a journal, letters, or fiction those striking characteristics of daily life in America which elude the native, the resident, or the visitor. Some examples (for the Polish immigrant) are: Mary Antin, *From Plotzk to Boston* (1889) and *The Promised Land* (1912), personal impressions of a Polish Jewish immigrant; Abraham Cahan, *The Rise of David Levinsky* (1917), a novel of the newly arrived immigrant; William I. Thomas and Florian Znaniecki, *The Polish Peasant in Europe and America* (2 vols.; 2d ed., 1927), translating and reprinting intimately revealing letters, journals, and other documents. The late nineteenth century produced a flood of realistic novels which are a valuable source. After the popularization of photography, the rise of photographic journalism, and the development of the motion picture film, additional rich sources became available, which are indicated in the General Section above.

On clothing we have better chronicles of the manufacturing than of the wearing. Even in great historical collections like those in The National Museum of History and Technology of the Smithsonian Institution in Washington, examples of everyday clothing and the work clothing of the common citizen are rare, while there are beautiful examples of costumes of elegance, including gowns actually worn by First Ladies at the Inaugurations. For the history of clothing manufacturing and distribution in general, the useful works include: Margaret L. Brew, "American Clothing Consumption, 1879–1909" (unpublished Ph.D. dissertation, Division of Biological Science, University of Chicago, Sept. 1945); Harry A. Cobrin, *The Men's Clothing Industry* (1970); Arthur H. Cole, *The American Wool Manufacture* (2 vols., 1926); Melvin T. Copeland, *The Cotton Manufacturing Industry of the United States* (1912); Kenneth Dameron, *Men's Wear Merchandising* (1930); Jesse E. Pope, *The Clothing Industry in New York* (Vol. I,

Social Science Series, University of Missouri Studies, 1905); Harry Simons, *The Science of Human Proportions: A Survey of the Growth and Development of the Normal and Abnormal Human Being* (1933); U.S. Department of Commerce, Bureau of Foreign and Domestic Commerce, *The Men's Factory-Made Clothing Industry*, (Misc. Series No. 34; 1916).

The history of labor in the clothing industry has brought us some especially useful volumes, above the level of writings on labor history in general, for example: J. M. Budish and George Soule, *The New Unionism in the Clothing Industry* (1920); Elden LaMar, *The Clothing Workers in Philadelphia: History of Their Struggles for Union and Security* (1940); Louis Levine, *The Women's Garment Workers: A History of the International Ladies' Garment Workers' Union* (1924); Joel Seidman, *The Needle Trades* (1942), especially valuable; Charles E. Zaretz, *The Amalgamated Clothing Workers of America* (1934). On the manufacture of particular garments, see: Milton N. Grass, *History of Hosiery* (1955); Blanche E. Hazard, *The Organization of the Boot and Shoe Industry in Massachusetts 1875* (1921); George A. Rich, "Manufacture of Boots and Shoes," *Popular Science Monthly*, XLI (Aug. 1892), 496–515; and various publications of the U.S. Department of Commerce, Bureau of Foreign and Domestic Commerce, including *The Hosiery Industry* (Misc. Series No. 31; 1915), *The Knit-Underwear Industry* (Misc. Series No. 32; 1915), *The Women's Muslin-Underwear Industry* (Misc. Series No. 29; 1915), *The Shirt and Collar Industries* (Misc. Series No. 36; 1916).

For the saga of the sewing machine, the following are useful: Charles K. Adams, "Sewing Machines," in *New Universal Encyclopedia* (8 vols., 1893–95); James Bolton, "Sewing Machines," Chicago World's Columbian Exposition, Committee on Awards, *Report* (1901), Vol. II; Grace R. Cooper, *The Invention of the Sewing Machine* (1968), an excellent monograph updating the story; Charles A. Durgin, *Digest of Patents on Sewing Machines, Feb. 21, 1842–July 1, 1859* (1859), a good starting point for further research; George W. Gifford, *Argument of Gifford in Favor of Howe's Application for Extension of Patent* (U.S. Pat. Off., 1860); George W. Gregory, *Machines, etc. Used in Sewing and Making Clothing*, Vol. VII of *Reports and Awards*, Philadelphia International Exhibition, 1876 (1880); C. B. Kilgare, *Sewing Machines* (1892); Frederick L. Lewton, "The Servant in the House: A Brief History of the Sewing Machine," Smithsonian Institution, *Annual Report, 1929* (1930); James Parton, "History of the Sewing Machine," *Atlantic Monthly*, XIX (May 1867), 527–44, a valuable early account by the eminent biographer; John Scott, *Genius Rewarded, or the Story of the Sewing Machine* (1880), a paean to Singer. Much unmined material is found in the nineteenth-century journals of the industry, for example in: *The Sewing Machine Advance*, 1879–1913; *The Sewing Machine Journal*, 1879–1884; *The Sewing Machine News*, 1877–1893; *The Sewing Machine Times*, 1882–1924. A too-little-used resource is the remarkable collection of early sewing machines in The National Museum of History and Technology of the Smithsonian Institution in Washington, D.C.

Of the numerous works on style and fashion, the following are helpful: M. C. C. Crawford, *The Ways of Fashion* (1948); Ruth E. Finley, *The Lady of Godey's: Sarah Josepha Hale* (1931); Oskar Fischel and Max von Boehn, *Modes & Manners of the Nineteenth Century* . . . (4 vols.; rev. ed., 1927); Claudia Kidwell, *Women's Bathing and Swimming Costume in the United States* (1968); Katherine M. Lester, *Historic Costume: A Resumé . . . from the Most Remote Time to the Present Day* (1925); Elisabeth McClellan, *History of American Costume, 1607–1870* (1937); Paul Nystrom, *Economics of Fashion* (1928);

Elizabeth Sage, *A Study of Costume* (1926).

Since marketing has become a major subject in American schools of business administration, numerous casebooks and textbooks have appeared, treating the subject from the point of view of the businessman seeking a market. And there are a few excellent monographs on the history of the marketing of particular products or services as well as on the history of particular firms. There still remains to be written a comprehensive social history of marketing in the United States.

For the history of the department store, a good starting point is Ralph M. Hower, *History of Macy's of New York, 1858–1919* (1943), readable and well-documented. A useful general introduction is H. Pasadermadjian, *The Department Store: Its Origins, Evolution and Economics* (1954). See also: Harry G. Baker, *Rich's of Atlanta, the Story of a Store since 1867* (1953); Edward A. Filene, *The Model Stock Plan* (1930); Herbert A. Gibbons, *John Wanamaker* (1926); Edwin P. Hoyt, *The Supersalesman* (1962); Tom Mahoney and Leonard Sloane, *The Great Merchants, America's Foremost Retail Institutions and the People who made them Great* (new ed., 1966); John Wanamaker, "The Evolution of Mercantile Business," *Annals of the American Academy of Political and Social Science*, XV (1900), Supplement, 123–35 (edited and with an introduction by Malcolm P. McNair) in *An American Primer* (ed. Daniel J. Boorstin, 1966), II, 630–40; Lloyd Wendt and Herman Kogan, *Give the Lady What She Wants: The Story of Marshall Field & Co.* (1952); Émile Zola, "Notes sur le 'Bon Marché,'" *Oeuvres Complètes*, XII, *Au Bonheur des Dames* (1927). On the earlier, small-scale merchandising there are a number of readable works: Lewis E. Atherton, *The Pioneer Merchants in Mid-America*, (Vol. XIV, U. of Mo. Studies, 1939), and his *Main Street on the Middle*

Border (1954), *The Frontier Merchant in Mid-America* (1971); Gerald Carson, *The Old Country Store* (1954); Thomas D. Clark, *Pills, Petticoats and Plows: The Southern Country Store* (1944).

On chain stores and five-and-ten's, an introduction is Godfrey M. Lebhar, *Chain Stores in America, 1859–1959* (1962), a thin authorized history. More helpful are the specific studies: Norman Beasley, *Main Street Merchant: The Story of the J. C. Penney Company* (1948); Ralph Cassady, Jr., and W. L. Jones, *Changing Competitive Structure in the Wholesale Grocery Trade* (1949); Malcolm P. McNair, "Trends in Large-Scale Retailing," *Harvard Bus. Rev.*, X (1931), 6; John K. Winkler, *Five and Ten: The Fabulous Life of F. W. Woolworth* (1940); *Woolworth's first 75 Years* (F. W. Woolworth Co., 1954); and a valuable series in *Fortune*: "A. & P. and the Hartfords," VIII (March 1933); "Woolworth's $250,000,000 Trick," VIII (Nov. 1933); "Case History of a Chain Store," X (Nov. 1934).

For the history of mail-order we are fortunate to have the copious, scholarly, and readable *Catalogues and Counters: A History of Sears, Roebuck and Company* (1950), by Boris Emmet and John E. Jeuck, which is indispensable for the student of the subject. The history of the mail, inextricable from the history of mail-order merchandising, can be explored in two admirable works by Wayne E. Fuller: *RFD, the Changing Face of Rural America* (1964); and *The American Mail: Enlarger of the Common Life* (1972), in The Chicago History of American Civilization. Other works I have drawn on include: Nina Brown Baker, *Big Catalogue, the Life of Aaron Montgomery Ward* (1956); Irwin M. Heine, "The Influence of Geographic Factors in the Development of the Mail Order Business," *Am. Marketing Journal*, III (April 1936), 127–30; Rae Elizabeth Rips, "An Introductory Study of the Role of the Mail Order Business in American History, 1872–1914," unpublished Master's thesis, Dept. of History, U. of Chicago, 1938; Carl H. Scheele, *A Short History of the Mail Service* (1970). Montgomery Ward and Company in Chicago possesses a detailed, closely documented unpublished history of the firm, which the firm generously allows historians to consult; and see my article "A. Montgomery Ward's Mail-Order Business," *Chicago History*, new series II (Spring–Summer 1973), 142–52. Early issues of Sears and Montgomery Ward catalogues have been reprinted and are available inexpensively, providing the best access to what these firms were doing in the heyday of mail order.

Advertising, one of the most characteristic and most vigorous of American institutions, has been less adequately chronicled than almost any other major institution. References useful for the history of advertising and brand-naming will be found appended to my book *The Image: A Guide to Pseudo-Events in America* (1961; Atheneum Paperback, 1972) in the Suggestions for Further Reading (and Writing), especially for chs. 5 and 6. On the early history of advertising in newspapers, an admirable introduction is Frederic Hudson, *Journalism in the United States from 1690 to 1872* (1873), especially Ch. 25 to end, an account by a thirty-year associate of James Gordon Bennett. And see also the indispensable writings of Frank Luther Mott, *American Journalism* (3rd ed., 1962), *The News in America* (1952), and *A History of American Magazines* (5 vols., 1957–68), for periodicals and their editors. Frank Presbrey, *The History and Development of Advertising* (1929), still provides the best general history (illustrated) of the earlier period, which can be supplemented by James Playsted Wood, *The Story of Advertising* (1958), a textbook, for the later period, and Martin Mayer's readable *Madison Avenue, U.S.A.* (1958), for a survey of the operating industry in the mid-twentieth century. Of the copious literature (mostly sensational, debunking, or defensive) the following is a sifted sample along with some how-to-do-it books and others providing essential facts for practitioners: American Association of Advertising Agencies, *The A.A.A.A. Study on Consumer Judgment of Advertising* (1965); N. W. Ayer & Son, *American Newspaper Annual* (1908–); Frank Leroy Blanchard, *The Essentials of Advertising* (1921); Leo Bogart, *Strategy in Advertising* (1967), and "Where Does Advertising Research Go From Here?," *Journal of Adv. Res.*, IX (March 1969); Neil H. Borden, *The Economic Effects of Advertising* (1942); Floyd Clymer's *Scrapbook of Early Advertising* (1955), reproducing notable advertisements from 1880 to 1912; Carl Crow, *Four Hundred Million Customers* (1937); Roy S. Durstine, *This Advertising Business* (1928); Blanche B. Elliot, *A History of English Advertising* (1962); The Editors of *Fortune*, *The Amazing Advertising Business* (1957), a selection of useful articles; Horace Greeley, "The Philosophy of Advertising," *Hunt's Merchants Magazine*, XXIII (1850), 580–83; John Lee Mabin, *Advertising: Selling the Consumer* (1914); Pierre Martineau, *Motivation in Advertising: Motives that Make People Buy* (1957); Harold J. Randolph, *Four Million Inquiries from Magazine Advertising* (1936); E. S. Turner, *The Shocking History of Advertising* (1952); George Wakeman, "Advertising," *Galaxy Magazine*, III (1952) 202–11.

There is a need for a social history of brand names in the United States, including a comprehensive guide and bibliography for the subject. Meanwhile, the literature is thin, but I have found the following useful: Leon H. Amdur, *Outline of Trade-Mark Law* (1934); Arnold B. Barach, *Famous American Trademarks* (1971); Jessie V. Coles, *Standards and Labels for Consumers' Goods* (1949); E. J. Kahn, Jr., *The Big Drink: The Story of Coca-Cola* (1960); Isaac E. Lambert, *The Public Accepts: Stories Behind Famous Trademarks, Names and Slogans* (1941); T. F. Schutte, "The Semantics of Branding,"

Journ. of Marketing, XXXIII (1969), 5–11; Clayton L. Smith, *The History of Trade Marks* (1923); Robert E. Witt, *Group Influence on Consumer Brand Choice* (U. of Tex. Studies in Marketing No. 13, 1970). And see the publications of the Brand Name Foundation.

The literature of market research (and its offshoot, opinion research), although recent, is vast and varied. A good introduction is Martin Mayer, *Madison Avenue, U. S. A.* (1958), Part IV, "Finding the Facts of Life." The professional and popular significance of the subject is attested by the range as well as the quantity of publications, which include statistical compendia, psychological treatises, debunking tracts, pedestrian textbooks, magic success-formulae, sensational exposés, etc. A sampling of this range might include: American Marketing Assn., *A Survey of Marketing Research* (1963), and *The Technique of Marketing Research* (1937); Ernest S. Bradford, *Marketing Research* (1959); British Market Research Bureau, *Readings in Market Research* (1956), a selection by British Authors; Lyndon O. Brown, *Market Research and Analysis* (1937), and *Distribution Research* (1949); Louis P. Bucklin, "Testing Propensities to Shop," *Journ. of Marketing*, XXX (1966), 22–27; Louis Cheskin, *Basis for Marketing Decision* (1961), and *Business without Gambling* (1963); Victor J. Cook and Thomas F. Schutte, *Brand Policy Determination* (1967); Richard D. Crisp, *Marketing Research* (1957), and *Marketing Research Organization and Operation* (1958); Ross M. Cunningham, "Brand Loyalty: What, Where, How Much?" *Harvard Bus. Rev.*, XXIV (1956), 116–28; George S. Day, *Buyer Attitudes and Brand Choice Behavior* (1970); Ernest Dichter, *The Psychology of Everyday Living* (1947), *The Strategy of Desire* (1960), and *Handbook of Consumer Motivation: The Psychology of the World of Objects* (1964), and on Dichter, see the article by Roger Ricklefs, *Wall Street Journal* (Nov. 20, 1972),

p. 1; C. S. Duncan, *Commercial Research* (1919); Robert Ferber and Hugh G. Wales (eds.), *Motivation and Market Behavior* (1958); Willard M. Fox, *How to Use Market Research for Profit* (1950); Myron S. Heidingsfield, *Marketing and Business Research* (1962); Hal Higdon, *The Business Healers* (1969); Donald M. Hobart, *Marketing Research Practice* (1950); H. Lawrence Isaacson, *Store Choice: A Case Study of Consumer Decison Making* (1966); Dexter Masters, *The Intelligent Buyer and the Telltale Seller* (1966); Vance Packard, *The Hidden Persuaders* (1957); Chester R. Wasson and David H. McConaughy, *Buying Behavior and Market Decisions* (1968).

On advertising agencies, the best introduction is the admirable monograph by Ralph M. Hower, *The History of an Advertising Agency: N. W. Ayer & Son at Work, 1869–1949* (1949). See also Burt F. Allen, *American Advertising Agencies . . . Their Origin, Growth, Functions and Future* (1940); Roger Barton, *Handbook of Advertising Management* (1970); Paul Harper, "The Advertising Agency—The Past," in *Advertising Today, Yesterday, Tomorrow* (75th anniversary publication of *Printers' Ink*, 1963), pp. 77–92. For outdoor advertising, see: Hugh E. Agnew, *Outdoor Advertising* (1938); E. Allen Frost, *Outdoor Advertising: Its Genesis, Development, and Place in American Life* (Outdoor Advertising Assn. of America, 1939–41); Harvey W. Root, *The Unknown Barnum* (1927); Frank Rowsome, Jr., *The Verse by the Side of the Road: The Story of the Burma Shave Signs and Jingles* (1965).

Biographical studies of special interest include: P. T. Barnum, *The Life of P. T. Barnum Written By Himself* (1855); Waldo R. Browne (ed.), *Barnum's Own Story: The Autobiography of P. T. Barnum, Combined & Condensed from the Various Editions* (1927); Edward L. Bernays, *Biography of an Idea* (1965); Fairfax Cone, *With All Its Faults; A Candid Account of Forty Years in Advertising* (1969); John Gunther, *Taken at the Flood: The Story of Albert D. Lasker* (1960); Claude C. Hopkins, *My Life in Advertising* (1927); David Ogilvy, *Confessions of an Advertising Man* (1963); Charles L. Pancoast, *Trail Blazers of Advertising* (1926); *Publishers' Advertising, Being the Reactions of a Practising Publisher-Advertiser to the Exhortations of Non-Publisher Theorists*, by "A Practising Publisher-Advertiser" (London, 1930); George P. Rowell, *Forty Years an Advertising Agent, 1865–1905* (1906); *The Men Who Advertise: An Account of Successful Advertisers, Together with Hints on the Method of Advertising* (a publication of Rowell's *American Newspaper Directory*, 1870).

For a selected reading list of the history of opinion polling, see my Suggestions for Further Reading in *The Image* (above), especially pp. 292 ff. Concise introductions are George Gallup and Samuel Forbes Rae, *The Pulse of Democracy: The Public Opinion Poll and How it Works* (1940), and Lindsay Rogers, *The Pollsters* (1949), which come from the early era; up-to-date innovations are reported, defended, and attacked in the *Public Opinion Quarterly;* see also *Group Research Report* (1961–) and *Gallup Opinion Index* (1965–).

The movement called "consumerism" by the 1970's was so new that the word in this sense had not yet entered the dictionaries. But in many respects it was simply a new name for an old movement which had gathered momentum. Its shibboleth remained the old maxim *Caveat emptor* ("Let the buyer beware!"). The roots go back at least to the muckraking movement of the 1890's and to such books as Upton Sinclair's *The Jungle* (1906) (an exposé of the exploitation of immigrant workers in the meat-packing industry) which helped lead to the Pure Food Legislation of 1906. Sinclair later complained that while he had hoped to strike Americans in their hearts, he had only succeeded in hitting them in their stomachs. The recent movement gained its momentum in the Depression of 1929 when the need to economize produced such organizations as the Consumers Union, which published reports at first only for members, later made available to the public. The prophet of the movement in the 1960's was Ralph Nader, whose *Unsafe at Any Speed* (1965), a best-selling attack on automobile manufacturers, brought him into the spotlight. In the late '60s and '70s the rational concern to inform the consuming public and organize consumers to improve the products offered them on the market became overshadowed—by a fanatical but secular Neo-Calvinist zeal that reversed the old Protestant ethic and now assumed that success and prosperity (for an American) were usually the wages of sin. This fanaticism threatened to numb the public conscience by its indiscriminate Nay-Saying.

We need a comprehensive and sophisticated social history of American holidays. On Christmas, consult the useful, if solemn, *The American Christmas: A Study in National Culture* (1954), by

James H. Barnett. Other helpful works include: John E. Baur, *Christmas on the American Frontier, 1800–1900* (1961), describing Christmas before it had become a festival of consumption; George Buday, *The History of the Christmas Card* (1954; 1971); Earnest Dudley Chase, *The Greeting Card Industry* (1946); Arthur D. Coleman, *Keeping Christmas Christian* (1957); Earl W. Count, *4000 Years of Christmas* (1957); T. G. Crippen, *Christmas and Christmas Lore* (1923); Maymie R. Krythe, *All About American Holidays* (1962); William DeLoss Love, *Fast and Thanksgiving Days of New England* (1895); Katherine L. Richards, *How Christmas Came to the Sunday-Schools* (1934); Robert H. Schauffler (ed.), *Our American Holidays: Christmas* (1916); Jane A. Stewart, *The Christmas Book* (1908); Arthur M. Sowder, "Christmas Trees—The Tradition," "Christmas Trees—The Industry," and "The Farmer and Christmas Trees," in United States Department of Agriculture, *Trees, The Yearbook of Agriculture, 1949.*

PART THREE

STATISTICAL COMMUNITIES

SINCE STATISTICAL COMMUNI-ties exist in that no-man's-land between "Intellectual History" and Social and Economic History, they have hardly been chronicled. The history of mathematics and the applications of mathematics in statistics have been recounted, we begin to have histories of the technology of computation, and there are, of course, histories of psychology. But the experience of the citizen, who lives out the by-products of the new sciences of statistics, remains a promising and largely unexplored territory for the historian.

For the history of statistics, a good starting point is the American pioneer S. N. D. North's *Seventy-Five Years' Progress in Statistics* (1914). Also useful

are the articles on statistics in the *Encyclopaedia of the Social Sciences* (ed. E. R. A. Seligman; 15 vols., 1930–35) and in the *International Encyclopaedia of the Social Sciences* (ed. Donald L. Sills; 17 vols., 1968). A perspective on the uses of statistics in social science is provided by Bernard Berelson and Gary A. Steiner, *Human Behavior: An Inventory of Scientific Findings* (1964), especially pp. 15–37, "Methods of Inquiry." Other useful works include: Raymond A. Bauer (ed.), *Social Indicators* (1966); John Koren (ed.), *The History of Statistics* (1918); F. S. Baldwin, "Statistics in the Service of the Municipality," Am. Stat. Assn. *Quarterly Pub.*, XIV (1914), 103; F. F. Stephan, "The History of the Uses of Modern Sampling Procedures,"

Am. Stat. Assn. Journal, XLIII (1948), 12; Helen M. Walker, *Studies in the History of Statistical Method, With Special Reference to Certain Educational Problems* (1913); Walter F. Willcox, "Lemuel Shattuck, Statistician . . ." *The Am. Statistician*, I (1947), 11–13. And consult other articles in the *American Statistical Association Journal* (1905–) and the *American Statistician* (1947–).

The history of the United States census is concisely surveyed in Ann Herbert Scott, *Census, U.S.A.* (1968). Other useful works include: Donald J. Bogue, *The Population of the United States* (1959); Hinton R. Helper, *The Impending Crisis of the South* (1860), an early example of the polemical uses of statistics in national politics; W. Stull Holt, *The Bureau of the Census* (1929); Otis C. Skipper, *J. D. B. De Bow* (1958); Carroll D. Wright and William C. Hunt, *The History and Growth of the United States Census* (1900); U.S. Bureau of Census, Dept. of Commerce & Labor, *A Century of Population Growth from the First Census of the United States to the Twelfth, 1790–1900* (1909). There is, of course, no substitute for consultation of the census reports themselves, which in one form or another are available in many libraries.

Literature on the history of insurance in the United States is spotty. There remains to be written a comprehensive history of the place of insurance in American civilization, but there are a number of valuable histories of particular companies, for example: R. Carlyle Buley, *The American Life Convention, 1906–1952: A Study in the History of Life Insurance* (1958), *The Equitable Life Assurance Society in the United States, 1859–1959* (1959), a concise centennial volume, and *The Equitable Life Assurance Society of the United States, 1859–1964* (2 vols., 1967); Shepard B. Clough, *A Century of American Life Insurance . . . The Mutual Life Insurance Company of New York, 1843–1943* (1946); Marquis James, *Biography of a Business, 1792–1942: Insurance Company of North America* (1942); Morton Keller, *The Life Insurance Enterprise, 1885–1910: A Study in the Limits of Corporate Power* (1963), a study of government regulation of the "Big Five"; Thomas I. Parkinson, *"Equitable" of the U.S.* (1950); Powell Stamper, *The National Life Story* (1968); Harold F. Williamson and Orange A. Smalley, *Northwestern Mutual Life* (1957), study of a smaller company. On insurance in general, works of interest include: James L. Ahearn, *Risk and Insurance* (1969), a textbook; Henry Darrach, *Insurance, 2285 B.C.–1906 A.D.* (1906); Insurance Information Institute, *Insurance Statistics* (1962); Edson S. Lott, *Pioneers of American Liability Insurance* (1938); G. A. MacLean, *Insurance up through the Ages* (1938); Morris Pike, *America Insures Itself* (1930); Prudential Insurance Co., *The Documentary History of Insurance, 1000 B.C.–1875 A.D.* (a Panama-Pacific Exposition Memorial Publication, No. 5; 1915); Josiah Royce, *War and Insurance* (1914).

On life insurance in particular, see: William J. Graham, *The Romance of Life Insurance* (1909); Equitable Life Assurance Society of the U.S., *Henry Baldwin Hyde* (1901), a memorial brochure; David N. Holway, *Life Insurance of the World, 1861–1889* (1889); George W. Johnson, *Some Evolutionary Developments in Life Insurance* (1914); Morton Keller, *The Life Insurance Enterprise, 1885–1910* (1963); Griffin M. Lovelace, *Life and Life Insurance* (1961); Terence O'Donnell, *History of Life Insurance* (1936); David Graham Phillips, *Light-Fingered Gentry* (1907; 1970), a muckraking novel of corrupt life-insurance executives; J. Owen Stalson, *Marketing Life Insurance* (1942; 1969); Mildred F. Stone, *A Short History of Life Insurance* (1942).

Elizur Wright is a many-sided figure who deserves a more prominent place in the American pantheon of organizers and reformers. The standard biography is Philip G. Wright and Elizabeth Q. Wright, *Elizur Wright, the Father of*

Life Insurance (1937), by members of the family. To grasp the cosmic significance that Elizur Wright saw in life insurance, consult one of his own works: *Politics and Mysteries of Life Insurance* (1873), *Elements of Life Insurance* (1876), *The Necessity of Reform in Life Insurance* (1878), *Insurance and Self-Insurance* (1880).

For the rise of liability and automobile insurance, see: Automobile Mutual Insurance Co. of America, *Pathway of Progress, 1907–1957* (1957); Walter G. Cowles, *What Is the Matter with the Automobiles?* (1921); Eugene F. Hord, *History and Organization of Automobile Insurance* (1919); Michigan University Survey Research Center, *Public Attitudes Toward Auto Insurance* (1970); H. Jerome Zoffer, *The History of Automobile Liability Insurance Rating* (1959); and, for fire insurance, Henry R. Gall, *One Hundred Years of Fire Insurance* (1919). For the growth of government-sponsored insurance programs, see, for example, Edwin E. Witte, *The Development of the Social Security Act* (1962).

References on the history of sizing will be found in the Bibliographical Notes for Part Two (above) on the history of the clothing industry. The essential introduction to the subject is Harry Simons, *The Science of Human Proportions* (1933).

A handy popular introduction to the history of the Bureau of Standards is John Perry, *The Story of Standards* (1955), which should be supplemented by Rexmond C. Cochrane, *Measures for Progress: A History of the National Bureau of Standards* (1966).

Although Statistical Quality Control is one of the most potent of the institutions shaping American production, it remains one of the most arcane. Here is another opportunity for a historian to introduce the nation to itself; on this subject we need a comprehensive book intelligible to the layman. I owe my introduction to the subject to Eugene S. Ferguson, especially to a brilliant un-published manuscript by him, "The History and Development of Statistical Quality Control," delivered to a conference at the Eleutherian Mills–Hagley Foundation on April 15, 1964, and to his other writings. Published works which I have found useful include: Dudley J. Cowden, *Statistical Methods in Quality Control* (1957); Federal Products Corporation, *Federal Dimensional Quality Control Primer* (Providence, R.I., a trade catalogue, 1946); J. G. Knapp, "Industrial Design, Its Role in Cost Reduction," *Mechanical Engineering*, XCIII, (Dec. 1971), 23–26; S. B. Littauer, "The Development of Statistical Quality Control in the United States," *Am. Statistician*, IV (Dec. 1950), 14–20; G. S. Radford, *The Control of Quality in Manufacturing* (1922); Walter A. Shewhart, *Economic Control of Quality of Manufactured Product* (1931) and "The Future of Statistics in Mass Production," *Annals of Mathematical Statistics*, X (1939); Robert C. Tumbleson, "Statistical Engineering," *Am. Statistician*, I (Aug. 1947), 7–11.

An up-to-date, scholarly, and comprehensive history of the cash register, of adding and calculating machines, and their place in American civilization is much needed. At the moment the literature is miscellaneous and inadequate, and consists mainly of the promotional publications of particular firms. Among the works I have found useful are: Burroughs Adding Machine Company, *A Better Day's Work at Less Cost of Time, Work, and Worry to the Man at the Desk* (1910); Roy W. Johnson and Russell W. Lynch, *The Sales Strategy of John H. Patterson, Founder of the National Cash Register Company* (1932); James H. McCarthy (ed.), *The American Digest of Business Machines* (1924); Isaac F. Marcosson, *Wherever Men Trade: The Romance of the Cash Register* (1945; 1972); J. A. V. Turck, *Origin of Modern Calculating Machines* (1921; 1972); and for later reports on the computer terminal as a successor to the cash register, see the useful article by

John A. Prestbo, "The Super Registers," *Wall Street Journal* (Nov. 20, 1972), p. 1, and "How Giant Sears Grows and Grows," *Business Week* (Dec. 16, 1972), 52–57. A valuable preliminary survey is Uta Merzbach, *Of Levers and Electrons and Learning and Enlightenment: Technological Augmentation of Cognition in the United States Since 1776* (1971). Interesting vistas are opened by Charles Eames, *A Computer Perspective* (1973), a graphic history of computers from 1890 to 1950. And see the relevant articles on the principal figures in *D.A.B.* and supplements. For I.B.M., see Saul Englebourg, "International Business Machines: A Business History," Ph.D. dissertation, Columbia University (1954). The National Museum of History and Technology in Washington, D.C., has a valuable collection of early cash registers and calculating machines.

The current literature on taxation and on the income tax is enormous. Tax law has become a major subject in American law schools; numerous textbooks and loose-leaf tax-information services have been provided for this market and for the growing number of tax lawyers and tax accountants. But we still need a comprehensive history of taxation in American civilization. A starting point is Sidney Ratner, *American Taxation, Its History as a Social Force in Democracy* (1942). And see also: James Don Edwards, "Some Significant Developments of Public Accounting in the United States," *Bus. Hist. Rev.*, XXX (1956), 211–25; Roy G. and Gladys C. Blakey, *The Federal Income Tax* (1940); Elmer Ellis, "Public Opinion and the Income Tax, 1860–1900," *Miss. Valley Hist. Rev.*, XXVII (1940), 225–42: Elmer L. Irey and William J. Slocum, *The Tax Dodgers* (1948); Delos O. Kinsman, *The Income Tax in the Commonwealths of the United States* (1903); Henry H. Smith, *Income Tax* (1893); and articles in *Law and Contemporary Problems* (1933–).

For statistics on individual and national income, see the *Statistical Abstract of the United States,* for the years since 1878. A handy introduction is the *Pocket Data Book,* published biennially since 1967. For a historical compilation, see *Historical Statistics of the United States,* described in the General Section above. Significant works on the subject include: Elizabeth E. Hoyt and others, *American Income and Its Use* (1954); Willford Isbell King, *The Wealth and Income of the People of the United States* (1915), a pioneer study; Simon Kuznets, *National Product Since 1869* (1946), *National Income: A Summary of Findings* (1946); Edgar W. Martin, *The Standard of Living in 1860* (1942); Robert F. Martin, *National Income in the United States, 1799–1938* (1939); National Bureau of Economic Research, *Retrospect and Prospect, 1920–1936* (1936).

THE BEST INTRODUCTION to the history of poverty in the United States is Robert H. Bremner's readable and vivid *From the Depths: The Discovery of Poverty in the United States* (1956), which can be supplemented by his *American Philanthropy* (Chicago History of American Civilization, 1960). And see also: Ben H. Bagdikian, *In the Midst of Plenty* (1964); Michael Harrington, *The Other America: Poverty in the United States* (1964); Robert P. Hunter, *Poverty* (1904; ed. Peter d'A. Jones, 1964); Raymond H. Mohl, *Poverty in New York: 1783–1825* (1971); Stephan Thernstrom, *Poverty and Progress: Social Mobility in a 19th Century City* (1964); William Graham Sumner, *What Social Classes Owe to Each Other* (1925), in which Sumner proposed the phrase "the forgotten man" in a context different from that later given it by F.D.R.; and the report "A Nation Within a Nation," *Time,* XCI (May 17, 1968), 24–32. One famous example of the temptation to offer panaceas for poverty is Henry George's *Progress and Poverty* (1879), which urged a tax on land as a sovereign solution and became the bible of a movement. For a lively account of the political cross fire which has plagued recent efforts to "solve" the problem of poverty, see Daniel P. Moynihan, *The Politics of a Guaranteed Income: The Nixon Administration and the Family Assistance Plan* (1973).

In the late 1960's and early '70's the subject of intelligence testing became clouded with passions. Chauvinist champions of disadvantaged "minorities" charged that intelligence tests, because they were culturally conditioned, were nothing but a scheme to discriminate against these minorities. The more moderate practitioners of intelligence testing had not denied that their "intelligence" tests simply tested "what intelligence tests test," nor had they claimed that it was possible to devise a test that was entirely culture-free. But they had suggested that since a reasonable purpose of such tests was to predict performance in a particular culture, the tests would have to be culturally conditioned, focusing on those forms of knowledge and skill which the culture most valued and rewarded. An admirable introduction to the history of this thorny subject is Richard Herrnstein, "I. Q.," *Atlantic Monthly*, CCXXVIII (Sept. 1971), 43–64. And for a clue to the passions aroused, see the sampling of readers' comments on that article in a later issue of *Atlantic Monthly*, CCXXVIII (Dec. 1971), 101–10. See also Arthur R. Jensen, "How Much Can We Boost IQ and Scholastic Achievement?" *Harvard Educational Review*, XXXIX (Winter 1969), 1–124. Another clue to the heat around the subject was that for a time the editors of the *Review* would not send out that article to would-be purchasers without insisting that they buy the next issue also, which included numerous articles in rebuttal, XXXIX (Spring 1969), 273–357. I do not know another recent example of similar conduct by a learned journal. If the reader needs further evidence of the atmosphere surrounding the subject in this era, he can find it in the articles in a special issue of *The Humanist*, XXXII (Jan.–Feb. 1972). A readable and scholarly introduction to the history of recent American attitudes toward inherited mental inferiority is Mark Haller, *Eugenics: Hereditarian Attitudes in American Thought* (1963), which I have found an indispensable guide.

The book and periodical literature on educational testing is vast, itself a testimony to the growth of public education in the United States, the concern with the democratizing of education, and the professionalizing of education in colleges and universities. Items of special interest include: Orville G. Brim, Jr., and others, *Experiences and Attitudes of American Adults Concerning Standardized Intelligence Tests* (1965); Walter F. Dearborn, *Intelligence Tests, Their Significance for School and Society* (1928); Joseph Peterson, *Early Conceptions and Tests of Intelligence* (1926; 1969); Victor Serebriakoff, *IQ, A Mensa Analysis and History* (1966); Robert M. Yerkes (ed.), "Psychological Examining in the United States Army," in *Memoirs of National Academy of Sciences*, XV (1921). For the history of the College Entrance Examination Board, begin with Claude Fuess, *The College Board: Its First Fifty Years* (1950); see also: College Entrance Examination Board, *The Work of the College Entrance Examination Board, 1901–1925* (1926) and Frank Bowles, *The Refounding of the College Board, 1948–1963* (1967).

To put American attitudes toward childhood in a wider historical perspective, the reader should not miss Philippe Ariès' delightful *Centuries of Childhood: A Social History of Family Life* (trans. from the French; Vintage Paperback, 1962). Robert H. Bremner and others (eds.), *Children & Youth in America: A Documentary History* (2 vols., 1970–71; Vol. II: 1866–1932), brings together illuminating materials nowhere else so conveniently available or so well edited. For G. Stanley Hall, we have an excellent biography (with critical bibliography) by Dorothy Ross, *G. Stanley Hall: The Psychologist as Prophet* (1972), which should be supplemented by a sampling of Hall's own writings, for example: *Adolescence* (2 vols., 1904), *Youth, Its Education, Regimen and Hygiene* (1906), *Aspects of Child Life and Education* (1907), *Educational Problems* (2 vols., 1911). For Hall's interesting relationship with William James, see the letters in Ralph Barton Perry, *The Thought and Character of William James* (2 vols., 1936). On Arnold Gesell, see National Academy of Sciences, *Biographical Memoirs,* XXXVII (1964), and his own writings, especially (with Frances L. Ilg) *Infant and Child in the Culture of Today* (1943) and *Youth, the Years from Ten to Sixteen* (1956). Other items of special interest include: David Bakan, "Adolescence in America: From Idea to Social Fact," *Daedalus* (Fall 1971), 979–92; Oscar Handlin and Mary F. Handlin, *Facing Life: Youth & Family in American History* (1971); Joseph F. Kett, "Adolescence and Youth in Nineteenth-Century America," *Journal of Interdisciplinary History, II (1971)*, 283–98; Roy Lubove, *The Professional Altruist: The Emergence of Social Work as a Career, 1880–1930* (1965); Anthony M. Platt, *The Child Savers: The Invention of Delinquency* (1969); Robert C. Sorensen, *Adolescent Sexuality in Contemporary America* (1973); William I. and Dorothy S. Thomas, *The Child in America* (1928; 1970).

For the changing American attitude to sexual morality, a good introduction is Nathan G. Hale, Jr., *Freud and the Americans: The Beginning of Psychoanalysis in the United States, 1876–1917* (1971). An admirable survey of the epoch is Henry May, *The End of American Innocence . . . 1912–1917* (1959). A vivid glimpse of how intellectuals viewed the "New Morality" in full flood is found in Freda Kirchwey (ed.), *Our Changing Morality: A Symposium* (1924), by an assortment of American social scientists and men of letters. On Alfred Kinsey and his work there are two essential books: Cornelia Christenson, *Kinsey: A Biography* (1971), by one of his assistants, and Wardell B. Pomeroy, *Dr. Kinsey and the Institute for Sex Research* (1972), by one of his collaborators. And, of course, Kinsey's own writings, especially: *An Introduction to Biology* (1926), a textbook; *The Gall Wasp Genus Cynips: A Study of the Origin of Species* (1930); *New Introduction to Biology* (1933); (with M. L. Fernald) *Edible Wild Plants of Eastern North America* (1943); (with W. B. Pomeroy and C. E. Martin) *Sexual Behavior in the Human Male* (1948); (with W. B. Pomeroy, C. E. Martin, and P. H. Gebhard) *Sexual Behavior in the Human Female* (1953); and the essays of Kinsey reprinted in Christenson, *Kinsey* (1971), particularly "Individuals," pp. 3–9, and pp. 207 ff. A useful general history is Edward M. Brecher, *The Sex Researchers* (1969).

For a sampling of other sexual research and its appraisals, see: Sophie D. Aberle and George W. Corner, *Twenty-five Years of Sex Research: History of the National Research Council Committee for Research in Problems of Sex* (1953); Hugo G. Beigel (ed.), *Advances in Sex Research* (pub. of the Society for the Scientific Study of Sex, 1963); Bernard Berelson and Gary A. Steiner, *Human Behavior: An Inventory of Scientific Findings* (1964), especially chs. 3, 7; Robert Latou Dickinson and Lura Beam, *A Thousand Marriages: A Medical Study of Sex Adjustment* (1931; 1970); J. R. Kantor, *The Scientific Evolution of Psychology*, Vol. II (1969); Kenneth M. Ludmerer, *Genetics and American Society* (1972); William H. Masters and Virginia E. Johnson, *Human Sexual Response* (1966), and *Human Sexual Inadequacy* (1970); Niles Newton, *Maternal Emotions: A Study of Women's Feelings Toward Menstruation, Pregnancy, Childbirth, Breast Feeding, Infant Care, and Other Aspects of Their Femininity* (1955); Lewis

M. Terman, *Psychological Factors in Marital Happiness* (1938); William S. Sahakian (ed.), *History of Psychology* (1968). On group sex, see the works by an anthropologist, Gilbert D. Bartell, *Group Sex: A Scientist's Eyewitness Report on the American Way of Swinging* (1971), and by a perceptive reporter, Jim Seymore, "Love Me, Love My Wife," *Washingtonian Magazine*, VII (February 1972), p. 44. A guide into the literature criticizing Kinsey's work (with samples) is found in Pomeroy, *Kinsey* (1972). Some of the more sophisticated critiques of Kinsey and of sex research might include: Committee on the College Student, Group for the Advancement of Psychiatry, *Sex and the College Student* (1966); James B. Conant,

"Scientific Principles and Moral Conduct," *American Scientist*, LV (1967), 311–28; Robert Latou Dickinson, "Truth and Consequences: Kinsey's Version," *American Scholar*, XVII (1948), 461–68; Morris L. Ernst and David Loth, *American Sexual Behavior and The Kinsey Report* (1948); Geoffrey Gorer, "Justification by Numbers," *American Scholar*, XVII (1948), 280–86; Jerome Himelhoch and Sylvia F. Fava, *Sexual Behavior in American Society, an Appraisal of the First Two Kinsey Reports* (1955); Russell Kirk, "Statistics and Sinai," *South Atlantic Quarterly*, XLVIII (1949), 220–28; Lionel Trilling, "Sex and Science: The Kinsey Report," *Partisan Review*, XV (1948), 460–76.

PART FOUR

THE URBAN QUEST FOR PLACE

IMMIGRATION AND CITIES, two of the most remarkable and most characteristic aspects of American history, have only recently begun to receive a serious and extensive scholarly treatment. This is another example of the dominance of American thinking by Old World categories. Immigration did not feature prominently in the modern history of Western European nations, nor were many great European cities founded within the last two centuries or even within the period of extensive historical records.

The pioneer historian of American immigration was Marcus Lee Hansen (1892–1938), who was born in Wisconsin, studied history and sociology at the University of Iowa and taught at the University of Illinois, and who, despite the brevity of his life, gave the subject the leadership and the literary models that it needed. Every student of the subject should read *The Immigrant in American History* (1940), a posthumous collection of his essays, and *The Atlantic Migration, 1607–1938: A History of the Continuing Settlement of the United*

States (1940), and also "The Problem of the Third Generation Immigrant," *Augustana Historical Society Publications* (Rock Island, Ill., 1938). While Professor Arthur Schlesinger, Sr., had long been urging the importance of this and other neglected topics of American social history, and therefore should be considered the godfather of the study, Hansen's work opened a new era of scholarship. Hansen had actually gone to the trouble of learning the relevant European languages, and he worked in the archives of the countries from which the immigrants came. He wrote with a rare grace and warmth, and with a sympathy that he did not allow to be monopolized by any sect or country.

This universality of Hansen's interest was especially important for a subject which was (and still is) cursed by filiopietism, and by ethnic, racist, and religious chauvinisms. These antihistorical diseases have generally been endemic, confined to particular places and groups aiming at self-praise. But from time to time one of them has taken on epidemic proportions, becoming so widespread that it is not even recognized as a disease. This has occurred in two recent epochs. One was the "Anglo-Saxon Superiority" epidemic, which became virulent in the 1880's and '90's. Its symptoms were talk of the White Man's Burden, the Yellow Peril, etc., with a whole vocabulary of ethnic and national derogation. An admirable introduction to the history of this phenomenon is Barbara Miller Solomon, *Ancestors and Immigrants* (1956). For some clues to the products of this way of thinking, see A. A. Roback, *A Dictionary of Ethnophaulisms* (1944), which brings together many of the derogatory slang terms for various groups; and see also Harold Wentworth and Stuart B. Flexner, *Dictionary of American Slang* (1960), preface and the numerous words there historically defined. A similar epidemic was the "Black is Beautiful" mania which from its relatively innocent antidefamation start became widespread and virulent in the 1960's and early '70's. Its symptoms were a whole vocabulary of indiscriminate indictment, accusation, and shallow self-praise, manifested in "Black Studies Programs" and in a flood of books and series of books, many of which had little or no scholarly or literary value. The people of the United States, then, no less than others, are the periodic victims of these epidemics. But there appear to be antibodies which cure such maladies. Sensible historians of later generations do not fail to note the epidemic—with the consequence (unhappy for the pathologically overpraised group) that historians then become wary of recognizing the unvarnished facts of the case. This is the familiar "revisionist" cycle.

A vivid introduction to the recent phenomenon of American immigration is the copiously illustrated *Strangers at the Door; Ellis Island, Castle Garden, and the Great Migration to America* (1971), by Ann Novotny. Bernard A. Weisberger, *The American Heritage History of the American People* (illus-

trated, 1971), offers a balanced and lively narrative with well-chosen selections from the writings of the immigrants themselves. Interesting pathways into specific topics in this period are: Oscar Handlin, *Boston's Immigrants, 1790–1865: A Study in Acculturation* (1941), whose *The Uprooted* (1951; 2d ed., 1973) gives a moving account of the whole story; John Higham, *Strangers in the Land: Patterns of Nativism, 1860–1925* (1955). On immigration in general, works of particular interest for this later period and its background include: Edith Abbott (ed.), *Immigration: Selected Documents and Cases* (1924), and *Historical Aspects of the Immigration Problem: Select Documents* (1926); Ray A. Billington, *The Protestant Crusade, 1800–1860: A Study of The Origins of American Nativism* (1938); Theodore C. Blegen (ed.), *Land of Their Choice: The Immigrants Write Home* (1955); Lawrence G. Brown, *Immigration: Cultural Conflicts and Social Adjustments* (1933); Rebecca Burlend, *A True Picture of Emigration* (1936); Niles Carpenter, *Immigrants and their Children, 1920: A Study based on Census Statistics* (1927); John R. Commons, *Races and Immigrants in America* (1907; 1920); Charlotte Erickson, *American Industry and the European Immigrant, 1860–1885* (1957); Harold Fields, *The Refugee in the United States* (1938); Oscar Handlin (ed.), *Children of the Uprooted* (1966), an anthology; Isaac S. Hourwich, *Immigration and Labor: The Economic Aspects of European Immigration to the United States* (2d. ed., 1922); Edward P. Hutchinson, *Immigrants and Their Children, 1850–1950* (in the Census Monograph Series, 1956); W. Jeremiah Jenks and W. Jett Lauck, *The Immigration Problem... American Immigration Conditions and Needs* (6th ed., 1926); Maldwyn A. Jones, *American Immigration* (Chicago History of American Civilization, 1960); Hugo Munsterberg, *The Americans* (1904), the views of an eminent immigrant; John P. Sanderson, *Republican*

Landmarks: The Views and Opinions of American Statesmen on Foreign Immigration (1856); George Stephenson, *A History of American Immigration, 1820–1924* (1926); W. Lloyd Warner and Leo Srole, *The Social System of American Ethnic Groups* (Yankee City Series, Vol. III; 1945).

Of the enormous literature on particular immigrant groups, a large proportion is self-serving, chauvinistic, antiquarian, or genealogical. The most detailed and best-documented accounts, of course, are the biographies of immigrants who were famous when they arrived or who became famous. The more useful of these would include: Robert G. Athearn, *Thomas Francis Meagher, An Irish Revolutionary in America*, account of one who became a Union brigadier-general in the Civil War and territorial governor of Montana; Bernard M. Baruch, *Baruch* (2 vols., 1957–60), an autobiography; Edward Bok, *The Americanization of Edward Bok* (1920), story of an immigrant from the Netherlands; Andrew Carnegie, *Autobiography* (1920), and the excellent *Andrew Carnegie*, by Joseph F. Wall (1970); Laura Fermi, *Illustrious Immigrants . . . 1930–41* (1968); Claude M. Fuess, *Carl Schurz* (1932); George Juergens, *Joseph Pulitzer and the New York World* (1966); Carl Schurz, *Reminiscences* (3 vols., 1907–1908); and Don C. Seitz, *Joseph Pulitzer, His Life & Letters* (1924). More revealing of the common immigrant experience are the reminiscences of less-eminent persons whose careers here made them self-conscious about their immigrant past, for example the delightful, if sentimental, works of the social worker Mary Antin, *From Plotzk to Boston* (1899), *The Promised Land* (1912), and *They Who Knock at Our Gates* (1914); or *The Rise of David Levinsky* (1917), a novel by Abraham Cahan, a leader of the American Yiddish press.

On the Irish we have an eloquent and brilliantly told (but unfortunately not explicitly documented) work by George

W. Potter, *To the Golden Door* (1960), which no one should miss. Other items of special interest on British immigration include: Rowland T. Berthoff, *British Immigrants in Industrial America, 1790–1850* (1953); Thomas N. Brown, *Irish-American Nationalism, 1870–1890* (1968); Terry Coleman, *Going to America* (1972); R. Dudley Edwards and T. Desmond Williams (eds.), *The Great Famine* (1957); Stanley C. Johnson, *A History of Emigration from the United Kingdom to North America, 1763–1912* (1913); Arnold Schrier, *Ireland and the American Emigration, 1850–1900* (1958); William V. Shannon, *The American Irish: A Political and Social Portrait* (1963); Carl Wittke, *The Irish in America* (1956).

On Jewish immigrants, a vivid introduction (focused on New York City) is Allon Schoener (ed.), *Portal to America: The Lower East Side 1870–1925* (1967), photographs and chronicles by and about the immigrants. And see: Rudolph Glanz, *Jews in Relation to the Cultural Milieu of Germans in America up to the 1880's* (1947); Oscar Handlin, *Adventure in Freedom: Three Hundred Years of Jewish Life in America* (1954); Milton Hindus (ed.), *The Old East Side, An Anthology* (1969); Oscar D. Janowsky (ed.), *The American Jew: A Composite Portrait* (1942), *The American Jews: A Reappraisal* (1964); Samuel Joseph, *Jewish Emigration to the United States from 1881 to 1910* (1914), a statistical study; Bertram W. Korn, "American Jewish Life a Century Ago," *Yearbook of Central Conf. of Am. Rabbis*, LIX (1949), 273–302; Moses Rischin, *The Promised City, New York's Jews 1870–1914* (1962); Marshall Sklare (ed.), *The Jews: Social Patterns of an American Group* (1954).

German immigrants are chronicled in: T. S. Baker, "America as the Political Utopia of Young Germany," *Americana Germanica*, I (1897), 62–102; Frederick Behlendorff, "Recollections of a Fortyeighter," *Deutsch Amerikanische Geschichtsblätter*, XV (1915), 310–51;

August Bondi, *Autobiography, 1833–1907* (1910); Ernest Bruncken, "Germans in America," *Am. Hist. Assn. Annual Report* (1898), 347–53, "Francis Lieber...," *Deutsch Am. Gesch.* XV (1915); Dieter Cunz, "Christian Mayer, Baltimore Merchant," *German-American Review*, X (1944), 11–13, *The Maryland Germans* (1948); Chester V. Easum, *The Americanization of Carl Schurz* (1929); Albert B. Faust, *The German Element in the United States, with Special Reference to Its Political, Moral, Social, and Educational Influence* (1927); Frank Freidel, *Francis Lieber, 19th Century Liberal* (1947); John A. Hawgood, *The Tragedy of German-America* (1940); Richard O'Connor, *The German-Americans: An Informal History* (1968); Joseph Schafer, "Carl Schurz, Immigrant Statesman," *Wis. Mag. Hist.*, XI (1927–28), 373–94; Carl Schurz, *Speeches, Correspondence and Political Papers . . .* (ed. Frederic Bancroft; 6 vols., 1913), "Intimate Letters . . .," ed., Joseph Schafer, State Hist. Soc. of Wis. Pub. *Colls.*, XXX (1928); George von Skal, *History of German Immigration to the United States and Successful German-Americans and Their Descendants* (1908); Frederick F. Schrader, *The Germans in the Making of America* (1924); Carl Wittke, *Refugees of Revolution: The Forty-Eighters in America* (1952).

On other groups, see for example: O. Fritiof Auder, *The Cultural Heritage of the Swedish Immigrant* (Augustana Lib. Pub. No. 27, n.d.); Theodore C. Blegen, *Norwegian Migration to America* (2 vols., 1931–40); Emil Lengyel, *Americans from Hungary* (1948); Oscar Lewis, *La Vida: A Puerto Rican Family in the Culture of Poverty—San Juan and New York* (1966); Henry S. Lucas, *Netherlanders in America: Dutch Immigration to the United States and Canada, 1789–1950* (1955); Theodore Saloutos, *The Greeks in the United States* (1964); Patricia Cayo Sexton, *Spanish Harlem* (1965).

For the comparative study of the assimilation of immigrants in the city, an admirable starting point is Nathan Glazer and Daniel P. Moynihan, *Beyond the Melting Pot: The Negroes, Puerto Ricans, Jews, Italians, and Irish of New York City* (2d ed., 1970). And see Oscar Handlin, *The Newcomers: Negroes and Puerto Ricans in a Changing Metropolis* (1965). These works provide a necessary gloss on the folklore of "The Melting Pot," popularized in a play of that name by Israel Zangwill (1909).

On the relation of the immigrant (especially the Irish immigrant) to city politics, I am especially indebted to the insights and information offered by Moynihan in *Beyond the Melting Pot* (1970). Other useful works on this subject include: H. J. Browne, *The Catholic Church and the Knights of Labor* (1949); James M. Burns, *John F. Kennedy: A Political Profile* (1960); James Michael Curley, *I'd Do It Again: A Record of All My Uproarious Years* (1957), and the novel based on Curley's career, *The Last Hurrah*, by Edwin O'Connor (1956); Philip H. Des Marais, "John Ireland in American Politics, 1886–1906," unpublished M.A. thesis, Georgetown Univ. (1951); James A. Farley, *Jim Farley's Story* (1948); Florence E. Gibson, *The Attitude of the New York Irish Toward State and National Affairs, 1848–1892* (1951); Oscar Handlin, *Al Smith and His America* (1958); Norman Hapgood and Henry Moskowitz, *Up From the Streets: Alfred E. Smith* (1927); Kenneth T. Jackson, *The Ku Klux Klan in the City, 1915–1930* (1967); Alfred Henry Lewis, *The Boss and How He Came to Rule New York* (1903); Dennis T. Lynch, *"Boss" Tweed* (1972), and *The Wild Seventies* (1941); Arthur Mann, *Yankee Reformers in the Urban Age* (1954), and *LaGuardia* (2 vols., 1959–65); Henry F. Pringle, *Alfred E. Smith* (1927); William L. Riordan, *Plunkitt of Tammany Hall* (intro. Arthur Mann, 1963); Lincoln Steffens, *Autobiography* (1931); John P. Roche (ed.), "Plunkitt of Tammany Hall," in *American Primer* (2 vols., 1966), II, 672–85; M.

R. Werner, *Tammany Hall* (1928), a popular history.

A GUIDE TO reading on the history of the American city is found in the Bibliographical Notes to *The Americans: The National Experience*, Part Three. The following notes will be confined to works especially useful on the modern period, to works on the topics on which I focus in my chapters, and works on urban history which have appeared since publication of my earlier volumes. The literature has proliferated in the last decades. Because the shaping of American cities has become a major issue of American politics, much of the writing has been polemical and partisan, expressing passions hardly less fervent than those of the abolitionist era.

A good starting point for the history and issues of American city life in this period are these three readable volumes: John W. Reps, *The Making of Urban America: A History of City Planning in the United States* (1965), a brilliant survey copiously illustrated with an illuminating text; Jane Jacobs, *The Death and Life of Great American Cities* (1961; Vintage Paperback), a lively exposition of the latent problems of all city planning, in the form of an attack on the American dogmas of city planning prevalent in mid-century; Sam Bass Warner, Jr., *Streetcar Suburbs: The Process of Growth in Boston, 1870–1900* (1962), an admirable introduction to the relation of city growth to the technology and economics of transportation. The most widely debated issues are posed in two sharp and readable books from opposing points of view: Edward C. Banfield, *The Unheavenly City* (1970), and Sam Bass Warner, Jr., *The Urban Wilderness* (1972). A world perspective (not unmarred by polemics) is found in Lewis Mumford, *The City in History* (1961).

The best work on the industrial utopia, American style, is Stanley

Buder, *Pullman: An Experiment in Industrial Order and Community Planning, 1880–1930* (1967), on which I have drawn. Of the many general works on the American city in the recent period (in addition to those mentioned in Bibliographical Notes to *The National Experience*) I have found the following especially useful: Charles Abrams, *The City is the Frontier* (1965); Alexander B. Callow, *American Urban History: An Interpretative Reader with Commentaries* (1969); Daniel J. Elazar, *Cities of the Prairie: The Metropolitan Frontier and American Politics* (1970); M. Mason Gaffney, "Urban Expansion—Will it Ever Stop?" in *Land: The 1958 Yearbook of Agriculture* (1958), pp. 503–22; the Editors of Fortune, *The Expanding Metropolis* (1958); Charles N. Glaab, *The American City: A Documentary History* (1963), and (with A. Theodore Brown), *A History of Urban America* (1967); Blake McKelvey, *The Urbanization of America* (1963); Jeffrey K. Hadden and others, *Metropolis in Crisis* (1967); Roderick D. McKenzie, *The Metropolitan Community* (1933; 1967); Page Smith, *As a City Upon a Hill* (1966), interpretive essays; Stephan Thernstrom and Richard Sennet (eds.), *Nineteenth-Century Cities: Essays in the New Urban History* (1969); Anselm L. Strauss, *The American City* (1968); Sam B. Warner, Jr., *The Private City: Philadelphia in Three Periods of its Growth* (1968). And see the volumes in the valuable Urban Life in America Series, published by the Oxford University Press and edited by Richard C. Wade.

On modern city planning and the aesthetics of the American city, see especially: William Ashworth, *The Genesis of Modern British Town Planning* (1954); Edmund N. Bacon, *Design of Cities* (1967), and "New-World Cities: Architecture and Townscape," in *American Civilization* (ed. Daniel J. Boorstin, 1972), Ch. IX; Daniel H. Burnham and Edward H. Bennett, *Plan of Chicago* (1909); John Codman, *Preserva-*

tion of Historic Districts by Architectural Control (1956); Constantinos A. Doxiadis, *Ekistics: An Introduction to the Science of Human Settlements* (1968); James Marston Fitch, *Architecture and the Esthetics of Plenty* (1961); Constance McL. Green, *The Rise of Urban America* (1965); Victor Gruen, *The Heart of Our Cities* (1965); Philip H. Hauser and Leo F. Schnore (eds.), *The Study of Urbanization* (1965); Werner Z. Hirsch (ed.), *Urban Life and Form* (1963); Ebenezer Howard, *Garden Cities of Tomorrow* (1898; new ed. 1965), the English classic; Sibyl Maholy-Nagy, *Matrix of Man: An Illustrated History of Urban Environment* (1968); Steen Eiler Rasmussen, *London, the Unique City* (1934; MIT Paperback, 1967); Montgomery Schuyler, *American Architecture and other Writings* (2 vols., 1961); Vincent Scully, *American Architecture and Urbanism* (1969); Anselm L. Strauss, *Images of the American City* (1961); Christopher Tunnard and Henry Hope Reed, *American Skyline: The Growth and Form of Our Cities and Towns* (New American Library Paperback, 1956); Raymond Vernon, *The Myth and Reality of Our Urban Problems* (1966), defining the problems which the author discovered in the New York Metropolitan Regional Study, summarized in *Anatomy of a Metropolis: The Changing Distribution of People and Jobs within the New York Metropolitan Region* (with Edgar M. Hoover, 1959).

For the basic facts on demography and the flow of the American people, the essential work is the massive three-volume *Population Redistribution and Economic Growth, United States 1870–1950* (American Philosophical Society, 1957) prepared under the direction of Simon Kuznets and Dorothy Swaine Thomas. A more accessible treatment of the consequences of this movement in one region of the nation is Jean Gottmann, *Megalopolis: the Urbanized Northeastern Seaboard of the United States* (1961). Some useful works on the

relation of these population movements to the growth and planning of cities and suburbs and to real estate values include: Charles Abrams, *Revolution in Land* (1939); Francis S. Chapin, Jr., *Urban Land Use Planning* (1957); Gordon R. Clapp, *The TVA: An Approach to the Development of a Region* (1955); Marion Clawson, *Man and Land in the United States* (1964); Pear Janet Davies, *Real Estate in the United States* (1964); Glenn S. Dumke, *The Boom of the Eighties in Southern California* (1944); Garnett L. Eskew, *Of Land and Men* (1959); Constance McL. Green, *American Cities in the Growth of the Nation* (1957); Homer Hoyt, *One Hundred Years of Land Values in Chicago* (1933); David Lavender, *California: Land of New Beginnings* (1972); J. C. Nichols, *Real Estate Subdivisions: The Best Manner of Handling Them* (American Civic Association, 1912); A. M. Sakolski, *The Great American Land Bubble, the Amazing Story of Land-grabbing, Speculations, and Booms from Colonial Times to the Present Time* (1932); Kevin Starr, *Americans and the California Dream, 1850–1915* (1973); Richard C. Wade, *The Urban Frontier: The Rise of Western Cities, 1790–1830* (1959; Phoenix Paperback), *Slavery in the Cities* (1964).

The various methods of slum clearance and of providing urban housing have been an arena of debate for varying social and economic philosophies. While the subject is involved with obscure technical questions of public finance, it has been clouded by passion. Among the more useful works for the history of the subject, I have found the following representative of the spectrum of interpretations: Leo Adde, *Nine Cities: The Anatomy of Downtown Renewal* (1969); Martin Anderson, *The Federal Bulldozer: A Critical Analysis of Urban Renewal, 1949–1962* (1964); Bryton and Ella Barron, *The Inhumanity of Urban Renewal* (1965); Clarence J. Davies, *Neighborhood Groups and Urban Renewal* (1966);

Robert E. Forman, *Black Ghettos, White Ghettos, and Slums* (1971); Leo Grebler, *Urban Renewal in European Countries: Its Emergence and Potentials* (1964); Scott Greer, *Urban Renewal and American Cities: The Dilemma of Democratic Intervention* (1965); Thomas F. Johnson and others, *Renewing America's Cities* (1962); Marshall Kaplan and others, *The Model Cities Program: A History and Analysis of the Planning Process in Three Cities: Atlanta . . . Seattle . . . Dayton* (1969); Langley Carleton Keyes, Jr., *The Rehabilitation Planning Game* (1969); Fred Powledge, *Model City, A Test of American Liberalism* (1970); *Renewal of Town and Village: A Worldwide Survey* (for the International Union of Local Authorities, 1965); Peter H. Rossi and Robert A. Dentler, *The Politics of Urban Renewal: The Chicago Findings* (1961); Twentieth Century Fund, *CDCs: New Hope for the Inner City* (1971); John B. Willman, *The Department of Housing and Urban Development* (1967); Edith E. Wood, *The Housing of the Unskilled Wage Earner: America's Next Problem* (1919), and *Recent Trends in American Housing* (1931).

Congressional hearings and the government documents compiled from them and from other sources provide an indispensable source for grasping both the state of American housing in the mid-twentieth century, and the facts (actual and presumed) on which government policy has been based. Among the more important of these are: *Study and Investigation of Housing, Hearings before Joint Comm. on Housing*, 80th Cong., 1st Sess., Sept. 10 and 19, 1947 (1948); *Housing in America,* a Joint Report prepared for the U.S. Congress Joint Comm. on Housing, pursuant to H. Cong. Res. 104, 80th Cong. (1948); *General Housing Legislation, Hearings before Subcom. of Com. on Banking and Currency,* U.S. Senate, 81st Cong., Feb. 1949 (1949); *Middle-Income Housing, Hearings before Subcom. of Com. on Banking and Cur-*

rency, U.S. Senate, 81st Cong., Jan. . . . . 1950 (1950). Government documents of the 1960's provide a survey of what had, and had not, been accomplished in the first decades of public housing: U.S. Gen. Accounting Office, Report to Congress, *Review of Policies and Procedures for Controlling and Sharing the Costs of Slum Clearance and Urban Renewal Administration Housing and Home Finance Agency, June, 1961* (1962) and review of *Selected Slum Clearance and Urban Renewal Activities under the Administration of the Philadelphia Regional Office Housing and Home Finance Agency,* March 1961 (1962); U.S. Cong. House, *Urban Renewal, Hearings before Subcom. on Housing of the Com. on Banking and Currency,* 88th Cong., Pt. 1, Oct. 22, 23, 24, 1963; Pt. 2, Nov. 19, 20, 21, 1963 (2 vols., 1963); U.S. Urban Renewal Administration, *Historic Preservation Through Urban Renewal* (1963); Comptroller Gen. of the U.S., *Savings Available in Federal Share of Cost of Demolishing Buildings* (1968).

On neighborhood life, especially as it has been affected by the rate of urban growth, by movements of population, and by urban renewal itself, see: Howard P. Chudacoff, *Mobile Americans: Residential and Social Mobility in Omaha, 1880–1920* (1972); Otis D. Duncan and Albert J. Reiss, Jr., *Social Characteristics of Urban and Rural Communities, 1950* (Census Monograph Series, 1956); Herbert J. Gans, *The Urban Villagers: Group and Class in the Life of Italian-Americans* (1962), a study of the effect of urban removal on the life of the Italian East Boston community; Jean Gottmann, *Megalopolis* (1961); Philip Hamburger, *An American Notebook* (1965), a shrewd reporter's view of towns from Bismarck, N.D., to Wilmington, Del.; Edgar M. Hoover and Raymond Vernon, *Anatomy of a Metropolis: The Changing Distribution of People and Jobs within the New York Metropolitan Region* (1959; 1962); John B. Lansing and others, *New Homes and*

Poor People: A Study of Chain Moves (1969); Oscar Lewis, *La Vida: A Puerto Rican Family in the Culture of Poverty —San Juan and New York* (1966); Gilbert Osofsky, *Harlem: The Making of a Ghetto* (1966); Robert E. Park, Ernest W. Burgess, and Roderick D. McKenzie, *The City* (new ed., intro. by Morris Janowitz, 1967); Leo F. Schnore, *The Urban Scene: Human Ecology and Demography* (1965); Patricia Cayo Sexton, *Spanish Harlem: The Anatomy of Poverty* (1965); Walter A. Terpenning, *Village and Open-Country Neighborhoods* (1931); NASA Conference, *Space, Science and Urban Life* (a NASA publication, 1963); Anda Ferrin Weber, *The Growth of Cities in the Nineteenth Century* (1899; 1963); Robert A. Woods, *The Neighborhood in Nation-Building; The Running Comment of Thirty Years at South End House* (1923), account of a pioneer social worker in Boston.

The sociology of suburban life has provided some of the most readable and most widely read books on American civilization in the twentieth century (along with a jargon of American self-description and self-derogation), and has focused attention on the suburb as a touchstone of American experience in the twentieth century. William H. Whyte's readable and suggestive book, *The Organization Man* (1956), began as a gloss on the life he found in Park Forest, a newly built Chicago suburb, and became a good starting point for his and our view of the new place of the suburb in American life. Some of the most popular works on suburbia (which in the 1930's was still called "the country-club set" and was still presumed to be the life of the upper-middle classes) are the novels of Scott Fitzgerald and John O'Hara. Among the more useful works, I have found: Herbert J. Gans, *The Levittowners: Ways of Life and Politics in a new Suburban Community* (1967), and "Park Forest: Butt of a Jewish Community," *Commentary*, IV (1951), 330–39; Park D. Goist, "Where Town and Country Meet: The Fusing of Urban

and Rural Images in Early Automotive Advertising," *Popular Culture* (April 1971); Virginia Taylor Hampton, "The Fabulous Van Sweringens: Empire-Building, 1915–1935," typed ms. in Library of Congress (1965); John Keats, *The Crack in the Picture Window* (1957); John R. Seeley, R. Alexander Sim, and Elizabeth W. Loosley, *Crestwood Heights: A Study of the Culture of Suburban Life* (1956); A. C. Spectorsky, *The Exurbanites* (1955); Graham R. Taylor, *Satellite Cities: A Study of Industrial Suburbs* (1915); Gibson Winter, *The Suburban Captivity of the Churches: An Analysis of Protestant Responsibility in the Expanding Metropolis* (1961); Robert C. Wood, *Suburbia: Its People and Their Politics* (1959), a useful corrective to the clichés of the emptiness of suburban life; Robert A. Woods and Albert J. Kennedy, *The Zone of Emergence* (new ed., 1962).

The internal life of modern American cities has been more obviously tied to systems of urban transportation than was the life of earlier cities, save perhaps a few dramatic exceptions like Venice, Amsterdam, and Bangkok. A good introduction to the story of streetcars is Sam B. Warner, Jr.'s readable *Streetcar Suburbs: The Process of Growth in Boston, 1870–1900* (1962). See also: Burton J. Hendrick, "Great American Fortunes and Their Making: Street-Railway Financiers," *McClure's Magazine*, XXX (1907), 32–48, a muckraking article illustrating incidentally what such writers did and did not offer; Edward S. Mason, *The Street Railway in Massachusetts: The Rise and Decline of an Industry* (1932); John A. Miller, *Fares Please! A Popular History of Trolleys, Horse Cars, Street-Cars, Buses, Elevated, and Subways* (1941; paperback 1960); Robert O. Schad, *Henry Edwards Huntington* (1931; rev. ed. 1963); Lincoln Steffens, *Autobiography* (1931), Part III; U.S. Dept. of Commerce and Labor (Bureau of the Census), *Special Reports: Street and Electric Railways, 1902* (1905). On highways and the demands of the automobile, see: Victor Gruen, *The Heart of Our Cities* (1965); Lawrence Halprin, *Freeways* (1966); Helen Leavitt, *Superhighway—Superhoax* (1970), on the perils and profits in the Interstate Highway System, which the author describes as "the largest single public works project ever undertaken by man."

Much of the literature which was a by-product of the Environmental Concern of the 1960's expressed the spirit of self-flagellation and utopianism that prevailed in other areas of American life. Despite the flood of polemics and muckraking, describing the allegedly insufferable evils of all American civilization in the twentieth century, there have been few serious and comprehensive works recounting the ways in which American city dwellers in the earlier past did (or did not) deal with their problems of water, sewage, sanitation, public health, etc.

To put the automobile and smog in perspective, we urgently need a solid book describing the place of the horse in urban life and the products and by-products of horses for health and disease, for odors, for clothing, and for street maintenance. An excellent start is Nelson Blake, *Water for the Cities: A History of the Urban Water Supply in the United States* (1956), but we need more of its quality. Some imaginative and industrious historian should be challenged by the need for a comprehensive history of American plumbing, which could provide an intimate glimpse of American manners, morals, cuisine, public health, and the American Standard of Living. Until now, a considerable proportion of the writing on the subject is in the spirit of Charles ("Chic") Sales's *The Specialist* (1929) and recalls the graffiti on lavatory walls.

A history of urban systems of waste disposal, for which there are copious printed sources, could be a touchstone, too, of the problems of community organization and urban politics. Meanwhile, I have found the following to be useful: American Industries Salvage Committee, *Scrap and How to Collect It* (1942), a wartime manual; Harold E. Babbitt, *Sewerage and Sewage Treatment* (1940); Battelle Memorial Institute, *Survey and Analysis of the Supply and Availability of Obsolete Iron and Steel Scrap* (1957); James H. Cassedy, *Charles V. Chapin and the Public Health Movement* (1962); Stuart Chase, *The Challenge of Waste* (1925), and *The Tragedy of Waste* (1925), on the wastefulness of the economic system; Morris M. Cohn, *Sewers for Growing America* (1966); David Cushman Coyle, *Waste: The Fight to Save America* (1963), on the economic system; H. R. Crohurst, *Sanitary Disposal of Sewage Through a Septic Tank* (1921); Leonard P. Kinnicutt and others, *Sewage Disposal* (1919); Monroe Lerner and Odin W. Anderson, *Health Progress in the United States, 1900–1960* (1963); Edgar W. Martin, *The Standard of Living in 1860* (1942); Forrest McDonald, *Let There Be Light: The Electric Utility Industry in Wisconsin, 1881–1955* (1957); Karl A. McVey, *Water Supply for Country Homes* (Univ. of Mo. Engineering Experiment Station, Bull. No. 2; 1910); Medical Assn. of the State of Alabama, *How to Secure a Safe Water Supply* (1924); Wilson G. Smillie, *Public Health . . . the Development of Public Health in the United States, 1607–1914* (1955); U.S. Bureau of Census, *Electrical Industries* (1902).

Some studies of particular cities which I have found of special value include: Nathaniel Burt, *The Perennial Philadelphians: The Anatomy of an American Aristocracy* (1963); Robert Cromie and Herman Kogan, *The Great Fire: Chicago 1871* (1971); Beverly Duncan and Philip M. Hauser, *Housing a Metropolis: Chicago* (1960); James Ford and others, *Slums and Housing with special reference to New York City: History, Conditions, Policy* (1971); Charles N. Glaab, *Kansas City and the Railroads* (1962); Constance McL. Green, *Washington* (2 vols., 1962–63), and *The*

Secret City (1967); Bessie L. Pierce, *Chicago* (3 vols., 1937–57); John W. Reps, *Monumental Washington* (1967); W. W. Robinson, *Los Angeles: A Profile* (University of Oklahoma Press Centers of Civilization Series, 1968); Stephan Thernstrom, *Poverty, Planning, and Politics in the New Boston* (1969); Sam Bass Warner, Jr., *The Private City: Philadelphia in Three Periods . . .* (1968); Walter Muir Whitehill, *Boston: A Topographical History* (new ed., 1963); *Boston in the Age of John Fitzgerald Kennedy* (U. of Okla. Press Centers of Civilization Series, 1966).

FUTURE HISTORIANS WILL doubtless begin to be wary of the books on the history of the Negro in the United States when they find the word "Negro" being displaced by the word "Black" in the 1960's and 1970's—just as they are wary of books in German history in the era when the word "Aryan" became fashionable. "Negro" is a neutral historical term. Many other groups have found it unobjectionable to accept a designation (even if, as with "Quaker" or "Tory," it began as a term of disparagement) when it has acquired a neutral and descriptive historical meaning. A perceptive portrait of how reverse discrimination has afflicted Americans of good will is Tom Wolfe's brilliant report "Radical Chic," on the party given in New York City by the Leonard Bernsteins for the Black Panther Defense Fund on January 4, 1970; reported in *Radical Chic and Mau-Mauing the Flak Catchers* (1971). For the reaction of less privileged Americans to "Black" Racism, see Louise Kapp Howe (ed.), *The White Majority: Between Poverty and Affluence* (1970).

The history of the Negro American began to be chronicled, and was being well chronicled in quite another spirit, before the word "Black" became fashionable. The pioneer book was John Hope Franklin, *From Slavery to Freedom: A History of Negro Americans* (1947; 3d ed. 1967), which did a great deal to define the subject and to mark off the tasks for future scholars, and which remains by far the best general guide into the subject. A selected bibliography is found in Franklin's book. But even before Franklin, there was much valuable scholarship, as indicated in Monroe N. Work, *A Bibliography of the Negro in Africa and America* (1928); updated by Elizabeth W. Miller, *The Negro in America, A Bibliography* (1966); and in the *Journal of Negro History* (1916–). The "Black Studies" movement has tended to inflame the subject without proportionately illuminating it, and has become the Trojan Horse of a new racism.

For a guide to the literature on the Negro in earlier periods of American history, see the Bibliographical Notes to *The Americans: The Colonial Experience* (Parts Three and Four) and *The National Experience* (Part Four). Here I offer only a selection of those works which I have found most useful for this part, which deal with the Negro in the city, or which have appeared since my earlier volumes.

A good starting point is Gilbert Osofsky, *Harlem: The Making of a Ghetto, Negro New York, 1890–1930* (1966), which relates the story both to the movement up from the South and to the internal history of the city. A monument to American social science in the early twentieth century is *An American Dilemma: The Negro Problem and Modern Democracy* (1944), by Gunnar Myrdal, with the assistance of Richard Sterner and Arnold Rose and the collaboration of a large staff. This 1,500-page volume, produced under a grant from the Carnegie Corporation, illustrates both the strength and weaknesses of collaborative scholarship. It brought into focus knowledge and expertise from the whole range of the social sciences, but the volume lacks unity and much of it reads like a memorandum. Nevertheless, it did a job which had not yet been done. And a by-product was to make many of the simple facts of American life more widely credible because this study had been directed by an internationally famous social scientist from abroad, and because the product was costly, ponderous, and collaborative. More widely quoted than read, the volume provided ammunition for the civil rights movement of the next two decades, and was cited by the United States Supreme Court in its epoch-making desegregation decision, Brown v. Board of Education of Topeka (1954), 347 U.S. 483.

On the movements of American Negroes, a basic book is Daniel O. Price, *Changing Characteristics of the Negro Population* (a 1960 Census Monograph, U.S. Bureau of Census, 1969). Other works that I have found especially valuable on the forming of "cities within cities" include: John H. Bracey, Jr., August Meier, and Elliott Rudwick (eds.), *The Rise of the Ghetto* (1971); St. Clair Drake and Horace R. Cayton, *Black Metropolis: A Study of Negro Life in a Northern City* (2 vols., rev. ed., 1970), on Chicago; Nathan Glazer and Daniel P. Moynihan, *Beyond the Melting Pot* (2d ed., 1970), on New York City; August Meier and Elliott M. Rudwick, *From Plantation to Ghetto* (1966); Robert C. Weaver, *The Negro Ghetto* (1948; 1967), by the scholar who became President Lyndon B. Johnson's Secretary of Housing and Urban Development.

For the "Harlem Renaissance," the best introduction is Nathan I. Huggins, *Harlem Renaissance* (1971). And see: James Weldon Johnson, *Black Manhattan* (1930); Alain Locke (ed.), *The New Negro: An Interpretation* (1925); Claude McKay, *Harlem: Negro Metropolis* (1940); and the numerous works by the leading figures in the Harlem Renaissance, whose works are mentioned in Huggins. To grasp the human meaning of life in the Negro's city-within-the-city, and the mark left by that experience, one must read autobiographies, for example: James Baldwin, *Notes of a Native Son* (1955), and *Nobody Knows my Name* (1960); Claude Brown, *Manchild in the Promised Land* (1965); Eldridge Cleaver, *Soul on Ice* (1968); The

Autobiography of Malcolm X (1965). Perhaps the best novel on the subject of the Negro in the United States, and one of the best American novels of this century is Ralph Ellison, *Invisible Man* (1953), but there are many others of interest; for example, Richard Wright, *Native Son* (1940). To place these in the context of recent American Literature, see R. W. B. Lewis, "Written Words: The Making of American Literature," in *American Civilization* (ed. Daniel J. Boorstin, 1972).

Other works which I have found most helpful on the Negro American in the modern period include: John H. Bracey, Jr., August Meier and Elliott Rudwick (eds.), *Black Nationalism in America* (1970), an anthology; George C. Cable, *The Negro Question* (ed. Arlin Turner, 1958); Edmund D. Cronon, *Black Moses: The Story of Marcus Garvey and the Universal Negro Improvement Association* (1955); Allison Davis and John Dollard, *Children of Bondage* (1940); Leslie H. Fishel, Jr., "The Negro in Northern Politics, 1870–1900," *M.V.H.R.*, XLII (1955), 466–89; John Hope Franklin, "The History of Racial Segregation in the United States," in *Racial Desegregation and Integration* (Annals of Am. Acad. of Pol. & Soc. Sci., 1956), and (ed.) *Color and Race* (1968); E. Franklin Frazier, *The Negro Family in the United States* (1939; rev. and abr. by Nathan Glazer, 1966), *Black Bourgeoisie: The Rise of a New Middle Class in the United States* (1957; 1962), and *On Race Relations* (selected by E. Franklin Edwards, 1968); Melville J. Herskovits, *The Myth of the Negro Past* (1958); Winthrop D. Jordan, *White Over Black, American Attitudes toward the Negro, 1550–1812* (1968), a scholarly study of some roots of the American Dilemma; Charles F. Kellog, *NAACP, 1909–1920* (1967), an authorized history; John Litwack, *North of Slavery: The Negro in the Free States, 1790–1860* (1961); August Meier and Elliott Rudwick (eds.), *The Making of Black America* (2 vols., 1969); I. A. Newby (ed.), *The Development of Segregationist Thought*

(1968); Gilbert Osofsky (ed.), *The Burden of Race* (1967), a documentary history; Talcott Parsons and Kenneth B. Clark (eds.), *The Negro American* (1967); *The Booker T. Washington Papers* (ed. Louis T. Harlan; 1972–); Arthur I. Waskow, *From Race-Riot to Sit-In, 1919 and the 1960's* (1966); C. Vann Woodward, *The Strange Career of Jim Crow* (2d ed., 1966), an influential revisionist study; T. J. Woofter, *Negro Problems in Cities* (1928; 1969). For biographies and autobiographies of leading Negro Americans, see the valuable series edited by John Hope Franklin for the University of Chicago Press, including lives of William Wells Brown, Henry Ossawa Tanner, Ida B. Wells, John Roy Lynch, and others.

Can there be a folklore in literate, urbanized United States? Some earlier peculiarities of American folklore are explored in *The Americans: The National Experience*, Part VII, and the accompanying Bibliographical Notes. Some questions for the modern period are suggested by Richard M. Dorson in *American Folklore* (1959), chs. 5–7, and are explored in more detail in Americo Paredes and Ellen J. Stekert, *The Urban Experience and Folk Tradition* (1971). See also: Roger D. Abrahams, *Deep Down in the Jungle: Negro Narrative Folklore from the Streets of Philadelphia* (1970; 1973); B. A. Botkin, *Sidewalks of America: Folklore, Legends, Sagas, Traditions, Customs, Songs, Stories, and Sayings of City Folk* (1954); H. Gaidoz and Paul Sebillot, *Blason Populaire de la France* (1884), an exploration of the ethnic slur as an expression of folklore; Hutchins Hapgood, *The Spirit of the Ghetto* (1902; 1966), on Yiddish folk theater in America; Bruce A. Rosenberg, *The Art of the American Folk Preacher* (1970).

The temptation of scholarly writers on all popular arts is to be oversubtle and overserious and so to dull the characteristic spontaneity, casualness, and vagrancy of their subject. Obviously the only way to capture the spirit of a music is to hear the music in its proper environment and then draw one's own conclusions. The opportunity to hear otherwise inaccessible American folk music and jazz is offered by the extensive musical archives of the Library of Congress. For blues, jazz, and the Negro musical achievement in the cities, a scholarly introduction is Wilfrid Mellers, *Music in a New Found Land* (1965), complemented by the acute popular essays of Martin Williams, *Where's the Melody? A Listener's Introduction to Jazz* (1966). Some of the best books written by Negroes on their special experience in the United States come to us through their writings on music, for example, LeRoi Jones (who changed his name to Imaru Baraka), *Blues People: The Negro Experience in White America and the Music that Developed From It* (1963). Other works, from the vast and uneven literature, which I have found useful include: Sterling Brown, "Negro Folk Expression: Spirituals, Seculars, Ballads and Work Songs," *Phylon*, XIV (1953), 45–61; Samuel B. Charters IV, *Jazz: New Orleans, 1885–1963* (1963); David Ewen, *American Popular Songs: From the Revolutionary War to the Present* (1966), an encyclopedia; Max Jones and John Chilton, *Louis: The Louis Armstrong Story* (1971); Charles Keil, *Urban Blues* (1966), useful despite its heavily psychoanalytic interpretation; Henry A. Kmen, *Music in New Orleans* (1966); Neil Leonard, *Jazz and the White Americans: The Acceptance of a New Art Form* (1962); Henry Pleasants, *Death of a Music: The Decline of the European Tradition and the Rise of Jazz* (1961); Gunther Schuller, *Early Jazz* (1968); Nat Shapiro and Nat Hentoff (eds.), *Hear Me Talkin' to Ya* (1955), a delightful collection of the words of jazz musicians on their jazz; Alec Wilder, *American Popular Song: The Great Innovators, 1900–1950* (1972); Martin Williams, *Jazz Masters of New Orleans* (1970).

BOOK TWO

THE DECLINE OF

THE MIRACULOUS

PART FIVE

LEVELING TIMES AND PLACES

THE GROWTH OF the historical profession in the United States seems only to have made more respectable and more rigid the bias toward writing about what historians have always written about—namely "important" events recorded in official records, governmental proclamations, legislation, archives, and the journals and biographies of famous men. Some of the most poignant and characteristic features of daily life remain unchronicled precisely because they are universal and commonplace. And since the transformation of everyday experience is one of the notable achievements of American civilization, we are inclined to underestimate the American achievement. The increase of history and historians has still not provided us the resources that we need. Therefore these Bibliographical Notes to Parts Five and Six are as much a description of territory still to be explored as a map of territory already charted.

One way to grasp the change in ways of daily living is to look at a homemaker's guide of a century ago—for example, *The American Woman's Home: or, Principles of Domestic Science; being a Guide to the Formation and Maintenance of Economical, Healthful, Beautiful, and Christian Homes* (1869), by Catharine E. Beecher and Harriet Beecher Stowe—and compare it with a modern survey, or what we know to be common in our own time. A point of comparison for our own time is any wide-circulating homemakers' magazine like *Woman's Day,* or *Better Homes and Gardens;* a convenient compendium, with statistics, is *This U.S.A.,* by Ben J. Wattenberg and Richard M. Scammon (1965), a view of American consumption levels from the census of 1960. An interesting popular history of the American household during this century is Russell Lynes, *The Domesticated Americans* (1963), which brings together much fugitive material. For the larger context, the reader should consult the two remarkable books by the Swiss scholar Sigfried Giedion, *Mechanization Takes Command* (1948; Norton Paperback, 1969) and *Space, Time and Architecture* (1949).

On the history of the American diet, the best available book is Richard O. Cummings, *The American and His Food* (1940), but it does not cover the most recent decades; for the later period, see Edward C. Hampe, Jr., and Merle Wittenberg, *The Lifeline of America: Development of the Food Industry* (1964), a useful textbook and reference work. A valuable comparative study is J. C. Drummond and Anne Silbraham, *The Englishman's Food . . . Five Centuries of English Diet* (rev. Dorothy Hollingsworth, 1957), but there is not to my knowledge a similarly comprehensive and well-documented account for the United States.

For Borden we are fortunate to have the excellent biography (with bibliography) by Joe B. Frantz, *Gail Borden: Dairyman to a Nation* (1951), which should be supplemented by Borden's own writings, especially *The Meat Biscuit* (1850; 1851). Other works on Borden, on milk processing and distribution include: Arvill W. Bitting, *Early History of the Production of Evaporated Milk* (Evap. Milk Assn., n.d.); Harold W. Comfort, *Gail Borden and His Heritage Since 1857* (Newcomen Society pub., 1953); Charles L. Flint, *Milch Cows and Dairy Farming* (1860); Paul W. Gates, *The Farmer's Age: Agriculture, 1815–1860* (1962); E. L. Roadhouse and J. L. Henderson, *The Market-Milk Industry* (1941); Joseph Schafer, *The Social History of American Agriculture* (1936); Clarence R. Wharton, *Gail Borden, Pioneer* (1941).

While, as indicated in the Bibliographical Notes to Part One, above, the literature on Western cattle raising is copious, much of the saga of meat packing and meat distribution remains to be told. But see Louis F. Swift, *The Yankee of the Yards: The Biography of Gustavus Franklin Swift* (1927). On other topics: R. A. Clemen, *The American Livestock and Meat Industry* (1923); James T. Critchell and Joseph Raymond, *History of the Frozen Meat Trade* (1912); Austin A. Dowell and Knute Bjorka, *Livestock Marketing* (1941), a textbook with selected bibliography; *The Packing Industry . . . Lectures Given under the Joint Auspices of the School of Commerce and Administration of the University of Chicago and the American Institute of Meat Packers* (1924); Theodore V. Purcell, *The Worker Speaks His Mind on Company and Union* (1953). And see Upton Sinclair's influential muckraking novel of immigrants and meat packers, *The Jungle* (1906). An interesting account of efforts to stop publication of that volume is found in Frank Nelson Doubleday, *Memoirs of a Publisher* (1972).

On food processing, canning, distribution, and marketing in general, see: E. A. Ackerman, *New England's Fishing Industry* (1941); A. W. Bitting, *Processing and Process Devices* (Natl. Canners Assn., 1916), and on particular vegetables, *Asparagus* (1927), *Corn* (1928), *Peas* (1909), *Spinach* (1926), and (with K. G. Bitting) *Canning and How to Use Canned Food* (1916); John G. Clark, *The Grain Trade in the Old Northwest* (1966); James H. Collins, *The Story of Canned Foods* (1924); Edward A. Duddy and David A. Revzan, *The Physical Distribution of Fresh Fruits and Vegetables* (1937); Edward C. Hampe, Jr., and Merle Wittenberg, *The Lifeline of America* (1964); Magnus Pyke, *Food Science and Technology* (1964); Wells A. Sherman, *Merchandising Fruits and Vegetables* (1928); George Rogers Taylor, *The Transportation Revolution, 1815–1860* (1951), and (with Irene D. Neu), *The American*

Railroad Network, 1861–1890 (1956), an important monograph showing how the numerous railroad gauges, and then the standardizing of gauges, affected transportation; U.S. Dept. of Commerce, *Canned Foods* (Misc. Series No. 54; 1917); Louis D. Weld, *Private Freight Cars and American Railways* (1908); F. Huntly Woodcock, *Canned Foods and the Canning Industry* (1938).

Refrigeration is a subject which has been neglected precisely because it touches so many different aspects of American life. But a start has been made in a few excellent works; for example, Oscar E. Anderson, *Refrigeration in America* (1953), and Richard O. Cummings, *The American Ice Harvests* (1949). For the earlier story of ice, see *The Americans: The National Experience*, Ch. 2, and Bibliographical Notes. And see: Edward A. Duddy, *The Cold Storage Industry in the United States* (1929); Clarence Francis, *A History of Food and Its Preservation* (1937); W. P. Hedden, "Refrigeration," in *Encyc. of Soc. Sci.* (15 vols. 1930–35), Vol. XIII, p. 196; J. S. Larson, J. A. Mixon, and E. C. Stokes, *Marketing Frozen Foods—Facilities and Methods* (1949); Alexander C. Twining, *The Manufacture of Ice on a Commercial Scale and with Commercial Economy* (1857); W. R. Woolwich, "Observations on Refrigeration in Great Britain and Western Europe," *Refrigerating Engineering*, LVII (1949), 658. Special topics can be followed in the periodicals of the industry, for example: *Ice and Refrigeration* (1891–); *The Ice Trade Journal*, for the late nineteenth century, and under later names *Cold Storage and Ice Trade Journal* (1899–1907) and *Refrigerating World* (1907–1934); *Quick-Frozen Foods and the Locker Plant* (1938–). An excellent brief sketch of Clarence Birdseye is in Alex Groner, *History of American Business and Industry* (1972), p. 257.

Other aspects of the history of food, food requirements, and preparation are touched on, for example, in histories of particular industries and products: W.

R. Aykroyd, *The Story of Sugar* (1967); Thomas C. Cochran, *The Pabst Brewing Company* (1948), a valuable wide-ranging study; William G. Panschar and Charles C. Slater, *Baking in America* (2 vols., 1956); John J. Riley, *A History of the American Soft Drink Industry* (1958; 1972). Numerous fugitive facts can be found in James Trager's whimsical and impressionistic *Foodbook* (1970), with bibliography. On the relation of food and food sanitation to public health, see, for example: Oscar E. Anderson, *The Health of a Nation* (1958); James H. Cassedy, *Charles V. Chapin and the Public Health Movement* (1962); René J. Dubos, *Louis Pasteur: Free Lance of Science* (1950); George Rosen, *A History of Public Health* (1958); Wilson G. Smillie, *Public Health . . . 1607–1914* (1955); John Snow, *Snow on Cholera* (1936). For the world context of the problems of food and diet, see: Club of Rome, *The Limits to Growth* (1972); Josue de Castro, *The Geography of Hunger* (1952); William and Paul Paddock, *Famine 1975!* (1967).

On the history of railroads and railroad cars, see *The Americans: The National Experience*, chs. 14 and 15, and Bibliographical Notes to Part Two. Of special interest on the history of the Pullman sleeping car and dining car are: Joseph Husband, *The Story of the Pullman Car* (1917; 1972); August Mencken, *The Railroad Passenger Car* (1957); John F. Stover, *American Railroads* (Chicago History of American Civilization, 1961), with bibliography; Jefferson Williamson, *The American Hotel* (1930). The novelist William Dean Howells was fascinated by the experiences encompassed in the latest modes of transportation; see his plays, *The Parlor Car* (1876), *The Sleeping Car* (1883), *The Elevator* (1885), *The Albany Depot* (1892), and *The Smoking Car* (1900).

FOR THE HISTORY of American building, we have numerous excellent books on the history of monuments, of public buildings, and of architectural styles, but fewer on the sorts of buildings that most Americans lived in, and almost none at all on the history of particular building materials. We are fortunate to have a scholarly and reliable guide into the subject in the writings of Carl Condit: *American Building* (Chicago History of American Civilization, 1968), the best brief introduction; *American Building Art: The Nineteenth Century* (1960), and *The Twentieth Century* (1961). For the earlier story, see *The Americans: The National Experience*, chs. 3, 18, 19, and Bibliographical Notes, pp. 441 f., 460 ff.

The very concept of "building materials" as the stuff that holds up a structure and holds it together became obsolete in twentieth-century American civilization, where construction aimed to create a whole environment, including the climate. By mid-century the mechanical and electrical utilities were commonly amounting to half of building costs and exacted the major resource of expert effort to shape temperature, light, and vision. Such apparatus came to dominate building considerations. For a lively, well-illustrated exploration of the new significance of mechanical environmental control (in contrast to structure), see Reynar Banham, *The Architecture of the Well-Tempered Environment* (1969), a work which transcends the familiar categories of architectural history and opens some interesting vistas.

The story of glass, for my purposes, has had to be approached through general histories of technology (e.g., Singer, et al., in General Section, above), through articles from popular, technical, and scientific journals, through biographies, trade periodicals, advertisements, company histories, and miscellaneous other sources. We need a comprehensive history of glass and its meaning for American civilization. Meanwhile, among the items I have found useful are: "The Colburn Window-Glass Machine," *Scientific Ameri-*

can Supplement, LXV (1908), 312–14; Arthur E. Fowle, *Flat Glass* (1924); J. F. McManus, *A Century of Glass Manufacture* (1918); Warren C. Scoville, *Revolution in Glassmaking: Entrepreneurship and Technological Change . . . 1880–1920* (1948); also, articles in *Architectural Record* (1891–), *Architectural Forum* (1892–), and *Journal of the Society of Architectural Historians* (1941–).

On other building materials, see: Turpin C. Bannister, "Bogardus Revisited, Part I: The Iron Fronts," *Journ. Soc. Arch. Hist.*, XV (Dec. 1956), 12–22; Kurt Billig, *Prestressed Concrete* (1953); James Bogardus, *Cast Iron Buildings: Their Construction and Advantages* (1856); William J. Fryer, Jr., "Iron Store-Fronts," *Architectural Review and American Builders' Journal*, I (1869), 620–22; Robert W. Lesley, *History of the Portland Cement Industry in the United States* (1924; 1972); Ernest L. Ransome and Alexis Sourbrey, *Reinforced Concrete Buildings* (1912); Charles van Ravenswaay, "America's Age of Wood," *Proc. Am. Antiq. Soc.*, LXXX, Pt. 1 (1970), 49–66; Arthur Woltersdorf, "The Father of the Skeleton Frame Building," *Western Architect*, XXXIII (1924), 75; *Report on the Building Stones of the United States and Statistics of the Quarry Industry* (Tenth Census of U.S., 1880). For the development of granite as a structural material and its place in the New England economy, see *The Americans: The National Experience*, ch. 3 and Bibliographical Notes.

The skyscraper has inspired a copious literature. Two good starting points are: *The Towers of New York* (1937), by Louis J. Horowitz and Boyden Sparkes, the informal memoirs of the Polish-born Horowitz, who was brought to the United States as a young man and became the building contractor for the Woolworth Building, the Equitable Building, and other skyscrapers; Carl Condit, *The Rise of the Skyscraper* (1952). Items of special interest include:

William Alex, "The Skyscraper: U.S.A.," *Perspectives U.S.A.*, VIII (Summer 1954), 86–103; Leopold Arnaud, "The Tall Building in New York in the Twentieth Century," *Journ. Soc. Arch. Hist.*, XI (May 1952), 15–18; William H. Berkmire, *Planning and Construction of High Office Buildings* (1898); Claude Bragdon, "Harvey Ellis," *Arch. Rev.* (Dec. 1908); W. C. Clark and J. L. Kingston, *The Skyscraper: A Study of the Economic Height of Modern Office Buildings* (1930); Carl Condit, "Sullivan's Skyscrapers as the Expression of Nineteenth Century Technology," *Technology and Culture*, I (1959), 78–93, and *Chicago Since 1910: Building, Planning, and Urban Technology, 1910–1929* (1973); H. W. Desmond, "Rationalizing the Skyscraper," *Arch. Rec.*, XV (1904), 361–84; Barr Ferree, "The High Building and Its Art," *Scribner's Magazine*, XV (Mar. 1894), 297–318, "The Modern Office Building," *Inland Architect and News Record*, XXVII (1896), 4–5, 12–14, 23–24, 45–47; Joseph K. Freitag, *Architectural Engineering with Special Attention to High Building Construction* (1895); Paul Holcombe, *Depreciation and Obsolescence in the Tacoma Building* (1929); David Loth, *The City within a City: The Romance of Rockefeller Center* (1966); Hugh Morrison, "Buffington and the Skyscraper," *Art Bulletin*, XXVI (1944), 1–2; Francisco Mujica, *History of the Skyscraper* (1929); Irving K. Pond, *The Origin of the Skyscraper* (1939); Frank A. Randall, *History of the Development of Building Construction in Chicago* (1949; 1972); Michael Rosenauer, *Modern Office Buildings* (1955); Montgomery Schuyler, "The 'skyscraper' up to date," *Arch. Rec.* (Jan.–Mar. 1899); Earle Shultz and Walter Simmons, *Offices in the Sky* (1959); Col. W. A. Starrett, *Skyscrapers and the Men Who Build Them* (1928); J. Carson Webster, "The Skyscraper: Logical and Historical Considerations," *Journ. Soc. Arch. Hist.*, XVIII (1959), 126–39; Winston Weisman, "New York and the Problem of the First

Skyscraper," *Journ. Soc. Arch. Hist.*, XII (Mar. 1953), 13–21; John K. Winkler, *Five and Ten: The Fabulous Life of F. W. Woolworth* (1940), and F. W. Woolworth Co., *Woolworth's First 75 Years* (1954), on the Woolworth Building.

On plumbing, plumbing fixtures, and water supply (in addition to references on urban and suburban water and sanitation for Part Four, above), see: M. N. Baker, *The Quest for Pure Water* (1948); Nelson M. Blake, *Water for the Cities* (1956); Glenn Brown, *Water Closets: A Historical, Mechanical and Sanitary Treatise* (1884); James P. Kirkwood, *Report on the Filtration of River Waters, for the Supply of Cities as Practised in Europe* (1869); James J. Lawler, *American Sanitary Plumbing* (1896); *The Way Things Work* (2 vols., 1969–72), for the mechanism of modern water closets; Lawrence Wright, *Clean and Decent* (1960); Louis P. Cain, "Raising and Watering a City . . . Chesbrough and Chicago's First Sanitary System," *Technology and Culture*, XIII (July 1972), 353–72.

We need a history of central heating and air conditioning. The following (among other works I have drawn on) are a beginning: Carrier Engineering Corporation, *The Story of Manufactured Weather* (1919); Carrier Corporation, *Twenty-Five Years of Air Conditioning, 1915–1940* (1947); Willis H. Carrier, "The Economy of Man-Made Weather," *Scientific American*, CXLVIII (1933), 199–202, and (with Realto E. Cherne and Walter A. Grant) *Modern Air Conditioning, Heating and Ventilating* (1940); Margaret Ingels, *Willis Haviland Carrier, Father of Air Conditioning* (1952); Ruth Eugenie Mier, "John Gorrie, Florida Medical Pioneer and Harbinger of Air Condition-

ing," unpublished M.A. Thesis (John B. Stetson Univ., De Land, Fla., 1938).

The general works on architecture especially relevant to this Part include: Wayne Andrews, *Architecture, Ambition, and Americans* (1955; Free Press Paperback, 1964), and *Architecture in Chicago and Mid-America* (1968); Walter C. Behrendt, *Modern Building* (1937); John Burchard and Albert Bush-Brown, *The Architecture of America: A Social and Cultural History* (1961); Carl Condit, *The Chicago School of Architecture* (1964); James M. Fitch, *American Building: The Forces That Shape It* (1948); Sigfried Giedion, *Mechanization Takes Command* (1948; Norton Paperback, 1969), and *Space, Time and Architecture* (1949); Hugh Morrison, *Louis Sullivan: Prophet of Modern Architecture* (1935); Lewis Mumford, *Sticks and Stones* (1924), *The Brown Decades . . . 1865–1895* (1931; Dover Paperback, 1955), *Technics and Civilization* (1934), *The City in History* (1961), and (ed.) *The Roots of Contemporary American Architecture* (1952); George Nelson, *The Industrial Architecture of Albert Kahn, Inc.* (1939); Mark L. Peisch, *The Chicago School of Architecture: Early Followers of Sullivan and Wright* (1965); Adolf K. Placzek, "A Brief Review of the Decade's Architectural Literature," *Journ. Soc. Arch. Hist.*, XXIV (Mar. 1965), 34–35; Montgomery Schuyler, *American Architecture and Other Writings* (ed. William H. Jordy and Ralph Coe, 1961); Arthur Siegel (ed.), *Chicago's Famous Buildings* (1965); Louis H. Sullivan, *Kindergarten Chats (Revised 1918) and Other Writings* (1947); Frank Lloyd Wright, *Modern Architecture* (1931) and *The Natural House* (1954).

PART SIX

MASS-PRODUCING THE MOMENT

WHATEVER ELSE can be said of Time, it is without doubt one of the most difficult subjects to talk or write

about. This perhaps explains why so much of the talk about Time consists of truisms such as "Time is money," "A stitch in time saves nine," etc., and why so much of the writing about Time is metaphysical, mystic, or unintelligible. It is difficult to describe an epoch's attitude toward time (even our own epoch's); and we take refuge in simple notions of haste and speed. A valuable introduction that gives us some perspective on our own peculiar view of time is found in Wyndham Lewis, *Time and Western Man* (1927; Beacon Paperback, 1957) and J. T. Fraser (ed.), *The Voices of Time: A Cooperative Survey of Man's Views of Time as Understood and Described by the Sciences and by the Humanities* (1966). Neither of these books is light reading, but even a brief perusal of them will suggest the elusiveness and subtlety of the subject, and remind us that, as times change, so "time" changes.

The best introduction to the modern American view of time is Daniel Bell's brilliant essay "Work and Its Discontents" (1956), reprinted in his *End of Ideology* (1960), at pp. 222–62, to which I am much indebted. An appropriate approach to "time" in the era of this volume is through the literature on efficiency and scientific management—which itself is a revealing fact. These works significantly deal with time as a stock of something to be "budgeted," scarce less because each fragment of it is unique than because the whole stock is scarce, i.e., an "economic good." The items I have found most useful and/or most revealing include: James P. Baughman (ed.), *The History of American Management* (selections from the *Business History Review*, 1969); Reinhard Bendix, *Work and Authority in Industry* (1956; Harper Torchbook, 1963); Samuel Haber, *Efficiency and Uplift: Scientific Management in the Progressive Era, 1890–1910* (1964); Roland Mann, *The Arts of Top Management* (1971); James E. Webb, *Space Age Management, The Large-Scale Approach* (1969), an important book by one of the most successful of twentieth-century large-scale managers; William

H. Whyte, *The Organization Man* (1956). On watch- and clock-making, see Henry G. Abbott (pseud. of G. H. A. Hazlitt), *The Watch Factories of America, Past and Present . . . from 1809 to 1888* (1888); Carl W. Drepperd, *American Clocks and Clockmakers* (2d ed., 1858).

Frederick Winslow Taylor (1856–1915), one of the most enticing and bizarre of the leading figures in this epoch, for some reason has not commanded the attention he and his ideas merit from historians. The basic work about him remains the naïve but well-documented biography by Frank B. Copley, *Frederick W. Taylor: Father of Scientific Management* (2 vols., 1923), which can be complemented by the fascinating, if oversubtle, *Frederick Taylor: A Study in Personality and Innovation* (1970), by Sudhir Kakar, who grasps the genius of Taylor which he interprets psychoanalytically. A convenient brief selection of Taylor's writings and statements is found in *An American Primer* (ed. Daniel J. Boorstin; 2 vols., 1966; New American Library Paperback, 1966), with a critical essay by Daniel Bell. The most accessible collection of Taylor's writings and views is Frederick W. Taylor, *Scientific Management: Comprising . . . Shop Management, Principles of Scientific Management, Taylor's Testimony before the Special House of Representatives Committee* (1947). For Brandeis' views of scientific management, see Alpheus T. Mason, *Brandeis: A Free Man's Life* (1947) and Alfred Lief (ed.), *The Social and Economic Views of Mr. Justice Brandeis* (1930). The principal writings of the Gilbreths include: Frank B. Gilbreth, *Primer of Scientific Management* (1912), and *Fatigue Study* (1919); Mrs. Lillian E. Gilbreth, *The Psychology of Management* (1914), *Time Study* (1920), *The Home-Maker and Her Job* (1927), and *Living With Our Children* (1928). Their principal collaborative book was *Time Study and Motion Study, as Fundamental Factors in Planning and Con-*

trol (1920). The home life of the Gilbreths was hilariously described in the best-selling novel (1948) and movie (1950), *Cheaper by the Dozen.*

A good introduction to the acute and imaginative ideas of Elton Mayo (1880–1949) is *The Social Problems of an Industrial Civilization* (1949), with a valuable appendix (pp. 132–40) surveying the studies of the Department of Industrial Research of the Graduate School of Business Administration of Harvard University, and providing a bibliography. And see the collection of suggestive essays, Clyde E. Dankert and others (eds.), *Hours of Work* (1965).

On the history of an American system of manufacturing and its earlier roots, see *The Americans: The National Experience*, chs. 4 and 5, and Bibliographical Notes.

AMONG THE MORE interesting phenomena in the sociology of knowledge is the fact that many of those remarkable and experience-changing developments of the twentieth century which I recount in Book Two as "The Decline of the Miraculous" have scarcely entered the history school books. The rigidity of the categories of academic history is nowhere better illustrated. And the writing of solid histories of the telephone, of the phonograph, of photography, of radio, and of television and allied topics has required of its authors a special independence of mind. The writings of Marshall McLuhan boldly forage across academic boundaries, providing brilliant insights and appealing slogans, in an often cryptic style: *The Mechanical Bride* (1951), *The Gutenberg Galaxy* (1962), and *Understanding Media* (1964). Many of the topics discussed in Part Six are illuminated by *The Lonely Crowd* (1950), by David Riesman (with Nathan Glazer and Reuel Denney). A convenient vista of how technological changes looked at the time is Ernest V. Heyn, *A Century of Wonders: 100 Years of Popular Science* (1972).

The best avenue into the history of the phonograph is Roland Gelatt's readable and well-researched *The Fabulous Phonograph* (2d ed., 1965). Other items of special interest include: Jacques Barzun, *Music in American Life* (1956); Semi J. Begun, *Magnetic Recording* (1949); Emile Berliner, *The Loose Contact Transmitter* (address before the Telephone Society of Washington, Dec. 1, 1910), *A Reminiscence* (address before the Telephone Pioneers of America, Nov. 14, 1912), and *The Development of the Talking Machine* (address to Franklin Institute of Philadelphia, May 21, 1913); George L. Frow, *Guide to the Edison Cylinder Phonograph* (1970); Cynthia Hoover, *Music Machines— American Style* (1971), catalogue of an Exhibition at The National Museum of History and Technology, Washington, D.C., which possesses a remarkable collection of early phonographs; Lawrence Lessing, *Man of High Fidelity: Edwin Howard Armstrong* (1956); Oliver Read and Walter L. Welch, *From Tin Foil to Stereo* (1959); John Philip Sousa, "The Menace of Mechanical Music," *Appleton's Magazine*, VIII (Nov. 1906), p. 7; Henry Swoboda (ed.), *The American Symphony Orchestra* (1967), especially chs. 3, 12–17; Frederic W. Wile, *Emile Berliner, Maker of the Microphone* (1926); *The Phonograph and How to Use It* (National Phonograph Company, 1900). For some further suggestions on the phonograph, see my book *The Image* (1962; Atheneum Paperback, 1972), especially Ch. 4, and bibliography. For other references specially related to music, see Bibliographical Notes, above, to Part Four; for references on Thomas A. Edison, see notes to Part Nine, below.

While the literature on the history of American photography is more copious than that on the phonograph, it tends to fall into two classes: works technical or antiquarian, for the professional photographer or the buff; or works treating photography as "art" in costly, oversize tomes, lavishly illustrated. Despite the number of first-rate volumes of both these sorts, we still need a comprehensive account of the place of photography in American civilization—of how it has been shaped, and of the reshapings of experience it has made possible. A modest experiment in this direction for the latest period is my book entitled *The Image* (1962; Atheneum Paperback, 1972), with accompanying bibliography. The best general introduction is Beaumont Newhall, *The History of Photography* (rev. ed., 1964), with bibliography. From the extensive literature, some of the works I have found especially useful include: Carl W. Ackerman, *George Eastman* (1930); C. E. K. Mees, *From Dry Plates to Ektachrome Film, A Story of Photographic Research* (1961); Richard Rudisill, *Mirror Image* (1971), the story of the daguerreotype; Robert Taft, *Photography and the American Scene: A Social History, 1839–1889* (1938; Dover Paperback, 1964). For references on Alfred Stieglitz and on photography as art, see Bibliographical Notes for Part Eight, below; for Thomas A. Edison, notes to Part Nine, below. The history of photography and cinematography can be envisaged in the excellent exhibits and collections of the Museum of Modern Art, New York City, N.Y., of Eastman House, Rochester, N.Y., and of The Library of Congress and The National Museum of History and Technology, Washington, D.C.

The movies have inspired a literature even more extensive than that on still photography. In addition to the two kinds of books which account for the bulk of books and journals on photography, there is a lively literature of biography—of directors, producers, cinematographers, and actors—and there begins to be a valuable library of books which use the movies as an index and source for social history. But we need histories of the effect of motion pictures on the tenor of daily life. The best way into the subject is still *A Million and One Nights* (1926), by Terry

Ramsaye (1885–1954), who was born in Tonganoxie, Kansas, began life as a journalist, produced Charlie Chaplin films, managed movie theaters, and eventually became editor of Pathé News and of the *Motion Picture Herald* (until 1941). Ramsaye communicates the rapture, suspense, and boundless optimism of the early days of film. A good short history is Arthur Knight, *The Liveliest Art* (1957), which can be complemented by the American Film Institute's *The American Film Heritage* (1972), a collection of illustrated, insightful essays on film-genres, on individual films and filmmakers. For research into the history of American films and to help us discover the film resources for American social history, we now have the incomparable *American Film Institute Catalog* (1971–) which in numerous volumes will offer essential information on American films (including features, shorts, and newsreels) since the beginning, with admirably complete indexes of names, credits, and subjects.

Of the vast and miscellaneous literature, the works I have found most useful include: Frank Capra, *The Name Above the Title* (1971); Charles Chaplin, *My Autobiography* (1964); "Mass Culture and Mass Media," *Daedalus*, XC (Spring 1960), a collection of essays; Raymond Fielding, *The Newsreel* (1972); Richard Griffith and Arthur Mayer, *The Movies: The Sixty-Year Story* (1957), copiously illustrated; Pauline Kael, *I Lost It At the Movies* (1965), and *Kiss Kiss Bang Bang* (1968); Paul Rotha and Richard Griffith, *The Film Till Now* (rev. ed., 1960); Richard Schickel, *The Disney Version: The Life, Times, Art and Commerce of Walt Disney* (1968), and *Second Sight: Notes on Some Movies, 1965–70* (1972); Gilbert V. Seldes, *The Movies Come from America* (1937); Paul Tabori, *Alexander Korda* (1966), esp. chs. 4 and 5; Elizabeth Taylor, *Elizabeth Taylor* (1965). Other insights into the meaning of filmmaking to its makers and to the nation are found in Leo Rosten's brilliant *Hollywood: The*

Movie Colony, The Movie Makers (1945) and in the better novels about Hollywood, including Budd Schulberg, *What Makes Sammy Run?* (1941) and Nathanael West's *The Day of the Locust* (1939).

For the history of radio and television we are fortunate to have the masterful three-volume work by Erik Barnouw, *A Tower in Babel: A History of Broadcasting in the United States to 1933* (1966), *The Golden Web: A History of Broadcasting in the United States, 1933–1953* (1968), and *The Image Empire: A History of Broadcasting in the United States from 1953* (1970), a pioneer survey which combines a perceptive and informed chronicle of the industry and its performers with suggestions on how broadcasting touched and shaped American life. Anyone seriously interested in the subject must read Barnouw's volumes; they will lead him into the other literature, which is not rich. Some other works which I have found helpful on radio, on television, and on the problems of broadcasting, include: Julian L. Bernstein, *Video Tape Recording* (1960); Leo Bogart, *The Age of Television: A Study of Viewing Habits and the Impact of Television on American Life* (1956); George Everson, *The Story of Television: The Life of Philo T. Farnsworth* (1949); Raymond Fielding (ed.), *A Technological History of Motion Pictures and Television* (1967), an anthology; Fred W. Friendly, *Due to Circumstances Beyond Our Control . . .* (1967); Kurt Lang and Gladys E. Lang, *Politics and Television* (1968), some illuminating case studies; Robert E. Lee, *Television: The Revolution* (1944); Lawrence Lessing, *Man of High Fidelity: Edward Howard Armstrong* (1956); *Life* magazine, LXXI (Sept. 10, 1971), an issue commemorating the twenty-fifth anniversary of television; Eugene Lyons, *David Sarnoff* (1966); W. Rupert Maclaurin, *Invention and Innovation in the Radio Industry* (1949); Newton N. Minow, *Equal Time: The Private Broadcaster and the Public Interest* (1964), essays by a vigorous chairman of the Federal Communications Commission, including his influential chapter "The Vast Wasteland"; Alfred P. Sloan Foundation, *On the Cable: The Television of Abundance* (1971), the report of the Sloan Commission on Cable Communications.

On the newly popular American visual and sound media as a touchstone of American civilization in the twentieth century, see Richard Schickel's illuminating "Entertainment Arts: Theater, Music, and Film," in *American Civilization* (ed. Daniel J. Boorstin, 1972), Ch. 10. Also helpful on the context are the writings of Gilbert V. Seldes, for example: *The Seven Lively Arts* (1924), *The Great Audience* (1950), *The Public Arts* (1956).

The new arts of copying still need their chronicler. By 1970 it appeared that xerography and similar techniques would have widespread effects on business and government, and might even make obsolete the existing laws of copyright. For an introduction to the subject, see John Dessauer and Harold E. Clark (eds.), *Xerography and Related Processes* (1965), a technical description, and John H. Dessauer, *My Years With Xerox: The Billions Nobody Wanted* (1971). On the history of the typewriter there are two especially useful works: Bruce Bliven, *The Wonderful Writing Machine* (1954), and Richard N. Current, *The Typewriter and the Men Who Made It* (1954).

The story of the search for the spontaneous touches so many aspects of American life that it is difficult to offer a helpful brief bibliography. Some of the subjects I discuss in the text are explored at greater length in my book *The Image* (1962; Atheneum Paperback, 1972), and its bibliography. For the history of American newsgathering and reporting, the best general introductions are: Frank Luther Mott, *American Journalism* (3d ed., 1962), *The News in America* (1952), and Bernard A. Weisberger, *The American Newspaperman*

(Chicago History of American Civilization, 1961), and their bibliographies. On Pulitzer, see George Juergens, *Joseph Pulitzer and the New York World* (1966). On sensational reporting and the relation of the press to fair trials, see: American Newspaper Publishers Assn., *Free Press and Fair Trial* (1967); Assn. of the Bar of the City of New York, *Freedom of the Press and Fair Trial: Final Report with Recommendations* (1967); Ronald H. Beattie, *Manual of Criminal Statistics* (1950); Allen Churchill, *A Pictorial History of American Crime, 1849–1929* (1964); Barbara A. Curran, *Fair Trial—Free Press* (Am. Bar Fdn., 1964); Bill Doherty, *Crime Reporter* (1964); Howard Felsher and Michael Rosen, *The Press in the Jury Box* (1966).

One of the most amusing, if not cheering, books on what television means to the viewer is the saga of the indomitable Charles Sopkin, who locked himself in his New York apartment, rented five television sets in addition to the one he owned, watched all sets steadily for a full week, and lived to tell the tale in *Seven Glorious Days, Seven Fun-Filled Nights* (1968).

Of the extensive and uneven literature on sports in the United States, I have found Harold Seymour, *Baseball* (2 vols., 1960–71) an indispensable history. A sampling of the most useful works on baseball includes: *The Baseball Encyclopedia: The Complete and Official Record of Major League Baseball, 1876–1968* (1969); Francis C. Richter, *Richter's History and Records of Base Ball* (1914); Hy Turkin and S. C. Thompson, *The Official Encyclopedia of Baseball* (1956); David Q. Voight, *American Baseball* (1966). And see: Allison Danzig, *Oh, How They Played the Game: The Early Days of Football and the Heroes Who Made It Great* (1971).

On weather forecasting, see Donald R. Whitnah, *A History of the United States Weather Bureau* (1965).

BOOK THREE

A POPULAR CULTURE

PART SEVEN

THE THINNER LIFE OF THINGS

IN THE VAST LITERATURE about democracy in America, too much has been written on the political mechanics of an equalizing society and too little on the consequences of the equalizing and diffusing of the Good Things of Life. One reason why the popularization and transformation of property in the United States have been so inadequately chronicled is that the story has been frozen in Old World categories of "capitalism" vs. "socialism." Whole libraries have been written offering interpretations and exegeses of the political and economic theorists from Locke to Marx. But there has been a quite astonishing neglect of some of the more obvious facts about economic goods and the life of "property" in America.

The transformation of property by the modern limited-liability joint-stock corporation, even by the late twentieth century, had barely reached public consciousness. Despite large expenditures promoting the virtues of American "capitalism" (which have centered around the virtues of "free enterprise" and competition), hints of the diffusion of ownership and of the transformation in its meaning had reached few Americans.

The basic book, required reading for anyone interested in the characteristics of modern American civilization, is

Adolf A. Berle and Gardiner C. Means, *The Modern Corporation and Private Property* (1934; rev. ed., 1968). Berle's *20th Century Capitalist Revolution* (1954) brilliantly and concisely puts the modern American corporation into the context of political theory and economic history. For some of the peculiar consequences of the novelties and ambiguities of law in America for education, for the legal profession, and for other aspects of American life, see *The Americans: The Colonial Experience,* especially Parts Six and Seven, and *The National Experience,* chs. 6, 11, 12, 25, 29, and Part Eight, and relevant Bibliographical Notes. For the legal profession and the opportunities of incorporation, see above, Bibliographical Notes for Part One.

While the literature on the social consequences of the rise of the modern American corporation is meager, the scholarly books on corporation law and its relations to constitutional history are numerous. The best introduction to the history of the business corporation in the United States is Edwin Merrick Dodd, *American Business Corporations until 1860* (1954). Other items (in addition to the works suggested in the General Section, above) that I have found of special interest include: Louis D. Brandeis, *Business—A Profession* (1914), *Other People's Money* (1914), and *The Curse of Bigness* (1934); James Burnham, *The Managerial Revolution* (1941), a stimulating, if somewhat sensational, account of the shifting centers of managerial power; Alfred D. Chandler, Jr., and Stephen Salsbury, *Pierre S. du Pont and the Making of the Modern Corporation* (1971); Francis L. Eames, *The New York Stock Exchange* (1968); J. Kenneth Galbraith, *The Affluent Society* (1958), *The Great Crash* (1955), and *The New Industrial State* (1967); Walton Hamilton, *The Politics of Industry* (1957, Vintage Paperback, 1967), brilliant and suggestive; James Willard Hurst, *The Legitimacy of the Business Corporation in the Law of the United*

States, 1780–1970 (1970); Matthew Josephson, *The Money Lords: The Great American Finance Capitalists, 1925–1950* (1972); Alfred Lief (ed.), *The Social and Economic Views of Mr. Justice Brandeis* (1930); E. Victor Morgan and W. A. Thomas, *The Stock Exchange* (1962); Humphrey B. Neill, *The Inside Story of the Stock Exchange* (1950); Robert Sobel, *AMEX: A History of the American Stock Exchange, 1921–1971* (1973). Accessible sources of recent information on corporations are the annual volumes of *Statistical Abstract of the United States.* News of the politics of corporations and the problems of shareholders' democracy is competently reported in the *Wall Street Journal;* readable and well-researched articles on corporations, their ownership, management and typology are found in *Fortune* (1930–).

On the history of installment selling, the basic work is Edwin R. A. Seligman's solid *Economics of Instalment Selling* (2 vols., 1927), but there is not to my knowledge a comparable study for the later period. Other useful works include: Robert H. Cole, *Consumer and Commercial Credit Management* (1968); *Instalment Credit* (Am. Inst. of Banking, 1954); Edgar R. McAlister, *Retail Instalment Credit: Growth and Legislation* (1964); Martin J. Meyer, *Credit-Cardmanship* (1971); Clyde W. Phelps, *The Role of the Sales Finance Companies in the American Economy* (1952). Essentials of the story of installment credit and of franchising will be found in histories of automobile companies and in biographies of their leaders; for example, in Allan Nevins and Frank Hill, *Ford* (3 vols., 1954–63), and Alfred P. Sloan, Jr., *My Years with General Motors* (1964).

A popular introduction to franchising is Harry Kursh, *The Franchise Boom* (rev. ed., 1968), which can be supplemented by the solid facts in publications of the U.S. Dept. of Commerce, for example, *Franchise Company Data* (1966), and later volumes. Much of the literature on franchising is sponsored by the franchisors themselves to create a market for their franchises, but there is a growing monographic literature which is not self-serving. A window to the franchising world is the classified advertising columns of the *Wall Street Journal*, where numerous opportunities for franchises are offered. And see: J. A. H. Curry and others, *Partners for Profit* (Am. Management Assn., 1966); Robert M. Dias and Stanley I. Gurnick, *Franchising* (1969); *Directory of Franchising Organizations* (1966); Charles M. Hewitt, Jr., *Automobile Franchise Agreements* (1956); Edwin H. Lewis, *The Franchise System of Distribution* (U. of Minn., for Small Bus. Adm., 1963); Management Conference on Franchising, *Franchising Today* (1968); Robert Rosenberg (with Madelon Bedell), *Profits from Franchising* (1969).

Packaging has been not only skimped, but virtually ignored as a historical phenomenon. Yet there are few developments more interesting or more suggestive for the sociology of knowledge, for the shaping of the consumer's world, and, in a word, for the transforming of everyday experience. The pioneer book, still the most revealing on the subject, is Richard B. Franken and Carroll B. Larrabee, *Packages That Sell* (1928), which should be complemented by Larrabee's *How to Package for Profit* (1935). Works of special interest include: Louis C. Barail, *Packaging Engineering* (1954), offering clues to the elaboration and professionalizing of packaging techniques; *Productivity Report: Packaging* (Anglo-American Council on Productivity, Sept. 1950); Alex Davis, *Package and Print, The Development of Container and Label Design* (1967), a useful avenue into the history of package design and materials; Milner Gray, *Package Design* (1955); Report to The American Foundation for Management Research, Inc., *The Role of Packaging in the U.S. Economy* (Arthur D. Little, Inc., 1966); Hearings before the Subcommittee on Antitrust and Monopoly of the U.S. Senate, published as *Packaging and Labeling Practices* (G.P.O., 1961).

The most comprehensive survey in print of the shifting motives, techniques, and materials of packaging can be found in the relevant publications of the American Management Association, which would include the following: *Profitable Packaging* (1932); *Changing Trends in Packaging* (1933); *Packaging Materials* (1935); *Packaging Engineering* (1935); *Packaging Design* (1937); *Merchandising Aspects of Packaging* (1938); *Changes in Packaging Technique* (1941)); *The Economics of Packaging* (1941); *Package Standardization and Simplification* (1942); *The Package as a Selling Tool* (1946); *Consumer Packaging—Its Technique and Psychology* (1948); *Increasing Packaging Effectiveness at the Retail Level* (1950); *Controlling Packaging Costs* (1952); *Advances in Packaging Material and Design* (1953); *Increasing Profitability Through Better Packaging* (1954); *New Potentials in Consumer Packaging* (1955); *Company Approaches to Better Packaging* (1956); *Developments in Automatic Packaging Equipment* (1956); *A Basic Guide to Preparing Packaging Specifications* (1956); *Marketing Research Reports on Packaging* (1957); *Packaging for Profits* (1960); *The Package: Key Component of Marketing Strategy* (1964); *Profitability and Penetration Through Packaging* (1965); *Consumer-Oriented Packaging* (1967). Additional references on the relation of packaging to advertising, on brand naming, consumer motivation, retailing, and consumption in general, are found in Bibliographical Notes to Part Two, above. For packaging developments in relation to food and diet, see Bibliographical Notes to Part Five, above.

A wide range of modern American developments take on a new aspect when one thinks of them as a kind of packaging. Examples include the rise of ready-made clothing (Part Two, above), housing and glass (Part Four, Part Five), the phonograph, photograph, and efficiency engineering (Part Six), etc. In fact, there are few characteristically modern developments which could not be treated as a kind of packaging.

THE AMERICAN ATTITUDE toward language in the years after the Civil War must be viewed as a later expression of distinctive developments reaching back to the years of the first settlements. For those earlier phases, see *The Americans: The Colonial Experience*, Parts Ten, Eleven, and Twelve and *The National Experience*, Parts Six and Seven, and their respective Bibliographical Notes. A basic guide to reading about the American Language is found there. Here I will mention works which relate specifically to the aspects of language treated in Part Eight of the present volume, or general works which have appeared since my earlier volumes.

The best general introduction to the subject, and a delight to read, is Raven I. McDavid, Jr.'s revision and abridgment into one volume, *The American Language* (1963), of H. L. Mencken's three volumes. A good short introduction is Albert Marckwardt, *American English* (1958; Galaxy Paperback). The layman interested mainly in the facts of the everyday usage of language needs again to be reminded that there is no subject more clouded by pedantic passions or more befuddled by the timid dogmas of the literati. The special character of the ever-more-democratized American language seems somehow—both among specialists and among laymen—to inflame these passions and freeze these dogmas. As a result, the problem of "proper" language has possessed a peculiar significance in American academic debate and has embroiled American men of letters in quarrels over questions of linguistic propriety which English literati, for example, have long assumed to be permanently settled beyond need of discussion. A handy and amusing introduction to the embattled linguists and their lay critics is *Dictionaries and THAT Dictionary: A Casebook on the Aims of Lexicographers and the Targets of Reviewers* (ed. James Sledd and Wilma R. Ebbitt, 1962), which collects reviews of *Webster's Third New International Dictionary* (1961). And see Raven I. McDavid, Jr., "False Scents and Cold Trails: the Pre-publication Criticism of the Merriam *Third*," *Journal of English Linguistics*, V (March 1971), 101–21, for a witty and dispassionate post-mortem on THAT dictionary.

The basic reference works for the later period, too, remain the great historical dictionaries. An indispensable volume is *A Dictionary of Americanisms on Historical Principles* (ed. Mitford M. Mathews; 2 vols., 1951; one-vol. ed., 1960). It can be supplemented by *A Dictionary of American English on Historical Principles* (ed. Sir William A. Craigie and James R. Hulbert; 4 vols., 1938). But there is no substitute for the monumental *Oxford English Dictionary . . . On Historical Principles* (ed. James A. H. Murray and others; 12 vols. and one supp. to date, 1933); the supplementary volume contains many items on American usage of interest for my chapters. A less costly small-print edition in two volumes appeared in 1971 with magnifying glass supplied. Especially useful for the rising power of the colloquial is the bold *Dictionary of American Slang* (ed. Harold Wentworth and Stuart B. Flexner, 1960), which chronicles and illustrates the emergence of American slang words and expressions on historical principles and offers a helpful general introduction, along with some suggestive discursive appendices on such topics as Children's Bathroom Vocabulary and Synonyms for Drunk, together with an invaluable bibliography.

The background in linguistic science for the transformed attitudes to grammar can be glimpsed conveniently in the selection of essays by Edward Sapir, *Culture, Language, and Personality* (ed. David G. Mandelbaum, U. of Cal. Press Paperback, 1956). For a more technical exposition, see Leonard Bloomfield, *Language* (1933), or *Language History* (1965). For an introduction to the newer approach to grammar, see Charles C. Fries, *American English Grammar* (1940), and (with Robert Lado) *English Sentence Patterns* (1947, 1958). And for samples of the new-style language textbooks, see the works of the popular and successful Paul Roberts: *Understanding Grammar* (1954); *Patterns of English* (1956); *Understanding English* (1958); *English Sentences* (1962); and *Modern Grammar* (1967, 1968). For the relationship between linguistic science and teaching, see: Harold B. Allen (ed.), *Applied English Linguistics* (1958); James J. Lynch and Bertrand Evans, *High School English Textbooks* (1963); Ruth G. Strickland, *The Contribution of Structural Linguistics to the Teaching of Reading, Writing, and Grammar in the Elementary Schools* (1963).

Other works on language of special interest include: C. Merton Babcock, *The Ordeal of American English* (1961); Carl Bode, *Mencken* (1969); Jack C. Gray, *Words, Words, and Words about Dictionaries* (1963); Robert A. Hall, *Leave Your Language Alone!* (1950); George P. Krapp, *The English Language in America* (2 vols., 1925); Donald J. Lloyd and Harry R. Warfel, *American English in Its Cultural Setting* (1956); Mitford M. Mathews, *Beginnings of American English* (1931; 1962); Mario Pei, *The Story of Language* (1957), and *The Many Hues of English* (1967); Thomas Pyles, *Words and Ways of*

American English (1952), and *The Origins and Development of the English Language* (1964); Douglas C. Stenerson, *H. L. Mencken: Iconoclast from Baltimore* (1971). And see the editor's introduction to each of the principal American dictionaries of the mid-twentieth century, for example: Philip B. Gove's introduction to *Webster's Third New International Dictionary* (1961); Jess Stein's introduction to *The Random House Dictionary of the English Language* (1966); William Morris' introduction to *The American Heritage Dictionary of the English Language* (1969). For special forms of American English, see: Ramon F. Adams, *Western Words* (1968); J. L. Dillard, *Black English: Its History and Usage in the United States* (1972), a volume of great interest in a new field the author calls "Social Dialectology," in which he argues that "lack of adequate structural and historical information about Black English . . . has been a major handicap to educational programs for Black children."

For delightful and amusing light on the immigration of language to the U.S.A., see the writings of Leo Rosten, especially *The Education of Hyman Kaplan* written under the nom de plume Leonard Ross (1937), and *The Joys of Yiddish* (1971).

I owe a great deal to the stimulus of conversations with Professor Edgar Dale of the Ohio State University and to the information he has given me about vocabulary studies, and the developing techniques of testing readability, in which he has been a leader. Of his numerous works, the following have been especially illuminating: Edgar Dale and Jeanne S. Chall, *A Formula for Predicting Readability* (Educational Research Bulletin, Ohio State Univ.), XXVII (1948), pp. 11-20, pp. 37-54, "Developing Readable Materials," Ch. IX of the *Fifty-fifth Yearbook of the National Society for the Study of Education*, in Part II, *Adult Reading:* 1956; Edgar Dale and Donald Reichert, *Bibliogra-*

phy of Vocabulary Studies (rev. ed., 1957).

In the era of Sputnik, a flurry of interest in the teaching of reading—halfway between faddish enthusiasm and reforming zeal—was sparked by Rudolf Flesch's *Why Johnny Can't Read* (1955), followed by Arthur S. Trace's *What Ivan Knows That Johnny Doesn't* (1961) and by a flood of other words of national self-flagellation, of hysteria, and of self-congratulation. A useful survey of these books is Selma Fraiberg, "The American Reading Problem," *Commentary*, XXXIX (1965), 56–65. This phenomenon—revealing the volatile character of educational passion and opinion in a democratic society—is itself an event of interest to the American historian. A by-product of this movement was the growth of enthusiasm for techniques of speed-reading, which became the foundation of new professional specialities in the 1960's and '70's. Some interesting observations on language and technological society are offered by Herbert Marcuse in his *One-Dimensional Man* (1964).

ON THE ORIGINS of American oratory, see *The Americans: The National Experience*, Part Six, "American Ways of Talking," especially Ch. 37, "A Declamatory Literature," and Bibliographical Notes. A clue to the significance and omnipresence of oratory in the United States in the late nineteenth and early twentieth centuries is the prevalence of multivolume sets of "Great Orators" in secondhand furniture stores and (when these still were common) secondhand bookstores. For some decades, sets of orations were a staple of the subscription-book publishers.

The best introduction to the once prominent place in American life of declamation and reading-aloud is to peruse one of William Holmes McGuffey's *Readers*. Fortunately one of these, *McGuffey's Fifth Eclectic Reader*, has recently been reprinted (New American Library Paperback, 1962; ed. with a helpful foreword by Henry Steele Commager) and is easily accessible. Richard D. Mosier's *Making the American Mind: Social and Moral Ideas in the McGuffey Readers* (1947) surveys the content of these books, and speculates on their effect from about 1837 to about 1900. And see: H. C. Minnich, *William Holmes McGuffey and His Readers* (1936); Melanchthon Tope, *A Biography of . . . McGuffey* (1929); Henry H. Vail, *A History of the McGuffey Readers* (1910).

The basic work on the movement from oratory to public speaking is Earl R. Wallace (ed.), *History of Speech Education in America* (1954). Rhetoric, the theoretical and philosophical framework for oratory, is a subject with a long and historic entanglement with philosophy, logic, metaphysics, aesthetics, theology, and (more recently) psychology. While this literature includes some of the most illuminating (and most stultifying) literary criticism, beginning with Aristotle's *Rhetoric*, much of the writing has been for other students of rhetoric. In the mid-twentieth century, interest in rhetoric in the United States was commonly associated with a neo-Aristotelian approach to education. The most respectable introduction to the American literature of rhetoric in the traditional mode is John Quincy Adams' *Lectures on Rhetoric and Oratory* (2 vols., 1810; and succeeding editions: a Russell and Russell reprint, 1962). A sampling of the literature on rhetoric (with American editions of British and continental rhetoricians) might include: Dudley Bailey (ed.), *Essays on Rhetoric* (1965); A. Craig Baird, *Rhetoric: A Philosophical Inquiry* (1965); Thomas W. Benson and Michael H. R. Prosser (eds.), *Readings in Classical Rhetoric* (1969); Hugh Blair, *An Abridgement of Lectures on Rhetoric* (1854), and *Lectures on Rhetoric and Belles Lettres* (new ed., 1865); George Campbell, *The Philosophy of Rhetoric*

(1963); Edward P. J. Corbett, *Classical Rhetoric for the Modern Student* (1965), and (with James L. Golden), *The Rhetoric of Blair, Campbell and Whateley* (1968); Thomas De Quincey, *Essays on Style, Rhetoric, and Language* (1893); Daniel Fogarty, *Roots for a New Rhetoric* (1968); Henry Hardwicke, *History of Oratory and Orators* (1896); Raymond F. Howes (ed.), *Historical Studies of Rhetoric and Rhetoricians* (1961); Samuel Neil, *The Elements of Rhetoric* (1854); Marie H. Nichols, *Rhetoric and Criticism* (1963); Mabel Platz, *Public Speaking* (1935); W. Ross Winterowd, *Rhetoric: A Synthesis* (1968). A lively account of the place of oratory in American education in the 1880's is found in Ray A. Billington, *Frederick Jackson Turner* (1973), chs. 1 and 2.

A vivid study of the contrast between the old and the new styles—between oratory and public speaking—is the contrast between the styles (and the concerns) of William Jennings Bryan and of Clarence Darrow, each spectacularly successful in his genre. More perhaps than any other nationally noted American politician, Bryan built his career, which can be followed in the popular biography by M. R. Werner (1920), on the shallow foundations of oratory. Darrow's autobiography, *The Story of My Life* (1932), can be supplemented by Irving Stone's lively popularization, *Clarence Darrow for the Defense* (1941), and Arthur Weinberg (ed.), *Clarence Darrow, Attorney for the Damned* (1957), and (ed. with Lila Weinberg) the interesting collection of Darrow's writings, *Verdicts Out Of Court* (1963). The confrontation of the two men and their two styles is dramatized in Jerome Lawrence and Robert Edwin Lee's play about the Scopes "Monkey" Trial of 1925, *Inherit the Wind* (1957), which became a successful movie and then entered American folklore as a staple of high school dramatic troupes. And see the account of that trial by the defendant: John T. Scopes

(with James Presley), *Center of the Storm* (1967).

For the development and the reach of the new style and its relation to technology, there is no more readable or more reliable source than Erik Barnouw's three volumes on the history of broadcasting in the United States (see above, Part Six). And then follow the speaking careers of successful practitioners of the new naturalistic art, for example: in Frank Freidel, *Franklin D. Roosevelt* (3 vols., 1952–56); Arthur M. Schlesinger, Jr., *The Age of Roosevelt* (3 vols., 1957–60); T. Harry Williams, *Huey Long* (1969). For the connections with the rise of public relations and the elaboration of press relations, see my book *The Image* (1962; Atheneum Paperback, 1972), especially chs. 1 and 2, and Bibliographical Notes. For the role of personality and public speaking in the press conference, see James E. Pollard, *The Presidents and the Press* (1947). Both the most popular evangelists and the most popular preachers of atheism offer interesting case histories of the techniques—old and new—of the public platform and the public microphone. See, for example: Orvin Larsen, *American Infidel: Robert G. Ingersoll* (1962); William G. McLoughlin, *Billy Sunday Was His Real Name* (1955); Bernard A. Weisberger, *They Gathered at the River: The Story of the Great Revivalists and Their Impact Upon Religion in America* (1958).

While academic historians when dealing with earlier periods are generally willing (however reluctantly) to admit to their ken writers and speakers who did not attain academic respectability in those earlier times, they have been noticeably snobbish about some of the most potent and significant figures of recent times. And while these academic historians have justified their studies of earlier figures (such as Ralph Waldo Emerson) by elevating publicists into philosophers, finding subtlety where there may have been only ambiguity, they have been much less generous to figures of their own era, especially to those who attained financial and popular success. A good example of this neglect is Dale Carnegie, whose books and programs have reached millions, shaping and expressing dominant attitudes of the age, but whose name does not appear in academic histories of public speaking. By the lucky chance of a long friendship with Dorothy Carnegie (Mrs. Dale Carnegie), a fellow Oklahoman and a Go-Getter in her own right, I have had an additional valuable perspective on the career of Dale Carnegie and on his remarkable enterprises. A short, authorized treatment (the only book on Dale Carnegie to my knowledge) is William Longgood, *Talking Your Way to Success: The Story of the Dale Carnegie Course* (1962). Among Dale Carnegie's writings are: *Public Speaking and Influencing Men in Business* (1926; 1937); *Lincoln the Unknown* (1932); *How to Win Friends and Influence People* (1936 and later eds.); *How to Stop Worrying and Start Living* (1944). See also Dorothy Carnegie (ed.), *Dale Carnegie's Scrapbook* (1959), *The Quick and Easy Way to Effective Speaking* (1962; a revision of Dale Carnegie's first book), and Dorothy Carnegie, *Don't Grow Old, Grow Up!* (1956).

FOR THE STORY of American education, especially higher education, in earlier times, see *The Americans: The Colonial Experience*, Part Six, and *The National Experience*, Ch. 20, and accompanying Bibliographical Notes. In my essay-review, "Universities in the Republic of Letters," *Perspectives in American History*, I (1967), 369–79, I have surveyed the bibliography of American higher education. In these notes I will mention only works which deal with this later period, or which have appeared since my earlier volumes went to press. A succinct and copiously illustrated survey of some of the distinctive characteristics of American education in the twentieth century is Marcus Cunliffe, "Teaching the Nation," Ch. VIII in *American Civilization* (ed. Daniel J. Boorstin, 1972).

The best book on American higher education since the Civil War is Laurence R. Veysey's masterful and readable *Emergence of the American University* (1965). On the history of land-grant institutions, the best introduction is Allan Nevins, *The State Universities and Democracy* (1962), and see also: Mary Turner Carriel, *The Life of Jonathan Baldwin Turner* (1961); Edward D. Eddy, Jr., *Colleges for Our Land and Time* (1957); Earle D. Ross, *Democracy's College: The Land Grant Movement in the Formative Stage* (1942). On Charles W. Eliot, see: Hugh Hawkins, *Between Harvard and America: The Educational Leadership of Charles W. Eliot* (1972); Henry James, *Charles W. Eliot* (2 vols., 1930); Edward A. Krug (ed.), *Charles W. Eliot and Popular Education* (1961). And see selections of Charles W. Eliot's writings; for example, *American Contributions to Civilization* (1907) and *A Late Harvest* (1924). On G. Stanley Hall, see Bibliographical Notes to Part Three, above.

For John Dewey, a convenient introduction is Joseph Ratner (ed.), *Intelligence in the Modern World: John Dewey's Philosophy* (Modern Library Giant, 1939), with introductory essay and a selection of Dewey's writings. A briefer selection is Martin S. Dworkin (ed.), *Dewey on Education* (1959). Of Dewey's numerous works, the following are among those most relevant here: *Democracy and Education* (1916); *Reconstruction in Philosophy* (1920); *The Quest for Certainty* (1929); *Experience and Education* (1938; 1963); *The Public and Its Problems* (1946). On higher education in this era, see also: Jacques Barzun, *We Who Teach* (1946), and *The House of Intellect* (1959); Carl L. Becker, *Cornell University; Founders and the Founding* (1943); Clarence F. Birdseye, *Individual Training in Our Colleges* (1907), and *The Reorgani-*

zaton of Our Colleges (1909); Philip Dorf, *The Builder, a Biography of Ezra Cornell* (1952); Abraham Flexner, *Universities, American, English, German* (1930); Nathan Glazer, *Remembering the Answers: Essays on the American Student Revolt* (1970); Oscar and Mary F. Handlin, *The American College and American Culture* (1970); Richard A. Hatch (comp.), *Some Founding Papers of the University of Illinois* (1967); Robert Maynard Hutchins, *The Higher Learning in America* (1936), and *Education for Freedom* (1943); Christopher Jencks and David Riesman, *The Academic Revolution* (1969); Howard H. Peckham, *The Making of the University of Michigan* (1967); Richard J. Storr, *The Beginnings of Graduate Education in America* (1953), and *Harper's University . . . a History of the University of Chicago* (1966); Thorstein Veblen, *The Higher Learning in America: A Memorandum on the Conduct of Universities by Business Men* (1918).

The best introduction to changing attitudes toward education in this period is Lawrence A. Cremin, *The Transformation of the School: Progressivism in American Education, 1876–1957* (1961), and the best brief survey of American secondary education at mid-century is James B. Conant, *The American High School Today* (1959). From the growing and notably uneven literature on American secondary education and its history, the descriptive works which I have found most valuable include: Bernard Bailyn, *Education in the Forming of American Society: Needs and Opportunities for Study* (1960), a bibliography and prospectus for further study on the early period; Paul E. Belting and A. W. Clevinger, *The High School at Work* (1939); Elmer E. Brown, *The Making of Our Middle Schools* (1902); John F. Brown, *The American High School* (1909); Lawrence A. Cremin, *American Education: The Colonial Experience, 1607–1783* (1970), the basic book for the early period; Merle Curti, *The Social Ideas of American Educators* (new ed.,

1959), a valuable survey; Walter J. Gifford, *Historical Development of the New York State High School System* (1922); H. G. Good, *A History of American Education* (1956; 1962); Orwin B. Griffin, *The Evolution of the Connecticut State School System, with Special Reference to the Emergence of the High School* (1928); Emit D. Grizzell, *Origin and Development of the High School in New England before 1865* (1923); G. Stanley Hall, *The New Movement in Education* (1891); Raymond P. Harris, *American Education* (1961); Silas Hertzler, *The Rise of the Public High School in Connecticut* (1930); Alexander J. Inglis, *The Rise of the High School in Massachusetts* (1911); Charles H. Judd, *The Evolution of a Democratic School System* (1918); Edward A. Krug, *The Secondary School Curriculum* (1960), and *The Shaping of the American High School* (1964); Marvin Lazerson, *Origins of the Urban School: Public Education in Massachusetts, 1870–1915* (1957); Martin Mayer, *The Schools* (1961), a survey by a skilled reporter; James McLachlen, *American Boarding Schools: A Historical Study* (1972); J. Murray Meiring, *The American High School* (Pretoria, South Africa; The Carnegie Corp. Visitor's Grant Committee, 1930); Adolphe E. Meyer, *An Educational History of the American People* (1957); Walter S. Monroe and Oscar F. Weber, *The High School* (1928); Richard D. Mosier, *Making the American Mind* (1947), on the McGuffey *Readers* and their influence; James Mulhern, *History of Secondary Education in Pennsylvania* (1969); National Congress of Parents and Teachers, *Golden Jubilee History* (1947); National Education Association, *Policies for Education in American Democracy* (1946); Robert E. Potter, *The Stream of American Education* (1967); Frank W. Smith, *The High School* (1916); William A. Smith, *Secondary Education in the United States* (1932); Harold Spears, *Secondary Education in American Life* (1941); Rena L. Vassar (ed.), *Social His-*

tory of American Education (2 vols., 1965), an anthology; Rush Welter, *Popular Education and Democratic Thought in America* (1962).

Of the extensive polemical literature (for or against American education as it is, or is supposed to be), the following is a mere sample: Donald Barr, *Who Pushed Humpty Dumpty? Dilemmas in American Education Today* (1971), by the headmaster of the Dalton School; Raymond E. Callahan, *Education and the Cult of Efficiency* (1962), an attack on the influence of fiscal decisions in educational policy; George S. Counts, *The Selective Character of American Secondary Education* (1969); Raymond P. Harris, *American Education: Facts, Fancies, & Folklore* (1961), a classroom teacher's defense of American education; Harry Kemelman, *Common Sense in Education* (1970), against the prevailing modes of higher education.

A BRILLIANT INTRODUCTION to art in twentieth-century America is Harold Rosenberg, "Aesthetic America: The Problem of Reality," Ch. XII in *American Civilization* (ed. Daniel J. Boorstin, 1972). In my interpretation I have been much influenced by Rosenberg and also by James S. Ackerman's writings, especially "The Demise of the Avant Garde: Notes on the Sociology of Recent American Art," *Comparative Studies in Society and History,* XI (1969), 371–84. A handy guide into the recent era is Barbara Rose, *America Art Since 1900* (1967). For the wider context, the earlier period, and the emergence of American styles in art, see: Virgil Barker, *American Painting: History and Interpretation* (1950); Henri Dorra, *The American Muse* (1967); James T. Flexner, *The Pocket History of American Painting* (1950; 1962), *That Wilder Image: The Painting of America's Native School from Thomas Cole to Winslow Homer* (1962), *Winslow Homer* (1966), *America's Old Masters* (rev. ed., 1967), and *Nineteenth Century*

American Painting (1970); Samuel M. Green, *American Art: A Historical Survey* (1966); Clement Greenberg, *Art and Culture: Critical Essays* (1961; 1967); Oskar Hagen, *The Birth of an American Tradition in Art* (1964); Hans Huth, *Nature and the American: Three Centuries of Changing Attitudes* (1957; Bison Paperback, 1972); John W. McCoubrey, *American Art 1700–1960: Sources and Documents* (1965); Jerome Mellquist, *The Emergence of an American Art* (1942; 1969); Sir Joshua Reynolds, *Discourses* (ed. Roger Fry, 1905); Edgar P. Richardson, *American Romantic Painting* (1944), an interpretive catalogue of paintings in American collections, and *The Way of Western Art, 1776–1914* (1939), *Washington Allston, A Study of the Romantic Artist in America* (1948), and *Paintings in America, from 1502 to the Present* (1965); John Ruskin, *Lectures on Architecture and Painting* (1853 and later eds.). Few other interpreters of the history of modern art are as perceptive, as original, and as persuasive as Harold Rosenberg, all of whose writings will reward and entice, for example: *The Tradition of the New* (1959), *The Anxious Object: Art Today and Its Audience* (1964), *Artworks and Packages* (1969), *Discovering the Present: Three Decades in Art, Culture and Politics* (1973). For some suggestions of the connection between the rising technology of repeatable experience (which I call "The Graphic Revolution") and art, see my book *The Image* (1962; Atheneum Paperback, 1972), especially Ch. 4, and appended bibliography.

A suggestive introduction to the problem of de-colonializing American art is Henry Cabot Lodge, "Colonialism in the United States," in his *Studies in History* (1884).

Among the histories of American art which try to define American-ness and modernity are: Virgil Barker, *From Realism to Reality in Recent Painting* (1959; 1968); Samuel L. M. Barlow, *The Astonished Muse* (1961); Martin Battersby, *The Decorative Twenties* (1969); Rudi Blesh, *Modern Art USA: Man, Rebellion, Conquest, 1900–1956* (1956); Milton W. Brown, *American Painting from the Armory Show to the Depression* (1955), and *The Story of the Armory Show* (1963); Henry Geldzahler, *New York Painting and Sculpture: 1940–1970* (1969); Neil Harris, *The Artist in American Society: The Formative Years, 1790–1860* (1966); Richard Kostelanetz (ed.), *The New American Arts* (1965); John Kouwenhoven, *Made in America* (1948; Norton Paperback under the title *The Arts in Modern American Civilization*, 1957); Russell Lynes, *The Art-Makers of Nineteenth Century America* (1970), and *Good Old Modern: An Intimate Portrait of the Museum of Modern Art* (1973); Lillian B. Miller, *Patrons and Patriotism . . . the Fine Arts in the United States, 1790–1860* (1966); Francis V. O'-Connor, *Federal Art Patronage, 1933 to 1943* (1966); Barbara Rose (ed.), *Readings in American Art Since 1900* (1968), a companion to her *American Art Since 1900* (1967); Aline B. Saarinen, *The Proud Possessors: The Lives, Times, and Tastes of Some Adventurous American Art Collectors* (1958), delightful and suggestive; Maurice Tuchman (ed.), *American Sculpture of the Sixties* (1967); Whitney Museum of American Art, *Pioneers of Modern Art in America* (intro. by Lloyd Goodrich, a catalogue of an exhibition, 1946); Frederick S. Wight, *Milestones of American Painting in Our Century* (1949), a catalogue of an exhibition at the Institute of Contemporary Art in Boston. For more philosophical or more personal efforts at definition: Rudolph Arnheim, *Art and Visual Perception* (1954); John I. H. Baur, *Revolution and Tradition in Modern American Art* (1951; 1967); George Biddle, *The Yes and No of Contemporary Art* (1957); *Camera Work* (1903–1917), a photographic quarterly, edited by Alfred Stieglitz; Waldo Frank, Lewis Mumford, Dorothy Norman, Paul Rosenfeld, and Harold Rugg (eds.), *America and Alfred Stieglitz* (1934); Lawrence Gowing, "Paint in

America," a review-article in the *New Statesman* (May 24, 1958); Robert Henri, *The Art Spirit* (1923; Lippincott Paperback, 1960); Gyorgy Kepes, *Language of Vision* (1944), *The New Landscape* (1956), and numerous works of his editing; Jackson Pollock, "My Painting," in *Possibilities: An Occasional Review* (Sept. 1947), p. 79. Among biographies and autobiographies of special interest: H. H. Arnason, *Calder* (1966); Thomas Hart Benton, *An Artist in America* (1968); Lloyd Goodrich and Doris Bry, *Georgia O'Keefe* (1970); George Grosz, *A Little Yes and a Big No* (1946); Dorothy Norman, *Alfred Stieglitz* (1960); Frank O'Hara, *Jackson Pollock* (1959).

BOOKS ON THE HISTORY of travel have too often left out the meaning of the travel experience for the traveler himself and his culture, for his notion of the commonplace, for his view of adventure, and for his ideas of how and where he can enlarge his knowledge of the world. Travel has been treated as an aspect of the history of transportation, of high finance (Why did Queen Isabella pawn her jewels? How did the railroad promoters secure their subsidies and their land grants?), of emigration, immigration, and the Westward movement. American travel to Europe has been treated as an aspect of "intellectual" history—e.g., Van Wyck Brooks, *The Pilgrimage of Henry James* (1925; 1972), and *The Dream of Arcadia: American Writers and Artists in Italy, 1760–1915* (1958)—or of reverse migration: Louis Adamic, *The Native's Return: An American Immigrant Visits Yugoslavia and Discovers his Old Country* (1934), and Theodore Saloutos, *They Remember America: The Story of Repatriated Greek-Americans* (1956). But by the mid-twentieth century, especially after the rise of photography and of air travel, travel abroad had become a new shaping influence on the American's view of the world. For earlier travel and travel literature, for travelers to America, and travel literature as a source of our knowledge of America, see Bibliographical Notes to *The Americans: The Colonial Experience*, General Section, and to *The Americans: The National Experience*, Parts Two and Five. For some suggestions of the meaning of innovating technology, see my book *The Image* (1962; Atheneum Paperback, 1972), Ch. 3, "From Traveler to Tourist: The Lost Art of Travel," and accompanying bibliography.

There is no better index to the increasing significance of overseas travel for Americans than the recent volumes of *Statistical Abstract of the United States* and the relevant maps in *The National Atlas of the United States*. The best available introduction to this history is Foster Rhea Dulles, *Americans Abroad: Two Centuries of European Travel* (1964). A vivid account of the experience of transatlantic steamship travel (1819–1968) is John Malcolm Brinnin, *The Sway of the Grand Saloon: A Social History of the North Atlantic* (1971). Other items of special interest include: Anna M. Babey, *Americans in Russia, 1776–1917* (1938); Harlan Cleveland, Gerard J. Mangone, John Clarke Adams, *The Overseas Americans* (1960), a survey which includes Americans teaching and doing business abroad; Alden Hatch, *American Express, 1850–1950* (1950); Christopher Hibbert, *The Grand Tour* (1969); Henry James, *The Art of Travel* (ed. Morton D. Zabel, 1958); Walter Johnson, *The Fulbright

Program: A History (1965); Louis H. Lehman, *Traveling to Prosperity* (1933), travel as a panacea for the problem of intergovernmental debts; Frank Matthews, "Our Annual Travel to Europe," *The Chautauquan* (1896), 569–72; Hiram Motherwell, "The American Tourist Makes History," *Harper's Magazine*, CLX (1929), 70–76; Philip Rahv (ed.), *Discovery of Europe: The Story of American Experience in the Old World* (1960); *Report to the President... from the Industry-Government Special Task Force on Travel* (1968); Louis Solomon, *Telstar: Communication Break-Through by Satellite* (1963); U.S. Congress, House of Rep., *Office of International Travel and Tourism*, Hearings before a Subcommittee of the Committee on Interstate and Foreign Commerce, H. of R., 87th Cong. 1st Sess., Mar. 28, 29, 30, Apr. 11, 12, 1961; Joseph Wechsberg, "The American Abroad," *Atlantic Monthly*, CC (1957), 264–68. Useful and accessible sources of American attitudes toward travel are the popular magazines for travelers, would-be travelers, or armchair explorers, e.g., *The National Geographic* (1888–); *Holiday* (1945–), and the promotional giveaway airline magazines, published monthly and found at passengers' seats.

For the history of the postcard, see Jefferson R. Burdick, *Pioneer Post Cards* (1964), and Frank Staff, *The Picture Postcard & Its Origins* (1966).

BOOK FOUR
THE FUTURE ON SCHEDULE

PART NINE

SEARCH FOR NOVELTY

THE STORY OF American invention has been told mainly from the point of view of the individual inventor. While this individualist emphasis has created a few folk heroes—Edison and Ford, for example—it has tended to ignore the impact of invention on the experience of the individual citizen. Emphasis on the heroic has led us to obscure some of the more distinctive features of the hopes and careers of the leading American inventors themselves, and sometimes even to overlook their own concern with the impact of their work on the lives of other individual Americans. It has also distracted us from one of the most remarkable characteristics of American civilization: the speed with which technological innovation becomes translated into novel experience for the millions.

Perhaps it would help us give our thinking about invention a focus appropriate to a wealthy, democratic society if we would think of Americans as not only adept inventors and organizers but also as "inventees" *par excellence.* By "inventees" I mean persons who are enriched, afflicted, or otherwise affected by an invention. For the literature on technology and innovation in general, see the General Section, above, and Bibliographical Notes to Parts Six and Seven. For the earlier period, see *The Americans: The National Experience,* Part One, and Bibliographical Notes.

Despite the fact that Thomas A. Edison was one of the most characteristic, most prolific, and most effective Americans of the age—his inventions reached from 1868, when he was only twenty-two and applied for his first patent, until nearly the day of his death in 1931—the serious literature about him and his work is sparse. The best introduction to the man and his work is Matthew Josephson, *Edison: A Biography* (1959), which draws copiously on Edison's notebooks and other unpublished materials. An interesting path into the story of electric lighting is Harold C. Passer's admirable monograph, *The Electrical Manufacturers, 1875–1900: A Study in Competition, Entrepreneurship, Technical Change, and Economic Growth* (1953; 1972). Other items of special interest here include: Arthur A. Bright, Jr., *The Electric-Lamp Industry: Technological Change and Economic*

Development from 1800 to 1947 (1949; 1972); George S. Bryan, *Edison, the Man and His Works* (1926); Frank L. Dyer and Thomas C. Martin, *Edison, His Life and Inventions* (2 vols., 1910; rev. ed., 1929); Henry Ford (with Samuel Crowther), *Edison as I Know Him* (1930); John W. Howell and Henry Schroeder, *History of the Incandescent Lamp* (1927); Forrest McDonald, *Insull* (1962); Malcom McLaren, *The Rise of the Electrical Industry in the 19th Century* (1943); Henry Schroeder, *Electric Light* (1923); Harold I. Sharlin, *The Making of the Electrical Age* (1963). Edison's original laboratory from Menlo Park can be seen where it has been rebuilt at the Greenfield Village museum at Dearborn, Michigan, and there are extensive Edison materials in the Henry Ford Museum Library at Dearborn, Michigan.

While numerous books have been written about individual universities and other research institutions in the familiar genres, institutions of Research and Development (R&D) have hardly begun to enter the history books. They seem to come into public consciousness when some of their papers are stolen, or when there are notorious cases of industrial espionage. But to get the increase of knowledge in the United States into perspective (historical and statistical) it is necessary to observe the story of the great industrial research laboratories, public, private, and semipublic.

In science and technology, the R&D Spirit was a counterpart to the Booster Spirit in city building. The R&Ders showed a similar belief in the reality of events that had not yet gone through the formality of taking place, and a similar refusal to make pedantic distinctions between the present and the future. The best introduction to this spirit is the writings of one of its most ingenious and most eloquent prophets, Arthur D. Little (1863–1935), which can be savored in a collection of his attempts "to preach the Gospel of Research," *The Handwriting on the Wall* (1928). The more prosaic administrative and organizational aspects are described in the works of Charles E. K. Mees (1882–1960), the pioneer director and (beginning in 1912) developer of the Eastman Kodak Company research laboratory in Rochester, N.Y.; for example, "Industrial Research Organization," *Trans. Am. Soc. Mech. Eng.*, XLI (1919), 83–90, and (with John A. Leermakers) *The Organization of Industrial Scientific Research* (1950). See also his chronicle of his own work, *From Dry Plates to Ektachrome Film, A Story of Photographic Research* (1961). On the adventurous career of Willis R. Whitney (1868–1958), see John T. Broderick, *Willis Rodney Whitney: Pioneer of Industrial Research* (1945), and Virginia V. Westervelt, *The World Was His Laboratory: The Story of Dr. Willis R. Whitney* (1964). For accounts of various types of research laboratories, see: Kendall Birr, *Pioneering in Industrial Research: The Story of the General Electric Research Laboratory* (1957); Lawrence A. Hawkins, *Adventure Into the Unknown: The First Fifty Years of the General Electric Research Laboratory* (1950); Bruce L. R. Smith, *The RAND Corporation: Case Study of a Nonprofit Advisory Corporation* (1966), a nonprofit enterprise supported largely by government contracts; and see Bibliographical Notes, above, to Part Three, for the Bureau of Standards, and to Part Six for the Weather Bureau. A readable and informative, if somewhat sensationalized, survey is Paul Dickson, *Think Tanks: An Inside Report on the Remarkable Idea Factories* (1971).

For additional information about the early days of American industrial research (especially on the role of Arthur D. Little) I am indebted to Mr. Raymond Stevens of Cambridge, Massachusetts, who was a long-time close personal associate of Little, and particularly to his letter to me dated March 9, 1970. Other items by Arthur D. Little include: *A Laboratory for Public Service* (1909); *Industrial Research in*

America (1913), presidential address to the American Chemical Society; *The Dyestuff Situation and Its Lessons* (1915), an address to the U.S. Chamber of Commerce; *The Relation of Research to Industrial Development* (1917), an address to the Canadian Manufacturers Association. For another light on the work of the laboratories, see the Arthur D. Little Laboratory Professional Papers (1908–), e.g.: E. G. Bailey, *Some Things Manufacturer Should Know about Coal;* Arthur D. Little, *The Chemist and the Community;* Harry S. Mork, *Selective Economy in Raw Materials*.

On the general development of industrial research, see, for example: Lawrence W. Bass, *The Management of Technical Programs, With Special Reference to the Needs of Developing Countries* (1965); William W. Buchanan (ed.), *Industrial Research Laboratories of the United States* (1965); Dwight T. Farnum and others, *Profitable Science in Industry* (1925); A. P. M. Fleming, *Science and Industry: Industrial Research in the United States* (1917; 1972), a British government publication, and (with J.G. Pearce) *Research in Industry —The Basis for Economic Progress* (1922); Courtney R. Hall, *History of American Industrial Science* (1954; 1972); Carl Heyel, *Handbook of Industrial Research Management* (1959); Frank B. Jewett, *Industrial Research* (1918); Richard L. Lesher and George J. Howick, *Background, Guidelines, and Recommendations for use in Assessing Effective Means of Channeling New Technologies in Promising Directions* (1965); T. S. McLeod, *Management of Research, Development and Design in Industry* (1969); National Research Council, *Research: A National Resource*, Vol. II, *Industrial Research* (1940); George Perazich and P.M. Field, *Industrial Research and Changing Technology* (1940); D. Duer Reeves, *Management of Industrial Research* (1967); Clayton H. Scharp, "Independent Laboratories in the Engineering

Industry," *Metallurgical and Chemical Engineering,* XVII (1917), 167–69; Edward R. Weidlein and William A. Hanor, *Glances at Industrial Research during Walks and Talks in Mellon Institute* (1936); Frederick A. White, *American Industrial Research Laboratories* (1961); Willis R. Whitney, "American Engineering Research," *Trans. Am. Inst. Elec. Eng.,* XXXVII (1918), 1709–19.

On the research laboratory for chemistry, a field in which many of the characteristic features of other R&D originated in the late nineteenth century, see: John J. Beer, *The Emergence of the German Dye Industry* (1949); William Haynes, *Chemical Pioneers: The Founders of the American Chemical Industry* (1939); "A Modern Steel Works Laboratory, The Bethlehem Steel Company's New Chemical and Physical Department, a Unique Model . . . ," *Iron Age,* XCIV (1914), 710–13; Robert P. Multhauf, *The Origins of Chemistry* (1967), and his forthcoming history of industrial chemistry; National Research Council, *A Reading List on Scientific and Industrial Research and the Service of Chemistry to Industry* (1920); F. Sherwood Taylor, *A History of Industrial Chemistry* (1957; 1972).

A suggestive introduction to the fashions of scientific collaboration and their effects on scientists and scientific progress is Alvin M. Weinberg, "Scientific Teams and Scientific Laboratories," *Daedalus,* XCIX (Fall 1970), 1056–75. An especially valuable survey of twentieth-century inventions, inventors, and how they did their work is John Jewkes, David Sawers, and Richard Stillerman, *The Sources of Invention* (2d ed., 1958). Other items on the nature of invention and discovery and their history in the United States include: George H. Daniels, "The Pure Science Ideal and Democratic Culture," *Science,* CLVI (1967), 1699–1705, and *Science and Society in America: A Social History* (1971); L. Sprague De-Camp, *The Heroic Age of American In-*vention (1961); Marvin Fisher, *Workshops in The Wilderness, the European Response to American Industrialization, 1830–1860* (1967); George Ernest Folk, *Patents and Industrial Progress* (1942); The Editors of Fortune, *The Mighty Force of Research* (1956); Clifford C. Furnas, *The Next Hundred Years: The Unfinished Business of Science* (1936); S. Colum Gilfillan, *Invention and the Patent System* (1964); H. J. Habakkuk, *American and British Technology in the 19th Century* (1962); H. S. Hatfield, *The Inventor and His World* (1933); P. d'A. Jones and E. N. Simons, *Story of the Saw* (1960), a well-illustrated account of the steps in improvement of a single tool; Thomas S. Kuhn, *The Structure of Scientific Revolutions* (1962); Fritz Machlup, *The Production and Distribution of Knowledge in the United States* (1962); Richard C. MacLaurin, "The Outlook for Research," *Clark Univ. Pub.,* II (1911); W. Rupert MacLaurin, *Invention & Innovation in the Radio Industry* (1949); Simon Marcson, *The Scientist in American Industry* (1960); National Academy of Sciences, *Basic Research and National Goals* (1965), and *Applied Science and Technological Progress* (1967), both being Reports to the Committee on Science and Astronautics of the U.S. House of Representatives; *Proceedings and Addresses at the Celebration of the Beginning of the Second Century of the American Patent System* (1891); Nathan Reingold (ed.), *Science in Nineteenth Century America, a Documentary History* (1964); Samuel Rezneck, "The Rise and Early Development of Industrial Consciousness in the U.S., 1760–1830," *Journ. of Ec. and Bus. Hist.,* IV (1932), 784–811; L. T. C. Rolt, *A Short History of Machine Tools* (1965); Jacob Schmookler, *Invention and Economic Growth* (1966); Leonard S. Silk, *The Research Revolution* (1960); W. Paul Strassmann, *Risk and Technological Innovation, American Manufacturing Methods during the 19th Century* (1959); Universities National

Bureau, Committee for Economic Research, *Rate and Direction of Inventive Activity: Economic and Social Factors* (1962); F. L. Vaughan, *The United States Patent System: Legal and Economic Conflicts in American Patent History* (1956); Edward R. Weidlein and William A. Hamor, *Science in Action . . . The Value of Scientific Research in American Industries* (1931); Willis R. Whitney, "Research as a Financial Asset," *General Electric Review*, XIV (1911), 325–30; Robert S. Woodbury's admirable monographs, scrupulously documented and copiously illustrated, *History of the Gear-Cutting Machine* (1958), *History of the Grinding Machine* (1959), *History of the Milling Machine* (1960), and *History of the Lathe* (1961).

The rise of the engineering profession is, of course, a measure of the importance the society attaches to the application of scientific knowledge. An illuminating introduction to this development is Daniel H. Calhoun, *The American Civil Engineer: Origins and Conflict* (1960), on the beginnings through the 1840's, and Raymond H. Merritt, *Engineering in American Society, 1850–1875* (1969). For the world context, See Richard S. Kirby and others, *Engineering in History* (1956).

On the rise of "Big Science" and the relation of government to the progress of science and technology, see: Lewis E. Auerbach, "Scientists in the New Deal," *Minerva*, IV (1965), 457–82; James Phinney Baxter 3rd, *Scientists Against Time* (1946; M.I.T. Paperback, 1968); J. D. Bernal, *The Social Function of Science* (1939; M.I.T. Paperback, 1964); Harvey Brooks, *Can Science Be Planned?* (Reprint No. 3, Harvard University Series from Program on Technology and Society, 1967); Vannevar Bush, *Science: The Endless Frontier* (1945); J. J. Carty, "Relation of Pure Science to Industrial Research," *Smithsonian Inst. Reports* (1916–1917), 523–31; I. Bernard Cohen, "Some Reflections on the State of Science in America During the 19th Century," *Proc. Nat. Acad.*

Sci., XLV (1959), 666–77; James B. Conant, *Science and Common Sense* (1951); A. Hunter Dupree, *Science in the Federal Government: A History of Policies and Activities to 1940* (1957); William Gilman, *Science: U.S.A.* (1965), a survey by a perceptive reporter; Gene M. Lyons, *The Uneasy Partnership: Social Science and the Federal Government in the Twentieth Century* (1969); National Research Council, *The National Importance of Scientific and Industrial Research* (1919); National Resources Committee, *Technological Trends and National Policy, including the Social Implications of New Inventions* (1937; 1972); Hasan Ozbekhan, *The Triumph of Technology: "Can" Implies "Ought"* (System Development Corp., 1967); M. E. Pickard, "Government and Science in the United States," *Journ. Hist. of Med.*, I (1946), 254–89, 446–81; Don K. Price, *Government and Science: Their Dynamic Relation in American Democracy* (1954), and *The Scientific Estate* (1965); Carroll W. Pursell, Jr., "A Preface to Government Support for Research and Development Research Legislation and the National Bureau of Standards, 1935–41," *Technology and Culture*, IX (1968), 145–64, and his *Readings in Technology and American Life* (1969); John E. Sawyer, "The Social Basis of the American System of Manufacturing," *Journ. Ec. Hist.*, XIV (1954), 361–79; Ronald C. Tobey, *The American Ideology of National Science , 1919–1930* (1972); Alvin M. Weinberg, *Reflections on Big Science* (1967), outspoken essays by the man who for eighteen years was Research Director and Director of the Oak Ridge National Laboratory.

For the careers of particular industrial research pioneers, see: Greville and Dorthy Bathe, *Jacob Perkins* (1943); Junius Edwards, *The Immortal Woodshed* (1955), an account of Charles M. Hall, the pioneer in the chemistry of aluminum; Maurice Holland (with Henry F. Pringle), *Industrial Explorers* (1928); Sigmond A. Lavine, *Kettering, Master Inventor* (1960); John A. Miller,

William David Coolidge, Yankee Scientist (1963), an account of the pioneer in X-rays who was a close collaborator of Willis R. Whitney at the General Electric Laboratories; Albert Rosenfeld, *The Quintessence of Irving Langmuir* (1966); C. Guy Suits, *The Collected Works of Irving Langmuir* (1961); David O. Woodbury, *Elihu Thompson, Beloved Scientist, 1853–1937: Inventive Genius of the Electrical Age* (1944).

ON THE RISE and special character of American manufacturing, see *The Americans: The National Experience*, chs. 3 and 4, and Bibliographical Notes to Part One. And for the later phase, see especially Parts Two and Three, above, and Bibliographical Notes. And for the role of highways and cities in the story, see Part Four, above, and Bibliographical Notes. John B. Rae, *The American Automobile, a Brief History* (Chicago History of American Civilization, 1965), provides a readable and reliable chronicle with a selected bibliography. For the larger context, see Sigfried Giedion, *Mechanization Takes Command* (1948; Norton Paperback, 1969), a brilliant account of how new techniques of manufacturing changed the worker's and consumer's point of view, and were reshaped by them. And for the relation of the new manufacturing technology to social ideals and standard of living, see my essay "Self-Liquidating Ideals," a statement to the Panel on Science and Technology of the Committee on Science and Astronautics of the House of Representatives, 91st Cong., 2d Sess., Jan. 28, 1970.

There is not, to my knowledge, a comprehensive history of the assembly line, although hints are found here and there (e.g., in Giedion, above, and in other items of the history of technology). Perhaps the best approach to the subject, in the present state of scholarship, is through the history of Henry Ford and the Ford Motor Company,

which is copiously chronicled in Allan Nevins and Frank E. Hill, *Ford* (3 vols., 1954–62). Other works especially illuminating for the development of flow technology and the annual model are: Horace L. Arnold and Fay L. Faurote, *Ford Methods and Ford Shops* (1915; 1972); James T. Flink, *America Adopts the Automobile, 1895–1910* (1972); Charles F. Kettering and Allen Orth, *The New Necessity* (1932), the credo of the automotive inventor, and long-time chief of research for General Motors; Mrs. Wilfred C. Leland and Minnie D. Millbrook, *Master of Precision: Henry M. Leland* (1966), a biography of the expert machinist who created both the Cadillac and the Lincoln, and elaborated the scheme of interchangeable parts for the automobile industry; John B. Rae, *American Automobile Manufacturers: The First Forty Years* (1959); Alfred P. Sloan, Jr., *My Years with General Motors* (1963), essential reading for the birth of the annual model, and (with Boyden Sparks) *Adventures of a White Collar Man* (1941); Theodore H. Smith, *The Marketing of Used Automobiles* (1941).

The organization of the automobile industry is chronicled and interpreted masterfully and subtly by Alfred D. Chandler, Jr., in his *Giant Enterprise: Ford, General Motors, and the Automobile Industry, Sources and Readings* (1964; Harcourt Brace & World Paperback), an application of some of the ideas and conclusions of his *Strategy and Structure: Chapters in the History of the Industrial Enterprise* (1962). And also helpful is Charles E. Edwards, *The Dynamics of the United States Automobile Industry* (1965).

The literature on Henry Ford is copious and varied. The books range from those which Ford himself wrote with collaborators, which present him as a kind of Horatio Alger Saint, to pamphlets like Upton Sinclair's *Flivver King* (1937) which make him a Horatio Alger Satan. A sampling of the literature might include: Harry Bennett, *We*

Never Called Him Henry (1951), a hostile biography by Ford's former confidant and personal assistant of thirty years; Roger Burlingame, *Henry Ford* (1957), brief and balanced; Anne Jardim, *The First Henry Ford: A Study in Personality and Business Leadership* (1970), a psychological study. Ford's own ideas and utterances can be found in: *Ford Ideals* (1926); *Today and Tomorrow* (with Samuel Crowther, 1926); *My Philosophy of Industry* (1929); *Moving Forward* (in collaboration with Samuel Crowther, 1930); *Things I've been Thinking About* (1936).

Of the growing literature (much of it for the home mechanic, the buff, the collector, or the racing-car enthusiast), the following have been particularly helpful: Rudolph E. Anderson, *The Story of the American Automobile* (1950); Automobile Manufacturers Association of America, Inc., *Automobiles of America* (1968); Anthony Bird, *Roads and Vehicles* (1969); T. A. Boyd, *Professional Amateur* (1957; 1972), a good biography of Kettering; Walter P.

Chrysler (with Boyden Sparks), *Life of an American Workman* (1937); David L. Cohn, *Combustion on Wheels* (1944); *The Complete Encyclopaedia of Motorcars* (1968), a European guide; Merrill Denison, *The Power to Go* (1956); James R. Doolittle (ed.), *The Romance of the Automobile Industry* (1916); R. C. Epstein, *The Automobile Industry* (1928; 1972); Frank E. Hill, *The Automobile* (1967); John Jerome, *The Death of the Automobile: The Fatal Effect of the Golden Era, 1955–1970* (1972), a slightly premature obituary, with interesting observations on some consequences of the annual model; Jean Labatut and Wheator J. Lane (eds.), *Highways in Our National Life* (1950; 1972), a symposium; Smith H. Oliver and Donald H. Berkebile, *The Smithsonian Collection of Automobiles and Motorcycles* (1968); L. T. C. Rolt, *Motoring History* (1964), a concise illustrated guide to the spectacular events and cars in the history of the automobile; Harless D. Wagoner, *The U.S. Machine Tool Industry from 1900 to 1950* (1968).

PART TEN

MISSION AND MOMENTUM

MUCH OF AMERICAN HISTORY —not only in the colonial period and in the era of Western settlement but also many of the later efforts to reshape and reform American life in the cities and the suburbs—could be chronicled as a history of the missionary spirit. For the promise, the performance, and the perils of this spirit in the early period, see *The Americans: The Colonial Experience*, Book One, "The Vision and the Reality," Parts One through Four, and *The National Experience*, Parts Two, Three, and Five, and Bibliographical Notes. Our tendency to view the American missionary spirit abroad as a diversion from the mainstream of our history is misleading.

The best approach to the story of American missions abroad is through

the writings of Kenneth Scott Latourette (1884–1968), an ordained Baptist minister, himself once a missionary in China, who became Professor of Missions and Oriental History at Yale in 1927, and remained interested in promoting missionary efforts during his long life. Despite his own firm convictions he remained critical of missionary efforts, and his assessment of the methods and products of those efforts have a magisterial detachment not easy to find in the other literature. A brief introduction to his work is his *Missions and the American Mind* (1949) or *These Sought a Country* (1950). Latourette's eighty-odd published volumes include: *The History of the Expansion of Christianity* (7 vols., 1937–45), with accounts of missions all over the world; *Christianity* in a Revolutionary Age: A History of Christianity in the 19th and 20th Centuries (5 vols., 1958–62). Especially interesting, in the light of the development of American foreign policy in the mid-twentieth century, are his *History of the Christian Missions in China* (1929) and *The American Record in the Far East, 1945–1951* (1952), a publication of the American Institute of Pacific Relations, which describes the "ever deepening entanglement" of the United States in that area, relates it to strong currents in American history (like the Westward movement), and assesses American policy in China as a failure.

To put the American mission movement in the context of American history and American philanthropy, we are fortunate to have Merle Curti's judicious, charitable, and readable *American Philanthropy Abroad* (1963), with an indispensable bibliographical essay. An interesting supplement is Scott M. Cutlip, *Fund Raising in the United States: Its Role in American Philanthropy* (1965). For the context of American religious history, see the admirable survey by Edwin Scott Gaustad, *A Religious History of America* (1966), with bibliography, and his *Historical Atlas of Religion in America* (1962). For the attitudes of the major denominations toward missions and philanthropy abroad, see the relevant volumes (all with bibliographies) in the Chicago History of American Civilization Series: Robert Bremner, *American Philanthropy* (1960); John Tracy Ellis, *American Catholicism* (2d ed., 1969); Nathan Glazer, *American Judaism* (2d ed., 1972); and Winthrop S. Hudson, *American Protestantism* (1961). Of the vast literature on American religious history, these volumes are especially helpful: Colin B. Goodykoontz, *Home Missions on the American Frontier* (1939); Will Herberg, *Protestant-Catholic-Jew* (rev. ed., 1960); Charles Johnson, *The Frontier Camp Meeting: Religion's Harvest Time* (1955); Layman's Foreign Mission Inquiry, *Re-Thinking Missions* (1932,

William E. Hocking, Chairman); Martin Marty, *The New Shape of American Religion* (1959), *The Modern Schism: Three Paths to the Secular* (1969), *Righteous Empire: The Protestant Experience in America* (1970), and his cogent and stimulating chapter, "Freedom and Faith: Spiritual Attitudes of a New World," in *American Civilization* (ed. Daniel J. Boorstin, 1972); Sidney Mead, *The Lively Experiment: The Shaping of Christianity in America* (1963); Anson Phelpes Stokes and Leo Pfeffer, *Church and State in the United States* (rev. ed., 1964); William Warren Sweet, *Revivalism in America: Its Origin, Growth, and Decline* (1944), *The Story of Religion in America* (2d ed., 1950), *Religion in Colonial America* (1942), *Religion in the Development of American Culture, 1765–1840* (1952), and *Religion on the American Frontier* (4 vols., 1931–46); Bernard A. Weisberger, *They Gathered at the River: The Story of the Great Revivalists and their Impact upon Religion in America* (1958); Gibson Winter, *The Suburban Captivity of the Churches* (1961).

On particular missionaries and leaders of the mission movement, especially for the early period, the *Dictionary of American Biography* remains an indispensable source, in some cases the only one in print. Items which I have found especially useful include: Rufus Anderson, *To Advance the Gospel* (1967); Samuel B. Capen, *The Next Ten Years* (1911), and *Foreign Missions and World Peace* (World Peace Foundation Pamphlet Series, 1912); Harriet Bronson Genung, *The Story of Cyrus Hamlin* (1907); Robert H. Glover, *The Progress of World-Wide Missions* (rev. and enlarged by J. Herbert Kane, 1960); Cyrus Hamlin, *Among the Turks* (1878), *My Life and Times* (1893); Chauncy J. Hawkins, *Samuel Billings Capen* (1914); Hiram C. Hayden (ed.), *American Heroes on Mission Fields* (1890); Peter G. Mode, *Source Book and Bibliographical Guide for American Church History* (1964); Thomas C. Richards, *Samuel J.*

Mills, *Missionary Pathfinder, Pioneer and Promoter* (1906); Gordon S. Seagrave, *Waste-Basket Surgery* (1930), *Tales of a Waste-Basket Surgeon* (1938), *Burma Surgeon* (1943), and *Burma Surgeon Returns* (1946); Frederic Shoberl (ed.), *Present State of Christianity and of the Missionary Establishments for Its Propagation in All Parts of the World* (1828); E. G. Stryker, *Missionary Annals* (1888); Barbara Tuchman, *Stilwell and the American Experience in China, 1911–1945* (1972); Francis Wayland, *A Memoir of the Life and Labors of the Reverend Adoniram Judson* (2 vols., 1853). For the work of Rockefeller and his Foundation, see Raymond B. Fosdick, *The Story of the Rockefeller Foundation* (1952).

Other items of special interest on American philanthropy include: Nolan Rice Best, *Two Y Men* (1925); Samuel Crowther, *John H. Patterson, Pioneer in Industrial Welfare* (1923); Lewis Tappan, *Is It Right To be Rich?* (1869); Joseph F. Wall, *Andrew Carnegie* (1970); Warren Weaver, *U. S. Philanthropic Foundations, Their History, Structure, Management, and Record* (1967); M. R. Werner, *Julius Rosenwald, the Life of a Practical Humanitarian* (1939).

THE LITERATURE OF "foreign relations" and "foreign policy" has suffered from excessively rigid definition and from compartmentalization into academic "subjects." Except in the Marxist literature (which purports to put the foreign relations of a nation into the whole context of the society, but then narrows the vision by mistaking the productive machinery for the whole society), there has been too little treatment of international relations as simply that aspect of a civilization in which a people are concerned with their relations to "others." In fact, international relations could be viewed as the counterpart in *space* for what history is in *time:* history shows that things can be otherwise in a society because

they *have been* otherwise; international relations shows that they can be otherwise because they *are* otherwise in other societies.

A good introduction to American international relations in the late era is Ernest R. May, "Missionary and World Power: America's Destiny in the Twentieth Century," in *American Civilization* (ed. Daniel J. Boorstin, 1972). On the theoretical implications of American foreign policy and the nation's freedom to shift its position, particularly illuminating are: Henry Kissinger, *The Necessity for Choice: Prospects of American Foreign Policy* (1961), *The Troubled Partnership: A Reappraisal of the Atlantic Alliance* (1965), and *American Foreign Policy, Three Essays* (1969); and Hans J. Morgenthau, *Politics Among Nations: The Struggle for Power and Peace* (rev. ed., 1954), a philosophical textbook pointing the connections between foreign policy and the aims of a civilization, and *A New Foreign Policy for the United States* (1969). From the extensive and controversial literature, the following items are of special interest: Dean Acheson, *Present at the Creation: My Years in the State Department* (1969); John R. Beal, *Marshall in China* (1970); Sidney Bell, *Righteous Conquest: Woodrow Wilson and the Evolution of the New Diplomacy* (1972); William A. Brown, Jr., and Redvers Opie, *American Foreign Assistance* (1953), a massive economic study; Lloyd C. Gardner, *Architects of Illusion: Men and Ideas in American Foreign Policy, 1941–1949* (1970); Michael A. Guhin, *John Foster Dulles: A Statesman and His Times* (1972); George F. Kennan, *American Diplomacy, 1900–1950* (1951), *Soviet-American Relations, 1917–1920* (2 vols., 1956–58), *Russia, the Atom and the West* (1958), *Russia and the West under Lenin and Stalin* (1961), *Memoirs* (2 vols., 1967–72), and " 'X' plus 25," an interview in *Foreign Policy*, VII (Summer 1972), 3–21; Gabriel and Joyce Kolko, *The Limits of Power: The World and United States Foreign Policy,*

1945–54 (1971); Sidney Lens, *The Forging of the American Empire from the Revolution to Vietnam: A History of American Imperialism* (1971); Walter Lippmann, *U.S. Foreign Policy: Shield of the Republic* (1943); Raymond F. Mikesell, *United States Economic Policy and International Relations* (1952); Robert E. Osgood, *Ideals and Self-Interest in America's Foreign Relations* (1953), and *Limited War, The Challenge to American Strategy* (1957); Forrest C. Pogue, *George C. Marshall* (3 vols., 1963–73); Walt W. Rostow, *The Stages of Economic Growth* (2d ed., 1960), *The Diffusion of Power, 1957–1972* (1972); Arthur M. Schlesinger, Jr. (ed.), *The Dynamics of World Power: A Documentary History of American Foreign Policy, 1945–1972* (5 vols., 1972); William Appleman Williams, *The Tragedy of American Diplomacy* (1960), and *The Shaping of American Diplomacy* (1960).

On the Peace Corps, see *Annals of the American Academy of Political and Social Science*, CCCLXV (1966), and Robert G. Carey, *The Peace Corps* (1970).

For the story of foreign aid and the Marshall Plan, see such items as: Lloyd D. Black, *The Strategy of Foreign Aid* (1968); John C. Culver, "U.S. Foreign Aid: Life or Death at 21?," *Harvard Law School Bulletin*, XIX (1968), 6–11; Herbert Druks, *Harry S. Truman and the Russians, 1945–1953* (1966); Robert A. Goldwin (ed.), *Why Foreign Aid?* (1963), messages by President Kennedy and essays by others; Harry B. Price, *The Marshall Plan and Its Meaning* (1955); Harry S. Truman, *Memoirs* (2 vols., 1955–56); Margaret Truman, *Harry S. Truman* (1973); Don Wallace, Jr., "The President's Exclusive Foreign Affairs Powers Over Foreign Aid," *Duke Law Journal* (Apr.–June 1970), 293–328, 453–94. Cogent statements putting the programs in perspective are found in *An American Primer* (ed. Daniel J. Boorstin, 2 vols., 1966; New American Library Paperback, 1968):

Hans J. Morgenthau (ed.), "George C. Marshall on the Marshall Plan, 1947," and Herbert Feis (ed.), "Harry S. Truman on the Point IV Program, 1949."

An obvious example of momentum in foreign policy, in addition to foreign aid, is the United States relation to the Far East, which has been the subject of countless volumes and bitter controversy. How momentum operates can be observed in two lively books: Barbara Tuchman, *Stilwell and the American Experience in China, 1911–45* (1972) and David Halberstam, *The Best and the Brightest* (1972), an account, emphasizing personalities, of American involvement in Vietnam.

ODDLY ENOUGH, the great national scientific enterprises which, for reasons of security, have sometimes been shrouded in secrecy, have been better chronicled than the myriad advances in the technology of everyday life. This is doubtless because the enormous costly enterprises have required presidential support and congressional appropriations, and so have been more obviously involved with political history, with the policies and positions of Presidents and Congresses, and hence fit into the familiar categories of academic history. Future historians will surely note the high quality of historical writing and the remarkable historical self-consciousness that have marked both the atomic enterprise and the space enterprise.

For the story of the atomic bomb, the essential, remarkably readable, and balanced resource is *A History of the U.S. Atomic Energy Commission*, Vol. I, *New World, 1939–1946* (1962), by Richard C. Hewlett and Oscar E. Anderson, Jr., and Vol. II, *Atomic Shield, 1947–1952* (1969), by Richard C. Hewlett and Francis Duncan. A briefer popular account is Stephane Groueff, *Manhattan Project: The Untold Story of the Making of the Atomic Bomb* (1967). The attitudes and participation of scientists in the project, and their reactions at several stages, are subtly and vividly chronicled by Alice Kimball Smith, who had the advantage of knowing personally many of the leading figures, in *A Peril and a Hope: The Scientists' Movement in America, 1945–47* (1965), a work which, so far as I know, has no close parallel in the historiography of modern technology. No one who is curious about the meaning of modern collaborative "Big Science" for the collaborators themselves should miss this book. A selected list of other works from the growing literature would include the following items of special value: James Phinney Baxter 3rd, *Scientists Against Time* (1946); Arthur Holly Compton, *Atomic Quest, A Personal Narrative* (1956); Laura Fermi, *Atoms in the Family: My Life with Enrico Fermi* (1954), and *Atoms for the World* (1957); Donald Fleming (ed.), "Albert Einstein, Letter to Franklin D. Roosevelt, 1939," in *An American Primer* (ed. Daniel J. Boorstin; 2 vols., 1966; New American Library Paperback, 1968); Leslie R. Groves, *Now It Can Be Told, The Story of the Manhattan Project* (1962); John Hersey, *Hiroshima* (1946); Henry Kissinger, *Nuclear Weapons and Foreign Policy* (1957); Robert J. Lifton, *Death in Life: Survivors of Hiroshima* (1968); David E. Lilienthal, *Change, Hope and the Bomb* (1963), and *Journals* (4 vols., 1964–69); Sam H. Schurr and Jacob Marschak, *Economic Aspects of Atomic Power* (1950); Henry D. Smyth, *Atomic Energy for Military Purposes: Official Report on the Development of the Atomic Bomb under the Auspices of the United States Government, 1940–45* (1945); Leo Szilard, *The Voice of the Dolphins and Other Stories* (1961), sparkling essays by one of the prime movers of the atomic enterprise; Edward Teller, "The Era of Big Science," *Bull. Atomic Scientists* (Apr., 1971), pp. 34–36, and (with Allen Brown) *The Legacy of Hiroshima* (1962); John Toland, *The Rising Sun: The Decline and Fall of the Japanese Empire, 1936–45* (1970), a brilliant account of World War II from the Japanese documents and the Japanese point of view, including the experience of the atomic bombs by their victims; Margaret Truman, *Harry S. Truman* (1973), for a more personal view of President Truman's decision and relations to the press concerning possible use of the bomb in the Korean War. Valuable articles on numerous related topics will be found in the *Bulletin of Atomic Scientists* (1945–).

The problems of those who would write about the space project are in many respects the opposite of those who would seek to chronicle the atomic enterprise. While in the chronicle of the atomic bomb the prime problem was secrecy, in the case of the space enterprise there has been an understandable desire to publicize activities in every way that would encourage public interest and congressional appropriations. Nevertheless, the publications sponsored by NASA have been impressively well balanced and free from advertising puffs. They are on the whole readable and well documented, revealing a sense of history which is rare even in accounts of less spectacular and more remote events. NASA has, however, been faced by the competition between the need to chronicle numerous particular events while they are still fresh and their participants are still available, and the need to offer a wider view and a larger understanding to the general public.

Future historians will be grateful to the historians and administrators of NASA whose Historical Series has provided such admirable monographs as: Loyd S. Swenson, Jr., James M. Grimwood, and Charles C. Alexander, *This New Ocean: A History of Project Apollo* (1966); Edwin P. Hartman, *Adventures in Research: A History of Ames Research Center, 1940–65* (1970); and the valuable, detailed NASA chronologies of each of its projects. The layman will find his bearings with the help of Richard S. Lewis' readable and balanced account of the space enterprise from Explorer I to the first moon landing: *Appointment on the Moon* (1969). Two valuable accounts of specific events which show the convergence of the forces of science, of politics, and of public opinion are Constance McL. Green and Milton Lomask, *Vanguard: A History* (1971), and John M. Logsdon, *The Decision to Go To the Moon* (1970). A wonderfully suggestive volume which opens myriad new paths for the historian is Bruce Mazlish (ed.), *The Railroad and the Space Program: An Exploration in Historical Analogy* (1965). For contemporary alarms at the consequences of the transcontinental railroad, see Charles Francis Adams, Jr., and Henry Adams, *Chapters of Erie and Other Essays* (1871), pp. 332 ff.

A vivid introduction to the new meanings of the earth when seen from space is *This Island Earth* (1971), a NASA publication. Some other items of special interest include: Tom Alexander, *Project Apollo: Man to the Moon* (foreword by Sir Bernard Lovell, 1964); Arthur C. Clarke, *Profiles of the Future: An Inquiry into the Limits of the Possible* (1962); Robert H. Goddard, *Papers* (ed. Esther C. Goddard and G. Edward Pendray; 3 vols., 1968); Milton Lehman, *High Man: The Life of Robert H. Goddard* (1963); Anne Morrow Lindbergh, *Earth Shine* (1969), a poem; Charles A. Lindbergh, *Wartime Journals* (1970), with some glimpses of Lindbergh's assessment of aeronautical progress in Britain and the United States by con-

trast with that in Nazi Germany; Norman Mailer, *Of a Fire on the Moon* (1970); The Martin Co. and United Aircraft Corp., *The Missile Industry—In Defense and the Exploration of Space* (1961); Bruce Mazlish, "The Idea of Progress," *Daedalus*, XCII (1963), 447–61; Eric G. Oakley, *Project Telstar: The Amazing Story of the World's First Communications Satellite* (1963); Eugene I. Rabinowitch and Richard S. Lewis (eds.), *Man on the Moon: The Impact on Science, Technology and International Cooperation* (1969); William R. Shelton, *American Space Exploration: The First Decade* (1967); Loyd S. Swenson, Jr., "The 'Megamachine' Behind the Mercury Spacecraft," *American Quarterly*, XXI (Summer 1969), 210–27; U.S. Congress, House of Rep., *The Next Ten Years in Space, 1959–69*, Staff Report of the Select Com. on Astronautics and Space Exploration (1959); *To Amend the National Aeronautics and Space Act of 1958*, Hearings before the House of Rep. Com. on Science and Astronautics, 86th Cong., 2d Sess. (1960); *Manned Space Flight: Present and Future*, Staff Study, Com. on Science and Astronautics, House of Rep., 91st Cong., 2d Sess. (1970); Vernon Van Dyke, *Pride and Power: The Rationale of the Space Program* (1964), a sociological study; Theodore von Kármán (with Lee Edson), *The Wind and Beyond: Theodore von Kármán, Pioneer in Aviation and Pathfinder in Space* (1967); James E. Webb, *Space Age Management: The Large Scale Approach* (1969).

Index

ABOUT THE AUTHOR

Daniel J. Boorstin is the Librarian of Congress. He has been senior historian of the Smithsonian Institution, Washington, D.C., director of The National Museum of History and Technology and Preston and Sterling Morton Distinguished Service Professor of American History at the University of Chicago where he taught for twenty-five years.

Dr. Boorstin has spent a good deal of his life viewing America from the outside, first in England where he was a Rhodes Scholar at Balliol College, Oxford, winning a coveted "double-first." More recently he has been visiting professor of American History at the University of Rome and at Kyoto University, consultant to the Social Science Research Center at the University of Puerto Rico, the first incumbent of the chair of American History at the Sorbonne, and Pitt Professor of American History and Institutions and a Fellow of Trinity College, Cambridge University, which awarded him its Litt.D. degree.